HISTORY OF THE BOOK IN CANADA

VOLUME III
1918–1980

HISTORY OF THE BOOK IN CANADA

VOLUME III
1918–1980

Edited by
Carole Gerson and Jacques Michon

General Editors:
Patricia Lockhart Fleming and Yvan Lamonde

UNIVERSITY OF TORONTO PRESS
Toronto Buffalo London

ISBN-10: 0-8020-9047-8
ISBN-13: 978-0-8020-9047-8

Cet ouvrage est également disponible en langue française aux Presses de l'Université de Montréal.
© Les Presses de l'Université de Montréal, 2007

ISBN-10: 2-7606-1998-2
ISBN-13: 978-2-7606-1998-2

Translations by/traductions par: Phyllis Aronoff and Howard Scott.

Printed on acid-free paper

Library and Archives Canada Cataloguing in Publication

History of the book in Canada / general editors: Patricia Lockhart Fleming and Yvan Lamonde.

Published also in French by Presses de l'Université de Montréal under title: Histoire du livre et de l'imprimé au Canada.
Published in cooperation with the History of the Book in Canada Project.
Includes bibliographical references and indexes.
Contents: v. 1. Beginnings to 1840 – v. 2. 1840–1918. – v. 3. 1918–1980.
ISBN-13: 978-0-8020-8943-4 (bound : v. 1)   ISBN-10: 0-8020-8943-7 (bound : v. 1)
ISBN-13: 978-0-8020-8012-7 (v. 2)   ISBN-10: 0-8020-8012-X (v. 2)
ISBN-13: 978-0-8020-9047-8 (v. 3)   ISBN-10: 0-8020-9047-8 (v. 3)

1. Books and reading – Canada – History.   2. Book industries and trade – Canada – History.
3. Book industries and trade – Social aspects – Canada.   4. Printing – Canada – History.
I. Fleming, Patricia   II. Lamonde, Yvan, 1944–   III. History of the Book in Canada Project.

Z206.H58 2004   002'.0971   C2004-901302-5

University of Toronto Press acknowledges the financial assistance to its publishing program of the Canada Council for the Arts and the Ontario Arts Council.

This book was made possible in part through the Canada Council for the Arts Translation Grant Programme.

This book has been published with the help of a grant from the Canadian Federation for the Humanities and Social Sciences, through the Aid to Scholarly Publications Programme, using funds provided by the Social Sciences and Humanities Research Council of Canada.

University of Toronto Press acknowledges the financial support for its publishing activities of the Government of Canada through the Book Publishing Industry Development Program (BPIDP).

CONTENTS

Illustrations   vii

General Editors' Preface   xxi

Acknowledgments   xxiii

History of the Book in Canada / Histoire du livre et de l'imprimé au Canada   xxv

Abbreviations   xxvii

Chronology   xxix

Editors' Introduction   3

PART ONE: THE CULTURAL INFLUENCE OF BOOKS AND PRINT IN CANADIAN SOCIETY

1   THE BOOK AND THE NATION

Imprinting the Nation in Words   13
A.B. MCKILLOP

Government Policy and Allophone Cultures   24
PAUL HJARTARSON

Intersections between Native Oral Traditions and Print Culture   29
BLANCA SCHORCHT

The State and the Book   34
PAUL LITT

Book Policy in Quebec   45
JOSÉE VINCENT

Translating the Two Solitudes   51
JEAN DELISLE AND GILLES GALLICHAN

Canadianization of the Curriculum   56
LUCIE ROBERT, CHRISTL VERDUYN, AND JANET B. FRISKNEY

Case Study: Canadian Content in Primary Textbooks in Quebec   63
JACQUES MICHON

Cohering through Books   64
JENNIFER J. CONNOR

Picturing Canada   70
JO NORDLEY BEGLO

2   SYMBOLIC VALUE OF BOOKS

Books and Reading in Canadian Art   75
CAROLE GERSON AND YVAN LAMONDE

The Image of the Book in Advertising   80
RUSSELL JOHNSTON, LYNDSEY NOWAKOWSKI-DAILEY, MICHELLE PRESTON,
AND JAIME SWEETING

Prize Books in Quebec   86
FRANÇOIS LANDRY

Marshall McLuhan and the History of the Book   88
RICHARD CAVELL

PART TWO: AUTHORSHIP

3   AUTHORS' CAREERS

Social and Cultural Profile of Writers   93
CAROLE GERSON AND MARIE-PIER LUNEAU

Allophone Authorship   100
CATHERINE OWEN

Economics and the Writer   103
FRANK DAVEY

    Case Study: Collecting Canadian Manuscripts at the University of
    Calgary   113
    APOLLONIA STEELE

    Case Study: The Canada Council for the Arts Writer-in-Residence
    Program   115
    NANCY EARLE

Celebrating Authorship: Prizes and Distinctions   116
MARIE-PIER LUNEAU AND RUTH PANOFSKY

Writers' Networks and Associations   122
PEGGY LYNN KELLY AND JOSÉE VINCENT

    Case Study: The CAA and Propaganda during the Second World
    War   129
    PETER BUITENHUIS

4   THE AUTHOR AND THE MARKET

Writers and the Market for Fiction and Literature   131
JANET B. FRISKNEY AND CAROLE GERSON

Writers and the Market for Non-Fiction   138
CLARENCE KARR

Sports Writing   142
MICHAEL A. PETERMAN

Children's Authors and Their Markets   145
FRANÇOISE LEPAGE, JUDITH SALTMAN, AND GAIL EDWARDS

    Case Study: Leslie McFarlane and the Case of Pseudonymous Children's
    Authorship   153
    JANET B. FRISKNEY

CBC Radio and Anglophone Authors   154
SHEILA LATHAM

Adaptations for Film and Television   157
PETER DICKINSON

PART THREE: PUBLISHING FOR A WIDE READERSHIP

5   TRADE AND REGIONAL BOOK PUBLISHING IN ENGLISH

The Agency System and Branch-Plant Publishing   163
GEORGE L. PARKER

Trade and Regional Publishing in Central Canada   168
GEORGE L. PARKER

Atlantic Canada   178
SANDRINE FERRÉ-RODE

Prairie Publishing   182
FIONA A. BLACK

    Case Study: 'Harlequin Has Built an Empire'   185
    ARCHANA RAMPURE

British Columbia and the North   188
PETER J. MITHAM

Organization and Training among Book Publishers   192
NANCY EARLE AND JANET B. FRISKNEY

    Case Study: From Tea Room to Top Floor: The Book Publishers' Professional
    Association   196
    NANCY EARLE

6   PUBLISHING BOOKS IN FRENCH

Book Publishing in Quebec   199
JACQUES MICHON

    Case Study: *Les insolences du frère Untel / The Impertinences of Brother
    Anonymous*   206
    JACQUES MICHON

Ontario   208
ROBERT YERGEAU

Acadia   210
DOMINIQUE MARQUIS

The West 211
DOMINIQUE MARQUIS

Francophone Organizations in the Book Trade 213
JOSÉE VINCENT

7 PUBLISHING FOR CHILDREN AND STUDENTS

Publishing for Children 216
SUZANNE POULIOT, JUDITH SALTMAN, AND GAIL EDWARDS

The Rise and Fall of Textbook Publishing in English Canada 226
PENNEY CLARK

   Case Study: Coles Notes 232
   IAN BROCKIE

   Case Study: McClelland and Stewart and the Quality Paperback 233
   JANET B. FRISKNEY

Textbook Publishing in Quebec 237
PAUL AUBIN

   Case Study: French-Canadian Classics from Fides 239
   JACQUES MICHON

8 THE SERIAL PRESS

Major Trends in Canada's Print Mass Media 242
MARY VIPOND

Women's Magazines 248
MARIE-JOSÉ DES RIVIÈRES, CAROLE GERSON, AND DENIS SAINT-JACQUES

   Case Study: Almanacs in French Canada 251
   FRÉDÉRIC BRISSON

   Case Study: Serial Pulp Fiction in Quebec 253
   JACQUES MICHON

   Case Study: Canadian Pulp Magazines and Second World War
   Regulations 255
   CAROLYN STRANGE AND TINA LOO

PART FOUR: PUBLISHING FOR DISTINCT READERSHIPS

9   GOVERNMENT AND CORPORATE PUBLISHING

Government as Author and Publisher   261
GILLES GALLICHAN AND BERTRUM H. MACDONALD

Case Study: The Federal Government's Advice to Mothers   267
KATHERINE ARNUP

The Publishing Activities of CBC / Radio-Canada   270
DOMINIQUE MARQUIS

CPR in Print   272
IAIN STEVENSON

10   ORGANIZED RELIGION AND PRINT

The Religious Press in Quebec   276
DOMINIQUE MARQUIS

Case Study: The Magazine *Relations*   278
SIMONE VANNUCCI

Catholic Publication and Distribution of Books in French   280
YVAN CLOUTIER

Case Study: A Catholic Best-Seller: The Journal of Gérard Raymond   282
SIMONE VANNUCCI

Print and Organized Religion in English Canada   283
BRIAN HOGAN

Publishing for Young Christians   288
DANIEL O'LEARY

11   PUBLISHING AND COMMUNITIES

Publishing and Aboriginal Communities   293
CHERYL SUZACK

Allophone Publishing   296
CATHERINE OWEN

Jewish Print Culture   305
REBECCA MARGOLIS

Case Study: The *Free Lance*   307
DOROTHY W. WILLIAMS

Small Press Publishing   308
DAVID MCKNIGHT

Publishing by Women   318
CAROLE GERSON

Publishing against the Grain   322
DONALD W. MCLEOD

12 SCHOLARLY AND PROFESSIONAL PUBLISHING

Scholarly and Reference Publishing   328
FRANCESS G. HALPENNY

   Case Study: R.E. Watters's *Check List of Canadian Literature*   336
   SANDRA ALSTON

Scientific Periodicals   337
BERTRUM H. MACDONALD

Legal Publishing   339
STUART CLARKSON AND SYLVIO NORMAND

   Medical Publishing   343
   JENNIFER J. CONNOR

PART FIVE: PRODUCTION

13 PRINTING AND DESIGN

The Canadian Printing Industry   349
ÉRIC LEROUX

   Case Study: Thérien Frères   354
   ÉRIC LEROUX

   Case Study: From Humble Beginnings: Friesens Corporation   355
   LINDA BEDWELL

Working in the Printing Trades   358
CHRISTINA BURR AND ÉRIC LEROUX

Case Study: Learning the Trade: The École des arts graphiques de Montréal   368
ÉRIC LEROUX

The Graphic Arts in Quebec   369
GUY DE GROSBOIS

Case Study: The *Livre d'artiste* in Quebec   372
CLAUDETTE HOULD

The Private Press   374
RICHARD LANDON

Case Study: The Alcuin Society   376
JIM RAINER

Book Design in English Canada   378
RANDALL SPELLER

Case Study: Cartier: Canada's First Typeface   385
ROD MCDONALD

PART SIX: DISTRIBUTION

14   SYSTEMS OF DISTRIBUTION

International Sources of Supply   389
FRÉDÉRIC BRISSON

The World of Bookselling   393
FRÉDÉRIC BRISSON

Case Study: The Book Room   401
GWENDOLYN DAVIES

Case Study: Librairie Tranquille   402
FRÉDÉRIC BRISSON

Control and Content in Mass Market Distribution   404
SARAH BROUILLETTE AND JACQUES MICHON

Book Clubs   408
ARCHANA RAMPURE AND JACQUES MICHON

Booksellers' Organizations   411
GEORGE L. PARKER AND PASCALE RYAN

PART SEVEN: REACHING READERS

15   LIBRARIES

Government Libraries   417
ROSS GORDON

The Canada Institute for Scientific and Technical Information   422
BERTRUM H. MACDONALD

National Library of Canada   424
PAUL MCCORMICK

Bibliothèque nationale du Québec   428
MARCEL LAJEUNESSE

The Rise of the Public Library in English Canada   429
LORNE BRUCE AND ELIZABETH HANSON

The Public Library in Quebec   435
MARCEL LAJEUNESSE

Academic Libraries   439
MARCEL LAJEUNESSE AND PETER F. MCNALLY

Special Libraries   445
ELAINE BOONE

The Profession of Librarianship   449
MARTIN DOWDING

16   READING HABITS

Measuring Literacy   453
MICHEL VERRETTE

Surveying the Habit of Reading   455
HEATHER MURRAY AND ANDREA ROTUNDO

Best-Sellers   459
KLAY DYER, DENIS SAINT-JACQUES, AND CLAUDE MARTIN

Fan Mail from Readers   463
CLARENCE KARR

Autobiographies of Reading: L.M. Montgomery and Marcel Lavallé   465
CLARENCE KARR

17 CONTROLLING AND ADVISING READERS

Government Censorship of Print   468
PEARCE CAREFOOTE

Religious Censorship in English Canada   473
DANIEL O'LEARY

From Censoring Print to Advising Readers in Quebec   475
PIERRE HÉBERT

'Read Canadian'   480
W.H. NEW

Encouraging Children to Read   484
LORNA KNIGHT

18 SPECIAL COMMUNITIES OF READERS

Reaching Out to Isolated Readers   491
LORNA KNIGHT

    Case Study: Libraries on the Move   496
    ERIC BUNGAY

    Case Study: Women's Institute Libraries   498
    JEAN COGSWELL

    Case Study: Wheat Pool Libraries   500
    ELISE MOORE

Reading on the 'Rez'   501
BRENDAN FREDERICK R. EDWARDS

Reading in Alternative Formats   505
JANET B. FRISKNEY

Reading and Study Clubs   509
DENEL REHBERG SEDO

    Case Study: Société d'étude et de conférences   513
    FANIE ST-LAURENT

Coda   515
CAROLE GERSON AND JACQUES MICHON

Notes   523

Sources Cited   565

Contributors   601

Index   613

ILLUSTRATIONS

1.1 Lionel Groulx, [1960]. 17

1.2 Men in Corner Brook, NF, reading the St John's *Evening Telegram*, July 1948. 20

1.3 *The Manitoba Ruthenian-English Readers*, I and II (London, [1913?]). 26

1.4 Robert La Palme, caricature of Jean Bruchési, 1938. 47

1.5 *Dutch Oven: A Cook Book of Coveted Traditional Recipes from the Kitchens of Lunenburg* (Lunenburg, NS, 1953). 65

1.6 *Le Passe-Temps* (Montreal), July 1946. 69

1.7 J.E.H. MacDonald, cover of *Canadian Section of Fine Arts, British Empire Exhibition, London, 1924*. 72

2.1 Edwin Holgate, *Mother and Daughter* (1926). 77

2.2 John Alexander Hall, *Lydia and Veronica* (1940). 78

2.3 Judith Copithorne, 'The telephone ringing it's changes in the evening light' (Vancouver, 1973). 80

2.4 Advertisement for du Maurier cigarettes, *Le Magazine Maclean* (Montreal), August 1964. 83

2.5 Advertisement for Lux soap, *Chatelaine* (Toronto), February 1941. 84

2.6 Advertisement for Molson's Golden Ale, *Maclean's* (Toronto), April 1956. 85

2.7 Examples of prize books from the Bibliothèque canadienne series published by Librairie Beauchemin (Montreal, 1924–7). 87

3.1 D.G. Jones, *Under the Thunder the Flowers Light Up the Earth* (Toronto, 1977); binding by Pierre Ouvrard. 118

3.2 Edwin Holgate, *Portrait of Stephen Leacock* (1943). 124

4.1 Still from *Le chandail/The Sweater* (1980). 145

4.2 Maggie Muggins doll, 1947. 149

4.3   Selected titles by Mary Grannan, 1942–58.   149

4.4   Sue Ann Alderson and Fiona Garrick (illus.), *Hurry Up, Bonnie!* (Edmonton, 1977).   151

5.1   Jack McClelland promoting books in Saskatoon, February 1976.   176

5.2   Karl Marx, *The Communist Manifesto* (Vancouver, 1919).   189

6.1   [Jean-Paul Desbiens], *Les insolences du frère Untel* (Montreal, 1960).   206

7.1   Pauline Lamy and Alec Leduc, *Journal de bord d'Alfred* (Montreal, 1942).   219

7.2   Andrée Maillet and Robert La Palme (illus.), *Ristontac* (Montreal, 1945).   220

7.3   Girl with textbooks during Education Week, Vancouver, March 1966.   228

7.4   Frank Newfeld, cover designs of the first four books in McClelland and Stewart's New Canadian Library, 1958.   236

7.5   Covers from three series of French-Canadian classics published by Éditions Fides, 1944–68.   240

8.1   Franklin Arbuckle, cover of *Maclean's* (Toronto), 10 November 1956.   246

8.2   *Almanach du peuple 1959* (Montreal, 1958).   252

8.3   Examples of serial pulp fiction from Montreal's Éditions Police Journal, 1955–64.   254

8.4   Adrian Dingle, *Nelvana of the Northern Lights* (Toronto, ca. 1943).   256

8.5   *Scoop Detective Cases* (Toronto), Nov.–Dec. 1943.   257

9.1   Composing room of *L'Action catholique*, Quebec City, 1925.   264

9.2   *Canadian Mother and Child* (Ottawa, 1953) / *La mère canadienne et son enfant* (Ottawa, 1963).   269

9.3   Canadian Pacific Railway Foundation Library bookplate, 1937.   275

11.1   Markoosie, *Harpoon of the Hunter* (Montreal, 1970).   296

11.2   *5 Latviešu Dziesmu Svētki Kanadā 1970* (Toronto, 1970).   304

11.3   The Canadian Small Press / Petites maisons d'édition et revues littéraires.   309

11.4   Byron Wall, ed., *Manual for Draft-Age Immigrants to Canada*, 5th ed. (Toronto, 1970).   314

13.1   Lionel Bisaillon, Linotypist, in the office of *L'Abeille*, Laprairie, Quebec, 1943.   351

13.2   *Das Bergthaler Gemeindeblatt*, Winkler, Manitoba, January 1936.   357

13.3   Albert Bisaillon, compositor, in the composing room of *L'Abeille*, Laprairie, Quebec, 1943.   366

13.4   Anne Trueblood Brodzky and others, *Corridart, 1976–* (Montreal, 1976), with illustrations by Pierre Ayot and others, binding by Pierre Ouvrard.   373

13.5   Bertram Brooker, ed., *Yearbook of the Arts in Canada, 1928–29* (Toronto, 1929).   380

13.6   Thoreau MacDonald, cover of the *Catalogue of Fine, Graphic, and Applied Arts, and Salon of Photography. Canadian National Exhibition, August 22nd to September 6th 1930* (Toronto, 1930).   381

13.7   Carl Dair. *Type Talks* (Hull, QC, 1948).   385

14.1   Librairie J.A. Pony, Montreal, 1950.   394

15.1   Interior of the Thomas Fisher Rare Book Library.   444

17.1   *Clarté, journal d'opinions et d'action populaire* (Montreal), 17 April 1937.   470

17.2   Pegi Nicol MacLeod, *Jane Reading* (ca. 1948).   486

17.3   Barbara Cooney, Brochure for Young Canada's Book Week / La semaine du livre pour la jeunesse canadienne, 1959.   487

18.1   *The Khaki Varsity Book of Songs and Yells* (Ripon, England, [1918?]).   492

18.2   Molly Lamb Bobak, *CWAC Reading a Book* [1943?].   494

18.3   Bookmobile, Prince Edward Island, ca. 1933–6.   497

18.4   Braille being stereotyped at the CNIB Library by Michael Bocian, supervisor of Braille production, 1959.   509

Charts

7.1   Sales of Saint-Denys Garneau in three series issued by Éditions Fides, 1950–79: BCF, Classiques, Nénuphar.   241

14.1   Principal importing countries of books and pamphlets, 1970–9.   390

14.2   Origin of books and pamphlets imported into Canada, 1913–79.   391

Map

I.1   Canada in 1950.   5

Tables

3.1   Production of members of the SÉC and of the UNÉQ.   99

3.2   Production of members of the WUC.   100

3.3   Selected writers' organizations, 1918–80.   126

13.1   Labour in the book trades.   364–5

GENERAL EDITORS' PREFACE

With publication of Volume 3, the final volume of *History of the Book in Canada /
Histoire du livre et de l'imprimé au Canada*, Canadian book historians continue their
dialogue with other scholars writing national histories of the book to define a field
of study, to set goals for further investigation, and to provide foundations for international exchange.

Ours has been a collaborative project of research and writing in French and
English based at sites in Vancouver, Regina, Toronto, Montreal, Quebec, Sherbrooke,
and Halifax. Volume 1, *Beginnings to 1840*, was published in 2004; and Volume 2, *1840–
1918*, in 2005. Each volume has been developed within an expanding community of
book historians, starting with an open conference where a draft table of contents
was presented for discussion. Editors and other members of the volume teams then
worked closely with the authors invited to write sections and case studies. A second
conference for authors of each volume, held after first drafts were received and
distributed, encouraged debate about the coherence of the narrative, the content
and balance of individual chapters, and appropriate documentation.

The team of Volume 3 authors, drawn from a broad range of disciplines, includes
pioneers who first began to investigate the history of books decades ago, as well as
emerging scholars who will carry the work forward. As a group, we have debated the
meaning of the book in Canada in English and in French. While we speak of print in
the lives of Canadians, we recognize the role of oral transmission as well as new
media and formats. In these pages, 'print' is not limited to the book in codex form;
instead it encompasses newspapers, magazines, public print, printed music, and
illustrations in books and periodicals. As each volume of HBiC/HLIC redefines its
'book in Canada,' the meanings shift. For the book trades, the years between 1918

and 1980 were a period of continual change. Nonetheless, patterns set in the early years were durable and define this project of Canadian book history: printing in many languages, the importance of regional presses, and a constant exchange between print and power.

In tandem with the three volumes, HBiC/HLIC has developed five databases to support the inquiries of authors and editors and to establish an infrastructure for ongoing research: Bibliography of the History of the Book in Canada / Bibliographie d'histoire du livre et de l'imprimé au Canada; Canadian Book Trade and Library Index / Index canadien des métiers du livre et des bibliothèques; Catalogues canadiens relatifs à l'imprimé / Canadian Book Catalogues; Imprimés canadiens avant 1840 / Canadian Imprints to 1840; and Manuels scolaires canadiens / Canadian Textbooks.

This volume is printed in Cartier Book, Canada's first roman typeface. Originally created by graphic designer Carl Dair, the proofs of Cartier were released on 1 January 1967 as his Centennial gift to the people of Canada. To ensure that the font made a successful transition into the age of computer typesetting, designer Rod McDonald worked closely with Dair's sketches, respectfully and elegantly interpreting them into Cartier Book.

ACKNOWLEDGMENTS

The project for a *History of the Book in Canada / Histoire du livre et de l'imprimé au Canada* is pleased to acknowledge the support of the Social Sciences and Humanities Research Council of Canada through the Major Collaborative Research Initiative Program for the years 2000 to 2006. This funding has enabled us to bring together editors, authors, students, and colleagues at conferences in Vancouver, Regina, Toronto, Montreal, and Longueuil. We have been able to recruit post-doctoral fellows for each volume and graduate research assistants at all of the sites. Their enthusiastic participation in the volumes and databases has animated every day of this project for the seven editors.

We also wish to thank the site universities for their generous support: Simon Fraser University, University of Regina, University of Toronto, McGill University, Université de Sherbrooke, and Dalhousie University, as well as the library of the National Assembly of Quebec. At the two sites for volume 3, Simon Fraser University and Université de Sherbrooke, we are particularly grateful for the ongoing assistance of support staff and librarians, and the generosity of senior administrators, notably President Michael Stevenson and Dean John Pierce at SFU, and at Université de Sherbrooke, the Faculté des lettres et sciences humaines and the Chaire de recherche du Canada en histoire du livre et de l'édition.

Among the colleagues named on the Project Advisory Board and the Project Editorial Committee, we wish to extend particular thanks to Leslie Howsam, Germaine Warkentin, and Bruce Whiteman, who were involved in the planning of this project, as well as to Sandra Alston, Eric Swanick, and Josée Vincent. We are especially grateful to George L. Parker for his generous consultations. We also thank the peer reviewers of the manuscript for their insightful comments. The work of translation for

Volume 3 has been funded by the Canada Council through the Translation Grant Programme and carried forward by Phyllis Aronoff and Howard Scott (French to English) and Dominique Bouchard, Jean Chapdelaine Gagnon, and Patricia Godbout (English to French). Our publishers, University of Toronto Press and Les Presses de l'Université de Montréal, have encouraged us since we began to plan this project. For their generous support we thank Antoine Del Busso (directeur général) and Yzabelle Martineau (éditrice) at PUM, and at UTP, Bill Harnum (senior vice-president, scholarly publishing), Siobhan McMenemy (editor), Frances Mundy (managing editor), and Ani Deyirmenjian (production coordinator). Ken Lewis was a meticulous copy editor and Val Cooke an inspired designer.

Throughout the project we have depended on the co-operation of libraries, archives, and museums across Canada and abroad. To the following individuals we owe a particular debt of gratitude: Suzanne Ledoux at the Bibliothèque nationale du Québec, Elaine Hoag and many other staff at Library and Archives Canada; Jeannine Green at the Bruce Peel Special Collections, University of Alberta; Richard Landon and Anne Dondertman at the Thomas Fisher Rare Book Library, University of Toronto; and Leslie McGrath at the Osborne Collection of Early Children's Books, Toronto Public Library. In addition we wish to thank Jim Allen and Tom Andrews at Thomas Allen & Son Ltd, and Evelyn Strahlendorf of Hamilton, ON.

We want to underline the special contribution of Janet Friskney, who has fulfilled the role of associate editor for Volume 3 at Simon Fraser University from 2001 to 2006, as well as the essential involvement of two graduate assistants: Frédéric Brisson at Université de Sherbrooke, and Nancy Earle at SFU, who participated in many facets of research and editing. At Sherbrooke, René Davignon meticulously checked citations and sources. Judy Donnelly, the project manager, worked at the heart of this project, dealing with administration and finance as well as research and communications. For Volume 3 she arranged permissions for the illustrations and cheered us on.

Our greatest debt is to the authors who agreed to write these three volumes. They have shared their methodologies and research and broken fresh ground. Together with the editorial team, they have set Canadian book history in new directions.

HISTORY OF THE BOOK IN CANADA / HISTOIRE DU LIVRE ET DE L'IMPRIMÉ AU CANADA

HBiC/HLIC Editorial Team

Project Director: Patricia Lockhart Fleming, Faculty of Information Studies, University of Toronto.

General Editors: Patricia Lockhart Fleming; Yvan Lamonde, Département de langue et littérature françaises, McGill University.

Volume 1 Editors: Patricia Lockhart Fleming; Gilles Gallichan, Reconstitution des Débats, Bibliothèque de l'Assemblée nationale, Québec; Yvan Lamonde.

Volume 2 Editors: Yvan Lamonde; Patricia Lockhart Fleming; Fiona A. Black, School of Information Management, Faculty of Management, Dalhousie University.

Volume 3 Editors: Carole Gerson, Department of English, Simon Fraser University; Jacques Michon, Canada Research Chair in Book and Publishing History, Faculté des lettres et sciences humaines, Université de Sherbrooke.

Editor of Electronic Resources: Bertrum H. MacDonald, School of Information Management, Faculty of Management, Dalhousie University.

Project Manager: Judy Donnelly, Faculty of Information Studies, University of Toronto.

HBiC/HLIC Volume 3 Team

Associate Editor: Janet B. Friskney.

English Text Editors: Elizabeth Hulse, Nancy Earle.

French Text Editors: René Davignon, Yzabelle Martineau.

Translators: Phyllis Aronoff, Howard Scott; Dominique Bouchard, Jean Chapdelaine Gagnon, Patricia Godbout.

Cartographer: Jane Davie.

Indexer: Elizabeth Macfie.

Post-doctoral Fellows: Éric Leroux, Dominique Marquis, Pascale Ryan, Simone Vannucci.

Research Associate: Josée Vincent.

Graduate Research Assistants (Université de Sherbrooke): Frédéric Brisson, Martin Doré, Isabelle Gagnon, Fanie St-Laurent.

Graduate Research Assistants (Simon Fraser University): Nancy Earle, Sarah Brouillette, Jef Clarke, Travis deCook, Jacqueline Hoekstra, Alison McDonald, Catherine Owen, Sandra Walker.

Multi-media Technician: Karel Forestal.

ABBREVIATIONS

ANQM   Archives nationales du Québec à Montréal
BNQ   Bibliothèque nationale du Québec (on 1 January 2006 became Biblio-
          thèque et Archives nationales du Québec)
CAA   Canadian Authors Association
CBC   Canadian Broadcasting Corporation
CE   *Canadian Encyclopedia*
CEGEP   Collège d'enseignement général et professionnel
CNIB   Canadian National Institute for the Blind
ECP   *Encyclopedia of Canada's Peoples*
GRÉLQ   Groupe de recherche sur l'édition littéraire au Québec, Université de
          Sherbrooke
HÉLQ   *Histoire de l'édition littéraire au Québec au XXe siècle*, ed. J. Michon
LAC/BAC   Library and Archives Canada / Bibliothèque et Archives Canada
OCCL   *The Oxford Companion to Canadian Literature*, ed. E. Benson and W. Toye
PBSC/CSBC *Papers of the Bibliographical Society of Canada / Cahiers de la Société
          bibliographique du Canada*
RHAF   *Revue d'histoire de l'Amérique française*
SÉC   Société des écrivains canadiens
SFU   Simon Fraser University
SRC   Société Radio-Canada
UNÉQ   Union des écrivains québécois
WUC   Writers' Union of Canada

CHRONOLOGY

1914–19   War Measures Act, which includes a clause controlling the publication and dissemination of print in Canada, is in force

1919   *Canadian Bookman* is launched in Toronto

1921   Canadian population is 8,787,949
Canadian Authors Association (CAA) is established
New Copyright Act is passed by the Canadian government and comes into effect in 1924

1922   CAA initiates the annual Canada Book Week
Creation of the Concours littéraires et scientifiques du Québec, commonly known as the Prix David

1923   Société des poètes canadiens-français is established in Montreal

1927   Repeal of Regulation 17, adopted by the province of Ontario in 1912, which limited French as a language of instruction to the first two years of primary school

1928   Canada becomes an independent signatory to the Convention of Rome, an amendment to the Berne Convention of 1886 on the international protection of literary and artistic works

1928–9   Royal Commission on Radio Broadcasting (Aird Commission)

1929   In response to a constitutional challenge on the part of five Canadian women, the Judicial Committee of the Privy Council in England recognizes women as 'persons' under the British North America Act, and therefore eligible to hold a seat in the Canadian Senate

1931   Statute of Westminster, passed on 11 December by the British Parliament, negates the Colonial Laws Validity Act of 1865 and establishes the supremacy of the Canadian Parliament. However, at Canada's request, repeal, amendments, or alteration of the British North America Act (which served as Canada's constitution until 1982) are exempted from the statute

1933   Société d'étude et de conférences is founded in Montreal

1935   *Quill & Quire*, English Canada's book-trade journal, is established in Toronto

1936   Canadian Broadcasting Corporation / Société Radio-Canada (CBC/SRC) is established, replacing the Canadian Radio Broadcasting Commission (est. 1932)
The CAA establishes the Governor General's Literary Awards. In 1959 they are taken over by the Canada Council for the Arts, with additional categories in French as well as English
Société des écrivains canadiens is established in Montreal
Maurice Duplessis is elected premier of Quebec, a position he holds from 1936 to 1939 and from 1944 to 1959
'Letters in Canada,' an annual review of Canadian writing, is initiated by the *University of Toronto Quarterly*

1937   Bank of Canada issues the first bilingual banknotes
The Padlock Law, making illegal the printing and distribution of Communist material, is passed in Quebec

1939   National Film Board of Canada is established

1939–45   War Measures Act is in force

1940   Women gain the provincial vote in Quebec, the last major jurisdiction in Canada to grant female suffrage

1943   Mandatory school attendance for children in Quebec comes into effect
École des arts graphiques is established in Montreal

Société des éditeurs canadiens du livre français is established, and will change its name several times: Société des éditeurs canadiens (1960), Association des éditeurs canadiens (1970), Association nationale des éditeurs de livres (1992)

Association des bibliothèques d'institution is founded, and will change its name twice – Association des bibliothèques catholiques (1945), Association canadienne des bibliothécaires de langue française (1948) – before being replaced by the Association pour l'avancement des sciences et des techniques de la documentation (ASTED) in 1974

1944   Académie canadienne-française is established. It is known today as Académie des lettres du Québec

1945   Canadian Conference of the Arts is established

1946   Canadian Library Association / Association canadienne des bibliothèques is established. In 1971 it ceases to be bilingual
Bibliographical Society of Canada / Société bibliographique du Canada is established

1949   Newfoundland enters Confederation

1949–51 Royal Commission on National Development in the Arts, Letters and Sciences (Massey Commission)

1951   The first Salon du livre de Montréal is organized by the Société d'étude et de conférences

1952   Television broadcasting begins, with English programming by the CBC and French programming by Radio-Canada
Canadian Booksellers' Association is established
Canada signs the Universal Copyright Convention (Geneva), which comes into effect in 1955

1953   National Library of Canada / Bibliothèque nationale du Canada is established in Ottawa. In 2004 it joins with the National Archives of Canada to form Library and Archives Canada / Bibliothèque et Archives Canada (LAC/BAC)

1954   Société des libraires grossistes canadiens is formed. It ceases in 1970

1955   Canadian Writers' Conference in Kingston, Ontario

1957   Canada Council for the Arts is established
        Rencontre des poètes is initiated. In 1959 its name changes to Rencontre des écrivains, and in 1972 it is replaced by the Rencontre québécoise internationale des écrivains

1959   Agence de distribution populaire (ADP) is established
        Canadian Literature, the first scholarly journal entirely devoted to Canadian writing, is established at the University of British Columbia

1960   Jean Lesage's victory in the Quebec provincial election marks the beginning of the 'Quiet Revolution,' a decade of transformation that witnesses the final retreat of the Catholic Church from its central role in Quebec society, the rise of the state as the primary force behind the province's political, social, and cultural direction, and the emergence of a new nationalism focused on the French language and the territory within the borders of Quebec
        Royal Commission on Publications (O'Leary Commission)
        Société des libraires canadiens is established in Montreal; it is replaced by the Association des libraires du Québec in 1969

1961   Quebec establishes the ministère des Affaires culturelles
        Commission royale d'enquête sur l'enseignement dans la province de Québec (Parent Commission)
        Conseil supérieur du livre (CSL) is established in Quebec and revives the Salon du livre de Montréal in 1962. The CSL is disbanded in 1980

1962   Canadian Book Publishers' Council becomes independent of the Toronto Board of Trade

1963   *Rapport de la Commission d'enquête sur le commerce du livre dans la province de Québec* (Bouchard Commission)

1963–9 Royal Commission on Bilingualism and Biculturalism (Laurendeau-Dunton Commission)

1964   Quebec creates the ministère de l'Éducation to replace the Department of Public Instruction, and ends the distribution of school prize books
        Société des librairies de détail du Québec is established

1965   Canada adopts its national flag, featuring a red maple leaf

1967   Centennial of Canadian Confederation
            Expo 67, the World's Fair in Montreal
            Bibliothèque nationale du Québec is established. In 2006 it joins with
            the Archives nationales du Québec to form the Bibliothèque et
            Archives nationales du Québec (BAnQ)

1969   Official Languages Act declares English and French to be the official
            languages of Canada, for all purposes of the Parliament and Govern-
            ment of Canada
            Collèges d'enseignement général et professionnel (CEGEPS) are initi-
            ated in Quebec, thereby consolidating the secularization of higher
            education
            Association des libraires du Québec (ALQ) is established

1970   October Crisis in Quebec. Two politically motivated kidnappings
            result in the imposition of the War Measures Act by the federal
            government of Prime Minister Pierre Elliott Trudeau

1970–2   Ontario Royal Commission on Book Publishing

1971   Independent Publishers' Association of Canada (IPAC) is formed. In
            1976 it becomes the Association of Canadian Publishers (ACP)
            Books in Canada, a review magazine dedicated to Canadian titles, is
            launched in Toronto

1972   Association for the Exportation of Canadian Books is established
            Canada Council for the Arts initiates its translation and block grant
            programs for publishers
            Ontario Arts Council initiates funding programs for publishers

1972–84   Commission on Canadian Studies sponsored by the Association of
            Universities and Colleges of Canada (Symons Commission)

1973   Association for Canadian Studies is established
            Corporation des libraires du Québec is established
            Writers' Union of Canada is established
            Canadian Multiculturalism Directorate is established within the
            Department of the Secretary of State following initiation in 1971 of a
            multiculturalism policy. Canada becomes officially multicultural in
            1988 with passage of the Multiculturalism Act

1975 Book and Periodical Development Council is formed

Le Livre d'ici, a weekly literary newsletter, is launched by the Société de promotion du livre (SPL), an organization created by the Canada Council for the Arts. In 1982 this publication becomes *Livre d'ici*, Quebec's monthly book-trade magazine

1977 Bill 101, making French the official language of Quebec, is introduced by the Parti Québécois government

Founding of the Canadian Society of Children's Authors, Illustrators, and Performers / Société canadienne des auteurs, illustrateurs et artistes pour enfants (CANSCAIP)

Société de développement des industries culturelles (SODIC) is formed. In 1995 it becomes the Société de développement des entreprises culturelles du Québec (SODEC)

Union des écrivains québécois (UNÉQ) is established. In 1991 it becomes the Union des écrivaines et écrivains québécois

1978 Association des distributeurs exclusifs de livres en langue française (ADELF) is established

1979 Book Publishing Industry Development Program (BPIDP) is introduced by the federal government

1979–82 Federal Cultural Policy Review Committee (Applebaum/Hébert)

1980 First Quebec referendum on the sovereignty issue

1981 Canadian population is 24,343,181

Loi sur le développement des entreprises québécoises dans le domaine du livre (Bill 51)

1982 Enactment of the Constitution Act and the Charter of Rights and Freedoms

HISTORY OF THE BOOK IN CANADA

1918–1980

EDITORS' INTRODUCTION

In Canada, the history of the book is part of the second revolution of the book, coinciding with the expansion of periodical publications in the eighteenth century.[1] Whereas in Europe books were among the first products of the printing press, in Canada the earliest presses, introduced in the eighteenth century, were used to produce posters and newspapers. In the nineteenth century, the Canadian book still often derived from periodicals. Only in the twentieth century did a book industry develop that was distinct from printing offices and newspapers. After 1918, with the emergence of independent publishing houses, authors' associations, literary and academic awards, and subsidies (the latter particularly notable in Quebec), books became increasingly important in the transmission and promotion of a national culture that was seen as both a heritage and a projection into the future. In the twentieth century, Canadian publishers became architects of culture.[2]

The material in this volume is organized into seven major sections: the role of books and print in Canadian society; authorship; publishing for a wide readership; publishing for distinct readerships; production and design; distribution; and libraries and readers. This order of presentation loosely follows Robert Darnton's model[3] as supplemented by that of Adams and Barker,[4] and it allows us to show how internal and external forces – social, political, intellectual, and commercial – have shaped the world of the book in Canada. Each section includes one or more articles concerning the role of government, a reflection of governments' decisive impact on print culture in Canada during the twentieth century.

The asymmetry of Canadian history is particularly evident in this last volume of *History of the Book in Canada*. In Volume 1, French Canada received substantial attention because of the primacy of French settlement. By Volume 3, English Canada dominates by virtue of its larger population and greater geographical spread, both of which increased when Newfoundland joined Confederation in 1949. The dual personality of the country consolidated as the two major linguistic groups developed separate cultural institutions. In the previous century, many publishers, printers, and booksellers had produced books in both of the country's main languages and often shared the same readership; after 1900 there was a clear division between French-language and English-language markets, and joint commercial publishing efforts were rare. Two production systems developed independently, based on distribution networks whose distinct publishing practices and traditions followed British and American methods in the case of English Canada, and French ones in the case of Quebec. Already visible in the material presentation of books – soft-bound in French and hard-bound in English – this difference was most evident in the types of books sold and in the evolution of the industry itself; engagement with national book policies on the part of English-language and French-language publishers reflected their specific ideological and commercial orientations.

The First World War proved a watershed in this evolution. Following the war, Canada realized that it was a country independent of the colonial empires with which it had previously identified. In English Canada this feeling was very strong, and Canadian participation in the Allied victory was perceived as equivalent to a coming of age. The situation was different in French Canada; after the failure of francophones to obtain recognition for French in the schools of the Western provinces and Ontario, Quebec once again found itself isolated and marginalized in its refusal to take part in what it perceived as an imperial war. This split crystallized in the conscription crisis of 1917–18. In the interwar period, English Canada and French Canada followed separate paths in politics and culture. Montreal and Toronto were confirmed as the country's two major cities, each the book centre of its dominant language group.

Aboriginal peoples, ethnic and religious groups, and visible minorities also continued to use the tools of print culture in order to express their values and affirm their social identities. Periodical publications were their most effective means for reaching their members and creating a sense of community. A distribution map of publications in languages other than English and French would reveal the complex identity of the country, officially bilingual but in reality multicultural. Beginning in the eighteenth century, as we have seen in Volumes 1 and 2 of *History of the Book in Canada*, immigration from Europe and Asia led to flourishing print production in German (since 1787), Gaelic (since 1835), Icelandic (since 1883), and Yiddish and Swedish (both since 1887). Before 1914, further immigration added Finnish, Danish,

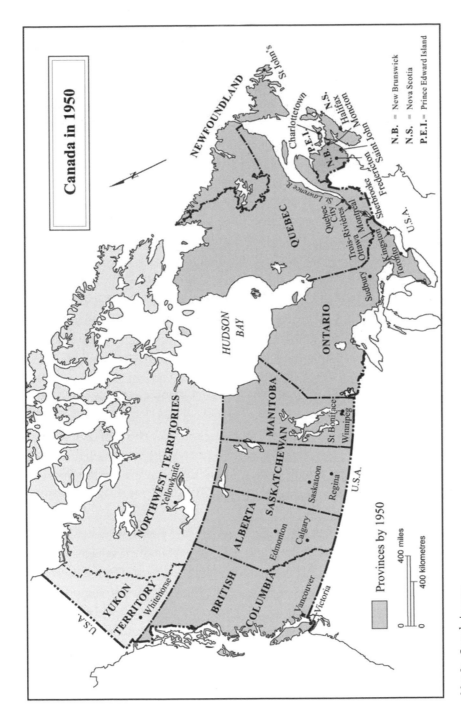

Map I.1 Canada in 1950

Ukrainian, Chinese, Japanese, Arabic, and Bulgarian. After the First World War, there were new waves of immigration from eastern Europe (Serbia, Macedonia, Greece, Poland, and Russia) and northern and central Europe (the British Isles, Scandinavia, and Italy). Immigrants from Asian countries (Japan, China, and India), who were not as well received as other groups, also put out newspapers reflecting their community life. The liberalization of Canadian immigration policy and, in 1971, the adoption of official multiculturalism encouraged the development of print production in a wide range of languages, from Arabic to Urdu; the multiculturalism policy also encouraged print production among the First Nations.

The Great Depression of the 1930s led to stagnation in publishing activity as some firms set up in the previous decade were forced to close. However, the decade also saw the development of new forms of solidarity as collective publications and small magazines brought together socially committed writers and artists, many of whom would become prominent during and after the Second World War. In Quebec there was a liberalization of the Catholic Church, which abandoned direct repression of writers and printed matter and began to give greater recognition to the role of secular writers in the exchange of ideas. However, it would take many years of ideological battle before the Quiet Revolution of the 1960s put a definitive end to the censorship that the church had imposed on the intellectual life of the province since the mid-nineteenth century.

Canada entered the Second World War in September 1939, one week after Great Britain and more than two years before the United States. Its geographic position between Europe and the United States, and the strategic role it played in the war, soon gave it a prominent place on the world stage. One positive consequence of this increased visibility was the start of a new era in its literary relationships with other countries. From June 1940 to May 1945, during the occupation of France, Quebec took over France's role in the publishing of French-language books and their worldwide distribution. Some francophone Montreal publishers responded to the appeal of General de Gaulle and placed their resources and their productive capacity in the service of the Free French, while other, more traditionalist, publishers provided a platform for supporters of the Vichy regime and Marshal Pétain. The war put local concerns on the back burner, and French-language publishing in Canada entered the international arena. While the Toronto book industry was already well integrated into the North American market, the war gave rise to greater national demand for Canadian books, and print runs increased, as did sales. Only the rationing of paper and the shortage of skilled labour slowed this expansion.

A major effect of the war was to shift the lines of international trade. North-south relations between Canada and the United States further developed at the expense of east-west relations between Canada and Britain and France. In Toronto, American publications supplanted those of British publishers when transatlantic shipping was endangered, and the transfer of cultural influence from Great Britain (the hallowed mother country) to the United States (the aggressively friendly neighbour) was accelerated. The penetration of American mass culture into Canada reached an unprecedented level, which was all the more apparent because popular publications were subject to special controls and restrictions during wartime. The country seemed flooded with mass market paperbacks, comic books, popular magazines, and the offerings of book clubs from the United States. Not far behind were the new media of the twentieth century: American movies reached an ever-increasing audience, and American radio entered most Canadian homes, soon followed by television.

In 1928 concern over radio had led to the Royal Commission on Broadcasting (the Aird Commission) and the resulting establishment of the Canadian Radio Broadcasting Commission (Commission canadienne de radiodiffusion) in 1933, followed by the Canadian Broadcasting Corporation (Société Radio-Canada) in 1936. The post-war situation further alarmed the politicians, and in 1949 a royal commission was formed under Vincent Massey, the former Canadian high commissioner in London; its mandate was quickly extended to all spheres of culture. The creation of CBC Television in 1952, the National Library of Canada in 1953, and the Canada Council for the Arts in 1957 were direct results of the Massey Commission's report and proved important steps in ensuring a Canadian cultural space. This movement intensified in the 1960s with the expansion of publishing, libraries, and post-secondary education.

The post-war baby boom led to the ballooning of elementary education in the 1950s, secondary education in the 1960s, and post-secondary education in the 1970s; this dramatic rise in school enrolments also encouraged the development of commercial publishing. Universities provided a favourable context for the expansion of book culture, fostering new publishing structures, such as small literary presses and university presses, as well as the development of scholarly associations in every field of research. In the 1970s the increase in the number of campus bookstores – which then accounted for over one-quarter of retail book sales in Canada – was another result of this unprecedented expansion.

Authors also benefited from the development of these institutions. In addition to enjoying new outlets for their work, they found employment in keeping with their skills; many literary and intellectual writers of the 1960s and 1970s belonged to the university and college community. The media also expanded in these two decades, providing additional job prospects for writers as well as venues for the dissemination of their work. Radio Canada's television series and plays were particularly lucrative for many Quebec writers. The Canada Council for the Arts also contributed to professionalization of authorship, establishing support programs for creators and financing writers' residencies in universities. Government funding thus made it possible for a larger number of authors to earn a living by their pens. Although writers' incomes remained relatively modest, and were often below the poverty line, the increasing number of literary prizes and support programs that were set up by provincial and municipal governments and professional associations allowed many to achieve sufficient autonomy to devote themselves entirely to their writing.

The 1960s was a period of transition for both major language groups. In English Canada, the demographic impact of the baby boom, reaction to the Vietnam War (and the American immigration it provoked), unprecedented economic prosperity, innovative government programs, liberal social policies, second wave feminism, and the nationalism surrounding the centennial of Confederation inspired a new boom in literary and publishing activity. In Quebec, the Quiet Revolution gave added meaning to all these changes, which affected the entire society. Books and printed matter were at the centre of a huge undertaking: a rereading of the past, a rewriting of history, and a reform of political and cultural institutions. Radio, films, and television played a decisive role while contributing to the development of print culture by inspiring and publicizing books and authors. In 1963 the Commission d'enquête sur le commerce du livre au Québec (commission of inquiry into the book industry in Quebec), chaired by Maurice Bouchard, an economics professor at the Université de Montréal, proposed a set of measures that led, among other things, to the withdrawal of religious organizations from education and thus from textbook publishing. Bouchard's main reforms would be implemented some fifteen years later, changing the balance of power between the Quebec industry and foreign companies in the 1980s.

Canada has long been one of the countries with the broadest range of books for sale. In the second half of the twentieth century, more than 70 per cent of its books came from abroad, primarily from France, Britain, and the United States. As a new wave of foreign publishers set up shop, increased protection for domestic companies became imperative. This situation became critical in 1970, when two Canadian companies that possessed symbolic as well as material value – Ryerson Press, in Toronto, and Librairie Garneau, in Quebec City – fell or risked falling under foreign control. These events produced a shock wave in public opinion and forced governments to react by providing financial support to Canadian publishing. In Ontario, the provincial government set up a royal commission on book publishing, which recommended that title grants be provided for Ontario's publishers. In Quebec, the Conseil supérieur du livre, which had instigated the creation of the Bouchard Commission, proposed that limits be placed on the share of foreign capital that could be invested in Quebec companies.

However, it was not until the late 1970s that permanent structures to aid the book industry were established, both federally (the Book Publishing Industry Development Program) and provincially (Act Respecting the Development of Quebec Firms in the Book Industry, RSQ, c. D-8.1). These measures were the result of more than a century of struggle and demands, of individual and collective action by writers, critics, publishers, booksellers, librarians, and readers, determined to create a distinct and viable book culture in Canada. The entire circuit of written communication, as described by Robert Darnton, took part in this undertaking.

Why does Volume 3 stop at 1980? Many factors led to this decision: the need to maintain a certain historical distance from the object of study, limitations of space, and, finally, the symbolic nature of that year, which coincided with the end of one cycle and the start of a new era in many sectors of the book world in Canada. At the beginning of the 1980s, the federal government established the Federal Cultural Policy Review Committee, chaired by Louis Applebaum and Jacques Hébert. There was a reconfiguration of the cultural and political stakes and a reconstitution of production and readership at every level as the generation that had sparked the developments of the 1960s grew older and shifted its focus. At the beginning of the 1980s, increasing economic globalization, the growing cultural dominance of mass media, developments in electronic communication, and the coming digital revolution marked another turning point in the book world. Change was coming not only in production, but also in values and genres, the scope and impact of which remain to be measured.

PART ONE

THE CULTURAL INFLUENCE OF BOOKS AND PRINT IN CANADIAN SOCIETY

chapter 1

THE BOOK AND THE NATION

Imprinting the Nation in Words

A.B. MCKILLOP

In 1918 Canadian intellectuals, politicians, journalists, and educators who imagined their nation in words had five primary vehicles through which to share their ideas: the classroom, the podium, the article, the essay, and the book. The last three, all presented in print, retained their cachet even after the introduction of broadcast media. While radio and television were broader in their immediate reach, their communicative power was less enduring. Print provided Canadian thinkers with a means of lengthier and more complex discourse on the nature of the country, and in turn gave their audience greater opportunity to study, reflect upon, and, in some cases, respond to the arguments put forward. Print's fundamental role as a medium of cultural expression and influence is writ large in the national narratives which construct Canada. Close study of such narratives reveals genealogical and antagonistic relationships among authors and texts. The most provocative and resonant of titles and phrases associated with such publications – *Canadian Mosaic, Colony to Nation, Refus global, Nègres blancs d'Amérique* – have entered the country's cultural lexicon, imprinting themselves so thoroughly on the national consciousness that few citizens feel the need to trace them back to their origins.

At the end of the First World War, Canadians recognized that a 'New Era' had dawned and that new ways must be found to deal with 'the upbuilding of the Canadian Commonwealth,'[1] but no consensus existed about the direction of this reconstruction. Canada was Janus-like, facing in two directions: urban and rural, future and past, English and French.[2] The primary concerns of key intellectual figures, from both English and French Canada, who would reflect on the nature of the country are captured in three words: Nation, Empire, Identity. The notions these words invoke – liberal autonomy, imperial connection, and the pursuit of identity – often framed issues and choices as Canadian intellectuals articulated their vision through the medium of print, pursuing lines of thought established toward the end of the nineteenth century and into the twentieth in influential works by Goldwin Smith, George Parkin, John Watson,[3] and Henri Bourassa. In the post-war period, those who used their knowledge and insight to imagine their nation in words almost always reflected one or another of these approaches, the shifting relations of the Canadian – and Quebec – state within the imperial triangle of Great Britain, France, and the United States forming an integral part of their discourse. Such intellectuals furthered an understanding not only of Canada but of modernity itself.

English Canada to Mid-Century

Until the mid-twentieth century, national narratives produced in English Canada were dominated by the work of professional historians, whose disciplinary training encouraged them to seek insight into the nature of Canada by turning a reflective gaze on the country's past and whose ideas appeared in book-length studies. George M. Wrong consistently argued that emotional loyalty to the British Empire had nurtured a distinctive Canadian 'national type.' While he concurred with Smith's view that English-speaking Canadians and Americans shared a cultural and linguistic bond, he emphasized the dissimilarity of their forms of government, the central message in his collection of lectures, *Canada and the United States: A Political Study* (1921). For Wrong, as for other imperialists in Canada, imperialism was its own form of nationalism.[4] A man who 'laid great stress on communicating the results of historical research to the general reading public,' Wrong also influenced the view of Canada disseminated in schools through his widely adopted textbook, *Public School History of Canada* (1921).[5]

Economic historian Harold A. Innis reinforced the justification for preserving British ties by introducing an important counter-argument to the continentalism of Smith. In *The Fur Trade in Canada* (1932), Innis explored the importance of staple industries as a determining factor in the economic, social, and political development of Canada. The country's geographical axis, he argued, was not north-south, as Smith had insisted, but east-west: the Canadian Shield and its river systems provided an underlying natural unity that made Canada possible as a political entity. Donald Creighton would develop this Laurentian thesis, as it came to be called, in another influential historical study, *The Commercial Empire of the St. Lawrence 1760–1850* (1937), a work that benefited from its inclusion in the prestigious – and well-funded – transnational series, The Relations of Canada and the United States.[6] From books by Innis and his followers, Canadians learned that history and geography situated Canada at the fulcrum of British and American influence, creating a kind of interpretive space that allowed the country's writers, scholars, politicians, and diplomats to occupy a mediating position between the two imperial powers.

To Canadian intellectuals of liberal descent, committed to an evolutionary progressivism, the meaning of Canada lay in the gradual removal of restrictive imperial ties and the growth of political autonomy. Political scientist O.D. Skelton, who became a major adviser to Prime Minister Mackenzie King in 1921, was persuaded by the argument for autonomy put forward in John S. Ewart's *The Kingdom Papers* (1912–17) and *The Independence Papers* (1932). Through Skelton and King, Ewart's ideas led to the reorientation of Canadian foreign policy away from Britain and toward closer co-operation with the United States.[7] John Wesley Dafoe, the influential editor of the *Manitoba Free Press*, popularized the equation of nationalism with autonomy and of liberalism with progress in his many editorials and through his popular prime ministerial biography, *Laurier: A Study in Canadian Politics* (1922). In his wake, historian Frank H. Underhill passed the interwar years writing barbed essays for the *Canadian Forum* (1920–2000) and other publications, providing a sustained critique of the imperial tie. Bruce Hutchison, a popular journalist with access to the inner circle of the Liberal Party, carried on this tradition, all but dismissing the British role in Canada's future in his lyrical meditation on the nation, *The Unknown Country* (1942).

In his survey history of Canada, *Colony to Nation* (1946), historian A.R.M. Lower offered an interpretation drawn from Social Darwinist assumptions: Canada had evolved from immaturity to maturity, oligarchy to meritocracy, dependence to independence. The primary dialectic of Canadian history, he wrote, was the coexistence, often uneasy, of English Canadians and French Canadians, mirroring the larger struggle in North America between material and spiritual values; Lower concluded that Canada was nothing less than an act of faith. The 'distillation' of many years of university lecturing, *Colony to Nation* dominated the English-Canadian textbook market and found a significant general audience. In Lower's words, the book 'descended into strata of Canadian life that [he] had never imagined would be penetrated by formal historical writing.'[8] Indeed, by 1957, historian Kenneth McNaught considered Lower's 'colony to nation' thesis 'the "received" Liberal version of Canadian history.'[9]

Other interpretations of Canada's past sought a middle way between the extremes of imperial allegiance and direct connection to the United States. At a philosophical level, Hegelian influences on Canadian thought held that the one and the many could be reconciled by means of rational dialogue. John Watson's influential and prophetic book *The State in Peace and War* (1919) argued this case, suggesting that the modern state was the best means of creating the conditions by which, in a pluralistic society, the unitary ideal of 'the highest human life' could be achieved.[10] This idealist creed echoes in the dialectical character of Mackenzie King's *Industry and Humanity* (1918), the blueprint for the Canadian future he wrote before becoming prime minister in 1921. Such commitment to the public good and vision of the State helps explain the extraordinary commitment of the public service under the 'Government Generation,' a cohort that came to maturity during and after the Second World War and continued through the years of Lester B. Pearson's prime ministership (1963–8). This wave of secularized Christians, who launched much of Canada's post-war social welfare legislation and peacekeeping diplomatic initiatives, also imprinted the nation in words – often in the official discourse of internal government memoranda and draft bills.[11]

French Canada to the Quiet Revolution

In French Canada prior to 1960, nationalist thought was most keenly expressed through articles, pamphlets, and essays, with the cumulative writings of figures like Henri Bourassa, Lionel Groulx, and Esdras Minville proving particularly powerful. Unlike their English-Canadian counterparts, after 1918 French Canada's intelligentsia did not struggle with any sentiment over the imperial tie, but rather with the difficult heritage it represented. The political meaning and cultural ramifications of Confederation were preoccupations of nationalist discourse, as was the place of French Canada's agrarian and Roman Catholic traditions.

Henri Bourassa established his credentials as a thinker well before 1918, taking up an anti-Empire, nationalist stance during Wilfrid Laurier's prime ministership (1896–1911) and vehemently opposing conscription during the First World War. Based on an excellent grasp of British constitutional principles and practices, Bourassa's anti-imperialism was as ardent as his Roman Catholicism. When it was published in 1902, his pamphlet *Grande-Bretagne et Canada* caused a sensation: it advocated a program of autonomy for Canada within the British Empire, and for the

1.1 Lionel Groulx, [1960]. Courtesy of LAC/BAC, C-16657.

individual provinces within Confederation; it insisted on equal rights and autonomy
of decision-making for his home province and for all Canadians, and promoted a
bicultural state that treated both French and English with respect and equality. As
founder of Montreal's *Le Devoir* (1910–), and editor until 1932, Bourassa was a figure
of great influence whose views circulated widely. Some of his articles were reprinted
in published collections.

In the 1920s, Roman Catholic priest, university professor, and historian Lionel
Groulx overtook Bourassa as the most influential advocate for French Canada (see
illus. 1.1, above). Groulx agreed with Bourassa's stance on participation in foreign
wars but differed with his analysis of Quebec's past, present, and future. For Groulx,
the entire history of Quebec after the Conquest of 1759 was disastrous. The Conquest itself was 'an invasion of barbarians,' while Confederation represented 'a geographical and political absurdity.'[12] Appointed in 1915 to a newly created chair in
Canadian history (a position Bourassa had long advocated), Groulx lectured at the
University of Montreal until he retired in 1949, the only professor to teach Quebec
history in the province for many years.[13] In 1917 he joined the influential nationalist

organization Action française and during the 1920s edited the journal bearing its name. Early in that decade, Groulx tentatively and briefly put forward in *L'Action française* the idea of French Canada working toward an independent state, a vision that was harshly attacked by Bourassa, who continued to see a place for Quebec within Canadian Confederation. From the 1920s to the 1940s, Groulx's influence was keenly felt by the upcoming generation of intellectuals in Quebec, including André Laurendeau, Jean Drapeau, and even Robert Charbonneau. In popular novels as well as weightier tomes, including his four-volume masterpiece *Histoire du Canada français* (1950–60), Groulx envisioned French Canadians as a people with an indomitable will to survive.

Influenced by Groulx, Esdras Minville, an economist, professor, and director of the École des Hautes Études commerciales, enhanced the vision of Quebec as French and Catholic. However, his work underlined the importance of economic development and technological progress for the future of the province. Beginning with *Invitation à l'étude* (1943), he argued that it was possible to link traditional nationalism with economic and social modernity,[14] and thus advocated a distinctly economic nationalism for French Canada. Moreover, as the dominance of British capital came to be replaced by that of American investment in the Canadian economy as a whole, Minville was the first to denounce the grip of U.S. companies in Quebec. Just five years later, *Refus global* sent a shock wave through Quebec's elite. A collection of mimeographed, typewritten pages gathered in a portfolio designed by Jean-Paul Riopelle and privately published in a run of four hundred copies, *Refus global* was a manifesto that attacked the clerical and capitalistic grips on Quebec society, and challenged Premier Maurice Duplessis' authoritarian rule over the province. The title essay was penned by painter Paul-Émile Borduas, and co-signed by fifteen other members of his artistic circle. For his audacity, Borduas was banned from his livelihood of teaching art in Quebec and would ultimately die in exile in France; however, the publication of *Refus global* was a signal moment, foreshadowing the transformation of the province that would occur during the Quiet Revolution of the 1960s.

Of equal significance during the 1940s and 1950s were the cumulative efforts of Dominican priest and professor Father Georges-Henri Lévesque, whose religious order and university affiliation helped him weather Duplessis' displeasure. A liberal Catholic and democrat, he wished to dissociate the church from French-Canadian nationalism. Lévesque expressed his opinions on religious and social matters in a variety of periodicals, including *La Revue dominicaine* (Montreal, 1895–61) and *Ensemble* (Quebec City, 1940–83). At Université Laval, he reorganized the school of social sciences, and under its auspices trained a new generation of sociologists (Maurice

Lamontagne, Arthur Tremblay, Fernand Dumont, Jean-Charles Falardeau, Guy Rocher, Léon Dion, and Gérard Dion) and labour organizers (Jean Marchand and Marcel Pepin), all of whom would become important figures in the Quiet Revolution.

Canada and Quebec after Mid-Century

After mid-century, serious problems in Canada's social, economic, political, and cultural institutions could no longer be ignored. Waves of immigration, especially after the mid-1890s, had transformed the country from Ontario westward into a sociologically heterogeneous mixture of Native peoples, settlers, urban workers, and new immigrants. In 1938 Canadian Pacific Railway employee and publicist John Murray Gibbon had published a book, *Canadian Mosaic*, whose title suggests a cultural ideal of tolerant pluralism and the peaceful commingling of peoples.[15] Yet the phrase more accurately reflected the failure of an assimilationist ideal that had been central to the socialization of immigrants for generations. The Depression, in turn, had exposed raw fissures in the country's social and regional equality, circumstances brought into relief by the influential Royal Commission on Dominion-Provincial Relations (1944). The first of three federal investigations that would imprint themselves on the structure of Canada at a fundamental level, the commission report was grounded in a statistical analysis and recommended fiscal solutions aimed at a greater degree of social and economic equality among provinces, including the idea of the federal government redistributing tax money more equally between the provinces. Joseph Smallwood considered Canada's fledgling efforts in this direction a strong point in the country's favour as he first set out to woo Newfoundland's population into Confederation in the mid-1940s (see illus. 1.2, p. 20).[16]

The shift in power and influence from Britain to the United States after the Second World War radically challenged perceptions of Canada's relation to both countries, as well as the nature of culture and cultural influence. Arnoldian humanism, with its aesthetic ideal of pursuing 'the best that is known and thought in the world,' slowly lost authority in Canadian universities, and the leviathan of mass media and American popular culture began to displace British literature from its role as the foundation of Canadian humanistic understanding.[17] Until the 1960s, the dominant response to such challenges was defensive, with the most comprehensive and imaginative countercharge arising out of the second federal investigation, the Royal Commission on National Development in the Arts, Letters and Sciences. Mandated to report on Canadian cultural and scientific institutions, in 1951 the

1.2 Men in Corner Brook, Newfoundland, reading the St John's *Evening Telegram*, its headlines announcing the result of Newfoundland's second referendum, held 22 July 1948, which brought the province into Confederation. Courtesy of LAC/BAC, Chris Lund / National Film Board, Photothèque collection / PA-128007. Reproduced with the permission of the Minister of Public Works and Government Services Canada (2005).

commission instead assessed the state of the national soul, an appraisal discussed in detail by Paul Litt later in this chapter. Historian Hilda Neatby, the commissioner who drafted much of the report, two years later published the provocatively titled *So Little for the Mind*, an indictment of the ideas of American progressivist education in Canadian schools. Allied in a rearguard battle against the threat of continental integration and the encroachment of republican values and American mass culture, another conservative historian, W.L. Morton, published in 1961 a series of lectures entitled *The Canadian Identity*; in this volume, he stressed Canada's commitment to monarchy and its northern nature, the latter an idea that journalist Pierre Berton, no conservative, had already popularized in his Governor General's Award–winning *The Mysterious North* (1956).

Canadian intellectuals in the 1960s, energized by the secularization of society, the Quiet Revolution in Quebec, the presence of the baby boom generation in college and university life, and the controversial decision to adopt a national flag for Canada, renewed the debate over Canadian nationalisms and American imperialism. While the indictment of Quebec's Department of Public Instruction voiced by *Les insolences du frère Untel* (1960) signalled an early tremor in the Quiet Revolution, Frank H. Underhill's cautionary yet optimistic Massey Lectures, published as *The Image of Confederation* (1964), chronicled the decline of British influence, echoing Bourassa's earlier critique of imperial ties and colonial status. Underhill's book marked the apotheosis of the liberal-autonomist view of Canada, with its gravitation toward continental integration, just as Carl Berger's seminal study of Canadian imperialists, *The Sense of Power*, would underpin the transatlantic imperial-nationalist vision when it appeared in 1970. Equally implicated in the English-Canadian nationalism that characterized the 1960s and 1970s was George Grant's new critique of liberal dominance, which he introduced in *Lament for a Nation* (1965), and elaborated upon in *Technology and Empire* (1969) and *English-Speaking Justice* (1974). In Grant's view, the conscription of science and technology by an instrumental reason – thinking that divorced ethical ends from technological advancement for the purpose of economic and political 'modernization' – had transformed liberalism from being simply one ideology among others into a world view protected and propelled by technology and from which there could now be no escape. To Grant, the impossibility of conservatism meant the impossibility, also, of Canada. The era of the 'universal and homogeneous state' had arrived.[18]

For those intellectuals focused on Canada's domestic milieu in the post-war period, however, the issue was not homogeneity but heterogeneity. A restrictive immigration policy between the wars had maintained the illusion of a country populated by two founding cultures, French and English, which themselves existed in uneasy balance. Although Hugh MacLennan's award-winning and widely circulated novel, *Two Solitudes* (1945; translated as *Deux solitudes*, 1963), had advocated greater accommodation between the two cultures, many felt that its title captured the tension of the nation in a phrase. In 1963 a third federal investigation, the Royal Commission on Bilingualism and Biculturalism (B&B), set out to determine how 'an equal partnership between the two founding races' might be achieved, without overlooking the cultural contributions of other ethnic groups.[19]

Co-chairman André Laurendeau brought definite ideas to the commission, having had frequent occasion to refine his vision of Canada through earlier positions as editor of *L'Action nationale*, leader of the Bloc populaire, editor-in-chief of *Le Devoir*, and contributor to *Le Magazine Maclean*. For Laurendeau the national question in relation to French Canada concerned the development of a collective identity, as well as the defence of rights and institutions. As the province of Quebec was the sole agency that could promote this cause, Laurendeau advocated shared sovereignty and political equality between federal and provincial powers, a view supported by the evident vitality of two distinct cultures.[20] Convinced that centralization of power at the federal level would only harm Canada, in reflections like those collected in *Ces choses qui nous arrivent: Chronique des années 1961–1966* (1970), Laurendeau promoted a renewed federalism in a profoundly reformed Canadian political system. A significant outcome of the commission he co-chaired was the federal Official Languages Act, which declared the 'equality of status' of English and French in Parliament and the Canadian public service. Adopted in 1969 under the new federalism of Prime Minister Pierre Elliott Trudeau, it was a point of agreement between two men whose opinions otherwise diverged over the future of Quebec. Trudeau's preference for a strong federal government and a pan-Canadian bilingualism – two ideas founded on the rejection of French-Canadian nationalism – had been articulated at length in his essay collection *Le fédéralisme et la société canadienne-française* (1967; trans. *Federalism and the French Canadians*, 1968), opinions he had first begun to refine while contributing to *Cité libre* in the 1950s.

The nationalist ideas of Claude Ryan, director of *Le Devoir* from 1964 to 1978, developed significantly following the definition of a bicultural society established by the B&B Report. As editor of *Le Devoir*, Ryan advocated modification of the Canadian constitution. Convinced of the special status of Quebec, he opposed Trudeau but defended the federal state because he felt that French Canadians would be better served by remaining within Canada. By contrast, Pierre Vallières's *Nègres blancs d'Amérique* (1968; trans. *White Niggers of America*, 1971) shocked readers with its assessment of the social status of French Canadians, though the author tempered his call to arms several years later in *L'urgence de choisir* (1971; trans. *Choose!*, 1972), opting instead to support the potential for political reform represented by René Lévesque's Parti Québécois. Lévesque, who believed the future of Quebec lay in political sovereignty in conjunction with an economic union with Canada, had published in 1968 *Option Québec*, the manifesto which became the political program of his party, founded the same year. Using the B&B Report as his foundation, Lévesque argued the presence of two nations and two societies in Canada to justify an utter revision of the role of Quebec in Confederation, a point of view that would be at the centre of the Referendum of 1980.

In English Canada the debate over empire, nation, and identity took a new turn after the self-congratulation of the Canadian Centennial, the success of Montreal's Expo 67, and the B&B Report, the fourth volume of which was devoted to other Canadian ethnic groups. Constitutionally bicultural as of 1969, Canada was also recognized to be sociologically multicultural. In 1971 the Trudeau government adopted an official policy of multiculturalism, a vision of Canada in which children of the 1970s would be schooled, and which would subsequently be enshrined in the Canadian Charter of Rights and Freedoms and in the Multiculturalism Act of 1988 as a 'defining feature of Canadian society.'[21] Canada's new generation of professional historians, the first whose own backgrounds mirrored the country's pluralistic reality, turned their attention to social history, heeding Ramsay Cook's call of 1967 to stop 'deploring our lack of identity,' and instead 'attempt to understand and explain the regional, ethnic and class identities that we do have.'[22] By the late 1970s, the magisterial edifice of the Laurentian interpretation of Canadian history, little willing to accommodate ethnic, gendered, or class-based diversity, crumbled as the governing interpretive paradigm of Canadian history offered within the universities. When it came to writing national historical narratives, journalists would take the lead for the remainder of the century. Heading this vanguard was Pierre Berton, whose bestselling *The National Dream* (1970) and *The Last Spike* (1971) built on English Canada's mythological investment in the Canadian Pacific Railway, the second book winning a Governor General's Award.

As Canada edged toward a new millennium, the country's intellectuals found it increasingly difficult to confine imaginings of empire, nation, and identity within borders of any kind. Symbolic of the new Canada was writer and literary critic Naïm Kattan, an Iraqi-born Jew who chose to write in French after he arrived in Canada in 1954. Kattan explored individual and national identity, usually within settings of displacement and exile. His autobiographical novel *Adieu, Babylone* (1975; trans. *Farewell Babylon*, 1976), portrayed the artist as a young emigrant, while his three volumes of criticism, *Ecrivains des Amériques* (1972–80), offered a comprehensive and coherent assessment of 'American literature' in its broadest sense, including Latin America and Canada. Appointed head of the Writing Section of the Canada Council in 1967, Kattan played a major role in furthering understanding and co-operation on several levels: between Muslims, Christians, and Jews; between Canadians and Americans; and between Canada's two traditional cultures. '[T]he only groups whose identity is clear and precise,' he wrote in 1977, 'are dead groups ... The history of Canada is made up not of the demarcation by each group of its own territory, but of compromise, of influences endured or accepted, of bonds one welcomes or to which one becomes resigned.'[23]

Government Policy and Allophone Cultures

PAUL HJARTARSON

In 1918 Canada was fighting two wars: one in Europe; and another at home against 'enemy aliens,' socialist revolutionaries, and militant labour activists. In the logic of the day, a view that held sway past mid-century, socialist revolutionaries and labour activists, like enemy aliens, were invariably foreign-born immigrants who spoke in languages other than French or English. Although the First World War ended in 1918, Canada's war against the enemy within continued for many decades and shaped the Dominion's understanding of, and relation to, allophones (persons whose first language was neither English nor French) and the print cultures to which these communities gave rise. Government documents record the history of Canada's attitudes toward, and regulation of, immigrant communities; they reveal that allophone newcomers were welcome more for their manpower than for their cultural diversity. Before the 1960s, English Canada conceived of itself as 'a monocultural, monolingual, single-nation state and made no apologies for being so.'[24] Despite the fact that one-third of Canada's population was French-speaking, Anglo conformity was the expectation for new immigrants, and 'ethnic identification' was perceived as 'at best a transitional stage, a way station on the road from immigrant to true Canadian.'[25] The history of Canada's relation to allophones is evident in such documents as the War Measures Act (5 George 5, 1914, c. 2), Criminal Code amendments, the Defence of Canada Regulations (1939), and various Immigration Acts. Allophone immigrants who sought to retain their languages and print cultures struggled against considerable odds. It was only in the 1960s that Canada began to value cultural pluralism.

Even before the war, the Canadian government was increasingly anxious about its ability to assimilate allophone immigrants. Three events turned that worry into near panic: the first was Canada's entry into the First World War, which, virtually overnight, transformed more than half a million allophone new Canadians into 'enemy aliens,' that is, nationals of countries with which Canada was now at war. The second was the success of the Bolshevik revolution of 1917 in Russia, which led to widespread fear of socialist revolutionaries within Canada's allophone communities. The third was increasing labour militancy, culminating in the Winnipeg General Strike of 1919. The War Measures Act, passed in 1914, granted the Governor-in-Council virtually unlimited powers of 'arrest, detention, exclusion, and deportation'[26] and was used to outlaw the printing, publication, or possession of documents in any enemy language or in Russian, Ukrainian, or Finnish. Although these measures were lifted in 1919, the Dominion revised the Immigration Act and the Criminal Code to strengthen the government's power to restrict immigration, deport undesirables, and arrest on mere suspicion anyone thought to be involved in an unlawful organization or in the importation, printing, publication, or distribution of any seditious material. Simple possession of such material also continued to be an offence. Those in power directed these measures largely against allophone communities believed to harbour threats to the country's welfare. At the same time, the Dominion redoubled its efforts to 'Canadianize' its allophones, focusing this assimilative work on the children of immigrants and on compulsory schooling in English language and culture (see illus. 1.3, p. 26). Although Anglo conformity had always been expected of allophone immigrants, post-war pressure to assimilate rapidly was intense. Even members of 'preferred' immigrant communities from northern Europe learned the wisdom of assimilating quickly. The print culture of all allophone communities suffered, and some, notably that of German-speaking Canadians,[27] never fully recovered.

In the immediate post-war years, social and political acceptability displaced economic factors as primary criteria in the selection of immigrants. As prosperity returned, agricultural and industrial demands for labourers became acute. Canada's inability to secure sufficient immigrants from Britain prompted the federal government to sign an agreement with the Dominion's two national railways to recruit from 'non-preferred' nations. The influx of immigrants under the Railway Agreement (1925), particularly from central Europe, sparked a national debate. Speaking in the House of Commons on 7 June 1928, opposition leader R.B. Bennett declared, 'We must still maintain that measure of British civilization which will enable us to assimilate these people to British institutions, rather than assimilate our civilization to theirs.'[28]

In the early 1930s, with the onset of the Depression, Canada restricted immigration to white British and American subjects and to agriculturalists with economic

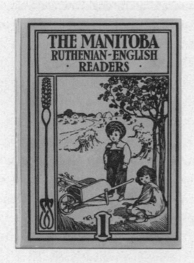

106   **Wheat.**

WHEAT.

My father is a farmer, and when I grow to be a man I shall be a farmer too. There is always something to see and something to do on a farm.

I have often seen my father sow the wheat. He sows it with a seed-drill. It takes him a long time to get it all into the ground.

When the wheat is in the ground the sun and the rain help it to grow. It grows very rapidly.

Пшениця.   107

ПШЕНИЦЯ.

Мій тато є фармером і коли я виросту, то буду фармером також. На фармі є завсїгди на що подивити ся і є що зробити.

Я часто бачив мого тата, як він сїяв пшеницю. Він сїє єї сївачкою. Єму забирає се довший час, аби все посїяти.

Коли пшениця в земли, то сонце і дощ помагають їй рости. Она росте дуже скоро.

1.3 *The Manitoba Ruthenian-English Readers*, I and II, detail from second reader (London: T. Nelson & Sons, [1913?]). By 1916 more than four hundred school districts in the Prairie provinces offered instruction in both English and Ukrainian (Ruthenian). Manitoba and Alberta abolished their programs that year, but Saskatchewan schools continued teaching in both languages until 1919. Courtesy of the Adam Shortt Library of Canadiana, Special Collections, University of Saskatchewan.

means, made the Communist Party illegal under the Criminal Code, and clamped down on allophone immigrant workers and activists, arresting and deporting thousands. Many Canadians considered allophones, even those born in Canada, as 'foreigners' who took jobs from members of the dominant community and whose print cultures were to be viewed with distrust. This exclusionary mode rendered Canada reluctant to accept refugees of any kind, including Jews fleeing Nazi persecution, whose plight was dismissed with the notorious statement: 'None is too many.'[29] When Canada entered the Second World War, it moved against enemy aliens under authority of the Defence of Canada Regulations (passed in 1939 pursuant to the War Measures Act), which empowered the government 'to detain without trial both immigrants and Canadian citizens on the mere suspicion of hostile intent, rather than on proof of such.'[30] Suspicion fell disproportionately on members not just of enemy alien communities but on any allophones suspected of harbouring fifth columnists, communists, or communist sympathizers. These regulations enabled the repression of the entire Japanese-Canadian community – the vast majority of whom were Canadian-born and therefore citizens – through interning them, closing down their newspapers, and seizing their property.

Early in the war, the Dominion decided not only to police allophone communities and print cultures closely, but also to educate their members in the virtues of Canadian citizenship, usually in English, as in Watson Kirkconnell's pamphlet *Canadians All: A Primer of Canadian National Unity*, issued in 1941 by the minister of public information (part of which also appeared in French as *Tous canadiens*). Hence, the government established the Nationalities Branch in the Department of National War Services and an advisory body, the Committee on Co-operation in Canadian Citizenship. In 1944 the Nationalities Branch was reorganized as the Citizenship Division. Unlike other wartime agencies, the latter was not disbanded at war's end but in 1950 was transferred to the Secretary of State and in 1993 moved to the newly created Department of Citizenship and Immigration.

Fearing a recession after the war, the federal government maintained restrictions on immigration until the post-war boom forced its hand. When Prime Minister Mackenzie King announced in 1947 that Canada was opening its doors to European immigrants, he promised to proceed cautiously and 'relate immigration to absorptive capacity.' 'The people of Canada,' he declared, 'do not wish to make a fundamental alteration in the character of their population through mass immigration.'[31] The same retention of earlier ethnic and racial priorities underscored the Immigration Act of 1952 (1 Elizabeth 2, 1952, c. 325). The first since 1910, the act codified existing practices and instituted Cold War security checks. Sustained post-war economic expansion, however, accentuated the need for immigrant labour and the influx of immigrants. The more than two million who arrived between 1946 and 1962[32] revitalized allophone communities, renewing both the supply of heritage-language speakers and the demand for allophone publications. The continuing economic growth of the 1950s pushed Canadian society toward a more tolerant view of immigrants and their many languages.

The United Nations' formulation of a universal declaration of human rights in 1948 (drafted by Canadian John Peters Humphrey) inflected Canada's treatment of its allophone communities. Prior to signing the declaration, in 1946 Canada passed the Canadian Citizenship Act (10 George 6, 1946, c. 15) and in 1947 repealed the Chinese Immigration Act of 1923 (2 George 6, 1947, c. 19). Transformation of the British Commonwealth, as colony after colony achieved independence, led the Canadian government in 1956 to loosen its immigration policies and slowly begin to admit immigrants from India, Pakistan, and Ceylon.[33] Following Soviet suppression of the Hungarian uprising of 1956, the strength of the Canadian economy and the sympathy created in the media for anti-communist 'freedom fighters' prompted a reluctant government to open its doors to Hungarian refugees. The success of that resettlement program shaped Canada's response to later refugee crises in Czechoslovakia, Uganda, Chile, Vietnam, Laos, Cambodia, and elsewhere. In 1962 Canada introduced new regulations designed to remove racial and ethnic discrimination from immigration policy. It was not until 1967, however, that 'all vestiges of racial and ethnic discrimination were officially expunged from Canadian immigration regulations and procedures,' the motivation being 'less to open the country to the arrival of non-whites than to clean up Canada's international image and bring immigration legislation into line with the focus on human rights in public policy more generally.'[34]

In the 1960s, perhaps the most pressing force for change was Canada's need to reconcile its long-standing demand for Anglo conformity with the concept of two founding nations and the aspirations of francophones, particularly in light of the Quiet Revolution in Quebec. In 1963 the federal government established the Royal Commission on Bilingualism and Biculturalism to examine relations between the two founding language groups. The Dominion's need to come to terms with its francophone population led to confirmation of official bilingualism at the same time as the growing political strength of 'other ethnic groups,' Canada's international commitments, and its continuing desire for immigrants led to adoption of multiculturalism as government policy in 1971 and to passage of the Canadian Multiculturalism Act in 1988 (35-36-37 Elizabeth 2, 1988, c. 31). According to Prime

Minister Pierre Elliott Trudeau, Canada had two official languages but no official culture, 'nor [did] any ethnic group take precedence over any other.'[35] This affirmation
of cultural egalitarianism was grounded in the separation of language from culture.
While allophone cultures were validated, multiculturalism was set firmly in a bilingual framework: Canada would conduct its business in English and French, and allophones would be expected to learn one of the official languages.

The year in which Canada announced its multiculturalism policy was also the
first year in which the majority of immigrants were of non-European heritage.[36] That
trend has continued, revitalizing older allophone communities, such as the Chinese,
and enabling new language groups, religions, and cultures to establish themselves.
These communities almost invariably organize print cultures in their heritage languages, a topic further discussed by Catherine Owen in chapters 3 and 11.

Intersections between Native Oral Traditions and Print Culture

BLANCA SCHORCHT

A tradition of textualizing Aboriginal discourses in Canada began in the seventeenth
century, with the apparently literal documentation of Native speech in the *Jesuit Relations*. A written Inuit literature commenced in 1745 with the London publication of
'A Greenland Ode,' an Inuit poem with an interlinear English translation. Sharing a
common language expressed in a number of dialects, the Inuit were taught to read
and write in Inuktitut by missionaries and were almost universally literate by the
turn of the twentieth century.[37] However, because First Peoples experienced the
power of print through a barrage of Christian materials translated into Aboriginal
languages, as well as in legal documents such as treaties, Native leaders generally
regarded the medium with feelings ranging from caution to suspicion.[38] Pauline
Johnson's Cree spokeswoman of 'The Cattle Thief' (1894) articulates the sense of
betrayal associated with print: 'How have you paid us for our game? how paid us for
our land? / By a *book*, to save our souls from the sins *you* brought in your other
hand.'[39]

The twentieth century witnessed a significant change in the interface between
indigenous oral traditions and print culture in Canada, a shift marked in terms of

genre, voice, and narrative authority. Over the decades Aboriginals achieved increasing prominence in many written genres, ranging from ethnographic story collections, autobiographies, and life narratives to poetry, drama, and fiction. The development of the latter three mirrored the so-called renaissance of Native literatures that occurred in the United States during the late 1960s and came to fruition in Canada in the early 1980s.

The autonomous Aboriginal literary activity in English that began in the 1960s deviated significantly from the previously dominant written forms associated with First Peoples, such as translations of the Bible into Inuktitut and Cree syllabics and, later, texts emerging from the practice of 'salvage anthropology.' The overall trends in the new written literature, moreover, reflect the oral traditions out of which this literature arose. While early collections compiled and edited by missionaries and anthropologists often preserved narratives as objects or print artifacts, later twentieth-century writing controlled by Aboriginal authors draws on the on-going genre conventions of oral storytelling performance. Translating features of oral narrative into mainstream forms such as the novel, contemporary First Peoples' literatures work to decolonize both the English language and its genres of literary expression, while transforming them into uniquely Aboriginal representations.

Until after the Second World War, interest in Indigenous oral traditions continued to be refracted through the romanticized and imperialistic ideals of the anthropology of the day. Such research led to seminal collections such as those of Franz Boas, who published widely in both English and German. Boas's major contribution to the study of First Peoples' narrative traditions lay in his insistence that, in order to understand a culture, one must develop a thorough understanding of its language and stories. His publications on the Canadian Northwest include *Bella Bella Tales* (1932) and *Kwakiutl Tales* (1935) as well as numerous, and comprehensive, ethnographic studies.

Despite widespread European interest in the Native peoples of North America, the majority of research publications appeared in English. These were the work of a fairly cohesive group of government-affiliated anthropologists in Canada, most of whom maintained close connections with Boas. Quebec-born Marius Barbeau wrote extensively on French-Canadian folklore and songs, as well as on Huron and Wyandot mythology. English was the preferred language for Barbeau's anthropological works on Native peoples, such as *The Downfall of Temlaham* (1928) and *Tsimsyan Myths* (1961). Most of the research of other anthropologists writing at this time, including the linguist Edward Sapir, James Teit, John Swanton, Harlan Smith, and Diamond Jenness, occurred in the West, particularly British Columbia, where it was believed that as a result of their later contact with Euro-Canadians, Native peoples were more likely to live in 'pure' and 'traditional' states. Jenness also spent three years in the Arctic, where he wrote several volumes on Inuit administration and governance. That white, male anthropologists mediated First Peoples' oral traditions remains problematic to this day.

Because the mandate of Boasian anthropology situated Native peoples in an imagined pre-contact past, anthropological collections of narratives often focused on the preservation of orally performed stories as 'myths' and 'legends.' The rush to capture these accounts in print accorded with the impetus to archive what were widely perceived as the disappearing cultures of Aboriginal peoples in Canada. Ironically, while anthropologists were busy 'salvaging' First Peoples' narratives and other cultural artifacts, governments were implementing explicit policies of cultural assimilation, through residential schools and other institutions, which were designed to eliminate Aboriginal languages and traditions.

In anthropological collections, more emphasis was placed on classifying recurring motifs for folkloric analysis than on distinguishing the original occasion and duration of each performed event – or its meaning. Creation stories or origin 'myths,' migration narratives, and stories of 'supernatural' power were emphasized in books like Jenness's *The Corn Goddess and Other Tales from Indian Canada* (1956). The 'authenticity' of such stories was generally determined by the collector, typically a scholar foreign to the culture and language. Other kinds of narratives (historical, personal, or contemporary) that might have provided a broader range of content tend to be absent from the printed record, or minimally represented. In the case of sexually explicit material, the extent to which these stories may have been edited or elided from the archive remains an interesting question. Despite its popularity, Herbert T. Schwarz's *Tales of the Smokehouse* (1974) remains one of the few published books of Aboriginal erotic stories – Ojibwa, in this instance.

Individual storytellers were seldom identified or recognized; in a few significant exceptions, however, the collector/anthropologist worked closely with an 'informant' who is identified in the written texts – Boas with George Hunt and John Swanton, for example, and Barbeau with the Tsimshian chief William Beynon. There are several possible explanations for the storytellers' anonymity. Anthropologists sought to construct their discipline as one based on neutral scientific observation; the contradictions inherent in 'participant observation' required them to distance both themselves and their informants from the subject material at hand. As well, within Native communities, there may have been questions concerning ownership of stories. In cultures where stories remain powerful entities, potential ethical problems could be avoided by protecting the storyteller's identity. However, the consequent lack of contextualization in these early print collections has led to on-going difficulties in interpreting these orally performed stories. Problems range from translation issues to the question of who was, in fact, controlling the recording process. Narrative authority potentially resides in both the storyteller and the person doing the recording: the collector holding the pen or operating the tape machine may have elicited the very stories that he/she *wanted* to record.

The process of translating orally performed stories into print was often twofold, from a Native language into English, and from oral dramatization into written genres of expression. Stylistic and literary qualities which informed the original meaning of stories were often overlooked in favour of emphazing social function and plot structure. Repetitions, paratactic language structures (the placing of clauses side by side, without linking words to indicate coordination or subordination), and other performative features coherent with oral genre conventions and integral to oral presentation seldom appeared in the written texts. The resulting narratives became print artifacts that retained little sense of their oral roots. Teit's *Mythology of the Thompson Indians* (1912; reprint, 1975), for instance, while bereft of any overt content that suggests European contact, reads more like Aesop's fables than like orally performed stories from an Aboriginal culture.

During the 1960s, as Canada shifted toward more inclusive multicultural attitudes and initiatives, interest in the artistic and literary productions of Aboriginal peoples also increased. The rise in Aboriginal writing led to the further development of First Nations publishing and increasing autonomy for Native writers, as discussed further by Cheryl Suzack in chapter 11. Between 1960 and 1980, Aboriginal writing in genres such as history, autobiography, and fiction, mostly in English, increased exponentially. Many popular early collections were reissued, often with new illustrations and formal recognition of the original storytellers. The stories in *The Adventures of Nanabush: Ojibway Indian Stories* (1979), as told by Sam Snake, Chief Elijah Yellowhead, Alder York, David Simcoe, and Annie King, for example, first appeared in the 1930s under the names of Emerson and David Coatsworth. Interest in Inuit writing also grew: Markoosie's *Harpoon of the Hunter* (1970) was eventually translated into more than a dozen languages (see illus. 11.1, p. 296). Such 'ethnographic' books contributed to a sense of Aboriginal identity and community during a period when the introduction of official multiculturalism policies encouraged public recognition of Native cultures.

By the 1970s, decisions about how to represent Aboriginal oral narratives in print were frequently shared between storyteller and editor, yet the nature of some of these decisions could still be obscured by the textualization process. In the case of the wildly popular *My Heart Soars* (1974), for instance, the reader is led to believe that the volume was indeed written by its putative author, Chief Dan George. As a collection of thoughts and story fragments presented in blank verse, the book appears to elucidate George's point of view as inherently Aboriginal and, therefore, in direct contrast with European written and philosophical traditions. But George's long-time friend and biographer, Hilda Mortimer, suggests that George's book was ghost-written and argues that writing was neither part of George's 'tradition' nor his mode of expression.[40]

In contrast, *The Days of Augusta* (1973) is one of the first books to represent a version of 'Rez English' dialect in written form in order to convey a sense of orality – and, perhaps, cultural authenticity – in the written text. The book includes a wide range of stories as told to Jean E. Speare by Mary Augusta Tappage, many represented in a blank verse that replicates the rhythms and conventions of oral storytelling. The book is a blend of Shuswap stories, Tappage's life history, and other recollections. The variety in the book's narrative formats and its preservation of features from oral storytelling give readers the sense that Tappage guided both the recording and textualization processes. Basil Johnston's *Moosemeat and Wild Rice* (1974) similarly insists on the use of dialect in represented speech in a manner that refuses to allow readers to stereotype Native peoples as simple, naïve, or uneducated. Such books reveal how First Peoples' writing resists the ideology of stereotyping often associated with the translation of spoken dialect into written forms.

The growing number of Native writers publishing in Canada during the 1970s makes it less easy to categorize their writing in terms of binary oppositions such as oral versus written. The idea that First Peoples remain immersed in orality, while mainstream Canadian culture is almost exclusively print-based, perpetuates outdated stereotypes. It also overlooks the fact that the Inuit have been translating foreign texts into Inuktitut syllabics (originally developed by missionaries) since the early eighteenth century. Regarding the oral as the opposite of writing further implies that translation between the two is impossible, and repeats essentialized ideas correlating language with identity.

Alma Greene's *Forbidden Voice: Reflections of a Mohawk Indian* (1971) and Maria Campbell's frequently reprinted *Halfbreed* (1973) reflect the rise of a new kind of multi-genred literature from Native writers. *Halfbreed* – part autobiography, part memoir, part fiction – is written in the first person using a narrative voice reminiscent of diary-writing, a genre that is closely linked to oral modes of expression. *Forbidden Voice* mixes Greene's personal narrative with inherited Mohawk stories, weaving together multiple traditions to blend an older history into present time.

Since the 1970s, as a result of the growing readership for Native texts, trade publishers such as McClelland and Stewart have been quick to pick up Inuit titles such as *Peter Pitseolak's Escape from Death* (1977). Alootook Ipellie, probably the best-known contemporary Inuit writer today, is famous for his use of 'modern' form and structure as well as a culturally specific, satiric wit. In their multiplicity and fluidity, these books resonate with the conventions of dynamic and vital oral storytelling traditions as well as more mainstream literary traditions.

Such books, like much of the literature of the 1980s and 1990s from writers like Lee Maracle, present readers with social commentary through literature and storytelling. They reveal the struggle of Aboriginal writers to define their sense of self in new languages and genres of expression, through translations and transformations between cultures, and between oral and written (literary) genres. The textualization of First Peoples' identities, it might be said, reflects the 'reinvention of the enemy's language'[41] in such a way that contemporary First Peoples' literatures are both part of and apart from the larger canon of Canadian literature. Refusing to be categorized as 'either/or,' Aboriginal writers insist instead on being viewed as 'both/and.'

The State and the Book

PAUL LITT

The Canadian government did little to support the book in the half century following the First World War. Dramatically, and famously, it imposed public ownership on broadcasting. Occasionally, and ineffectually, it meddled with other media, but displayed comparatively little interest in the book. The explanation for this negligence begins with the nature of government involvement in cultural matters during this period. There were, on the one hand, general government policies that had cultural ramifications and, on the other, government initiatives that had explicit cultural goals. The history of government investigation and support for the book can be viewed in three phases: an initial phase in which government policies, principally economic in nature, indirectly affected the book; a middle phase in which the government developed new policies with cultural objectives but paid little attention to the book; and a third phase in which the government explicitly targeted book production as part of a broader cultural industries policy strategy. Layers of policies accumulated as each of these regimes supplemented rather than replaced its predecessor.

Indirect Effects

The Canadian publishing industry developed along classic National Policy lines, with producers based in Central Canada selling to a nationwide market. They were protected by a tariff on book imports that was part of the government's broader protectionist system rather than a unique treatment applied to the publishing industry, and was not high enough to keep cheap American books off the Canadian market. American publishers enjoyed a domestic market ten times the size of that available to Canadian publishers and could easily extend their print runs to sell into Canada at prices that, even with the added cost of shipping and duty, Canadian publishers could never match. Canadian publishers might have been able to compete had they had access to the American market, but the United States protected its publishing industry with copyright legislation and high tariff barriers. When Canada tried to do the same, its protectionist measures were vetoed by Britain for fear they would jeopardize Anglo-American trade relations. As Canada gained more autonomy from Britain, it developed and passed its own Copyright Act, proclaimed in 1924. Since Canada was a net importer of books, the government opted to keep tariffs low, which helped its balance of payments at the expense of Canadian authors. The Canadian Authors Association was formed in 1921 to press for revisions, some of which it obtained in the 1930s, but it failed to alter the fundamental economic logic that shaped Canadian copyright policy.

The First World War stimulated Canadian nationalism and channelled it toward achieving greater independence within the British Empire, which in the process was redefined as the Commonwealth. Yet even as Canadians thrilled to newfound political autonomy, their cultural distinctiveness was challenged by a burgeoning continental mass culture. American cultural products flowed north across the border through new mass media – the ever-expanding popular press, movies after the turn of the century, and radio following the end of the war. Pressured to institute protectionist measures, the federal government responded in a piecemeal fashion with mixed success. In 1917 it helped break Canadian newspapers' dependence on American news services by providing a $50,000 annual subsidy to support a national service, Canadian Press, whose French-language operation would begin in 1951.[42]

While the federal government did nothing to support a Canadian feature film industry, documentary film units were created by both federal and provincial governments. In 1931 the federal government imposed a tariff on American magazines which was effective but short-lived. Its most radical intervention came in the field of radio, where, after a royal commission and much debate, it created a public broadcasting system in 1932.

These government initiatives had indirect benefits for writers, who could earn some income from writing for Canadian magazines, public radio, or documentary films. Direct support, however, was incidental and paltry. Sometimes the government commissioned books to recognize significant events or promote government objectives, but government patronage usually took the form of public memorialization or beautification,[43] projects of greater benefit to sculptors, dramatists, composers, or architects than to writers. Amid all the pioneering interwar activity in cultural policy, there was no nationalist agitation or government intervention on behalf of the book. As George L. Parker elaborates in chapter 5, the main subsidizers of books were a handful of Canadian publishers who, as good corporate citizens moved by nationalist ideals, published Canadian works, and more often than not lost money doing so.

High Culture Nationalism and the Missing Book

The prevailing discourse surrounding culture accounts for the book's curious exceptionalism in the decades following the First World War. A blend of elitist, liberal, and romantic ideas shaped the thinking of Canadian leaders in relation to culture: elitist, because they thought of culture as the traditional knowledge and values of the educated; liberal, because they thought of culture as the product of individual learning, inspiration, or creative genius; romantic, because they were inspired by idealistic notions of how things should be rather than how they actually were. According to this set of beliefs, which can be summarized as high culture nationalism, individual self-improvement through culture would bring social progress. High culture precepts transferred easily from social improvement to nation-building. As both a sign and disseminator of national identity, culture was recognized as a key ingredient of nationalism. In the climate of the 1920s, in which mass culture appeared to be invading Canada from the United States, high culture and nationalism melded in a defensive posture.

The absence of the book from government cultural policy in this period is understandable in the context of the defensive response to the rise of continental mass culture. The book predated the mass media that threatened high culture and, despite having become a mass-produced commodity in its own right, was traditionally the privileged medium which stored and perpetuated the educated classes' cultural capital. Ironically, the book was disregarded because it was highly regarded. The Second World War reinvigorated Canadian cultural nationalism, stimulating even greater resolve to assert and safeguard a Canadian national identity than had been engendered by the First. Artists and writers lobbied for state support, buttressing traditional high culture-nationalist rationales with the argument that, during post-war reconstruction, culture played an essential role in articulating the values of liberal democracy in its international confrontations with fascism and communism. The Parliamentary Committee on Reconstruction and Re-establishment (Turgeon Committee), established in 1944, gave their claims a prominent public forum. Sixteen cultural groups, including the Canadian Authors Association, contributed to a brief that called for a government body to sponsor the arts and establish community arts centres nationwide. Encouraged by their positive reception, the originators of this brief established an umbrella organization which became the Canadian Arts Council (CAC) in 1945.

In 1946 Alberta became the first Canadian jurisdiction to respond to these concerns when it set up a series of arts boards to support cultural activities. Saskatchewan established its own Arts Board two years later. In Nova Scotia, New Brunswick, British Columbia, and Ontario, provincial departments in various fields also began to support cultural programming. These offices assumed responsibility for libraries, a sector which had received increasing provincial support over the previous decade. In 1939 supporters of libraries had secured from the federal government a postal subsidy allowing books to be sent between libraries at a discounted rate (a similar subsidy for newspapers and magazines had existed for decades; it was extended to the book late and in a limited fashion).[44] Support for libraries by both levels of government, which increased sevenfold between 1937 and 1957, came through incremental commitments and represented the first direct subsidy for the book in the history of Canadian cultural policy.[45]

The federal government was, meanwhile, initially disinclined to act on the main recommendations of the CAC. The British North America Act made jurisdictional clashes with the provinces a possible consequence of any federal cultural initiative. Moreover, laissez-faire and freedom of expression were still influential political principles, particularly as the Western world felt besieged by alternative, authoritarian political systems. However, times were changing. Anticipating a reward for wartime sacrifices and dreading a return of the Great Depression, Canadian public opinion pushed governments to implement extensive new social programs. Post-war expectations paved the way for state intervention in areas that had been out of bounds during the rule of laissez-faire. Under these conditions, the federal government found it hard to resist deploying its spending power to consolidate the supra-constitutional power it had exercised during the war.

The immediate stimulus to action came, however, from the federal government's existing cultural responsibilities. Private radio station owners were campaigning against regulation by the Canadian Broadcasting Corporation (CBC) even as the government confronted public broadcasting underfunding and considered whether to extend the public system to the new medium of television. Unsure of how to deal with these issues, the government established the Royal Commission on National Development in the Arts, Letters and Sciences, known as the Massey Commission, after its chairman, Vincent Massey. To mask the political motives behind the commission, Prime Minister Louis St Laurent instructed it to investigate the full range of the government's involvement in culture. As well, Canadian universities were squeezed for cash as enrolments skyrocketed with the influx of veterans who were given free access to post-secondary education. Eager to help, even though education was a provincial matter, the federal government instructed the commission to investigate scholarships for higher education, and waited to see where this would lead it.

Although references to the book were nowhere to be seen in the Massey Commission's instructions, writing and publishing were affected by a wide range of issues touched on by the commission. In hearings conducted in 1949 and 1950, commissioners collected the opinions of cultural producers and consumers across Canada. Statistics showed that while American and British firms were publishing thousands of books every year, Canadian publishers were issuing only a few dozen Canadian literary and trade titles. Equally damning was the estimate that there were only about two dozen bookshops in the country that survived by selling books alone. The commission heard that individual Canadian books often sold as well as American or British books in Canada, yet Canadians read three foreign books for every one written by a compatriot. The size of the market for Canadian books was the problem. Publishers claimed they could not find enough buyers in Canada alone to make money on books by Canadian authors, while little international demand existed for their work. Hence publishers asked that books be exempted from the 8 per cent federal sales tax and be given a preferential postage rate similar to that available for books in the United States and France.

The commission's report raised public alarm about the vulnerability of Canadian culture to American cultural influences. It articulated the romantic nationalist

belief that a prime function of a nation's literature was to express the special character of its people, but found that literature had 'taken a second place, and indeed
has fallen far behind painting' as a medium of national expression in Canada.[46]
Despite this dire assessment, the commission's recommendations paid less attention to books than to other arts and media. Writers were considered within the
broad category of scholars and artists, while the report's section on the mass media
entirely overlooked publishing. Instead, the Massey Report's recommendations
concentrated on the political issues that had led to the commission's establishment.
It defended the existing system of broadcasting regulation for radio and suggested
it be extended to television as well. It called for the government to establish secure,
enhanced government funding for the CBC and other government cultural institutions and to establish an arts funding agency. Stepping boldly into provincial jurisdiction, it also recommended federal funding for universities. The only direct help
the Massey Report offered for the book came in two areas: its call for the establishment of a National Library, and its recommendation that diplomatic posts expand
their libraries and distribute Canadian books abroad.

Although the problems of the book and publishing were largely absent from its
recommendations, the Massey Commission's legacy would lead to aid for Canadian
books and authors through the government's subsequent support of the CBC, the
National Library of Canada, and the Canada Council for the Arts. Moreover, the
acceptance of its proposal that the federal government fund universities paved the
way for a significant expansion of post-secondary education, which would increase
the study of Canadian subjects and boost demand for Canadian books for classroom
use. University presses would grow apace, a story recounted by Francess G. Halpenny in chapter 12. Most significantly, university education would steep young
Canadians more deeply in print culture, expanding the Canadian market for books.

The arts council recommended by the Massey Commission almost failed to see
the light of day, but dogged lobbying by the cultural community and some unexpected tax windfalls finally led to its creation in 1957. Half of the original $100 mil-
lion endowment grant of the Canada Council went to a University Capital Grants
Fund, which further assisted university expansion. When the council began to distribute money for culture, most of it went to performing arts companies. In its first
year it provided $639,300 in grants to the performing arts, compared to only $10,000
to support academic publication and writing.

At first the council's policy was not to subsidize fiction and other non-academic
writing except through facilitating translation. This began to change in 1959, when
it took over administration of the Governor General's Literary Awards, establishing

French categories and substantially increasing the accompanying cash prize. In 1960 it formally initiated a program of grants for writers, a practice that would be imitated by provincial arts councils. By the end of its first decade, the Canada Council had distributed $1 million for literary activities, mostly as grants. In 1968 the council launched the Writer-in-Residence Program, described by Nancy Earle in chapter 3. While the total dollar figure directed toward literary interests rose each year, it remained miniscule compared to the funding of high-overhead ballet companies and symphonies. In 1968–9 the Canada Council granted $544,000 to literary activities out of $8,766,000 in disbursements to the arts. The Ontario Council for the Arts (later the Ontario Arts Council / Conseil des arts de l'Ontario), established in 1963, showed a similar bias.[47]

Cultural Industries Policy and the Discovery of the Book

As the 1960s progressed, the high culture–nationalist strain of government policy would be displaced by a cultural industries strategy that treated cultural activities as an economic sector. The rise of the mass media made cultural production an increasingly important part of the Canadian economy. In the information age, culture was a sophisticated form of information that had economic value as content for multiplying media outlets. As Marshall McLuhan observed, Western civilization was moving 'from an era when business was our culture to one in which culture is our business.'[48]

At the same time, Canadian nationalism surged, buoyed on the one hand by reaction to the troubled American civil rights movement and the Vietnam War, and on the other by the Centennial celebrations of 1967 and Trudeaumania. Cultural issues were re-sensitized, with initiatives to Canadianize school classrooms, university faculties, the airwaves – indeed, any and all means by which knowledge, information, and values were disseminated – yet Canadian publishers, nonetheless, continued to subsidize Canadian literature far more than the government.

With attention accorded to the information age and Canadian nationalism, it was small wonder that the post-war years saw a succession of high-profile federal royal commissions exploring issues involving culture, the media, and Canadian sovereignty. Broadcasting, a central concern of the Massey Commission, was taken up again by the Fowler Commission during 1955–7. In 1960 came the federal Royal Commission on Publications, which, despite its name, dealt exclusively with the continuing tribulations of Canadian magazines and paid no attention to books. A Special Senate Committee on the Mass Media, chaired by Senator Keith Davey, tackled the magazine issue again in 1969.[49] It also looked at newspapers, but not books, which apparently still did not qualify as mass media.

This spate of inquiries exhibited the new focus on cultural industries. Policymakers had become wary of weaknesses in the high culture approach. To begin with, the dire predictions had not come true: civilization had not collapsed under the onslaught of mass culture. Instead, the definition of culture had broadened. The modern cultural scene offered a smorgasbord of cultural products and pastimes, few of which fitted comfortably into the categories of high culture versus mass culture. As well, the book sector was growing both larger and more complex along with the country as a whole. Consequently, the Massey Commission's focus on individual creators and edification of the average citizen gave way to the provision of subsidies for all producers in certain cultural sectors. This approach could be justified in economic terms and defended as equitable.

While significant new policies for the Canadian television, film, and music industries developed in the 1960s, the federal government was still struggling toward conceptualizing the book trade as a cultural industry. The first sign of change came in 1969 when the federal Ministry of Industry, Trade and Commerce commissioned a study of the publishing industry by a private consulting firm. The result, *The Book Publishing and Manufacturing Industry in Canada: A Statistical and Economic Analysis* (1970), provided an overview of the industry's sales, revenues, and significance in relation to Canada's economy as a whole.

Then came a sudden wake-up call in 1970, when Gage and Ryerson, two venerable Canadian publishers, were sold to American interests. This crisis, described by George L. Parker in chapter 5, secured for the book industry what most other Canadian cultural industries had already enjoyed: its own royal commission – albeit a provincial one, established by Ontario, home to most of the large Canadian-owned, English-language publishers. The Ontario Royal Commission on Book Publishing (ORCBP) was officially established on 23 December 1970. No sooner had it begun than a new emergency flared. In February 1971, Jack McClelland declared that he had to sell his family firm, McClelland and Stewart, or go bankrupt for lack of access to capital at reasonable rates. Rising to the occasion, the royal commission issued an interim report recommending that the Ontario government bail him out. In a rare example of a government acting immediately on a royal commission recommendation, the province did just that, loaning McClelland close to one million dollars on generous terms. This measure was later extended, following the recommendation of another interim report, to provide similar assistance for other Ontario-based, Canadian-owned publishers.

The commission's final report maintained that a balance between Canadian- and foreign-owned publishing firms would be ideal. It noted that Canadian book publishers had an even smaller portion of their domestic market than did Canadian magazines. Moreover, while foreign-owned firms accounted for 70 per cent of sales in English Canada, they produced only 15 per cent of all new books about Canada and just 3 per cent of all works of Canadian literature. These last two statistics reflected the fact that Canadian books published by foreign-owned firms tended to be for the reliable and relatively lucrative textbook market, and that many of these were adaptations of foreign texts.

The recommendations of the commission's main report were destined, like those of most official inquiries, to be ignored by the government that had asked for them. Nevertheless, the crisis of the early 1970s was a turning point. It made it clear that the book was a product not just of literary genius but of a healthy publishing industry as well. Like other cultural industries, the book trade was to be fortified as a line of defence against Americanization. Unlike others, it had significant existing Canadian production, distribution, and public demand for a Canadian product. This belated official recognition of the book as a particularly significant bastion of Canadian culture ensured that there would henceforth be government policies that focused directly on the cultural industry of publishing.

The cultural industries approach to the book was reinforced by foreign ownership controversies throughout the 1970s. The Trudeau government established the Foreign Investment Review Agency (FIRA) in 1974 in response to anxieties about foreign ownership across all sectors of the economy. Its powers were quite limited: it could not do anything about the fact that most Canadian publishing operations were already foreign-owned, but could only patriate foreign-owned subsidiaries when their corporate parents changed ownership. Nevertheless, FIRA's existence, and the political sensitivities it symbolized, may have had some deterrent effect, prompting U.S. firms to make arrangements with Canadian firms rather than trying to take them over or muscle them out of the marketplace.

At the Canada Council, grants for writers and individual publications were supplemented from 1972 with a cultural industries policy of block grants to publishers who were actively producing and marketing Canadian books. Subsequently the council built on this approach with a Book Purchase Program, export marketing assistance, and a co-publishing policy. In 1975 the council established a Book Promotion and Distribution Program. Two years later, in the wake of the election of the Parti Québécois in Quebec, the council accepted an infusion of 'national unity' money, which it directed to its Book Purchase Program, translation assistance, a National Book Week, and a special fund for children's literature.[50] By 1979–80, the Canada Council was allocating $3.8 million for translation grants, promotion assistance, publication subsidies, and the purchase and distribution of Canadian-authored books to non-profit institutions in Canada and abroad. In the 1970s the Multiculturalism Directorate of the Secretary of State also began to serve as a kind of Canada Council for allophone communities, funding literature not written in one of Canada's official languages.[51]

While any industry-targeted assistance was welcome, the publishing industry was not perfectly happy with the way in which federal assistance was developing. It did little to improve Canadian publishers' competitiveness with foreign firms because funding was piecemeal and tied to particular projects. The federal government finally addressed this criticism in the late 1970s, introducing a program that offered the type of industry-wide support it provided for other cultural industries. The Canadian Book Publishing Industry Development Program, initiated with $5.7 million in fiscal year 1979–80, provided annual subsidies for Canadian-owned publishers at levels calculated according to their size and budgets.[52]

As the 1970s came to a close, the federal government established the Federal Cultural Policy Review Committee, instructing it to review the federal government's increasingly diverse array of cultural programs. The committee heard about the many ailments afflicting Canadian publishing: corporate concentration of book retailing, foreign ownership, insufficient funding for libraries, and public sector book-purchasing policies that failed to support public policy objectives for Canadian publishing. In this sector, as in others, the committee found itself snowed under by the minutiae of myriad interests created by the government's now extensive involvement in the field and hard pressed to discriminate between competing claims. In this sense, the cultural sector had become a victim of its own success. Offered no clear strategic direction by the committee, the federal government largely ignored its recommendations.

Meanwhile, some provincial governments were offering more support for the book, much of it related to libraries and schools, institutions for which they were responsible. British Columbia, for example, developed the Library Bulk Purchase Programme, which bought titles for distribution to local libraries. Under the Wintario Lottery Program in Ontario, libraries were given between one and two million dollars a year to purchase books by Canadian authors. Ontario also tested a system that purchased certain approved titles and distributed a free copy to every school, but it had mixed success targeting Canadian- over foreign-owned publishers. The ample Alberta Heritage Fund developed books and distributed them free to schools in the province, although this did little for existing publishers.

Other provincial programs addressed the retail book market. By 1980 every province but Prince Edward Island was funding writers and publishers, either through an arts council or a ministry. In many cases, the grants were small and few in number, reflecting the relative insignificance of the industry outside central Canada. Ontario was responsible for well over 80 per cent of the grant funds distributed to publishers outside of Quebec. It took the lead in other forms of aid as well. For three months in 1978, Ontario's Wintario Lottery ran a rebate program whereby a lottery ticket could be redeemed at half value toward the purchase of a Canadian book or magazine subscription. That same year, Ontario followed up on the earlier precedent of the *ad hoc* loans it had made on the recommendation of the ORCBP with the Ontario Guaranteed Loan Program, and also encouraged publishers to apply for assistance under its Small Business Development Corporation. These measures allowed many Ontario-based publishers to reinvest in and expand their businesses.[53]

The 1970s were a critical decade for the relationship between Canadian governments and the book. For the first time the book had attracted more attention than either newspapers or magazines – if somewhat less than the electronic media. It was now the beneficiary of an array of government programs. Despite the protracted foreign ownership crisis, Canadian books were growing in quantity and sophistication, earning increasing international attention. The Massey Commission's observation that literature was overshadowed by painting no longer held: writing was undisputedly the standard bearer of Canadian cultural nationalism, a success story that filled nationalists with hope for Canada's future.

Although publishers' and writers' associations continued to lobby for more and better government aid, in retrospect the 1970s would be seen as the heyday of governmental support for the book. Ahead lay the Canada–United States Free Trade Agreement, with its restrictions on new government cultural initiatives, deficit-fighting that would cut deeply into cultural programs, and an ascendant neo-liberal ideology, all of which combined to impair government cultural programs. However, the history of government support for the book over the previous seventy years suggests that the Canadian nation-state's concerns for its cultural and economic sovereignty, the nationalism and self-interest of Canadian publishers and writers, and the responsiveness of the Canadian public to nationalist appeals were all factors with the staying power to fight another day.

Book Policy in Quebec

JOSÉE VINCENT

Quebec had no official book policy before 1960. This does not mean, however, that nothing was done on behalf of the book sector before the Quiet Revolution – from the end of the nineteenth century there were various forms of government intervention to support authors and publishers. More inclined to intervene in culture than their anglophone counterparts, French-Canadian politicians were motivated by the rise of nationalist sentiment, which in the 1920s became widespread in both the political arena and the intellectual community. Subsequently the protection and development of the book milieu were closely linked to the definition of French-Canadian identity. Early independent publishers such as Albert Lévesque and Édouard Garand used patriotic arguments to promote their books and, like authors, did not hesitate to appeal directly for the support of political leaders. The laissez-faire approach in English Canada in the first half of the twentieth century thus contrasted with policies in Quebec, where two government bodies, the Department of Public Instruction and the Department of the Provincial Secretary, had supported books since the beginning of the century, the former in the area of education and the latter in the area of literature and the humanities.

The Department of Public Instruction

The Department of Public Instruction (DPI) was responsible for the approval of textbooks and the distribution of book prizes in public schools, and imposed its choices on Quebec school boards until the early 1960s. This represented a form of religious control since the DPI's Council for Public Instruction was made up of Catholic and Protestant committees composed of members of the clergy and representatives of the education system, who shared the work and enjoyed broad latitude regarding textbook approval.[54] The committees wielded considerable power, which publishers well understood. The voluminous correspondence of religious communities, who, as outlined by Paul Aubin in chapter 7, were the major publishers of textbooks before 1960, clearly demonstrates their close relationships with the political authorities.[55] While some people questioned the choices of the DPI, others profited from the system. For example, before the Quiet Revolution, the friendships that formed between the directors of Librairie Beauchemin and members of the Catholic committee did not hurt the publisher's business.[56] Criticism of these practices, raised by Maurice Bouchard in the commission of inquiry into the book industry in Quebec in 1963, led to the disappearance of such privileges for certain publishers.

The DPI also chose the books given as prizes at the end of the school year, which represented a sizeable portion of the publishing market, as described by François Landry in chapter 2. In 1925 an amendment to the law governing schools forced the school boards to purchase at least 50 per cent of their prize books from Canadian companies.[57] This created a market that many publishers exploited by designing series essentially for the schools.

The Department of the Provincial Secretary

Soon after Louis-Alexandre Taschereau was elected premier of Quebec in 1920, the government undertook a series of measures to support and develop education. The founding of an autonomous Université de Montréal in 1920, the creation of schools of fine arts in Montreal and Quebec City in 1922, the granting of subsidies to classical colleges starting in 1922, and an increase in the number of fellowships for study abroad stimulated cultural development, which benefited the book world as well.

The Department of the Provincial Secretary primarily supported literary publishing. Under Athanase David, who was secretary of the province in the Taschereau government, subsidies for publishing, which had been rare before the First World War, increased and took several forms. At the request of authors and publishers, the Department of the Provincial Secretary purchased part of the print run of selected titles, thereby enabling the publisher to cover printing costs and avoid losses. These books were then distributed in schools, municipal and ministerial libraries, and the offices of the Province of Quebec in foreign countries. Such purchases were significant, particularly in the case of literary books, for which sales were always unreliable. This relatively effective system was proposed to the federal government by the Société des écrivains canadiens (SÉC) in its brief to the Massey Commission in 1950[58] and reiterated at the end of the decade, when the mandate of the Canada Council for the Arts was being defined.

Occasionally, the Department of the Provincial Secretary also helped with cultural activities. In the 1920s and 1930s, it regularly funded poetry evenings, exhibitions, and authors' banquets organized during Canada Book Week by the French section of the Canadian Authors Association, which in 1936 became the SÉC. It also gave the SÉC an annual grant to cover its administrative expenses – essentially

1.4 Robert La Palme, caricature of Jean Bruchési, 1938. Bruchési (1901–79), undersecretary for the Province of Quebec from 1937 to 1959, was a staunch advocate for the arts and literature under the governments of Maurice Duplessis (Union nationale) and Adélard Godbout (Liberal). Reproduced from *Le Bien public* (Trois-Rivières, 1938). Courtesy of the Succession de Robert La Palme.

office rent and one permanent employee – which rose from $1,000 in 1936 to $2,000 in 1955. The fact that Jean Bruchési, undersecretary of the province, was on the board of directors of the SÉC partly accounts for this generosity (see illus. 1.4, above). In the 1940s and 1950s, the Department of the Provincial Secretary also funded the Société des éditeurs canadiens du livre français and the Association des bibliothécaires de langue française for Canada Book Week and Young Canada's Book Week, which the provincial government saw as an opportunity to support the development of French-Canadian culture. This assistance nurtured the cultural community, even during the term of Premier Maurice Duplessis, who was known for his suspicion of artists and intellectuals.

The province's literary and scientific prizes were no doubt the most coveted forms of assistance before 1960, yet were paradoxically the least costly.[59] On 8 March 1922, on the initiative of Athanase David, provincial literary and scientific competitions were legally established (George 5, 1922, c. 56). The creation of these prizes marked an important step in the history of the book in Quebec because they were the first instance of literary recognition that was entirely French-Canadian and secular. In addition to cash, the winners received substantial publicity, and their subsequent publications had a better chance of being recognized and purchased by the government.

Until the 1960s, the Department of the Provincial Secretary provided subsidies for book purchases, promotional activities, and literary prizes. While the sums invested were not large, this ongoing support made it possible to maintain a literary life, however fragile, and to improve conditions for authors. However, because of the lack of official regulation, the province's generosity was usually subject to the discretion of the presiding secretary. The creation of the department of cultural affairs in 1961 completely changed the picture, through the establishment of new programs with more objective criteria.

The Welfare State in the Service of Quebec Culture

At the beginning of the 1960s, while the federal government was setting up the Canada Council for the Arts programs to fund Canadian culture, French-Canadian culture also became the subject of government attention in Quebec. The priorities of the government of Premier Jean Lesage were health, the economy, and education, but after the stagnation of the Duplessis period, the creation of the ministère des Affaires culturelles in itself heralded a renewal. Although its budgets were still modest, much to the chagrin of Georges-Émile Lapalme, the first minister of cultural affairs, other initiatives in tune with the social and cultural changes in Quebec contributed to the modernization of the province. Under the direction of Deputy Minister Guy Frégault and his right-hand man, Clément Saint-Germain, himself a former publisher at Éditions Fides, the ministère des Affaires culturelles and its literature and publishing section developed programs of grants, prizes, and support for publishing. To carry out their work, civil servants consulted the cultural community and the leaders of the Conseil supérieur du livre (CSL).[60]

One of the first actions taken by the provincial government to support publishing was the adoption of the Publishers' Loss Insurance Act (Elizabeth 2, 1962, c. 14). Based on the old system of book purchases by the Department of the Provincial Secretary, this legislation was prepared by representatives of the CSL and one of its main leaders, Pierre Tisseyre.[61] To help publishers cover their expenses, the government committed itself to buying part of their print runs. While the idea seemed promising, its application was subject to constraints and deadlines that slowed the program and discouraged publishers. They preferred the program of grants by title, which encouraged the publication of scholarly books, and was inaugurated by the same department in 1965. For literary books, financial assistance came mostly from the Canada Council.

Promotion and distribution of books in Quebec and abroad was also among the objectives of the ministère des Affaires culturelles, which supported major events such as the Salon du livre de Québec (1959–), the Salon du livre de Montréal (1962–6), and the Montreal International Book Fair (1975–7). Following agreements in 1965 between France and Quebec, the ministry also encouraged the export of books to France. The Centre de diffusion du livre canadien-français (1967–73), which had offices in the Librairie de l'École in Paris, for several years received an annual grant allowing it to maintain an outlet in France. Similar initiatives were tried in Belgium and in the United States. The Librairie du Québec in Paris, subsidized by the Department of Industry and Commerce, took over from the Librairie de l'École from 1978 to 1985. While book fairs were increasingly successful with the public over the years, attempts to export Quebec books proved disastrous.[62] Only the subsidized participation of publishers in the international book fairs in Frankfurt, Nice, Paris, and Brussels produced positive results in the long term.

During the 1960s, several large municipalities became patrons of the arts. According to their means, the cities of Quebec and Montreal contributed to significant literary events, subsidizing annual book fairs and special exhibitions, as on the occasion of Expo 67. Montreal established the Metropolitan Montreal Arts Council in 1962 and created the Grand Prix littéraire de la Ville de Montréal in 1964. Sherbrooke, Hull, and Trois-Rivières also began to promote occasional literary activities in their regions, largely through special events.

Though grants and subsidies from the provincial government or municipalities were an important form of assistance, they were nonetheless limited by a lack of resources and could not compete with the larger budgets of the federal government. In compensation, the Quebec government emphasized legislative measures, which were less costly but very effective. It wanted to defend and preserve cultural production in Quebec, and identified regulation of markets as the most appropriate type of intervention. In 1954 the Société des éditeurs canadiens du livre français had proposed a draft action plan for the book trade to the Royal Commission of Inquiry on Constitutional Problems, chaired by Judge Thomas Tremblay. The group's basic idea was very simple: it asked that the provincial government take 'urgent new action to see that libraries, school boards, and educational institutions place greater emphasis on Canadian books, and that government subsidies be given to these organizations, which are educational in nature, only if they show they are aware of the role they need to play in French-Canadian culture.'[63] Another request was that all cultural organizations, including schools, be obliged to buy books from Quebec booksellers instead of dealing directly with foreign firms. These two recommendations, formulated by Pierre Tisseyre, underpinned the book policy that was to develop over the following two decades. In the short term, however, they went unheeded because the report of the Tremblay Commission was quickly shelved by the Duplessis government. It was not until the 1960s that the entire book industry mobilized behind the CSL to demand regulation of the book market.

In January 1963 the CSL presented Georges-Émile Lapalme with a 'Mémoire sur la crise de la librairie au Canada français au début de 1963.' In this document, the CSL bemoaned the plight of Quebec's bookstores, which were being undermined by the institutions' practice of buying directly from European publishers. The CSL called on the government to carry out a broad consultation and to create a regulatory authority for books, a Régie du livre. Government intervention was common at the time, as exemplified by the nationalization of the power companies in 1962–3. But while the provincial government saw the advantages of controlling the sale of electricity, it did not feel the same way with regard to books, a sector in which profits were minimal and government intervention was always suspect. However, the Lesage government agreed to the first proposal and in 1963 created the Commission d'enquête sur le commerce du livre dans la province de Québec, chaired by Maurice Bouchard. All the professional associations, as well as such publishers as the Centre de psychologie et de pédagogie and Éditions Fides, submitted briefs. It soon became clear that the regulation of business practices was necessary, especially concerning the sale of textbooks.

Toward the end of the 1960s, the situation was further exacerbated as publishers from the United States and France set up branch plants in Montreal. McGraw-Hill, Holt, Rinehart and Winston, and Prentice Hall opened offices, where they began to translate their textbooks into French. The owners of Encyclopaedia Britannica bought Centre de psychologie et de pédagogie, and Hachette announced the opening of a second bookstore in Montreal and the creation of the Messageries internationales du livre, with exclusive distribution rights to its mass-market series. In 1969 the CSL, reacting quickly, sent the premier its *Livre blanc sur l'affaire Hachette*, urging him to intervene to prevent the control of culture by foreign firms. Long discussions ensued between the government and representatives of the book trade.[64] The government tried to ease the situation, announcing a new book policy through its minister of cultural affairs, François Cloutier, in 1971, but it failed to achieve significant change as the law accrediting booksellers still permitted foreign interests to control the textbook market.

During the 1970s, the perception of books by both the trade and the government altered. While books were still associated with culture, the notion of a book industry was growing. In demanding protection for 'national culture,' members of the book trade were seeking as well to defend their share of the market; despite appearances, the provincial government was not completely insensitive to this change in discourse. In 1976 a Green Paper by Jean-Paul L'Allier, the minister of cultural affairs, *Pour l'évolution de la politique culturelle*, recognized the need to support cultural industries and to establish a policy on reading. The idea received support and was taken up by the new government of the Parti Québécois, specifically by Denis Vaugeois, who initiated the Act Respecting the Development of Quebec Firms in the Book Industry (*RSQ*, c. D-8.1), enacted on 21 December 1979, which gave government-accredited retail bookstores the exclusive right to sell to institutions and required Quebec ownership of all book-related businesses that sought government support. This new law, which finally led to the consolidation of the distribution network, rounded out the province's book policy.

Translating the Two Solitudes

JEAN DELISLE AND GILLES GALLICHAN

The ramifications of translation are political as well as literary and linguistic. Translation embraces cultural and social realities and touches the heart of interaction with the Other; thus it is hardly surprising that the prevailing metaphor for translation in Canada is that of a bridge between two solitudes.[65] This metaphor became rooted in Canada's collective imagination after Hugh MacLennan selected the phrase as the title of his novel about English-French relations, which was published in New York in 1945. Eighteen years passed before the French translation by Québécoise Louise Gareau-DesBois appeared in Paris. The temporal and geographical circumstances surrounding the publication and translation of *Two Solitudes* are far from unique: before 1982, approximately 75 per cent of the French translations of English-Canadian literary authors appeared in Paris. Government translation, by contrast, has always been performed in Canada.

Government Translation

Section 133 of the British North America Act of 1867 recognized Canada as a bilingual country with French and English as its two national languages. Prior to 1980, however, bilingual production of official documents and other government publications was essentially confined to the federal government, the Quebec government, and, after 1969, the New Brunswick government. Elsewhere in Canada, government translation was marginal or non-existent.

Translation services related to the federal government in Ottawa were decentralized in the 1910s, with Parliament, the Post Office, and the Secretary of State producing the bulk of translations. Translators enjoyed enviable working conditions and were considered privileged;[66] sometimes a position as translator was passed down from generation to generation within a family. In 1920 some ninety translators were affiliated with the federal government. Their efforts were supplemented by a further thirty when Parliament was in session, mainly to facilitate the publication of bills, proceedings, and debates.[67]

Under the British North America Act, Quebec was required to publish its laws and parliamentary proceedings in French and English. In 1920 the Legislative Council and Legislative Assembly had a team of about a dozen translators for both French and English. In addition to laws and parliamentary journals, the Quebec government translated official reports, tourist guides, and other documents for the general public. Most permits and forms were also printed in both languages. These translations were done by the staff of the relevant department or contracted out.

In the 1920s the status of French began to improve. With communication increasingly facilitated by radio and cinema, more and more francophones were demanding bilingualism. In 1927 Ontario repealed Regulation 17, legislation which since 1912 had restricted teaching in French to the first two years of primary education. At the federal level, bilingual postage stamps (1928) and currency (1937) were adopted. In 1934 the Conservative government created the Translation Bureau to bring all federal translators together. Many francophones expressed misgivings about this approach; they would have preferred to see a more generalized presence of French in all departments. Not until the Second World War did the bureau become fully functional. It employed 175 translators in 1948, a number that soon increased to 300.[68] In addition to producing translations, the bureau also issued many guides to Canadian usage of bilingual terminology.

The Royal Commission on Bilingualism and Biculturalism (1963–9), whose recommendations gave rise to the Official Languages Act (17-18 Elizabeth 2, 1969, c. 54), established the translation of all federal publications as standard practice. Political will was the determining factor in this expansion.[69] Between 1965 and 1975, the number of translators rose from 350 to 1,300, and university language programs underwent a similar expansion. Nonetheless, the federal government remained an essentially English-speaking institution that communicated only partially in both languages.[70] Although a quarter of the public service was French-speaking, relaively few of these employees produced materials in their first languages. Indeed, only 10 per cent of the translation was done from French into English.

In 1964 a translation service was established by the Department of the Provincial Secretary of Quebec. It started slowly because of the difficulty of recruiting professional translators, whose services were needed by the federal government, the private sector, and the Montreal World's Fair, Expo 67.[71] The law making French the official language of Quebec (LQ, 1974, c. 6) and the Charter of the French Language (LQ, 1977, c. 5) did not reduce official publication in English, nor the need for government translators. In New Brunswick the legislation that made the province bilingual (18 Elizabeth 2, 1969, c. 14) gave a strong impetus to the publication of official French translations. In 1972 Quebec and New Brunswick were the provinces employing the largest numbers of translators, twenty-five and twenty-four respectively. Ontario at the time had eight translators and Saskatchewan one, while the six other provinces had none.[72] After 1980, following a ruling by the Supreme Court and a reawakening of the francophone communities in the West, Manitoba had to catch up.[73] At the provincial level, bilingualism in official publishing thus appears to be a phenomenon essentially related to French Canada, with little penetration of English Canada.

Bridging the Two Cultures

Before 1920, two English-Canadian literary works were translated into French, while ten French titles were translated into English. Of 48 works translated in Canada between 1920 and 1960, 39 were translations into English and 9 into French.[74] In addition, during the 1930s and 1940s, all books by Grey Owl (Archibald Belaney), the popular pseudo-Indian, were translated in France. By 1981 there were 300 French translations of books by 240 English authors, more than a third of them (115) novels.[75] Five of Canada's best-known writers – Stephen Leacock, Mazo de la Roche, Malcolm Lowry, Leonard Cohen, and Mordecai Richler – were translated and published in France. In the 1970s, Canadian translations of Margaret Atwood, Margaret Laurence, and Robertson Davies began to appear.

It was rarer for English-Canadian poets to be translated into French in Canada; Leonard Cohen, John Robert Colombo, and Dennis Lee were among the lucky few before the situation changed radically in 1969 with the creation of *Ellipse* at the Université de Sherbrooke. This journal's mission was to present the works of English-Canadian and Quebec poets in translation; by 1980, after twenty-six issues, *Ellipse* had published some fifty translated poets. The journal instigated a new mode of poetry translation in Canada, creating a space for dialogue and networks of sociability between pairs of literary writers from the two main linguistic groups, such as Gaston Miron and F.R. Scott. In the 1970s, a truly bilingual community arose among authors and translators, particularly feminists, with anglophones translating francophone novelists and theorists. This *complicité*, sense of common cause, which gave rise to some very original thinking about translation, would peak in the following decade.[76]

Theatre presented an entirely different situation: until the 1980s, French Canada displayed very little interest in English-Canadian drama. Only eleven plays by nine authors, including David Fennario, John Herbert, and John Thomas McDonough, were translated, almost all of them dealing with Quebec or Montreal.[77] Many more French plays were translated into English, especially those of Michel Tremblay.

Non-fiction – biography, history, and literary criticism – was the only genre in which the number of titles translated from English to French exceeded the number translated from French to English. Of the 170 known titles in this category, the majority date from the 1960s and 1970s, and were predominantly historical, cultural, or socio-political studies dealing with aspects of Quebec. Books by Northrop Frye, Peter C. Newman, Marshall McLuhan, Marius Barbeau, Stanley B. Ryerson, and Merrill Denison were also translated into French.

On average, one literary translation from French into English was published per year from the beginning of the century to the 1960s.[78] Two-thirds of this meagre output consisted of novels by such authors as Louis Hémon, Maurice Constantin-Weyer, Roger Lemelin, and Gabrielle Roy. Often criticized for their poor quality, many of these translations were by foreigners and reflected a lack of familiarity with Canada. It was not until the mid-1970s that better translations appeared, thanks in part to the financial assistance of the Canada Council. In the 1960s the rate of literary translation into English increased sixfold; translations included twenty-seven novels, five collections of poetry, three plays, and nine works of history and literary criticism.[79] Philip Stratford observed significant progress with regard to the novel: '... prior to 1900 seven Quebec novels were translated; in the next sixty years 36 titles were added, a little more than one every two years; in the next decade, 1960–70, twenty new novels were translated, an average of two a year; from 1973 to 1982, 89 translations of Quebec novels were undertaken, almost nine per year.'[80]

Significance of the Canada Council

The landscape changed radically in 1972 with the establishment of the Canada Council's translation grants. Conceived in a spirit of national unity, this program incited major advances in the practice of translation in Canada. As Philip Stratford recounted in 1983:

> Since the Canada Council's programme began in 1972, almost five hundred new literary titles have been translated, more than all the years before. Forty-five French publishers have been involved, fifty English ones. The work was done by 110 Francophone translators and 100 Anglophones, a third of whom now have two or more translations to their credit. A significant change, whose results may be far-reaching, is that the old 2-to-1 ratio (two French books translated for every English title) no longer applies: in five of the past ten years more books were translated into French than into English, and the overall totals are equal.[81]

The Canada Council program inspired related initiatives and developments: the creation of the Canada Council Translation Prizes in 1973; the founding of the Literary Translators' Association of Canada in 1975; the first edition of the *Bibliography of Canadian Books in Translation: French to English and English to French,* by Maureen Newman and Philip Stratford (1975); the introduction, in 1977, of a translation section in the annual 'Letters in Canada' issue of the *University of Toronto Quarterly*; improvement in the quality of criticism, which now took into account the specific nature of translations; the initiation of serious discussion of the meaning of literary translation in Canada; and the creation of several publishers' series devoted to translations of Canadian literary works. Individual translators such as Sheila Fischman became known in their own right.

In the fall of 1972, Montreal publisher Pierre Tisseyre initiated the Collection des deux solitudes to acquaint French-speaking readers with the most significant works of English-Canadian literature. The first title to appear, Emily Carr's *Klee Wyck* (1973), was translated by Michelle Tisseyre, editor of the series, who also issued French editions of titles by Morley Callaghan, Robertson Davies, Margaret Laurence, Mordecai Richler, Brian Moore, and W.O. Mitchell. In 1977 the same publisher launched the Collection des deux solitudes, juvénile, the first title of which was *Jacob Deux-Deux et le vampire masqué,* Jean Simard's translation of Mordecai Richler's captivating children's story. In 1978 this series was renamed the Collection des deux solitudes, jeunesse; its new editor, Paule Daveluy, published *Chemins secrets de la liberté,* her translation of Barbara Smucker's historical novel of the Underground Railway.

Also in Montreal, Harvest House, which in 1965 had issued *Ethel and the Terrorist,* David S. Walker's translation of Claude Jasmin's novel, established its French Writers of Canada series in 1973. Its titles included Jacques Ferron's *Dr Cotnoir: A Novel,* translated by Pierre Cloutier, and Anne Hébert's *The Torrent: Novellas and Short Stories,* translated by Gwendolyn Moore. Other publishers followed suit, including McClelland and Stewart, Oberon Press, Coach House Press, and Talon Books, and on the French side, Les Éditions Héritage, Hurtubise HMH, and Québec Amérique. In addition to the substantial financial assistance provided by the Canada Council, this vitality reflected the increased interest in translated works arising out of developments in the political situation in Quebec.

If it is true that literary translation offers a site for meeting and dialogue, it still remains difficult to assess accurately the cross-cultural repercussions of translations. The quantitative evidence shows that, in literature and in the humanities, Canada's 'two solitudes' significantly expanded their interest in one another through the 1970s.

Canadianization of the Curriculum

LUCIE ROBERT, CHRISTL VERDUYN, AND JANET B. FRISKNEY

The issue of presenting Canadian material in all subject areas and at all levels of education came to a head in two separate documents: the report of the Royal Commission of Inquiry on Education in the Province of Quebec (1963–6), better known as the Parent Report, and *To Know Ourselves* (1975), written by T.H.B. Symons for the

Association of Universities and Colleges of Canada. Symons argued that 'the most valid rationale for Canadian studies is not any relationship that such studies may have to the preservation or the promotion of national identity, or national unity, or national sovereignty, or anything of the kind. The most valid and compelling argument for Canadian studies,' he emphasized, 'is the importance of self-knowledge, the need to know and to understand ourselves: who we are; where we are in time and space; where we have been; where we are going; what we possess; what our responsibilities are to ourselves and to others.'[82]

While some advocates of Canadian curricular materials would have placed more weight on the issues of preservation and promotion of identity, unity, and sovereignty, all would have concurred with the designation of self-knowledge as a compelling reason for the Canadianization of school curricula. In both French and English Canada, this desire was evident by the end of the First World War; by mid-century, the question became even more pressing. A research focus in education, this debate was documented in print at the same time as advocates strove to make published works about Canada – as well as other curricular materials of Canadian origin – an integral part of Canadian schooling. Throughout the century, the issue of Canadian content in the country's education system involved such concerns as classroom teaching materials, library resources, and funding.

Prior to the Second World War, most of the discussion about Canadian content in school curricula centred on the teaching of Canadian literature and history, core subjects that lent themselves readily to the study of Canada and which were clearly linked to the shaping of cultural identity. In English Canada, history fared far better than literature in finding a place on the curriculum and by 1918 was taught regularly at elementary, secondary, and post-secondary levels. Canadian literature, in contrast, had achieved only sporadic representation, a situation that would prevail for some decades to come. Lorne Pierce, editor at Ryerson Press, showed a commitment in both domains. During the 1920s, he initiated such series as The Ryerson Canadian History Readers, 'an inspirational, whiggish series of dozens of booklets on heroes and events from Canadian history,' and added Canadian literary items to the expected British literature contained in The Treasury Readers and The Canada Books of Prose and Verse.[83] At the post-secondary level, Canadian literature would remain a marginal area of study until the 1940s. Although a handful of Canadian universities offered a course on the topic in the 1920s, Canadian literature was typically pursued as an extracurricular activity by the few scholars who felt some interest in the subject. Labelled 'immature' in comparison to the work of British writers, Canadian literature struggled for curricular acceptance within its own country.

In Quebec during the early twentieth century, the inculcation of national values was directed primarily at children. As demonstrated by Jacques Michon's case study in this chapter and François Landry's article in chapter 2, elementary textbooks and prize books, as well as children's literature in general, featured heroes of national history. However, such was not the case at higher levels of education. Unlike nineteenth-century historians François-Xavier Garneau and Abbé Jean-Baptiste-Antoine Ferland, few of the new generation of scholars were prepared to write textbooks. In October 1913 a strenuous debate broke out in the pages of *Le Devoir* regarding the sorry state of research and education on Canadian history. Henri Bourassa, Émile Chartier, and Lionel Groulx[84] demanded the creation of a chair in Canadian history, which was achieved in 1916 at Université Laval in Quebec City and its branch in Montreal. During the early decades of the century, Quebec universities developed professional programs and public courses on history and literature, whereas after the Second World War, new research interests led to the establishment of the folklore archives at Université Laval in 1944 and the Institut d'histoire de l'Amérique française in 1946. Although these institutions laid the foundations for the renewal of programs starting in 1970, they lacked adequate funding and were not organized to promote pedagogy.

At the beginning of the century, the teaching of French-Canadian literature fared better. A conference on secondary education in Quebec City in 1906 passed a motion calling for the inclusion of Canadian literature in the examinations required for graduation. Abbé Camille Roy, a professor at the Petit Séminaire de Québec and Université Laval, who had previously published his famous essay 'La nationalisation de la littérature canadienne' in 1904, responded to this new requirement with his *Tableau de l'histoire de la littérature canadienne-française,* which went through eleven editions from 1907 to 1939, and continued to be reprinted until 1962. A special edition was also prepared for the students of the Sisters of St Anne. In spite of this success, the teaching of French-Canadian literature at the secondary level remained marginal. Although French literature replaced Latin literature as the primary subject in 1920, the new program focused on writing from France.

The Massey Commission (1949–51) raised public awareness of Canadian cultural life. Although education, strictly speaking, was beyond its purview, the commission asserted that the strong U.S. influence on academic institutions in the English-speaking provinces, particularly through American teacher training and the extensive use of American textbooks, was having a deleterious impact. 'But for American hospitality,' it ironically stated, 'we might, in Canada, have been led to develop educational ideas and practices [and materials] more in keeping with our own way of

life.'[85] This report was followed in 1955 by a conference of prominent English-Canadian writers at Queen's University, which resolved 'to give a more prominent place
to Canadian literature in school curricula, textbooks, colleges, and universities and
to support Canadian libraries.'[86] Delegates also advocated the reprinting of Canadian works in inexpensive editions, an idea seconded two years later by the Ontario
Library Association, which arranged a debate on the matter between publisher Jack
McClelland and Canadian literary scholar Robert McDougall. Although McClelland
took up the nay position in the debate, he was already on the cusp of launching the
New Canadian Library (est. 1958), a series of affordable, paperback reprints under
the general editorship of Malcolm Ross that would enable the teaching of Canadian
literature in a substantial way.[87] McClelland followed up this initial venture with a
second paperback series, the Carleton Library (est. 1963), a joint initiative with
Carleton University's Institute of Canadian Studies, which included biographies,
memoirs, journals, and government documents in support of teaching and research
about Canada across a variety of disciplines.[88]

In Quebec, until 1960, the Canadianization of education occurred in fits and
starts, relying on the initiative of a few teachers and administrators, without systematic coordination or lasting impact. In 1963–6, the report of the Royal Commission
of Inquiry on Education in the Province of Quebec, which led to a complete restructuring of the school system, noted the use of outmoded teaching methods and textbooks that still promulgated agrarian and old-fashioned religious values. Although
the commission recognized the education system's history of dependence on
imported materials, it did not recommend the immediate Canadianization of textbooks. Instead, it advocated importing better-quality European textbooks from
France or Belgium, but accorded them a secondary role in schools. By recommending the replacement of textbook-based education with a pedagogy that was to focus
on the needs of the student and take into account both national culture and popular culture, the commission changed the rules of the game. While students' books
were mostly imported from France, procedures for distributing them within the
school system nonetheless benefited the domestic industry by providing business
opportunities for many publishers, distributors, and booksellers. Beyond the production of new textbooks, which were still subject to approval by the government,
an important local children's book industry evolved, with titles distributed by the
schools even though they were not part of the curriculum. In the teaching of literature, a trend to replace textbooks and anthologies with complete works gave a
boost to the distribution of paperbacks in pocket-book format.

French courses in the CEGEPs (collèges d'enseignement général et professionnel), which were founded in 1967, also had an immediate impact on the dissemination of Quebec books. From the outset, the teaching of French in the CEGEPs was organized around a common core of four separate compulsory courses devoted to poetry, the novel, drama, and non-fiction. Beginning in 1973, the provincial coordinating committee on French proposed that the curriculum focus on contemporary Quebec works, with the choice of authors and titles left to teachers. This measure dramatically boosted the book market: it is estimated that between 1967 and 1987 nearly 2.8 million books were sold solely to meet the needs of this curriculum.[89] No similar measures for history were instigated. With no consensus on the nature of the history to be taught, philosophy was chosen instead as a compulsory subject.

Despite notable signs of change at the post-secondary level through the 1950s and 1960s, the type and presentation of Canadian curricular materials at earlier levels of education remained an issue in English Canada. In the second volume of the report of the Royal Commission on Bilingualism and Biculturalism, published in 1968, Canadian history was identified as a contentious area. A survey of textbooks on Canadian history confirmed that the approach to the subject in elementary and secondary schools tended to maintain and even strengthen cultural stereotypes.[90] Pointing out that '[s]tudents are taught history because societies believe that it provides a desirable and necessary training for future citizens,' the report recommended that in the future, without ignoring the cultural differences between the French and the English, 'the study of our history should also make students aware of the positive values of the other culture and of our common cultural heritage.'[91] That same year, A.B. Hodgetts's *What Culture? What Heritage?* offered a harsh critique of how Canadian history was being taught in schools. The result of a 'two-year fact-finding investigation into the teaching of Canadian history, social studies and civics in the elementary and secondary schools of all ten provinces,' his study confirmed that at the elementary level, for example, American or British history continued to dominate classrooms, and documented 'very infrequent use of Canadian materials on bulletin boards, the failure to take advantage of the paperback revolution, and other details.' He reiterated the need, already stressed in previous studies by provincial and federal governments, for a review of textbooks. Meanwhile, 'in school libraries, American magazines and newspapers outnumbered Canadian by almost three to one,' while 'only 10 percent of the classrooms visited contained Canadian historical maps.' Finally, many academic historians and political scientists candidly expressed lack of interest in the curriculum at earlier levels of education and in Canadian content in general, indifference that translated into university graduates ill-prepared to teach elementary and high school students.[92]

What Culture? What Heritage? proved instrumental in the creation, in 1970, of the Canada Studies Foundation, an organization designed to foster ways to improve the quality of Canadian studies in the elementary and secondary schools through the creation of curricular materials and other initiatives.[93] Unfortunately, many of these materials were not widely used because they did not obtain the status of officially authorized resources at the provincial level. Nonetheless, when Hodgetts and Paul Gallagher issued a follow-up study, *Teaching Canada for the '80s* (1978), they noted a substantial increase in Canadian studies during the 1970s, crediting 'the work of the Foundation and the activities and interests of a great many other organizations and dedicated individual educators.'[94]

In *The Struggle for Canadian Universities* (1969), Robin Mathews and James Steele called for the Canadianization of the country's universities, beginning with increased hiring of Canadian academics, who would be more convinced of the relevance and legitimacy of Canadian materials. In combination, the two books encouraged the creation of the Association for Canadian Studies (est. 1973), a society intended to initiate and support research, publication, teaching, communications, and the training of students in Canadian studies at the university level, with special emphasis on interdisciplinary and multidisciplinary perspectives. Similarly, a paper presented by Mathews in 1972 on the state of teaching and research in Canadian literature at the post-secondary level contributed to the founding, in 1973, of the Association for Canadian and Quebec Literatures, an organization devoted to the promotion of research in both languages.[95]

As chairman of the Commission on Canadian Studies (1972–84), T.H.B. Symons was asked to 'study, report, and make recommendations upon the state of teaching and research in various fields of study relating to Canada,' including the 'number and content of courses' and the 'location and extent of library holdings.'[96] Because he received his mandate from the Association of Universities and Colleges of Canada, Symons had the latitude to make assessments of a trans-provincial nature. In his extensive, three-volume report, *To Know Ourselves*, he documented Canadian content in an array of university disciplines and college programs, including the sciences. He found ongoing neglect of teaching and research about Canada in many areas, an assessment that triggered curriculum changes at schools, colleges, and universities across the country. For example, supported by more than $8 million from its Heritage Trust Fund, Alberta developed a range of Canadian instructional materials which provided opportunities for authors, illustrators, editors, and regional publishers. This funding included grants to the University of Alberta Press to aid increased publication of titles on Canada. The Manitoba and Prince Edward Island education departments published *In Search of Canadian Materials* (1978) and *Readings in Prince Edward Island History* (1976) respectively.

One of the major research gains to arise out of *To Know Ourselves* was the creation, in 1978, of the Canadian Institute for Historical Microreproductions / Institut canadien de microréproductions historiques (CIHM / ICMH), known today as Canadiana.org. Funded with an initial grant of $2 million from the Canada Council, it was created to preserve Canada's print heritage and build library holdings through a large-scale microfilming project of Canadian imprints and books relating to Canada issued prior to 1900.[97] Also notable was the Department of External Affairs' creation, for distribution abroad, of several bibliographies citing Canadian studies resources, and the National Library of Canada's strengthening and enlarging of its 'bibliographic, reference and lending services ... in order to facilitate the development of Canadian studies.'[98] Even so, when James Page reviewed the situation at the end of the decade in *Reflections on the Symons Report: The State of Canadian Studies in 1980*, he concluded that, despite a remarkable response to the recommendations of *To Know Ourselves*, much remained to be done, especially at the university level. Page joined Symons in completing volume 3 of the Report of the Commission on Canadian Studies. *Some Questions of Balance: Human Resources, Higher Education and Canadian Studies* (1984) addressed concerns in higher education, notably the human resources required to support Canadian teaching and research. It concluded that 'few areas of teaching and research about Canada have been more neglected than the state of Canadian higher education itself.'[99] If university students had only minimal exposure to Canadian content, then how were the future teachers among them to obtain adequate training for elementary and high school instruction?

In Quebec, the restructuring of the school system in the 1960s led to increased possibilities for post-graduate study abroad, in Europe and in the United States. When they returned to Canada, these graduates radically reconsidered university education, principally in the social sciences but also in arts and literature. They applied their international experience to extensive research programs and, in keeping with the political climate of the time, refocused the content of teaching on national issues. In 1971 Université Laval welcomed its first cohort of students in programs in Quebec literature. In 1977, following the lead of other universities, the Université du Québec à Montréal created a doctoral program in Canadian history. The movement was also felt in Acadia and French-speaking Ontario, although in those cases it was more a matter of special courses than complete programs. The French-language universities subsequently founded scholarly journals devoted to Quebec culture and opened specialized research centres. Through their participation in the creation of the Association for Canadian Studies (1973), the American Council for Quebec Studies (1980), and the Association internationale des études québécoises (1997), the French-language universities also contributed to the development of Canadian and Quebec studies abroad.

Born of a particular situation in which the reorganization of educational structures coincided with the rise of modern nationalism, considerable advances were made between 1960 and 1980 in the Canadianization of school curricula. In both Quebec and English Canada, many of these gains resulted from the initiatives of individual teachers, from elementary school to university. Such individuals would continue to support Canadian content during the final two decades of the twentieth century, despite the absence of consistent political will on the part of municipal, provincial, or federal governments.

CASE STUDY
Canadian Content in Primary Textbooks in Quebec
– Jacques Michon

Canadianizing education through the content of textbooks was among the strategies of French Canada's clerical elites in the first half of the twentieth century. While students in the classical colleges benefited from Camille Roy's *Tableau de l'histoire de la littérature canadienne-française* (1907) and, especially, his *Morceaux choisis d'auteurs canadiens* (1934), elementary school students encountered texts by French-Canadian authors in their regular French textbooks. In books published by Catholic congregations in Quebec, the presence of the national literature increased steadily from 1918 to 1960. Excerpts from works by Canadian authors were provided for reading and analysis or recitation in class, or as illustrations of the rules of grammar and composition. These excerpts appeared side by side with texts by French authors, without being distinguished in any way. For example, in *Langue française, code grammatical et préceptes littéraires* (Montreal, 1929), a textbook for the senior elementary grades compiled by the Brothers of the Christian Schools, there were excerpts from works by Philippe Aubert de Gaspé, Louis Fréchette, Pamphile Le May, and Camille Roy, as well as writing by Jean Racine and Jean de La Fontaine.[100] Pieces by French-Canadian authors appeared in all elementary school textbooks for French, from grades one to seven; before 1960, such material represented between 25 per cent and 75 per cent of the content. This approach, which exposed students to French-Canadian literature from a very young age, supplemented the system of book prizes distributed at the end of each school year, a phenomenon discussed in chapter 2 by François Landry.

With the creation of the Quebec Department of Education in 1964, secondary education was no longer confined to classical colleges and instead became accessible to everyone. This change required a revision of the elementary curriculum, including the content of textbooks. Excerpts from the corpus of great literary writers were abandoned in favour of selections from children's literature, material often written specifically for pedagogical purposes. Elementary school students were thus no longer exposed to works from their literary heritage but, instead, to texts adapted for their age group. Furthermore, the French program of the Department of Education in 1979 relegated Quebec literature to a marginal position, leaving the decision to include it to the discretion of secondary school and CEGEP teachers. Nonetheless, in the late 1970s and early 1980s, publishers who produced texts for the CEGEP market offered many anthologies of Quebec literary texts covering every century and a wide range of genres; such variety indicates that instructors at these institutions continued to favour Quebec literature in the classroom.

Cohering through Books

JENNIFER J. CONNOR

'The cooperation of the whole community was necessary to compile this book,' declare the editors of *Dutch Oven: A Cook Book of Coveted Traditional Recipes from the Kitchens of Lunenburg* (See illus. 1.5, p. 65).[101] Issued by the Ladies Auxiliary of the Lunenburg Hospital Society in 1953, this title exemplifies one community's self-representation through print. Whether local, regional, or national, the collection and publication of personal recipes, historical narratives, and traditional stories and songs contribute to the formation of identity. Compilers have ranged from patent medicine firms that disseminate local culture in order to promote their products,

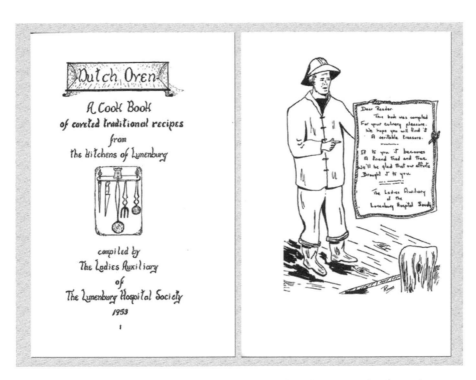

1.5 *Dutch Oven: A Cook Book of Coveted Traditional Recipes from the Kitchens of Lunenburg* (Lunenburg, NS: Lunenburg Hospital Society, Ladies Auxiliary, 1953). The fiftieth anniversary of this cookbook was celebrated in 2003. Copies are still sold at the hospital gift shop and at bookstores across the country. Courtesy of the Fishermen's Memorial Hospital Auxiliary and the Una Abrahamson Canadian Cookery Collection, University of Guelph Library.

through scholars who view folk culture as a topic for academic analysis, to community enthusiasts eager to share their material in order to preserve their traditions for future generations. While some collectors believed they were returning lore to the community to be shared anew through its presentation in books,[102] community members have occasionally regarded the static nature of print as antithetic to the vitality of oral practices.[103]

For francophone Canadians, long-standing scholarly interest inspired half a dozen important collectors whose efforts in the 1918–80 period have ensured that more material has been preserved about French-Canadian traditions than about any other group.[104] Canada's best-known pioneer in folklore studies was Marius Barbeau, an ethnologist employed by the National Museum of Canada in Ottawa, who forged a national sense of Canada's folkloric heritage. Collecting widely from Native peoples in addition to French- and English-speaking Canadians, he published books that earned the Prix David six times, and in 1950 he received the Royal Society of Canada's Lorne Pierce Medal for his outstanding contribution to Canada's critical and imaginative literature. The museum was the usual publisher of Barbeau's work, providing a solid foundation for a long-term anthropological series. For instance, his *Folk-songs of Old Quebec* (1935), issued as Bulletin No. 75, presented fifteen songs in French with English translations. The museum published bulletins solely in French as well, such as *La littérature orale en Gaspésie* (1955) by museum employee Carmen Roy; in addition to scholarly discussion, this Bulletin No. 134 included a catalogue of songs along with sayings, tales, beliefs, and medical practices. Other collectors included Luc Lacourcière and Germain Lemieux, who in addition to collecting stories and songs in Quebec and northern Ontario, produced two periodicals: *Les archives de folklore* (Montreal, 1946–50) and *Les vieux m'ont conté: contes franco-ontariens* (Montreal, 1973–). One of the most enduring francophone collections was La bonne chanson, ten volumes for schoolchildren and the general public culled from a variety of print sources and published by Charles-Emile Gadbois in St Hyacinthe in the 1940s.[105]

In English-speaking Canada, the systematic collection of local culture for regional and national distribution began to take hold in the 1920s, resulting in volumes issued by established scholarly and trade presses as well as the federal government through the National Museum of Canada. Collectors gathered materials primarily from the longer-settled central and eastern regions. Harvard University Press published W. Roy Mackenzie's *Ballads and Sea Songs from Nova Scotia* (1928), while in Toronto, Dent produced Helen Creighton's *Songs and Ballads from Nova Scotia* (1932). Creighton's collection, in particular, was deployed to promote Canadian identity. It was adopted in Nova Scotia schools, presented to visiting dignitaries, and displayed in government offices abroad.[106] Over the next thirty years, Creighton produced eight more song and tale collections from the region, including one collaboration in Gaelic. In compiling the National Museum of Canada's *Come A Singing! Canadian Folk-Songs* (1947, Bulletin No. 107), Barbeau, Arthur Lismer, and Arthur Bourinot drew on works collected by Creighton and Mackenzie, as well as those held by the museum. This selection created a strong sense of Canadian place, highlighting such locations as Barrington Street and Citadel Hill in Halifax, and the Red River Valley in Manitoba.

In the 1950s, Edith Fowke emerged as the leading collector for English-speaking Canada. Her first titles, *Folk Songs of Canada* (1954) and *Canada's Story in Song* (1960), were jointly compiled with musicians in the hope that they would 'enliven the teaching of Canadian history.'[107] Among her many books (and records) were

Traditional Singers and Songs from Ontario (1965) and *Lumbering Songs from the Northern Woods* (1970). By the late 1970s, Fowke held an academic appointment at York University and was publishing books on tales and other forms of Canadian folklore for both scholars and general readers. Fowke's books represented important reference works for teachers in elementary and secondary schools, and they advanced knowledge of Canadian lore in post-secondary institutions.

From the 1960s, the National Museum's anthropological bulletins increasingly presented the songs of smaller regions and specific ethnic groups. Kenneth Peacock's *Songs of the Newfoundland Outports* appeared in three volumes in 1965; that same year saw MacEdward Leach's *Folk Ballads and Songs of the Lower Labrador Coast*. Peacock's collection of *Twenty Ethnic Songs from Western Canada* (1966) featured Doukhobor, Mennonite, Hungarian, Ukrainian, and Czech songs in their original languages with English translations. In 1970 Robert Klymasz's *An Introduction to the Ukrainian-Canadian Emigrant Folksong Cycle* took a similar approach, the impact of the songs enhanced by the inclusion of a recording. Following the renaming of the museum in 1968, a new series was made available from the Centre for Folk Culture Studies / Centre d'études sur la culture traditionelle;[108] among its original studies was Paper No. 26, a synthetic work of scholarship by Carole Henderson Carpenter, *Many Voices: A Study of Folklore Activities in Canada and Their Role in Canadian Culture* (1979).

Folklore publications are shaped by collectors' motives and intended audiences. The most ubiquitous commercial distributors of community lore were patent medicine firms. To appeal to customers, these companies added local tales, songs, and testimonials to the usual mix of cure claims, household tips, recipes, calendars, and brief essays in their pamphlets and almanacs. For example, Gerald S. Doyle's *Old-Time Songs and Poetry of Newfoundland*, published in five editions from 1927, consolidated a strong sense of identity among Newfoundlanders. Distributed free throughout the island by Doyle's patent medicine company, these books became 'prized possessions in many households.'[109] Drawing from earlier broadsides and songsters published in St John's, Doyle's collection revived interest in local songs.

Alongside commercial and scholarly collectors, community members published their own lore and history. An example that blends local history, French-Canadian tradition, and English-Canadian popularization concerns the Ottawa Valley strongman Joseph Montferrand, who became Joe Mufferaw in legend. Local resident Bernie Bedore published his own tall tales about Mufferaw in the 1970s, while Joan Finnigan drew on Bedore's tales and compiled anecdotes from other residents in various publications, such as *'I Come from the Valley': The Ottawa Valley* (1976), issued in Toronto by NC Press.[110] Around the same time, Newfoundland's Breakwater Books began a series entitled Canada's Atlantic Folklore and Folklife, issuing unedited collections to reflect 'more honestly the culture which we are striving to preserve,' according to the jacket of Len Margaret's *fish & brewis, toutens & tales: Recipes and Recollections from St. Leonard's, Newfoundland* (1980).

Folklore also appears in the serials issued by regional and local history societies, such as the annual reports and volumes of the Waterloo Historical Society (1913–). The Pennsylvania German Folklore Society of Ontario issued *Canadian German Folklore* (Kitchener, 1961–89), and created a sense of cohesion for this ethnic group, in part through historical studies of German-language publishing in the Kitchener-Waterloo area. Perhaps taking advantage of Canada's strengthened sense of national identity following the Centennial celebrations of 1967, as well as contributing to it by evoking a nostalgic sense of place, in the 1970s Ontario-based publishers began to issue facsimile reprints of early Canadian historical imprints. In Toronto, Coles produced many titles in paperback such as C.S. Clark's *Of Toronto the Good* (1898; 1970), W.H. Smith's *Smith's Canadian Gazetteer* (1846; 1972), and Newton Bosworth's *Hochelaga Depicta, Or the Early History of Montreal* (1846; 1974). In Belleville, Ontario, Mika Press specialized in local history, issuing a facsimile reprint of William Canniff's *The Settlement of Upper Canada* (1869; 1971) and reprints of county atlases along with new historical studies.

Throughout rural Canada, the compilation and publication of book-length local histories have often been inspired by forthcoming jubilees or centenaries and undertaken by local women's groups, some of whose efforts have been guided by printing companies such as Friesens, discussed by Linda Bedwell in chapter 13. Writing collectively of the more than one thousand volumes of this nature found in the Saskatchewan Legislative Library, Barbara Powell noted: 'They celebrated the pioneer past and consolidated community identity through communal authorial effort.'[111]

Community collections are often pamphlets produced by local printers in small print runs, with minimal attention to aspects of format, such as dates or pagination. Distributed through local outlets, these ephemeral publications are thus more likely to be found in regional archives than on the shelves of major libraries. Throughout the twentieth century, members of smaller, specialized communities – particularly church and hospital volunteers – continued a practice established in the nineteenth century by printing collections of their own recipes, usually for fund-raising purposes.[112] To return to the example cited earlier, it was the Ladies Auxiliary of the Lunenburg Hospital Society in Nova Scotia that produced *Dutch Oven*, a cookbook so popular that it enjoyed seventeen reprints by 1983. Gathering recipes from mem-

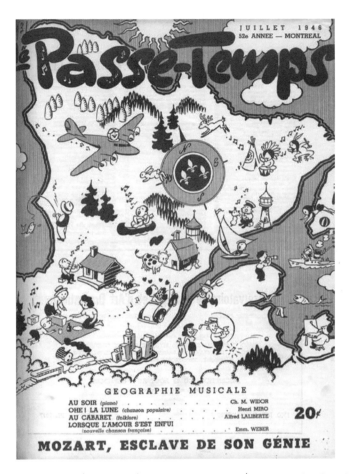

1.6 *Le Passe-Temps*, July 1946 (Montreal: Éditions du Passe-temps). Designed for the whole family, *Le Passe-Temps*, published in Montreal from 1895 until 1949, was the longest-lived Canadian musical periodical. Courtesy of LAC/BAC, Music Division, e003895007.

bers, who generally were identified, such efforts often included household hints and advertisements from local merchants. Sometimes a cookbook noted a community goal: proceeds from the sale of *Our Ladies' Choice Cook Book*, for example, which was compiled by the Girls Friendly Society in Bonavista, Newfoundland (ca. 1978), went toward the building fund for the new Anglican church. Typically typeset in the 1920s and 1930s, later community publications (like later bulletins of the National Museum) were produced from typewritten text with paper covers. Some, like *Dutch Oven*, collated the signed handwritten recipes of contributors; in the *Guelph Commu-*

nity Cookbook (1977), handwritten recipes joined typewritten household hints in a book whose apparatus included a table of contents page and acknowledgments.

Throughout the twentieth century, book and pamphlet collections of local information and traditions, as well as some magazines (see illus. 1.6, p. 69), promoted and maintained the identity of communities across Canada. Familiar publications such as community cookbooks were joined by collections of songs and stories issued by scholars and community histories that marked chronological milestones. Together, these genres fortified a sense of national unity by building a cross-Canadian familiarity with far-distant regions and different cultural groups. From the local to the national, printed documents helped to construct a complex identity that was characterized by John Murray Gibbon, colleague of Marius Barbeau and CPR publicist who organized many folk festivals at CPR hotels,[113] as a *Canadian Mosaic* (1938).

Picturing Canada

JO NORDLEY BEGLO

Canadian art books and exhibition catalogues have captured and disseminated enduring images of Canada: the land, cities and monuments, and the people, represented by painters and other visual artists. The activities and publications of the country's developing cultural institutions played a significant role in the early recognition of images that would come to define Canada. Incorporated by an Act of Parliament in 1913, the National Gallery of Canada quickly implemented a loan exhibition program that was unprecedented among national galleries worldwide. The period between the two world wars was an optimistic era for the visual arts with the expansion in 1926 of the Art Gallery of Toronto, the construction in 1931 of a new public gallery in Vancouver, and the opening in 1933 of the Musée de la Province de Québec. Well-established institutions such as the Art Association of Montreal, the Royal Canadian Academy of Arts, and the Ontario Society of Artists were joined by new art societies founded in Ontario, Manitoba, Alberta, and the Maritimes. These bodies supported increasing numbers of exhibitions and publications. By 1980 images such as Cornelius Krieghoff's *Habitant Farm* (1854), Tom Thomson's *Jack Pine* (1916–17), and Emily Carr's *Big Raven* (1928) had become part of a shared visual vocab-

ulary, recognized at home and abroad as quintessentially Canadian, and disseminated in formats ranging from costly volumes to calendars and postage stamps.

Before the First World War, nineteenth-century European paradigms of subject
and technique influenced not only painting but also photography, particularly in a
distinctive genre of publication: the Canadian souvenir view album. Often illustrated by anonymous photographers and aimed at tourists, potential settlers, and
investors, these volumes were popular from the 1880s through the 1930s, presenting 'utopian views of the potential and progress' of cities across the Dominion during a period of rapid growth and grand ambition.[114] As the century progressed,
books of photographs focusing on the land and people of Canada were issued under
the auspices of the Still Photography Division of the National Film Board as well as
by commercial publishers.[115] A masterpiece of the genre, Lorraine Monk's *Canada:
The Year of the Land*, celebrated Canada's Centennial in 1967.

A new direction in Canadian art was announced in 1920 when the Group of
Seven's first exhibition, held at the Art Gallery of Toronto, proclaimed an inherently
Canadian iconography in the northern landscape. The National Gallery introduced
this vision to Europe in 1924, when it organized the Canadian Section of the first
British Empire Exhibition at Wembley Park, London. Canada was the only dominion to produce its own catalogue as well as an accompanying *Portfolio of Pictures*. The
covers, designed by J.E.H. MacDonald, established enduring Canadian images: a
canoe navigating a rugged landscape dominated by a twisted pine (catalogue; see
illus. 1.7, p. 72); a lone tree set against a starry sky ablaze with northern lights (portfolio). The portfolio's full-page illustrations showcased a distinctive Canadian school
of painting. The foreword by Eric Brown, director of the National Gallery, attributed
the vigour of Canada's artists to the 'tremendously intense character' and seasonal
colour of the country.[116] In 1927 Canada sent a major exhibition to Paris accompanied by a catalogue resplendent with cover images by J.E.H. MacDonald. The same
year, the National Gallery and the National Museum in Ottawa mounted Canadian
West Coast Art, Native and Modern, to explore relationships between Canadian
painters and Aboriginal arts. This exhibition marked the national debut of Emily
Carr, who contributed twenty-six works and designed the catalogue cover, featuring
a totem pole and decorative border inspired by Northwest Coast traditions.

In addition to the publication of catalogues, the National Gallery, through its
Canadian art reproduction program, initiated in the 1920s, placed thousands of
Canadian images in schools, libraries, public buildings, and private homes.[117] Reproduced as prints and postcards, images such as Thomson's *Jack Pine* were widely distributed across the country and, along with study guides prepared by Arthur

1.7 J.E.H. MacDonald (designer), cover of *Canadian Section of Fine Arts, British Empire Exhibition, London, 1924.* Collection of Richard Landon.

Lismer, incorporated into public school curricula. This ferment also prompted the first illustrated monographs on Canadian art. Reflecting the controversies of the time, in *The Fine Arts in Canada* (1925) Newton MacTavish retained the criteria of nine-teenth-century academic traditions while denying the existence of art that was 'peculiarly Canadian.'[118] F.B. Housser's passionate rejoinder, *A Canadian Art Movement: The Story of the Group of Seven* (1926), championed the Group as a distinctly Canadian phenomenon, 'drawing its inspiration from the backwoods.'[119] In the *Yearbook of the Arts in Canada* for 1928–9 (see illus. 13.5, p. 380), Bertram Brooker strenuously defended modern art, while Lismer credited the National Gallery's Canadian art reproduction program with providing 'a source of educational enlightenment to thousands.'[120] The second *Yearbook*, delayed by the Depression until 1936, reproduced more than a hundred works of Canadian painting, sculpture, architecture, and photography.

In Quebec during the same era, signs of new vitality were evident in publications such as Jean Chauvin's *Ateliers* (1928). With the acumen of a journalist sympathetic to modern art, Chauvin presented twenty-two painters, sculptors, printmakers, and architects in an illustrated volume, published by Louis Carrier, with a title page designed by Thoreau MacDonald. Beginning with *Peintres et tableaux* (1936), Gérard Morisset issued groundbreaking studies of the traditional arts of New France and Quebec. Monographs on modern Quebec artists such as James Wilson Morrice, John Lyman, Goodridge Roberts, Alfred Pellan, and Paul-Émile Borduas followed in the 1940s, in the Collection art vivant series from Les Éditions de l'Arbre in Montreal.

The publishing program of Ryerson Press, guided by Lorne Pierce, was a vital force in promoting Canadian art. Beginning in the 1930s, Ryerson issued volumes on many individual artists as well as collective studies such as *Group of Seven* (1944) and *Painters of Quebec* (1946). Ryerson's Canadian Art series, launched in 1937 in collaboration with A.H. Robson, made illustrated art books accessible in a compact, standardized format. Robson's *Canadian Landscape Painters* (1932) was a tour de force, illustrated with seventy-five colour plates of works by fifty artists. His foreword argued that 'in the artists of today, Canada has a school of Canadian painters, rapidly growing in proportions and importance.'[121] Ryerson also published watershed works by Marius Barbeau, whose Cornelius Krieghoff biography and catalogue raisonné appeared in 1934, and Donald W. Buchanan, whose illustrated biography and catalogue raisonné of Morrice followed in 1936. This phase of publishing activity culminated in the first edition of Graham McInnes's *A Short History of Canadian Art* (1939), which included a bibliography of some sixty items. For the frontispiece, he selected Tom Thomson's *Spring Ice* (1916), followed by familiar landscape scenes ranging from those of Krieghoff to J.E.H. MacDonald.

By the time the country entered the Second World War, a distinct canon of images had been firmly established, powerfully consolidating Canada's identity as a rugged northern nation. This canon was further reinforced by an ambitious project, undertaken in 1942 by the Toronto printing firm of Sampson-Matthews in partnership with the National Gallery, to produce large-scale silkscreen prints of Canadian art for widespread distribution to military bases and schools. The resulting series of thirty-six wartime (1942–5) and eighty-one post-war (1945–63) prints by more than fifty artists depicted the landscape from coast to coast.[122]

During the post-war period, Canadian art publishing and the dissemination of images increased dramatically in the wake of the Massey Report of 1951 and the Symons Report of 1975. R.H. Hubbard's catalogue of the National Gallery's permanent collection, *Canadian School* (1960), as well as J. Russell Harper's *Painting in Canada* (1966), Dennis Reid's *Group of Seven* (1970), and Charles Hill's *Canadian Painting in the Thirties* (1975), created new standards for scholarship and set the foundations for ongoing research. With the introduction of Canadian art history into university curricula, iconic images were analyzed in studies such as François-Marc Gagnon's *Paul-Émile Borduas, 1905–1960: Biographie critique et analyse de l'oeuvre* (1978). Expanded exhibition programs in Canadian museums prompted an array of publications in both official languages, including catalogues of travelling exhibitions, among them the Vancouver Art Gallery's *Emily Carr: A Centennial Exhibition Celebrating the One Hundredth Anniversary of Her Birth* (1971), and the Musée du Québec's *L'art du paysage au Québec, 1800–1940* (1978). Post-war publications also captured new artistic interpretations in Joyce Wieland's *Reason over Passion* quilt (1968), Ken Danby's images of sport, and the realist visions of Alex Colville and Christopher Pratt. As the century drew to a close, 'picturing Canada' became possible not only through a rich repertoire of published materials, listed in *Art and Architecture in Canada: A Bibliography and Guide to the Literature to 1981* (1991), but also with the aid of digital resources, provided under the auspices of agencies such as the Canadian Heritage Information Network (CHIN).

chapter 2

SYMBOLIC VALUE OF BOOKS

Books and Reading in Canadian Art

CAROLE GERSON AND YVAN LAMONDE

As Canada entered the modern era, artists retained earlier patterns of representing books and reading, including the use of books in portraits and in still-life arrangements.[1] However, the growing dominance of representations of wilderness and landscape as Canada's hallmark features, described in chapter 1 by Jo Nordley Beglo, led to critics' marginalization of art depicting social topics.

While the book remained a significant feature in Canadian portraiture after 1918, its symbolism altered. Less a general marker of social or intellectual class than in the nineteenth century, images of books in twentieth-century art instead strengthened links between reading and gender. The earlier practice of using books to signal social status did not disappear entirely – witness Ozias Leduc's painting of businessman Frederick Bindoff in the classic pose of the interrupted reader (1935). However, a photograph of medical writer Dr Earle P. Scarlett carefully posed in his book-lined Calgary study (1961)[2] demonstrates that when books appear in formal portraits of men, their usual role is to identify the subject as an author, as in Adrien Hébert's portrait of Marcel Dugas (ca. 1923), Edwin Holgate's portrait of Stephen Leacock (1943) (see illus. 3.2, p. 124), and Yousuf Karsh's two photographs of Marshall McLuhan taken in 1974, one with him holding a closed book and the other with open books on his desk.[3] In paintings by Hébert, books also enhance artists' studios, following the example of still-life settings by Leduc.[4]

Although the intellectual or literary abilities of women were likewise occasionally signalled by the presence of books,[5] it has been far more common to depict women as readers. Analysis of the biographical connections between artists and their subjects suggests that the image of the solitary reader implies intimacy. In these paintings, the book simultaneously represents 'a text, the act of reading, and a personal experience.'[6] Images of men engaged in reading are relatively rare and are usually created by friends or relatives: Marian Scott's undated sketch of her husband *F.R. Scott Reading in Bed*,[7] Holgate's portrait of his close friend, critic Jean Chauvin (1933), Hébert's affectionate picture of his brother, *Henri Hébert lisant* (1938), and John Lyman's respectful portrait of his father (1922).[8] When the reader is an unnamed man, the preferred genre is the newspaper.

Representations of newspapers and magazines may invoke social commentary, as in images of the Depression that depict unemployed men reading newspapers in public places, often out of doors, in an urban setting.[9] Newspapers also occasionally appear in work by Canadian war artists, whose scenes of battle-fatigued soldiers at rest or in transit suggest that reading had to compete with card-playing and napping.[10] However, because most readers are female, most scenes of reading occur in domestic spaces – usually indoors in a boudoir or a living room or at a table, sometimes by a window. Scenes of outdoor reading involving women tend to relate to social occasions such as a summer picnic or a beach holiday.[11]

Whereas the standard use of books in formal portraiture is to present the subject either gazing outward while holding a closed book that connotes education or social status, or as an interrupted reader glancing up from an open book, thereby bringing the full face into view, most depictions of the woman reader present a different image. Sometimes she gazes dreamily away from her book, as in Jeanne Rhéaume's *Portrait of a Woman* (1947),[12] but usually she is utterly absorbed. With her eyes hooded and her face shadowed, the solitary woman reader embodies the pleasure of reading as a fulfilling experience in itself. We occasionally learn her name, but more often than not both the text and the woman remain anonymous, as in Molly Lamb Bobak's powerful wartime sketch simply titled *CWAC Reading a Book* (see illus. 18.2, p. 494). The erotic potential of the pursuit receives unexpected expression in Holgate's *Mother and Daughter* (1926) (see illus. 2.1, p. 77), in which both the woman and the child are so attentive to their book that the mother's nakedness goes unnoticed. This painting partakes of two conventions – the reading nude[13] and the intimacy of shared reading, the latter also a feature of Lyman's *The Serial Novel* (ca. 1935) and John Alexander Hall's *Lydia and Veronica* (1940) (see illus. 2.2, p. 78).[14]

2.1 Edwin Holgate, *Mother and Daughter* (1926). Courtesy of the Estate of Edwin Holgate and the McMichael Canadian Art Collection, Gift of Mr Syd Hoare, 1971.16.

Child readers of both sexes are likewise depicted as deeply absorbed, as in Pegi Nicol MacLeod's picture of her daughter, *Jane Reading* (ca. 1948) (see illus. 17.2, p. 486). While representations of small boys reading are more frequent than those of young men, portraits of female readers are dispersed across all age groups. The convention of representing women as readers takes on additional resonance when adopted by the female painter for her own self-portrait as did Christiane Pflug in *Self Portrait in a Window Pane* (1962) and Betty Goodwin in *Self-Portrait Three* (ca. 1954–5).[15]

Rather than the act of reading, it is the symbolic weight of the material book as

2.2 John Alexander Hall, *Lydia and Veronica* (1940). Courtesy of Pauline Hall and the Art Gallery of Ontario, Toronto. Gift of the artist, Newmarket, 1996.

cultural artifact and repository of knowledge that accounts for its continuing presence in still-life paintings. Goodridge Roberts frequently used an unidentified book to invoke the life of the mind, letting a volume sit in its hard-edged solidity beside sensuous fruit that connotes the life of the body.[16] In the paintings of Paul-Émile Borduas, the image of the book alters from a concrete object in an early still life (1923) to a fluid abstraction in *Composition in Blue, White and Red* (1944).[17]

Books whose titles are identified – a long-standing practice in European art[18] – add further meaning, as in some canvases of Leduc.[19] Alfred Pellan's *La table verte* (ca. 1934) provocatively cites Proust as the author of the book sitting open on the table.[20] The naming of a book's author or title may be whimsical, as in Norman Bethune's 1935 watercolour of himself reading Marx in bed,[21] or it can provide a narrative for a painting. Maxwell Bates's *Modern Olympia* (1969) centres on a coquette lying on a bed, framed by a flyer displaying the words 'Olympia – 1969' under her right forearm, while Émile Zola's *Nana* lies closed beside her left thigh. In Bates's *Reception #4* (1971), depicting a group of prostitutes waiting for clients in a hotel, the viewer's eye is drawn to the word 'Movie' on the magazine being read by the woman displaying the most flesh.[22]

As the artistic experimentation of the 1960s and 1970s swept through Canada, books began to appear in sculptures and installations, as in the work of Pierre Ayot. Artists envisioned new relationships among books, images, and words, questioning traditional generic distinctions by turning paintings, drawings, and even quilts into texts to be read. In chapter 13, Claudette Hould describes the growth of the genre of the *livre d'artiste* in Quebec. A concrete poem such as Judith Copithorne's untitled 1973 drawing narrates a lovers' relationship by uniting visual images of a ringing telephone and books by William Blake, Karl Marx, and Anaïs Nin with the words of her own poem (see illus. 2.3, p. 80). Joyce Wieland transformed books into art and art into books with her exhibit True Patriot Love / Véritable amour patriotique in 1971. To create her exhibition catalogue, she appropriated an existing technical tome, *Illustrated Flora of the Canadian Arctic Archipelago* (1964, Bulletin No. 146 of the Department of the Secretary of State), into which she paper-clipped images of her own work, including stills and text from her film on Tom Thomson. The resulting catalogue, reproduced in multiple photocopies, is itself an artistic statement (as well as a challenge to library catalogues), merging official print discourse with Wieland's nationalistic images. Further artistic play with the concept and form of the book appears in Michael Snow's *Cover to Cover* (1975), an unpaginated bound volume whose text consists of photographs arranged to subvert conventional notions of the orderly book. The work of Wieland and Snow in Toronto in the 1970s was a quiet prelude to the developments of the 1980s, when textualizing of the canvas, by adding long written passages to visual images, would become a major political strategy of feminist and First Nations artists. Charles Rea, working in Vancouver, dreamed up yet another innovation. He created three-dimensional artworks by nailing discarded books onto boards and thickly painting the resulting structures to represent architectural spaces such as cathedrals,[23] thereby taking one step further the artistic trend to simultaneously hallow and challenge the sanctity of the material book.

2.3 Judith Copithorne, 'The telephone ringing it's changes in the evening light,' as published in *Arrangements* (Vancouver: Intermedia Press, 1973). Courtesy of Judith Copithorne and the Thomas Fisher Rare Book Library, University of Toronto.

The Image of the Book in Advertising

RUSSELL JOHNSTON, LYNDSEY NOWAKOWSKI-DAILEY, MICHELLE PRESTON, AND JAIME SWEETING

Advertising is a form of mediated communication intended for mass persuasion. Because an advertisement has mere seconds to sell a product, its words and images are manipulated to present instantly recognizable scenes that show the product in a desirable light. Modern Canadian advertising emerged early in the twentieth century when advertising agents mastered this technique in the print media.[24] While never a predominant element in Canadian advertising, images of books and other reading material have occasionally appeared as simple yet powerful symbols. Just as Canadian artists for many centuries featured books in the visual vocabulary of their work, advertisers have employed the iconic value of books for their own ends. Through much of the twentieth century, in both French and English Canada, advertisements featured books in four common scenarios: schooling, the pursuit of leisure, appeals to authority, and the display of cultural capital.

Early in the period, books were predominantly incorporated into advertising to identify students and school settings and to signify diligent preparation for life and a successful career. Children were depicted with textbooks to suggest eager learners filled with innocence and hope for a better future. After 1945, books also marked young adults as ambitious, upwardly mobile university students. A typical scene revealed a youth studying by the dim light of a table lamp while an anxious parent hovered in the shadows. Readers were prompted to ask: how could a caring mother help her hard-working son? The advertiser always had an answer. This use of the book was favoured in advertisements for products ranging from insurance to prepared foods.

Reading as an idyllic adult pastime comprised a second significant representation. A solitary figure, book in hand, relaxing in a serene, appealing setting, such as a cozy den or sunlit beach, was one common image. Alternatively, small groups, such as a couple or family, might be seen intimately sharing a newspaper or storybook, drawn together, both literally and figuratively, around the printed page. In both depictions, the book, or some other source of reading, suggested that comfort and happiness would be attained by using the advertised product. In the years immediately after the Second World War, images of books were manipulated in this way to structure advertisements for building supplies and household conveniences; later, this representation appeared in advertisements for vacation destinations and financial services.

Advertisements often exploited the popular belief that books represent truth and knowledge. Objective sources of authority can reinforce an advertiser's claims, and scientific research is often used in this respect. Images of books, however, can suggest authority visually without reference to actual research. Any bound sheaf of papers may connote facts and learned opinion, even if the text is never named, opened, or quoted. An apt example of this strategy appeared in a 1953 advertisement for the federal Progressive Conservative Party, which depicted twenty hardcover volumes representing the history of Canada and proclaimed that 'the record speaks' on the party's behalf. Precisely what it said was left to the imagination.

The most common use of books in advertisements has been to deploy them more subtly to complete a setting and serve as a signifier of class or gender. Sometimes these advertisements include individuals whose reading material conveys something about their personality. In advertisements that depict unpeopled rooms, books enhance the setting's desirability, giving it more warmth than could be achieved with static arrangements of furniture. In both scenarios, the advertised product is marked with the signs of class and gender created by its association with reading materials and their implied cultural capital. The audience is encouraged to identify with and emulate the cultural tastes depicted in the advertisement, and therefore to purchase the featured product. Leather-bound books and recognized classics (though titles are rarely legible) or multiple bookshelves heavy with volumes continued to connote traditional values by suggesting edification, high culture, permanence, 'old money,' power, and masculinity. Advertisements depicting executives or professionals drew upon this representation, as did those for liquor, tobacco, and goods designed for men (see illus. 2.4, p. 82). In contrast, a scene including paperbacks and magazines signified modern sensibilities by suggesting diversion, popular culture, transience, suburbia, freedom, and femininity. Advertisements evoking these concepts sold personal hygiene products, home appliances and cleansers, and home decor.

These four major categories do not account for every way in which books and other reading materials were portrayed in advertisements before 1980. Nonetheless, their ubiquity is evidenced by advertisers' occasional ironic inversion of these representations. Advertisements for personal hygiene products in the 1930s fostered anxiety about individual desirability by picturing lonely individuals whose only companions were books (see illus. 2.5, p. 84). In such advertisements, a book may be cast aside by a doleful character mooning over a silent telephone. In 1956, a Molson's Golden advertisement playfully inverted a standard representation by depicting a sombre library reading room to indicate how an ale could taste 'dry.' The authoritative nature of the setting was undercut by the product's spokesperson, a smirking cartoon lion (the product logo) in pince-nez (see illus. 2.6, p. 85). Both this willingness to poke fun at authority and the suggestion that bookish people are unhappy accelerated after 1960, in keeping with broader cultural trends that celebrated hedonistic youth culture and the relaxation of formal social codes.

2.4 Advertisement for du Maurier cigarettes, *Le Magazine Maclean* (Montreal), August 1964. Courtesy of Imperial Tobacco, *Maclean's,* and the Toronto Public Library (TRL).

2.5 Advertisement for Lux soap, *Chatelaine* (Toronto), February 1941. Courtesy of Unilever Canada, *Chatelaine*, and the Thomas Fisher Rare Book Library, University of Toronto.

"The French have a word for it" said Goldie

"But how can an *ale* be *dry?*" demanded Goldie's friend.

"Let's not quibble," said the Golden Ale lion, "Molson's Golden is a delightfully smooth and satisfying liquid. But the big news is that each sip leaves behind it a refreshingly clean taste that has been described as *dry*. Just enough hops are used to keep it from being too sweet — yet Golden is never, never bitter. The French say *sec* of a fine dinner wine. Canadians say *dry* of this perfect ale."

Lighter than most, smoother than any, Molson's Golden retains all the zest and authority of a traditional ale.

You'll find every mellow swallow tastes the same in any language — a golden, gratifying delight.

BREWERS SINCE 1786

MOLSON'S GOLDEN ALE

LIGHTER, MUCH SMOOTHER, AND A MITE "DRIER"

2.6 Advertisement for Molson's Golden Ale, *Maclean's* (Toronto), April 1956. Courtesy of Molson Canada, *Maclean's*, and the Thomas Fisher Rare Book Library, University of Toronto.

Prize Books in Quebec

FRANÇOIS LANDRY

In 1856 Pierre-Joseph-Olivier Chauveau, Quebec's superintendent of public education, instituted the distribution of book prizes through the Department of Public Instruction (DPI), awarding them to top students at the end of every school year. A tradition imported from France, its purpose was to encourage the reading of 'good books' by young people and to provide the basis of small family libraries in their homes. Heavily bound in imitation linen and red percaline, sporting gilt-edged pages, and embossed with Quebec's coat of arms, these books were trophies to be exhibited by children who came first in their classes.

Beginning in 1876, Quebec placed its own cultural stamp on the practice of awarding school book prizes. To educate the nation and support the provincial book industry, the government encouraged the publication of series of works by French-Canadian writers. Abbé Henri-Raymond Casgrain, the first editor chosen to oversee these publications, issued such works as Philippe Aubert de Gaspé's *Les Anciens Canadiens* and Patrice Lacombe's *La terre paternelle*. Between 1876 and 1886, the government distributed an estimated 175,000 books in the Casgrain series through the school book prize program.[25] At the end of the 1880s, Casgrain's series was replaced by the ultramontane Bibliothèque religieuse et nationale, published by Cadieux & Derome. More than 335,000 volumes in this series were sold in Quebec between 1882 and 1912,[26] before it was superseded by Librairie Beauchemin's Bibliothèque canadienne.

Supported by the religious and political elites, the Bibliothèque canadienne also highlighted the patriotic and religious values of French Canada, but it was considered better suited to the needs of the school system. Divided into six series named after heroes of New France – Dollard, Montcalm, Maisonneuve, Laval, Champlain, and Jacques Cartier – with a different format for each series and a choice of eight bindings, the Bibliothèque canadienne offered an impressive range of books for every taste and budget (see illus. 2.7, p. 87).[27] At its inception, the Bibliothèque canadienne published the authors of the 'patriotic school' of Quebec, whose books soon attained the status of classics. The posthumous fame of such authors as Abbé Casgrain, Joseph Marmette, Antoine Gérin-Lajoie, Hubert LaRue, Laurent-Olivier David, and Laure Conan was largely due to the dissemination of these Beauchemin editions. From 1912 to 1929, the DPI alone purchased nearly half a million volumes in the series. Patrice Lacombe's *La terre paternelle,* which sold 20,000 copies, topped

2.7 Examples of prize books from the Bibliothèque canadienne series published by Librairie Beauchemin (Montreal), 1924–7. Top (l. to r.): Françoise, *Fleurs champêtres* (Coll. Maisonneuve), 1924, paperback edition, 21 x 13 cm; Hector Berthelot, *Montréal, le bon vieux temps*, 2nd series (Coll. Laval), 1924, in red cloth with a fleur de lys and the arms of the Province of Quebec, 23 x 16 cm; Georges Bellerive, *Artistes-peintres canadiens-français, les anciens*, 2nd edition (Coll. Laval), 1927, in half leather and marbled boards, 23 x 16 cm. Bottom (l. to r.): Henri-Raymond Casgrain, *F.-X. Garneau et Francis Parkman* (Coll. Montcalm), 1926, in imitation linen decorated with the arms of the Commission des écoles catholiques de Montréal, 21 x 13 cm; Laurent-Olivier David, *Tribuns et avocats* (Coll. Montcalm), 1926, in red cloth with maple leaves and the arms of the Province of Quebec, 20 x 13 cm; L.-O. David, *La jeunesse et l'avenir* (Coll. Montcalm), 1926, in ochre cloth, 20 x 13 cm. Courtesy of Librairie Beauchemin and private collection.

the list.[28] By 1940, the Bibliothèque canadienne comprised 161 titles. In addition to the DPI, schools, colleges, school boards, and libraries purchased these books. While new Quebec titles had print runs of a thousand copies during this period, a book in one of these series could easily have a print run ten times higher.

Between the two world wars, Granger Frères, the Librairie générale canadienne, the Bibliothèque de l'Action française, and Éditions Albert Lévesque followed Beauchemin's example, creating competing series for the prize-book market. A closely related development was the emergence of a French-Canadian children's literature in the early 1920s, for these series included the earliest books written especially for young people. In the 1940s and 1950s, Éditions Variétés and Fides followed suit with the publication of additional series. With the dissolution of the DPI in 1964, and the creation of the Department of Education, which ended the school book prize program, the market for these books collapsed, leading to the disappearance of all series that Quebec publishers had established for that purpose.

Marshall McLuhan and the History of the Book

RICHARD CAVELL

Winner of the Governor General's Award for non-fiction in 1962, Marshall McLuhan's influential volume *The Gutenberg Galaxy* has never been out of print. Its telling subtitle, *The Making of Typographic Man*, signals its concern with printing and social change and with the psychological effects of print technology. An English professor at the University of Toronto, McLuhan developed an analysis of the relations among orality, print, and electronic communications that also anticipated many concerns that would be raised by scholars of book history and print culture.

McLuhan's interest in the material and cultural significance of the book was indebted to earlier research, such as H.J. Chaytor's study of script and print, David Diringer's account of the alphabet, and Lucien Febvre and Henri-Jean Martin's notion of eye and ear cultures, as well as Harold A. Innis's concept of media biases.[29] *The Gutenberg Galaxy* asserts that cultural history is recursive, rather than linear; McLuhan thus posits the book within a series of historical eruptions from orality to script to print to electronic media, which, in their non-linear organization, have much in common with oral modes. Arguing for the intermediation of media, McLuhan notes the formulaic quality of oral texts, the attempt of printed texts to duplicate scribal ones, and the ways in which electronic 'texts' configure themselves in terms of the book.

The Gutenberg Galaxy challenges the conventions of the book and of the printed page, in Raymond Williams's view self-consciously deconstructing itself to illustrate its argument that the linearity of print imposes its own teleologies on the material it communicates, so that they become naturalized as inherent to thought rather than understood as dependent upon conformity to a specific medium.[30] In its material form, *The Gutenberg Galaxy* radically disrupts the integrity of the book as medium, presenting itself as 110 asterisked footnotes to an absent text – that of The Book itself, rendered culturally marginal, according to McLuhan's theories, in the electronic era. With its introduction at the end, and having no conclusion, *The Gutenberg Galaxy* at once testifies to its status as 'non-book,' to which McLuhan insisted it belonged,[31] and to the exigencies of the book as medium. This focus on the medium made possible McLuhan's analysis of how the book had been complicit in the creation of the notion of the individual, the construction of the nation, the fragmentation of sensibility, and the breakdown of the *sensus communis*. In his view, the process of book printing was prototypical of assembly-line technology in its dependence on a few infinitely substitutable parts to mass-produce identical consumer objects.

The formal and methodological brilliance of *The Gutenberg Galaxy* ensured that it was at once groundbreaking and a dead end, in that its arguments could not be built upon within a research context. The volume's most serious critic, Elizabeth L. Eisenstein, sought, thus, not to extend McLuhan's research, but to adapt its insights to a more conventional historical model. A significant text in the field of book history, *The Printing Press as an Agent of Change* (1979) credited McLuhan as an inspiration but argued that McLuhan's macro-historical concerns with aspects of mediation resulted in a lack of detailed historical analysis.[32] In reviewing Eisenstein's book, McLuhan argued that it was precisely the notion of historical *change* that eluded her study, in that it posited the book as a static entity rather than one that both produced and was the product of historical change.[33]

A generation of critics schooled in the complexities of poststructuralism have tended to agree on McLuhan's primal significance. Jacques Derrida develops the dynamics of orality and literacy, book and writing, into the methodology of deconstruction in *De la grammatologie* (1967). D.F. McKenzie's *Bibliography and the Sociology of Texts* (1986) cites *The Gutenberg Galaxy* as a foundational work. Adrian Johns, in *The*

Nature of the Book (1998), returns to McLuhan's historical model through the articulation of a 'network' theory of production, whereby the book is understood as functioning epistemically, ordering knowledge according to its own dictates.

Perhaps McLuhan's greatest legacy has been his insistence on the materiality of the book as signifier, and hence, in books such as *The Medium Is the Massage* (1967), his empathy with the tradition of the *livre d'artiste*. John Robert Colombo has suggested that the typographical experiments of McLuhan's work, especially *Verbi-Voco-Visual Explorations* (1967), has had a profound effect on the development of typography in Canada.[34] That influence extends to concrete poets such as bpNichol and their bookish experiments, as well as to the history of book design.[35] In retrospect, McLuhan emerges as a historian of the book *sui generis* whose work inspired innovation in multiple fields, many of which emerged only after his death in 1980, including critical and spatial theory, as well as the media studies with which he is most often associated.

McLuhan understood that the materialities of the book, far from being outmoded or obsolete in electronic culture, would remain prototypical: the book's volumetric compaction returns in the boxes for video cassettes and DVDs; its pages become the model for the Internet screen. No longer the ground of cultural production, the book has become the figure, studied by academics as an object of major research in and of itself, apart from its content, thus giving further credence to McLuhan's insistence that the medium is the message.

PART TWO

AUTHORSHIP

chapter 3

AUTHORS' CAREERS

Social and Cultural Profile of Writers

CAROLE GERSON AND MARIE-PIER LUNEAU

When La Grande Sauterelle asks the narrator of *Volkswagen Blues* what he does for a living, he answers without hesitation:

> 'I'm a writer,' said the man. 'What are you?'
> 'A mechanic,' she said. 'I studied automobile mechanics.'
> 'Do you have a diploma?'
> 'No. You?'
> 'Me neither,' he said, smiling.[1]

The identity of writers is complex and intangible. With few opportunities for certification, they must wait until others confer recognition. After winning the Governor General's Award for fiction, Alice Munro finally possessed sufficient confidence to identify herself as a writer rather than a housewife on the 1971 census.[2] Nathalie Heinich has recently devoted a book to exploring 'under what conditions a subject can say "I am a writer," what is meant by uttering this phrase and how it is received – without too many misunderstandings – by others.'[3] Because it is important to know who authors are before attempting to understand how they define themselves, a demographic approach similar to the one applied to French authors by Michèle Vessillier-Ressi shapes the following discussion.[4]

The most accessible corpus of demographic information regarding Canadian authors is to be found in the membership lists and records of their major professional associations: the Canadian Authors Association (CAA, est. 1921), the Writers' Union of Canada (WUC, est. 1973), the Société des écrivains canadiens (SÉC, est. 1936), and the Union des écrivains québécois (UNÉQ, est. 1977). Not all authors were members, and a number of important writers refused to join. Moreover, membership lists exhibit a bias toward literary authorship. However, these organizations were more inclusive than most literary histories of the period, and to varying degrees their records allow the researcher to track specific writers over time. With respect to the SÉC, 'from 1936 to 1965, the average membership of the Société was 220, and for the period from 1940 to 1959 it was 233, which represents 24 per cent of the writers listed in volume three of the *Dictionnaire des œuvres littéraires du Québec*.'[5] Equivalent data for English-language writers of the middle decades of the twentieth century is unavailable.[6] Basing this profile of Canadian authors on members of writers' organizations, despite their limitations, has a precedent in Brian Harrison's 1979 survey of freelance writers. Commissioned by Statistics Canada, it defined authorship in a self-referential fashion by drawing its data from 1,045 members of '18 writers' associations and unions thought to be representative of the population of Canadian writers.'[7]

To determine the demographic evolution of Quebec authors from a diachronic perspective, samples for each decade were taken.[8] Over the years, the SÉC membership lists reveal an aging population of authors: the average age of members was 49 in 1936 and 58 in 1978. However, these figures should be compared with those for the members of UNÉQ, unquestionably a younger association, where in 1978 the average age was 43. This finding accounts for Jacques Godbout's satirization of the SÉC as 'an organization wearing slippers' in 1962.[9] If membership lists of the UNÉQ and the SÉC are combined for 1978, the average age is 51, a figure that destroys the myth of the marginal young poet, represented by Émile Nelligan.

Members of the WUC also seem a domestic lot, despite their popular image as young Turks who disdained the CAA. Although information about marital and family status was inconsistently recorded, in 1980 over half described themselves as parents, the majority with two or three children. Data are lacking for longitudinal analysis of the median age of Canada's anglophone authors, but it is evident that in 1980 they did not differ substantially from their francophone colleagues. In the WUC the median age for both genders was 50, with the bulk in their forties. However, Harrison's 1979 survey, which looked at both language groups and included periodical writers and scriptwriters, found the largest bulge in 'male full-time writers aged 30–39.' He also noted a high proportion of writers in their 60s and 70s.[10]

Women were well represented in the SÉC. Although they represented only '15 to 20 per cent of [Quebec's] writing population'[11] in the period 1945–69, they constituted 18 per cent of the SÉC's membership in 1936, 25 per cent in the 1940s, 1950s, and 1960s, and reached 52 per cent in 1978.[12] This last figure is much higher than the actual proportion of women authors, as is made clear by a comparison with the membership of the UNÉQ. In 1978 women accounted for 26 per cent of its members, although that organization included many more literary authors than the SÉC.

In English-speaking Canada, the question of gender representation is equally complex. In the interwar period, women dominated the membership of the CAA, rising from 45 per cent of the more than 800 English-speaking members in 1924, to 58 per cent by 1933, thereby arousing the mockery in F.R. Scott's 1929 poem 'The Canadian Authors Meet,' where they are ridiculed as 'virgins of sixty who still write of passion.'[13] But this percentage does not represent their proportion of activity in genres other than cookbooks and writing for children; a more consistent figure for the entire period of 1920–80, based on the volume of books produced, would be around 31 per cent.[14] Harrison, whose data combined anglophones and francophones, found that in 1979, '58 per cent of all writers were men, and if we consider full-time writers only, the percentage climbs to 64 per cent.'[15] Yet in 1980 women comprised 44.5 per cent of the members of the WUC, indicating that the affiliative tendencies of women writers transcended language boundaries.

In the first half of the twentieth century, religion remained a crucial feature of English-Canadian life, and many authors who were known for writing in secular genres also carried ministerial qualifications, sometimes evident in the spiritual content of their published work. Novelists Charles W. Gordon ('Ralph Connor'), Hiram A. Cody, and Basil King, poets E.J. Pratt and Robert Norwood, editor Lorne Pierce, and critic Northrop Frye were all ordained Protestant ministers, as were about a dozen of the men named on the published membership lists of the CAA in the 1920s.[16] Religion figured in both the content and social values of many of the era's popular women authors, such as Nellie McClung, a deaconess in the United Church, and L.M. Montgomery, who married a Presbyterian minister. However, most Canadian authors who were clerics or missionaries did not join literary associations, and hence are not easily analyzed as a group (other than being predominantly male). Best-known were those who produced autobiographies and memoirs, such as Sir Wilfred Grenfell, whose narrative of forty years as a mission doctor, first issued as *A Labrador Doctor* (1919), reappeared in many editions under different titles. Less visible beyond their own denominational communities were hundreds of authors of church-published accounts of missions on Canada's western or northern frontiers, denominational histories, sermons, inspirational poetry and prose, theological analyses, and similar specialized genres. The formation of the United Church of Canada in 1925 produced a flurry of publications from prominent theologians and clergymen, while the Depression inspired writing that was consolatory or activist, in the tradition of the social gospel. By the 1940s, the growing secularization of English-Canadian society sequestered religious writers as a specialized (albeit large) group that seldom identified with the popular sphere. Many Canadians avidly read popular religious texts, but most of these were imported, such as editions of the works of evangelist Aimee Semple McPherson, who, despite her Canadian birth, is more commonly perceived as American. Hence, former evangelist Charles Templeton stands almost alone with his best-selling *Jesus* (1973), a paraphrase of the Gospels.[17]

Similarly in Quebec, authors who were members of writers' associations tended to be laypersons, a pattern that intensified over the years. From 26 per cent in the 1930s, the proportion of religious authors in the SÉC dropped to 10 per cent in 1978; in the same year, they made up only 2 per cent of the membership of the UNÉQ. Lucie Robert has shown that in the twentieth century 'the clergy, members of the liberal professions, and children of farmers gradually disappeared from the profession [of writer],'[18] an observation that largely holds true for English-speaking Canada. Using a list of publications issued between 1918 and 1980, compiled by the Bibliothèque nationale du Québec (BNQ) for this project, it is possible to create a composite sketch of the francophone religious author for the entire period. Such writers were mostly male, and members of the regular or secular clergy. Nuns belonging to congregations were much less numerous. Women often wrote for young readers and mostly produced edifying biographies and catechisms. Regardless of gender, virtually all these authors used writing as a vehicle for propaganda, education, or evangelism. Their output includes biographies, obituaries, histories, and commemorative books. Most produced only a single publication, but some were more prolific, with over twenty titles. These writers, who toiled in obscurity, with their work subject to the approval of church authorities, form a separate category.

Canada's much vaunted multiculturalism has produced writers whose roots emanate from scores of countries, and who have chosen to write in English not only to assimilate into the dominant national culture but also to join the global literary marketplace. It is not possible to quantify their presence and activities, as many authors known for their ethnic affiliation were born in Canada, into immigrant families. For example, Winnipeg-born Laura Goodman Salverson, who won the Governor General's Award for non-fiction for her memoir *Confessions of an Immigrant's Daughter* (1939), achieved prominence for voicing the experiences of Icelandic Canadians. Before 1945, English Canada's Anglo-Saxon ideology welcomed few alternative voices. Jewish poet A.M. Klein established his credentials through his affiliation with the McGill modernists. Novelist Frederick Philip Grove, a German masquerading as a Swede, and Archibald Belaney, an Englishman masquerading as the Indian 'Grey Owl,' were exceptions whose appeal lay in their ability to play the exotic outsider while displaying the manners of gentlemen.

After the Second World War, new sensitivity to alternative cultural values made it possible for outsiders to break into the English-Canadian literary field. The Jewish community gained increasing prominence through the English writings of child immigrants such as Irving Layton and Peter C. Newman and second-generation authors such as Adele Wiseman and Leonard Cohen. Rudy Wiebe was the first significant Mennonite writer to publish in English, and Austin Clarke was the first notable author to emigrate from the Caribbean. In the 1970s, greater social tolerance and government policies favouring multiculturalism brought literary results, first visible in anthologies based on various combinations of ethnicity, race, and gender, such as *I Am an Indian* (1969), *Harvest: Anthology of Mennonite Writing in Canada, 1874–1974* (1974), *One Out of Many: A Collection of Writings by 21 Black Women in Ontario* (1975), and *Inalienable Rice: A Chinese and Japanese Canadian Anthology* (1979). However, only a handful of these authors joined the mainstream of English-Canadian culture or national writers' organizations. While it is no surprise that the 1980 membership of the WUC was dominated by native-born Canadians (65 per cent), it is significant that the vast majority of immigrants hailed from major English-speaking countries (Britain, the United States, Australia), with only a sprinkling from other constituents of the 'Canadian mosaic.' Harrison's survey found that in 1979, 29 per cent of the freelance writers polled had been born outside Canada, a higher proportion than the general adult Canadian population (20 per cent in the 1971 census). This he interpreted as confirmation that writers 'are a nomadic group.'[19]

With francophone authors, France was the country of origin of most immigrants, irrespective of the year.[20] Not all these writers joined authors' associations. In 1978, 84 per cent of the authors in the SÉC were born in Quebec, compared to 87 per cent in the UNÉQ. These figures acquire further meaning when we take into account authors' places of residence. The proportion of authors living in Montreal grew from 37 per cent in 1936 to 49 per cent in 1954. Although some were born in rural areas, during the twentieth century some 69 per cent of Canada's francophone authors lived in major cities, including Quebec and Ottawa, as well as Montreal.[21] Nevertheless, in the 1960s, some decentralization took place, which suggests a degree of literary life or, at least associative activity, outside the major cities and towns.

Parallel to the way francophone authors moved to the urban centres of literary activity and production, anglophone authors who remained in Canada likewise chose to locate themselves strategically close to their publishers. Many Canadian-born authors represented in the WUC's membership in 1980 had migrated from the Prairie and Atlantic provinces to Ontario and British Columbia, with increasing numbers living in the urban centres of Toronto and Vancouver. Harrison's tabulations also discerned a concentration of authors in central Canada, especially Ontario, which in 1979 was home to 43 per cent of the writers in his study, at a time when just 36 per cent of the national population lived in this region.[22] These figures do not take into account authors who chose to reside outside the country between 1918 and 1980, from the heady Paris days of the 1920s, enjoyed by Morley Callaghan and John Glassco, to the British residencies of Norman Levine and Margaret Laurence for extensive periods during the decades following the Second World War. Screenwriting opportunities outside of Canada often supported the mobility of Canadian authors, from Winnifred Eaton's days in Hollywood in the 1920s to Mordecai Richler's years in London in the 1950s and 1960s. On the francophone side, the best-known case is that of Anne Hébert, who lived in Paris from 1967 to 1997. Did thirty years of 'exile' in the country long regarded as a literary mecca by Quebec writers make her a French writer? This is one example that highlights the problem of how to define the migrant author.

While the data are not exhaustive, the predominance of creative genres among the work produced by writers belonging to the major associations is clearly evident. This phenomenon is particularly striking in the case of the UNÉQ, whose members' publications denote it as essentially an association of literary authors. While the SÉC in 1978 included all kinds of writers, the UNÉQ apparently focused on bringing together only true 'écrivains,' that is, those aspiring to literary recognition (see table 3.1, p. 99).

Literary writing also dominated the output of the WUC (see table 3.2, p. 100), albeit less overwhelmingly than was the case with the UNÉQ. The WUC attracted a larger proportion of scholarly writers (humanities, social sciences, criticism) as well as authors of non-fiction (biography, autobiography, travel) and children's authors. However, writers working in such fields as business, science, and technology seem vastly under-represented, although they could meet the eligibility requirement of a trade book published by a commercial or university press. Even humour – a genre with a prize of its own (the Stephen Leacock Memorial Medal) – had few practitioners in the WUC.[23] Yet among the participants in Harrison's survey (which included periodical authors), non-fiction was the principal field of activity for 48 per cent of all freelance writers, followed by fiction (24 per cent), with poetry and

Table 3.1
Production of members of the SÉC and of the UNÉQ

Genre	Percentage of members					
	SÉC					UNÉQ
	1936	1944	1954	1963	1978	1978
Literature	55	57	53	57	42	94
Social sciences						
History	36	29	27	29	15	3
Geography	3	4	4	2	2	0
Law	0	2	3	3	1	1
Economics	3	1	1	2	1	0
Other genres						
Religion	23	23	14	14	6	2
How-to books	10	13	7	7	6	2
Textbooks	4	7	5	4	4	2
Politics	3	5	4	5	1	2
Art and music	4	2	4	3	3	2
Health	1	3	4	3	4	1

Sources: ANQM, fonds Société des écrivains canadiens; V. Barbeau, *La Société des écrivains canadiens* (1944); *Répertoire bio-bibliographique de la Société des écrivains canadiens, 1954*; *Annuaire des membres de l'UNÉQ* (1978); biographical dictionaries of Canada and Quebec authors. Table compiled by Josée Vincent.

Notes: 1. Not all members of the SÉC and the UNÉQ are covered in this compilation as 10 to 15 per cent do not appear in dictionaries and other reference sources that identify their output.
2. As many authors work in more than one genre, the total percentages exceed 100.

drama tied at 14 per cent each. This distribution, he surmised, reflected the realities of the marketplace. Full-time writers, who supported themselves by their pens, had a greater tendency than part-time writers to produce fiction, whereas poetry was a genre favoured by part-timers.[24] This discrepancy between the wider field of writing and the genres practised by members of the WUC suggests that in English Canada the generic term 'writer' carries an increasingly literary signification unless modified by a qualifier, in parallel with the term 'écrivain' in Quebec, which definitively refers to a literary writer.

As outlined later in this chapter by Peggy Lynn Kelly and Josée Vincent, from the 1970s the rise of alternative associations for writers of specific genres such as periodical articles, science, crime fiction, children's literature, romance, and speculative fiction has not only created opportunities to share genre-specific marketing and

Table 3.2
Production of members of the WUC

Genre	Percentage of members
Literature	59
Social sciences and humanities	27.7
History	(12.5)
Law	(1.5)
Children's books	20.7
Biography and autobiography	18.5
Geography, travel, and regional studies	7.3
Literary criticism	6.7
Art, architecture, and music	5.5
Education and textbooks	4
Reference books	3.6
Lifestyles	3
Humour	2.7
Science and medicine	2.7
Industry and commerce	1.5
Religion	<1

Source: Writers' Union of Canada, *The Writers' Union of Canada: A Directory of Members* (1981). Table compiled by Nancy Earle.

Note: As many authors work in more than one genre, the total percentages exceed 100.

mentoring opportunities, but also reflects a desire to claim identity and validity. This development returns us to the problem posed by our opening quotation, in which Jacques Poulin's characters discuss the credentials of authorship. In Canada, they have shifted over time, in relation to the larger cultural milieu.

Allophone Authorship

CATHERINE OWEN

The vital contribution of allophone authors – those who write in languages other than French or English – to the Canadian literary scene was acknowledged each year from 1935 to 1965 in Watson Kirkconnell's reviews of 'Publications in Other Languages' in the 'Letters in Canada' summary published by the *University of Toronto Quarterly*.[25] Official recognition of 'The Cultural Contribution of Other Ethnic

Groups' in volume 4 of the report of the Royal Commission on Bilingualism and Biculturalism in 1970 was followed by a policy of multiculturalism adopted by the federal government in 1971. Despite these gestures, in 1978 Chilean immigrant poet Ludwig Zeller noted, 'At present writers in languages other than the official ones ... are little heard of or ignored here.'[26] Whether these writers came to Canada as refugees from war-torn homelands, to avoid political persecution, or to seek new economic or professional opportunities, once arrived they faced similar challenges in writing and publishing in their first languages. Many diasporic writers have struggled with questions of language retention, audience, critical reception, and government support.

Poetry has generally been the most common and valued form of literary writing practised by immigrants, from Icelandic poet Stephan G. Stephansson in the early part of the twentieth century to the 'Chilean Emergent Promotion' poets in the 1970s. Having arrived in Alberta in 1889, Stephansson published in his native tongue in both Reykjavik and Winnipeg, with his last work appearing in print in 1938, more than a decade after his death.[27] Unconcerned with reaching a wider Canadian audience and fiercely attached to Old Norse, Stephansson – whose verse centred on such common themes arising from the immigrant/exile experience as love, nostalgia, gratitude, patriotism, and grief – was content to have his collections circulate in Iceland and the small Icelandic communities of North America. His reputation among anglophone readers benefited from posthumous translation and promotion by Watson Kirkconnell.

Other poets have grappled with their need for an audience. Andrew Machalski's study of 1988, which surveyed Hispanic poets' feelings toward the Canadian literary environment, encountered responses ranging from frustration to despair, with the most common reaction being a deep sense of isolation.[28] These emotions stem from the hybrid nature of allophone literature. Immigrant writers compose in their native language to draw on the more cogent lexical intent of their mother tongue, yet they also aim to communicate Canadian imagery and values. Seeking to reach an audience beyond their own communities, they are often disappointed to discover that the larger Canadian public is inaccessible. Furthermore, as publisher Ann Wallace notes, allophone communities 'are not necessarily book buyers.'[29] Often, writers must work for years in more public roles as journalists or critics to build a readership for their work. Journalist Zbigniew Waruszyński of the *Polish Voice* (Toronto) edited or authored several histories of Canadian Polish associations in Quebec published between 1952 and 1966.[30] Viennese art and music critic Carl Weiselberger, who came to Canada from England in 1940, was well known to the readers of the Ottawa *Citizen* during his lifetime.[31] His successful German collection of stories, *Der Rabbi mit der Axt* (Victoria), was published posthumously in 1973.

Collectively authored publications, ranging from newspapers and periodicals to cookbooks, travel guides, and practical pamphlets, have often proven the most sustainable mode of textual production in immigrant languages. Some such specialized and professional publications have reached international audiences. In 1952 four Belarusian authors founded the Kastus Kalinouski Research Institute in Toronto and New York and began issuing a periodical on Belarusian history, *Dokumenty i fakty* (Toronto, 1952–);[32] the Association of Latvian Engineers, based in Montreal, started a long-lived international technical review in 1954.[33] Other writers have achieved a wide audience when their grammar texts or children's books were purchased by community groups or schools with language programs. Ber Sheinson, a Lithuanian essayist who was interned in a concentration camp before escaping to Quebec in 1948, devoted his writing life to the production of grammar and language texts in Hebrew, such as the three-volume *Sefat Yisra'el* (1951).[34] Nina Mudryk-Mryts, who came to Toronto following the Second World War, found her niche in the field of children's literature, publishing many poems, legends, and tales in Ukrainian between 1955 and 1983.[35] A widely read genre in many languages has been the personal memoir, whose typical evocation of nostalgia for the homeland and narrative of hardship experienced during the journey to Canada resonate for immigrants. Danes have produced many such titles, among them Idun Engberg's 1950 memoir of her marriage to a Danish settler in Ontario of the 1930s.[36] Further outlets for artistic expression exist through the strength of a culture's orality. After arriving in Vancouver in 1966, Punjabi poet and playwright Ajmer Rode produced dramas with the theatre group Vancouver Sath in order to reach an audience beyond the narrow scope of literacy.[37]

However, skeptical critics and limited government support have hindered allophone authorship. Many mainstream critics, especially before the 1970s, dismissed allophone writing as being of 'sociological rather than literary interest'[38] and denigrated ethnic language retention as a 'cultural fetish.'[39] Allophone texts were thus viewed as signs of a lack of interest in their authors' adopted culture, rather than as rich contributions to Canada's diverse cultural heritage. While critical attention gradually increased in the 1970s, partially as a result of grants allotted to academics studying allophone literature, direct funding to allophone authors remained low. Moreover, an insidious connection between 'cultural policies' and 'political interests' in some of the homelands of immigrant authors has deterred them from seeking government aid in Canada.[40]

For the majority of allophone authors desiring a channel of communication with Canadian society as a whole, translation of their often self-published texts remains a primary objective. Such efforts require a rare combination of talent and dedication, as exhibited by Watson Kirkconnell's forty-year career as a translator of verse from many European languages into English.[41] Consequently, most of the impetus, and much of the translation, have come from authors themselves. However, as the Italian axiom 'traduttore, traditore' indicates, to translate is to betray: a translated work can never capture the full resonance of the original text, while the very need for translation can signify an erosion of the author's language community. Despite their limitations, however, such translations broadened and deepened the literary wealth of twentieth-century Canada.

Economics and the Writer

FRANK DAVEY

Authors who were able to support themselves or their families through their writing have been sufficiently rare in Canada to become the subject of gossip and legend. Charles G.D. Roberts has been cited as such a writer, although throughout the 1920s he was recurrently in debt and in 1931 he was rescued from poverty by supporters who obtained for him a government pension.[42] Al Purdy has been described as self-supporting, although in the 1940s and 1950s his wife, Eurithe, provided significant household income, and from the late 1960s most of his earnings came from grants and positions as a writer-in-residence, rather than from sales of his poetry.[43] Apart from journalists and a few novelists, such as L.M. Montgomery, Mazo de la Roche, Gabrielle Roy, and Yves Thériault, who achieved international success and benefited from royalties earned by foreign sales and film rights, most Canadian writers in the 1920–80 period needed to augment substantially their earnings from writing in order to meet life's basic needs. The biography of Leslie McFarlane, best known for ghost-writing many titles in the Hardy Boys series, illustrates the energy and versatility required of a 'journeyman writer' whose goal of maintaining middle-class family comfort led him to the editorial offices of the National Film Board and the CBC.[44] Two best-selling non-fiction authors of the post-war era, Farley Mowat and Pierre Berton, first achieved financial stability through print journalism before branching into book publication, and parlaying their distinctive personalities into public images with media appeal.

Income from Writing

Government methods of reporting the income of writers during much of the period under discussion make it difficult to establish definitive financial figures for those engaged in a writing life of any description. From 1921 to 1961, the Dominion Bureau of Statistics (later Statistics Canada) grouped the earnings of editors and reporters with those of writers engaged in all other forms of writing activity. Reporting improved somewhat in 1971, when the census divided 'Occupations in writing' into three categories, 'Writers and editors,' 'Translators and interpreters,' and 'Occupations in writing, n.e.c. [not elsewhere classified].' The difficulty with these categories is that they could as easily include writers of advertising copy as writers of articles and books.

Hard figures on the state of professional authorship are to be derived from a Statistics Canada study of 1978, the precision of which underlines the inadequacy of earlier statistics.[45] In 1978 the median income for all members of the Canadian labour force was $11,400. Writers surveyed for this study reported an average income from writing of $6,761 with a median of $2,500. Those writing full-time had an average income of $14,095 with a median of $7,000, while for part-time writers the average was $3,628 and the median $1,380.[46] In addition, the study's analysis of full-time writers by genre revealed significant disparities in all categories between the average reported income and the median: book sales ($6,077 and $1,050), sales to periodicals ($4,392 and $2,500), sales to radio and television ($13,591 and $6,000), writing for cinema ($8,710 and $2,000), and writing for the theatre ($3,110 and $800). The striking differences between the average and the median indicate that the former was being elevated by a few exceptionally well-paid individuals, and that most writers surveyed were earning considerably less than the 'average.'

Anecdotal sources offer significant insights, if not comprehensive data, about the finances of Canadian writers during the twentieth century. E.K. Brown declared in 1938 that the economic base of literature in Canada was 'unsound,' and that the only three options for Canadian writers were to emigrate, take secondary employment, or 'while continuing to reside in Canada, become, economically at least, a member of another nation and civilization,' and that none of these was likely to lead to substantial *Canadian* literary production.[47] Reflecting on both commercial and literary writing in 1955, publisher John Morgan Gray estimated that a Canadian writer selling to American mass-market magazines could earn more than $18,000 a year, a significant income at that time. However, a best-selling Canadian novel would bring its author only $1,000 to $1,500, unless it found a publisher in Britain and the United States, in which case it would produce 'much more satisfactory' returns.[48] Yet, the experiences of Hugh MacLennan reveal that exceptionally lucrative writing did not necessarily provide financial independence. Although his *Barometer Rising* (1941) was a best-seller in Canada, the United States, and Britain, the Canadian government taxed his foreign earnings so heavily that MacLennan was unable to leave his teaching post. In addition, in the 1940s Canadian taxation laws did not allow a writer to spread a book's earnings over several tax years, even though the volume might have taken several years to write. Consequently, although MacLennan's *Two Solitudes* (1945) also proved an international best-seller, by March 1946 the book had earned him $3,354.21 in secondary rights and $12,000 in royalties after taxes.[49] A year later, Gabrielle Roy fared much better with secondary rights, receiving $67,000 for the film rights to *The Tin Flute*, and 50 per cent of the $110,000 reprint fee paid by the Literary Guild of New York, a book club that ordered 700,000 copies.[50]

Genre has been a considerable factor in Canadian writers' incomes. Journalism, especially salaried work for a newspaper or magazine, has provided much economic security for writers. As an alternative to full-time employment, print journalists have sometimes done part-time or freelance writing, producing a regular column for a particular newspaper or magazine, or undertaking journalistic writing in tandem with creative writing. Freelance or salaried writing for film, radio, and television also paid the bills. Journalism has been a significant component in the writing careers of authors ranging from Pierre Berton and Scott Young to poets Clément Marchand and Jovette Bernier. For poets, public readings became a significant source of income during the 1970s, welcome compensation from a genre for which royalties remained minimal.

For playwrights, there were very few sources of income until the establishment of public broadcasting in the 1930s, which led to the purchasing and commissioning of radio plays and, later, television scripts. In Quebec, the need for French-language radio and television programs created lucrative opportunities for several writers whose novels became serial dramas broadcast from the 1930s through the 1960s – Claude-Henri Grignon's *Un homme et son péché* (1933) and Roger Lemelin's *Les Plouffe* (1948). In the 1970s, Victor-Lévy Beaulieu continued this pattern by adapting many of his novels for the small screen. Authors for children, such as Tante Lucille (Lucille

Desparois), Grand-père Cailloux (André Cailloux), Maman Fonfon (Claudine Valle-rand), and Henriette Major, also adapted their stories for radio and television. After 1960, the vitality of live and televised theatre in Quebec enabled several franco-phone playwrights, including Marcel Dubé, Françoise Loranger, and Michel Trem-blay, to live off their royalties. In English Canada, script-writing for the CBC was a major source of income for Gwethalyn Graham from 1958 to 1965, while the prolif-eration of small theatre companies in the late 1960s and 1970s enabled popular play-wrights, such as David French, to acquire a liveable annual income from repeated performances, both national and international.

An intermittent and unreliable source of income for writers has arisen out of contests and prizes, the impact of which is discussed in greater detail by Marie-Pier Luneau and Ruth Panofsky later in this chapter. After the First World War, the earli-est recorded annual prizes were the Concours littéraires et scientifiques du Québec (first awarded in 1923), known as the Prix David, and the Imperial Order Daughters of the Empire (IODE) Awards for the short story and one-act play (1923–33). Although prizes have been relatively numerous – Statistics Canada reported in 1976 that Canada had as many literary and journalistic prizes as did each of Britain, Aus-tria, and Switzerland (but fewer than France)[51] – the vast majority offered less than $1,000. Some lucrative prizes did become available in the 1970s, when the Governor General's Award was raised to $5,000 in 1975 and the Seal First Novel Award of $50,000 was established in 1976. Apart from the Seal award, prizes have not been conceptualized as purchasing time for writers to create. While many early contests sponsored by newspapers or magazines encouraged new writers and provided a bit of income for the winners (for example, the *Maclean's Magazine* Short Story Awards, 1927–55), their purpose was also to create a news event for the sponsor. Later prizes, such as the Ryerson Fiction Awards (1942–60), the Doubleday Canadian Prize Novel Award (1961–7), the Seal, and the Prix du Cercle du livre de France (1949–87), gener-ated publicity for book publishers and often encouraged more substantial sales – and therefore greater royalties – for winning authors.

Newer resources for writers arose from various state interventions, many directly or indirectly resulting from the Massey Report of 1951 and the subsequent creation of the Canada Council for the Arts in 1957. Further improvements to the economic situation of writers developed through a series of post-1960 government inquiries – into culture, copyright, the arts, publishing, and what became known as the 'cultural industries.' Juried granting programs, offering monies to writers on the basis of past accomplishment and programs of current work, were first intro-duced by the Canada Council in 1960, and replicated by several provincial arts coun-cils founded soon afterward (Ontario in 1963, Manitoba in 1965). These grants offered writers substantial blocks of unencumbered time. During the 1960s, however, these programs were relatively small; H.R. Percy complained in 1964 that only $30,000 of the Canada Council's 1962–3 grant budget of $1.6 million had gone to writers – an amount equal to the Winnipeg Symphony Orchestra's grant that same year.[52] In the mid-1960s, the Canada Council created further initiatives: its Writer-in-Residence Program, which is described in the following case study by Nancy Earle; its funding of public readings; and its grants to Canadian periodicals and book publishers, which in later years would require publishers to pay royalties to authors. The council's financial support of new writers' organizations, such as the Writers' Union of Canada (WUC), the Union des écrivains québécois (UNÉQ), and the League of Canadian Poets, led indirectly to greater income from public readings, to contract reform, and to progress toward the public lending right and copyright collectives, both of which would become significant sources of income for writers in the 1990s. By the early 1970s, the number of granting agencies had multiplied, and the funds available had greatly increased. For example, many writers in this decade were eligible for grants from the federal Local Initiatives Program and Opportunities for Youth; in some provinces, younger writers could count on up to four years of continuous grant support. As well, the Canada Council Public Readings Program enabled popular writers – Susan Musgrave and Al Purdy among them – to give up to twenty council-funded readings per year at universities and public libraries, and additional readings through the council-funded League of Canadian Poets.

In the late 1960s writers' manuscripts and other archival materials became another potential source of income. While a few university libraries had accepted occasional donations before this period, the systematic building of Canadian manuscript collections for research purposes did not begin until Canadian literature was established as a doctoral program field. The first significant purchase by the Thomas Fisher Rare Book Library at the University of Toronto was an accession of Earle Birney's papers in 1966. The National Library of Canada's collection began with the Arthur Bourinot fonds in 1969. The University of Calgary inaugurated its Canadian Collection, described in the following case study by Apollonia Steele, with the purchase of Hugh MacLennan's papers in 1973.

Most acquisitions of writers' papers in the 1965–80 period were by purchase rather than donation. This was partly because federal tax provisions regarding the donation of literary materials were unfavourable until the Cultural Property Export and Import Act of 1975 (23–4 Elizabeth 2, 1975, c. 50) came into effect in 1977. For income tax purposes, cash sales before 1977 were treated as capital gains. Under the 1975 legislation, the appraised value of manuscripts sold or donated was exempt from capital gains tax and, in the case of a donation, 100 per cent deductible from the writer's taxable income. However, a writer who donated under the act could, depending on his or her tax bracket, and the taxation rates of that year, receive at best 43–5 per cent of the appraised value. Under the somewhat less generous 1985 legislation, a writer who donates receives a tax credit of approximately 30 per cent of the appraised value.

Most writers, who do not have substantial incomes against which to use tax credits, have not benefited from the two cultural property acts, and have remained better off selling rather than donating their papers. A few who have built lucrative writing careers, or who have had high-paying secondary careers, have made better use of the acts – Margaret Atwood, for example, who sold her early manuscripts to the University of Toronto in 1969 and again in the early 1970s, has since made additional donations. In Quebec, the selection of a home for a writer's papers can be a delicate topic. In 1980, after being courted by many institutions, Gabrielle Roy arranged for her papers to go to the National Library of Canada after her death, with posthumous payment to the Fonds Gabrielle Roy. The main beneficiaries of the federal legislation have been libraries, who, by negotiating various permutations of cash payment and tax credits, have been able to acquire significant collections at very little expense to themselves and modest benefit to the writers.

Other Sources of Income

Few Canadian authors of either language enjoyed the advantage of Alain Grandbois, whose personal wealth enabled him to travel the world and write to his own schedule. With the notable exceptions of journalists and a few commercially successful novelists, until 1960 Canada's best-known writers all followed other careers. The challenge for a writer was to find a congenial career that left time for writing, or that did not interfere, physically or psychologically, with the energy required to write.

For Canadian writers unable to live solely by their pens, principal areas of employment have been education, broadcasting, government, publishing, and the legal and medical professions. The cultural pattern of women beginning professional writing while living – and often raising children – in households nominally financed by their husbands existed throughout the period, as in the early years of the careers of Margaret Laurence, Alice Munro, Marian Engel, and Jane Urquhart. In the world of paid employment, even journalists like Scott Young often had an editorial component built into their salaried positions. F.P. Grove taught public school from 1909 to 1923, failed as a farmer in southern Ontario in the early 1930s, and was then supported by his wife's private teaching. Lucie Robert has shown that in Quebec, before 1920 writers' vocations were nearly equally divided between the Catholic Church and the professions (42.8 per cent) and teaching and journalism (43 per cent); after 1920, teaching and journalism prevailed (73 per cent).[53] Similar patterns of professionalism obtained in both language communities: Montreal poets F.R. Scott and A.M. Klein were practising lawyers; Ringuet (Philippe Panneton) and Jacques Ferron were medical doctors. Québécois children's authors Marie-Claire Daveluy and Claude Aubry were librarians, while their anglophone counterpart Janet Lunn worked as an editor of children's books. Sinclair Ross and Raymond Souster, by contrast, held relatively low-level jobs in Canadian banks until retirement.

Authors found some of their most congenial livelihoods in broadcasting, film, and government. During the 1950s and 1960s, many Québécois poets (Jean-Guy Pilon, Paul-Marie Lapointe, Fernand Ouellette) and novelists (Robert Charbonneau, Gilles Archambault, André Langevin, Hubert Aquin, Wilfrid Lemoine) worked as producers, editors, or directors in radio or television for Radio-Canada, and Phyllis Webb was a producer with the English-language CBC. Morley Callaghan buttressed his writing career with a forty-year relationship with CBC radio and television, beginning in 1943 as a paid participant in various programs on current and cultural affairs, such as *Citizens' Forum*, *Fighting Words*, and *Now I Ask You*. In 1957, Jacques Godbout joined the National Film Board, where Anne Hébert worked briefly in 1953 and 1954, as had Leslie McFarlane and Irene Baird in the 1940s. Some writers worked in the civil service: Quebec's Ministry of Cultural Affairs, established in 1961, created administrative positions in the arts and letters that were filled by poets and writers, while Naïm Kattan became head of the Canada Council's Writing and Publication Section in 1967.

For writers who placed their focus on an academic career, and whose primary output would be scholarly in nature – such as Northrop Frye, A.G. Bailey, and Roy Daniells – a university appointment was essential. Robertson Davies' twenty years as master of Massey College (1961–81) provided an opportunity for colourful leadership. However, university teaching was a mixed blessing for many creative writers. Following the examples of E.J. Pratt and A.J.M. Smith, and influenced by the professionalizing of poetry and criticism by the New Critics, many English-speaking poets from the 1940s onward obtained tenured university positions – Earle Birney, Ralph Gustafson, Louis Dudek, James Reaney, and Eli Mandel foremost among them. The frustrations that a parallel career in the university could bring to creative writers were voiced by Birney, who in the late 1950s wrote several scholarly articles and won a Nuffield grant to complete a book on Chaucer, but complained to a friend that the 'academic chains' were 'almost crushing' and that he had 'written nothing of a creative nature for nearly four years.' Yet Birney's academic post was a financial necessity: in 1957, when his salary rose from $8,500 to $10,000, his income from 'royalties, radio work and permissions' was $557.43.[54] Novelists were less likely to make long-term commitments to teaching – possibly because the genre requires long uninterrupted periods of writing, and possibly also because the economic potential of fiction was greater. Before 1980 male writers were more likely to secure university positions than were women, although in the 1970s they were joined by novelists Aritha Van Herk and Bharati Mukherjee.

With the tremendous expansion of post-secondary education across the country in the 1960s, university or teaching careers, often part-time, became almost the norm for literary writers in both official languages. The growth of creative writing courses in universities in the 1960s and 1970s not only opened new employment opportunities for writers, but also guided many aspiring authors toward university study, thereby equipping them with credentials for at least the part-time teaching of creative writing or positions in community colleges. The many teaching positions opened by the initiation of Quebec's CEGEPs in 1967 likewise produced good jobs for the generation of young poets who filled the little magazines and ran the new publishing houses of the 1970s.

The Business of Writing: Copyright, Literary Agents, and Contracts

Copyright was a complicated business in Canada until 1911, when the United Kingdom passed a revised Copyright Act (1–2 George 5, c. 46), which allowed its 'self-governing' dominions to repeal imperial copyright legislation and pass new legislation without the threat of imperial disallowance. Canada's first effective copyright act was realized a decade later, when a new act (11–12 George 5, c. 24) was passed in 1921 and proclaimed in 1924. Although largely modelled on the British act of 1911, it gave Canadian authors important new protections, extending the term to life plus fifty years, granting protection to works by Canadians in other countries, granting authors various secondary rights such as film and radio adaptation, setting penalties of fines and/or imprisonment for infringement, and prohibiting the commercial importation of books into Canada to compete with Canadian-licensed printings. The act, however, also specifically denied that copyright was a 'natural' right, declaring it to be only a creation of 'statutory enactment' – a view that would be disputed in later copyright discussions.

While this act remained substantially unrevised for sixty years, copyright issues arose periodically. In 1928 Canada formally ratified the Rome text of the Berne Convention, a convention which respected copyrights internationally and to which Canada had become a member indirectly in 1886 through Britain's adhesion. In 1954 the St Laurent government appointed a Royal Commission on Patents, Copyright, Trade Marks, and Industrial Design, giving it a mandate to seek a balance between the rights of creators and the public benefits of access. The commission's report of 1957 had little effect on legislation, although its recommendation that Canada join the Universal Copyright Convention was enacted in 1962, giving Canadian authors important 'national-treatment' protections in the United States. In 1966 the Pearson government asked the Economic Council of Canada to undertake a further study, but with emphasis on economic policy and the well-being of consumers. The council's 1971 *Report on Intellectual and Industrial Property,* while making significant mention of the cultural goals of copyright legislation, recommended that there be little change to present protections. Much more influential was the Keyes-Brunet report of 1977, *Copyright in Canada: Proposals for a Revision of the Law,* commissioned by the Department of Consumer and Corporate Affairs, although it too did not lead – at least directly – to legislation. Keyes-Brunet argued that it was inconsequential whether copyright was a natural property right or a statutory privilege – effectively validating the former by the back door – and implied as well that the rights of the creator, together with the national cultural interest, could outweigh any right of public access. The Trudeau government's response to Keyes-Brunet was the white paper *From Gutenberg to Telidon* (1984), which proposed to expand creators' rights in the context of new technologies, to balance the rights of creators and the needs of users, and to strengthen Canadian culture.

The election of the Mulroney government later that year resulted in the abrupt replacing of the white paper in 1985 with the *Charter of Rights for Creators.* The *Charter,* and subsequent copyright legislation, moved in much different directions, defining copyright as containing both property rights and moral rights, allowing corporations and co-operatives to possess such rights, expanding the rights of creators without expanding those of users, encouraging copyright collectives, and raising the financial penalties for infringement to a maximum of $1 million dollars. While the federal government oversaw the collective rights of authors through copyright legislation, it was left to authors and their agents to monitor the copyright and other contractual arrangements made with publishers.

Before the 1970s, most of the literary agents who represented Canadian writers were based in New York, along with a few in London. In the 1920s and 1930s, the established agencies of A.P. Watt and Paul Reynolds represented best-selling writers like Robert Stead and Arthur Stringer.[55] Gabrielle Roy understood the importance of an agent; in 1945 she retained as her business manager Jean-Marie Nadeau, a brilliant lawyer and copyright specialist, who for the next ten years expertly steered her professional transactions. In the early 1950s, Farley Mowat broke into the major American periodicals such as *Saturday Evening Post* under the guidance of a New York agency.[56] However, many American agents did not grasp the cultural or literary goals of their Canadian clients. MacLennan's agent, Blanche Gregory, advised him after the success of *Barometer Rising* to write articles for *Reader's Digest*, while Alice Munro's American agent, Virginia Barber, urged her to write novels instead of stories.[57]

Although a few Canadians advertised editorial and agency services in the *Canadian Author and Bookman* in the 1930s, probably the first anglophone Canadian literary agent of note was Matie Molinaro, who began working out of her Toronto home in 1950 and pioneered the concept of agents within Canadian publishing. Most of her business before 1970 focused on arranging lectures rather than placing manuscripts. With the expansion of writing and publishing in the 1970s, new agencies emerged, including those of Nancy Colbert and Lucinda Vardey, and book manuscripts and book contracts became agents' primary business. The new agencies helped to internationalize Canadian writing, it being more lucrative for both writer and agent to place a manuscript first with an American publisher, and to split off the Canadian rights for separate sale and thus better domestic royalties. In the 1970s, John Goodwin was the agent for many internationally known francophone authors who were widely translated, including Marie-Claire Blais, Roch Carrier, and Michel Tremblay.[58]

Prior to the 1970s there had been very little change in publishing contracts in Canada – partly because there was so little money to be made in the Canadian market by either publisher or author, but also because few Canadian writers used literary agents. The introduction of agents caused an increase in the royalty advances paid by Canadian publishers and generated contracts that committed publishers to spending certain amounts on promotion. By contrast, the standard contracts of earlier years had been highly restrictive in favour of the publisher: they granted the publisher world rights rather than ones to particular markets, and substantial percentages of all possible subsidiary rights; they specified a deadline by which the author was to deliver the manuscript but no deadline by which the publisher was required to publish; they contained no reversion clause for the return of copyright to the author should the publisher allow the book to go out of print; and they granted the publisher first refusal rights on the author's next book, regardless of its genre. The Canadian Authors Association (CAA) had routinely warned its members to challenge contract terms and, in the 1940s, at the initiative of Gwethalyn Graham developed its own 'Standard Book Contract,'[59] which, however, received little acceptance. Small presses founded in the late 1960s and early 1970s frequently copied the established publishers' standard contracts, even though they had no staff or expertise for the sale and management of subsidiary rights, and no ability to distribute outside of Canada.

Although individual authors with access to lawyers were able to have contracts rewritten, it was through the efforts of the WUC and UNÉQ, as well as the interventions of agents, that industry-wide changes to publishing contracts began to be made in the 1970s. With better financing and more high-profile authors among its membership than the CAA, the WUC was able to publicize contract inequities, offer contract-evaluation services to members, and propose a set of 'minimum terms,' many of which became part of the WUC's own model contract and were widely adopted by publishers. These included a fixed date for the publisher to publish, fixed terms for subsidiary rights, and reversion of rights on a work's going out of print.

The trajectory, over the course of the twentieth century, was clearly toward greater economic stability for Canada's writers. This development arose through increased sales of their work, and also through a growing infrastructure of support that included grants, congenial post-secondary teaching posts, employment in broadcasting and film agencies, and sales or donations of their papers to archives. These opportunities have been supported by a network of social and government commitments – at both federal and provincial levels – that underscore a belief that Canada's cultural industries are too important – and too fragile – to be left to the whims of the global marketplace.

CASE STUDY
Collecting Canadian Manuscripts at the University of Calgary
– Apollonia Steele

The wave of nationalism that crested with Canada's 1967 Centennial and swept through the 1970s, combined with growing academic interest in the serious study of the country's literatures, encouraged the collection of Canadian authors' papers by government archives and universities, and made the sale of papers a potential source of income for writers. While institutions such as the National Archives of Canada and the libraries at the University of Toronto substantially increased their acquisitions in this area, it became the 'special mission' of Rare Books and Special Collections at the University of Calgary, a library department established in 1971, 'to collect the papers of contemporary Canadian authors.'[60] During the 1970s, the university's chief librarian, Kenneth M. Glazier, joined forces with Ernie B. Ingles to build a significant and diverse collection.

The department's first major acquisition came in 1973 when Glazier paid $15,500 for a collection of Hugh MacLennan's papers sold at public auction.[61] The purchase, which was funded by private donations and matching grants from the province of Alberta, elicited national media attention and the applause of the university's English Department, which had just sponsored the landmark Canadian Conference of Writers and Critics. The appointment of Ingles as head of Special Collections in 1974 enhanced a zealous campaign for Canadian manuscripts. Papers of leading anglophone novelists Mordecai Richler, Brian Moore, W.O. Mitchell, Robert Kroetsch, and Rudy Wiebe soon joined the collection, alongside those of influential dramatists George Ryga, Joanna Glass, and Michael Cook. The strong western component represented by many of these names was reinforced by papers of non-fiction authors James Gray, Grant MacEwan, and Bruce Hutchison, as well as those of Christie Harris, an interpreter of West Coast Native legends. Sharing Glazier's conviction that 'no one [could] claim to have a Canadian collection of literary manuscripts unless French Canadian authors were represented,' Ingles sought out papers of francophone writers and, after some effort, acquired material from Claude Péloquin and André Langevin.[62]

Rapid acquisition of literary manuscripts in the late 1970s was facilitated when the Canadian Cultural Property Export and Import Act came into effect in 1977, providing donors with advantageous tax benefits. It would compensate somewhat for the cessation of matching provincial grants in 1980. That year, papers of Alice Munro and Clark Blaise came to Calgary, bringing to twenty-one the number of major literary collections acquired between 1973 and 1980. By 1980 the Rare Books and Special Collections Department of the University of Calgary Library had become an internationally recognized research centre for Canadian literary and cultural studies. In the mid-1980s it would begin to publish detailed finding aids to specific collections in order to further facilitate research.

CASE STUDY ———————————————————————————————
The Canada Council for the Arts Writer-in-Residence Program
– Nancy Earle

The Canada Council for the Arts Writer-in-Residence Program was created in 1965 in order to support authors and heighten the profile of Canadian literature. Drawing matching grants from host institutions, author residencies have provided nationally recognized authors with time to devote to their own writing projects, as well as mentoring aspiring writers. While the council has emphasized the priority of the authors' creative work, it has also encouraged attempts to increase resident writers' profiles through university classroom visits and public appearances.

During the program's first fifteen years, between 1965 and 1980, the council helped to support ninety writer-in-residence appointments at twenty-five institutions in eight provinces. The institutions were typically universities, though by the late 1970s Mohawk College (Hamilton) and the Regina Public Library had also hosted residencies. Sixty-one authors of fiction, poetry, and drama participated during this period, including eight francophone authors, the majority of whom were based at the University of Ottawa. Many of the country's most prominent authors, such as Austin Clarke, Claire Martin, and Alice Munro, have been writers-in-residence at least once in their careers.

Residencies provide authors with prestigious, if short-term, employment. Norman Levine, who returned from England to be the first writer-in-residence at the University of New Brunswick in 1965, encapsulated the contradictory emotions engendered by such fleeting moments in the public eye. His short story 'Thin Ice' tells of a writer, still warm from the glow of the university hearth, who, en route to an ill-fated reading engagement, finds himself unknown and destitute in a small, wintry Canadian town, reflecting bleakly on the uncertainties inherent in his chosen profession.[63] Many writers-in-residence have experienced something of a nomadic existence. Dorothy Livesay held residencies in four universities in as many provinces between 1966 and 1980. Marian Engel also travelled, children in tow, between appointments at the University of Alberta and the University of Toronto. Accepting the latter, she wrote that the year-long position in her hometown offered 'a security I hadn't dreamed of.'[64] The chance to write full-time, in or out of town, was sufficient inducement for many authors to interrupt other careers. Michael Ondaatje, Robert Kroetsch, and Jack Hodgins all sought leaves-of-absence from stable teaching positions to become resident authors.

Despite their brevity, writer-in-residence appointments have strengthened ties between specific authors and institutions and, more generally, between creative and academic circles. Alden Nowlan began his long association with the University of New Brunswick in 1968 through Canada Council funding. Gaston Miron's *Courtepointes* was published by the University of Ottawa's French Department in 1975, four years after Miron's residency. Ralph Gustafson, who retired from a teaching position at Bishop's University in 1977, returned there as writer-in-residence for another two years. The residency activities of these and other authors typically attracted attention beyond the campus, involving local and oftentimes province-wide writing communities.

Between 1965 and 1980 the increasingly visible Writer-in-Residence Program, representing both direct support to authors and a vehicle for 'artist-audience communication,'[65] steadily expanded. In 1977, in co-operation with the Scottish Arts Council, the Canada Council established the Canada-Scotland Writer-in-Residence Exchange, which continued for twenty years. Drastic government cutbacks in the early 1990s resulted in a three-year suspension of domestic author residencies. They were reinstated in 1997, when they became open for the first time to writers of non-fiction.

Celebrating Authorship: Prizes and Distinctions

MARIE-PIER LUNEAU AND RUTH PANOFSKY

Literary awards and prizes do more than recognize the achievement of a writer. They also confer power on those positioned to judge the value of a literary work and bring 'into relief the continuing evaluative process by which the literary text is constructed as an object of negotiation'[66] through various legitimizing authorities, including publishers, booksellers, reviewers, the media, and the audience. Hence any consideration of literary awards and prizes will reflect the biases of the prevailing literary industry, whose very nature often renders it conservative in taste and cautious in judgment. Some prizes appear to have been designed at least in part to raise the profile of a national literature, such as the Governor General's Literary Awards (1936–), the Médaille de l'Académie des lettres du Québec (1946–), the Prix Athanase-David (1968–), and the CBC Literary Awards (1979–). Others assert the significance of Canadian writing, such as many of the awards offered over the years by the Canadian Authors Association (CAA), or celebrate a region, such as the Grand Prix littéraire de la Ville de Montréal (1964–) and the City of Toronto Book Awards (1973–). More minor are those created to support an ethical position – for example, from 1923 to 1933 the Imperial Order Daughters of the Empire (IODE) gave prizes to unpublished short stories deemed 'wholesome in treatment or subject matter'[67] – or to argue a particular literary viewpoint, as when in 1975 the CAA re-established a program of national literary prizes in order to honour 'writing that achieves literary excellence without sacrificing popular appeal.'[68] The political implications of literary prizes are highlighted when a winner declines, as occurred when several francophone authors expressed their objections to the federal government by rejecting Governor General's Awards in the early 1970s.

Prizes for English-Canadian Authors

In the 1920s, given the dearth of Canadian awards for literature in English, authors sought recognition in the United States. Two international successes marked the decade: Martha Ostenso's 1925 novel *Wild Geese* won the U.S. $13,500 prize for a best first novel offered jointly by the *Pictorial Review*, the Famous Players–Lasky Corporation, and Dodd, Mead and Company; and Mazo de la Roche's 1927 novel *Jalna* won the inaugural *Atlantic Monthly* contest for a best first novel, which brought a cash prize of U.S. $10,000. In both cases, the awards for unpublished manuscripts were offered by American publishers seeking potential best-sellers, whereas the most notable Canadian awards have been conferred by juries seeking to distinguish literary merit. De la Roche's victory established her reputation as a writer of international stature, and she went on to publish fifteen more titles in the Jalna series.

In 1938 de la Roche became the first woman to receive the Royal Society of Canada's prestigious Lorne Pierce Medal. Established in 1926 to recognize merit in imaginative or critical literature in English or French, by 1980 it had gone to just six women, in contrast to thirty-nine men. This award, as well as fellowship in the Royal Society, constituted the highest honours available to English-Canadian authors until the launch in 1936 of the Governor General's Literary Awards (affectionately known as the GGs) as the first national literary prizes, originally administered by the CAA.

3.1 D.G. Jones, *Under the Thunder the Flowers Light Up the Earth* (Toronto: Coach House Press, 1977), binding by Pierre Ouvrard, winner of the 1977 Governor General's Literary Award for poetry. Reproduced from *Pierre Ouvrard, Master Bookbinder, Maître relieur* (Edmonton: University of Alberta Press, 2000). Courtesy of Pierre Ouvrard and the University of Alberta Libraries (Bruce Peel Special Collections).

The Canada Council for the Arts became the sponsor of the GGs in 1959, adding categories for French-language authors. Eight awards were offered: for the best works written in English and in French in fiction, non-fiction, poetry, and drama. In 1987 the number of awards expanded to fourteen with the addition of categories in children's literature (text and illustration) and translation. Since 1974 winners have received a commemorative copy of their book hand-bound by master-binder Pierre Ouvrard (see illus. 3.1, above).

Despite the GGs' prestige, until 1950 winners received only a medal. From 1951 to 1958 a small cash prize of $250 was added. In 1959 the value of the GG increased to $1,000; in 1966, to $2,500; in 1975, to $5,000; and in 1989, to $10,000. It is not surprising, then, that upon winning the GG for her 1956 novel *The Sacrifice*, twenty-eight-year-old Adele Wiseman, a cash-strapped writer, was struck by the absence of a significant financial component. Fortunately, her publisher paid for an overseas flight from London, where she was living, so that she could attend the awards ceremony in Winnipeg. Later, when Wiseman was surprised to discover her medal sewn into a collage made by her artist mother, Chaika Wiseman responded ironically: 'Why should it just lie around the house?'[69] In fact, the GG helped to launch Wiseman's career and brought her international acclaim, culminating in an honorary D.Litt. awarded in 1989 by her alma mater, the University of Manitoba.

Other writers whose early careers were boosted by a GG include Hugh MacLennan, who went on to become English Canada's most lauded mid-century writer after *Two Solitudes* received the fiction award in 1945,[70] and Margaret Atwood, whose star rose quickly after *The Circle Game* won the poetry award in 1966. Non-fiction awards have gone to an array of genres, ranging from the autobiography of Laura Goodman Salverson, who won in 1939 for *Confessions of an Immigrant's Daughter*, to the political writings of F.R. Scott, who received the 1977 prize for *Essays on the Constitution*. Cultural analysis was recognized when the prize went to Marshall McLuhan for *The Gutenberg Galaxy* (1962) and to George Woodcock for *The Crystal Spirit: A Study of George Orwell* (1966). History has often been honoured, in books by academic writers such as Donald Creighton (1952, 1955) and Carl Berger (1976), and by popular authors like Thomas Raddall (1948, 1957) and Pierre Berton (1956, 1958, and 1971). From 1936 until 1980, across all categories and languages, men outnumbered women by a ratio of three and a half to one. Hugh MacLennan topped the list with a total of five GGs; three-time winners included Pierre Berton, Bruce Hutchison, E.J. Pratt, Thomas Raddall, James Reaney, and Gabrielle Roy, who was honoured for two books in English translation, as well as one in French.

Following their winning of GGs, MacLennan, Alice Munro, and Robertson Davies later received the Lorne Pierce Medal, and Scott, MacLennan, McLuhan, Woodcock, Atwood, Margaret Laurence, Munro, and Davies each received the prestigious Molson Prize (worth $15,000 before it was increased to two prizes of $50,000 in 1983). Also administered by the Canada Council, the Molson Prize recognizes outstanding cultural achievement in the arts (a second Molson Prize is awarded annually for achievement in the social sciences and humanities). Further recognition of writers' achievements and contributions to the cultural life of Canada takes the form of honorary degrees, fellowship in the Royal Society of Canada, and companionship in the Order of Canada.

Since 1947 the Stephen Leacock Memorial Medal has annually rewarded the country's best humorous writing. Although the GGs honour outstanding achievement in drama, separate national awards administered by the Ontario Arts Council Foundation, the Floyd S. Chalmers Canadian Play Awards ($10,000 each), also honour original plays by Canadian playwrights. David French won a Chalmers Award in 1973 for *Of the Fields, Lately*, his sequel to the successful *Leaving Home*, produced the previous year at Toronto's Tarragon Theatre. James Reaney received a Chalmers Award in 1974 for the second in his landmark trilogy of Donnelly plays, *The St Nicholas Hotel* (1976), and David Fennario's career was given a boost when *Balconville* was awarded a Chalmers in 1980. A variety of smaller awards – regional, provincial, municipal, institutional, generic, and thematic – also encourage authors' careers.[71]

In 1977 the W.H. Smith / *Books in Canada* First Novel Award (later the Chapters / *Books in Canada* First Novel Award) was established to recognize the best first novel by a Canadian writing in English. A cash prize of $5,000 and the esteem conferred by the award serve to promote both the author and the publisher of a first novel, providing encouragement in a market resistant to books by unknown writers. The inaugural W.H. Smith Award was given to Michael Ondaatje for *Coming through Slaughter* (Toronto, 1976), a novel that broke new literary ground in Canada and anticipated his eventual receipt of the international Booker Prize in 1992 for *The English Patient*. While awards for published books have dominated the landscape of Canadian literary prizes, several major publishers created great fanfare when they established literary contests like those won by Ostenso and de la Roche in the 1920s. During the 1930s and 1940s, the Ryerson Press issued highly publicized novels from prize-winning manuscripts, a practice also followed by Pierre Tisseyre in Quebec in the late 1940s and revived by Jack McClelland in 1978 with the first Seal Book Award of $50,000. Won by Aritha Van Herk for her novel *Judith*, the Seal prize launched her on an illustrious career as an author and critic.

Prizes for French-Canadian Authors

In contrast to the situation for authors writing in English, during the second half of the twentieth century, the number of literary prizes available to authors writing in French has been critized as excessive. By 1980 more than seventy different prizes (regional, municipal, provincial, or national) had been created, and more than seven hundred honours had been bestowed on French-language authors. While the vast majority of prize-winning English-language authors were male, the two French-language authors who won the most awards were women, Anne Hébert and Gabrielle Roy; moreover, authors of children's books and of books in the humanities and social sciences, which are often considered marginal to the literary canon, were frequently honoured.[72] Few important authors seem to have been forgotten in the francophone awards system. Even Yves Thériault, who described himself as 'the most harshly criticized and frequently attacked writer in Quebec,'[73] was often recognized.

While literary competitions existed in the nineteenth century, the first important Quebec prize, the Prix David, was created in 1922. Until the 1950s, this prize, along with the Prix d'Action intellectuelle, created in 1919 by the Association catholique de la jeunesse canadienne-française, was the only honour to which French-Canadian authors could aspire. Although the Royal Society of Canada began to award the Lorne Pierce and Tyrrell medals in the 1920s, francophone winners were extremely rare. The Prix Ludger-Duvernay, created in 1944 by the Société Saint-Jean-Baptiste, provided some balance.

In 1949 the literary prize of the Cercle du livre de France (CLF) substantially changed the picture. Created by Montreal publisher Pierre Tisseyre in order to recruit new authors, this accolade helped publicize the young generation of novelists of the 1950s: André Langevin, Françoise Loranger, Claire Martin, and Claude Jasmin. In the 1960s, eight new provincial prizes were added to the seven created in the 1950s. Between 1970 and 1980, twenty-two other major prizes came into being. But these initiatives, which were intended as a form of support for literary creation, were disparaged by critics, a response that in the long run undermined their credibility.

In the 1960s and 1970s, controversy over the system of awards was in part related to political disagreements between the province of Quebec and the federal government. Initially excluded from the GGs, French-language authors finally became eligible in 1959, when the management of the prizes was transferred from the CAA to the Canada Council for the Arts. Ten years later, Hubert Aquin initiated a political protest movement among writers by refusing the GG conferred on his novel *Trou de mémoire* (1968). After the October Crisis of 1970, many other winners, including Fernand Dumont, Fernand Ouellette, Roland Giguère, Victor-Lévy Beaulieu, Nicole Brossard, Michel Garneau, and Gilbert Langevin, disputed the legitimacy of awards given by a government they saw as the oppressor of the Quebec people. Other, more neutral, prizes compensated for this rejection and were often awarded to the same authors. Of the sixty French-language authors who received the most awards between 1918 and 1980, 43 per cent received both the Prix David and a Governor General's Award. A frequent comment was that these literary prizes did more to promote institutions than authors.[74]

In such a context, what effect can a literary award have on the career of the winner? With respect to prizes given for new works, the impact on sales can be significant. The prize of the Cercle du livre de France, in the 1950s, and the Prix Robert-Cliche, starting in 1979, generated sales of between 6,000 and 10,000 copies for the chosen books. After 1980 some national prizes included such handsome monetary awards – notably, the Molson Prize and the Prix Gilles-Corbeil (created in 1990, with an award of $100,000 given every three years to a francophone author residing in Canada or the United States) – that they freed the winners from financial need, at least for a while. Sometimes, however, the books had reached their readership before the prizes were awarded, and the impact on sales was relatively modest. Paradoxically, Gilbert Larocque described the Canada-Switzerland Literary Prize, which he received for his novel *Les masques* in 1982, as a veritable 'curse,' since none of his previous books had sold so badly.[75]

International prizes give their recipients fame and visibility that often transform their lives. The Prix Goncourt, awarded to Antonine Maillet in 1979 for *Pélagie-la-Charrette,* almost guarantees sales of over 100,000 copies. Success obtained through winning a prestigious prize often permitted authors to live from their writing. Gabrielle Roy, after receiving the Prix Femina in 1947, and Anne Hébert, after receiving the Prix des Libraires de France in 1971, achieved a degree of financial autonomy they had not previously known. An international prize can also launch the career of a young, relatively unknown writer, both abroad and in the author's own country, as was the case for Marie-Claire Blais after she won the Prix Medicis in 1966.

Growth in the number of prizes and medals awarded since the 1950s has enhanced the visibility and symbolic capital of Canadian authors, while enabling some to improve their financial situation. While the impact of Canadian awards on the literary marketplace remains unpredictable, the political dimension of prizes awarded by government bodies is obvious, insofar as they are often the most visible aspect of state patronage.

Writers' Networks and Associations

PEGGY LYNN KELLY AND JOSÉE VINCENT

The material and social conditions of their profession were of vital importance to Canadian authors in the twentieth century. The expansion of writing markets, as well as shifts in legislation that affected their work and income, led authors to form organizations for mutual support, professional development, and political influence. Such bodies also served as forums for debates over literary standards and as platforms from which to promote books and reading. Although anglophone and francophone authors held many preoccupations in common, language proved a fundamental divide. Anglophone and francophone authors organized separate collective structures that nonetheless followed similar paths.

Anglophone Writers' Associations

By the end of the First World War, Canadian authors were quite familiar with the concept of a writers' organization. Concerns about copyright had inspired the establishment of the Canadian Society of Authors (CSA) in 1899. Modelled on the Society of Authors in the United Kingdom, the CSA enjoyed about ten highly active years before fading in influence.[76] In the 1910s, Ottawa-based novelist and journalist Madge Macbeth turned to the Authors' League of America, convinced that '[a]uthors must have a common meeting ground.'[77] When the Canadian Authors Association (CAA) was formed in 1921, Macbeth abandoned the American organization to become an active member in the Canadian body. Like the CSA, the CAA was inspired by authorial concerns over new copyright legislation, in this case spearheaded by a new generation of writers. Many sources cite Stephen Leacock (see illus. 3.2, p. 124), Pelham Edgar, J.M. Gibbon, and B.K. Sandwell as the founders, but the CAA's papers provide several other names, including Nellie McClung, Bliss Carman, Sir Charles G.D. Roberts, Florence Randal Livesay, and Robert Service.[78] In 1933 the CAA absorbed what remained of the earlier CSA.[79]

While the CAA carried out policy work from its central office in Ottawa, it developed a network of regional branches to support promotional and professional activities and even considered establishing an American branch to reach expatriate Canadian authors.[80] Fledgling and professional writers, as well as associates such as booksellers and publishers, were eligible for membership. During the 1920s, the CAA promoted initiatives such as Canada Book Week and national reading tours to develop a market for Canadian literature. From the beginning it issued a regular newsletter, whose most enduring title was the *Canadian Author and Bookman* (Toronto), in which members debated cultural nationalism, free verse, literary standards, and literary movements, and found practical advice about writing and marketing. Many Canadian writers, especially modernists, also reached out to the international literary arena by joining Poets, Essayists, and Novelists (PEN), an international authors' organization dedicated to writers imprisoned for political reasons, which established a bilingual branch in Montreal in 1926.

3.2 Edwin Holgate, *Portrait of Stephen Leacock* (1943). Humorist and political economist, Leacock was one of the founders of the Canadian Authors Association. Courtesy of the Estate of Edwin Holgate and the National Gallery of Canada, Ottawa.

Notwithstanding the devastating effects of the Depression on the market for their work, the 1930s proved a decade of significant collective activity for anglophone writers. Inspired by Sir Charles G.D. Roberts's financial plight, the Canadian Writers' Foundation was instituted in 1931 by Pelham Edgar to provide aid to sick and elderly Canadian authors no longer able to support themselves. In 1936 the CAA itself initiated both the *Canadian Poetry Magazine* (Toronto) and the Governor General's Literary Awards. CAA branches, such as those in Montreal, Edmonton, and Toronto, held national poetry contests that resulted in anthologies under their imprints. Edmonton was the most active, from 1930 to 1990 publishing the *Alberta Poetry Year Book*, which culminated in the retrospective anthology *Sixty Singing Years* (1990).

The crisis of the 1930s and 1940s led some Canadian authors to join overtly political writers' and arts associations. Committed to developing a grassroots movement for social change, the Progressive Arts Club and the Workers' Theatre Movement were organized by members of the Communist Party of Canada, whose ranks included poet-journalist Dorothy Livesay. Also partisan, the Writers, Broadcasters, and Artists War Council sought to improve relations between Canada and the USSR by arranging wartime cultural donations. At the other end of the political spectrum was the Writers' War Committee, described in the following case study by Peter Buitenhuis, which briefly assisted the federal government's propaganda program during the early 1940s. In the 1940s, politicization within the profession led anglophone writers to lobby for the standardization of writing contracts and income averaging for tax purposes, both under the auspices of the CAA. Then in the late 1940s and early 1950s, writers' groups such as the CAA and the Canadian Writers' Committee began to influence cultural policy by submitting briefs to government investigations such as the Massey Commission. In spite of protests from CAA members, in 1959 the Governor General's Literary Awards were transferred to the Canada Council, an organization representing one of the most concrete outcomes of the commission's investigation.

The resurgence of cultural nationalism in the mid-twentieth century made government funds available to diverse writers' organizations which sprang up through the 1970s and 1980s. Starting with the Saskatchewan Writers' Guild in 1969, writers in each province and one territory founded regional organizations to serve writers of all genres of literature. Genre-based writers' groups represented a move toward professional specialization and also responded to an increasingly sectored marketplace. The trend toward national organizations based on specific literary genres began with the founding of the League of Canadian Poets in 1966.

The establishment of the Writers' Union of Canada (WUC) in 1973, under the leadership of F.R. Scott, Margaret Laurence (its first chair), and Marian Engel, was a major development. Operating as a centralized national organization based in Toronto, the WUC favoured the literary over the popular and restricted its membership to professional writers in all genres, defined as those who had published a trade book. During the 1970s the WUC was instrumental in settling grievances between writers and publishers and in promoting the public lending right, legislation which was passed in 1986. In co-operation with the Canada Council, the WUC began to administer several projects to support and publicize professional writers, such as the National Public Readings Program and the Writers-in-the-Schools Program.

Between 1918 and 1980 many anglophone writers held multiple memberships in professional organizations. For example, poet Hilda Ridley belonged to both the CAA and the Writers' Craft Club, CAA member Lyn Harrington served on the WUC's Task Force on the Canada Council, and Margaret Atwood was active in PEN and the WUC. In addition, writers created formal associations and informal writing circles at

Table 3.3
Selected writers' organizations, 1918–80

Dates	Organization
1921	Canadian Authors Association*
1921–35	Section française de la Canadian Authors Association
1922	Société des poètes canadiens-français
1925	Writers' Craft Club
1926	PEN (Poets, Essayists, and Novelists)*
1931	Progressive Arts Club
1932	Workers' Theatre Movement
1936	Société des écrivains canadiens*
1940	Bliss Carman Society
1943	Writers, Broadcasters and Artists War Council
1948–54	Association des écrivains pour la jeunesse
1954–68	Union des jeunes écrivains
1957–58	Rencontre des poètes canadiens
1959–61	Rencontre des écrivains canadiens
1968–71	Rencontre des écrivains
1972–92	Rencontre québécoise internationale des écrivains
1966	League of Canadian Poets*
1966?–71?	Syndicat des écrivains du Québec
1968	Newfoundland Writers' Guild*
1969	Saskatchewan Writers' Guild*
1971	Canadian Science Writers Association*
	Communication-jeunesse*
	Guild of Canadian Playwrights*
1973	Writers' Union of Canada*
1975	Literary Translators' Association of Canada / Association des traducteurs et traductrices littéraires du Canada*
	Writers' Federation of Nova Scotia *
1976	Periodical Writers' Association of Canada*
1977	Association des auteurs des Cantons de l'Est*
	Canadian Society of Children's Authors, Illustrators and Performers*
	Union des écrivains québécois*
1978	Academy of Canadian Writers
	Canadian Association of Journalists*
	Société des écrivains de la Mauricie*
1980	Island Writers Association (PEI)*
	Writers' Guild of Alberta*

*Organization still in existence in 2005.

the local level. In the early part of the century, the latter included the Vancouver Poetry Society (est. 1916), the Song Fishermen of Nova Scotia (est. 1928),[81] and the Toronto Writers' Club (1920s). A desire for formal associations based in the community became increasingly evident in the century's final decades, with the proliferation of groups like the Flin Flon Writers Guild (est. 1983) in Manitoba. As well, informal writers' circles provided opportunities for writers to share drafts and receive constructive criticism. Some writers preferred such groups to the CAA, which was never joined by either Sinclair Ross, who found his support in the Phoenix Club, which started up in Winnipeg in 1932, or Ethel Wilson, who preferred to participate in Authors Anonymous, organized in Vancouver by Earle Birney around 1950.[82] In Atlantic Canada the Bliss Carman Society, formed by historian and poet A.G. Bailey at the University of New Brunswick in 1940, functioned as both a writing circle and a formal organization, and established *Fiddlehead Magazine* (Fredericton) in 1945.[83] Since the development of the World Wide Web, many Canadian writing circles have operated on the Internet, especially those associated with creative writing courses in post-secondary educational institutions.

Francophone Writers' Associations

In French Canada the socio-economic conditions necessary for the emergence of a professional writers' association did not exist before the First World War. Even the École littéraire de Montréal (est. 1895), as organized as it was, did not claim to be a professional organization. Only the Association des journalistes canadiens-français (AJCF, 1903–6),[84] and some fashionable salons and social networks where writers gathered, had shown any concern for the professional aspects of writing. The professionalization that had occurred among journalists through the second half of the nineteenth century had not yet reached the literary arena and ran counter to the way the majority of writers perceived their place in society. Authors found themselves few in number, and with a limited market. Forced by an inadequate publishing infrastructure to supervise the entire production and distribution process, if they did issue their work in book form, they were unable to earn a living by their pens. Nonetheless, the AJCF's 1904 campaign against literary piracy, rife in Quebec at the turn of the century, had helped to raise writers' awareness of the need to assert their rights.

When the federal government began to plan a change to copyright legislation after the war, it became clear that writers needed to form an organization capable of representing their interests. In 1921, encouraged by their English-speaking colleagues, French-Canadian writers joined the Canadian Authors Association (CAA), creating a French section within its ranks. Since advocacy work on matters such as copyright was the responsibility of the central council of the organization, individual sections devoted much effort to literary and promotional activities, the best known of which was Canada Book Week. The French section, most of whose members were prominent Montrealers, professionals, and teachers, functioned largely as a social club. In 1936, as a result of the rise of nationalist sentiment among French-Canadian intellectuals, who were unhappy with their subordination to the English-language organization, the Société des écrivains canadiens (SÉC) was formed to provide francophone writers with a credible organization while respecting their desire for cultural autonomy. Based on the model of the CAA, the SÉC established a central council in Montreal, with regional sections in Quebec City, Ottawa, Sherbrooke, and Trois-Rivières.[85] Thanks to an annual grant from Quebec's Department of the Provincial Secretary, the SÉC had a permanent office, which was run by Germaine Guèvremont from 1938 to 1948. Under the leadership of Victor Barbeau, its first president, the SÉC published anthologies, directories, terminology guides, and a *Bulletin bibliographique,* which listed new French-Canadian titles. It also organized many promotional activities, literary evenings, exhibitions, competitions, and commemorations, soon becoming the major cultural organization of the period.

The end of the Second World War marked a new stage in the history of the SÉC when, in 1946, under the presidency of Jean Bruchési, under-secretary of the Province of Quebec, its lobbying activities intensified. Bruchési put the SÉC at the centre of the debates of the time, instigating its membership in the Canadian Arts Council and making it a signatory to briefs presented to the Massey, Tremblay, and Fowler commissions. The SÉC demanded recognition of the rights and social status of authors, and promoted the writer as a purveyor of national identity. However, the SÉC held an elitist view of the mission of the writer. In 1955 it refused to associate itself with the Association des écrivains pour la jeunesse, an organization discussed in the next chapter. The SÉC also kept its distance from the Union des jeunes écrivains, considering it unworthy of its interest. Although by 1957 the SÉC could no longer ignore the growing importance of the new generation of poets published in Éditions de l'Hexagone and gathered under the banner of the Rencontre des poètes,[86] its attitudes remained unchanged, with no effort to develop closer relations.

In the early 1960s, a sombre, unstable period began for the SÉC. Undermined by a series of presidential resignations, deprived of the annual grants it had formerly received, and unable to renew itself, the SÉC, despite the support of the Conseil supérieur du livre, became incapable of adopting a consistent course of action. In 1967, under the presidency of Robert Charbonneau, it undermined its status as a professional organization by recruiting most of its new members among unestablished writers.

In the 1970s, the affirmation of Quebec literature and government support for the book trades and publishers gave the literary community a new impetus and led to increased professionalization among writers. More authors were able to live by their pens. Lively discussion about the status and rights of authors occurred at the Rencontre des écrivains, which brought together a younger generation of writers, most of them contributing to the journal *Liberté* (Montreal, 1959–). This group, led by Jacques Godbout, who disparaged the SÉC, envisaged a new professional association more reflective of the social reality of contemporary Quebec writers. When the Union des écrivains québécois (UNÉQ) was founded in 1977, its members immediately asserted their professional status, requiring writers to have published at least two books in order to be admitted.

By the 1970s, books and literature were no longer associated with a cultivated elite, but with a profession represented by a formal association. The existence of universities and colleges throughout Quebec and the adoption of a provincial policy to support cultural development in the regions also favoured the emergence of new structures outside the major urban centres. In the late 1970s, authors from the Estrie and Mauricie regions formed their own autonomous organizations, a trend that intensified after 1980.

CASE STUDY——————————————————————————————————
The CAA and Propaganda during the Second World War
– Peter Buitenhuis

During the Second World War, Canada needed an effective, centralized propaganda office to boost morale at home and publicize the country's war effort abroad. But Prime Minister Mackenzie King, 'profoundly suspicious of any proposal for a ministry of information and, indeed, of any organized effort to provide so-called public information,' was reluctant to act.[87] Canadian authors, many of whom had served with distinction in the propaganda services of the First World War, were annoyed at being shut out by the state.[88] When the Wartime Information Board (WIB), headed by Charles Vining, was finally established on 9 September 1942, Canadian authors were eager to offer their services. The following day, delegates gathered at the annual Canadian Authors Association (CAA) convention unanimously resolved to establish the Writers' War Committee (WWC). Their enthusiasm was encouraged by Carl Carmer, president of the Authors' League of America, who spoke about the activities of the Writers' War Board in the United States, the organization on which the Canadian committee would be modelled.[89] 'When the whole of civilization is at stake in a conflict of spiritual principle, the writer, whose very phrases are weapons forged by the resolute mind, cannot afford to doze in his sentry-box or loiter on the line of march,' stated Watson Kirkconnell, incoming CAA president and newly appointed WWC chair.[90]

Although formed under the auspices of the CAA, the WWC board drew on writers from across the country, not all of them CAA members, while the Société des écrivains canadiens created a separate French section under the wing of the committee. When Kirkconnell formally offered the services of the WWC to the WIB, Vining responded positively but could offer only a meagre $200 per month to defray the committee's administrative costs. Nonetheless encouraged, the WWC executive surveyed its participating writers to produce a National Service Register, a volume listing the literary genres and published titles associated with each author, and presented Vining with a reference copy.[91] The executive also identified topical targets, such as nutrition, War Saving Certificates, and Victory Loans, which it passed along to members, 'who were [then] expected to [write and] market their own work in the usual way.' Finally, the WWC organized a series of subcommittees, including those on songs, radio, and morale-building. Authors associated with the song subcommittee produced a number of popular tunes, such as John Murray Gibbon and Murray Adaskin's 'Back the Attack,' which supported the fourth Victory Loan campaign, and Gordon V. Thompson's 'Cross of Red on a Field of White,' created in aid of the Red Cross campaign.[92]

The WWC's achievements of 1942–3 occurred in a context of diminishing financial and moral support from the WIB. Reimbursement for administrative expenses proved difficult to collect, and specific writing assignments from the WIB were rare, Vining having discovered that his office was more limited in scope than it first appeared. When he resigned on 26 January 1943, he was replaced by John Grierson, commissioner of the National Film Board (est. 1939).[93] Grierson did not embrace the WWC and its objectives, placing more faith in the efficacy of film and radio propaganda.[94] By autumn 1943, loss of the WIB's minimal support, coupled with the resignation of the WWC's energetic secretary, ground the committee to a halt. '[W]e simply parked our vehicle for the duration,' Kirkconnell recalled in his memoirs, and so ingloriously ended Canadian writers' official part in the propaganda of the Second World War.[95]

chapter 4

THE AUTHOR AND THE MARKET

Writers and the Market for Fiction and Literature

JANET B. FRISKNEY AND CAROLE GERSON

For most of the twentieth century, Canadian authors of fiction and poetry recognized that a readership sufficient to sustain them financially was not to be found in Canada, a country with a relatively small, dispersed, and linguistically divided population. Professional authors either resigned themselves to writing part-time or sought to advance their work in the major English- and French-language markets of the United States and Europe. Thus they not only had to negotiate different ideas of the social and cultural role of the writer generally, and of the Canadian author specifically, but also had to navigate the expectations of foreign as well as domestic publishers. The period saw dramatic changes in the venues through which Canadians could publish at home and abroad, as a distinct market emerged first nationally and eventually internationally for 'CanLit' – Canadian fiction and poetry defined as 'literary' by its authors, publishers, and critics. In English-speaking Canada the schism between Canada's popular and literary writers, as well as between the audiences they addressed, was acknowledged by prolific novelist Dan Ross in 1972: 'Maybe I could do better than Mordecai Richler ... Maybe he could write my stuff ... But you know we're both like the oboe and the flute, we both function in the same orchestra of literature. You don't reach a popular audience unless you're able to communicate with people.'[1]

Advice from the publications of the Canadian Authors Association, as well as the more obscure *Writers' Studio* (Toronto, 1933–44), made it clear that before the 1950s, book publication offered less financial stability for fiction writers than did the magazine market, itself divided into the 'slicks' and the 'pulps' (in Quebec, the latter took the form of serial pamphlets known as *fascicules*, described in the case study by Jacques Michon in chapter 8). During the early decades of the century, novels were often serialized in both elite and popular magazines before appearing as books. Arthur Stringer was especially adept at exploiting 'the potential of pre-publication serialization,' thanks to the expert guidance of literary agent Paul Reynolds.[2] However, magazine editors had distinct notions regarding suitable types of fiction. With their publications' financial health dependent on advertising income, which was calculated on the basis of circulation, editors couldn't afford to misinterpret their readers' interests.

The situation of Canadian writers of magazine fiction was complicated by the fact that domestic periodical publishers desperately tried to compete with the volume of imported magazines flooding the Canadian market. Although Canada's English-language magazines generally paid less than American publications, writers were expected to submit work of competitive type and quality. Nor could they hope to separate rights for the Canadian and American markets, and thus profit from both. As *Maclean's* editor H. Napier Moore explained in 1929, 'Most of the United States magazines would not agree that when they bought United States rights in a Canadian story, Canadian publication could purchase the Canadian rights, with simultaneous publication.'[3] This situation led domestic editors of periodicals to purchase much foreign fiction, a practice regularly denounced by Canadian authors. In 1938 the literary editor of the *Canadian Home Journal*, Margaret Lawrence, responded that 'Canadian editors are always specially interested in the work of their own writers,' but 'they find a dearth of really acceptable material that will stand up against the pressure of competition from across the line, and ... they like a Canadian locale if it is authentic and not just "dragged in."' Lawrence further detailed what she desired in magazine fiction. Although stories focussed on sex, race, religion, or economics made her readers 'see red,' she advised that 'any subject can be treated if carefully handled' in a 'tone [that] is lifting.' She also sought to reduce a split in readership: 'while the field of the big popular magazines prohibits it being "high-brow," the tendency is in the direction of the less ephemeral and artificial work.'[4] Her cautions and her advocacy of an uplifting tone applied equally to the American slicks. Canadians who proved particularly capable of writing for this North American market included Isabel Ecclestone Mackay, Ernest Buckler, Brian Moore, and Scott Young.

Before 1939, fiction writers working in French had fewer opportunities than their English colleagues as many Québécois publishers of magazines and books were content to reprint fiction by popular authors from France. Édouard Garand represented a notable exception. He maintained the series Le roman canadien (est. 1923) by buying each copyright outright for a price that never exceeded $50 – not a princely sum, but enough to maintain the loyalty of authors with few other options.[5] In 1931 Robert Choquette presented a bleak analysis, claiming that French-Canadian authors worked 'practically for nothing. An English-Canadian author sees open before him, besides England, the whole Dominion, not to speak of the possible market of the United States. He can deal with magazines that pay. All this is out of the question as far as we are concerned ... Our authors cannot, therefore, live on their writings. They must earn their living by some other means, allotting to their literary efforts their spare time only. They remain hardly more than amateurs.'[6]

The disadvantage of a restricted language community became an advantage with the advent of new media. Choquette was one of the first authors to benefit from the genre of the 'radioroman,' inaugurated in Quebec in 1936 when he published Le curé de village, a book based on a radio serial.[7] With the introduction of television in 1952 came the téléroman and télétheâtre. These new forms of popular culture created a huge audience for Quebec writers that enabled authors like Claude-Henri Grignon, Marcel Dubé, and Roger Lemelin to bridge the gap between the popular and the literary. Francophone writers for both broadcast media and the live stage drew on a long-standing tradition of play publication that was more lucrative than the production of books in other genres. Garand's series of Canadian novels had been partnered by a series of plays that numbered some twenty-nine titles from 1924 to 1931.[8] After the Second World War, the success of Gratien Gélinas's plays Tit-coq (staged 1948, published 1950) and Bousille et les justes (1960) was followed by the immense impact of Michel Tremblay's Les belles sœurs (1968). In contrast, neither the popular culture nor the serious stages of English-speaking Canada could sustain local authors because most comedies and plays were imported from the United States and Great Britain. However, there were such notable exceptions as Canadian Theatre of the Air, which acquired forty-seven of its sixty-five scripts from Canadians after the radio show's producers recognized the quality of domestic talent.[9]

By the 1930s an emergent group of modernist English-speaking writers with lofty aspirations, including F.R. Scott, A.J.M. Smith, and Morley Callaghan, were distancing themselves from 'professional' Canadian writers such as Mazo de la Roche who earned often substantial incomes from mass-market magazine fiction or book publication of popular genres. In 1938, Callaghan regretted Canada's lack of 'quality' magazines like the American *Harper's* and *The New Yorker*, which published literary fiction; the only domestic aspirant he identified was the *Canadian Forum*, which could not afford to pay contributors. Callaghan also noted the preference of Canadian book publishers for sharing the risk of publication with a foreign publisher on those occasions – rarer during the Depression – when they did engage in original publishing.[10] This practice endured past mid-century: for example, in 1959, Margaret Laurence's *This Side Jordan* was accepted by McClelland and Stewart with the proviso that a British or American publisher be found to share costs.[11] However, writers of Laurence's post-war generation benefited from the significant growth of Canada's little magazines. Authors who subsequently published books drew on this established audience, as well as the one they gained through literary broadcasts on CBC Radio.

The agency system that characterized Anglo-Canadian book publishing through much of the twentieth century, along with the country's small domestic market, created an unusual book publishing environment. As John Morgan Gray of Macmillan of Canada explained in 1955, the Canadian book publisher did not derive 'any important part of his revenue (or *any* net profit) from Canadian general publishing'; the only reasons to engage in original Canadian trade publishing were those of 'pride and prestige.'[12] Before 1960, neither Canadian literary fiction nor poetry had much international appeal; consequently, only Canadian publishers with a substantial nationalist commitment engaged in these areas of trade publishing, often entirely at their own risk. In 1954 Macmillan of Canada, for example, independently published Charles Bruce's *The Channel Shore* and Ralph Allen's *The Chartered Libertine* – 'good novels making an important and clarifying statement about life in Canada' – when it 'found no publishers in the United States or England' for either title.[13] To foster a larger market for Canadian literature, Ryerson Press emulated a publicity gambit of American and British publishers, mounting annual novel contests between 1942 and 1957; the strategy may have done some good, for several winning titles, among them G. Herbert Sallans's *Little Man* (1942) and Evelyn M. Richardson's *Desired Haven* (1953), were picked up by foreign publishers or went into second editions.[14]

In such a difficult domestic publishing environment, authors in English Canada resorted to various alternatives to get their work into print. While the recourse of poets included chapbooks and self-publication, novelists often bypassed Canadian publishers entirely and submitted their manuscripts directly to foreign companies. Morley Callaghan, Sinclair Ross, Hugh MacLennan, and Mordecai Richler all pursued the latter option. For Callaghan and MacLennan, foreign publication proved a conundrum. Callaghan often obscured the Toronto locale of his stories in favour of a generic North American urban setting, thus making his work more appealing to a broader audience. Convinced he could assume no prior knowledge of Canada on the part of international readers, MacLennan self-consciously addressed himself to two audiences.[15] When MacLennan's *Each Man's Son* was issued by Boston's Little, Brown in 1951, explication of its Canadian setting appeared in the text while an introduction describing Cape Breton prefaced the work. Even co-publishing between a Canadian and a foreign house did not resolve these difficulties. John Morgan Gray revealed in 1955 that in such an arrangement the foreign publisher was dominant: 'The big decisions, editorial and commercial, are made in New York and London and in the interest of his author a Canadian editor dare not forget it.'[16]

For Québécois writers, success in France was largely determined by the name, prestige, and specialization of the publisher. The pattern that began in 1938, when Flammarion issued Ringuet's *Trente arpents* and Gallimard issued Léo-Paul Desrosiers's *Les engagés du grand portage*, was disrupted by the outbreak of the Second World War. Interest in Canadian authors resumed in the late 1940s and was greatest for authors consecrated by major French literary prizes. Gabrielle Roy's *Bonheur d'occasion* was an instant best-seller when it was first published in Montreal in 1945. Issued by Flammarion in 1947 after selling 750,000 copies in the United States in its English translation as *The Tin Flute*, the book garnered the Prix Fémina and ongoing success with Parisian readers. However, that same public was not ready for Marie-Claire Blais, whose first novel, *La belle bête*, met with failure in France in 1961, despite its appearance under the Flammarion imprint. Similarly, major novelists of the Quiet Revolution – André Langevin, Claude Jasmin, Claire Martin, and Hubert Aquin – sold poorly in France. All were published in Paris by Robert Laffont in his series Les jeunes romanciers canadiens, but their reception was undermined by the commercial reputation of the publisher and their lack of appeal to a readership that wanted grand narratives reminiscent of *Maria Chapdelaine*. Editions du Seuil kept canny control over the elite image of its list by publishing just two Canadian authors, Jacques Godbout and Anne Hébert. Hébert's *Kamouraska* (1970) proved a great success, promoted through clever marketing that evoked 'grand passion and exoticism,' two favourite themes with readers in France.[17] Efforts of the Canadian and Quebec governments to reach French readers in Europe through the distribution of books from Québécois publishers began in the 1960s. Despite the opening of the Centre de diffusion du livre canadien-français in Paris in 1967 and a heroic series of agreements, participation in international book fairs, and production of catalogues, sales failed to meet expectations. The federal government's 'Livres du Canada – Books from

Canada' program, launched in 1972, was equally ineffective in penetrating the French marketplace, especially for literary work.[18]

During the middle decades of the century, North American English-language book publishing was transformed by the paperback revolution. Marketed through the established magazine network, paperbacks quickly made their way into Canada to become an integral part of the domestic book market. The public delighted in these inexpensive books, slowly abandoning its former allegiance to story magazines. The short shelf life of mass-market paperbacks made the new industry voracious for 'product.' Reprints of older hardback titles could not satisfy the demand, and, as a result, paperback publishers produced original works in this format and acquired the paperback rights to recent hardback publications.

Canadian authors suffered, adjusted, or took advantage of this new reality. Scott Young, who through the late 1940s and early 1950s had made a living by writing fiction for the slicks, returned to journalism.[19] Under both his own name and the pseudonyms of Bernard Mara and Michael Bryan, Brian Moore penned seven mass-market thrillers during the 1950s: two for Canadian-owned Harlequin, and others for American and British publishers, in order to 'earn money that would buy him time to work on serious novels.'[20] Hugh MacLennan, who did not see writing original mass-market novels as an option, identified a double impact of the paperback revolution on the finances of writers who sought initial publication in hardback: first, many book buyers waited for cheaper paper editions, which paid lower royalties to the author; second, paperbacks destroyed the North American rental library system, in which, in the 1940s, a book 'picked up anything from 4,000 to 6,000 sales automatically,' with each copy read 'by anything from 30 to 100 people,' thus enabling the author to become 'more widely known.'[21] After 1962 Dan Ross, on the other hand, made the original paperback market his primary target. As he explained in 1971, 'An average hardcover book with a printing of 3000 copies, could, if it sold every copy ... bring in $18,000 and net the writer $1,800 which is hardly a princely sum.' By contrast, 'the lowest advance paid in the most lowly of paperback markets today is $1,000 and it goes sharply up from there.'[22]

In Quebec, the local publishing of titles from France that had flourished during the war resulted in French authors continuing to dominate popular reading material in magazines, pocketbooks, and book clubs. However, wartime restrictions also facilitated the domestic production of pulp serials written by Quebec authors, which remained part of the market until the 1960s. Thus Yves Thériault established economic security by answering a 1945 newspaper advertisement headed 'Writers Wanted.' He and his wife, Germaine-Michelle Blanchet, embarked on the production of anonymous or pseudonymous 'ten-cent novels' for Edgar Lespérance, together penning three detective stories and three romances a week for $20 apiece.[23]

As the general magazine and newspaper markets for short stories and poems shrank in the 1950s, anglophone authors found their economic role replaced by the anthology – sometimes intended for general readers (e.g., *Stories with John Drainie* [1963]), sometimes for university students (e.g., Klinck and Watters, eds, *Canadian Anthology* [1955, 1966, 1974]). The literary anthology, a long-standing classroom staple, was to prove a growing source of income as Canadian literature became an established area of study. Poets and authors of short stories were the main beneficiaries, along with the publishers who supplied texts for the baby boomers swelling Canada's post-secondary classrooms through the 1960s and 1970s. In the mid-1950s, Phyllis Webb shrewdly noted that the economic value of poems accrued through reprintings in anthologies;[24] author John Metcalf would subsequently make a viable living by having his stories regularly appear in anthologies, and from 1967 to 1980 edited some twenty-four of them himself.[25] The 1970s were a boom decade for English-Canadian literary anthologies, producing three and a half times the number of titles that appeared during the 1960s.[26] While anthologies have been valued by writers for the support they provide for shorter literary forms, critics note the 'power of the anthology not only to canonize but also to determine ways of reading,' especially in relation to poets such as Anne Wilkinson, whose known oeuvre has been reduced to several frequently reprinted texts.[27]

The paperback literary anthology represented one genre within the larger phenomenon known as the 'quality paperback.' A substantial market for paperback literary reprints began in the United States in the late 1940s when New American Library established Mentor Books, a more expensively priced paperback line. Marketed through trade and college bookstores, these titles quickly became popular as teaching texts. Canadian publisher McClelland and Stewart joined this field in 1958 when it launched the New Canadian Library (NCL), a series of Canadian literary reprints, further discussed in Janet B. Friskney's case study in chapter 7. Novels dominated the titles in the NCL as well as its domestic competitors such as Macmillan's Laurentian Library (est. 1967) and the 'collections de poche' issued by Fides (beginning in 1960). These publishing ventures revived many literary works or kept them in print, and helped to raise the profile of numerous Canadian and Quebec writers among a new generation of readers. Although the royalties such series generated were initially small, the consistency with which some authors' titles were chosen for the classroom, substantial expansion of the teaching of Canadian literature between the 1950s and the 1970s, and significant increases in paperback royalty rates in the 1970s translated into good income for some writers. Through the 1970s, Margaret Laurence came to rely on NCL sales, and she was angered in 1978 when she discovered that the new mass-market Seal editions of her Manawaka titles, whose lower price resulted in smaller royalties, were undercutting sales of the NCL editions to the college trade.[28]

Laurence's ability to earn a living as a Canadian literary author represented the outcome of expanded domestic markets and new infrastructure support, such as Canada Council programs, that enabled writers of her generation to create a fresh wave of literary excitement in the 1960s and 1970s. Although Laurence always found her keenest reading public at home, other major Canadian literary figures of this period, such as Margaret Atwood, Robertson Davies, and Anne Hébert, garnered international success. Leonard Cohen's poetry and songs performed a similar feat, gathering a national and international following, and uniting the oboe and the flute in the orchestra of literature envisioned by Dan Ross.

Writers and the Market for Non-Fiction

CLARENCE KARR

Through the twentieth century, the market open to Canadian writers of non-fiction embraced publishing venues ranging from newspapers through consumer and trade magazines to books, while the new media of film, radio, and television offered additional opportunities. Some writers pursued non-fiction alongside professional careers or as part-time work, while for others – including many who proceeded through the journalistic ranks – writing was a full-time occupation. An immensely broad category, non-fiction included current affairs, history, biography, politics, economics, science, nature, travel, sports, and self-help and instruction manuals.

During the interwar period, periodicals provided the most lucrative market for non-fiction writers. Newspapers and magazines comprised about 75 per cent of the listings in the *Canadian Writer's Market Survey* of 1931; those devoted to Canada subdivided into general (47), agricultural (35), financial (19), and religious (11) magazines, as well as leading daily (56) and weekly (8) newspapers. With 128 publications, the category for trade and related magazines was the largest. Payment rates varied:

Canadian Homes and Gardens offered 1½ cents per word; the *Canadian Baker and Confectioner* $5 per printed page; the *Western Farmer* $3 per 16–inch column; and *La Tribune* (Sherbrooke) $40 for 10,000 lines. Many American consumer magazines had a base rate of 2 cents per word, although 'serious' slicks like *Collier's* and *Harper's Magazine* started at 5 cents per word.[29]

Success in magazines did not naturally lead to books, and collections of articles were usually regarded as unmarketable.[30] For example, despite its author's high profile as a Toronto editor and columnist, William Arthur Deacon's *Pens and Pirates* (1923), an assortment of comic, literary, and nationalistic essays issued by Ryerson Press, sold only 276 copies in two years.[31] Well-known periodical writers fared better with memoirs, travel narratives, biographies, and histories. Hector Charlesworth published three thick volumes of reminiscences, beginning with *Candid Chronicles: Leaves from the Note Book of a Canadian Journalist* (1925). In the 1920s and 1930s, 'Katherine Hale' (Amelia Garvin) and Blodwen Davies both produced travel narratives, while E. Cora Hind, an internationally recognized agricultural reporter, issued *Seeing for Myself: Agricultural Conditions around the World* (1937), based on articles she originally wrote for the Winnipeg *Free Press.*

The market for the linked genres of biography and history attracted clerics, professors, librarians, and journalists. The Reverend Roderick G. MacBeth, son of one of Lord Selkirk's Red River settlers, recalled Louis Riel and Manitoba's pioneer past in *Romance of Western Canada* (1918). His *Policing the Plains* (1922), a history of the Royal Canadian Mounted Police issued in New York and London as well as Toronto, and his *The Romance of the Canadian Pacific Railway* (1924), championed the peaceful development of the nation. In Quebec, Abbé Lionel Groulx used history to instill pride in identity, bringing the past to life in vigorous, eloquent prose. Foremost among his heroes was Dollard des Ormeaux, whose rescue of Montreal from an Iroquois attack in 1660 he addressed many times, from *Si Dollard revient ...* (1919) to *Dollard est-il un mythe?* (1960) (see illus. 1.1, p. 17). Non-conformist in spirit and author of incisive pamphlets like those earlier written by Claude-Henri Grignon, Victor Barbeau published many essays during the 1930s and 1940s in which he tried to awaken his fellow citizens from their torpor of mediocrity. During the Depression, in titles like *Pour nous grandir* (1937), he spurred them to follow the path of corporatism, which he saw as preferable to the current alternatives of undisciplined liberalism and paralyzing conservatism.

While professors A.R.M. Lower and Marcel Trudel recalled difficulties in publishing serious historical studies in the interwar period,[32] University of Toronto librarian W. Stewart Wallace worked the whole range of the history market, from his popular volume, *By Star and Compass: Tales of the Explorers of Canada* (1922), through his *Dictionary of Canadian Biography* (1926), a Macmillan of Canada publication that went into multiple editions, and *Documents Relating to the North West Company* (1934), edited for the Champlain Society. Wallace also tapped the textbook market, writing *Sir John Macdonald* (1924) for Macmillan's Canadian Statesmen Series as well as titles for Ryerson's Canadian History Readers (1925–31), a venture which attracted professional authors such as Agnes Laut. Merrill Denison benefited from the market for accessible history when he was commissioned to write twenty-five instalments at $250 per script – ten times the going rate – for *The Romance of Canada*, a program broadcast on the radio facilities of Canadian National Railways, a system which preceded the CBC; six were later published as *Henry Hudson and Other Plays* (1931).[33]

Through the 1930s many writers expanded from print into radio: Thérèse Casgrain wrote and hosted *Femina* on Radio-Canada, while Joseph Smallwood broadcast *The Barrelman* (1937–43) on Voice of Newfoundland Radio, his show's title echoing the byline of his column in the St John's *Daily News*. Kate Aitken, who disseminated practical information, reversed this pattern by building her daytime radio audience before moving into print.[34] When television arrived in Canada in 1952, writers more visibly combined print and broadcasting, giving rise to multimedia stars like Pierre Berton, Laurier LaPierre, Lister Sinclair, Fernand Seguin, and Peter Gzowski. No one was more surprised than Gzowski himself when the 1974 book based on his radio show *This Country in the Morning* sold nearly 40,000 copies.[35]

After the Second World War, with the market for short and serial fiction all but vanquished by the rise of the paperback, non-fiction filled consumer magazines. Even so, Ralph Allen, editor of *Maclean's*, declared in 1955 that it would be 'almost impossible' for a freelancer 'to make a living [solely] from Canadian magazines' and noted that American periodicals paid about triple the usual Canadian rates. In addition, American competition within the Canadian market led to the demise of a number of Canada's larger consumer magazines, thus shrinking domestic opportunities. In Allen's view, at mid-century many of Canada's best writers were 'doing the great bulk of their writing in creative articles, ranging in form from the reportorial to the essay-like opinion piece.'[36] Prominent at the time were June Callwood, Blair Fraser, André Laurendeau, Christina McCall, Gérard Pelletier, and Pierre Elliott Trudeau. Less celebrated writers found steady work in trade publications, penning 'informative articles, clearly written ... and liberally sprinkled with authoritative quotes [and facts]' for the 430 Canadian and approximately 1,500 American papers circulating in Canada.[37] In the 1970s a new market arose as small, special interest consumer magazines proliferated; in 1976 freelance writers formed the Periodical Writers' Association of Canada to represent their collective interests.

At mid-century English Canada's book publishers described the domestic periodical industry as 'the training ground available and apparently essential to the writing of books in Canada.'[38] Journalistic collections had become marketable, an early example being *The Voice of Dafoe: A Selection of Editorials on Collective Security, 1931–1944* (1945) by the late Winnipeg *Free Press* editor and Liberal power-broker John W. Dafoe. After the war and before settling down as a publisher, Jacques Hébert was a globe-trotting journalist whose accounts of travels in South America, Africa, and Asia appeared in the Montreal newspapers *Le Devoir* and *La Patrie*. Collected into volumes published by Fides, these narratives sold like hotcakes at his popular lecture tours throughout Quebec. From 1948 to 1961, Hébert produced at least ten such books, some reaching print runs of 10,000; best known was *Two Innocents in Red China* (1961), co-authored with Pierre Elliott Trudeau.

The readership for books about Canada swelled after 1950, led by Bruce Hutchison's Governor General's Award winners, *The Unknown Country* (1943) and *Canada: Tomorrow's Giant* (1957). Mingling historical and contemporary content, Hutchison introduced Canada to its citizens and challenged them to take hold of their country's destiny. Léandre Bergeron, first known for his work in *Parti Pris*, proposed an alternative future in his best-selling *Petit manuel d'histoire du Québec* (1970), a terse anti-imperialist challenge to the British and Canadian occupation of Quebec. Translated as *The History of Quebec: A Patriote's Handbook* (1971) and produced in cheap paperback editions, it sold widely in French and English Canada, finding a receptive audience among a younger, more radical generation of readers. André Laurendeau's *La crise de la conscription, 1942* (1962), of which 15,000 copies were printed in its first year of publication, and Trudeau's *La grève de l'amiante* (1956; *The Asbestos Strike*, 1974), focused on politically charged historical events.

Colourful personalities Pierre Berton and Farley Mowat proved particularly successful in the non-fiction market as it expanded after mid-century. Berton exploited post-war nationalism in grand style, particularly through detailed, engaging, and best-selling Canadian historical narratives such as *Klondike* (1958) and *The Last Spike* (1971). While Berton's audience was largely Canadian, Mowat was the country's most internationally successful non-fiction writer, selling more than four million copies in twenty-two languages other than English by the early 1980s.[40] Pursuing concerns raised earlier by 'Grey Owl' (Archibald Belaney), Mowat contributed to the growing environmental movement. In *People of the Deer* (1952) and *Never Cry Wolf* (1963), he tapped into modern society's increasing unease with bureaucracy, experts, and corporate capitalism through a clever blend of satire, humour, pathos, and personal experience. Peter C. Newman took his fascination with Canadian capitalism to the bank with *The Canadian Establishment*; it became the Christmas blockbuster of 1975 and in 1978 launched McClelland and Stewart's Seal mass-market imprint in an initial printing of 100,000 copies.[40] In 1979, Morton Shulman similarly struck gold with *How to Invest Your Money and Profit from Inflation*, selling about 70,000 copies in Canada, and penetrating British and American markets.[41] As well, books by or about Canadian policy and politicians represented an important staple of these years, such as *Deux prêtres dénoncent l'immoralité politique dans la province de Québec* (1956), by lay priests Gérard Dion and Louis O'Neill, Walter Gordon's *Troubled Canada: The Need for New Domestic Policies* (1961), Pierre Laporte's *Le vrai visage de Duplessis* (1962), and Judy LaMarsh's *Memoirs of a Bird in a Gilded Cage* (1968).

Whatever their topic, the most successful of Canada's non-fiction authors produced engaging prose and possessed a shrewd ability to respond to the preoccupations of the day or anticipate new trends. While a tone of optimism characterized the work of many writers prior to the Second World War, in the latter half of the century many readers were more attracted by skepticism or scandal concerning the environment, business practices, political affairs, and even the future of the nation itself.

Sports Writing

MICHAEL A. PETERMAN

In the early decades of the twentieth century, newspapers were the ready medium to encourage growing public interest in sports stories and athletes. Even as print continued its role of enabling 'the very definition of sport in Canada,'[42] sporting contests, game statistics, and athletic personalities provided entertainment value and dramatic interest for growing numbers of people. Journalists adulated prowess in organized competition, developed the language of athletic achievement and hero worship, and encouraged rivalries created by entrepreneurs who fed the public appetite for competitive leagues and events. Pioneering journalists such as Lou Marsh and Ted Reeve in Toronto and Baz O'Meara, Elmer Ferguson, and Charles Mayer in Montreal, and their like across the country, became the agents of this contagious enthusiasm as newspapers in cities and towns, in daily issues and weekend supplements, reported on sports in increasing detail. Radio and television followed suit in their respective evolutions.

Sports writing quickly became a more sophisticated field as journalists sought to be more reflective and probing in their responses to football, hockey, baseball, lacrosse, water sports, horse racing, and track and field. However, they found little opportunity in sports magazines. With variations in title, *Rod and Gun* (Woodstock, Montreal, 1899–1973) did offer a dedicated domestic venue for stories about hunting and fishing, but for the most part the most reliable market for sports topics was the diverse American periodical industry, including *Collier's* and *American Magazine*. English Canada's dominant consumer magazine, *Maclean's*, was receptive to sports material and encouraged writers like Scott Young to investigate the darker side, giving rise to articles such as 'Hogtied Hockey,' an early exposé about the exploitation of players by owners.[43] Sports stories were also included in *La Revue populaire, La Revue moderne* – where Roland Beaudry wrote about hockey – and *Le Magazine Maclean* – where Louis Chantigny reported on boxing.

Along with fellow Manitobans Trent Frayne, Ralph Allen, and Jim Coleman, Young was part of a new generation of male sports writers, born in the 1920s and 1930s, who began to make their marks by mid-century. Their formative experiences in boyhood competitions inspired the kind of popular, celebratory, enthusiastic, and sometimes hard-boiled writing that attracted a growing readership. For women, entry into the field was typically preceded by a notable athletic career. After track stars Fanny 'Bobbie' Rosenfeld and Myrtle Cook won medals at the 1928 Olympics, they were hired respectively by the *Globe and Mail* and the *Montreal Star*. Significantly outnumbered by their male colleagues, most female sports writers found themselves confined to covering women's events.[44]

Some of the earliest books by and about Canadian sports figures focused on women champions such as Barbara Ann Scott and Marilyn Bell. Scott's best-selling titles, *Skate with Me* (1950) and *Skating for Beginners* (1953), both appeared in the United States. *Swim to Glory: The Story of Marilyn Bell and the Lakeshore Swimming Club* (1954) was the fifth sports book that Ronald McAllister published with McClelland and Stewart. McAllister's success, paralleling the overall expansion of the Canadian publishing industry, signalled a new level of market interest for sports writing in its many forms. Readership studies attuned to sports have been few to date, but there is some evidence that, since the 1950s, male readers with a wide range of educational backgrounds have made sports reading in both newspapers and books a priority in their lives.[45]

Anticipation of the Montreal Olympics, held in 1976, inspired a surge of sports books from Quebec publishers. In 1968, Les Éditions de l'Homme initiated a sports series that exceeded a hundred titles and included original works and translations of American books. Sports journalists took advantage of the moment to collect their best columns into volumes such as Louis Chantigny's three books published by Leméac: *Mes grands boxeurs* (1973), *Mes grands du cyclisme* (1974), and *Mes grands joueurs de hockey* (1974). Another major event, Canada's dramatic success in the USSR-Canada hockey summit of 1972, spawned a dozen books and a wave of magazine pieces.

Many of the sports books written in English between 1950 and 1980 were non-fiction works, quickie portraits or biographies lionizing prominent teams, entrepreneurs, and sports personalities. Few rose above their subject or occasion. More enduring books like those of Roderick Haig-Brown on fishing, Jim Coleman on horse racing, John Craig on baseball, Scott Young and Brian McFarlane on hockey, and Paul Ohl on the martial arts sought to interpret the culture and practice of their sports. Indeed, by 1980 Canadian readers found themselves inundated by an unprecedented range of sports books, many offering new levels of analysis and reflection coincident with the revolution in interest in sports that marked the latter half of the twentieth century. Literary writers such as Jack Ludwig, Mordecai Richler, Hugh Hood, Roch Carrier, and Rick Salutin included sports in both their fiction and magazine articles.

Although not officially named one of Canada's national sports until 1994, hockey's primacy marked this period. Toronto journalist Foster Hewitt, who became the English radio voice of *Hockey Night in Canada*, wrote several books, including *He Shoots, He Scores* (1949), its title based on one of his trademark phrases. Trent Frayne penned *The Mad Men of Hockey* (1974), while Scott Young captured the nation's love affair with the sport in his trilogy of boys' stories beginning with *Scrubs on Skates* (1952). The colourful antics of owner Conn Smythe and players like Charlie Conacher, King Clancy and 'Teeder' Kennedy drew the attention of writers covering the Toronto Maple Leafs. In French Canada, hockey also dominated the field of sports books, especially following Maurice Richard's mid-century rise to stardom. Biographies ran from the translation of Edward Fitkin's *Maurice Richard, Hockey's Rocket* (1961; *Le Rocket du hockey, Maurice Richard*, 1962) to Jean-Marie Pellerin's *L'idole d'un peuple, Maurice Richard* (1976). Books about the Montreal Canadiens such as Yvon Pednault's *Les Canadiens, nos glorieux champions* (1977) and another under 'Rocket' Richard's own name, *Les Canadiens sont là! La plus grande dynastie du hockey* (1971), proliferated in the 1970s. Also very popular were biographies and autobiographies of other Montreal hockey stars, such as Jean Béliveau and Jacques Plante. The country's most beloved hockey story, 'Le chandail,' was penned by Roch Carrier in 1979. Translated into English the same year as 'The Hockey Sweater,' and subsequently rendered as a short film by the National Film Board, it continues to delight young readers across the country (see illus. 4.1, p. 145).

4.1 A quotation from Roch Carrier's *The Hockey Sweater* now circulates in millions of copies on Canada's five-dollar bill: 'The winters of my childhood were long, long seasons. We lived in three places – the school, the church, and the skating-rink – but our real life was on the skating-rink.' Still from *Le chandail/The Sweater* (1980), the National Film Board of Canada's adaptation of Carrier's story. Image used with permission of the National Film Board of Canada and David Verrall.

Children's Authors and Their Markets

FRANÇOISE LEPAGE, JUDITH SALTMAN, AND GAIL EDWARDS

Although Canadian literature for children really came into its own in the twentieth century, acquiring literary, cultural, and economic significance, it did not develop symmetrically in Quebec and English Canada. In Quebec, children's literature received attentive support from publishers, nationalist associations, and public authorities as early as the 1920s, while in English Canada there were few new initiatives before the 1960s. The late 1970s marked the beginning of a period of exceptional growth on both sides of the linguistic boundary, as children's writers and illustrators achieved official recognition, thanks in part to the creation of national prizes. The Amelia Frances Howard-Gibbon Award was initiated in 1971 to honour illustrators, followed by the Canada Council Prizes for Children's Literature in 1975.

Established to celebrate authors and illustrators in both French and English, the latter became Governor General's Awards in 1987.

Writing for Young Francophones

Before 1920, apart from school books, the few publications specifically intended for children were produced by religious communities and several lay authors, such as Napoléon Legendre, Louis-Philippe Fournier, and Emma-Adèle Lacerte, whose juvenile work was sporadic. Most authors read by young people had in fact written for the adult market, but their works were regarded as suitably enriching for young minds.

A distinct literature for children arose between 1920 and 1940 as a result of the intervention of institutions and individuals who, convinced of its importance, invited literary people and colleagues to write specifically for young readers. The illustrated Contes historiques (1919–20), the first major series intended for children, was initiated by the Société Saint-Jean-Baptiste de Montréal (SSJBM). Most of the contributors were prominent citizens – judges, authors, librarians, historians, male and female members of religious communities – and, not surprisingly, thirty-two of the thirty-seven published stories were signed by men. Issued in collections or distributed in loose-leaf as prizes in schools or premiums in stores, sales of titles in this series ran to hundreds of thousands of copies.[46]

The SSJBM, represented by sociologist Arthur Saint-Pierre, also founded the magazine L'Oiseau bleu, which, in January 1921, definitively launched children's literature in Quebec. Here, too, most authors were recruited by invitation, beginning with Marie-Claire Daveluy, a well-known historian and librarian, who was asked to write a serial reflecting the prevailing nationalistic values of homeland, religion, and language. The result was Les aventures de Perrine et de Charlot. Subsequently published as a book in 1923, it was French Canada's first historical novel written for children. Daveluy, Michelle Le Normand, and Marie-Rose Turcot, as well as other women journalists and historians, went on to pen further serials, while men were recruited to write on specialized subjects, with the exception of the natural sciences, which was the province of Marcelle Gauvreau. These authors were paid until 1933, when the magazine began to experience the financial difficulties that led to its demise in 1940.[47] L'Oiseau bleu, like the Contes historiques, appealed to schoolchildren of all ages.

In the 1940s, children's literature found new champions in Jeanne and Guy Boulizon, two teachers at Collège Stanislas in Montreal, who recruited authors from among the priests and laypersons with whom they taught. This group produced adventure novels, many of which were published by Beauchemin, where Guy Boulizon served as a series editor. This writing was unpaid volunteer work, arising from the authors' personal commitment to the promotion of children's reading. Eugène Achard, in contrast, derived his livelihood in part from the many juvenile books he wrote and issued from his own publishing house, the Librairie générale canadienne, founded in 1927.[48] The readers of this new juvenile literature were mostly urban children whose families could afford to send them to school – school attendance did not become mandatory in Quebec until 1943 – and those who belonged to youth organizations, such as the Guides and the Scouts, in which a number of these authors were also active.

Radio and television broadcasting, which established themselves in the 1920s and 1950s respectively, helped to free youth literature from the ghetto of the school system and the ideological control of the clergy. New personalities from the broadcast media, such as Lucille Desparois, André Cailloux, and, later, Michel Cailloux, could reach a broader public, especially in terms of age. Children's literature became more democratized, and a wider occupational and ideological range of authors gave rise to greater variety in literary production.[49]

In 1948 the establishment of the first organization of French-speaking children's authors, the Association des écrivains pour la jeunesse (AÉJ), substantiated the presence of books for young French Canadians. The association made its members known by issuing a catalogue and placing biobibliographic articles in *Le Front ouvrier*. It founded a publishing co-operative that operated until 1952, and the Institut culturel Jeunesse to train new authors and improve the skills of those who were already established. Although short-lived, the AÉJ helped increase appreciation for members' work, enabled them to polish their skills, and raised public awareness concerning the need for literature written especially for young people.[50]

In the 1950s and 1960s, the pronounced gender division of youth readership invited more women to take up writing. Male authors such as Michel Chalvin, Maurice Gagnon, and Yves Thériault penned adventure novels for boys, while women such as Berthe Potvin and Reine Malouin created traditional stories for girls. This pattern was altered when Paule Daveluy wrote the first modern novel for adolescent girls, *L'été enchanté* (1958), antecedent of the contemporary socio-historical novel. Her book won a major award from the newly established Association canadienne d'éducation de langue française, one of three prizes given for different categories of children's books. Two other awards were created in the 1960s: the Prix Maxine, given just once, in 1966, and the Prix de la province de Québec, which was awarded from 1964 to 1966, in 1968, and in 1970. The latter was won by the most prolific and well-known writers: Paule Daveluy, Suzanne Martel, Monique Corriveau (twice), and Cécile Gagnon.[51] At the end of the decade, women were estimated to constitute 60 per cent of French Canada's children's authors.[52] Most were mothers and homemakers with a talent for writing, although some, such as Cécile Gagnon and Simone Bussières, also practised other professions.

This feminization of children's literature may account for the low esteem in which it was held in the late 1960s. Contributing to this situation was the decision, in 1965, of the Quebec Department of Education to stop buying books for school prizes. The elimination of this practice dramatically affected not only sales, but also the entire production cycle of children's literature. Led by Suzanne Rocher and Paule Daveluy, authors rallied in 1971 to create Communication-Jeunesse, an organization to promote French-language children's literature. Still flourishing today, its program of activities designed to encourage young people to read led to a gradual increase in the number of readers and the establishment of authors' visits to schools and libraries. As well, authors became better informed about their readers' interests and wrote books more consistent with young people's concerns at different stages of their lives. The founding, in 1974, of Éditions Le Tamanoir, which became La Courte Échelle in 1978, also invigorated francophone children's literature. Specializing in children's books, this new firm quickly established itself as Quebec's leading and most prestigious juvenile publisher. Moreover, during the 1970s the number of literary prizes began to increase. The creation of the Prix Alvine-Bélisle, the Prix Marie-Claire-Daveluy, and the Canada Council Prizes for Children's Literature heralded the proliferation of awards that would coincide with a boom in publishing in the 1980s.[53] No longer a female preserve, francophone children's literature was to see a dramatic return of male authors with the publication of books such as *Le dernier des raisins,* by Raymond Plante, in 1986.

Writing for Anglophone Children

In contrast with the inauguration of children's literature in French Canada in the 1920s, English-Canadian children's authors faced limited publishing opportunities, particularly within their own domestic market, until well after the end of the Second World War. Unusual was the success of Mary Grannan, known to her avid young audience as 'Just Mary' (see illus. 4.2 and 4.3, p. 149). During the 1940s and 1950s, daily CBC Radio broadcasts of her stories led to their published versions becoming Canadian best-sellers: in 1947, *Quill & Quire* reported that 'Just Mary, in her

4.2 Mary Grannan's popular CBC broadcasts and best-selling story collections inspired Maggie Muggins dolls, manufactured by the Reliable Toy Company of Toronto in the late 1940s and 1950s. The example shown here is a composition doll issued in 1947. Doll courtesy of Evelyn Robson Strahlendorf, Hamilton; photograph by Jim Chambers.

4.3 Selected titles by Mary Grannan: covers of *Maggie Muggins and Mr. McGarrity* (1952) and *Maggie Muggins Tee-Vee Tales* (1958); title page and interior page from *Just Mary Stories, Combining Just Mary and Just Mary Again* [1942] (all Toronto: T.H. Allen & Co.). Books courtesy of Thomas Allen & Son, Ltd and the Thomas Fisher Rare Book Library, University of Toronto.

various editions (one put out by the CBC at cost), has sold over 120,000.'[54] However, for most Canadian authors, writing was an adjunct to their primary careers, whether their readership was adult or juvenile. For example, Jean Little taught school when her first book, *Mine for Keeps* (1962), was published, and for many years thereafter, she identified herself as a teacher rather than as a writer.[55] From 1952 to 1962, Scott Young created his trilogy of hockey novels to supplement his income as a sports reporter and short-story writer at the suggestion of his savvy American literary agent, who told him: 'The only way I know for a writer to get a pension is to write a good juvenile, because the good ones just keep on selling forever.'[56]

Young's recourse to an American agent and publisher was typical of the period. Until the mid-1960s, the few English-Canadian publishers who produced books for children largely confined themselves to well-established genres, such as the domestic fiction of L.M. Montgomery and romanticized retellings of Aboriginal stories. Also popular were animal, adventure, and historical narratives, often by writers who usually wrote for adults, such as Roderick Haig-Brown, Farley Mowat, and Pierre Berton. With little financial or creative incentive to publish locally, Canadian writers with a serious commitment to young readers looked abroad for better-established markets, particularly to the United States, although some authors felt they had little chance of having their manuscripts considered unless they were represented by a New York agent.[57] Additionally appealing was the fact that many large American publishing houses employed children's book editors who had the mandate and the expertise to work with authors to refine their writing, a situation that would not prevail in Canada until the 1970s. Jean Karl, editor at Atheneum, provided Christie Harris with helpful feedback on the manuscript for *Once upon a Totem* (1963) after it had been rejected by a Canadian publisher with no explanatory note.[58] One potential drawback of foreign publication was a demand for changes in content, setting, or language. For example, when Janet Lunn's *Double Spell* appeared in an American edition from Harper & Row in 1968, the title was altered to *Twin Spell*, while in the text 'Marmite' was replaced by 'Oxo' and a footnote was added to explain that 'chesterfield means sofa.'[59]

While the American children's book scene of the 1960s was characterized by controversial fiction that dealt with contemporary social issues, the Canadian children's market remained conservative, favouring outdoor survival sagas, family stories, and historical fiction. In the late 1960s and early 1970s, when reawakened Canadian nationalism intersected with Canadian publishing, a robust market began to develop for a distinct and diverse Canadian children's literature. Aboriginal writers such as George Clutesi (*Son of Raven, Son of Deer: Fables of the Tse-Shaht People*, 1967) were published for the first time. New authors such as Ian Wallace, Sandy Frances Duncan, Kevin Major, and Brian Doyle explored the social and personal issues of contemporary children living in Canada's cities and rural communities. In the 1970s, picture books became an emerging genre for Canadian authors and illustrators as new specialist publishers encouraged authors to experiment in their approach to books for very young children, such as Sue Ann Alderson's Bonnie McSmithers series (see illus. 4.4, p. 151) and Robert Munsch's *Mud Puddle* (1979).

While poetry gained ground as a genre for children through the tremendous success of works such as Dennis Lee's whimsical *Alligator Pie* (1974), the more staple genre of historical fiction followed the contemporary trend toward social history,

4.4 Sue Ann Alderson and Fiona Garrick (illus.), interior page from *Hurry Up, Bonnie!* (Edmonton: Tree Frog Press, 1977). Courtesy of Tree Frog Press, Sue Ann Alderson, and Fiona Garrick.

focusing on details of everyday life and immigrant experience, as exemplified by Barbara Smucker's story of escaped American slaves, *Underground to Canada* (1977). By the late 1970s the relative success of these trade ventures was encouraging Canadian textbook publishers to acquire and reprint some of these works, thus buttressing the financial fortunes of Canadian children's authors.[60] Branch-plant publishers such as Scholastic, which had strong sales in the school market, began to accept manuscripts by Canadian authors for the first time.[61] The rise of Canadian children's magazines such as *Magook*, *Chickadee*, and *Owl* also provided an important market as well as a vital training ground for some writers.[62]

A notable shift in the cultural value invested in children's authorship character-ized the 1970s. Canadian children's authors had complained in earlier years about the isolation in which they worked and the lack of respect they received from pub-lishers, funding agencies, and authors of works for adults. As Sue Ann Alderson explained, children's authors had 'less access to grants and less ability to negotiate contracts. We were beggars, scratching at doors.'[63] While some praised the Writers' Union of Canada (est. 1973) for its political engagement and camaraderie, others felt disparaged by certain members who contemptuously described writing for children as 'kiddy litter.'[64] The formation in 1977 of the Canadian Society of Children's Authors, Illustrators and Performers (CANSCAIP) reflected a wish to address the specific needs of children's writers by providing opportunities for networking and support. According to one of its founders, CANSCAIP was 'a kinship connection, and felt like a family. The bond was one of struggling against an oppressor – the publisher. We were out to claim our rights and find our identity.'[65]

In the 1970s, other organizations arose that provided authors with opportunities to meet with teachers, librarians, academics, publishers, writers, illustrators, students, booksellers, and the general public. The Canadian branch of the International Board on Books for Young People (IBBY-Canada) was founded in 1973 to encourage the writing, publishing, selling, and reading of Canadian children's books domestically, while promoting Canadian and international children's books around the world. In 1975 the National Library of Canada inaugurated its Canadian Children's Literature Service, headed by Irene E. Aubrey. Its 1973 exhibit, Notable Canadian Children's Books / Un choix de livres canadiens pour la jeunesse, led to the publication of a frequently updated catalogue under the same title. The Canadian Children's Book Centre, established in Toronto in 1976, played a critical role in publicizing children's literature through its activities and publications such as *Children's Book News* and the annual *Our Choice* catalogue. The centre's biographical *Meet the Author* kits, film strips, and videos introduced children's writers to new audiences. Financial support from the Canada Council helped the centre to organize Children's Book Week, during which authors and illustrators visited classrooms and libraries across the country. Some authors found that their annual income was significantly enhanced by the Book Week tours, and the opportunity to travel and promote their books provided a stimulus to their writing, but illustrators were restricted by their inability to apply for Canada Council touring grants.[66] Judy Sarick's Children's Book Store (est. Toronto, 1974) similarly raised the profile of Canadian children's authors by organizing readings, signings, and other promotional events that brought together the children's literature community and the general reading public.[67] By the end of the 1970s, specialist children's bookstores were located in major cities across Canada, while the Canadian Booksellers' Association felt sufficient commitment to co-sponsor the Ruth Schwartz Children's Book Award (est. 1976) with the Ontario Arts Council.

Children's authors also found validation in increased scholarly interest in their work through the 1970s, a sea change that began with the publication in 1967 of Sheila Egoff's *The Republic of Childhood: A Critical Guide to Canadian Children's Literature in English*, an influential text subsequently consulted by librarians, academics, and parents. While the library community enhanced its ongoing services, academics sponsored courses, conferences, and a scholarly journal, *Canadian Children's Literature/ Littérature canadienne pour la jeunesse* (Guelph, 1975–). In 1980 the creation of an accredited program in children's writing in the University of British Columbia's Creative Writing Department further affirmed the academic validity of children's literature. A new generation of writers would emerge from this program, inspired by their opportunity to write a children's book as a thesis for a B.F.A. or M.F.A. degree.

By 1980, after decades of struggle, Canadian children's authors writing in both French and English were benefiting from the growth of local publishers, the expansion of markets for Canadian books, and a national audience composed of baby-boomer parents and the generation of their offspring. Public and school libraries were purchasing Canadian children's books, and librarians and teachers were eagerly promoting Canadian books in their classrooms and story times. The sense of possibility that had earlier inspired many authors to write for children was about to bloom into a robust national literature for young readers.

CASE STUDY
Leslie McFarlane and the Case of Pseudonymous Children's Authorship
– Janet B. Friskney

'Stay out of that business and don't even talk about it or you'll run into a lot of trouble,' a menacing voice advises Joe Hardy in *The Sinister Sign Post* (1936).[68] Teenage sleuths Joe and Frank Hardy, who entered the world of American juvenile literature in 1927, were the imaginative offspring of Edward Stratemeyer, owner of the Stratemeyer Syndicate (est. early 1900s, New York), an organization that specialized in series fiction for children. Stratemeyer drafted brief story outlines and then contracted out the writing of many of his syndicate's books. Leslie McFarlane, the Canadian who as 'Franklin W. Dixon' wrote about two-thirds of the twenty-six Hardy Boys books issued between 1927 and 1946, and as 'Carolyn Keene' penned the first four Dana Girls titles in the 1930s, recalled that Stratemeyer had authors sign a contract that paid a flat fee, insisted on the use of 'house names,' relieved writers of all rights, and constrained them from divulging their authorship. McFarlane agreed without hesitation, viewing the work simply as a steady source of income. During the 1920s he earned from $125 to just over $150 for each Hardy Boys title, an amount that dropped as low as $85 during the Depression.[69] His connection with the syndicate ceased in

1946, after he had begun working as a director with the National Film Board of Canada.[70]

Born in Carleton Place but raised in Haileybury, Ontario, McFarlane was a young journalist with the *Republican* (Springfield, Massachusetts) and a part-time writer of short fiction when he became a Stratemeyer author in 1926 after responding to an advertisement in *Editor and Publisher*. Initially, he produced titles for the Dave Fearless series, 'hack work' lucrative enough to allow him to return to northern Ontario, where he wrote full-time, interspersing his syndicate assignments with magazine fiction issued under his own name.[71] Stratemeyer subsequently commissioned him to write the initial three Hardy Boys books, to be set in a small, mythical east-coast American city called Bayport. Offered the opportunity to enter the series from the beginning and seeing qualitative potential in the first outline, McFarlane approached the adventures of Frank and Joe with attention to style and humour. In the first three volumes, he exploited the comic aspect of local policemen Chief Collig and Detective Smuff, but Stratemeyer soon restrained him to avoid suggesting disrespect for authority. However, the syndicate owner was sufficiently taken with the author's amusing interpretation of Aunt Gertrude (introduced in *The Missing Chums,* 1928) to make her a permanent minor character, and he raised no objections when McFarlane diverged occasionally from story outlines.[72]

The Hardy Boys titles, issued originally in red cloth bindings dressed in colourful dust jackets, proved a best-selling series and remain in print to this day: by mid-1929 about 116,000 copies had sold, a figure that increased to 26 million by the 1970s.[73] The stories penned by McFarlane endured as he had written them until 1959, when the syndicate began shortening and revising them in an effort to update the series for youth of the next generation.

CBC Radio and Anglophone Authors

SHEILA LATHAM

In 1929 the Royal Commission on Radio Broadcasting recognized the civic role of the new medium as 'a great force in fostering a national spirit and interpreting national citizenship.'[74] This nationalist mandate for radio influenced print culture in Canada in ways that differed from other countries, such as Britain, where radio was simply another medium added to a well-established literary culture, and the United States, where radio developed into a commercial entertainment business, separately from a government-protected publishing industry. The establishment of the Canadian Broadcasting Corporation (CBC) in 1936 nurtured Canadian print culture on many levels. The CBC encouraged the production of original texts by Canadian writers, developed an audience for programs featuring books and authors, transmitted unpublished and published texts over radio airwaves, published some texts under its own imprints or in collaboration with independent publishers, and celebrated original literature with awards. Its broadcasts of readings from books, dramatizations of fiction and poetry, interviews with authors, critical reviews, and academic lectures encouraged the listening public to buy, borrow, and read books and magazines.

Two of the outstanding CBC Radio producers – Andrew Allan and Robert Weaver – were as influential as any publisher. During Canada's 'Golden Age of Radio' in the 1940s and 1950s, for the programs *CBC Stage* and *CBC Wednesday Night*, Allan commissioned hundreds of original plays, as well as dramatizations from such books as Stephen Leacock's *Sunshine Sketches of a Little Town*, Louis Hémon's *Maria Chapdelaine*, and Hugh MacLennan's *Two Solitudes*. As a product of 'a Depression and a War,' he encouraged writers like Len Peterson, Joseph Schull, W.O. Mitchell, and Patricia Joudry to present progressive and controversial 'social content.'[75] Robert Weaver's equally legendary career, from 1948 to 1985, exemplified the symbiotic relationship between books and broadcasting. Believing that effective radio depended upon a healthy literary community, he worked tirelessly to nurture that community. Alice Munro recalled that after Weaver purchased his first story from her in 1951, '[f]or the next dozen or so years he was almost the only person I knew who had anything to do with the world of writing.'[76] As the producer of *Anthology* (1954–85) and co-editor of *Tamarack Review* (1956–82), Weaver printed poetry, fiction, and criticism originally commissioned for *Anthology* and broadcast texts that initially appeared in *Tamarack Review*. Though a leading literary quarterly, *Tamarack Review* had a print run of just 1,500 copies, whereas *Anthology,* CBC's 'Little Magazine of the Air,' was heard each week by fifty thousand listeners. In 1979 Weaver initiated the CBC Radio Literary Competition, which attracts several thousand manuscripts annually. By 1980 when Peter Gzowski's radio show *Morningside* was reaching over a million listeners, Phyllis Yaffe, director of the Association of Canadian Publishers, cited it as a major influence on book sales: 'Without CBC radio, the publishing industry in this country would be in despair.'[77] The educational program *Ideas*

(1965–), developed by poet Phyllis Webb, first edited by novelist Timothy Findley, and hosted for years by Lister Sinclair, exemplifies the CBC's role as a disseminator of original research and innovative thinking. *Ideas* spawned many influential books, including those published annually in the Massey Lectures series, which is discussed by Dominique Marquis in chapter 9.

The pervasive influence of CBC Radio on print culture is as subtle as it is broad. The author's relationship with a radio producer as well as a book editor extends the collaborative process in the social production of the text, marking a paradigmatic shift from individual identity to social community, from writing for isolated private readers to writing for a large public audience of listeners, and from the traditional literary genres to the experimental formats of the broadcast media. W.H. New noted radio's influence on the short story, and on the validation of Canadian dialects in published literature, citing W.O. Mitchell and Ray Guy as examples.[78] In 1948, after hearing Canadian stories read on CBC Radio, Mavis Gallant described the 'valuable lesson' she learned: 'There is something relentless about a story being read aloud. Lack of rhythm, vagueness and faulty characterization are glaringly obvious because you can't skip and you can't reread.'[79] In a similar vein, Milton Acorn revealed how radio can affect poetic composition: 'I decided to use the soap opera rule: Write a poem ... [such] that anyone tuning in at any time would soon get a good idea as to what was going on ... between various voices.'[80]

Though much of its programming is produced in Toronto, CBC Radio has strengthened both national and regional identities. Northrop Frye observed that the 'instant world of communications' leads to a 'uniform international way of seeing and thinking ... Regional developments are a way of escaping from that, developing something more creative.'[81] Don Domanski is a case in point: 'I began listening to [the CBC] while I was a high school student in Sydney, Cape Breton, and ... it was not a teacher or a book or a magazine but rather ... it was *Anthology* that made me realize that it was possible to be both a poet and a Maritimer.'[82] The CBC continues to recognize that cultural renewal comes from the margins of society, shifting its focus since the 1970s from rural regional diversity to the ethnic and social diversity of urban centres.

As a government-funded institution with a national mandate, using twentieth-century technologies to bring innovative thinking and literature by Canadians to Canadians, the CBC stands alone in the scope and influence of its book-related activities. From authorship to reception, the CBC's collaboration with writers and publishers in nearly every facet of production and dissemination has helped to inspire, develop, publish, promote, and critique Canada's authors, books, and magazines.

Adaptations for Film and Television

PETER DICKINSON

As Peter Morris demonstrates in *Embattled Shadows: A History of Canadian Cinema, 1895–1939*, book and film history have been linked since the silent era. For example, Morris notes that in 1919 producer Ernest Shipman signed a contract with Ralph Connor, then English Canada's best-known and best-selling author, granting Dominion Films exclusive rights to twelve of Connor's works. Announcing the deal to the Winnipeg Board of Trade in May 1920, Shipman stressed that Connor would contribute to 'story construction';[83] it remains unclear, however, what role, if any, the author played in adapting his work. In the end, between 1920 and 1924, Dominion Films released four films based on Connor's novels – *God's Crucible*, *Cameron of the Royal Mounted*, *The Critical Age*, and *The Man from Glengarry* – all directed by Henry MacRae.

During the silent and early talkies era, the Canadian writer whose work was featured most prominently on screen was, strictly speaking, not Canadian. Beginning in 1915, the Scottish-born former banker Robert W. Service saw the release of eleven Hollywood films adapted from his work, culminating in 1933 with a twelve-part serial based on the poem 'Clancy of the Mounted Police' (dir. Ray Taylor). In 1934 the work of an incomer to Quebec received similar treatment when French director Julien Duvivier released his adaptation of Louis Hémon's *Maria Chapdelaine* (1914). The novel would eventually be brought to the screen twice more: in 1950 in another French production, directed by Marc Allégret, and in 1983 in a Quebec production directed by Gilles Carle.

Coincidentally, 1934 also saw the release of George Nichols Jr's 'Hollywood-ization' of L.M. Montgomery's *Anne of Green Gables* (1908). Starring Anne Shirley, the actress who in real life adopted the name of the book's main character, the film is notable for inventing a miraculous deathbed recovery for Matthew Cuthbert. An earlier silent version, directed by William D. Taylor, had been released in 1919. Montgomery liked neither movie. Nevertheless, furious at having received no share of the $40,000 paid to her Boston publisher, L.C. Page, for the initial film rights for this book, she was determined to profit from her later titles, and to this end she wrote *Anne of Windy Poplars* (1936) with a view to its being adapted for the screen, as indeed it was in 1940 by director Jack Hively.[84] In 1935 Mazo de la Roche also received the Hollywood treatment with *Jalna* (dir. John Cromwell), based on the first four novels in her Whiteoaks saga. Like Montgomery's and Hémon's work, de la Roche's novels have given rise to their own version of filmic serialization; the CBC broadcast a live theatrical adaptation called *Whiteoaks* in January 1957, and the BBC produced several television episodes based on de la Roche's books in 1954 and 1955. The CBC returned to the material in 1972, commissioning Timothy Findley to write a miniseries called *The Whiteoaks of Jalna*.

Findley, who started his professional career as an actor, was one of the few high-profile English-Canadian authors to have written regularly for television. In 1974 he scored his greatest success adapting, together with partner William Whitehead, three of Pierre Berton's non-fiction books on the Canadian Pacific Railway – *The National Dream* (1970), *The Last Spike* (1971), and *The Impossible Railway* (1972) – for the CBC miniseries *The National Dream* (dir. James Murray and Eric Till). Findley also collaborated with Alice Munro in scripting episodes of the television series *The Newcomers* between 1977 and 1978. For his part, Berton, who decried in print Hollywood's 'de-Canadianization' of literary classics by Connor, Service, Montgomery, de la Roche, and others,[85] also maintained a keen involvement with television, serving as narrator on the 1978 documentary *The Dionne Quintuplets* (dir. Donald Brittain), based on his book *The Dionne Years* (1977), and acting as a consultant on the American television series *Klondike* (1960–1). However, Findley and Berton are the exception rather than the rule among English-Canadian writers. In contrast, their Québécois counterparts have routinely worked in multiple media, including television and film. This involvement is partly related to two important developments in Canadian media history.

The first was the creation of the National Film Board of Canada (NFB) in 1939. While documentaries and animated shorts governed the NFB's mandate during its early years, the institution quickly developed a parallel tradition of theatrical shorts and mid-length features, many of them adaptations of Canadian literary works. These include *Each Man's Son* (1954; dir. Roger Blais), based on the novel by Hugh MacLennan, and *La canne à pêche* (1959; dir. Fernand Dansereau), from a screenplay by Anne Hébert. Hébert, along with fellow future novelists Jacques Godbout and Hubert Aquin, worked as a scriptwriter at the NFB, during the 1950s and early 1960s, a period of exceptional creativity and collaboration in Québécois cultural production, especially after 1956, when the NFB moved its headquarters to Montreal. There it quickly became the training ground for a generation of bold new filmmakers and screenwriters. Hébert and Claude Jutra, for example, collaborated on the screenplay for the big-budget adaptation of Hébert's novel *Kamouraska* (1970) in 1973. Jutra admired Hébert's complex use of flashbacks in the novel and encouraged the author to retain this quintessentially cinematic device in her screen treatment.

Audiences expecting to see an historical epic, however, were confused by the film's art-house style. Moreover, Jutra, who did not have final cut over his film, saw his three-hour-plus picture edited severely for theatrical release. In 1983, three years before his death, he was able to return to his original negative and 'prepare a new 173–minute video version' for release on Canadian pay television.[86]

The second major development during this period, emerging directly from the Massey Report in 1951, was the creation of a national public television system, which immediately began to tap Canadian literature for source material. In 1952 *La famille Plouffe*, based on Roger Lemelin's 1948 novel, became the first *téléroman* broadcast on the Société Radio-Canada. The next year, the soap opera debuted in English on the CBC, and the series ran on the two networks until 1959, attracting weekly audiences in the millions. During the same period, a musical adaptation of *Anne of Green Gables* and a serialization of Stephen Leacock's *Sunshine Sketches of a Little Town* (1912) appeared on the CBC. Although difficult to measure exactly, these broadcasts had a definite impact on future editions and sales of the source texts. Among the authors to make the successful transition to *auteur* at this time was Gratien Gélinas, who brought his hugely popular play *Tit-coq* (1950) to the screen in 1953.

As feature filmmaking progressed through the 1960s and 1970s, aided in part by the establishment in 1968 of the Canadian Film Development Corporation (CFDC, the forerunner of Telefilm), questions of authorship became increasingly contentious. One thinks, in this regard, of the debate that erupted over the release of Arthur Lamothe's high-profile treatment of André Langevin's *Poussière sur la ville* (1953) in 1967, which succeeded in polarizing critical opinion both on the state of Québécois filmmaking, in general, and on the merits of fidelity to source material, more specifically. However, the role of the author was not yet obsolete. In 1974 André Brassard's *Il était une fois dans l'est* allowed Michel Tremblay to bring characters from the first six plays in his 'Belles-soeurs' cycle together on screen. That same year, Ted Kotcheff's adaptation of Mordecai Richler's *The Apprenticeship of Duddy Kravitz* (1959) appeared, with a script by Richler and Lionel Chetwynd. Richler and Kotcheff had worked together on several previous pictures in Britain and Hollywood, but they were unable to secure funding for *Duddy* from any major American studio. Instead, resources were cobbled together from the CFDC and the CBC, an impressive international cast and crew assembled on the fly, and shooting was completed during a particularly cold winter in Quebec, resulting in that rare Canadian film phenomenon, a box-office hit that also scored highly with critics. The film was awarded the Golden Bear at the Berlin International Film Festival, and Richler and Chetwynd received an Academy Award nomination for best adapted screenplay.[87]

Since 1980 the domestic film industry has been reinvigorated by a new generation of *auteurs* who have consistently turned to works by some of this country's most distinguished authors.

Nonetheless, the film adaptations that have registered most with viewers are those that have emanated from Hollywood. Worth noting, in this regard, is Paul Newman's 1968 Oscar-nominated *Rachel, Rachel*, based on Margaret Laurence's *A Jest of God* (1966). While many, including Berton, decried the transposition of Laurence's Manawaka into the quaint New England hamlet represented on screen, the film is a sensitive and skilful rendering of the novel, one that met with Laurence's approval. More to the point for a working author who was as practical as Montgomery, Laurence received $30,000 for the sale of the film rights, and the mass-market paperback, retitled *Rachel, Rachel* and released to coincide with the film, ensured substantial sales of the novel.[88] Understanding precisely how book history and film and television history are intertwined in Canada means, among other things, paying attention to such economic realities.

PART THREE

PUBLISHING FOR A WIDE READERSHIP

chapter 5

TRADE AND REGIONAL BOOK PUBLISHING IN ENGLISH

The Agency System and Branch-Plant Publishing

GEORGE L. PARKER

Because Canada has always depended upon imported books, the control over distribution and ownership of foreign copyrights is a fundamental component of our publishing industry. Throughout the twentieth century, the marketing of these imports under English Canada's distinctive agency system imperilled local book manufacturing and may well have delayed the development of original publishing. While publishers claimed, with some truth, that their agency profits were used to publish Canadian authors,[1] the agency system's *raison d'être* was to distribute American and British authors and protect copyrights on behalf of foreign owners. In 1972 David McGill, an executive at McClelland and Stewart, estimated that 'approximately 23,500 new titles from the United Kingdom, 24,300 from the United States ... and about 2,000 from Canada' were available in the Canadian market.[2] The system was relatively efficient in the pre-electronic age, but by the 1970s it was on the verge of collapse.

The terms 'agency system' and 'branch-plant publishing' are not synonymous, but both describe the mode by which a publishing house distributes its books in someone else's market through arrangements with a local company. Agency arrangements became formalized around 1900 as the expanding Canadian market was restructured after international piracy was eliminated by the 1891 agreement between the British and Americans to protect each other's copyrights. The 1897 tariffs and the 1900 Copyright Act amendment favoured a system whereby Canadians were appointed either exclusive agents covering the entire Dominion of Canada for foreign houses (known as 'principals') or as managers of local branches of foreign houses. In the twenty-five years before 1918, Toronto publishers accumulated agencies by the handful, while a number of British houses, such as Oxford University Press and Macmillan, established branch operations in the city.

The agents promoted their principals' books, for which the contracts, editing, design, production run, royalties, and occasionally the Canadian marketing were decided elsewhere. Normally Canadian publishers held only Canadian rights for foreign *and* Canadian authors because British and American publishers, with or without pressure from literary agents, retained world rights, which included lucrative reprint, theatrical, and motion picture rights. Foreign publishers preferred to export manufactured books to colonial markets because it was more cost effective than printing copies in Canada that could be sold only within Canada. Under the tariffs in place until the 1930s, imported bound books entered at a low duty of 10 per cent, but problems over authors' royalties often encouraged Canadians to import sheets (20 per cent) or plates (duty free) for a Canadian edition. Under certain conditions, then, the principal recognized the publicity value of a local edition for a Canadian author like Ralph Connor or a best-selling foreign author like Zane Grey. Unless one has access to publishers' and authors' records, the lines between an 'agency book,' a so-called 'Canadian Copyright Edition,' and a 'co-publication' begin to blur.

Strictly speaking, an agency book sold in Canada carries only the foreign publisher's imprint on the title page. A special category between the 1890s and the 1940s, the 'Canadian Copyright Edition,' with the Canadian imprint on the title page, carried a notice that it was 'For Sale in Canada only' or a warning, 'Not for Export Abroad.' During the same period there also evolved co-publication ventures. Because Canadian law, unlike American law, did not require typesetting or manufacture as a condition of copyright protection, co-publication or original publication editions could be manufactured in the United Kingdom or the United States. In 1919, for example, George Doran of New York appointed McClelland and Stewart (M&S) his Canadian agents but excluded his Canadian authors (such as Ralph Connor), for whom separate contracts were made. The Connor books distributed in Canada were printed in both the United States and Canada. It was the exception for a foreign author to sign an agreement with a local publisher.

Because book shipments from Britain were curtailed by the First World War, some British authors were distributed in American editions, to the chagrin of British publishers, who saw their slipping Canadian position through the 1920s as symptomatic of their loss of overseas markets to the Americans, a phenomenon analysed by Frédéric Brisson in chapter 14. The war also brought an upsurge in Canadian editions of British authors, whose excellent sales prompted Macmillan, McClelland and Stewart, Musson, and Ryerson Press to publish Canadian authors and considerable numbers of foreign authors in Canadian Copyright Editions in the 1920s. The Canadian Copyright Act of 1921 (11–12 George 5, c. 24) encouraged further accumulation of agencies, an outcome that exacerbated some of the difficulties of agency publishing. Booksellers regularly accused 'jobbers' (that is, agency-publishers) of driving up prices on foreign books, but publisher George J. McLeod claimed that imposition of a 40 per cent discount for retailers in 1920 gave him a smaller profit on agency books than before the war.[3] In addition, retailers and libraries would often 'buy around' the agent and order directly from abroad. Soon many in the trade questioned whether there were too many publishers (that is, agencies) and whether a 'real' publishing trade existed.[4] By 1928 Hugh Eayrs of Macmillan of Canada considered the business of the agent a greater 'gamble' than ever before.[5]

The Depression forced Canada and the United States into protectionist measures. In 1930 Canada raised the tariff on American goods by 50 per cent, which caused a drop in importation from the United States and a slight increase in British imports. However, American books produced for the U.S. domestic market were routinely dumped on the Canadian market, thereby transgressing Canadian copyright arrangements. 'Buying around' emerged as a permanent problem, and in 1939 the Book Publishers' Branch of the Toronto Board of Trade complained when libraries and departments of education applied to Ottawa to have tariffs rescinded on books they had imported directly.[6] It was a decade when bankruptcies and reorganization among the foreign principals involved transfers among the agencies, and confusion arose over agencies that shared different lines from the same principal. For example, the British house of John Murray was simultaneously represented in Canada by William Bell, Longmans Canada, and Ryerson.[7] Some agents such as Bell carried no stock but merely processed orders. Even so, at the end of 1939 McClelland and Stewart represented twenty-three foreign houses and had a 'connection' with the Canadian subsidiaries of Cassell, Dent, and both Dodd, Mead, and Little, Brown. This was the beginning of the era of blockbusters like *Gone with the Wind* (published in Canada by Macmillan of Canada), which remained so long at the top of the best-seller lists that other titles – and hence their agents – suffered.

Despite improved sales during the Second World War and an increase in Canadian editions of foreign and local authors, publisher S.J. Reginald Saunders

wondered in 1945: 'Are we to slip back to 1939, to the status of agents and distributors of the British and American books we are offered by our Principals in those two
great publishing centres – books in *their* format? Or, are we going to go forward by
printing and binding in Canada titles by leading English and American authors, and
by our Canadian authors who have so ably proved themselves?'[8] Between 1945 and
1970, as Canada became a 'battleground' between the British and Americans in the
'struggle for export markets,'[9] many Canadian arrangements were not respected by
wholesalers and jobbers in other countries. Much of the Canadian market was in the
hands of three wholesalers – Baker & Taylor of New York, Simpkin-Marshall of London, and W.H. Smith of London and its Canadian subsidiary. Economist J.N. Wolfe
blamed this situation partly on inefficient wholesale distribution and the existence
of too many small agencies, with approximately ninety publishers across Canada
representing some five hundred foreign firms. He noted that in the 1950s only one-
tenth of the books sold in Canada were produced here, while sixth-sevenths of the
imports came from the United States and the remainder from Britain.[10]

Because Canadian copyright permitted the importation of two copies for private
use, libraries justified 'buying around' agency-publishers when they needed small
quantities of many titles, claiming they received better service and discounts by
purchasing such orders through one jobber or library supply house. The agencies
maintained that their 'markups' reflected high overhead costs for transportation,
currency devaluations, and *ad valorem* tariffs that varied on different shipments of
the same title. It was difficult to estimate how much stock to keep on hand when
warehouse and insurance costs were skyrocketing. When fourteen British publishers formed the British Book Service (Canada) in 1949, they immediately severed
their agencies in Canada. Toronto publishers retaliated with their own Co-Operative
Book Centre (1954–70), a central ordering house that did not stock books, and was
used more for special orders than routine ones. It went into receivership and was
purchased by Maclean-Hunter in 1970. The Publishers' Academic Library Service
(PALS) was formed in 1966 to compete with British booksellers that supplied the
academic market; American books were added to the service in 1969. Two years earlier, however, *Quill & Quire* had declared, 'The agency system is dying.'[11] The old
colonial phase in Canadian publishing closed as the new global dispensation
evolved.

The end came when Doubleday, Houghton-Mifflin, McGraw-Hill, Prentice-Hall,
and Van Nostrand cancelled their agencies and established subsidiaries that developed Canadian programs aimed at the rapidly developing school and post-secondary educational markets. In 1964 McClelland and Stewart dropped all but its four

closest agencies to concentrate on original publishing, but it and other Canadian-owned houses could hardly compete on the same scale as the subsidiaries and soon experienced financial difficulties. The worst crisis of the century saw the sale through the early 1970s of Ryerson Press to McGraw-Hill Company of Canada, Gage to Scott-Foresman, Macmillan of Canada to Maclean-Hunter, and the near-bankruptcy of McClelland and Stewart. Demands for economic autonomy and cultural nationalism to counter the barrage of American products so beloved by Canadians – movies, television, sports, appliances, magazines, and books – forced Ottawa and Ontario to subsidize Canadian-owned firms that published Canadian authors. Dave Godfrey, president of the Independent Publishers' Association (IPA; later the Association of Canadian Publishers), urged Ottawa to regulate the distribution system by forcing distributors to give preference to Canadian stock.[12] In 1975 Paul Audley, the executive director of the IPA, estimated that 87 per cent of the books sold in Canada were imported, or adapted from imported books, and that only about 10 per cent of those imports entered through agency agreement, while the rest arrived through the foreign-owned subsidiaries. Indeed, those subsidiaries now constituted about 84 per cent of the book publishing industry in Canada.[13]

The advent of the computerized single order, single billing system implemented by British and American distributors in the late 1970s was a boon for Canadian retailers and libraries, which preferred dealing with one distributor rather than twenty to thirty publishers, each with its own system. As a result the share of the $600 million domestic book market held by imports would increase beyond its current 72 per cent. A new problem was to have Canadian books listed in the foreign systems. 'The threat is not inherent in the technology but in the control of the systems,' explained bookseller William Roberts.[14] The traditional agency system withered away, unable to handle the vastly increased importations entering the enlarged market; its place was taken by a handful of foreign and domestic wholesalers, and by a second wave of subsidiaries in the 1980s, among them Random House Canada and Harper Collins Canada, themselves subdivisions of international conglomerates. As the subsidiaries and Canadian-owned firms competed for publishing rights at international book fairs, a clearer demarcation developed between publishers and agency-distributors.

Arguments against the agency system arose out of disputes over distribution and 'buying around,' complaints over jacked-up book prices, and the negative impact the system had on original ventures by Canadian houses. Were Canadian writers denied publication, except in the 1930s? Foreign publishers have always issued Canadian authors, and some subsidiaries, such as Macmillan of Canada, actively promoted Canadian writing in competition with Canadian-owned houses. More problematic is the charge of economic imperialism: that the agency system and the multinational subsidiaries have exercised an excessive amount of foreign control and – in the post-colonial, globalized world after 1970 – ownership. Such accusations nowithstanding, the agency system brought a wide range of international books to Canadian readers.

Trade and Regional Publishing in Central Canada

GEORGE L. PARKER

In 1917 Canadians celebrated the fiftieth anniversary of Confederation mired in a European war and polarized by conscription, yet they soon emerged from these experiences with a new sense of pride founded on the country's military accomplishments and a coveted seat at the Paris peace talks. Canada's political autonomy was secured between the First World War, which ended the Victorian age, and the Second World War, which transformed the old British/French dispensation into a multicultural society. Cultural autonomy, however, proved more elusive: the agency-publishing industry that had emerged in English Canada around 1900 ensured a continued dependency on the distribution of foreign books. While prosperity in the 1920s encouraged a handful of Canadian houses and one British branch, Macmillan of Canada, to publish many Canadian writers, their books were only exported in small quantities, and normally American and British publishers insisted on retaining the lucrative foreign and subsidiary rights to Canadian authors. The trend to publish Canadian books almost disappeared during the Depression, as local houses fell back on agency profits to sustain them. During the Second World War, increased revenues and a new, broader readership laid the groundwork for developments after the mid-1950s. For the rest of the century there was an unprecedented increase in the volume and quality of Canadian writing published. Through the 1960s and 1970s, as the publishing industry in English Canada expanded domestically and internationally, it faced domination by aggressive American subsidiaries. Attracted by the prosperity of the Canadian trade, these subsidiaries initiated well-financed Canadian programs, launching into an area of publishing that had traditionally been the preserve of Canadian-owned firms. Over-expansion among Canadian-owned houses created a major crisis after 1970 that, despite government intervention, was not resolved by 1980 and continued to cause ripples into the twenty-first century. During the recession of the 1980s, the industry witnessed government cutbacks, even more takeovers, and the bankruptcy of publishing houses across the land.

The Interwar Years

The First World War brought votes for women, the Americanization of urban life, modernism in art and literature, and optimistic vision statements from the three Toronto-based publishing houses that dominated Canada's English-language industry for the next sixty years. John McClelland, co-owner of McClelland and Stewart (M&S), announced in 1918 that he was 'specializing as far as possible on the works of Canadian writers ... We have yet to lose a dollar on any Canadian book that we have ever published.'[15] His edition of Ralph Connor's *The Sky Pilot in No Man's Land* (1919), which achieved extraordinary sales of 40,000 copies, was a success that would not be duplicated by a Canadian-authored book published in Canada until the 1960s. Similarly, Hugh Eayrs, president of the British subsidiary Macmillan of Canada, declared that his house 'takes the stand that by what it publishes ... it may conceivably alter the viewpoint and outlook of the people of Canada ... It believes it has a serious purpose and mission in the interests of Canadian letters.'[16] His publication of Louis Hémon's *Maria Chapdelaine* in English translation was an unexpected international hit in 1921. Lorne Pierce, who joined Ryerson Press in 1920 and soon became its literary editor, made no apology for his messianic 'self-conscious Canadianism.' As he later recalled, in the 1920s he, McClelland, and Eayrs 'were at the beginning of things as a nation, and we felt under the obligation to assist as many spokesmen of our time as we could,' and with hard work 'were prepared to make great sacrifices to see that Canadian writers had a chance.'[17] In 1921 all three supported both the new Canadian Authors Association and the new Copyright Act, which brought Canada in line with the Berne Convention.

The positive outlook toward original Canadian publishing with which McClelland, Eayrs, and Pierce entered the 1920s was buoyed by an economic upturn after 1923. At M&S literary editor Donald French embarked on the reprinting of appealing early Canadian writers such as Susanna Moodie and Catharine Parr Traill, while McClelland reeled in Ralph Connor, Arthur Stringer, Stephen Leacock, and L.M. Montgomery, all of whom were current Canadian best-selling novelists.

Through the 1920s, the M&S list also included two prestigious poets, Bliss Carman and Duncan Campbell Scott, and a gaggle of mid-list writers. Although McClelland co-published Martha Ostenso's prize-winning *Wild Geese* (1925) with the New York firm of Dodd, Mead, most of his younger writers would not be remembered. While Montgomery would achieve posthumous fame as one of the world's most popular authors, by the 1930s McClelland's most illustrious authors were all middle-aged and past their best writing and greatest sales.

At Ryerson, the renamed trade division of the Methodist Book and Publishing House (itself after 1925 retitled the United Church Publishing House), ordained minister Pierce 'took to publishing ... like a duck to water,'[18] reinvigorating the firm's tradition of social and cultural activism. Pierce crammed Ryerson's lists with Canadian writers and devised endless schemes to promote them. Among the most significant was the biographical/critical Makers of Canadian Literature series, a venture that included both English-Canadian authors and several French-Canadian authors such as Antoine Gérin-Lajoie and Louis Fréchette.[19] The only other publisher of the 1920s to share this commitment to bridging English and French cultures was Louis Carrier of Montreal, whose English-language titles included works by Frederick Philip Grove, Watson Kirkconnell, and Sir Andrew MacPhail. Although occasionally accused of publishing anything Canadian, over the course of his forty-year career Pierce attracted critically acclaimed poets Raymond Knister, Dorothy Livesay, A.J.M. Smith, P.K. Page, and Earle Birney. The Ryerson Poetry Chapbooks, another series he initiated in the 1920s, would in the 1930s and 1940s represent one of the few outlets of book publication for many poets. Although the chapbooks relied on financial input from their authors, Pierce dealt with most Ryerson authors on a royalty basis. Many of the literary works on Ryerson's list were supported by revenues from textbook sales, another area of publication to which Pierce was devoted.[20] Hugh Eayrs similarly relied on educational and agency sales to support an original Canadian publishing program. The parent company permitted him to expand beyond the branch distribution of educational works by publishing Marius Barbeau, Morley Callaghan, Frederick Philip Grove, E.J. Pratt, and two of Canada's international best-selling authors, the environmentalist Grey Owl (Archibald Belaney) and novelist Mazo de la Roche, whose enduring Whiteoaks saga bolstered the firm's fortunes beginning in 1927 with the prize-winning first book in the series, *Jalna*. In their dark polished-wood offices, McClelland, Pierce, and Eayrs oversaw operations that were normally not hectic, except in September and before Christmas. Between the annual trips to New York and London to make agency and other publishing arrangements there were long summer vacations and literary events that made the society pages. Their activities were matched by other Toronto publishers, notably Thomas Allen and the Musson Book Company, firms that also engaged to a lesser degree in original Canadian publishing. Although this genteel life survived among Toronto publishers until the 1960s, the Depression marked an important transition, bringing with it a downturn in Canadian publishing.

Within two years of the 1929 crash, reforms in the American industry had repercussions in Canada. Ottawa raised the sales tax on all goods and increased both the tariff and valuations on foreign printed materials. Department stores stunned retailers by offering discounts of one-third or one-half on new books. American-owned book clubs, which are discussed by Archana Rampure and Jacques Michon in chapter 14, cut into publishers' and booksellers' sales. Remaindered books originally produced in the United States for American readers were dumped on the Canadian market. Four American publishers and their Canadian agents issued new series of novels that sold for one dollar or $1.50, half the previous normal price. By the end of the decade, the Penguin series from Allen Lane of London and Robert de Graff's Pocket Books of New York had entered the domestic market, captivating Canadian readers and heralding the arrival of the paperback revolution in Canada.

Mergers among American houses caused frequent shifts among the Toronto agencies, undermining the very survival of the companies that held them. One new firm, Clarke, Irwin (est. 1929), survived the Depression by its alliance with S.B. Gundy, who ran the Canadian branch of Oxford University Press and was a partner in the Canadian subsidiary Doubleday, Doran and Gundy. A promising Ottawa house, Henry Miller's Graphic Publishers (est. 1925), which issued only Canadian writers, went bankrupt in 1932, just two years after Louis Carrier had met a similar fate in Montreal. In 1935 British publisher J.M. Dent bailed out M&S, which agreed not to publish school textbooks until the end of the arrangement (1946). At Macmillan, textbook salesman John Gray advised Eayrs to expand the company's educational department, seeking stability in the promise of high-volume textbook sales.[21] Toronto houses also relied on popular blockbusters such as Margaret Mitchell's *Gone with the Wind* and Hervey Allen's *Anthony Adverse* to improve their financial positions.

In the face of these economic difficulties, Canadian publishers that did engage in original publishing cut back their lists. Ryerson and Musson issued fewer Canadian trade books. At Macmillan, Eayrs received over two thousand manuscripts in 1939 but published only thirty-six books, not all of them by Canadian authors.[22] Prose writer Morley Callaghan and poet Dorothy Livesay documented the disquiet of the 1930s, but neither achieved a wide audience for Macmillan of Canada. However, de la Roche and Grey Owl helped keep Macmillan in the black.

The Second World War was profitable for booksellers and publishers, even though printing for the war effort took precedence over other projects, and restrictions on paper, materials, and gasoline, as well as labour shortages and taxes, placed a premium on trade books. As described by Lorna Knight in chapter 18, men and women in uniform constituted a new reading public, and publishers supplied books at cost to Canadian military bases.

Although a nascent small-press community appeared in Montreal during the war, original trade book publishing in English remained largely confined to Toronto. Despite wartime restrictions, the William Collins subsidiary expanded its Canadian program, producing some cloth-bound books of exceptional design, many the work of artist Franklin Carmichael, and venturing into the mass market with its White Circle paperbacks, which the branch produced at a rate of eight a month under the supervision of Margaret Paull.[23] Now women assumed executive positions: Ellen Elliott was appointed a director at Macmillan soon after Hugh Eayrs's death in 1940, and in 1945 Mrs Reginald Saunders became president of her late husband's company of the same name. British publishers visited Canada in 1943, promising support for a real Canadian industry with Canadian-produced editions of British authors. Thus encouraged, the Publishers' Section of the Toronto Board of Trade undertook the first extended analysis of the book trade. However, when British and American publishers divided the world's post-war English-language market, each preferred to retain rights over the Canadian market whenever possible. A prosperous Christmas season in 1945 pointed to a post-war publishing revival, which materialized a decade later. *Quill & Quire* proclaimed 1955 the year that the book business came of age, stating it was 'undoubtedly the best, from a financial point of view, that Canadian publishers and booksellers have ever enjoyed.'[24]

Developments after the Second World War

The decade between 1945 and 1955 prepared the ground for change. Canada emerged from the Second World War with (temporarily) the fourth largest navy in the world, a new role as a middle power, and a reinvigorated self-reliance. Returning veterans John Morgan Gray (Macmillan), Jack Stoddard Sr (General), Gage Love (W.J. Gage), Jack McClelland (M&S), and Marsh Jeanneret (Copp Clark) were determined to be more than agent-publishers. In company with William Toye of Oxford

University Press, a driving force behind the subsidiary's handsome poetry volumes, its movement into children's publishing, and its Canadian *Companions* to history and literature, these innovators showed Canadians the breadth of the contemporary literary scene. Even so, in the 1950s, Gray observed, 'the principal business of most Canadian Publishers is still the buying and selling of British and American books,' although he recognized that the stability traditionally provided by the agency system was being undermined by the increasing influence of foreign wholesalers in the Canadian market.[25] In addition, the post-war emergence of the United States as the dominant economic and cultural force in the world had begun to make an impact.

As described by Paul Litt in chapter 1, state intervention into cultural affairs was one response to American ascendancy as Ottawa and the provinces moved to protect Canadian culture and media against encroaching and popular American movies, books, magazines, and television. From the recommendation of the Massey Report of 1951 came the Canada Council for the Arts in 1957, which provided funds for writers and publishers. Equally remarkable was the response of Toronto publishers to the paperback revolution. Jack McClelland's relative success with the New Canadian Library (est. 1958), a quality reprint series of Canadian literary titles, encouraged subsequent paperback series from Ryerson, Macmillan, University of Toronto Press, Oxford, and General Publishing.

In the early 1960s, publishing Canadian books was a growth industry, but within ten years over-expansion connected to the 1967 Centennial, inefficient distribution, poor service, inflated prices, cash-flow problems, and competition from distributors in the United States and from international subsidiaries in Canada created a crisis for Canadian-owned firms. The first to go into decline was Ryerson Press. Despite its revived book designs, and a list that included Hugh Hood and Alice Munro, the obligation to use the house's own production facilities rather than go outside for competing bids, and the heavy expense of a new colour press weighed on the directors. In 1970 the bank refused further loan extensions, and that December McGraw-Hill Company of Canada purchased Ryerson, agreeing to retain its trade division, authors, and paperback lists for at least five years. Earlier that same year, the educational firm of W.J. Gage had been sold to its American principal, Scott-Foresman. Although Gage would be repatriated six years later, the public outcry over the sale of these historic publishing icons forced Ontario to launch a royal commission, which ended up investigating the book trade throughout Canada. The hearings brought forth more bad news from venerable houses.

Under the presidency of John Morgan Gray, post-war Macmillan of Canada had enjoyed the 'most prosperous and successful period' of its history, with books by Donald Creighton, Robertson Davies, Hugh MacLennan, and James Reaney highlighting its list.[26] However, in the 1960s the firm's annual revenues began to decline, successively suffering inroads by American jobbers into the Canadian market, substantial drops in textbook purchases by provincial departments of education, and a general decline in the conditions of the Canadian book trade.[27] Toward the close of the decade, as part of shakeups in their worldwide holdings, the London directors of Macmillan pressed Gray to account for his steadily dropping annual revenues. Rejecting a purchase bid from a group headed by Gray and Jack McClelland, the Macmillans sold the Canadian branch to Maclean-Hunter, the Canadian magazine and communications giant. Under the presidency of Hugh Kane from 1969 to 1976, successful memoirs by political figures Grattan O'Leary and John Diefenbaker appeared, as well as the runaway best-seller for children by Dennis Lee, *Alligator Pie* (1974). Consequently, Maclean-Hunter caused shock waves when in 1980 it suddenly sold Macmillan to Ron Besse, the new president of Gage, who had previously managed Prentice-Hall of Canada. The respected Macmillan of Canada name finally disappeared in 2002.

'One of the keys to a successful book publisher is a total recognition of the author as the important part of the equation and he'd better keep this in mind in everything he does as a publisher,' said Jack McClelland, the publisher who most famously symbolized the glory days of the 1960s and 1970s.[28] His commitment to Canadian writers began when he joined his father's firm in 1948. Although it would take him until 1964 to divest all of his agencies, by 1954 40 per cent of McClelland's book business was Canadian in origin,[29] and the following year he would state unequivocally that 'the publisher is to great extent responsible for the recording and preserving of our cultural heritage.'[30] McClelland's major literary authors included Margaret Atwood, Leonard Cohen, Margaret Laurence, Irving Layton, Al Purdy, Mordecai Richler, and Gabrielle Roy, while extraordinarily successful non-fiction authors such as Pierre Berton, Farley Mowat, and Peter Newman also studded his list. Following the New Canadian Library and the Carleton Library, which are discussed by Janet B. Friskney in chapter 7, McClelland embarked on the Canadian Centennial History Series and the Canadian Illustrated Library. These costly series sold well but left him short of capital. In 1971 M&S achieved its biggest revenues, about one-fifth of its profits coming from the sale of 100,000 copies of Berton's history of the Canadian Pacific Railway, *The Last Spike*; yet that year McClelland placed his firm on sale and was only saved from bankruptcy by a loan of $960,000 from the Ontario government.

McClelland's financial problems continued through the 1970s and into the economic downturn of 1980–1, which also wounded University of Toronto Press and dealt Clarke, Irwin its first critical blow. When McClelland became CEO in 1982 and appointed Linda McKnight as publisher, Margaret Laurence wrote him, 'Damn near singlehandedly, you transformed the Canadian publishing scene from one of mediocrity and dullness to one of enormous interest and vitality.'[31] By 1984 he complained that publishing is 'a terrible business in this country,'[32] although he remained faithful to his authors. He sold out to Avie Bennett in 1985 and retired in 1987. By that time his torch had passed to Douglas Gibson, who moved from Macmillan with his authors to become publisher at M&S. The McClelland legacy – the outrageous promotions, the big parties, the care and nurture of his writers, and, above all, the thousands of titles – represents one of the outstanding eras in Canada's cultural annals (see illus. 5.1, p. 176).[33]

The publicly chronicled struggles of prominent houses like Ryerson, Macmillan, and M&S in a period of heightened nationalism brought new political attention to the publishing industry. A report commissioned in 1969 by the federal Department of Industry, Trade, and Commerce identified an export market worth $5.5 million. Of the $222 million domestic market, 65 per cent were imported books, 25 per cent were Canadian, and 10 per cent were adapted for manufacture in Canada.[34] Threats of bankruptcy and collapse and foreign takeovers all exacerbated nationalist feelings and intense debates over ownership of the cultural industries. The Independent Publishers' Association (IPA), which formed in 1971 in the wake of the sale of Ryerson Press, argued that only Canadian-owned firms publishing Canadian titles should be supported by public funds. Under the IPA's auspices, publishers lobbied Ottawa to develop stringent policies on foreign ownership and foreign investment in the cultural industries. Following Ontario's loan guarantee program in 1972 – one of the province's concrete responses to its royal commission on the industry – the federal government set up Block Grants to Publishers through the Canada Council and the Association for the Export of Canadian Books in 1973, and soon created the Foreign Investment Review Agency (FIRA) to regulate takeovers in the book industry. Ottawa subsequently established the Canadian Book Publishing Development Program in 1979 to provide support for Canadian-owned publishers. These programs were substantially revised in the 1980s by the Mulroney government as it negotiated the Canada-U.S. Free Trade Agreement, which fortunately excluded the cultural industries. Cabinet ministers Marcel Masse, Flora MacDonald, and Perrin Beatty fought to reinstitute funding and safeguards for the Canadian industry in the face of intensifying American and

5.1 Known for theatrical publicity stunts, publisher Jack McClelland is pictured here promoting a paperback giveaway in Saskatoon in February 1976. In 1972, Pierre Berton's *The Great Railway Illustrated* was publicized with a press kit containing moustache wax, a poker deck, a stereoscopic card, a cigar, buffalo meat, champagne, and cut plug tobacco. McClelland's most memorable stunt was a chariot ride with author Sylvia Fraser down Toronto's Yonge Street to promote her book *The Emperor's Virgin* on the Ides of March, 1980. A broken axle derailed the chariot and a blizzard dogged the determined, toga-clad publisher and author as they walked the route, accompanied by two shivering centurions. Courtesy of the William Ready Division of Archives and Research Collections, McMaster University Library. © Creative Professional Photographers Ltd.

European cultural hegemony. Often faulted, even damned, government intervention has proved a godsend for many publishing ventures that otherwise might not have seen the light of day. Nor did crises deter industry growth: in 1983 the domestic book market was $309.3 million and the value of imports, $735 million.[35]

One of the major outcomes of these interventions, most particularly that of funding, was to create a viable environment for English-language publishing in smaller Ontario centres, where new publishers invested in titles that were neglected by the large Toronto houses. Ottawa was home to Oberon Press, begun in 1967 by Michael Macklem and his wife, Anne Hardy, who authored the successful annual *Where to Eat in Canada*. Known for excellent book design, Oberon has published Hugh Hood, David Adams Richards, and W.P. Kinsella. Borealis Press, founded in 1972 by Glenn Clever of the University of Ottawa, specialized in poetry and books for children. Near Kingston was Camden House, founded in 1977 by James Lawrence of *Harrowsmith* magazine; under Frank Edwards, its list emphasized environmental issues.

Prior to 1970, Montreal's anglophone publishing community continued to develop. In 1959 a new trade publisher, Harvest House, was founded by Maynard and Anne Gertler to produce French-Canadian books in translation, while its titles on history, science, and biography achieved international sales. After 1970, other Montreal literary and political ventures courted audiences that were overlooked or ignored by larger houses. Black Rose Books (est. 1970) espoused the radical Left. Founded by Cesar Alba as a co-operative 'venture in brotherhood economics,'[36] it attacked American imperialism and social inequities. Véhicule Press (1973) emerged from the art gallery of the same name to issue cultural and social works related to Montreal. Antonio D'Alfonso founded Guernica Editions (1978) to focus on works on ethnicity, identity, and gender by allophone writers, occasionally publishing in the first languages of its authors.

While Toronto remained the centre for major houses and national distributors, beginning in the 1960s the city also supported a lively culture of small presses, a topic developed by David McKnight in chapter 11. Many of these houses issued the early works of writers who would later win national and international acclaim. From the 1970s to the turn of the century, a new generation of enthusiastic young Toronto editors and publishers, including Anna Porter, Louise Dennys, Jack Stoddard Jr, Anne Collins, and Patrick Crean, also emerged out of the training ground of the established trade houses, where they fostered their commitment to Canadian writing and in some cases went on to create their own firms. Lester, Orpen and Dennys (1973–91), directed by Malcolm Lester and Louise Dennys, developed an impressive list of Canadian and international authors, but failed in the depression of 1991. Key Porter Books, established by Anna Porter and Key Publishers in 1979, has had greater longevity, remaining under Porter's direct control until 2005.

Although Toronto retained the densest concentration of English-language publishers throughout the period and would remain dominant at the end of the twentieth century, the changes experienced by the central Canadian industry were also felt in other parts of the country. In effect, nineteenth-century regionalism was resurrected, but with a vitality and variety that gave proof of nationwide creativity.

Atlantic Canada

SANDRINE FERRÉ-RODE

Publishing in Atlantic Canada is extremely diverse, reflecting the complex nature of the regional context in which it developed. The Atlantic region – encompassing Newfoundland and the Maritime provinces of Nova Scotia, New Brunswick, and Prince Edward Island – is not a homogeneous unit. Each of its four component provinces lays claim to a distinct identity, though economic necessity has required them to act together on numerous occasions. Located on the periphery of Canada and home to a small population, Atlantic Canada must constantly reaffirm its local cultures in opposition to national and international influences. In addition to the practical difficulties of publishing at a distance from large urban centres, these competing cultural traditions have made the production, distribution, and reception of books within the region a challenge. East Coast publishers have been acutely aware of their vulnerability yet, at the same time, have been convinced of the crucial role of publishing in the affirmation, preservation, and recognition of regional culture.[37]

In the eighteenth and nineteenth centuries, the Atlantic region enjoyed a rich literary life, but that vitality faded by the First World War. In the interwar period – which Nova Scotian novelist Thomas H. Raddall would later describe as a 'cultural ice age' in which 'the pace [of change] was glacial'[38] – publishing activity was largely confined to newspapers, with the notable exception of the *Busy East of Canada* (1910–33; later the *Maritime Advocate and Busy East*, 1933–56; and the *Atlantic Advocate*, 1956–92), a New Brunswick magazine that exhibited a strong regional consciousness throughout its life. With the possibilities for publishing books locally in both the Maritimes and Newfoundland extremely limited, authors typically took on the expense of publication themselves and, to get their books printed, turned to the presses of local newspapers such as the *Tribune* (Sackville, NB, 1902–) and the *Herald* (Halifax, 1875–), or to commercial printers, such as Imperial[39] in Halifax, Irwin in

Charlottetown, and Robinson in St John's. Some even relied on the odd bookshop or stationery store, such as T.C. Allen in Halifax, which boasted a press on site.[40] The editorial quality of such books was often rudimentary. More professional were the publications of Halifax's Royal Print and Litho Limited. A division of the *Herald*, which was owned by the influential Dennis family, this commercial printing firm took over the publication of some of the directories of the region, as well as the famous *Belcher's Almanac*, in 1914. However, writers with serious ambitions, such as Raddall, Ernest Buckler, Hugh MacLennan, and Evelyn Richardson, found it necessary to 'publish in exile,' seeking out firms in Toronto, Boston, or New York where their work could be professionally edited, published, and distributed, as well as have some hope of critical and public recognition.

Universities became centres of intellectual, literary, and commercial publishing activity in Atlantic Canada after the First World War. The *Dalhousie Review* (Halifax, 1921–), a university journal intended for a broad readership, had a two-pronged publishing policy divided between locally produced literature and articles on scientific, literary, political, and historical subjects not limited to the region. A second journal, *The Fiddlehead* (Fredericton, 1945–), founded at the University of New Brunswick (UNB) by historian and poet A.G. Bailey, initially published poetry by teachers and students; later, under Fred Cogswell, another UNB professor, it became a well-known literary journal. By the late 1940s, Cogswell had also begun a modest publishing program, issuing collections under the imprint Fiddlehead Poetry Books. The region's first publishing conglomerate was the University Press of New Brunswick, founded by Michael Wardell in Fredericton in 1951. Its holdings included a daily newspaper, the *Daily Gleaner* (1889–), the *Atlantic Advocate*, a printing operation, and a publishing house, Brunswick Press, which focused on local history.

Outside the university milieu, Andrew Merkel, a former journalist and an influential member of the Nova Scotia arts community, revived the Abanaki Press imprint, which in the 1920s had experienced a short-lived association with a circle of poets known as the Song Fishermen, who wrote in a romantic mode. The resurrected Abanaki, an imprint that built on folk themes, lasted from the late 1940s until the mid-1950s, and represented the return of an anti-modernist trend within the provincial cultural establishment. The anti-modernist movement, which attracted many creative people, including publishers, reacted to the supposed ills of modern times by glorifying the past, promoting a cult of traditional values, and advocating a pastoral ideal, principles on which its advocates hoped to build a lasting regional culture.

By the 1960s, poetry and regional history had become the cornerstones of East coast publishing. At UNB, Fred Cogswell entrusted *The Fiddlehead* to colleagues so that he could further develop Fiddlehead Poetry Books. New faculty members at the university, including several Americans, were equally committed to literature and ensured that the university remained a centre of the literary community. In 1967 the New Brunswick Chapbooks imprint was initiated by a circle of poets made up of professors and students. That same year, William H. McCurdy, having inherited a printing company, founded Petheric Press in Halifax and began to publish books on Nova Scotian history. In Newfoundland, Premier Joseph R. Smallwood also created a publishing house, Newfoundland Book Publishers Ltd, in 1967, one which, despite its obvious partisan aims, served the cause of Newfoundland culture, culminating in a major encyclopedia project.

The centennial year of 1967 represented a watershed in Atlantic publishing. As part of the celebration, Ottawa subsidized many cultural initiatives, including works of local history and literature. In this atmosphere of cultural ferment, regional production further increased. New publishing houses appeared, including the scholarly presses ISER Books (est. 1967), established by the Institute of Social and Economic Research at Memorial University of Newfoundland, and UCCB Press (est. 1974) at the University College of Cape Breton, as well as publishing arms of provincial museums and other cultural institutions. Small presses multiplied and self-publishing increased. At the same time, publishing activity diversified and periodicals proliferated: in 1971 the scholarly journal *Acadiensis* was launched; literary magazines such as *The Antigonish Review* (Antigonish, NS, 1970–) and *TickleAce* (St John's, 1977–) appeared; as well there were student magazines such as *Alpha* (Wolfville, NS, 1976–90), arts and culture magazines such as *ArtsAtlantic* (Charlottetown, 1977–), popular history magazines such as *Cape Breton's Magazine* (Sydney, NS, 1972–) and *The Island Magazine* (Charlottetown, 1974–), news magazines such as *Atlantic Insight* (Halifax, 1979–89), and a journal of literary criticism entitled *The Atlantic Provinces Book Review* (Halifax, 1974–91; later *Atlantic Books Today*, 1991–). Carried along by the general upswing in publishing, writers and publishers in the area founded provincial and regional associations such as the Writers' Federation of Nova Scotia, in 1975, and the Atlantic Publishers' Association, in 1976.

Over the next decade, continued financial support from the Canada Council helped to build an infrastructure for regional publishing. Among literary publishers, Fiddlehead Poetry Books, producing a record number of collections during the 1970s, greatly enhanced its profile, as did Square Deal Publications, founded by Reshard Gool in Charlottetown in 1971, and Pottersfield Press, founded by Lesley Choyce in Halifax in 1979. The latter publisher was instrumental in the renaissance of Black Nova Scotian writing. At the same time, general-interest publishers like Jes person Press, founded in 1969 on Fogo Island, Newfoundland, combined literary publishing with a strong interest in history and folklore. Lancelot Press (est. 1968) in Nova Scotia began with a religious orientation, while others, such as Ragweed Press in Prince Edward Island, founded in 1973 by Harry Baglole, and Breakwater Books in Newfoundland, founded by Clyde Rose, also in 1973, initially adopted an educational focus, heralding the future development of educational publishing in the region. Breakwater became central in Newfoundland's writing boom and quickly gained the favour of readers in the province, as demonstrated by the success of its children's book *Down by Jim Long's Stage* (1976), written by Al Pittman and illustrated by Pam Hall, which sold thousands of copies and was named the Canadian Library Association's Book of the Year for Children.

The 1970s witnessed the greatest investment in Atlantic publishing since before the First World War, a phenomenon exemplified by Fred Cogswell's prolific publishing activity during this decade. Cogswell's retirement from publishing in 1980 symbolized the end of one era and the beginning of another, one that would be marked by tight budgets and cutbacks in cultural production. By the end of the 1970s, efforts by publishers to reveal the many facets of a regional culture had brought positive results, but cultural validation at the national level remained limited. The predilection for producing genres with limited commercial appeal, such as poetry, and for books with a strong regional flavour, such as folk tales and regional history, examples of which were issued in abundance, was detrimental to penetrating markets outside the region. The phenomenon of 'publishing in exile' has persisted: though writers from Atlantic Canada can now launch careers in the region, they almost inevitably later turn to firms in larger centres, seeking a wider audience and greater remuneration. David Adams Richards, for instance, published an early volume of poetry, *Small Heroics* (1972), with New Brunswick Chapbooks, but his novels have appeared under the imprint of Oberon (Ottawa) and McClelland and Stewart (Toronto).

The dilemma of regional publishing in Atlantic Canada is inescapable. Entrenched very early in a strong regionalist mandate that was the basis of its legitimacy and originality, and concerned from the outset, out of both desire and necessity, with preserving its regional distinctness, publishing in Atlantic Canada set its own limits on expansion. In addition, it was supported by cultural institutions capable of ensuring its development according to its own dynamics. The survival of regional culture seems assured, but its capacity for coordination with other regional, national, and even international milieux remains uncertain.

Prairie Publishing

FIONA A. BLACK

From poetry written under the stars by cowboys to the stirring political rhetoric of Tommy Douglas, publishing in Alberta, Saskatchewan, and Manitoba has been rich in distinctive content. With a collective population well below that of Central Canada in numbers, yet highly diverse in ethnicity, language, and religion, the three provinces share an open landscape criss-crossed by endless miles of rail-lines connecting communities remote from the centres of Canadian power and production. Into this geography, publishers' representatives from Ontario and elsewhere have travelled regularly; over time the products of their presses have been increasingly supplemented by local publications.

As with other regions, the Prairies' principal publishers, in terms of quantity and range of materials, have been provincial and municipal governments. Their output reflects such developments as the movement in the 1950s and 1960s toward public health care and hospital insurance. The fight for these benefits was led by Saskatchewan's popular socialist premier Tommy Douglas, some of whose published speeches were eagerly sought after. Alongside the typical variety of government documents, between 1918 and 1980 privately owned regional presses produced a wealth of newspapers and books. Textbook printing and publishing, which had been carried out in the Prairies since earlier in the century by companies such as School Aids and Text Book Publishing of Regina and the Western Canada Institute in Calgary, expanded greatly in the second half of the century, as the provincial departments of education offered more local contracts.

Western Producer Prairie Books (WPPB) has been one of the region's most notable economic success stories. Founded in 1954 by the Saskatchewan Wheat Pool at the Saskatoon offices of the *Western Producer,* the pool's weekly paper, its list was very strong on Prairie themes and issues.[41] WPPB specialized in paperbound books with colourful covers and line-drawing illustrations, thus providing inexpensive and appealing sources of information about the history of the region on topics ranging from Métis and French affairs to agricultural fairs and cattle ranching. WPPB was perhaps best known as the publisher of Grant MacEwan's hugely popular historical works, including *Fifty Mighty Men* (1958), later followed by *And Mighty Women Too* (1975). Many farm families collected books by MacEwan, an agricultural expert who became Alberta's lieutenant-governor from 1965 to 1974. His readers learned in advance the dates of publication for his books through advertisements in the *West-*

ern Producer, and public libraries purchased multiple copies of his titles in order to cope with the volume of requests.

Prairie book publishers built lists focused on particular subjects and genres of writing, redirecting manuscripts that fell outside their interests and conscientiously developing their reputations as competent producers of books as they proceeded. Peguis Publishers, established in 1967 by Mary Scorer, owner of Winnipeg's first independent bookstore, Mary Scorer Books, 'was among the first in Canada to publish native authors, particularly biographies, autobiographies and history.'[42] Peguis expanded its scope to issue women's history and regional history more broadly, with successful textbook endeavours in the 1980s.[43] In Alberta, cookbooks and works of poetry emerged from Red Deer College Press, founded in 1971 by a group of 'faculty flakes,' in the words of P.G. Boultbee.[44] Coteau Books in Moose Jaw, run by the 'typically Saskatchewan' Thunder Creek Co-operative, issued literary works, as did NeWest Press in Edmonton, founded in 1977 by George Melnyk following the success of his *NeWest Review*. While NeWest's initial book was printed on newsprint, by the end of its first year Miriam Mandel's *Station 14* (1977) had appeared sporting 'high quality paper, design and illustrations.'[45] In 1980 Pemmican Publications started in Winnipeg as 'the only Métis book publishing house in Canada.'[46]

Local print helped anchor a sense of Prairie community. From early official publications exhorting farm families to practise certain agricultural methods, print output peaked around centennial and jubilee years (1967, 1970, and 1980) with a flowering of small, and often short-lived, ventures that produced collectively written community histories for hundreds of villages and rural municipalities in all three provinces.[47] As many families purchased copies of the resulting volume because they had contributed genealogical and business information or photographs, print runs could be substantial. Linda Bedwell's case study in chapter 13 describes how the Mennonite printing company of Friesens in Altona, Manitoba, developed a niche market in printing such local histories.

Particularly notable in the twentieth century was the photographic travel or view book. Some of these titles fell squarely into the category of booster literature. For example, during the Depression, Angus W. Macpherson, a businessman in Saskatoon with connections to the Saskatchewan Motor Club, encouraged the club to publish the heavily illustrated *Northern Summers: Saskatchewan's Resorts, Sports and Cities of 1931*. Other photographic books were based on personal odysseys, such as Everett Baker's *Trails and Traces of Rupert's Land and the North-West Territories as Seen from 1940–1955*. Everett's widow, Ruth, who lived in Shaunavon, had this forty-page illustrated work printed in 1955 by the Modern Press in Saskatoon, 378 kilometres away. The 1960s saw the emergence of sophisticated natural history works such as Doug

Gilroy's *An Album of Prairie Birds* (1967), published by WPPB in 1976 in an expanded second edition titled *Prairie Birds in Color*. The Saskatoon firm also issued R.H. Macdonald's much larger and glossier work *Four Seasons West: A Photographic Odyssey of the Three Prairie Provinces* in 1975. By this time, Courtney Milne and other noted photographers had begun to transform printed images of the Prairies from stereotypical snaps of Prairie sentinels (grain elevators) to art photographs of the hidden hues of blue in snowdrifts and the glories of canola and flax planted in adjoining fields. Such books required advanced technology, which Prairie printing operations now handled with ease. Nonetheless, William Kurelek's haunting text and evocative images for *A Prairie Boy's Winter* (1973) and *A Prairie Boy's Summer* (1975) were issued in Montreal by Tundra Books because publishing from the centre, which held the potential of national distribution, continued to affect authors' decisions.

Mel Hurtig of Hurtig Publishing, based in Edmonton, was not a typical 'regional publisher' and refused to allow his company's physical distance from Toronto to cloud his national perspective or affect his publishing decisions. He entered the book trade in 1956 as a young bookseller in his hometown of Edmonton, and by the time he sold his bookstore chain in 1972, in order to concentrate on publishing, he owned one of the largest book retailing companies in the country. As a bookseller, he had learned much about marketing and distribution, knowledge he put to excellent use as he developed the country's only national trade publishing business outside central Canada.[48] Hurtig Publishers produced numerous award-winning titles, and in 1980 the company launched the most ambitious project in Canadian trade publishing, *The Canadian Encyclopedia*. When completed in 1985, it engendered a form of 'national community' through its inclusive scope and broad discussions of many themes in Canadian culture, politics, and society. Published initially in three volumes, in English and French, the set became a familiar sight in homes and libraries across the country. A man with political ambitions and a founding member of the Council of Canadians, Hurtig employed national marketing strategies very different from those of other Prairie publishers who envisaged a smaller geographic sphere of operations.

Prairie publishers of all sizes eagerly sought federal funding opportunities available to Canadian publishers in the wake of the crisis among Toronto publishers in 1970, discussed by George L. Parker earlier in this chapter. However, many publishers could not qualify for the grants. The immensity of the problem was demonstrated by Manitoba's publishers, for 'even collectively, the Manitoba industry [was] so undercapitalized' that it could not raise the equity investment required. The Canada Council's Block Grant Program imposed 'ever increasing annual production thresholds and minimum performance thresholds based on titles rather than sales,' which, along with other factors, favoured larger houses.[49] However, federal funds were not the only ones available: the Province of Manitoba created publishing-specific block and project grant programs which were accessed more readily, if smaller in scope. Thus government funding helped to maintain regional publishing endeavours at a time when 'the English language publishing activity outside Ontario [consisted] almost entirely of several small firms and one large publisher of trade books in Montreal.'[50]

By the late 1970s, government surveys of the Canadian publishing industry indicated a healthy surge in houses across the Prairies; in 1980, the seventy-eight businesses recorded represented over 11 per cent of the country's total.[51] Using revenue dollars as an indicator of market and advertising share, Manitoba considerably outstripped the other two provinces from at least the mid-1960s, when Harlequin, which is discussed by Archana Rampure in a case study below, was still based in Winnipeg. Alberta took over first place by 1978, as a result of the influence of Hurtig.[52] All three provinces experienced fluctuation in the size of their publishing industries as measured by establishments, revenue, and employees.

Throughout the twentieth century, Prairie publishers confronted challenges similar to those faced by central and eastern Canadian companies in the eighteenth and nineteenth centuries, especially economies of scale and size of market. It is no coincidence that one of Canada's best-loved novels, W.O. Mitchell's *Who Has Seen the Wind* (1947), has never been published in the Prairies. As a young writer with literary ambitions, Mitchell had to look outside his region for publication of this fiction; only his play, *The Black Bonspiel of Wullie MacCrimmon*, received local publication when it was issued by Frontiers Unlimited in Calgary in 1965, many years after its original broadcast on CBC Radio in 1951 and CBC television in 1955. Over the decades, the interests and contributions of Prairie publishers adapted and evolved, always in service to a fluctuating population which remained heavily rural and which bought or borrowed the rich array of imaginative and non-fiction publications from the small firms grounded in the Prairie community.

CASE STUDY ─────────────────────────────────
'Harlequin Has Built an Empire'
– Archana Rampure

The story of Harlequin resembles a business romance, one in which a cheap reprint house transforms itself into a multinational corporation controlling a quarter of the world's multi-billion-dollar romance fiction market. It is an example of what Eva Hemmungs Wirtén calls 'localized globalization,' a process through which a 'product ... emanating from an Anglo-American horizon' comes to be 'sold and marketed all over the world.'[53]

In 1947, the man who would later become mayor of metropolitan Winnipeg and chancellor of the University of Winnipeg, Richard Bonnycastle, in co-operation with several other Winnipeg businessmen, bought a printing firm that occasionally produced twenty-five-cent paperbacks for Collins's White Circle Pocket Editions, a series patterned after the famous Pocket Books that kick-started the paperback revolution in North America. Inspired by the White Circle example, Bonnycastle felt sufficient faith in the paperback revolution to start his own line of reprint titles. With editorial advice and access to the mass market provided by Jack Palmer, manager of Canadian operations for Curtis Distributing, then a major powerhouse in North American serial distribution, Bonnycastle in May 1949 issued his first reprint title, Nancy Bruff's *The Manatee*; it was subtitled *Strange Loves of a Seaman* and appeared under the imprint of 'A Harlequin Book.'

Over the next few years, Harlequin published a range of paperbacks, including a handful of the romances that would become synonymous with the company's name. According to company lore, Harlequin made a deliberate move into the genre only after Bonnycastle was advised by his wife, Mary, Harlequin's first 'editor,' and his secretary, Ruth Palmour, that the books with the lowest rate of returns were the 'sweet little doctor-and-nurse romances.' Having established that Mills & Boon, a small English company, published many such novels, Palmour wrote an historic letter on 8 May 1957 to acquire Canadian rights to these Mills & Boon titles.[54] Later that year, the house reprinted for the Canadian market two Mills & Boon novels that set the tone for Harlequin romances: Anne Vinton's *The Hospital in Buwambo* (no. 407) and Mary Burchell's *Hospital Corridors* (no. 409). Burchell's novel, set in a Montreal hospital, was reprinted many times for a female readership eager for narratives with which they could identify. The popularity of both books was such that in the 1960s Harlequin primarily dedicated itself to reprinting Mills & Boon titles, most of which were British-authored and set outside Canada. The firm entered the U.S. market in 1963.

In 1971, just three years after he had assumed control of Harlequin, Richard Bonnycastle Jr engaged in his own empire-building: to 'secure the stable' of Mills & Boon's writers, he purchased the English firm for $4 million. In doing so, he signalled the beginning of Harlequin's global consolidation. During the rest of the 1970s, the company reached outward to the world market, seeking countries with strong domestic publishing and distribution networks in which local partnerships could be formed for the purpose of distributing Harlequin titles in translation. Translations undertaken in France and introduced there in 1978 were reprinted in Canada for the French-language market,[55] where they quickly displaced the imported 'eau de rose' tales published by Delly and Magali, previously popular with Quebec's readers of romance. By 1989 Harlequin was in a position to celebrate its fortieth anniversary with the simultaneous release in eighteen languages in a hundred markets of *A Reason for Being* by best-selling British author Penny Jordan.[56]

Even as it made international gains in the 1970s, Harlequin faced its most significant challenge in its established North American market. During the 1960s and early 1970s, when most Canadian-owned publishers could not get their books on domestic mass-market racks, Harlequin had prospered through astute distribution arrangements. The connection with Curtis Distributing sustained the company in its early years, and a later deal with Pocket Books resulted in the Simon & Schuster-owned company distributing Harlequin titles across North America alongside its own publications. After the purchase of 51 per cent of Harlequin's stock in 1975 by the Canadian media conglomerate Toronto Star Limited (now Torstar Corporation), the romance publisher risked its unparalleled access (for a Canadian publisher) to distribution by giving Pocket Books notice that it was going to set up its own sales force. It was a decision that in Paul Grescoe's estimation ultimately cost the firm $100 million,[57] for Simon & Schuster responded by creating a competing romance imprint, Silhouette. Over the next few years, Harlequin engaged in a costly battle with Silhouette that no other Canadian publisher could have sustained. Ultimately realizing the futility of these 'Romance Wars,' in 1984 Harlequin struck a deal with Simon & Schuster, buying out Silhouette with the proviso that it would keep its competitor's romance lines alive and return Harlequin's distribution rights to Pocket Books. A by-product of that merger was a substantial increase in the representation of North American authors and settings among Harlequin's titles.

Expanding international operations became crucial for Harlequin in the latter part of the century when the North American market showed itself as both finite and susceptible to other purveyors of romance such as Avon, Bantam, and Silhouette. While explanations for Harlequin's global popularity have often gestured vaguely toward some 'international appeal of romance,'[58] other observers have credited the publisher's savvy in catering to the particularities of diverse national markets.[59] The fact remains that Harlequin built a global empire out of fantasies of love everlasting. It is the extraordinary success story of a small-time Canadian publisher gone global, one that can be measured by the Harlequin Web site's claim in 2003 of selling 5.5 romance novels every second.

British Columbia and the North

PETER J. MITHAM

During the twentieth century, trade book publishing in British Columbia, the Yukon, and the North came into its own, evolving from a sideline of newspapers and commercial printers to a free-standing business boasting some of Canada's leading book publishers. At the end of the 1970s, because educational books were typically purchased outside the region, trade books – those marketed to the general public primarily for leisure reading – represented a far greater share of new books issued by the region's publishers each year than the Canadian norm of 26 per cent.[60]

Prior to 1950, book publishing in British Columbia was minimal, leading ambitious authors such as Ethel Wilson and Roderick Haig-Brown to seek established publishers outside the province. A specialized venture of the interwar period was the Whitehead Library, produced in Vancouver, beginning in 1919. This series of six pamphlets, issued by the Socialist Party of Canada, was supported by a bequest from the late George Whitehead. It included reprints of Karl Marx's *The Communist Manifesto* (see illus. 5.2, p. 189) and Friedrich Engel's *Socialism, Utopian and Scientific*, making these texts available in Canada when their importation was banned under the lingering imposition of the War Measures Act. In a more literary vein, Lions' Gate Publishing issued Annie H. Foster's *The Mohawk Princess, Being Some Account of the Life of Tekahionwake* (1931) and a poetry collection by Vancouver's Alice Harper, *Coloured Sand* (1938).

The 1950s witnessed important developments. Vancouver commercial printer Mitchell Press broke into book publishing in the 1950s with two opportune titles: an English course for the wave of Hungarian immigrants who had arrived in 1956 and a sailing guide.[61] However, these titles were secondary to Mitchell's commercial printing activities. Indeed, because owner Howard Mitchell placed a priority on job

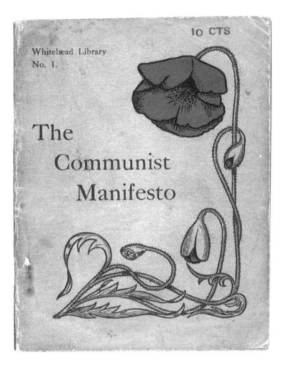

5.2 Karl Marx, *The Communist Manifesto* (Vancouver: Whitehead Estate, 1919). This Canadian edition of Marx's manifesto was the first in a series of pamphlets issued by the Socialist Party of Canada under the terms of a bequest from George Whitehead of Vancouver. Courtesy of the Thomas Fisher Rare Book Library, University of Toronto.

printing, the two or three books he issued each year tended to be released 'just in time to miss the major Christmas market.'[62] It was not until the success of R.E. Watters's *British Columbia: A Centennial Anthology* (1958) and similar celebratory volumes that regional publishers began to realize the potential scope of the local market. Although the British Columbia Provincial Museum and nascent presses such as Heritage House similarly helped to feed regional demand for locally authored and produced books after 1958, it was Gray's Publishing of Sidney and Vancouver-based J.J. Douglas Limited that would emerge as the first prominent BC trade publishers.

Launched in 1962 by Gray Campbell, Gray's Publishing debuted with John Windsor's Second World War memoir *Blind Date* (1962). The initial print run of 3,000 copies sold quickly and won Campbell enough attention that he began to receive unsolicited manuscripts.[63] The press would publish about sixty titles before Campbell's retirement in 1977, developing a regional list of works that sometimes attracted international attention, such as Amy Wilson's *No Man Stands Alone* (1965), which was reissued by Dodd, Mead of New York as *A Nurse in the Yukon* (1966). Gray's set the model for a generation of BC publishers whose first goal was to serve a local market that the major Toronto publishers had largely ignored.

Similarly J.J. Douglas, which issued its first list in 1971, was the brainchild of James J. Douglas. He capitalized on his experience of distributing books and finding new titles for McClelland and Stewart to make the leap into publishing proper. To a backlist of agency titles, Douglas initially added volumes that produced solid sales, such as John B. Harrison's *Good Food Naturally* (1971) and Norah Mannion Wilmot's *Cooking for One* (1971), both previously rejected by McClelland and Stewart.[64] The house rapidly secured a joint-publishing arrangement with University of Washington Press, and in its second year it issued Jack Richards's best-selling *Johann's Gift to Christmas* (1972), which demonstrated a western publisher's ability to produce children's books to rival those from Ontario. The house, which began issuing under the imprint of Douglas & McIntyre in 1978, when Scott McIntyre became a partner, eventually developed a general list that included books on First Nations culture as well as art books and regional titles.[65]

Concurrent with the rise of Gray's and J.J. Douglas there emerged literary presses: Klanak, founded in 1958 by William and Alice McConnell; Blewointment Press, launched by bill bissett in 1967; David Robinson's Talon Books, which issued its first poetry chapbooks in 1967; and the feminist collective, Press Gang, established in 1970. Robert Bringhurst noted that the writers published by these presses saw themselves as part of a 'larger historical whole.'[66] Talon subsequently broadened its activities to embrace non-fiction trade titles that supported its literary endeavours. Its failure to secure provincial funding in 1974 coincided with the arrival of Karl Siegler, who introduced fiscal discipline. By the end of the decade, he had published the first of three cookbooks, the success of which helped Talon to qualify for monies from the federal Department of Communication's Canadian Book Publishing Development Program. Susan Mendelson's *Mama Never Cooked Like This* (1980) would propel Talon to its most financially successful quarter to date in early 1981.[67]

During the early 1970s, the growth of BC trade publishers led to efforts to organize. Noting the formation of the Independent Publishers' Association in 1971 and its aim to foster Canadian writing and Canadian-owned book publishing, eleven publishers largely from the Vancouver area joined in 1974 under Douglas's leadership to form the British Columbia Publishers' Group, known today as the Association of Book Publishers of British Columbia.[68] By 1980 the association counted eighteen active members and twelve associate and supporting members.[69]

Collectively they published a wide range of genres, from International Self-Counsel Press's guides to legal issues, through New Star Books' works of social and political commentary, to UBC Press's scholarly titles, and Aboriginal titles from Theytus Books. The association lobbied governments, organized seminars, fielded queries, and perhaps most importantly, issued an annual catalogue of all books published in British Columbia, whether by association members or not. For some small houses, this represented 'the only catalogue promotion or advertising' they enjoyed.[70] The increasing scale of the BC book industry was evidenced as well in the formation of the distributor Book Express in 1979.[71]

The 1970s also saw the rise of trade publishing north of the sixtieth parallel. Northern ingenuity had earlier produced such ventures as the *Aklavik Journal* (1955–7), a mimeographed monthly that called itself 'Canada's most northern newspaper,' whose typewritten and hand-drawn contents included local news, advertisements, and lively cartoons. Mitchell Press printed *Tiara and Atigi* (1971) for the government of the Northwest Territories to commemorate the visit of Queen Elizabeth II during the territory's centenary in 1970. Local trade publishers were virtually non-existent in the Territories until Marion Lavigne launched Outcrop in 1975. Primarily a communications firm, it entered book publishing with Frederick B. Watt's *Great Bear: A Journey Remembered* (1980). Since then, Outcrop has regularly published titles of interest to northerners, and in December 1984 it launched *Up Here* magazine.[72]

The situation was similar in Yukon, but the presence of established newspaper offices led to local book production much earlier than in the Northwest Territories. As early as 1909, the Dawson *Daily News* issued a souvenir publication for distribution at the Alaska Yukon Pacific Exposition in Seattle.[73] The *Daily News* also produced the first major Yukon imprint, Marie Joussaye Fotheringham's *Selections from Anglo-Saxon Songs* (ca. 1916–18).[74] The relocation of the territorial government to Whitehorse in 1953 drew the centre of territorial publishing south.[75] A decade later, the *Whitehorse Star* published a lithographed collection of Old Crow correspondent Edith Josie's writing, *Old Crow News: The Best of Edith Josie 1963*, a title popular enough to spawn subsequent annual collections. Capitalizing on their success, Clarke, Irwin of Toronto produced its own compilation of Josie's work, *Here Are the News* (1966). In the late 1970s, the Council for Yukon Indians issued an illustrated volume of stories by Angela Sidney and others.[76] But as in the Northwest Territories, local trade publishing came into its own only at the end of that decade. Though *The Lost Whole Moose Catalogue* (1979), an irreverent but comprehensive catalogue of particularly northern information (from salt-curing food to building log homes and keeping kitchen stovepipes clean), was intended as a single venture, the producers came together in

1989 to publish a second volume, leading to the formation of Lost Moose Publishing in 1991.[77] Like trade publishers in British Columbia, and despite appearing relatively late in comparison to their counterparts in Ontario, houses operating in Yukon and the Northwest Territories became an integral part of Canada's publishing landscape by the end of the 1970s.

Organization and Training among Book Publishers

NANCY EARLE AND JANET B. FRISKNEY

During the twentieth century, collective activity among book publishers in English Canada became widespread and complex. As the pre-existing publishers' organization reconfigured in the face of a changing business environment, new associations, including umbrella organizations with allied trade groups, emerged. Professional development of their memberships became a priority for most organizations by the 1970s, a decade in which the first post-secondary program devoted to publishing appeared.

Book Publishers' Organizations

The early twentieth century witnessed a significant restructuring among book publishers in Toronto. Responding to the shift toward agency publishing and anticipating new copyright legislation, in 1910 the Wholesale Booksellers' Section of the Toronto Board of Trade reinvented itself as the Book Publishers' Section.[78] Under the section chairmanship of prominent publishers such as S.B. Gundy of Oxford University Press, John McClelland of McClelland and Stewart, and Hugh Eayrs of Macmillan Company of Canada, this group adjusted its name several times, sequentially identifying itself as the Book Publishers' Branch, the Book Publishers' Association Branch, and the Book Publishers' Association of Canada, before leaving the Board of Trade and becoming the Canadian Book Publishers' Council in 1962. Until the close of the 1960s, this group included most English-language book publishers in Canada, its membership encompassing Canadian-owned houses variously engaged in educational, agency, and original trade publishing, as well as foreign subsidiaries.

During its first decade, the Book Publishers' Section focused it efforts on copyright, postal and freight rates, tariffs, and wartime taxes. 'Buying around' – the direct purchase of foreign books that bypassed Canadian agencies – also registered as an ongoing concern.[79] In the two decades following the First World War, the section embarked on a series of projects and negotiations with legislators that were intended to stimulate the market and improve the general business climate for books. By the mid-1920s the group was producing annual catalogues featuring its members' publications. In 1925 it initiated the 'Canadian Copyright Bulletin' to alert customs officials to books whose Canadian rights were held by domestic publishers, and in 1928, without success, it lobbied the federal government to remove the sales tax on books.[80] As part of its promotional efforts, the branch spearheaded the formation in 1925 of the Association of Canadian Bookmen (ACB), a collective of publishers, authors, critics, librarians, and booksellers dedicated to promoting books and reading.[81] In the mid-1930s, the ACB organized several book fairs and other publicity ventures.[82]

From the early 1930s, the Book Publishers' Branch emphasized promotion abroad, taking out intermittent membership in the International Congress of Publishers and participating in book exhibits in Britain and France. One of its most important international initiatives was to dispatch a trade delegation to Britain in 1945.[83] Some of this overseas promotion, as well as its lobbying of government, was pursued in co-operation with the Société des éditeurs canadiens du livre français (SÉCLF).[84]

Well aware that the industry it represented played a cultural role in Canada, in the early 1950s the branch made submissions to the Massey Commission on culture and the Ilsey Commission on copyright. Although it did not advocate direct public subsidy for publishers, the branch's submission to the Massey Commission did recommend the establishment of grants for authors.[85] During these years, the branch's internal efforts on behalf of its members included a survey of wages within the industry and development of a standard scale of fees to be applied to sales to broadcasters.[86] Acknowledging the particular concerns of educational publishers, the Canadian Educational Book Publishers' Institute was established in 1953 under the branch's auspices. Late in the decade, the branch addressed the growth of its organization, and the English-language publishing industry in general, by initiating dedicated subcommittees on issues such as market research, censorship, and public relations. When it became independant of the Board of Trade in 1962, the branch adopted the name Canadian Book Publishers' Council (CBPC). At its inception, the CBPC structured its organization into two divisions: the Canadian Textbook

Publishers' Institute (for educational publishers) and the Book Publishers' Association of Canada (for trade publishers).

The surge in economic and cultural nationalism in the 1960s, coupled with the controversial sales of Gage and Ryerson to American companies in 1970, gave rise to a new organization, the Independent Publishers' Association (IPA), in 1971. Frustrated by the perceived inaction of the CBPC regarding the economic plight of Canadian-owned publishers, the IPA brought the financial crisis to the attention of the mainstream media.[87] With a small membership composed of young presses, such as Peter Martin Associates and House of Anansi Press, as well as several older and well-established Canadian-owned houses, notably Clarke, Irwin and University of Toronto Press, the IPA called for the implementation of federal policy and financial programs to protect and promote the domestic industry. Underlying the association's objectives was the conviction that 'a vigorous, Canadian-owned and -controlled book publishing industry is essential to the educational, cultural, social, and economic life of a united Canada.'[88]

The regional book publishing associations that emerged in the 1970s shared this vision. The British Columbia Publishers' Group (est. 1974), the Alberta Publishers' Association (est. 1975), and the Atlantic Publishers' Association (est. 1976) affiliated with the IPA with the aim of strengthening their member firms' local and national profiles. The Manitoba Independent Publishers' Association (est. 1976) and the Saskatchewan Publishers' Group (est. 1980), which began as more informal collectives, were similarly motivated. These regional groups lobbied provincial governments for public support, investigated textbook purchasing, and co-operated in matters of warehousing, distribution, and promotion. The Literary Press Group (est. 1975), another IPA subgroup, conducted a national market survey and issued catalogues featuring member presses from coast to coast. Regional and specialized publishers were also marketed through the IPA's Canada Books and Canadian Book Information Centre, which promoted educational and trade materials, respectively.

By the time the IPA became the Association of Canadian Publishers (ACP) in 1976, it had undergone a shift from a largely Ontario-centred lobby group to a multi-faceted trade organization with national representation. With over a hundred active and associate members, it rivalled the CBPC, with approximately fifty members, in political activities, if not in market share. Despite intermittent co-operative projects, the ACP and the CBPC remained divided on the key points of the necessity of a Canadian-owned industry and the appropriate level of government involvement in the sector.[89] The ACP was steadfast in its political goals, as evinced by its 1980 publication, *Canadian Publishing: An Industrial Strategy for Its Preservation and Development in the Eighties*, which reiterated demands for interventionist policies similar to those it proposed to the Ontario Royal Commission on Book Publishing in 1971.

While some publishers remained staunchly devoted to one association or the other (Jack McClelland, for example, refused to join the IPA/ACP), others, such as University of Toronto Press (UTP), found value in belonging to both. In 1972, UTP also led organizational efforts in the field of scholarly publishing. Three years after the press's launch of its international journal *Scholarly Publishing* in 1969, UTP director Marsh Jeanneret took a leading role in founding both the Association of Canadian University Presses / L'Association des presses universitaires canadiennes and the International Association of Scholarly Publishers.[90] The Canadian organization, which brought together English- and French-language scholarly presses, envisioned a collaborative relationship with existing trade associations and aimed to provide 'a basis for co-operation and exchange of information to aid publication of the results of scholarship, and of Canadian scholarship in particular.'[91]

The proliferation of associations in English Canada in the 1970s, while indicative of a diversified publishing sector, produced what has been called an 'alphabet jungle' of conflicting mandates.[92] In 1975 the Book and Periodical Development Council (BPDC) was formed as an umbrella group to encourage communication between organizations across the trade and to present a coordinated lobby to government.[93] Originally consisting of the Canadian Booksellers' Association, the Canadian Library Association, the Canadian Periodical Publishers' Association, the IPA/ACP, the CBPC, and the Writers' Union of Canada, the BPDC advocated on many fronts to increase the cultural and market profile of Canadian publications; many of its early initiatives remain active, including the Canadian Children's Book Centre and Freedom to Read Week.

Professional Development and Formal Training

Until mid-century, most training of publishing personnel took place on the job. Prior to that time, publishers occasionally visited university campuses to outline the general contours of the trade for the benefit of potential future employees. In 1928, for example, Hugh Eayrs, president of Macmillan Company of Canada, addressed a group of business students on the topic of 'The Printing and Publishing Industries as a Field of Employment for University Graduates.'[94] Some addresses were tailored for individuals already employed in the book trade, such as Jack McClelland's overview of 'Book Publishing in Canada' delivered to the Booksellers' Staff Training Course in Toronto in 1956.[95] Professional development workshops aimed at those working in publishing were pioneered by the Book Promotion and Editorial Club (est. 1951; later the Book Publishers' Professional Association), an organization Nancy Earle's case study discusses in detail below. Other professional associations followed the club's lead, offering workshops on subjects ranging from production to promotion. In 1979 freelance editors, a substantial part of the publishing workforce, created their own organization devoted to professional concerns, the Freelance Editors' Association. It was the forerunner of the Editors' Association of Canada / Association canadienne des réviseurs.

Formal accreditation for those entering the publishing industry began when Toronto's Centennial College launched a program in 'Industrial Editing and Book Publishing' in 1972 under the direction of Craig Barrett. To provide a 'working lab' for students, Barrett established the Centennial College Press in 1973.[96] In the following two decades, further accredited programs would emerge, including the Banff summer publishing workshops in Alberta, as well as certificate or degree programs at institutions such as Ryerson University in Toronto and Simon Fraser University and Langara College in Vancouver.

CASE STUDY
From Tea Room to Top Floor: The Book Publishers' Professional Association
– Nancy Earle

From 1951 to the present day, the activities of the Book Publishers' Professional Association (BPPA) have reflected the self-directed efforts of publishing personnel to overcome professional isolation, improve professional standards, and promote the book trade overall. What began as a small club for 'editorial and publicity types' – the majority of them women holding non-executive positions in trade and educational houses – developed by the 1970s into the Canadian publishing industry's main provider of professional development opportunities.

Women's contributions to publishing in the years following the Second World War have been described as under-recognized and under-remunerated. Unlike male employees, the most dedicated of whom progressed through clerical and sales positions to executive appointments, women typically worked in-house, under a glass ceiling.[97] Despite the scarcity of advancement and training opportunities, however, publishing was an appealing prospect for career-minded women, offering them intellectual and prestigious work at a time when universities were less welcoming to female professionals.[98]

The BPPA began at the Hearthstone Tea Rooms in Toronto in May 1951 as the Book Promotion and Editorial Club (BPEC). Addressing this gathering of thirty-six women and one man, founding president Barbara Byam of McGraw-Hill observed, 'We do different sorts of jobs, editorial, advertising, and promotion, and some of us are jacks-of-all-trades.' Describing the participants' common ground, she pointed to the specificity of their interests and skills: 'We are a very rare people – we not only read books, which automatically puts us in a minority, but we also help make and distribute them; what is more, we are doing it in Canada. This makes us a minority of a minority of a minority.'[99]

These 'very rare people' envisioned the club as a forum for discussions primarily focused on book advertising and promotion. Unlike the executives who attended the Canadian Book Publishers' Council, members did not represent their firms in an official capacity, but met on a voluntary basis as 'a community of interest.' Having established an eight-woman executive, the following month the BPEC presented two lectures – Kay Mathers of Clarke, Irwin on publicity and promotion, and Eleanor Harman of University of Toronto Press on the role of scholarly publishing – as well as a report on the recent convention of the American Booksellers Association by the British Book Service's Evelyn Weatherall.[100] The tone was immediately set for the club's wide-ranging investigations into the theory and practice of publishing. Lectures and debates would remain a mainstay of the BPEC's activities in the decades to come.

Through the 1960s and '70s, the group attracted dozens of new members, men and women working in publishing and the allied trades of printing, graphic design, and bookselling. Design became a major focus in these years, and the club invited commercial artists as guest speakers and sponsored The Look of Books, a touring exhibition of Canadian-produced titles chosen for their design merit.[101]

Despite the record of their professional activities, members observed a lingering perception of the BPEC as primarily a social club. In 1974, under the presidency of Angela Rebeiro, the group adopted a new name, the Book Publishers' Professional Association, and renewed its emphasis on professional development.[102] Recognizing the lack of formal training opportunities, the BPPA administered an annual series of professional development workshops open to anyone working in the industry. Practical seminars on subjects such as contracts, trade and educational editing, typography, and marketing were regularly offered alongside the continuing program of speakers and panels addressing issues facing the industry. The BPPA also continued to work toward strengthening relations across the trade, creating the Roy Britnell Award for booksellers in 1974.[103] Three years later, the group honoured one of its own with this award: Peggy Blackstock, who like co-recipient Bill Roberts was proprietor of Shirley Leishman Books in Ottawa, had been a founding member and early president of the BPEC.

By the 1970s, women were gaining more prominence in the industry, which itself had witnessed substantial development and growth. At the close of the decade, the BPPA – now 'an organization of approximately 275 men and women, most of whom are employed in executive, editorial, sales or promotion capacities in Canadian houses'[104] – had also changed considerably, reflecting the profession it had served for over a generation.

chapter 6

PUBLISHING BOOKS IN FRENCH

Book Publishing in Quebec

JACQUES MICHON

During the twentieth century, French-language publishing in Quebec witnessed a decline of wholesale bookseller-publishers, a system that had been in place since the end of the nineteenth century, and the slow emergence of independent publishing houses, most located in Montreal. Prior to 1960, books were typically published and distributed in French Canada by book wholesalers. Through their revenue from importing books, wholesalers were able to fund publications and series such as Librairie Beauchemin's Bibliothèque canadienne. Unlike the publisher-agents who handled English-language books, wholesalers did not hold exclusive rights to the books they sold. In addition to facing competition among themselves for the same titles, their sales were often undercut by institutions that imported books directly from overseas. In order to reduce the resulting financial risks, book wholesalers developed other commercial activities, such as bookbinding, selling stationery and office supplies, printing books and magazines, printing self-published books and textbooks, and even selling religious items and manufacturing church vestments, as did Joseph-Pierre Garneau in Quebec City.

The Beginnings of Independent Publishing Houses

After the First World War, independent publishing houses, which specialized in the production of books and pamphlets and were completely divorced from the traditional wholesaler-publisher system, began to emerge in Montreal. The repeated failure of French Canadians to gain official recognition for their language in Ontario and the western provinces, compounded by the imposition of conscription during the war, had generated a wave of nationalism in Quebec that provided the impetus for this new type of business. Such independent publishing houses relied on the support of readers loyal to the nationalist cause.

The first publishing house of this kind was the Bibliothèque de l'Action française, founded in 1918 by the Ligue des droits du français (after 1921 the Ligue d'Action française) to issue fiction, novels for young people, and large numbers of patriotic pamphlets. Inspired by the ideas of Lionel Groulx and devoted to the defence of French Canada, the Ligue's membership of prominent citizens and intellectuals had earlier initiated the *Almanach de la langue française* (1916–37) and the magazine *L'Action française* (1917–27; later *L'Action canadienne-française*, 1928–9). These propaganda efforts, which remained independent of specific political parties, culminated in the creation of the Bibliothèque.

The first trade publishing houses to produce and promote French-Canadian books and authors were run by people affiliated with this nationalist movement: Albert Lévesque, Édouard Garand, Eugène Achard, Albert Pelletier, and Louis Carrier. Carrier was the only one to seek a relationship with English Canada, developing a bilingual and bicultural catalogue. In promoting Canadian books exclusively and introducing new authors, the publishers of the interwar period initiated a decisive shift in the profession.

Albert Lévesque, who acquired *L'Action française* and the Bibliothèque de l'Action française in 1926, ran a publishing house devoted to general literature. It was known successively as the Librairie d'Action française (1926), the Librairie d'Action canadienne-française (1928), and Éditions Albert Lévesque (1930).[1] The most important house of its time, it covered all fields of intellectual and literary activity in French Canada. By 1936 Lévesque had issued more than 280 titles in some thirty series,[2] ranging from children's picture books to works on political economy. Surpassing the efforts of his predecessors, he introduced young writers committed to freeing French-Canadian literature from the didactic novel and pastoral poetry, and raised the status of the profession of publishing, of which he was the most eminent representative during the period between the wars. Writers Alfred DesRochers, Jovette Bernier, Harry Bernard, Louis Dantin, Albert Pelletier, Eva Sénécal, and Édouard Montpetit established the house's reputation.

Édouard Garand made his mark in the field of popular books in 1923, when he launched the series Le Roman canadien, which featured historical novels and adventure stories by local authors. Presented in the form of garishly illustrated magazines (26 × 18 cm), the series was similar to those popular in France before the war and which made the reputation of Fayard and Flammarion. Adapted to the Canadian context, the format under Garand's hand conveyed an unabashed nationalist message, as illustrated by Le Roman canadien's logo, which showed Jean-Olivier Chénier, a hero of 1837, wearing a ceinture fléchée and carrying a rifle. The series reached a broad public and was extremely successful.

Eugène Achard took advantage of the growth of children's literature in the 1920s to create the Librairie générale canadienne, a publishing house devoted solely to stories for young people, with an emphasis on the heroes of New France. In the same period, Louis Carrier founded a bilingual and bicultural publishing house, Les Éditions du Mercure / The Mercury Press, which co-published a number of titles with Ryerson Press of Toronto. Like his Toronto colleague Lorne Pierce, Carrier tried to break through the barrier between the 'two solitudes,' and promoted Canadian literature not only in Canada but also abroad, with representatives in London and New York.[3] The publisher's French-language catalogue listed books by Louis Dantin, Camille Roy, Maurice Hébert, and Robert Choquette, while his English-language offerings included titles from Lorne Pierce and Sir Andrew Macphail, and English translations of works by Georges Bouchard and Georges Bugnet.

Merely to publish Canadian books at this time was an act of cultural patriotism. Quebec's Department of the Provincial Secretary supported the endeavour by making bulk purchases from the print runs of such books. However, the Depression put an end to this collaboration. Éditions du Mercure closed down, and Éditions Édouard Garand reduced its production before finally ending operations in the early 1930s.

In 1933 Albert Pelletier, Lévesque's friend and collaborator, founded a small Montreal publishing house, Éditions du Totem, which by 1938 had published a dozen titles, including two very successful novels, Claude-Henri Grignon's Un homme et son péché (1933) and Jean-Charles Harvey's Les demi-civilisés (1934). However, the magazine Les Idées, established in 1935, exhausted Pelletier's energies, forcing the closure of his entire publishing operation in 1939.[4] In the interim, Albert Lévesque sold his business to his manager, Roger Gagnon, who was not able to save it.[5]

The Impact of the Second World War

The Second World War firmly established and consolidated the position of independent French-Canadian publishing houses. After the interruption of trade relations with France in June 1940, Quebec became a world centre of French-language publishing, a position that allowed its own industry to grow rapidly while raising its international profile. In order to meet the needs of French-language booksellers outside France, as well as the demands of Quebec schools and the general public, several publishing houses were founded and rapidly expanded. In Montreal, new houses such as Éditions Fides, Éditions de l'Arbre, Éditions Bernard Valiquette, and Éditions Variétés each issued hundreds of titles per year. To meet the ever-growing demand, many printing offices and booksellers also began producing books and establishing their own imprints. An estimated 10,000 titles were pub-lished by Quebec's French-language publishers between 1940 and 1946,[6] two-thirds of them reprints of French and Belgian books and the other third new works by Quebec authors or Europeans writing in exile.

The post-war period, by contrast, was a difficult time for most literary publish-ers, and many went out of business. From 1946 to 1950, membership in the trade organization, the Société des éditeurs canadiens du livre français, dropped by half, from twenty-seven to thirteen.[7] Writers took refuge with Librairie Beauchemin, in the book clubs of Pierre Tisseyre (Le Cercle du livre de France [CLF]) and Paul Michaud (Institut littéraire du Québec), or in new small Montreal houses such as Éditions d'Orphée and Éditions de l'Hexagone. The post-war period was marked mainly by expansion in educational publishing, children's books, and mass-market titles.

The Publishers of the Quiet Revolution

In the 1960s, Quebec was shaken by the Quiet Revolution, and its publishing indus-try was transformed. The new social climate fostered a questioning outlook and the discussion of ideas, leading to the emergence of new publishers. Éditions de l'Homme, Éditions du Jour, Éditions Hurtubise HMH, Éditions Leméac, and Édi-tions Parti pris were founded and gave voice to a new generation of writers. Estab-lished houses, such as L'Hexagone, Fides, and Le Cercle du livre de France, also took part in the redefinition of Quebec's identity. Supporting this production of Cana-dian books were grants from the Canada Council for the Arts (est. 1957) and the min-istère des Affaires culturelles du Québec (est. 1961).

Jacques Hébert, crusading journalist and co-founder of Éditions de l'Homme, published books to stimulate social change. The one-dollar book 'distributed every-where, like a newspaper' was his most spectacular innovation.[8] With these low-cost books, he gained a broad readership for exposés of the failings of Quebec society. By forming a partnership with Edgar Lespérance, a publisher and distributor of dime novels, Hébert was able to free books from the ghetto of an underdeveloped retail book trade and reach a wider public. From the outset, books from Éditions de l'Homme sold in tens of thousands of copies, sometimes surpassing even the most optimistic predictions, as in the case in 1960 of *Les insolences du frère Untel*, discussed in the following case study by Jacques Michon.[9]

Hébert also had plans for literary publishing projects; however, these were not shared by his associate Lespérance. Consequently, in May 1961 he left Éditions de l'Homme and founded Éditions du Jour, which subsequently introduced the young writers of the 1960s. While Lespérance continued to develop Éditions de l'Homme, putting out journalistic non-fiction and how-to books, Hébert at Éditions du Jour applied the one-dollar-book formula to fiction and introduced original literary works to the mass market. He sold 10,000 copies of a collection of stories by Jean-Louis Gagnon, *La mort d'un nègre* (1961), and 6,000 copies of Marie-Claire Blais's third novel, *Le jour est noir* (1962), in just a few weeks. Even poetry collections, modestly presented, attracted thousands of readers: in three years, 4,000 copies of Gatien Lapointe's *Ode au Saint-Laurent* (1963) and 6,000 copies of *Le premier mot* (1967) were printed. Hébert also recruited writers who were just starting out, among them Roch Carrier, Jean-Marie Poupart, and Jacques Poulin; in a few years, they became leading authors.[10] In order to support the publication of avant-garde literary work, which sometimes failed to cover its costs, Hébert issued more popular works on current events as well as cookbooks by Sister Berthe and Janette Bertrand.

Hébert's instincts were confirmed in 1966 when Marie-Claire Blais was awarded France's Prix Médicis for *Une saison dans la vie d'Emmanuel*. This novel, which was translated into many languages, opened the door to international publishing for Hébert. In 1969 he passed the literary editorship of the publishing house to Victor-Lévy Beaulieu, who attracted the avant-garde poets of the time and a few well-known authors. But the October Crisis of 1970 soon dealt a hard blow to the director of Éditions du Jour; its writers took a dim view of Hébert's friendship with Prime Minister Pierre Elliott Trudeau, who had imposed the War Measures Act on Quebec. In 1973 Victor-Lévy Beaulieu's resignation for explicitly political reasons led to the departure of other authors.[11] Also faced with administrative problems, Hébert withdrew in 1974. From then on, production at Éditions du Jour gradually declined, and its remaining authors moved over to Éditions Quinze, Éditions Alain Stanké, and Leméac, the last of these well known for publishing Michel Tremblay and Antonine Maillet.

Éditions HMH, founded by Claude Hurtubise in 1960, also excelled in the dissemination of new ideas. After serving as co-director of Éditions de l'Arbre in the 1940s, Hurtubise was involved in propagating the ideas of the *Cité libre* generation, including Pierre Elliott Trudeau, Jean Le Moyne, Gilles Marcotte, and Robert Élie, all of whom were published in Constantes, HMH's prestigious non-fiction series of the 1960s, which also included all of Marshall McLuhan's books in French translation.

Éditions Parti pris, founded in 1964, was run by a group of young intellectuals, recent graduates of Collège Sainte-Marie or the Université de Montréal who, like their elders, were involved in the political debates of the Quiet Revolution, campaigning for secularism, socialism, and Quebec independence. They also published a magazine of the same name, which helped establish the credibility of the new French-Canadian identity, one which was no longer defined in terms of ethnicity and religion, but of a space, a 'nation' – Quebec. Under the influence of Parti pris, within a few years the term 'French Canadian' was gradually displaced in Quebec's social discourse by 'Québécois.'

Although Éditions Fides stopped publishing magazines during the 1960s, it doubled its revenues by creating series of pocketbooks and reference books on Quebec literature.[12] The CLF, under Pierre Tisseyre, became a full-fledged publisher, and issued almost a quarter of all new novels in the 1960s, including works by Claude Jasmin, Claire Martin, Hubert Aquin, André Langevin, Gérard Bessette, and Gilles Archambault. In 1973 the CLF started its Deux solitudes series, publishing some thirty English-Canadian novels in French translation.

Éditions de l'Hexagone also went through a period of expansion during the 1960s. Its Rétrospectives series, in which it reissued works by several contemporary poets, was a remarkable success: *Poèmes* (1963), by Alain Grandbois, *L'âge de la parole* (1965), by Roland Giguère, and *Le réel absolu* (1971), by Paul-Marie Lapointe, enjoyed cumulative printings ranging from 8,000 to 13,000 copies.[13]

A Period of Transition

After a decade of relative prosperity, when the number of active publishers more than doubled, Quebec's book industry experienced a slowdown. The most significant contributing factor was the shortcomings of the distribution system. By the mid-1970s, many houses were in difficulty. Éditions du Jour, Éditions HMH, and Éditions Fides were showing losses, and their respective founders, Jacques Hébert, Claude Hurtubise, and Father Paul-Aimé Martin, CSC, were forced out. The industry as a whole witnessed a drop in productivity as well as decreases in print runs and the number of titles published. The book world was changing, and, in fact, the distribution system had undergone profound changes since the war. The wholesale bookseller-publisher was a thing of the past. The Commission d'enquête sur le commerce du livre au Québec, chaired by Maurice Bouchard, identified the problem in 1963. The commission's report criticized the unfair practices of the wholesalers, both lay and religious, who had imposed their rules on the book trade and hindered the development of retail booksellers.

In addition, the rapid development of the Quebec book market after the Second World War had opened the way for Parisian publishers to set up in Quebec. Even more aggressive than Quebec's book wholesalers, these firms initiated their own distribution systems in direct competition with them. Librairie Hachette, whose influence extended throughout the industry – publishing, bookselling, and distribution – took the lead. The exclusive distribution of books that it established in the 1960s reduced the wholesalers' influence, and at the beginning of the 1970s, Hachette acquired a large interest in the Centre éducatif et culturel, an important textbook publisher, which in turn became a significant shareholder of Librairie Garneau.

To counter this expansionism, as early as 1961 people in the Quebec book industry mobilized under the banner of the Conseil supérieur du livre and called on governments to put an end to foreign control.[14] These demands went unheeded until after the Parti Québécois came to power. In 1979 the Quebec government passed the Act Respecting the Development of Quebec Firms in the Book Industry (LRQ, D-8.1). Known as Bill 51 and presented by the minister of cultural affairs, it gave publishing houses wholly owned by Canadian citizens resident in Quebec the exclusive right to sell books to educational institutions. From then on, local firms were once again able to prosper and to compete with the European distribution giants. However, between 1975 and 1979, several publishers paid the price for this period of transition.

Almost twenty years passed between the Bouchard Report of 1963 and Quebec's enactment of a new book trade policy that favoured the development of independent bookstores, free of control by the wholesalers. Implemented in 1981 after approval in 1979, the same year the federal government created the Book Publishing Industry Development Program (BPIDP), this policy would result in a new balance among the various players – publishers, local booksellers and distributors, and foreign firms. Under the combined effects of these provincial and federal actions, the Quebec book industry would rapidly recover and experience a period of unprecedented growth during the 1980s.

6.1 [Jean-Paul Desbiens], *Les insolences du frère Untel* (Montreal: Éditions de l'Homme, 1960). Courtesy of Éditions de l'Homme.

CASE STUDY
Les insolences du frère Untel / The Impertinences of Brother Anonymous
– Jacques Michon

At the beginning of the Quiet Revolution, Éditions de l'Homme became known for its one-dollar exposés of the abusive regime of Quebec premier Maurice Duplessis. Among these titles were Jacques Hébert's *Scandale à Bordeaux, Le chrétien et les élections*, by Abbés Gérard Dion and Louis O'Neill, and Gérard Filion's *Les confidences d'un commissaire d'école*. However, Éditions de l'Homme's greatest success was *Les insolences du frère Untel* (see illus. 6.1, above).[15] Published in September 1960, just two and a half months after the provincial election victory of Jean Lesage's Liberal Party, the book criticized the incompetence and social irresponsibility of the Department of Public

Instruction (DPI) and demanded nothing less than its abolition. For proponents of educational reform, it came at just the right time.

In November 1959, two months after Duplessis's death, Brother Pierre-Jérôme (born Jean-Paul Desbiens) sent a letter to the editor of *Le Devoir*, André Laurendeau, who immediately published it under the pseudonym 'Frère Un Tel.' The young brother's attack on the pitiful state of the French language in Quebec, which he blamed on the highest authorities in the education system, immediately gave rise to lively discussion among readers of *Le Devoir*. Recognizing a potential best-seller, Jacques Hébert, publisher of Éditions de l'Homme, approached Brother Pierre-Jérôme in July 1960 and proposed to issue a volume of his writings. The fledgling author agreed, but his superior general got wind of the affair and forbade the book. Hébert proceeded in spite of this edict, releasing the book that September on the very first day of school. It was an immediate success: 17,000 copies were snatched up in ten days; 100,000 were sold in four months. The mystery surrounding the book's author, whose identity was gradually revealed in the media, kept the public's interest engaged, its curiosity already having been aroused by the brother's provocative writing.

The young brother attacked not only the shortcomings of the education system but also the cultural alienation of French Canada, as represented by the decline of the French language into an anglicized dialect. 'Our pupils speak joual because they think joual,'[16] he wrote. The book struck a chord throughout Quebec. Some workers demonstrated their support by sending the author a poster comparing him with the major hockey star of the era: 'Frère Untel, je vous aime encore plus que Maurice Richard' (Frère Untel, I love you even more than Maurice Richard).[17] A mother declared that she had purchased a copy of the book for each of her children. People identified with Frère Untel, who articulated the frustrations they had accumulated during the period they termed the 'Grande Noirceur.' The English translation, *The Impertinences of Brother Anonymous*,[18] was also a big success, selling 15,000 copies.

Frère Untel's book quickly became the symbol of the Quiet Revolution and its social reforms, particularly in education. The most noteworthy result was the abolition of the DPI and the creation, in 1964, of the Department of Education. Recruited by Quebec's major architect of educational reform, Minister Paul Gérin-Lajoie, Jean-Paul Desbiens held an executive position in the ministry from 1964 to 1970.

Ontario

ROBERT YERGEAU

Francophones in Ontario, who make up approximately 5 per cent of the province's population, have benefited from a small but vital provincial publishing industry since early in the twentieth century. Although much of this population has been located in eastern and northern Ontario, particularly in towns along the border with Quebec and in northern communities such as Sudbury and Hearst, Ottawa represented the only centre of French-language publishing in the province until 1973, when Éditions Prise de parole was founded in Sudbury.

Franco-Ontarian print culture has been inextricably linked to the struggle for the preservation and advancement of French-language education. While the Association canadienne-française d'éducation de l'Ontario (ACFÉO) was founded in 1910 in general defence of this cause, the Oblates of Mary Immaculate (OMI) of Ottawa played a decisive role as well by establishing several major Franco-Ontarian publishing institutions, including the newspaper Le Droit and the Centre catholique and Éditions de l'Université d'Ottawa at the University of Ottawa.

In 1913 Father Charles Charlebois, OMI, initiated Le Droit specifically to fight Regulation 17, provincial legislation which prohibited teaching in French beyond the second grade. From the beginning, this daily also exhibited a general concern for francophone culture in the province. With job printing providing a means of support, the newspaper began to publish books and pamphlets of a religious and patriotic nature, including two English titles on the schools issue in 1914. By 1927 a sales counter within the office had grown into a full-fledged bookstore. By the end of the 1940s, some forty booklets, ranging from printed speeches to manifestos, had appeared; another ten were issued in the 1950s and 1960s. According to François Paré, 'Any history of literary writing in French-speaking Ontario must take into account these sometimes unorthodox manifestations of the written word, since they are essential to understanding sites of collective representation in literature.'[19]

The OMI's second initiative, the Centre catholique de l'Université d'Ottawa, emerged in December 1935. Founded by Father André Guay, OMI, the Centre catholique became one of the largest religious publishing houses in Canada. Its Prie avec l'Église (1936; Prions en église after 1965), a 'missalette' distributed before Sunday mass for use during the service and throughout the following week, was the most widely disseminated of its publications. Familiar to Catholics across Canada, this periodical, which was translated into English (*Pray with the Church*, 1936; *Living with Christ*, after 1948), reached weekly print runs of 200,000 copies in 1960.

In 1965, when the religious faculties and institutes of the University of Ottawa became Université Saint-Paul / Saint Paul University (named in honour of Pope Paul VI), the Centre catholique moved with them, changing its name in September 1969 to Novalis, from the Latin *novalis*, meaning 'freshly ploughed field ready for seeding.' From its offices at Saint Paul University, Novalis presently oversees the editorial content of the books, magazines, and bulletins published under its imprint, while production and marketing services are provided by Bayard Presse Canada.

Éditions de l'Université d'Ottawa, the OMI's third publishing initiative, began under the direction of Father Raoul Leblanc, OMI, who in 1937 issued the house's first book, Father Louis Le Jeune's *Le Chevalier Pierre Le Moyne, sieur d'Iberville*. In 1946, Father Leblanc was replaced by Father Léopold Lanctôt, OMI. After the university's religious faculties were reconstituted as Saint Paul University, and a new secular institution under the name of the University of Ottawa was formed, Lanctôt remained with the press at the University of Ottawa, occupying the position of director until 1982. Under Lanctôt, the house's list consisted mainly of scholarly works, with some 400 titles – 75 per cent in French and 25 per cent in English – issued by the late 1970s.[20] In 1987, on the occasion of its fiftieth anniversary, Éditions de l'Université d'Ottawa changed its name to Presses de l'Université d'Ottawa / University of Ottawa Press.

Until the 1970s there were no French-language literary publishing houses in Ontario. Although the Imprimerie Beauregard (1907–2003), a family printing firm located in Ottawa, had published such creative writers as Jules Tremblay (seven titles) and Emma-Adèle Lacerte (six titles) prior to the Second World War, the founding in 1973 of Éditions Prise de parole, in Sudbury by poets Denis St-Jules and Gaston Tremblay, marked the real beginning of Franco-Ontarian literary publishing. The house's first title, *Lignes-signes* (1973), a collection of four suites of poems by Tremblay, St-Jules, Placide Gaboury, and Jean Lalonde, reflected the spirit of the 1970s. Prise de parole lived up to its name, operating as a collective and 'speaking out' through its emphasis on oral forms such as theatre, music, and poetry. The founding of several more literary publishers in the 1980s and 1990s consolidated this movement and introduced a new generation of Franco-Ontarian authors.

The first Franco-Ontarian venture into educational publishing emerged in 1974 when the Centre franco-ontarien de ressources pédagogiques (CFORP) was founded in Ottawa with a mandate to make educational materials available to French-language schools in Ontario. Defining itself as a multi-service centre, this house had its own press and bookstore, and produced books and managed projects for French-language school boards in Ontario. Under the leadership of Gisèle Lalonde until 1985, the CFORP became the major French-language educational publisher in Ontario. One of its significant accomplishments in 1982 was to issue two study guides to *Anthologie de textes littéraires franco-ontariens*, the first collection of Franco-Ontarian literature. Published by Fides that same year, this four-volume anthology represented a watershed in establishing the French-language literary corpus of Ontario.[21]

Acadia

DOMINIQUE MARQUIS

The emergence of Acadian publishing largely depended upon *L'Évangéline* (Digby, NS, 1887 – Moncton, NB, 1982), a daily newspaper which had a significant impact on its community and whose presses occasionally printed books. Local and religious histories, such as Désiré-François-Xavier Léger's *Histoire de la paroisse de Saint-Pierre de Cocagne* (1920) and Antoine Bernard's *Histoire de l'Acadie* (1938), typified titles to appear under its imprint. Occasionally *L'Évangéline* produced or reprinted polemical texts; for example, in 1929 it reprinted two earlier works by James E. Branch whose titles speak for themselves: *L'émigrant acadien: Drame social acadien en 3 actes* (18--?) and *Jusqu'à la mort! ... pour nos écoles! Drame canadien de la 'question des écoles'* (189?). The weekly *Le Madawaska* (Edmundston, NB, 1913–) also published Acadian writing on local history and society, including *L'Éducation des petits acadiens* (1934), by Calixte F. Savoie, and *Mère Maillet* (1934), by the Religious Hospitallers of Saint-Joseph. Books occasionally appeared from Imprimerie acadienne in Moncton, including Antoine J. Léger's *Une fleur d'Acadie: Un épisode du grand dérangement* (1946). Such volumes from newspaper or commercial presses were usually published at the author's expense.

Like many francophones in the West and Ontario, Acadian authors often looked to Quebec for publication. Most notably, beginning with her first novel, *Pointe-aux-Coques*, in 1958, all of Antonine Maillet's books were issued in Montreal. Éditions des Aboiteaux, the first true Acadian publishing house, which was founded in Moncton by Anselme Chiasson in 1961, attempted to remedy this situation.[22] An expert in folklore, Father Chiasson published some fifteen volumes of his own collections of Acadian historical materials and folk traditions.

However, Éditions des Aboiteaux did not satisfy the aspirations of the poets and other authors of the Acadian literary renaissance of the early 1970s, a period of unprecedented cultural ferment. To meet this demand, Éditions d'Acadie was created in 1972 under the aegis of the Université de Moncton and quickly became a cultural beacon for francophones in the region.[23] Its first title was Raymond Le Blanc's *Cri de terre* (1973), a collection of poems which enjoyed an exceptional print run of 3,500 copies, and was heralded as an 'essential work' and a manifestation of 'the cultural renaissance of an Acadia that flourishes in secret and refuses to let itself die.'[24] Other poetry volumes followed this first success: Acadian literature, like many national literatures, marked its entry into modernity through poetry. In 1974 Éditions d'Acadie received its first grant from the Canada Council and its first significant order from the New Brunswick Department of Education.

Through the remainder of the 1970s, Éditions d'Acadie enjoyed strong public support and such major successes as Melvin Gallant's children's book *Ti-Jean* (1973), the abundantly documented *La cuisine traditionnelle en Acadie* (1975), by Marielle Boudreau and Melvin Gallant, and Louis Haché's *Adieu, P'tit Chipagan* (1978), which won the first Prix France–Acadie in 1979. The press introduced many new writers, contributing to the emergence of Acadian voices, and by 1980 its catalogue listed nearly fifty titles, including poetry, novels, non-fiction, children's books, and textbooks. Éditions d'Acadie set an example for subsequent publishing houses, including Éditions Perce-Neige (1980), Bouton d'or Acadie (1996), and Éditions de la Francophonie (2001). These emerged in Moncton as Éditions d'Acadie itself began to decline, finally declaring bankruptcy in 2000.

The West

DOMINIQUE MARQUIS

The story of French-language print culture and publishing in the Western provinces begins with the Oblate Missionaries of Mary Immaculate. These priests, who had established themselves on the Prairies in 1845, spared no effort in providing local French-speaking communities with effective means of communication. In 1928 they lent their financial support and expertise to the creation of the newspaper *La Survivance* (Edmonton), which became *Le Franco-albertain* in 1967 and *Le Franco* in 1979. The Oblates financed and managed these papers, contributing articles and sometimes undertaking typesetting and printing.[25] Their publications spread a Catholic message and defended the French fact in the Prairies, thus playing a decisive role in the affirmation of French-Canadian identity in Manitoba, Saskatchewan, and Alberta.

The Oblates also published books. In Edmonton, Imprimerie La Survivance issued thirty-eight titles between 1929 and 1979, twenty-five of them in French.[26] Other community newspapers, *La Liberté* in St Boniface and *Le Patriote de l'Ouest* in Duck Lake, Saskatchewan, occasionally produced pamphlets such as *Les droits du français en Saskatchewan* (Prince Albert, SK, 1919), commemorative volumes such as *Souvenir des fêtes de la consécration épiscopale de Son Excellence Mgr Émile Yelle* (St Boniface, 1934), and devotional works. Still, in order to publish their books, many authors had to look to Quebec, as did Jean Féron in the 1920s.[27]

Éditions du Blé was the first distinctive literary publisher to emerge west of Ontario. Founded in St Boniface, Manitoba, in 1974 by two historians, Lionel Dorge and Robert Painchaud, a poet, Paul Savoie, and a teacher of French literature, Annette Saint-Pierre, Éditions du Blé was a non-profit co-operative supported by grants from the Canada Council. It focused on works by writers from Manitoba and the other western provinces and books about these regions, thereby offering French-speaking writers their own outlet for cultural expression. During its first year, Éditions du Blé produced three books: *Salamandre*, a poetry collection by Paul Savoie, *Les éléphants de tante Louise*, a children's play by Roger Auger, and *Salut les amis! Visitons le Manitoba avec Nico, Niski et ...*, a children's activity book by Claude Dorge. Through the 1970s, the house published an average of five titles a year in a variety of genres, with an emphasis on poetry and children's literature. In 1979 internal conflict at Éditions du Blé led to the creation of another literary publishing house, Éditions des Plaines. Founded as a commercial enterprise in St Boniface by Annette Saint-Pierre and Georges Damphousse, it proved successful, publishing more than 160 titles over the next twenty years and introducing many new writers.

French-language publishing houses were slower to take hold in the other Western provinces. Between 1975 and 1978, Éditions de l'Églantier, founded by Jean-Marcel Duciaume in Edmonton, tried to lay the foundations for literature in French in Alberta with the publication of three poetry collections, but financial problems put an untimely end to the venture. In 1984 Éditions Louis Riel was established in Regina; it would become Éditions de la Nouvelle Plume in 1996. On the West Coast, francophone publication began in 1858 with the newspaper *Courrier de la Nouvelle Calédonie* (Victoria). However, significant serial publication in French did not appear until after the Second World War, originating in the small French-speaking community of Maillardville (now part of Coquitlam) and in Victoria. The weekly *Soleil de Vancouver* (later *Soleil de Colombie*), founded in 1968, endured for three decades. The Société historique franco-colombienne began to issue documents in 1977, but there was no francophone trade book publishing in British Columbia until 1994, when several titles were launched by the province's brilliantly named Éditions du Phare ouest.[28]

Over the years, and particularly from the 1970s, French-Canadian publishing emerged in the West, struggling to free itself from the influence of Quebec and affirm its own identity. Thanks to new publishers, young authors acquired a place to express themselves and to promote the values that differentiated them from earlier generations, for whom the survival of the French language had been inextricably linked to the Catholic Church.

Francophone Organizations in the Book Trade

JOSÉE VINCENT

In Quebec, the first association of book publishers came into being with the Second World War. Before establishing their own organizations, some publishers were members of the Montreal and Quebec City chambers of commerce, while others, such as Albert Lévesque and Édouard Garand, who were active in authors' associations, independently took part in promoting local production. Starting in 1940, as the profession developed and the book trade grew, regulation became necessary. Problems related to the supply of paper and to reprint rights led to the creation in 1943 of the Société des éditeurs canadiens du livre français (SÉCLF), whose members were mostly Montreal firms.[29] The SÉCLF took over the organization of book weeks from the Société des écrivains canadiens in the 1940s and 1950s. A post-war recession in the trade forced the SÉCLF to cut back its activities; by 1952 it was down to about a dozen members, booksellers and textbook publishers who had difficulty agreeing because of their divergent interests. However, there was unanimity on one issue: the need for public support for book publishing. To give more weight to their demands, in 1956 this group, under the presidency of Paul Michaud of the Institut littéraire du Québec, considered the possibility of including other book professionals, such as retail booksellers, librarians, and writers, in their organization. This project fell through for lack of funding.

With the Quiet Revolution, the entire book industry went through a period of restructuring. Textbook publishers and wholesale booksellers who sold directly to institutions without going through retail bookstores were accused of discriminatory practices. The government was asked to adopt a coherent book policy, to regulate the trade, and to create programs to support publishing. The textbook publishers, led by Louis-Philippe Boisseau of the Centre de psychologie et de pédagogie, were the first to distance themselves from the demands of the general publishers, who supported the establishment of a book commission. In 1960 these dissidents founded their own association, the Société des éditeurs canadiens de manuels scolaires, which led the SÉCLF to change its name, in 1961, to the Association des éditeurs canadiens (AÉC).

The proliferation of book publishing, as well as bookselling, organizations during this period was offset by the creation of a central body in 1961, the Conseil supérieur du livre (CSL), whose purpose was the promotion and defence of the book trades. The CSL was led by some of the most dynamic publishers and booksellers of the time: Jacques Hébert, Claude Hurtubise, Jean Bode, and, especially, Pierre Tisseyre, who was its president from 1961 to 1977, with one interruption when he was replaced by Victor Martin in 1963. Between 1962 and 1977, J.-Z.-Léon Patenaude was its secretary and then director general. In addition to providing its members with an office, the CSL published the *Catalogue de l'édition au Canada français* and the magazine *Vient de paraître*. From 1965 to 1978, the magazine covered professional news and activities in the book world, paying special attention to promotional efforts by Quebec publishers in Canada and abroad. It ceased publishing shortly before the dissolution of the CSL and was not replaced until 1982, with the creation of a new professional magazine *Livre d'ici*.

The most significant CSL activities involved promotion: it organized the Salon du livre de Montréal from 1962 to 1966, and then the Montreal International Book Fair from 1973 to 1976. The CSL also coordinated Quebec publishers' participation in major international events such as the Frankfurt Book Fair, the Salon du livre de Nice, and the Foire du livre de Bruxelles. In 1969, to provide follow-up with foreign partners, the CSL created the Agence littéraire des éditeurs canadiens-français. Finally, in collaboration with the AÉC, the CSL was involved in various initiatives to export books to France, Belgium, and the United States, including the creation of the Centres de diffusion du livre canadien-français (1967–74) and *Books from Canada / Livres du Canada* (1972–6).[30] Although these activities varied in their success, they nevertheless contributed to the promotion of the book trades in Quebec and abroad.

From 1961 to 1980, the CSL established itself as the main intermediary with governments. The numerous battles it waged for the regulation of bookselling, against foreign domination of the market, and for public investment in book publishing and promotion convinced the provincial and federal governments to take concrete measures to support the industry. However, at the end of the 1970s, dissension arose in the ranks of the organization, as publishers and booksellers did not see eye-to-eye on their priorities. The dissolution of the CSL in 1980 marked the end of these joint efforts.

chapter 7

PUBLISHING FOR CHILDREN AND STUDENTS

Publishing for Children

SUZANNE POULIOT, JUDITH SALTMAN, AND GAIL EDWARDS

Children's publishing developed differently in Canada's two major linguistic communities. In French Canada, it flourished in the first half of the twentieth century. In English-speaking Canada, while the model established before 1918 remained stable and the authors examined by Leslie McGrath in Volume 2 continued to publish, there were few new developments until the 1960s. Beginning in the mid-1970s, national structures that were established to support cultural production and reading made a decisive contribution to the publishing of children's literature in both communities.

Children's Publishing in French Canada

Publishing for children and young people soared in Quebec at the beginning of the 1920s, and until the end of the 1950s was one of the most profitable sectors of the book industry. After a slowdown caused by the abolition of the system of book prizes in 1964, there was another period of significant growth in the 1970s, resulting in part from the founding of Communication-jeunesse in 1971, a non-profit organization dedicated to promoting children's books.

At the beginning of the 1920s, three magazines – *L'Oiseau bleu* (1921–40), created by the Société Saint-Jean-Baptiste de Montréal, *L'Abeille* (1925–47), published by the

Brothers of Christian Instruction, and *La Ruche écolière* (1927–34), founded by Eugène Achard, the publisher of the Librairie générale canadienne – contributed to the development of children's literature and the promotion of children's authors and illustrators. After the adoption in 1926 of a government regulation requiring school boards to reserve 50 per cent of their book purchases for Canadian books,[1] publishers such as Granger Frères, Albert Lévesque, and Eugène Achard initiated new juvenile series. In 1926, Granger Frères published *L'Annuaire Granger pour la jeunesse*, an annual children's magazine, and in 1930 it established the Collection canadienne, which, following the example of Beauchemin, reissued nineteenth-century books originally intended for an adult readership. Subsequently, Granger Frères developed a 'younger' catalogue, recruiting authors who wrote especially for youth, such as Tante Lucille, Cécile Lagacé, and Marie-Claire Daveluy, whose Perrine et Charlot series it reprinted.

In the interwar period, publishers developed age-specific series for young readers. In addition to stories and legends, they introduced novels for adolescents and non-fiction series about geography and the natural sciences. Albert Lévesque, the most innovative publisher in this area, encouraged his authors of books for adults – Lionel Groulx, Harry Bernard, and Louis Dantin – to write for young people. He created eight series by these writers and also recruited new authors, including Maxine (pseudonym of Marie-Caroline-Alexandra Bouchette) and Odette Oligny. Eugène Achard of the Librairie générale canadienne published large numbers of patriotic series as well as historical novels, biographies, travel memoirs, and stories, all associated with the history of Canada. He wrote most of these himself and later brought them together in the Collection pour la jeunesse canadienne.

The expansion of publishing, the adoption of a law on compulsory school attendance in 1943, the curriculum reform of 1948, and the development of public readings were the main factors favouring the development of children's literature in the 1940s and 1950s. The publishers Variétés, L'Arbre, Fides, Apostolat de la presse, and Éditions jeunesse created series that included European books and translations of American picture books and periodicals. Éditions Fides, which focused on moral and religious education, offered books by writers belonging to Jeunesse étudiante catholique (JÉC) or the Scout movement, such as Félix Leclerc, Ambroise Lafortune, Guy Boulizon, Suzanne Lamy, and Alec Pelletier. In order to counteract the influence of comic books, Fides published a very successful Catholic comic strip magazine, *Hérauts* (1944–65), which was a French translation of *Timeless Topix*, by the Catechetical Guild of St Paul, Minnesota. The house also issued the educational periodicals *L'Élève* (1951–66), *Le Maître* (1951–66), *Lectures* (1946–66), and *Mes fiches*

(1937–65), and magazines such as *Claire* (1957–61), *Le Petit Héraut* (1958–9), *Fanchon et Jean-Lou* (1960), and *L'Escholier* (1960–5). In 1959 the circulation of all these publications totalled 750,000 copies a month.[2]

Another religious publisher, Apostolat de la presse, which was run by the Society of St Paul, published books for adolescents in the 1950s. Its catalogue included the series Jeunesse de tous les pays and Romans missionnaires, which were presented as adventure stories and featured characters travelling around the world to convert various peoples to Catholicism.

Éditions jeunesse, a co-operative founded in the late 1940s and run by the Association des écrivains pour la jeunesse, published lay writers; its titles included *Parade historique* (1950–1), three volumes written by Béatrice Clément and illustrated with comic strips drawn by Daniel Lareau. After the publishing house ceased operations in 1952, it was revived in 1962 through the efforts of the director at Éditions du Pélican, Réal D'Anjou, who issued some forty titles. In 1969 its list was sold to Entreprises de l'éducation nouvelle.

In 1964 the abolition of the system of book prizes, described by François Landry in chapter 2, destabilized the publishing industry and caused a drastic drop in book production in Quebec. European series took the place of those from Quebec in the book market, and many, such as Éditions Marabout's Bob Morane series, were very successful. To compete with the imports, the Librairie des écoles chrétiennes (Lidec) started the series Lidec-Aventures (1965–8), which was divided into three sub-series: Volpek, written by Yves Thériault, Unipak, by Maurice Gagnon, and Capitaine Jolicoeur, by Robert Hollier. Despite this initiative, the decline in local production continued.

By promoting Quebec books, Communication-jeunesse, discussed by Françoise Lepage in chapter 4, created in 1971, helped to reverse this trend. The change began with children's picture books published by Éditions Leméac. Éditions Paulines also started its Jeunesse-pop series of novels for young people nine to sixteen years of age and published the magazine *Video-presse* (1970–95), which was a great success. During the same period, Éditions Héritage published short novels in its series Pour lire avec toi, Hurtubise HMH issued adventure and science fiction novels for young people ten to eighteen years old, and Pierre Tisseyre put out translations of English-Canadian novels in a series entitled Deux solitudes–jeunesse. In 1978 Éditions de la Courte Échelle, founded by Bertrand Gauthier, introduced game books and revitalized the picture book with its Jiji series, written and illustrated by Ginette Anfousse. In the 1980s, Éditions Ovale introduced another innovation, creating series of picture books such as Légendes du Québec, Bébés-livres, Plimages, and Imagimots. The

7.1 Pauline Lamy and Alec Leduc, *Journal de bord d'Alfred* (Montreal: Éditions Fides, 1942). Courtesy of Éditions Fides.

remarkable revival of children's publishing in the 1970s, and its continuing growth in the following decades, led to the diversification of production, with books for both young children – board books, pop-up books, and picture books – and for adolescents and young adults – comic strips, novels, and non-fiction.

At the same time, illustration, which had been important since the 1920s, also underwent major changes, moving from the most traditional realism to the most daring fantasy. Colour was introduced, starting with book covers. Books were now soft-bound, an innovation made possible by the use of paper or cardboard covers. Illustrations inspired by the great Romantics accompanied the text, expressing it in images. The best-known illustrator of the time was James McIsaac, whose drawings and engravings enhanced the major historical series of the interwar period. In the 1940s, new artistic trends emerged; illustrators who were also artists, such as Sim (pseudonym of Jean Simard), Robert La Palme, and Jean-Paul Lemieux, freed illustration from historical realism and explored new avenues. Printing techniques were

7.2 Andrée Maillet and Robert La Palme (illus.), *Ristontac* (Montreal: Éditions Lucien Parizeau, 1945). Courtesy of the Succession de Robert La Palme.

modernized, and the development of photoengraving led to the reproduction of more elaborate images, as seen in Fides's Alfred series (see illus. 7.1, p. 219), illustrated by Maîtrise d'arts, an artisans' co-operative founded in 1939 by Louis Parent, who taught wood carving at the École du meuble. This series, written by Pauline Lamy and Alec Leduc, was started in 1942 and had large print runs.

The post-war period saw a stylization of form and colour, a move toward abstraction, and the influence of cubism and futurism. Technically, the medium for the images became more refined with books being printed on quality papers. In picture books, the images became increasingly important. The plastic experiments of modern painters exercised an influence, as shown in Robert La Palme's illustrations for *Ristontac*, by Andrée Maillet (1945) (see illus. 7.2, above). In 1967 *Un drôle de petit cheval*, by Henriette Major, illustrated by Guy Gaucher and published by the Centre de psychologie et de pédagogie, contributed to a renewal of attention to illustration: images now engaged in dialogue with the text instead of simply repeating it. Children's books were also influenced by comic strips and images from movies and television. In spite of these significant artistic advances, it was only in the late 1970s and early 1980s, with the emergence of publishers specializing in picture books, that illustration really took off again, drawing on artistic innovations and technical advances to enhance the pleasure and comfort of reading. Sometimes comical, sometimes satirical, and often original, the multi-faceted images were now telling the story as well as decorating it.

Children's Publishing in English Canada

While vitality characterized children's publishing in Quebec during the first half of the twentieth century, the English-Canadian industry did not come into its own until the second half. Until the 1960s, the reading of young anglophones consisted almost entirely of American and British imports, for in addition to the usual challenges of population, distribution, and capital, domestic publishers who issued children's titles in English had to contend with the high cost of producing illustrated books in colour for a small market, limited editorial specialization in the field, minimal reviewing of domestic titles, and the preference of school and public libraries for more widely reviewed foreign imprints. Consequently, general-interest trade publications for children were limited and largely confined to titles on Canadian topics that could supplement school readers, thereby tapping into the lucrative educational market.[3]

The majority of children's books published in English Canada during the interwar years were sparsely illustrated, with minimal attention to design and paratextual elements. However, a few works of notable artistry did appear, such as *A Canadian Child's ABC* (1931), designed and illustrated with hand-lettering and woodblocks by Thoreau MacDonald, and Hazel Boswell's *French Canada: Pictures and Stories* (1938), which contained stylized illustrations inspired by traditional Québécois hooked rugs. After a worldwide slump in English-language children's publishing caused by the Depression and the Second World War, the general situation began to improve in the late 1950s, when a growing interest in Canadian literature emerged. Macmillan of Canada, Oxford University Press, and McClelland and Stewart took the lead in upgrading their children's lists; they were followed to a lesser degree by a number of other publishers.[4]

However, the output remained small: 30 to 40 original English-language and 40 to 80 original French-language children's books were issued annually in Canada between 1952 and 1964. While 90 appeared in French in 1957 and 61 in English in 1965,[5] by contrast, in 1969 American publishers produced about 1,300.[6] Canadian publishers cited a dearth of talented writers and illustrators, a scarcity of publishable manuscripts, and the lack of valuable backlist titles that could underwrite new ventures as the reasons behind this small output.[7] Dominant among those that did appear were adventure stories. Biographies and historical fiction were also issued, but often in textbook-like series to exploit institutional sales to libraries and schools. Typical was Macmillan's Great Stories of Canada (33 volumes, 1953–74), which included Pierre Berton's *The Golden Trail: The Story of the Klondike Rush* (1954). Because of the limited market, original imaginative fiction such as Catherine Anthony Clark's *The Golden Pine Cone* (1950) appeared infrequently on domestic publishers' children's lists. Most of the popular writers of this period, including Roderick Haig-Brown, James Houston, Christie Harris, Jean Little, and Farley Mowat, sought first publication outside Canada.

Innovation in the field began in the mid-1950s, when William Toye, editor at Oxford University Press Canada in Toronto and a self-taught book designer, set out to develop a Canadian children's book program similar to the parent company's acclaimed children's list, but with a particular focus on Canadian content. He felt that while 'there were a number of Canadian children's books … they weren't very good ones.'[8] To remedy the situation, he recruited book illustrators and designers such as Theo Dimson, Donald Grant, John A. Hall, Arthur Price, and Leo Rampen, and developed a small but strong list of attractive books for children on Canadian themes, including Aboriginal stories, Canadian history, and poetry. The style of illustration varied from Dimson's abstracted modernist play of black and white for James McNeill's *The Sunken City and Other Tales from round the World* (1959) to Frank Newfeld's European graphic modernism for *The Princess of Tomboso: A Fairy-Tale in Pictures* (1960). Under his guidance, Toye's stable of designers and illustrators revolutionized standards of design, typography, layout, and illustration. Frank Newfeld, Elizabeth Cleaver, and Laszlo Gal, in particular, produced integrated picture books that balanced text and illustration. Oxford's *The Wind Has Wings: Poems from Canada* (1968), compiled by Mary Alice Downie and Barbara Robertson and illustrated by Elizabeth Cleaver, established a landmark as the first Canadian children's book with full four-colour illustration. Despite these achievements, in 1971 Toye still regretted Canada's 'lack of first-rate writers who are interested in writing for children,' noting that few of the unsolicited manuscripts he received 'would justify a first printing of 5000 for Canada,' let alone 'interest a publisher in London and/or New York.'[9] In the early 1970s, foreign imports continued to dominate Canadian bookstore and library shelves for children, and during the first few years of the decade, domestic production of English-language children's books ranged between 37 and 116 annually.[10]

Toye uttered his gloomy reflection on the cusp of change. The late 1960s and early 1970s constituted an era in Canadian publishing during which concerns about cultural sovereignty were gaining urgency as a general rise in nationalism intersected with controversy over the sale of Canadian-owned publishers Gage and Ryerson to American interests. The resulting Ontario Royal Commission on Book Publishing in 1970 did not target children's book publishing in its recommendations, but the commission did inspire briefs and an important background paper that subsequently encouraged further development of independent local children's publishing. The established Toronto firm of Clarke, Irwin, for example, appointed Janet Lunn as its children's book editor in 1973. Although children's editors had existed in American and British houses since the 1930s, Lunn's was the first such appointment in the history of the English-Canadian trade, signifying 'a rare commitment and an understanding that publishing children's books wasn't a spare-time activity for editors with other priorities.'[11] 'My editorial position had some impact on the community,' recalls Lunn. 'I didn't have an influence on mainstream publishers because they didn't add children's book editors till later.' However, emergent publishers and writers did consult her.[12] Other significant initiatives of the period were the founding in Toronto of the Children's Book Centre and the Children's Book Store, and the launch of two review journals, *In Review: Canadian Books for Children* (Toronto, 1967–82) and *CM: Canadian Materials* (Ottawa, 1971–), as well as the academic journal *Canadian Children's Literature / Littérature canadienne pour la jeunesse* (Guelph, 1975–), the first venue to support serious and sustained examination of Canadian writing for children. Finally, the Canadian Library Association's Book of the Year for Children Award (est. 1947) was joined by the association's Amelia Frances Howard-Gibbon Illustrator's Award (est. 1971) and the Canada Council Prizes for Children's Literature (est. 1975).

Innovative, specialized presses, devoting all or part of their lists to children's books, characterized the 1970s. Peter Martin Associates (Toronto, est. 1967) published a small but distinguished selection of Canadian-themed children's publications and served as a training ground for Patsy Aldana, Michael Solomon, Tim Wynne-Jones, Peter Carver, Shelley Tanaka, and Valerie Wyatt, who went on to become children's book editors, publishers, designers, and writers. Alternative presses, often organized as collectives and funded by small federal government granting programs, principally Opportunities for Youth (OFY) and Local Initiatives Program (LIP), took greater risks than the larger publishers. All worked closely with new writers and illustrators to create a literature that reflected images of Canadian childhood, history, and place, and all participated in the ideological currents of the

1970s. The Women's Press (Toronto), funded by an OFY grant in 1972, issued non-sexist, non-racist children's books of contemporary family life. Kids Can Press (Toronto), established as a collective in 1973 and supported by OFY and LIP grants, likewise produced books with non-sexist, multicultural, urban content. Kids Can's first publications, extremely basic in construction, were typed or hand-lettered, illustrated in black and white or in one colour, printed on Gestetner machines, saddle-stitched (stapled), and given away rather than sold. Annick Press similarly began as an LIP-sponsored program in 1975 under the imprint Books by Kids (Toronto). It published handmade books of stories, pictures, and poetry by children reflecting Canadian and urban sensibilities. Annick's philosophy melded themes of Canadian nationalism, child empowerment, and multiculturalism. By 1979 Valerie Hussey at Kids Can and Rick Wilks and Anne Millyard at Annick would take their presses in a commercial direction. Two Aboriginal-owned publishing houses that issued children's books on Aboriginal themes by Native writers were launched in 1980: British Columbia's Theytus Books, founded by Randy Fred, which began in Nanaimo and later moved to Penticton as part of the En'owkin Centre, and Pemmican Publications, a Métis house in Winnipeg.

While some presses put more emphasis on content than on physical format in their early years, from the outset influential publishers such as May Cutler at Tundra Books (Montreal, est. 1967) and Patsy Aldana at Groundwood (Toronto, est. 1978) considered high production values integral to children's publishing. Cutler's commitment to fine production and design resulted in award-winning picture books that sold internationally and fulfilled her desire to publish 'Canadian Children's Books as Works of Art.'[13] When she began issuing children's picture books in 1971, she commissioned gallery artists to create memoirs of cultural diversity and regionalism, such as Shizuye Takashima's *A Child in Prison Camp* (1971) and William Kurelek's *A Prairie Boy's Winter* (1973), despite the fact that it was enormously expensive and technically difficult to reproduce illustrative art at that time.[14] Cutler was the first Canadian children's publisher to attend the Bologna Children's Book Fair and pursue international co-publication and rights deals. Kurelek's books eventually sold more than half a million copies in ten countries.[15] Ann Blades's *Mary of Mile 18* (1971) and *A Boy of Taché* (1973) were published internationally, including British, Swedish, Finnish, German, and Danish editions.[16] Cutler was also the first to distribute directly in the United States, establishing Tundra Books of Northern New York. A committed bilingual and dual-language publisher, Tundra produced some simultaneous English and French editions.

Macmillan's phenomenal success in 1974 with Dennis Lee's *Alligator Pie* proved that Canadian content, canny promotion, and a lively touring author could make Canadian children's books commercially viable. In the mid-1970s, publishers were aided in this ambition by the slow improvement of printing operations in Canada and the introduction of Canada Council block grant funding, an intervention that diminished but did not entirely offset the high production costs of heavily illustrated books. Many publishers used foreign printers, and by 1980 they turned to inexpensive and superior printing available in Hong Kong. Increased interest from Canadian media and the general public and expanding school and library budgets stimulated many of the larger publishing houses to develop children's lists for the first time. Simultaneously, Toronto-based companies such as McClelland and Stewart, Macmillan, Dent, Fitzhenry and Whiteside, Longman, Oxford, and Methuen expanded their children's publishing programs. By the mid to late 1970s, the number of English-language children's books being published annually was growing steadily. Nonetheless, in 1977 Statistics Canada noted that only 7 per cent of the children's books bought in Canada originated in the country.[17]

Concomitant with these developments in book publishing, serial publishing aimed at children was also on the rise in the 1970s. Typically targeted at seven- to twelve-year-olds, these regional and special-interest magazines included poetry, cartoons, crafts, games, puzzles, jokes, articles, and stories. *Canadian Children's Magazine* (Victoria, 1976–9), a quarterly, included features on children in society, history, and different cultures. Some magazine publishers experimented with different formats. Each issue of McClelland and Stewart's *Magook* (Toronto, 1977–9), for example, combined a picture book and a separately bound, sixteen-page magazine featuring stories, author profiles, poetry, and cartoons. *Owl* (Don Mills, ON, 1976–), which superseded the *Young Naturalist* (Don Mills, 1959–75) and included wildlife stories, science experiments, puzzles, comic strips, and feature articles, was the most successful full-colour monthly children's magazine. Co-editors Mary Anne Brinckman and Annabel Slaight built up the magazine's subscription base to 100,000 after three years and added a French edition, *Hibou*, in 1980. *Owl*'s format was adopted by *Chickadee* (Toronto, 1979–), a spin-off magazine designed for primary and preschool children. In a case of successful branding, publisher Greey de Pencier was also able to issue children's books based on *Owl*'s columns and articles.

By 1980 English-Canadian publishing for children was on the edge of maturity as a generation of publishers, editors, designers, writers, and illustrators, who were focused on both commercial survival and national self-definition, faced the future with creativity, courage, and guarded optimism. In both French and English Canada, growth in the quality and quantity of children's books and periodicals during the 1970s was attributable to culturally committed domestic publishers and government financial programs, as well as to institutional and public support from concerned librarians, teachers, and parents.

The Rise and Fall of Textbook Publishing in English Canada

PENNEY CLARK

The visible and concrete symbols of an education system that can be both opaque and abstract, textbooks provide a focus for concerns about schooling at all levels. Textbooks hold status by virtue of having been chosen by senior agents such as provincial educational authorities, school boards, or faculty in post-secondary institutions. Unlike most reading material, educational texts are normally 'selected by someone other than the reader to whom they are addressed,' having first been 'planned and promoted [by publishers] with the purpose of persuading instructors or other educational authorities to prescribe them.'[18] That they have long been a sensitive area of public consciousness is evident in a letter sent from Ladle Cove, Newfoundland, in 1945. Writing on behalf of his two nephews, who had not yet received their government-issued textbooks, Lewis H. Wellon told the secretary for education, 'A great change [has] taken place since my school days fifty odd years ago, but the change seems to me to be for the worse.'[19] The government official promptly assured the disgruntled taxpayer that the books were indeed on their way to their outport destination.

Textbooks played a core role in elementary and secondary classrooms until the early 1970s when a pedagogical shift began to undermine their traditional status. From the 1920s through the 1960s, children in elementary school typically read in sequence from readers, as well as science, history, and geography textbooks, and followed lessons based on these books.[20] In other words, the curriculum and the single, authorized textbook were one and the same (see illus. 7.3, p. 228). Major beneficiaries of this pedagogical approach were Canadian-based publishers engaged in educational publishing.

During the first half of the twentieth century, the practice of developing textbooks under the supervision of the Ontario Department of Education slowly disappeared.[21] Although education was a provincial jurisdiction, in the nineteenth century the sheer volume of textbooks used in Ontario led to its Department of Education holding *de facto* authority over the development of Canadian textbooks in English, with other provinces simply making selections from Ontario's lists of authorized titles. As the twentieth century unfolded, curriculum committees were put in place in each province with a mandate to develop curriculum guidelines, rather than textbooks. Publishers were then invited to submit review copies of any books on their backlists that appeared to fulfill these guidelines. If no suitable books were available, they were asked to develop new books. Again, because of the size of the market, Ontario textbooks prevailed.

In 1954 William Henry Clarke, co-founder of one of Toronto's prominent educational publishers, Clarke, Irwin, captured the current structure of the English-Canadian publishing trade when he likened it to a pyramid, 'the broad base of which is formed out of the solid mass of the educational book market – a market which in its volume and extent and in its continuity of demand affords almost the only permanent or reasonably dependable factor in a publisher's sales budget and forecast.'[22] Reading series proved particularly lucrative for educational publishers. In the 1920s, Macmillan of Canada printed 100,000 copies of its Canadian Readers; after the war, Copp Clark's history text *The Story of Canada* (1949) sold over a million copies, a consequence of being adopted in most provinces. In the 1950s, when the average print run for a Canadian novel was 2,000 copies, school readers and spellers were issued in runs of 50,000.[23] For many publishers, textbook sales provided the financial base for the publication of original trade books, the risky pinnacle of Clarke's publishing pyramid. Pursuing the educational field, recalled John Morgan Gray of Macmillan of Canada, required that one be 'at once diplomat, politician, educator, and salesman.'[24]

The Canadian-owned firms active in educational publishing were all based in Toronto. These included venerable houses such as Ryerson Press, Gage, and Copp Clark, all of which had roots in the nineteenth century, as well as younger firms like Clarke, Irwin (est. 1930) and the Book Society of Canada (est. 1945). McClelland and Stewart (est. 1906) entered the textbook market in 1946 after an agency arrangement prohibiting its activity in this sector came to an end. Textbooks also came from major British houses with Canadian subsidiaries – Oxford University Press (est. 1904), Macmillan of Canada (est. 1906), Thomas Nelson (est. 1913), J.M. Dent & Sons (est. 1913), Longman, Green (est. 1922) – and American branch operations such as Ginn (est. 1929), McGraw-Hill (est. 1947), Doubleday (est. 1948), and Collier-Macmillan (est. 1956). Other American publishers chose to use Canadian firms as agents to market their books. In the realm of 'college' sales – the trade designation for text-

7.3 Girl with textbooks during Education Week, Vancouver, March 1966. Courtesy of *The Province*, and Vancouver Public Library, Special Collections, VPL 2276.

books marketed to post-secondary institutions – agency arrangements with American houses were prevalent.[25] Even as late as 1970, the university book market was 87 per cent imported and 13 per cent domestic, with Canadian companies and subsidiaries originating Canadian-specific materials only in fields such as the social sciences. Foreign firms had little interest in publishing such texts since demand for them was limited in their domestic markets.[26]

A notable phenomenon of the Canadian textbook trade at both the elementary and secondary level was the 'Canadianization' of American texts. Under this practice, which became increasingly common after 1940, portions of American publications were replaced with Canadian content. American publishers found these substitutions cost effective, enabling them to recover the bulk of their production outlay in their domestic market while increasing their profit margin in the secondary Canadian market. In 1939, when Ontario chose for its grade two program an Alice and Jerry reader originated by Row, Peterson of Evanston, Illinois, and distributed in Canada by Copp Clark, about half the content was replaced with Canadian or British narratives and poems and American spellings were similarly altered. In such cases, production values often suffered. At the secondary level, those adapted texts that were manufactured in Canada were 'usually printed on poorer paper (made in Canada) and bound in a Canadian pyroxylin-coated cloth of stodgy appearance, carrying an unimaginative Canadian cover design.'[27]

Disapproval of American textbooks, which had been vigorously expressed in the nineteenth century, was more muted during the first half of the twentieth, a result of the increased output of both Canadian publishing firms and British subsidiaries in Canada, as well as the willingness of American firms to Canadianize their texts. According to John Morgan Gray, in the early 1930s the response of educators to Canadian textbooks was 'striking and heartening.'[28] However, by the late 1930s, Canadian curriculum developers were embracing American ideas of progressive education, a circumstance that saw American texts outselling British, sometimes by as much as 19 to 3. Ironically, although progressive education de-emphasized a textbook-based approach to teaching, it made American books more acceptable when texts were needed.[29] Moreover, throughout the Second World War the purchase of educational materials was not a top priority.[30] The Massey Commission's condemnation in 1951 of the 'lazy, even abject, imitation' of American educational practices, and its prediction that American textbook use could lead to retardation of Canada's cultural growth, signalled a re-emergence of earlier concerns about American textbooks.[31] C.J. Eustace of Dent estimated that by that time about 60 per cent of Canada's English textbooks were either direct American imports or Canadianized versions of American texts. Most popular were the Dick and Jane readers distributed by Gage.[32]

Notable exceptions to the dominance of American publications were history and geography textbooks. Because they required Canadian content, they tended to be written by Canadians and published by Canadian-owned firms or British subsidiaries. Dent issued popular Canadian history and geography textbooks, as well as readers, by Canadian educators such as Donalda Dickie and George Cornish. The BC edition of Cornish's *Canadian Geography for Juniors*, a revised version of the volume issued in Ontario in 1927, was prescribed in British Columbia from 1928 to 1946. The *Canadian Oxford School Atlas*, which was developed by the parent company in Britain and first issued in 1957, became, according to an Oxford University Press manager, 'probably the best-selling Canadian textbook ever.'[33] Ryerson and Macmillan had also self-consciously integrated Canadian material into their co-published and enduring Canadian Treasury Readers and Canada Books of Prose and Verse, two series launched in the 1930s. Also notable was Macmillan's *Dominion High School Chemistry* (1935), by Harold E. Bigelow and Fred G. Morehouse, a volume Gray described as 'a Canadian book relating chemistry to Canadian research and industry with appropriate Canadian illustrations.'[34]

In the 1960s, Canada's educational publishing industry entered a significant period of change, as more American publishers abandoned the practice of using Canadian agents and instead set up branch plants. Prentice-Hall (est. 1960), Addison-Wesley (est. 1966), John Wiley (est. 1968), and Allyn & Bacon (est. 1974) established subsidiaries in Toronto; several opened offices in Vancouver and the Atlantic region. In 1973, $87.3 million was spent on educational texts in Canada, but only $2.6 million went to Canadian-owned publishers.[35] The small percentage of the educational market controlled by domestic publishers in 1973 was due in part to the sale in 1970 of two of the largest Canadian-owned publishers, Gage and Ryerson Press, to American interests. These transactions, which made Clarke, Irwin the largest Canadian-owned textbook publisher, prompted the creation of the Ontario Royal Commission on Book Publishing in 1970.

According to the commission, educational publishing, 'long the most secure department in book publishing ... [entered] an economic cul de sac [in] 1968, its fuel running lower and lower, and unable to reverse gears.'[36] The commission's report of 1973 outlined the circumstances that had undermined the traditional stability of the educational publishing sector. By that year the only provinces still relying on an authorized text in the sense of one copy per pupil were Prince Edward Island, British Columbia (in some subjects), and Nova Scotia, and the last of these was in the process of abandoning the approach.[37] In addition, textbook sales were challenged by increases in manufacturing costs, declining enrolment, a new emphasis on multimedia resources, and the cessation in 1968 of Ontario's textbook stimulation grants, a subsidy that had provided school boards with a set amount per pupil to be spent on books. Once they were free to allocate their budgets where they saw fit, Ontario school boards reduced textbook expenditures from 2.5 per cent of their budgets in 1967 to 1 per cent in 1978.[38] Since this province accounted for half the English-Canadian textbook market, the change was critical. Based on the commission's recommendations, Ontario developed new policies to stimulate textbook publishing, including guaranteed loans to publishers and targeted development grants to stakeholders such as authors, book industry organizations, and publishers. However, textbook publishers were also up against a significant pedagogical shift toward neo-progressivism, an educational approach in evidence by the late 1960s and early 1970s that toppled the textbook from its throne.[39] As early as 1970, text-book print runs were reduced to 5,000 or fewer, while some titles were cancelled outright as a result of declining demand.

Through the 1970s, publishers also struggled with criticism about the content of textbooks, particularly with respect to ethnic and gender stereotyping and lack of Canadian content. Garnet McDiarmid and David Pratt's seminal study of history textbooks, *Teaching Prejudice* (1971), a review co-sponsored by the Ontario Human Rights Commission and the Ontario Institute for Studies in Education, was followed by further content analyses by provincial human rights commissions, women's and Aboriginal organizations, and provincial departments of education. The selection criteria which resulted, such as Ontario's *Race, Religion, and Culture in Ontario School Materials* (1981), began to influence authors, publishers, and provincial textbook selection committees.

T.H.B. Symons's sweeping survey of Canadian content in the post-secondary cur-riculum, *To Know Ourselves* (1975), was similarly momentous, raising awareness of the crisis at all educational levels. Through the mid to late 1970s, nearly every province promoted the development of Canadian materials for Canadian schools, either under contract with a publisher or by self-publishing.[40] Ontario was at the forefront of these efforts, giving schools free copies of new Canadian textbooks and providing subsidies for the development of materials which would not be profitable to pub-lish otherwise. *Circular 14*, Ontario's list of authorized materials, excluded all books that were not Canadian, including those published by American-owned firms, unless the writing, printing, and binding were done in Canada. In spite of such efforts, the dominance of American textbooks continued. In 1979 only about one-fifth of one per cent of the total textbook budget in the Atlantic provinces was spent on materials published in Atlantic Canada.[41]

By 1980 textbook publishing in English Canada was on the brink of another transformation, with the advent of small regional publishers, on the one hand, and the growth of multinationals, on the other. The market for social studies textbooks at first encouraged regional publishers in the West, such as Arnold Publishing (est. 1967), Weigl Publishing (est. 1979), Douglas & McIntyre (Educational) (est. 1980), and Duval House (est. 1985). By 2006, however, a series of buyouts and mergers had resulted in Douglas & McIntyre (Educational) and Arnold Publishing, as well as Harcourt Canada and Duval House, becoming part of the Canadian-owned multinational Thomson Nelson. The British-owned multinational Pearson Education Canada similarly took over the Canadian subsidiaries of many educational publishers, including Addison-Wesley, Collier-Macmillan, Ginn, GLC, and Prentice-Hall.[42] In 2005 Pearson's Web site claimed that the company's combined educational and trade-publishing operations ranked it the largest publisher in Canada. Over the course of the twentieth century, the economic power and the cultural significance of educational publishing ensured it was a focus of ongoing public debate.

CASE STUDY ────────────────────────────────
Coles Notes
– Ian Brockie

It is difficult to imagine a time when Coles Notes – those ubiquitous and pedagogically controversial booklets – were not part of student culture. Inspired by the little black notebook of 'key words and salient points' maintained by his teacher in the 1930s, Toronto bookseller Jack Cole published the first Coles Notes in 1948, literally reproducing a history teacher's notebook in mimeographed form. When that venture 'achieved sufficient sales,' Cole issued a printed version. 'After that, the scheme just took off,' Cole recalled in 1970. 'I found that *all* teachers had these little books ... and they were ideal for students to review a subject in the sudden-death atmosphere of examinations.'[43] The earliest publications, which sold for between 50 cents and one dollar, were small orange booklets (21.5 × 14.5 cm), some devoted to specific courses in Ontario high schools, others to individual texts. In 1955 they were reclothed in the series's signature black stripes on yellow – 'bumblebee' – covers. In the late 1960s, the price of a typical Notes was $1.25, a figure which crept up to $2.95 by 1979. By that time, the covers sported variously coloured panels; in the late 1990s, Coles's new corporate owner, the bookstore chain Chapters, adopted a uniform green colour.

Coles made use of both reprinted and original titles to keep pace with developments in the secondary and post-secondary student markets. The series reprinted titles from the Pennant Key-Indexed Study Guides and Forum House (a Coles university-oriented imprint), as well as from its American imitator, Cliffs Notes (est. 1958). The relationship between Coles and the American company was especially congenial: Jack Cole and Cliff Hillgass, CEO of Cliffs, were friends who had agreed not to compete in each other's domestic markets for twenty-five years and to share manuscripts. Original Coles guides for Canadian works first appeared in the 1970s and burgeoned during the 1980s with the addition of notes for novels by Morley Callaghan, Margaret Atwood, Hugh MacLennan, and Mordecai Richler. By this time, Jack Cole had developed markets throughout the Commonwealth, ensuring that students around the world could tap into his Canadian innovation.

Among educators, the reputation of Coles Notes has ranged from firm denigration to grudging acceptance. Hence many who authored Notes have preferred anonymity, although recognized writers such as Phyllis Grosskurth and Eli Mandel contributed to the series. Today, the majority of Coles Notes titles examine books commonly studied in literature classes. They typically contain a brief biography of the subject author and an overview of his/her cultural context, as well as a short introduction to the text, a plot summary, a list of major characters, and commentary on the major sections of the work. Some also provide study questions and sample responses; others include charts, bibliographies, and short analytical essays. Most Coles Notes reflect their mid-twentieth century origins, leaning toward rudimentary New Criticism. While their value as educational resources has been contested, their popularity among students has never been in doubt. Sales have been massive; by 1998 the notes to Margaret Laurence's *The Stone Angel*, the leading Canadian title, had sold 100,000 copies, and the guide to *Macbeth* over half a million.[44]

CASE STUDY ───
McClelland and Stewart and the Quality Paperback
– Janet B. Friskney

Although a few Canadian publishers experimented in 'pocket books' for the mass market as early as the 1940s, the English-language trade did not express substantial interest in the format until the 1960s, when it became evident that the 'quality' paperback (sometimes known as the 'trade' or 'egghead' paperback) held market potential for domestic publishers, particularly in the educational sector. A preference on the part of professors and students for quality paperbacks as course texts, substantial expansion of post-secondary institutions across the country, and a rising interest in Canadian topics – thanks in part to the reverberations of the Massey Commission – encouraged publishers to take a risk. While quality paperbacks were similar in size to mass-market titles, they distinguished themselves in a number of ways: produced in significantly smaller print runs, they appeared in more conservative covers, exhibited better production values, sported higher price tags, held backlist potential, and were marketed through trade and college bookstores.

McClelland and Stewart (M&S) pioneered the quality paperback in English Canada. Its first venture, the New Canadian Library (NCL), was launched on 17 January 1958 under the general editorship of Malcolm Ross, the English professor at Queen's University who first proposed the idea of a reprint series of Canadian literary titles.[45] Although most appeared with an introduction by a professor or other literary specialist, NCL volumes were envisioned as practical teaching texts rather than scholarly editions and, save for two original translations, were produced virtually without subsidy. Issued initially in distinctive covers designed by Frank Newfeld (see illus. 7.4, p. 236), the NCL proved invaluable to an emergent group of scholars who were eager to make Canadian literature a substantial part of their teaching and research careers.

While the series struggled financially through its early years, a circumstance that provoked several cost-saving abridgements which later proved controversial, its publisher and general editor persevered, as post-secondary institutions in Canada showed a steady increase in courses in Canadian literature and NCL titles were widely adopted. By the end of its first decade, with over 65 titles drawn from the eighteenth to the twentieth centuries and cumulative sales of more than 585,000 copies,[46] the series had become a valuable part of the M&S backlist and inspired other Canadian publishers to join the quality paperback field. Such initiatives, which, unlike the NCL, drew largely or entirely on fiction or non-fiction titles from their publishers' own backlists, included University of Toronto Press's Canadian University Paperbacks (est. 1963), Oxford in Canada Paperbacks (est. 1965), Clarke Irwin Canadian Paperbacks (est. 1965), Ryerson Paperbacks (est. 1967), and Macmillan of Canada's Laurentian Library (est. 1967). These ventures created competition in terms of sales and the acquisition of reprint rights. The latter circumstance ensured that in the 1970s the NCL became more reliant on the M&S backlist and titles in the public domain. Nonetheless, it was a decade of steady production and sales for the series, and by the time Ross retired as general editor in 1978, more than 180 titles had been issued in its main and subsidiary lines (the NCL Original series and the Canadian Writers series), while cumulative sales had exceeded 3 million copies. Following Ross's departure, the series went into hiatus for several years, but in 1981 new titles began to be added at the sole discretion of M&S. In 1988 the series was revised and relaunched under the auspices of a new general editor, David Staines of the University of Ottawa, and an editorial board. The NCL remains a vital publishing property for M&S to the present day.

M&S's second quality paperback initiative, the Carleton Library, had roots in its first; not long after the NCL's launch, its publisher and general editor began to receive suggestions for reprints of non-literary titles. In 1960, M&S approached Robert McDougall at the Institute of Canadian Studies at Carleton University about a Canadiana reprint series of significant history and social science works aimed at the post-secondary market. After several years of discussion and some surveying undertaken by the institute with the aid of a Canada Council grant, the Carleton Library was launched on 25 May 1963. Unlike the NCL list, which Ross selected in close consultation with the publisher, the Carleton Library utilized an editorial board that operated in an arm's-length arrangement with M&S. The series achieved respectable sales through the 1960s, but by 1970 it faced the same struggles as the NCL over reprint rights and market share.[47] Consequently, it became more reliant on the M&S backlist, titles in the public domain, and original compilations, and even began to originate some complete works. Nonetheless, discontent over the Carleton Library's general profitability, a scarcity of financially viable titles to add to the series, and disagreements with the editorial board over pricing policy all contributed to M&S's decision to cease acting as publisher in the late 1970s, by which time more than 100 volumes had appeared.[48] Over the next few years, the Carleton Library's editorial board made short-term arrangements with Macmillan and Gage, but its need for a long-term and stable publishing arrangement ultimately inspired the creation in 1981 of Carleton University Press (CUP), under whose imprint Carleton Library titles appeared until CUP's closure in 1999. McGill-

7.4 Although bearing a copyright date of 1957, the first four titles of McClelland and Stewart's New Canadian Library series, illustrated above, were issued in Toronto on 17 January 1958. In conceptualizing the look of the New Canadian Library, designer Frank Newfeld determined there were three things to keep in view: a distinctive format that would also suggest the Canadian content of the series; an element that highlighted the author of each volume; and visibility in the bookstore. The torn strip motif was 'intended to convey somehow both the rugged orderliness of the country and its unexplored possibilities.' He varied the images of authors depending on the type of prose they wrote; hence, Stephen Leacock's and Frederick Philip Grove's portraits were 'more strictly representational than [that] of Morley Callaghan.' (Source of quotations: McMaster University Library, William Ready Division of Archives and Research Collections, McClelland and Stewart fonds, series Ca, box 2, file 7, typescript description.) Covers reproduced with the permission of McClelland and Stewart Ltd.

Queen's University Press, which took over CUP's entire backlist, currently publishes the Carleton Library.

Textbook Publishing in Quebec

PAUL AUBIN

Textbook publishing in Quebec grew steadily from 1918 to 1960, declined during the next two decades, and then enjoyed a resurgence after 1980. From over 700 textbooks published in the 1920s (including reprints), the number rose to over 1,700 in the 1950s, with 160 titles published in 1957 alone.[49] Three main factors account for this increase: the law of 1943 on compulsory school attendance (George 6, c. 13), the development of secondary school education, and the post-war baby boom. The drop in textbook production in the 1960s and especially the 1970s resulted from both the effects on publishers of the report from the Parent Commission,[50] which recommended major reform of the education system, and a new pedagogical trend that de-emphasized the importance of textbooks in education.

The dominance of religious communities in textbook production, which was established in the nineteenth century,[51] continued into the twentieth. In the 1920s, 69 per cent of new textbooks were published by religious communities.[52] Although their market share steadily decreased in subsequent years, these communities remained the main producers of educational books until the 1950s, a decade in which they still wrote, printed, and published half of all French-language textbooks sold in Quebec.

The Brothers of the Christian Schools (BCS, est. 1838), the oldest surviving and largest religious community in French Canada, was the most prolific textbook publisher, followed by the Brothers of Christian Instruction (BCI) and the Clerics of St Viator (CSV). Among women's religious orders, it was also the oldest community, the Congregation of Notre-Dame (CND), that predominated. Each community had a speciality: the BCS published accounting textbooks; the BCI, English textbooks; and the CND, books on home economics and cooking.

Secular textbook publishers were also active, with over a hundred different firms entering the field over the course of the twentieth century. Many published only a few titles, while others, such as Librairie Beauchemin and Granger Frères, played a major role. Coexistence between secular and religious publishers was not always peaceful, and friction increased over the century. In 1938 there was public criticism of unfair competition on the part of the religious publishers, who enjoyed undeniable economic advantages over their secular counterparts.[53] The situation began to change with the creation of the Centre de psychologie et de pédagogie (CPP), a textbook publishing house founded by a group of lay teachers in 1945. After the CPP entered the market, some sixty new secular publishing houses were founded. From 1960 to 1962, the CPP dominated the market, with 35 per cent of total sales.[54] After the onset of the Quiet Revolution, which saw a sharp decline in their numbers, religious communities gradually withdrew from educational publishing or sold their lists to lay publishers.

Textbooks were an important part of Quebec's book trade. Indeed, half the report of the Commission d'enquête sur le commerce du livre dans la province de Québec, published in 1963, was devoted to the topic. The commissioner of the inquiry, Maurice Bouchard, criticized the high cost of textbooks and the absence of real competition in the textbook market, which was dominated by a few major players. He especially castigated the Department of Public Instruction, which had turned a blind eye to dubious practices in the textbook approval process.[55] These accusations forced both secular and religious publishers to curtail their activities for a time, while the Department of Education, created in 1964, contracted with the Quebec branch of Hachette to translate American textbooks into French for the Quebec market.[56]

Of about 3,000 titles printed in Quebec between 1918 and 1979, only 5 per cent were reprints, adaptations, or translations of foreign school books. Quebec publishers were relatively autonomous in textbook publishing and dominated the elementary school market, turning to foreign sources for only a few subjects and under specific circumstances. For example, during the Second World War, the need for secondary school textbooks led the BCS to reprint some imported titles.[57] It is hardly surprising that France was the major source, accounting for about 68 per cent of imported textbooks.[58] Belgium supplied titles on catechism, while books on mathematics came from Germany.

Until the 1960s, francophones outside Quebec produced very few textbooks, opting to purchase educational works from Montreal publishers. The national French-Canadian market provided an outlet for surplus titles even though the texts did not always suit local needs.[59] For example, Canadian history textbooks published in Quebec required adaptation elsewhere in Canada, and complaints were particularly vocal from the Acadians.[60]

At the centre of important economic and ideological issues, textbooks provided a site where various external forces converged, requiring authors and publishers to adapt their product to the market. While the Quebec government's role is well known, textbook publishers also had to reckon with other intervening forces that emerged in public discussion of education. This was seen, for example, following the creation of Quebec's Department of Education. A new approach, expressed unofficially by government bodies and implicitly supported by the department's adoption of a Core Program curriculum in the early 1970s, no longer promoted the use of textbooks in the classroom and resulted in a substantial decline in the number of textbooks produced in the 1970s. But the decrease proved only temporary, and textbooks made a strong comeback in the 1980s.[61]

CASE STUDY
French-Canadian Classics from Fides
– Jacques Michon

Three series issued by Fides, the Collection du Nénuphar, the Classiques canadiens, and the Bibliothèque canadienne-française, enjoyed resounding success in the 1960s. Aimed at the educational market, they played a major role in the formation and renewal of the Quebec literary canon during the Quiet Revolution (see illus. 7.5, p. 240).

The Collection du Nénuphar, edited by Luc Lacourcière, represented a turning point in the publication of French-Canadian literature. Before its creation in 1944, only historical and edifying works from the nineteenth century were reprinted. In the Collection du Nénuphar, however, Fides offered contemporary French-Canadian works printed with care on high-quality laid paper (21 × 14 cm). In 1952 Lacourcière issued the first critical edition of Émile Nelligan's *Poésies complètes, 1896–1899*, which became the series's most popular title. Reprints of works originally published in the 1930s and 1940s, including Félix-Antoine Savard's *Menaud, maître-draveur*, Léo-Paul Desrosiers's *Les engagés du grand portage*, Alfred DesRochers's *À l'ombre de l'Orford*, Hector de Saint-Denys Garneau's *Poésies complètes*, Germaine Guèvremont's *Le survenant*, and Ringuet's *Trente arpents*, quickly

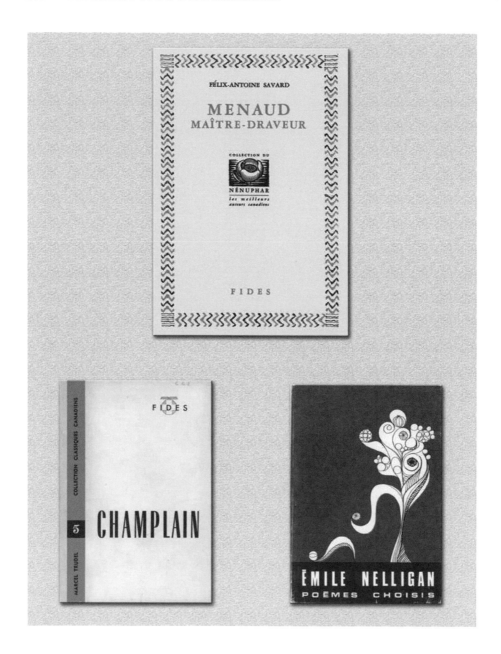

7.5 Sample covers from three series of French-Canadian classics published by Éditions Fides (Montreal). Top: Félix-Antoine Savard, *Menaud maître-draveur* (Collection du Nénuphar, 1944). Bottom (l. to r.): *Champlain*, edited and annotated by Marcel Trudel (Collection Classiques canadiens, 1968); Émile Nelligan, *Poèmes choisis*, selected and edited by Éloi de Grandmont (Bibliothèque canadienne-française, 1966). Courtesy of Éditions Fides.

Chart 7.1   Sales of Saint-Denys Garneau in three series issued by Éditions Fides, 1950–79: BCF, Classiques, Nénuphar.

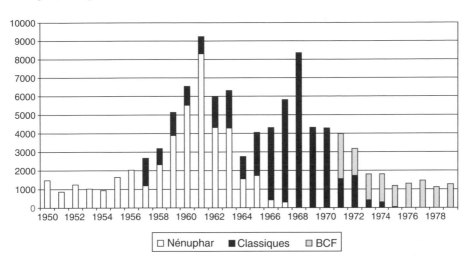

Source: Archives of the Corporation des Éditions Fides.

gained the public's favour.[62] From 1944 to 1979, some sixty titles were issued, and nearly half a million copies sold.

In 1956 Fides launched Classiques canadiens. Designed to provide students with selected texts at affordable prices, these paperbacks in the pocket book format (17 × 11 cm), each less than a hundred pages, contained extracts from works by writers of New France (Samuel de Champlain and Pierre-François-Xavier de Charlevoix), the nineteenth century (Octave Crémazie, Arthur Buies, and Pamphile Le May), and the twentieth century (Louis Dantin and Rina Lasnier). From 1956 to 1972, forty-five titles were published, with three contemporary poets achieving the greatest sales – Saint-Denys Garneau (42,900 copies), Alain Grandbois (17,500 copies), and Robert Choquette (13,600 copies).[63]

In 1960, on the strength of this success, the publisher launched a second pocket book series, Alouette bleue, which in 1965 became the Bibliothèque canadienne-française. It consisted of the most popular titles of the Collection du Nénuphar, such as Le survenant and Menaud, maître-draveur as well as many titles by Félix Leclerc. Over more than forty years, through the systematic distribution of these publications, Fides ensured the longevity of the books then considered most representative of contemporary Quebec.

chapter 8

THE SERIAL PRESS

Major Trends in Canada's Print Mass Media

MARY VIPOND

For much of the twentieth century, questions of ownership and competition dominated the serial press in Canada. For newspapers, the rise of chains and conglomerate ownership which resulted in one-newspaper cities provoked alarm and official investigation. For periodicals, where the greatest concern was competition from American magazines, various measures were introduced by the federal government to bolster the Canadian industry. While ownership and competition drew the most attention, other transformations were significant as well. The newspaper industry diversified as it consolidated, with the appearance of the tabloid format and more community newspapers; periodicals also diversified, and by 1980 what had formerly been a market dominated by large consumer magazines now included a wide range of special-interest publications.

At the end of the First World War there were approximately 135 daily newspapers in Canada, with the same number of owners. Newspapers faced very little competition from outside the country, and virtually all were locally owned. Most cities of any size had two or three dailies. The industry enjoyed a low second-class postal rate, only a fraction of the actual cost of carriage, which enabled urban dailies to reach many rural readers. The federal government had introduced this subsidy immediately after Confederation, on the grounds that it was necessary 'to encourage the dissemination of news to all parts of the new federation.'[1] While the justification for the subsidy decreased over the years as other media facilitated national communication, it remained in place, costing the post office, when combined with a similar subsidized rate for periodicals, close to $120 million per year by the early 1980s.[2] Both print mass media were also exempted from the manufacturers' sales tax (federal excise tax), which was worth more than $100 million to them in 1980.[3]

Despite such indirect aid, increasingly costly technology led proprietors to seek economies of scale. Canadian Press, created as a newspaper-owned co-operative in the 1920s, distributed common national and international stories to papers throughout the country.[4] The Sifton and Southam families established Canada's first newspaper chains in the same decade. The latter remained one of the most important chains in the English-language market, and over the succeeding decades was joined by Thomson Newspapers Limited and the *Sun* group. These three corporations together controlled 67 per cent of the circulation of English-language dailies in 1980. The French-language market, predominantly in Quebec, was even more concentrated, with Quebecor alone having 46.5 per cent of circulation and Paul Desmarais's Gesca another 28.8 per cent.[5] Consequently, although there were 117 urban dailies active late that year, genuine competition existed in only seven Canadian cities.[6] The Royal Commission on Newspapers (Kent Commission), formed in 1981 in response to the 'shock and trauma'[7] that followed the closure of the Winnipeg *Tribune* (est. 1890) and the Ottawa *Journal* (est. 1885) by the Thomson and Southam organizations, recognized that the search for more profits would lead newspaper proprietors to create further mergers and acquisitions and even less competition. Decreased attention to local editorial content in the major dailies aroused strong criticism, although the expansion of community newspapers was one response. The other principal concern was the increasing ownership of newspapers by conglomerates with diversified business interests, including other media holdings, which the commissioners linked to a decline in public service.[8] However, the government took no action.

An industry that had been run along fairly traditional lines for decades confronted significant changes in the 1970s. One was the rise of the crime- and sex-filled daily tabloid newspaper, pioneered by Pierre Péladeau's Quebecor in Montreal and Quebec City and developed in several English-Canadian cities by the *Sun* group. Tabloids had been part of the Toronto newspaper scene from before the Second World War; by the mid-1950s the city's big three – *Flash* (1936?–72), *Hush* (1927–37; 1941–73), and *Justice Weekly* (1946–72) – achieved national distribution.[9] However, the 1970s were a decade of substantial growth. By 1980 the *Journal de Montréal* (1964–) had captured almost 62 per cent of the Montreal French-language market, and the Toronto

Sun (1971–) held almost 22 per cent of the market in Toronto.[10] The success of the tabloids changed the landscape of the Canadian newspaper industry, while their morning appearance signalled a general trend from evening to morning papers. Another innovation was an emphasis on weekend papers and the introduction of Sunday editions. The arrival of computers in press and newsrooms presented changes that Peter Desbarats has rightly called 'revolutionary' for newspaper practice.[11]

The periodical industry faced a very different and much less prosperous situation. By 1918 the Canadian periodical market was already swamped with American publications, and throughout the 1920s and 1930s Canadian periodical publishers lobbied the government for more protection than the established postal subsidy. In the late 1920s the Liberal government reduced tariffs on some of the paper and other products the periodical publishers had to import; in the early 1930s a Conservative government introduced, for a short period, a tariff on imported periodicals. That, in turn, inspired the launch of Canadian split-run editions of American periodicals (printed in Canada from plates shipped across the border, sometimes with Canadian content added), which had the considerable advantage of being able to cover their overhead in the large U.S. market and therefore to charge lower advertising rates in Canada. The federal government eventually addressed that issue in the late 1950s, by which time 80 per cent of the total Canadian market share for general-interest consumer magazines went to U.S. publications, both directly imported (overflow) and split-run editions. By that time, the Canadian editions of *Reader's Digest* (both French, est. 1947, and English, est. 1948) and *Time* (English only, est. 1943) garnered 37 per cent of magazine advertising revenues.[12]

A Royal Commission on Publications (O'Leary Commission) was established in 1960 to investigate the Canadian magazine situation. As a result of the commission's recommendations, the Income Tax Act was amended in 1964 to prevent advertisers from deducting the costs of advertising in non-Canadian periodicals, with the exception of Canadian editions of American magazines already in existence. Schedule 5 of the Customs Tariff was also amended to prohibit the importation of split-run editions of non-Canadian periodicals if the advertising was aimed at the Canadian market. Nevertheless, by the end of the 1960s the Canadian magazine industry was in dire straits. Although *Maclean's* (see illus. 8.1, p. 246) enjoyed a solid readership, in general Canadians were reading fewer magazines in total and an increasing percentage of imports; national advertisers were switching from periodicals to the electronic media. The exceptions were *Time* and *Reader's Digest*, which enjoyed continuously expanding readership and revenues.

The Special Senate Committee on the Mass Media (Davey Committee) of 1968, in

its examination of the periodical situation, focused on the 'bad decision' of exempt-
ing *Time* and *Reader's Digest* from the previous legislation and recommended removal
of the exemption and possibly requiring both magazines to become Canadian-
owned.[13] Bill C-58, a further amendment to the Income Tax Act passed in 1975,
defined a Canadian magazine in a way that led *Time* to cease publishing its Canadian
edition as such and *Reader's Digest* to alter its ownership structure in order to qualify.[14] As a result of this measure, which improved revenues for domestic serials, by
1980 Canadian periodical publishers were feeling somewhat optimistic. Nevertheless, the industry was even more concentrated than its newspaper counterpart and
still operated in an environment where 71 per cent of consumer magazine circulation in the country, and a considerably higher percentage on newsstands, was of
periodicals with content 'produced originally for a foreign magazine.'[15] Moreover,
when second-class postal rates were raised substantially in 1969, the subsidy, much
more important to periodical than to newspaper publishers by this time, was
increasingly at risk. From the mid-1960s on, it was under attack for its inefficiency (it
subsidized foreign periodicals as well as Canadian) and for its contribution to Canada Post's deficit.[16]

The case of Quebec serials was somewhat different because of the protection
from the United States provided by their distinct language and by physical and cultural distance from French-speaking European competition, although neither factor
ensured profitability. Throughout the period, the proportion of French-language
material available on the Canadian serial market was consistently under-represented
relative to the francophone population of the country. Economic incentives led to
both innovation (tabloids) and even more concentration in the French-language
newspaper field than in English Canada. An unusual element in the French-language
press was the existence of the independent, non-profit *Le Devoir* (est. 1910), which,
despite its small circulation, was very influential among Quebec elites. The French-
language periodical press was smaller and weaker, and by 1980, 100 per cent of the
market was in the hands of four companies, none of them Québécois. The largest
publisher of French-language periodicals was Maclean-Hunter, whose French versions of *Maclean's* and *Chatelaine*, *Le Magazine Maclean* (est. 1961; after 1976, *L'Actualité*)
and *Châtelaine* (est. 1960), captured over 44 per cent of the market.[17]

Whether issued in French or English, in the twentieth century newspapers and
periodicals faced a new challenge from the broadcast media. As the Kent Commission put it, 'The reader from the beginning of the century has gradually become not
merely a reader but also a listener and a viewer.'[18] By 1980 newspapers and magazines
shared with radio and television their functions of informing, enlightening, and

8.1 Franklin Arbuckle, cover of *Maclean's* (Toronto), 10 November 1956. This issue shows Joe Pedlar, editor of the *Herald* in Oxbow, Saskatchewan, in his newspaper office. The woman, and the sign in the foreground that states 'poetry no longer accepted,' jokingly allude to Sarah Binks, the title character of Paul Hiebert's 1947 parodic novel. Courtesy of *Maclean's* and the Estate of Franklin Arbuckle.

entertaining Canadians, and they competed with these newcomers for advertising dollars. The Kent commissioners expressed considerable alarm that newspaper concentration was reducing the credibility of the press as a news source: in 1980 only 29 per cent of Canadians felt that newspapers offered the fairest and most unbiased news, while television scored 53 per cent.[19] While newspapers and magazines remained the preferred venue for in-depth coverage and analysis, they were being pushed both by competitive forces within their own industries and by competition with other media to 'dramatize, simplify, or trivialize,' as the rise of the tabloids revealed.[20] Not only was the economic structure of these two industries transformed over this period; so too was the appearance and content of their products.

The underlying factors affecting serials and other mass media in Canada changed little between 1918 and 1980. The newspaper and periodical press are cultural industries: that is, their cultural product is carried in a large technology-dependent and profit-driven vehicle. Their profit derives, not from the sale of the publications to readers, but from the sale of audiences to advertisers.[21] In 1980 advertising constituted about 70 per cent of total revenues for periodicals and just less than 80 per cent for newspapers.[22] Canada's contiguity to the largest producer of mass culture in the world, combined with social and (for most Canadians) language similarities, has undermined the ability of Canadian products to compete in their own market. In response, various waves of cultural nationalism have arisen, promoted sometimes self-interestedly and focusing on some cultural industries more than others.

The nationalist argument is that cultural products are not like other goods, in that they are instrumental in creating a sense of identity and national consciousness in enabling Canadians to speak to one another. They therefore need special protection in the marketplace, and the various measures described above resulted from this belief. On the other hand, there has always been considerable reluctance to have the state intervene in the free market of ideas, for similarly principled reasons. Thus protectionist measures have been debated, introduced, withdrawn, and tinkered with many times through the twentieth century. Because of their substantial Canadian content and ownership, newspapers have generated less concern, while periodicals have rung the alarm bells for a hundred years. Nonetheless, laments about newspapers have arisen from intellectual and cultural nationalist sources, with an emphasis on the need for a diversity of voices on the Canadian scene. The title to a Quebec report on press concentration expressed the key idea: 'De la précarité de la presse ou le citoyen menacé' ('The Vulnerability of the Press, or, The Threat to Citizenship').[23]

Women's Magazines

MARIE-JOSÉ DES RIVIÈRES, CAROLE GERSON, AND DENIS SAINT-JACQUES

While periodicals for women began in Europe in the eighteenth century, modern, family-oriented, mass-market women's magazines – characterized by a large format, glossy paper, full-page illustrations, and copious advertising – first appeared in the United States in the late nineteenth century, and soon spread throughout the Western world. In both English and French Canada, the early years of women's magazines were marked by trial and error. In Toronto, *Everywomen's Journal* (1914–22), and, in Montreal, *Le Coin du feu* (1893–6), *Le Journal de Françoise* (1902–9), *Le Foyer* (1903–27), and *La Femme* (1908–12), were short-lived and faced strong competition from American publications that flooded Canada. More enduring were *Canadian Home Journal* (Toronto, 1896–1958), *Mayfair* (Toronto, 1927–61), *Canadian Homes and Gardens* (Toronto, 1924–62), and *National Home Monthly* (Winnipeg, 1932–60), but all were dwarfed by the success of *Chatelaine*, in English (1928–) and French (1960–).

Modern Women's Magazines in French Canada

The establishment of women's magazines in Quebec came with the founding of *La Revue moderne* (Montreal, 1919–60). Its first editor, Madeleine (pseudonym of Anne-Marie Gleason), an experienced journalist, wanted to create a general circulation cultural publication similar to the enduring Parisian *Revue des deux mondes*. That it catered to a strong female readership was evident in the table of contents: the section entitled 'Femina' demonstrated the extensive appeal to women's interests. *La Revue moderne* regularly published French-Canadian writers as well as established French authors, mainly in the realm of romantic fiction. Articles typically focused on French Canada. In 1922 the magazine was subtitled *Organe de la section française de la société des auteurs canadiens*. As *La Revue moderne* increasingly addressed a female readership, its monthly circulation quickly rose to more than 20,000.[24]

Since most general magazines of the era contained women's sections, female readers wielded considerable influence on the whole magazine market. For example, expansion in the circulation of *Le Bulletin des agriculteurs* (Montreal, 1915–) was mainly due to its increasing appeal to women, its subscription list growing from 12,000 at the end of the 1920s to reach more than 60,000 at the end of the 1930s and over 140,000 in the late 1940s.[25] As a result of a new editorial policy, articles and advertising for farmers were supplemented with substantial material for women: fiction, fashion and cooking advice, and columns on recreational activities comprised nearly half of every issue. This development demonstrates the predominant role played by women in the success of mass-circulation magazines.

Even so, all these periodicals presented themselves primarily as 'family' magazines, and it was some time before any enduring French-language magazine overtly addressed a female readership, as did the *Ladies' Home Journal* (1883–) in the United States and *Chatelaine* (1928–) in English Canada. Nascent efforts included *Paysana* (Montreal, 1938–49) and *Jovette* (Montreal, 1941–52), the latter created by the publishers of *La Revue moderne*. The turning point occurred when *La Revue populaire* (Montreal, 1907–63) – the most important French-Canadian magazine of the period, along with *Le Samedi* (Montreal, 1889–1963) – gradually evolved into the 'Magazine de la Canadienne,' a subtitle finally adopted in 1958, when its monthly circulation exceeded 100,000. Along similar lines, in 1960 the French *Chatelaine* replaced *La Revue moderne*, which had been bought by Maclean-Hunter Publishing in Toronto.

Châtelaine (1960–), whose monthly circulation quickly reached 112,000, became the most important large-circulation magazine in Quebec.[26] Its first editor, Fernande Saint-Martin, made it a venue for the dissemination of women's views on a wide range of issues. Her editorials dealt with such subjects as feminism and social action, education, laws, and language and culture. *Châtelaine* also introduced new writers. Women journalists managed editorial and production processes in Montreal and determined the magazine's content, although they did not control the business operations, which were located in Toronto. Women readers in Quebec adopted *Châtelaine* as an important vehicle for women's social concerns in the 1960s and 1970s. Subsequently, *Châtelaine* became less of an educational or literary magazine and more oriented toward health, fashion, and entertainment. Moreover, beginning in the 1960s, topics that had been discussed in specific sections in *Châtelaine* became the basis for new and specialized periodicals.

Thus, over the course of the twentieth century, French-Canadian magazines evolved from 'family' publications to 'women's' publications. Through editorial content and targeted advertising that addressed female consumers, they contributed to defining a public space specifically for women.

Women's Magazines in English Canada: The Success of *Chatelaine*

Canada's most prominent women's periodical – and perhaps all-time magazine success story – was launched in March 1928 by the J.B. MacLean Company (owner of the flourishing *Maclean's Magazine*) as a general-interest publication for middle-class

Canadian women. Engagement with readers appeared at the outset; a 'name the magazine' contest with a prize of $1,000 received more than 75,000 entries,[27] leading to an initial print run of 60,000. By 1950 *Chatelaine* enjoyed an annual circulation of nearly 380,000. After its purchase in 1958 of the subscription list of *Canadian Home Journal* its circulation nearly doubled.[28] It subsequently became the largest paid-circulation magazine in Canada, exceeding one million subscribers in 1986,[29] as well as maintaining a prominent newsstand presence. As noted above, the French counterpart appeared in 1960 when the Maclean-Hunter Publishing Company purchased *La Revue moderne.* This strategic move was designed to create an inclusive national market for advertisers, and thereby forestall the threat of a major American women's magazine establishing a Canadian edition. The editor of the French edition, Fernande Saint-Martin, was a friend of the current English editor, Doris Anderson. The two versions shared some advertisements and articles. Although they carried separate editorials, they fulfilled parallel cultural roles and often held similar positions.[30]

Alongside the fashion columns and family advice typical of women's magazines, in its first decades *Chatelaine* published articles by the major proponents of maternal feminism. Judge Helen Gregory MacGill exhorted women to participate in public life (1928); Emily Murphy described the significance of the Persons Case (the 1929 landmark ruling of the British Privy Council declaring that, in Canada, women were 'persons' eligible to run for the Senate); and Nellie McClung advocated the ordination of women (1934). Women's work outside the home was a recurring theme; during the Second World War, Lotta Dempsey provocatively asked, 'Will the women workers go back home when it's over?'[31] In the 1950s the magazine's focus narrowed to post-war domesticity. It provided entertaining fiction, spiced with frank medical advice from Dr Marian Hilliard, whose columns ran from 1954 until her sudden death in 1958.

When Doris Anderson became editor in 1957, *Chatelaine* was 'a thin magazine devoted primarily to fiction, departmental features, and cheerful editorials.' She transformed it into 'an important resource for Canadian women which emphasized general feature articles, opinionated and often feminist editorial essays, and reader participation.'[32] Anderson highlighted Canadian topics and controversial issues. In 1959 she justified restricted legal abortion and then published an array of readers' letters. The following year, she ran 'the first article in North America on battered babies.'[33] After exposing the hypocrisy of Canada's divorce laws (1961), *Chatelaine* tackled pay equity in an article entitled 'All Canadians Are Equal except Women' (1962). In addition to featuring readers' letters, Anderson invited women to submit accounts of their experiences: 'In 1971 forty-eight stories in *Chatelaine* were written by people who had never before been published in a national publication.'[34]

Anderson summarized her magazine's success as both material and social: 'When I took over *Chatelaine*, the circulation was 480,000. By the end of the 1960s, the magazine was being read by 1.8 million women – one of every three in Canada. No magazine in the U.S. had anything like that penetration ... What we [accomplished] – besides putting out a good solid magazine with lots of Canadian content – was ... [to] help launch in North America the second stage of the women's movement.'[35] Moreover, *Chatelaine*'s administrative structure promoted women's professionalism: 'At a time when only two [American] magazines – *Woman's Day* and *Cosmopolitan* – had women editors, *Chatelaine*'s masthead was almost entirely filled with women's names.'[36]

Although Anderson claims to have pitched the magazine at 'a whole new generation of younger women ... bright homemakers, many with a university education,'[37] subsequent research indicates that in the 1950s and 1960s *Chatelaine*'s readership mirrored the Canadian average with regard to most demographic categories.[38] Readers' loyalty was maintained by answering their letters, publishing their views, and upholding the sense that 'from the Jazz Age to the New Age, *Chatelaine* has belonged to its readers ... They wanted a meeting place where grown women could connect as friends ... a Canada-wide kitchen table where no-holds-barred conversation ranged from what's wrong with health care to what's for dinner.'[39] Though totally independent of one another, the English and French magazines issued under the title of *Chatelaine/Châtelaine* recorded and influenced the lives of women during the 1960s and 1970s.

CASE STUDY
Almanacs in French Canada
– Frédéric Brisson

The almanac in French Canada is a distinct phenomenon. Whereas in the United States and English Canada, almanacs became advertising vehicles[40] in the early twentieth century and lost much of the popularity they had enjoyed in the nineteenth, they reached their peak in French Canada in the 1920s. The *Almanach du peuple Beauchemin* (1855–62, 1869–), the *Almanach Rolland* (1867–1936), and the *Almanach de la langue française* (1916–37), the three most popular during that decade, together sold over 200,000 copies annually, an extraordinary number for a population of less than two million.[41]

Oldest and best-known was the *Almanach du peuple.* Its cover, designed by Henri Julien at the end of the nineteenth century, remained unchanged

8.2 *Almanach du peuple 1959* (Montreal: Librairie Beauchemin, [1958]). The Montreal Canadiens celebrate the fourth of five successive Stanley Cup victories. Courtesy of Groupe Polygone and Club de hockey Canadien Inc.

for several decades, while the almanac's contents gradually expanded. Its pages included calendars, weather forecasts, horoscopes, ecclesiastical dates, lists of elected federal and provincial representatives and cabinet ministers, and laws relating to hunting and fishing. In the early twentieth century, substantial sections on education, agriculture, entertainment, sports, medicine, and hygiene were added, as well as literary stories and women's issues, enlarging the publication from some 130 pages in 1896 to 480 pages in 1914, a size that then remained stable for many years.[42] The *Almanach du peuple* was very different from its nearest English-language counterpart, the *Canadian Almanac and Directory* (1848–). The former, with its varied texts and illustrations, was intended for a very broad readership, while the latter more closely resembled a reference book.

At the end of the 1930s, the *Almanach du peuple*'s two main competitors ceased publication, yet it continued to grow, largely because the resources of its publisher, Librairie Beauchemin, included printing facilities and a broad distribution network. A low price of 25 to 35 cents between 1913 and 1940 also contributed to its widespread popularity. From about mid-century, coverage of sports (see illus. 8.2, p. 252) and women's issues expanded significantly. Between 1970 and 1980, the publication grew from 512 to 832 pages, a result, in part, of the addition of large sections bought by the Quebec and Canadian governments to publicize their ministries and services. From 1956 until it ceased publication in 1994, the *Almanach Éclair,* which became the *Almanach moderne,* published by Distributions Éclair, represented a serious competitor for Beauchemin; in the 1970s, each had print runs of some 125,000.[43] The *Almanach du peuple,* which had belonged to Beauchemin since its founding, was sold to the Groupe Polygone in 1982.

The *Almanach du peuple* is so deeply rooted in Quebec popular culture that it has survived the development of modern communication technology. Halfway between a book and a magazine, offering practical advice, diverse information and entertainment, and a review of the previous year, the *Almanach du peuple* continues to appeal to readers today.

CASE STUDY
Serial Pulp Fiction in Quebec
– Jacques Michon

The temporary halt of imports from France during the Second World War inspired Quebec's publishers to launch their own popular serials based on American pulp fiction. From 1940 to 1966 tens of thousands of westerns, spy stories, detective novels, and romances were offered to French readers every week in the form of booklets of 16 to 32 pages. Written by local authors, these episodic tales were printed on newsprint with garishly illustrated covers. American influence was evident not only in their content, format (17 × 12 cm; 22 × 15 cm), and methods of production, but also in the advertising strategies employed by their publishers. Issued in print runs of 10,000 and priced at 10 cents apiece, these serials were distributed through newsstands in Quebec and French Canada.[44] A single author such as Pierre Daignault, writing under the pseudonyms Pierre Saurel and Hercule Valjean, produced more than two thousand stories over a period of more than twenty years.

8.3 Four examples of serial pulp fiction published by Montreal's Éditions Police Journal. Top (l. to r.): Rita Lebrun, *Rêves d'amour*, 'Le Roman d'amour' series, no. 400, [1955]; Pierre Saurel, *Tu viens chéri*, 'Les aventures policières d'Albert Brien, détective national des Canadiens français' series, no. 805, [1963]. Bottom (l. to r.): *Sept gouttes de sang: Un autre épisode de la périlleuse carrière d'Alain de Guise*, 'Les exploits policiers du Domino noir' series, no. 392, [1955]; Pierre Saurel, *Le sérum miracle*, 'Les aventures étranges de l'agent IXE-13, l'as des espions canadiens' series, no. 851, [1964]. Courtesy of Sogides Ltée.

At the end of the war, most of the publishing houses producing this kind of material belonged to printers in Montreal and Berthierville; however, they were soon supplanted by the Imprimerie judiciaire (Court House Printing Reg'd), which belonged to Edgar Lespérance, the owner and founder of Éditions Police Journal in Montreal. In 1946, when Lespérance acquired Éditions du Bavard from Eugène L'Archevêque, his main competitor, he became the dominant figure in this market. Over some twenty years, he published five series that were especially popular with young readers and enjoyed lasting success: 'Aventures de cow-boys,' 'Les aventures étranges de l'agent IXE-13, l'as des espions canadiens,'[45] 'Les aventures extraordinaires de Guy Verchères, l'Arsène Lupin canadien-français,' 'Les aventures policières d'Albert Brien, détective national des Canadiens français,' and 'Les exploits policiers du Domino noir' (see illus. 8.3, p. 254).

Building on this success, in 1958 Lespérance formed a partnership with Jacques Hébert to found Éditions de l'Homme. The following year, he set up the Agence de distribution populaire, which supplied his publications to more than 1,800 retail outlets across the country.[46] However, at the beginning of the Quiet Revolution, the penetration of pocket-book series from Librairie Hachette and Éditions Marabout hurt the market for fiction published in weekly series; Éditions Police Journal closed down, whereas Éditions de l'Homme went on to flourish by producing one-dollar paperbacks.

CASE STUDY
Canadian Pulp Magazines and Second World War Regulations
– Carolyn Strange and Tina Loo

The Canadian pulp-magazine industry boomed in the 1940s thanks to a wartime austerity act that reduced American competition. In 1940 Mackenzie King's Liberal government prohibited the importation of non-essential goods for the war's duration when it passed the War Exchange Conservation Act (4–5 George 6, 1940, c. 2). Along with other leisure and luxury items, such as playing cards and champagne, the act proscribed periodicals that featured 'detective, sex, western, and alleged true or confession stories.' Canadian producers stepped in to fill the void.

Popular presses, which had turned out such tabloids as *Jack Canuck* (Toronto, 1911–18), as well as comic books (see illus. 8.4, p. 256) and Mountie

8.4 Adrian Dingle, *Nelvana of the Northern Lights*, 'Queen of the Crystal World' in 'The Unmasked Claw!' (ca. 1943). During the Second World War, when access to American comics was restricted, Canadian superheroes had their day. From 1941 to 1947, a series of Nelvana comics written by Adrian Dingle and published by Triumph Comics (Toronto) featured a semi-divine Arctic heroine able to travel at the speed of light on a giant ray of the Aurora Borealis. © Nelvana Limited. Used with Permission. All Rights Reserved. Copy courtesy of the Toronto Public Library, Osborne Collection of Early Children's Books.

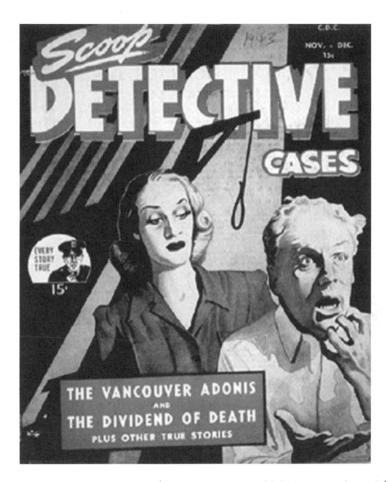

8.5 *Scoop Detective Cases*, Nov.–Dec. 1943 (Toronto: Magazine Publishing House of Canada). Courtesy of LAC/BAC.

dime novels, expanded, and several Toronto businesses, including Super Publications, Alval Publishers, Daring Productions, and the Norman Book Company, and others in Vancouver and Montreal, added new titles to their lists, issuing these publications in print runs substantial enough to meet the demands of Canada's mass-market distribution network. With names such as *Burlesque* (1942?–?), *Best True Fact Detective Cases* (Toronto, 194?–?), and *Sensational Love Experiences* (Toronto, 194?–?), they mimicked their banned U.S. pulp counterparts in both content and format.[47]

Wartime restrictions also created opportunities for writers and artists. Canadian popular fiction writers had been selling stories (particularly

Mountie tales) to American and British publishers for decades. Contributors to Toronto's Depression-era tabloids also found more work as a result of the act. These writers of true crime and crime fiction, who included such authors as Philip Godsell, C.V. Tench, and W.W. Bride, joined romance, science fiction, adventure, and horror writers in the stable of contributors to the Canadian pulps of the 1940s, earning from $50 to $400 per story.

The newly energized Canadian pulp industry published material from several sources: stories lifted from U.S. magazines, American manuscripts sent by writers stationed in the United States, and original, Canadian-authored stories. Sporting garish cover art in imitation of their American counterparts, despite poorly printed interiors, these magazines were cheap and bold (see illus. 8.5, p. 257). Available on newsstands, in drugstores, and at train stations, they targeted people with a taste for sensation and a dime or two to spare.

The heyday of Canadian pulps was short-lived. By the early 1950s, pulp publications featuring stories with Canadian content, particularly true crime magazines, were hard to find. One explanation is the passage of the 'Fulton Bill,' which led to a 1949 amendment to the Criminal Code prohibiting the publication of '*any* magazine, periodical or book which exclusively or substantially comprises matter depicting pictorially the commission of crimes, real or fictitious.'[48] Yet pulp magazines of all genres saw declining sales by the 1950s. The rise of the paperback novel, not government censorship, spelled the end of a publishing era, turning the pulps into nostalgic and highly collectible items by the 1960s.

PART FOUR

PUBLISHING FOR DISTINCT READERSHIPS

chapter 9

GOVERNMENT AND CORPORATE PUBLISHING

Government as Author and Publisher

GILLES GALLICHAN AND BERTRUM H. MACDONALD

By the second decade of the twentieth century, governments, especially at the federal level, had become the largest publisher in Canada. After the First World War, the number of government ministries, departments, agencies, commissions, Crown corporations, boards, task forces, committees, courts, and other offices proliferated. Through the Queen's/King's Printer or other arrangements, each produced numerous publications in order to advance government or political agendas, to inform Canadian citizens and international readers, and to support the functions of a modern state. Canadians expected their governments to communicate with them on many subjects; in response, governments turned out thousands of titles both ephemeral and substantial, usually authored anonymously in the name of the unit which published them.

Government Printing and Publishing at the Federal Level

In Canada the federal government, like those of each of the provinces, confers its official publishing upon a designated printer, known as the Queen's or King's Printer, depending upon the identity of the reigning sovereign. The Queen's/King's Printer has long been under the jurisdiction of the Secretary of State. Its responsibilities include the design and production of official government notices, advertisements, and publications, reports of commissions of inquiry, public notices, election returns, and statistical reports. Provision of photographic services for the government also falls under its purview. Finally, it has overseen the deposit of these documents in designated libraries and institutions, as well as their sale and dissemination to the public, using its own offices, distribution centres, and bookstores to meet these objectives.

The increase in print production by the federal government in the twentieth century naturally followed the demographic and economic growth of the country, as well as advances in printing technology. Times of war were busy periods in the production of particular types of printed matter, such as leaflets, ration coupons, military posters, and public notices. In 1939, in anticipation of urgent printing work during the Second World War, the budget of the King's Printer was increased from $700,000 to $2 million, while the government's total expenditure grew from nearly $5 million in 1939 to about $12 million in 1945. After the war, the Mackenzie King government sought to maintain this increased budget, believing that the needs would continue to grow. In Parliament, however, the Opposition became suspicious of this expansion. The Conservative MP for Peel (Ontario), Gordon Graydon, noted that an 'enormous amount of money is being spent by the government upon all kinds of informational and publicity work,' and declared: 'If there ever was a government that seemed to be printing-ink conscious, it is this one.'[1] Over the next two decades, the government was also criticized for engaging in unfair competition with private enterprise.[2]

The National Printing Bureau was one area of federal government printing that functioned largely as an internal service. Founded in the 1890s under the jurisdiction of the Secretary of State, the bureau's work included government publishing that was coupled with a large amount of translation, especially the record of debates of the House of Commons and the Senate (*Hansard*), which had to be published daily. The teams doing the transcription, editing, translation, and printing of the debates had long been accustomed to this demanding work. In 1949, the day after the budget speech, MPs leafing through the voluminous *Hansard* produced overnight expressed their amazement at the work that had been accomplished, comparing the job of the National Printing Bureau to that of putting out an issue of the *New York Times* and calling the printers and translators 'unsung heroes' preparing documents for the historical record.[3]

In 1951 the National Printing Bureau had more than a thousand employees. In the decade that followed, its facilities improved and its budget increased. The old presses, worn out by increased production, were replaced.[4] In response to the growing awareness of the importance of advertising, particularly during periods of armed conflict, colourful posters were produced while illustrations were increasingly used in reports and in publications for the public. By mid-century, the National Printing Bureau could no longer meet the entire demand from government departments. In the 1950s, and even more so after 1968, when the federal government contracted some of its printing to private businesses, it endeavoured to spread its orders throughout the country. In 1980 the federal government had a budget of $140 million for printing, only $57 million of which was spent in the Ottawa region.

Government Printing and Publishing at the Provincial Level

Provincial governments have similarly placed their Queen's/King's Printer under the jurisdiction of their Secretary of State or another appropriate ministry. For example, in Nova Scotia, the position of King's Printer, established at the beginning of the nineteenth century, was assigned after 1934 directly to a cabinet minister or even to the premier. The responsibilities of the Queen's/King's Printer include the publication of laws and executive documents, though provincial parliaments have also maintained the right to publish their materials autonomously. During the twentieth century, nonetheless, the use of independent printers by the provincial legislatures diminished.

When the established British colonies of British Columbia and Newfoundland joined Confederation in 1871 and 1949, each already had a King's/Queen's Printer in operation. The situation was different for the provinces of Alberta and Saskatchewan, which were created out of the North-West Territories in 1905. In Edmonton, the government of Alberta had to establish its own King's Printer, whereas in Regina, which had been the Territorial capital, the new provincial government took over the printing services of the previous administration. It was not until the late 1940s that the Manitoba government established its own government printer. In the early 1950s, government publishers and printers formed the Queen's Printers Association of Canada, whose members meet annually to exchange information. In the 1960s and 1970s, official publication, including the office of the Queen's Printer, often came under the jurisdiction of newly created provincial communications departments. These departments also provided printing and photocopying services, which expanded substantially during this period.

Although the Quebec legislature appointed a committee on printing, until 1968 legislative publications were usually produced by government printers. As in the other provinces, printing contracts under all jurisdictions were traditionally

9.1 Composing room of *L'Action catholique*, Quebec City, 1925. This office was awarded the government printing contract for the Province of Quebec in 1936. Reproduced from *L'Almanach de l'Action catholique* (Quebec City: Action catholique, 1926). Courtesy of the Bibliothèque de l'Assemblée nationale, Quebec City.

awarded at the discretion of the ministers, who favoured printers who were friends of the current government. To justify this practice, ministers argued that the printing of laws was extremely demanding, necessitating a relationship of trust between the government and its suppliers, who were chosen not only for their competence, but also for their respect for professional secrecy. It was feared that tendering in this very specialized sector would lead to collusion among companies and increase costs. Before 1936, *Le Soleil* and *The Quebec Chronicle Telegraph*, both Liberal newspapers in Quebec City, received lucrative printing and binding contracts;[5] under Duplessis's Union national government, the contracts went to the printing office of *L'Action catholique* (see illus. 9.1, above).

With the abolition of the Secretary of State in 1968, Quebec's Queen's Printer was replaced by the Quebec Official Publisher, which functioned under the Speaker of the National Assembly until 1971, when it was placed under the jurisdiction of the minister of communications. Since then, it has become a true publisher, named Publications du Québec. Its production became more diversified, including illustrated albums and coffee-table books, and its series were very popular with the general public. Since a 1967 agreement with France, stores run by Publications du Québec have distributed materials from the French government.

At the provincial level, Ontario issued the largest number of provincial publications between 1918 and 1980. Its Department of Education accounted for the lion's share, with such documents as laws and regulations on education, programs, educational material, directories of educational institutions, and pedagogical periodicals. Its Departments of Transportation and Agriculture were also major producers. In the 1930s and 1940s, Health and Labour were the departments with the largest increases in publications. In Quebec, the largest numbers of publications were issued in the sectors of agriculture and land settlement, natural resources, and lands and forests. Specific series also accounted for a great many publications. For example, between 1920 and 1975, provincial archivists Pierre-Georges Roy and Antoine Roy reproduced documents from Quebec's history in a series of books totalling some 50,000 pages, a veritable monument of documentation. The governments of Newfoundland and the Maritime provinces published regularly in the areas of tourism, public utilities, health, and fisheries. In the Western provinces, agriculture dominated government publishing. After 1960, in all provinces, tourist publications (regional attractions, itineraries, pamphlets, accommodations directories, etc.) became important.

Government Authorship

The *Canada Year Book*, issued by the Dominion Bureau of Statistics (later Statistics Canada), exemplifies federal government authorship. This long-running serial, primarily an annual compilation from a wide range of statistical reports, encapsulated the activities of the nation in demographic, social, educational, environmental, political, and economic terms. In 1920 attention was placed on post-war reconstruction; sixty years later, the volume for 1980–1 characterized the nation in twenty-three chapters that included 'Communications' and 'Cultural Activities and Leisure,' documenting newspaper and book publishing and reporting on a national survey of reading habits. In 1930 a companion handbook series, *Canada*, was initiated, revealing Canada through narrative and pictures interspersed with statistics. Both federal and provincial governments created many royal commissions, whose reports could be brief synopses, such as the *Report of the Manitoba Royal Commission on Adult Education* (1945), or lengthy productions, such as the six-volume *Report of the*

Commission of Inquiry into The Pas Forestry and Industrial Complex at The Pas, Manitoba (1974).

Annual reports, often mandated by legislation, were common publications for government agencies and departments. Their structure and content varied widely depending on the government unit and political agendas. The federally issued *Canadian Mineral Industry* report (est. 1956) offered a detailed analysis of the industry. In contrast, the *Annual Report* of the Manitoba Water Supply Board (est. 1960) was typically fewer than twenty-five pages in length. The impermanent nature of some reports is suggested by the mimeographed *Annual Report Covering the Operation and Enforcement of Liquor Laws in Manitoba* (1953).

Executive branches of both federal and provincial governments were the most prolific authors.[6] Some turned out a wide variety of publications in formats ranging from pamphlets to multi-volume bound reports. The federal Department of Agriculture, for example, produced a vast number of instructive publications, such as *Thrifty Meals with Canned Vegetables* (1969), *What You Should Know about Wheat* (1969; rev. 1975, 1977), and *Handling Eggs from Producer to Retailer* (1969; rev. 1975). This department also issued many substantial works, such as *The System of Soil Classification for Canada* (1970; rev. 1974). The federal Department of Finance prepared the weighty *Public Accounts*, which grew from a 156-page document in 1920 to three volumes in 1980, numbering more than 1,230 pages.

The mandate of a government department and its subsidiary units influenced both the quantity of publications generated each year and the degree to which corporate authorship was applied. A substantial department like Agriculture, which existed at both federal and provincial levels throughout the twentieth century, fulfilled multiple roles, one of which was to educate and inform the public. Canadians everywhere encountered publications prepared for this latter purpose, many of which were written under the name of the corporate body. Long-running serials produced by provincial bodies often used corporate authors. The *Analyse budgétaire des municipalités du Québec*, initiated by the Bureau de la statistique du Québec in 1969, is one example. In addition to such series, 'one-off' publications were common in every province, such as *Matrimonial Property Reform for New Brunswick* (1978). Since the Canadian parliamentary system of government has the flexibility to create and disband departments and subordinate units with relative ease (without requiring constitutional amendments), changes and variations of corporate authorship were common at all levels of government.

By mid-century, municipal governments, with all their subsidiary bodies, had begun to swell the ranks of prolific government authors. Some larger cities rivalled the smaller provincial governments in their total annual output. In 1968 Metropolitan Toronto had close to one hundred special-purpose bodies in addition to the city and five borough governments. The departments and councils of cities, counties, boroughs, towns, villages, and municipalities (regional and metropolitan governments) prepared publications to meet local needs. Since municipalities are the creatures of provincial governments, the Municipal Act in each province set the parameters of the publications that municipal governments issued. These included administrative documents, such as bylaws and minutes and agendas of council meetings, often accompanied by reports from civic departments, like the Vancouver City Planning Department's *Analysis and Forecast of Motor Vehicle Travel* (1959). Cities also created official plans and engineering documents, such as Montreal's *Plan directeur de Montréal – Espaces libres* (1955). Voters' lists, zoning bylaws, departmental annual reports, financial reports and audited statements, and maps of public and private lands constitute other kinds of documents frequently created by towns and cities.[7] The highest production values were often reserved for publicity and public relations materials, such as the Halifax Recreation Department's *Recreation in Halifax: Parks & Playgrounds, Schools, Other Recreational Opportunities* (1976). As Canada's cities became more multicultural, municipalities began to print utilitarian documents in the various languages of their residents.

Over the course of the twentieth century, all levels of government produced increasing numbers of publications, ensuring that Canadians had access to a vast diversity of printed materials which could affect their lives locally, nationally, or internationally. After 1980, desktop publishing replaced traditional techniques, and some series, such as statistics, became accessible only in electronic format. Virtual communication via the Internet added to the range of services provided by governments, but it did not replace the printed page.

CASE STUDY
The Federal Government's Advice to Mothers
– Katherine Arnup

In the early decades of the twentieth century, concern developed in Canada, as elsewhere in the Western world, over national health. Despite improvements in the health of the general population, infant mortality rates remained alarmingly high.[8] That fact, combined with a decreasing birth rate among Canadian-born citizens, increasing non-British immigra-

tion, and the deaths caused by the First World War and the Spanish influ-
enza epidemic of 1918–19, fuelled anxieties about the potential decline in
Canada of a predominantly white society of British and French cultural heritage. Hence, during the interwar years, governments at all levels began to
sponsor maternal advice literature. Although advice manuals were already
an established genre, direct government involvement in their production
was an innovation. Written almost exclusively by physicians, these publications were produced, funded, and distributed by government departments
and agencies. This literature, sanctioned by both the medical profession
and the state, held a legitimacy and authority not enjoyed by previous
publications.

Believing that mothers were responsible for national health, women's
groups, public health reformers, physicians, and government officials
launched campaigns to educate women for motherhood. At the forefront
was Dr Helen MacMurchy, first chief of the federal Department of Health's
Division of Child Welfare (est. 1920), a body that during its first year distributed 365,503 pieces of literature. Upon her appointment, MacMurchy wrote
The Canadian Mother's Book (1921), published in French as *Le livre des mères canadiennes.* Initially 86 pages in English and 118 in French, it went into six editions and eventually expanded to over two hundred pages. By the time the
division was briefly disbanded in 1933, approximately 800,000 copies had
been distributed. MacMurchy's staff also produced a series of pamphlets in
English and French known as the Little Blue Books / Petits livres bleus.
Launched in 1921, the series covered topics ranging from infant care to food
preparation and household management.[9] When the division was re-established in 1937, its new chief, Dr Ernest Couture, produced *The Canadian
Mother and Child* (1940), published simultaneously in French under the title
La mère canadienne et son enfant. Like its predecessor, this book proved to be
extremely popular (see illus. 9.2, p. 269). Demand constantly outstripped
supply: the initial run of 90,000 copies was distributed within the first year,
and a second run of 38,000 copies was depleted within three and a half
months of receipt from the printer. The division maintained a waiting list of
several thousand names pending the next printing.[10] In December 1948 the
minister of health, Paul Martin, presented the one-millionth copy of the
book.[11]

Demand for the division's publications was especially high in Quebec.
Federal literature was translated into French and distributed through

9.2 *The Canadian Mother and Child* (Ottawa: Department of National Health and Welfare, 1953) / *La mère canadienne et son enfant* (Ottawa: Ministère de la santé nationale et du bien-être social, 1963). Courtesy of Toronto Public Library and private collection.

various provincial agencies. Of the 72,346 mothers who in 1926 received *The Canadian Mother's Book* (almost one-third of all Canadian women giving birth that year), nearly 40 per cent requested the French edition, a high figure, given that the 1921 census had registered only 27.9 per cent of the population as French-speaking.[12]

In addition to copies sent in response to direct requests, government publications were distributed by public health nurses, doctors, magazines, and department stores. Throughout the interwar period, the federal government relied almost exclusively on publications to influence maternal and child health, citing federal-versus-provincial jurisdictional issues determined by the British North America Act (1867) as an impediment to providing direct aid to facilities such as well-baby clinics. Federal publications were distributed free until 1955, when a minimal charge began to be levied.

While mothers were inundated with information from many sources, the message they received during the 1920s and 1930s was uniform: follow your physician's directives and raise your children in accordance with the principles of scientific child-rearing. That advice discounted traditional information-sharing among women and implemented rigid regimes concerning the feeding, bathing, holding, comforting, and toilet training of infants and small children.[13] Such strictures engendered a measure of guilt and anxiety among mothers, who struggled to maintain standards that often lay beyond their reach. Nonetheless, through these publications they received valuable information about nutrition and hygiene that, coupled with general improvements in sanitation, refrigeration, and pasteurization, may have contributed to a notable decline in the infant mortality rate.

The Publishing Activities of CBC / Radio-Canada

DOMINIQUE MARQUIS

In November 1936 the Canadian Broadcasting Act (1 Edward 8, 1936, c. 24) gave the Canadian Broadcasting Corporation (CBC) / Société Radio-Canada (SRC) a mandate to develop and manage radio broadcasting in Canada. The planning of national programming proved difficult, because tensions between anglophones and francophones regarding the place of French seemed unavoidable. In 1937 a solution was found through the creation of a French-language station, CBF (Canadian Broadcasting in French), which provided French-language broadcasts in the greater Montreal region. From then on, the two networks developed in parallel. National programming in English provided a counterbalance to American broadcasts, while a French-language network was gradually established that attempted to meet the needs of all francophones in Canada.[14]

The CBC/SRC was established with a multi-faceted mandate: to inform, to entertain, and to educate the population, with an emphasis on Canadian content. It offered many programs in fulfillment of its educational mission: literature, science, philosophy, and history were among the subjects discussed on radio and, later, television. Largely as a public service, CBC's Publications Branch produced books and pamphlets based on broadcasts. Between 1939 and 1942 about a dozen English titles appeared;[15] by 1980 over a hundred titles had been issued by each of the networks, the majority during the 1960s and 1970s. Although the CBC/SRC was legally a single administrative entity, the two networks were relatively autonomous and adopted different broadcasting strategies, a circumstance that was reflected in their publishing activities. Only a few of their titles appeared in both languages, among them *From Sea to Sea / D'un océan à l'autre* (1961), and *Thirty-four Biographies of Canadian Composers / 34 biographies de compositeurs canadiens* (1964).

The English-language network published transcripts of radio programs such as *CBC University of the Air* and *Ideas*, which served the network's educational mission especially well. Many other CBC programs inspired appealing books, including some two dozen collections of Mary Grannan's best-selling children's stories (see illus. 4.3, p. 149) as well as volumes of literary stories emanating from the adult programming described by Sheila Latham in chapter 4. Due to copyright concerns, these volumes usually appeared under the imprint of Toronto trade publishers such as Thomas Allen, Ryerson, or Macmillan.[16] This situation changed with the establishment of CBC Enterprises; founded in 1982 to commercialize CBC recordings, it subsequently became the standard imprint on CBC publications.[17]

The prestigious Massey Lectures, initiated in 1961 and broadcast annually on *Ideas* since 1965, were regularly published. Named for former Governor General Vincent Massey, this series has included such internationally renowned guests as Northrop Frye (*The Educated Imagination*, 1962), Martin Luther King (*Conscience for Change*, 1967), and Claude Lévi-Strauss (*Myth and Meaning*, 1977). Other topics ranged from Canadian constitutional law to Christian philosophy, geology, and English literature. The presentation of all these books was sober, almost austere: small in format, they included a brief portrait of the author, a table of contents, and a bibliography. By 1969 many titles had sold over 10,000 copies, and Barbara Ward's *The Rich Nations and the Poor Nations* (1961) had reached 20,000. In general, the CBC envisioned an educated readership, noting with pride that 'there is a C.B.C. book being used as supplementary material at every English language university in Canada.' During the 1960s, books arising from the CBC's science programs, such as *Darwin and the Galapagos*, sold some 15,000 copies at the price of $1.00.[18]

Like the CBC, the French-language network fulfilled its educational mission with scholarly books on history, religion, and language. Both networks also offered a broad range of less formal materials, including transcripts of interviews, travel writing, poetry, stories, and recipes, all based on radio and television programs. The SRC often entrusted production and distribution to independent publishing houses such as Leméac, Hurtubise HMH, Héritage, and Éditions de l'Homme. For example, some of the major interviews done by Fernand Seguin for the television program *Le sel de la semaine* were co-published with Éditions de l'Homme. Issued in an unusual, very narrow format (25 × 10 cm), the abridged published interviews did their best to capture the spirit of the original broadcasts and extend their life in the viewers' memory.[19]

The SRC occasionally published books independently. Transcriptions of some forty radio interviews broadcast on the program *Portraits d'écrivains québécois* (1979–80) fell within this category, as did books on the technical aspects of radio and television broadcasting. Radio-Canada also had a long-standing reputation for the quality and number of its children's programs, as shown by the substantial list of its titles in this area. In 1967 the first nine episodes of the popular television series *D'Iberville* were reworked and co-published by Ici Radio-Canada and Leméac in an illustrated fifty-page book. In the 1960s and 1970s, children's programs by two star writers of the SRC, Michel and André Cailloux, were published jointly by Ici Radio-Canada or the SRC and Éditions Héritage. Young readers were thus able to rediscover the adventures of *Bobino* and *Nic et Pic* in picture books.

Although the French and English networks operated as separate entities, they both used print to extend and supplement their broadcasting mandate. This strategy resulted in hundreds of books that enabled listeners and viewers to catch up with broadcasts they had missed, or revisit those they had enjoyed.

CPR in Print

IAIN STEVENSON

The Canadian Pacific Railway (CPR) expanded from a transcontinental railway which linked eastern Canada to the Pacific Coast, starting in 1886, to a complex multinational corporation providing rail transport, shipping, air travel, hotels, and telecommunications, as well as engaging in land settlement, mining, and other businesses. Its hotels and train stations helped to create a distinctive Canadian cityscape, and its iconic use of natural scenery in its advertising communicated an enduring image of Canada as a land of pristine beauty and boundless opportunity.

At its height in 1945, the CPR employed close to ninety thousand people, or more than one in sixty of all Canadians in employment.[20] It also engaged in a vast publishing venture. From its headquarters at Windsor Station in Montreal, the company produced an unending stream of print: operating manuals, annual reports, magazines, brochures, maps, playing cards, greeting cards, telegrams, menus, games, tickets, postcards, and calendars. Publications were distributed by the CPR News Department through bookstalls in its stations and hotels, as well as on ships, trains, and aircraft.[21] Over nearly a century, the CPR's 'Herculean efforts' and 'innovations in silk screen production' also fostered 'a rich heritage' of Canadian poster art.[22]

The most basic publications of any railway are its timetables. Every six months, from 1886 until 1981, the CPR issued paper-bound timetables of its passenger services. By 1900 these were encased in the corporate livery of yellow covers, and in a standard size (23.5 × 20.5 cm). By 1916 they filled almost 100 pages, shrinking to 64 pages by 1938 and 32 pages by 1961. Timetables did not become bilingual until the 1960s.[23]

More elaborate was the *Annotated Time Table*, a souvenir guide for passengers travelling from Quebec City to Vancouver that provided distances, schedules, and descriptions of the sights en route. By 1912 it had grown to the 10-cent *Across Canada*, a 120-page volume in two colours with line drawings throughout and a three-colour cover. The title changed in 1927 to *Your Journey through the Canadian Pacific Rockies*, with a focus on the landscape between Calgary and Vancouver. The introduction of 'The Canadian' transcontinental train in 1955 launched *Across Canada by Canadian Pacific*, a full-colour, 28-page large-format souvenir guide to the entire route from Montreal to Vancouver.

To develop its market further, the CPR also published a wide range of tourist handbooks and publicity material. The most famous title is *The Challenge of the Mountains*, frequently reprinted following its initial appearance in 1903; its iconic cover image of a young female mountaineer contributed to the book's fame as a model of tourist literature. Perhaps the apotheosis of this kind of publication was *The Game Fishes of Canada* (1928), a 46-page hardback containing fifteen full-colour, full-page drawings. As well, multilingual brochures advertised transatlantic voyages in both directions; for example, *To and from Europe: Shortest Ocean Route, Large Fast Steamships* (July 1938) features panels in eight eastern European languages.[24]

Since a primary business objective of the CPR was to encourage immigration to the lands it owned along its tracks, it issued numerous titles extolling settlement opportunities, particularly in Western Canada. Typical is *British Columbia*, which appeared in many editions between 1900 and the 1930s as a handbook of 'trustworthy information'[25] for immigrants. With highly coloured covers often derived from posters designed by artists, the corporation's promotional literature targeted specific social groups, as in its brochure *Canada for Women* (1912).

Marketing to the wealthy, CPR steamships from 1920 offered cruises ranging from an annual, four-month circumnavigation of the globe to shorter Mediterranean or Baltic vacations. Passengers, who often paid fares over $2,000, were pampered with impeccable service, including specially printed handbook-itineraries. At first simple pamphlets, these quickly became elaborately designed hardbacks with 'the most exotic and colourful commercial artwork ever produced.'[26] During the 1920s and 1930s, travellers voyaging on CPR liners could purchase Katherine Hale's commissioned children's book *Legends of the St. Lawrence*, also issued in French as *Légendes du Saint-Laurent*, whose illustrations promoted bucolic images of rural Quebec. Interrupted by the Second World War, cruises recommenced in the 1950s, but the handbooks never again matched the style or lavishness of such titles as *Storied Coasts of the Mediterranean* (1930).

Characteristic of the CPR's paternalism toward its employees was a series called the Foundation Library. The goal was to provide 'a focal point for voluntary study among members of the great Canadian Pacific family' by publishing a set of subsidized books covering business, geography, history, railway operation, and language, in order to create the 'desire for self-improvement ... [and] ... a community spirit throughout the company ... tend[ing] to increased efficiency.'[27] Written by CPR managers or compiled from British or Canadian textbooks, the ten titles were printed in uniform gold-stamped red linen bindings with a bookplate reading 'Books are the Foundation of Knowledge' (see illus. 9.3, p. 275), and were sold by subscription to employees for $2 a set, less than half the production cost.[28] They proved extremely popular, with 14,000 sets going to anglophone staff across the country. The subject matter of the first nine volumes was serious and earnest, covering public speaking, French conversation, and parliamentary democracy, with a switch in genre for the final volume, *Canada Sings!*, a collection of popular songs. Sold out by 1940, the library subsequently lost its appeal. Only one volume, *Canadian Pacific Facts and Figures*, was republished in a second edition in 1946.

Despite this proliferation of print materials, the CPR did not set up its own printing arm but preferred to work in co-operation with established printers, mainly in Canada and Britain. This appears to have been a deliberate policy on the part of the company to support local industry. Following the termination of passenger services in 1981 and the CPR's focus on freight, its publishing output diminished, although annual reports and other corporate publications still appear. Now as then the com-

9.3 Canadian Pacific Railway Foundation Library bookplate, 1937. This specially designed book-plate was printed on the front endpaper of each book published in the CPR Foundation Library Series. Its design artfully combines the tree of knowledge with the CPR crest and a locomotive and an ocean liner that represent the corporation's two major enterprises. Courtesy of Canadian Pacific Railway Archives, A.37404.

pany's publishing displays two common characteristics: cutting-edge design that makes use of leading artists and innovative printing, and a pride in Canada and its landscapes, people, and resources.

chapter 10

ORGANIZED RELIGION AND PRINT

The Religious Press in Quebec

DOMINIQUE MARQUIS

At the beginning of the twentieth century, the Roman Catholic Church in Quebec, increasingly confronted with the changing realities of modern life, was impelled to address the needs of a population that was now mainly working-class, urban, and literate. To maintain its influence, the church deployed the press as a propaganda tool 'in the work of restoring all things in Christ,' an objective set out by Pope Pius X in 1905.[1]

Early in the century the church's newspapers and magazines were designed to support the faith and steer the population away from 'unhealthy' ideas. Between 1918 and 1980, more than seven hundred periodicals on Christian activities and the Christian message were published by the church in Quebec.[2] Approximately 30 per cent of these serials survived less than two years, while 25 per cent endured for over a quarter of a century. Quebec's multi-faceted Catholic publication activities may be divided into four broad categories corresponding to specific realms of church interest: devotional works, expressions of spirituality, foreign missions, and Catholic organizations.

The devotional press was by far the most stable. Congregations responsible for pilgrimage sites and dedicated to cults of particular saints published magazines, some of which lasted for more than a century. The *Revue Sainte-Anne*, issued by the

Redemptorist Fathers of the basilica of Saint-Anne-de-Beaupré since 1873, is among the oldest.[3]

To guide the reflections of the faithful, the church also published many magazines devoted to spirituality, thus providing models for a life in harmony with Catholic doctrine. The writers who contributed to these periodicals commented on current events from a Christian perspective, interpreted upheavals in society, and outlined changes in the liturgy and new pastoral approaches to society. These publications went through major adjustments as the century unfolded, and developed considerably after 1960 under the influence of the Quiet Revolution and the Second Council of the Vatican (1962–5). More than 40 per cent were established during the 1960s and 1970s.

Catholic religious communities with foreign missions were less affected by the changes of the twentieth century. The missionary press continued to reflect the proselytization of the Catholic Church, zealously spreading its values to faraway peoples. Periodicals issued by these communities typically served as forums for publicity and fundraising and praised the work of religious orders in foreign lands. About sixty of these magazines were published for a French-Canadian readership between 1918 and 1980.

Catholic associations proliferated in twentieth-century Quebec, issuing nearly one-quarter of the French-language Catholic periodicals surveyed. Newsletters, in particular, were published from the 1930s onward by specialized Catholic groups such as Jeunesse étudiane catholique, Jeunesse ouvrière catholique, and Jeunesse agricole catholique. These publications show how the faithful, both lay and clerical, coped with social change. Starting in 1965, when lay and non-denominational organizations took up the torch of social debate, the influence of association periodicals dwindled, and many ceased publication.

The Catholic Church also invested in daily and weekly newspapers, which it considered the best weapon against undesirable reading. 'Let us fight writing with writing,' wrote Pope Pius X in 1907.[4] Responding to this appeal, the bishop of Quebec City, Mgr Bégin, that year launched a major daily, L'Action sociale, which became L'Action catholique in June 1915. Although the routines of the newspaper press were foreign to the traditions of the church, the staff of the publication succeeded in meeting the challenge of producing a daily comparable to its main rivals, La Presse, Le Soleil, and La Patrie.[5] Other Quebec bishops followed Mgr Bégin's example. In Trois-Rivières in 1909, Mgr Cloutier founded Le Bien public. In 1912, Le Progrès du Saguenay became the organ of the diocese of Chicoutimi. In 1917, Le Messager de Saint-Michel, a parish newsletter, was founded in Sherbrooke; the following year, it became a weekly and the official organ of the diocese. In 1918, Mgr F.-X. Piette, the bishop of Joliette, became the owner of *L'Action populaire*. In Montreal, Mgr Bruchési preferred to encourage a project run by a layman and approved Henri Bourassa's creation of the major Catholic daily, *Le Devoir*, in 1910.

These newspapers, which represented only a fraction of the periodicals issued by Quebec's Catholic press in the twentieth century, were the most influential. While a newspaper like *L'Action catholique* demanded considerable effort and resources from religious authorities, the strong readership it maintained until the 1950s made it worthwhile. During that decade, the advent of television began to modify reading habits, while the rise of tabloid newspapers provided fierce competition for the Catholic press, which was increasingly out of touch with contemporary social and political realities. The church's efforts to modify its business practices to meet industry norms proved insufficient, and in 1971 the archdiocese of Quebec City had to sell its daily paper. Other Catholic newspapers also had to review their strategies and, in order to survive, gradually lessened their religious focus. After 1960, although it was becoming more difficult to sustain regional dailies or weeklies, the Catholic press succeeded in renewing itself. In 1968 the editors of these publications created the Association canadienne des périodiques catholiques to help them develop new directions, adapt their content, and improve the quality of their presentation.

During the twentieth century, to maintain its established position in Quebec, the Catholic press had to respond to pressures of social change. Certain categories of periodicals, such as devotional publications and missionary magazines, sailed through the period with few difficulties, while others, which were more closely tied to the church's engagement in everyday society, became more marginal, particularly after 1960.

CASE STUDY
The Magazine *Relations*
– Simone Vannucci

Relations, a magazine intended for the French-Canadian elite, was one of the major cultural periodicals of the 1940s issued by Catholic congregations in Canada. Others included *Culture* (Quebec City, 1940–70), a Franciscan publication, the *Revue dominicaine* (St Hyacinthe, QC, 1915–61), issued by the Dominicans, and *Carnets viatoriens* (Joliette, QC, 1939–55), produced by the Clerics of St Viator. According to the first editor of *Relations*, Jean-d'Auteuil Richard, the idea of creating a major Jesuit magazine on the model of *La Civiltà cattolica*, *Études,* and *America*, prestigious publications issued by the Society of Jesus in Italy, France, and the United States respectively, was first proposed in the early 1930s. *Relations* augmented the propaganda activities of the publishing arm of the Canadian Jesuits, located at the Centre de l'Immaculée-Conception in Montreal, which assembled a variety of services under one roof: a seminary; the Imprimerie du Messager, which printed periodicals; and a residence for writers connected to the community's publications. It was as part of this complex that *Relations* was established in January 1941.

Publishing monthly, with a format of 11 × 8.5 cm and an austere design, *Relations* replaced *L'Ordre nouveau* (1936–40), the organ of the 'semaines sociales,' annual conferences based on the church's social doctrine. It was intended as a high-quality magazine and had a special place in the Jesuits' 'arsenal of information.' The magazine's vocation was essentially social, covering all aspects of civic life. The industrial world, trade unionism, education – an eminently Ignatian concern – and health were the subjects most frequently discussed. From the outset, the editors took an interest in the burning questions of the day, such as the Arvida strike in 1941 (July-August issue) and the problem of asbestosis in 1948 (March); in fact, its coverage of the latter cost Jean-d'Auteuil Richard his job. The magazine also included book reviews aimed at its generally well-educated readership. Published under the aegis of the École sociale populaire, *Relations* saw its circulation increase from year to year, from 5,300 copies in 1942 to more than 15,000 in 1948.

The magazine has remained faithful to its social commitment and continues to participate in the major debates of the day. Supported by a team of laypersons and published by the Centre justice et foi under the responsibility of the Society of Jesus, *Relations* is available on newsstands throughout Quebec, or by subscription. Its current circulation, which has been stable for many years, is 4,000.

Catholic Publication and Distribution of Books in French

YVAN CLOUTIER

In the twentieth century, the major secular publishers in French Canada, unlike such houses as Desclée de Brouwer in Belgium and Lethielleux in France, invested little in religious books. At Librairie Beauchemin, the leader in Quebec's book trade up to 1960, religious titles represented only 6 per cent of total production: 110 out of 1,769 titles published between 1918 and 1980. At Granger Frères, the proportion was 11 per cent.[6] The participation of Catholic dioceses in publishing religious books was also negligible. In fact, the development of religious publishing in French Canada depended mainly on Catholic congregations established at the end of the nineteenth century, which initially preferred to issue periodicals, annuals, magazines, and calendars to disseminate their devotions.[7] In the 1930s, the huge growth of such publications[8] led to the adoption of more complex editorial structures, which were organized around printing offices, publishing houses, or bookstores.

In response to the social encyclicals of Popes Léon XIII and Pius XI, which resulted in the first activities of the specialized Action catholique in Belgium in 1925, some Canadian congregations extended their activities to publishing general literature. Religious books were produced mainly by five orders: the Dominican Order, the Congregation of Holy Cross, the Society of Jesus, the Society of St Paul, and the Missionary Oblates of Mary Immaculate. The last was active mainly outside Quebec, and its publishing activities are discussed by Dominique Marquis and Robert Yergeau in chapter 6.

In 1931 the Dominicans, who were located in Ottawa and Montreal, consolidated their activities around the Oeuvre de presse dominicaine and Éditions du Lévrier. Their production consisted of both scholarly books and those for a general readership. More than 42 per cent of the Lévrier catalogue consisted of religious books, but the importance of these books for the publisher was shown less in the number of titles than in the size of the print runs: *L'amour à l'âge atomique* (1950), *Le coeur et ses trésors* (1951), and *La vie en rose* (1952), all authored by Father Marcel-Marie Desmarais, each enjoyed cumulative printings of 150,000 copies.[9]

In 1937, under the direction of Father Paul-Aimé Martin, the Congregation of Holy Cross in Montreal launched *Mes fiches* (1937–66), a bimonthly newsletter on reading. This very successful publication was soon followed by a publishing service for the Jeunesse étudiante catholique organization, which in January 1941 became

Éditions Fides.[10] The new publishing house took advantage of the growth of Catholic action groups in Quebec, as well as the demand generated by the Second World War for French-language books. These markets supported the expansion of Fides, which in the 1940s and 1950s quickly became the foremost publisher of religious books and a major publisher of general literature in Quebec. Through this publishing house, the congregation participated in an innovative way in the moral and doctrinal renewal of the era. From the beginning, a third of its titles were religious in nature, a proportion that remained fairly constant until the 1970s. Fides enjoyed some major successes, such as Joseph Stedman's *Mon missel dominical* (1941), as well as many editions of the New Testament, which by 1978 had sold a total of two million copies. The rapid expansion of Fides outstripped the publishing activities of other congregations, and also discouraged secular publishers from entering this market.

Early in the century, the Society of Jesus set up a publishing network around the Imprimerie du Messager, an establishment located in Montreal. Beginning in the 1940s, the Jesuits gradually ceased publishing popular leaflets and books, and instead chose to concentrate on scholarly publishing, issuing such titles under the imprint Éditions Bellarmin.[11] However, the Society remained active in publishing religious magazines for the general public, such as *Relations* (1941–), discussed in this chapter by Simone Vannucci, and *Actualité: Ma paroisse* (1960–76).

Between 1920 and 1949, religious books represented on average 19 per cent of the total number of titles published by French-language publishers in Quebec. The arrival of the Society of St Paul in Sherbrooke in 1947, and its creation of Apostolat de la presse, a publishing house specializing in books for young people, was significant; however, its activities did not increase the overall proportion of French-language religious publishing as the introduction of its publications was countered by a general decrease in religious publishing. This decline began in the 1950s and became more pronounced over the course of the next two decades, as the proportion of religious books dropped to 10 per cent and then 5 per cent.

With the Quiet Revolution and the reforms resulting from the Second Council of the Vatican, which in 1962 began to modernize the Catholic Church, religious publishing underwent a crisis and had to face competition from secular publishers. Apart from Fides, Éditions Bellarmin, and Apostolat de la presse, which took part in public discussion of the issues arising from Vatican II, most congregations ceased issuing publications for the general public. Even Apostolat de la presse (Éditions Pauline after 1971) did not escape the decline: the religious portion of its production dropped from 62 to 24 per cent. However, the house distinguished itself in children's literature with the creation of the series Jeunesse-pop and the magazine

Vidéo-presse (1971–95).[12] Fides and Bellarmin both became testing grounds for new thinking on theology, while commercial publishers such as Éditions de l'Homme, Éditions du Jour, and Éditions Stanké entered the market with books on personal growth and secular spiritualities. In 1975, Éditions Anne Sigier began to publish religious books intended for the French-speaking world as a whole. This house focused on Christian spirituality and Bible publishing for the general public. Its first successes occurred in the 1980s with *Je rencontre Jésus* (1981), by Jean Vanier, and *Paroles d'un pèlerin* (1984), the Canadian speeches of Pope John Paul II.

Until the 1960s, French-language publishing of religious books in Quebec was dominated by Catholic congregations. Their roots in specialized Catholic action, their influence on intellectual life, and their numerous personnel and substantial financial resources enabled them to establish effective publishing structures at a time when independent publishers were just finding their feet. The hegemony of these communities delayed the development of lay Catholic publishing houses while giving rise to a varied production, according to the different natures of the communities. The priority that congregations placed on their religious mission and their capacity to adapt shaped their growth as publishers, and enabled some to maintain a strong position in today's market for religious books, which has broadened to include new forms of spirituality.

CASE STUDY
A Catholic Best-Seller: The Journal of Gérard Raymond
– Simone Vannucci

A monument of Catholic virtue, the *Journal de Gérard Raymond* represents the moral, literary, and religious ideal of devout youth in the 1930s. Born in Quebec City on 20 August 1912, Raymond died of tuberculosis on 5 July 1932, at the age of nineteen, in the city of his birth. He kept a diary along the lines of the writings of Thérèse de Lisieux, whose autobiography he had read and contemplated. Found after his death, Raymond's journal was a revelation to his family and friends. The priest of the parish in which he had lived, Israël Laroche, saw the diary as an exemplary inspirational document. He passed it on to Cardinal Villeneuve, the archbishop of Quebec City, who in turn asked the father superior of the Séminaire de Québec, where Raymond had studied, to make the work known to the students. Raymond, who came from a modest middle-class family in Quebec City, had been a gifted student who received many prizes in school and had stated in his diary that he wanted to become a Franciscan priest and a 'missionary' and 'martyr.'[13]

Long excerpts from the diary, annotated and accompanied by a biography, were published by the Séminaire de Québec in December 1932 under the title *Une âme d'élite : Gérard Raymond*. Distributed in colleges and parishes, the book was extremely successful and aroused a great deal of enthusiasm. To meet the demand, two editions were issued in successive years, with translation into English and other languages. In April 1933, a beatification investigation of the young man was approved by Cardinal Villeneuve. Raymond was then entrusted with prayer intentions, that is, written requests for personal benefactions directed to a holy figure. Testimonies attributing to him conversions, healings, and other temporal favours subsequently flooded in. The complete text of the diary was finally published in 1937 with a short introduction by Cardinal Villeneuve.

In his novel *Au pied de la pente douce* (1944), Roger Lemelin wittily described the fascination of the ordinary folk of Quebec City's Lower Town with the 'heavenly stripling'[14] and his fervent support by the Latruche sisters. Thirty years later, Victor-Lévy Beaulieu gave Raymond considerable attention in his *Manuel de la petite littérature du Québec* (1974). There is now a page on the Web site of the Diocese of Edmundston, New Brunswick, devoted to the memory of this young candidate for sainthood,[15] and an association, 'Les amis de Gérard Raymond,' which presents him as a model for youth and campaigns for his beatification.

Print and Organized Religion in English Canada

BRIAN HOGAN

In 1918 organized religion was a prominent feature of Canadian life.[16] Ninety per cent of Canadians were members of a Christian church, most of them routinely active in their observance. At the very least, life passages of birth, marriage, and death were accompanied by formal religious ritual. Reflecting this reality, Christian themes were pervasive in print, finding voice in overtly religious publications as well as literary works. Judaism also had a small but well-established presence, particularly in Montreal, Toronto, and Winnipeg. Immigration patterns after the Second World War contributed to Canada's growing mixture of faiths, as did the mushrooming of new spiritualities in the 1960s. Such demographic change would lead to increasing diversification in publishing and distribution by organized religious groups, particularly in the final two decades of the century. This shift occurred alongside the waning of active religious observance by the established Christian majority, and an accompanying decline in some sectors of denominational publishing.

Sacred texts, particularly the Torah, the Bible, and the Quran, have provided Canadians with the fundamental source for the experience and expression of faith, and have represented the most ubiquitous genre of religious print. Editions of these sacred works have typically been imported into Canada. Throughout the century, the Canadian Bible Society (CBS) served as a primary domestic agency for distribution of Bibles, New Testaments, and scriptural portions in a multiplicity of languages. Distribution efforts of the CBS included placing Scripture into the hands of immigrants as they disembarked onto Canadian soil and, in the tradition of the agency's nineteenth-century antecedents, facilitating its translation into Native languages. As well as distributing the many texts it imports, the CBS has annually published tens of thousands of volumes, particularly the versions of the Bible for which it holds Canadian copyright.[17] Gideons International represents another major distributor of Bibles and New Testaments in Canada; prior to 1980, it regularly handed out New Testaments to children in school, and it has ensured the presence of the Bible in virtually every hotel room, prison cell, and military barracks.

Cognate to sacred texts are the normative liturgical texts framing formal worship, as well as dozens of smaller texts, including personal prayer books and standardized prayer forms. Domestic publication of cognate works has varied from group to group – Anglicans, for example, used imported editions of *The Book of Common Prayer* until a first Canadian edition was printed in 1918 – and typically emanates from official publishing arms, such as the Anglican Book Centre and the United Church Publishing House, both located in Toronto, or the Publications Service of the Canadian Conference of Catholic Bishops in Ottawa. Promotion and distribution have also relied on formal institutional structures, among them the diocese, parish, and chaplaincies, as well as bookshops, religious goods stores – many non-denominational, as for example, the CBS – and wholly commercial enterprises, such as the former Landy's store in Toronto.

The hymnal, the most prominent cognate text for every Christian and Jewish congregation, has seen much domestic production. The most successful type of religious publication in economic terms, hymn books generate profits that support other works or church initiatives.[18] As a genre, hymnals reflect the prevailing preferences and preoccupations of sponsoring churches and synagogues at specific historical moments, and are revised at regular intervals. They also provide concrete examples of national expression and ecumenical collaboration. The Baptist Hymnary Committee of Canada, a national team established in 1932, developed the first common hymnal for the three regional Baptist bodies of Canada. Testifying to the efficacy of ecumenical effort represented by the creation of the United Church of Canada in 1925, this Baptist committee took that body's hymnal, *The Hymnary of the United Church of Canada* (1930), as the basis for its own. After appropriate revision and consultation with several other sources, *The Hymnary for Use in Baptist Churches* appeared in 1936.[19] Several decades later, the Anglicans, who had produced several editions of their *Book of Common Praise* (1918, 1938, 1959), joined with the United Church to issue *The Hymn Book of the Anglican Church and the United Church of Canada* (1971).

Catholic authorities in Canada were equally attentive to this genre, producing upwards of a dozen editions of *St Basil's Hymnal* after a major reworking of the volume in 1918.[20] By contrast, its successor of 1958, the *New St Basil's Hymnal*, underwent only one revision. This difference was due to the impact of the Second Council of the Vatican (1962–5), which undertook the first thorough pastoral and theological review of Roman Catholic liturgy and ecclesiology in the modern period. Over the following generation, all official ecclesiastical texts saw major revisions and reprinting, spurring the largest production of publishing in Canadian Catholic history. Rapid expansion in the forms and style of liturgical music resulted from the council, precipitating the development of a new national hymnal, the *Catholic Book of Worship* (1972), which was followed by *Catholic Book of Worship II* (1980).

Catechetical and religious educational materials have represented a regular undertaking for denominational publishers. Produced for initial or ongoing instruction in the faith, or to preserve and transmit a denomination's religious principles and practice across generations and cultures, this genre of religious print has ranged from small booklets characterized by a basic question and answer format, such as the Pentecostal Assemblies of Canada's *Learning God's Truth: A Catechism for Boys and Girls* (1954), to full-size books featuring more sophisticated texts distinguished by contemporary pedagogical methodologies, critical scriptural commentary, and modern historiographical perspectives. Religious groups normally maintain close control of the content of such texts, which have been produced in Canada for use in religious-based schools, Sunday schools, family-based education, and distance learning programs.

In response to significant changes in epistemology and pedagogy as the century unfolded, this sector experienced a huge increase in domestic production after mid-century. Fulfilling a fundamental formative role, such texts have frequently proven controversial, particularly in transitional times, when they often articulate the first formal literal expression of new emphases or adjusted statements of faith or understanding of scriptural and doctrinal teachings. For example, the Come to the Father series of catechism texts, launched in the late 1960s by the Canadian Catholic Church to incorporate many of the theological perspectives formally pioneered at the Second Council of the Vatican, occasioned great controversy. Critics objected to the series' emphasis on theological anthropology, which stressed the primacy and uniqueness of the human person, as well as the greater attention devoted to social justice and other global issues. Some felt these departures detracted from a focus on the divine as transcendent and other. However, advocates of the series insisted that Christianity, a religion based on the mystery of the incarnation – the embodiment of the son of God in human flesh as Jesus Christ – must necessarily, and essentially, concern itself with matters of space and time. The social gospel concerns of the late nineteenth and early twentieth centuries, which had waned in the 1930s and 1940s, similarly found new life after mid-century in the catechetical and educational materials of the Protestant churches, publications that Daniel O'Leary discusses in greater detail later in this chapter. Attention to social questions is hardly limited to Christian churches, however, and many of the emerging faith groups in Canada have found it impossible to separate religious questions and practices from normative cultural practices, particularly with respect to pressing issues relating to gender, relationships, labour, and leisure.

By virtue of the material's popularity among adherents, denominational publishers have also produced or distributed publications that introduce, explain, or promote ritual observance, pious devotion, spiritual themes, and cultic convention ancillary to core beliefs and practices. Such texts range from those found on parish pamphlet racks and tables, to retreat, devotional and sermon literature, and monographs focusing on spirituality and biography.[21] Over time the secondary rituals described in these publications have often supplanted or significantly modified traditional practices, as, for example, has been the case with Marian devotions. Russian-born Catherine de Hueck Doherty, who lived her long and productive adulthood in Canada, established the Madonna House Apostolate, based in Combermere, Ontario. Here she developed a well-structured, enduring organization for celibate men, women, and clergy. The many books she wrote dealing with spirituality, community, and service were published in a variety of countries and languages. An early work, *Stations of the Cross: A Meditation* (1954), appeared under the imprint of Madonna House, as have many others since 1980.

Most pervasive among denominational publications have been the calendars, bulletins, newsletters, newspapers, magazines, journals, directories, and formal printed pronouncements that have fuelled the regular patterns of observance and socialization for faith communities. In the mid-1920s, the Anglicans routinely produced pamphlets and circulars in print runs of 65,000 to 70,000 copies.[22] Such publications provide the factual and interpretive glue that binds and guides the committed into communities. The writing, publication, and distribution of these materials are substantially Canadian. Some are specifically local in their publication and audience, while others are produced for all adherents within a faith community throughout the country, and even abroad. Bulletins and journals have been particularly characteristic of the first phase of publishing when newly arrived organizations establish themselves in Canada.

All major groups have published monthly or weekly newspapers. Even with an incomplete response, a survey of 1958 which attempted a profile of English-language Catholic publishing identified seventy-three newspapers and journals, with a combined subscription list of 1,674,748.[23] Prior to mid-century, almost every Catholic diocese in Ontario issued its own newspaper at one time or another; however, a trend toward amalgamation characterized the years after the Second World War. Representative national papers, such as the *United Church Observer* (Toronto, 1939–), the Anglican *Canadian Churchman* (Toronto, 1876–1988), and the Salvation Army's *War Cry* (Toronto, 1884–), as well as two Roman Catholic periodicals, the *Ensign* (Montreal, 1948–56) and the *Catholic Register* (Toronto, 1893–), were distributed through local churches and by post. While these publications addressed topical events concerned with religious questions, they also considered current political, social, economic, and global matters.

Communities within the Catholic Church, as well as committees and societies affiliated with Protestant denominations and other religious groups, have also been significant publishers. Particularly committed among Catholic communities have been the Congregation of St Basil, whose imprint is the Basilian Press headquartered at the University of St Michael's College in Toronto, and the Oblates of Mary Immaculate, who pursued their work at both St Patrick's College and the University of Ottawa, and later at St Paul University. There the imprint Novalis remains among the most active and successful in the country for religious publishing. In Saskatchewan, the Oblates also founded the Marian Press. Here the central periodical of their minor publishing empire was the popular *Our Family* (Battleford, SK) magazine; launched in 1949, it reached a circulation of some 15,000 by the 1970s and continued publication until 2002.[24] Another Catholic newspaper out of Saskatchewan, the *Prairie Messenger* (1923–), was issued initially in German, and later in English, by St Peter's Benedictine Abbey in Muenster. The affiliated bodies of Protestant groups, in turn, have produced a vast array of printed materials. Within the United Church of Canada, prolific publishers included the Woman's Missionary Society, which had its own literature department, and the Board of Evangelism and Social Service: between 1925 and 1986, the former issued 43 separate imprints, the latter 194.[25] The Women's Missionary Society of the Presbyterian Church in Canada similarly produced a substantial number of titles.

Since mid-century, a number of small, independent publishers with a strong religious orientation, and sometimes a specifically denominational one, have also been active. From the late 1960s to the mid-1980s, Griffin House, an independent, family-owned Catholic publisher in Toronto, issued about one hundred titles, including instructional materials for teachers and students. Palm Publishers of Montreal ranged more widely across religious ground. Its publications include the two-volume *Theology of Renewal* (1968), the proceedings of the Canadian Centenary Congress on the Renewal of the Church, perhaps Canada's most outstanding theological event of the century. The productions of such private companies, alongside the official publications of Canada's numerous religious communities, made an enormous and often overlooked contribution to the print culture of this country in the twentieth century.

Publishing for Young Christians

DANIEL O'LEARY

Publishing for the instruction and wholesome diversion of children was a well-established practice of Canada's churches and affiliated organizations by the early twentieth century, reflecting the collective conviction that commitment to a Christian life was best instilled in childhood. Basing its analysis on statistics gathered in

1914, a Presbyterian Church in Canada report of 1918 declared the years between twelve and twenty-four to be the 'Church's harvest time for decisions for Christ and for Christian Training and Service'; it further noted that 68.5 per cent of individuals joined the church between the ages of thirteen and twenty, while 75 per cent of those who took up a religious calling made 'the decision during these strategic years.'[26] As the common belief that children were susceptible to negative influence through reading endured well into the twentieth century, Christian organizations were encouraged to issue prescriptive literature about reading and to publish 'wholesome' alternatives.

Materials issued with these concerns in mind varied in format, genre, and subtlety. Many publications were to be placed directly in the hands of children, but others were designed for adults. For instance, *A Fourfold Programme for Canadian Girls*, produced by the Anglicans in the 1920s, encouraged group leaders to pursue a miscellany of activities, interspersed by Bible readings; as well, it included a list of 'suggested books for reading' that covered missionary literature, poetry, drama, and fiction. Girls were advised to read such works as Basil Matthews's *Book of Missionary Heroes,* Christina Rossetti's *Goblin Market*, Louisa May Alcott's *Little Women*, and Robert Louis Stevenson's *Treasure Island*.[27]

In the 1920s and 1930s, children were exposed to religious principles through publications issued by national bodies, including the United Church of Canada (UCC), the Church of England in Canada, the Congregational Missionary Society, the Forward Movement of the Missionary Society of the Methodist Church, and the Presbyterian Board of Home Missions and Social Service. In addition, regional and local organizations, like the Baptist Home Mission Board of Ontario and Quebec and the Women's Baptist Missionary Society of Ontario West, sponsored and distributed religious print for children, as did American-based groups, including the Missionary Education Movement of the United States and Canada, and the Protestant Christian Forces of the United States and Canada. At the same time, British organizations, especially the London, Colonial and Continental Church Society, and the Society for the Propagation of the Gospel in Foreign Parts, continued to circulate material in Canada, supported by activist itinerant teachers like Eva Hasell, and by programs like the Church of England's Sunday School by Post. In the 1970s, outside of Quebec, Catholic materials issued from the Canadian Catholic Conference. In general, Sunday schools and denominational schools facilitated children's access to these publications, the Catholic Church being the dominant beneficiary of separate school legislation in most provinces.

Among Canadian churches, the UCC and Anglican presses produced the widest variety of titles. Sunday-school periodicals such as the weekly *Onward* (Toronto, 1891–1968) emanated from the United Church Publishing House, and through the mid-1920s the Anglicans issued 115,000 copies weekly of their *Lesson Helps and Story Papers*.[28] In 1934 an Anglican-Lutheran Joint Committee on Summer Schools and Institutes published accounts of Asian, Jewish, and First Nations missionary work to inspire young Christians. The General Board of Religious Education (GBRE) oversaw Anglican youth publishing throughout this period and produced a wide variety of manuals, histories, textbooks, kits, and readers containing religious fiction, biography, and poetry. By mid-century the Anglican and UCC imprints began to recognize and reflect the pluralist nature of the country. From the 1940s forward, the GBRE issued religious textbooks with increasingly ecumenical overtones. Written especially for young people by Anglican Archbishop of Quebec Philip Carrington, *A Church History for Canadians to 1900 A.D.* (1946) provided a friendly survey of Lutheran, Presbyterian, Methodist, Roman Catholic, and Jewish beliefs. In a similarly ecumenical spirit, between 1920 and 1950 the Religious Education Council of Canada issued songbooks, Trail Rangers Manuals, prayer books, children's games, and materials for the National Girls' Work Board and National Boys' Work Board.

The Baptist Publications and Home Missions Committees were also responsible for numerous religious publications for youth. During the Second World War, for example, the Baptist Publications Committee of Canada issued an eight-page weekly newspaper, *Girls of Canada,* which focused on wartime social issues. In the 1950s, the committee collaborated with the UCC to produce materials for Sunday schools, including the Workbook and Teacher's Guide series, which addressed the Bible, Christology, and Christian social teachings.

One of the longest-running of all the Christian youth serials was the UCC Woman's Missionary Society monthly magazine *World Friends: A Magazine for Boys and Girls* (1929–67). Newfoundland native and UCC moderator Marion Pardy recalled that *World Friends* gave 'a sense of belonging, not just to our own group, but of being connected with children around the world.'[29] The magazine fostered youthful interest in the romance of missionary enterprise, long an important focus of Canadian religious publishing. In the 1920s, social gospel concerns infused the popular missionary literature of the Canadian Protestant churches, and works stressing a self-abnegation rooted in social responsibility proliferated. Northern and Aboriginal evangelization was especially prominent in such titles, and the wide popularity of wilderness memoirs and novels extended to Britain. Nigel B.M. Grahame's *Bishop Bompas of the Frozen North: The Adventurous Life Story of a Brave & Self-Denying Missionary amongst the Red Indians & Eskimos of the Great North-West* (1925), issued in London and distributed in Canada, provides a typical early example. The UCC Committee on Young People's Missionary Education published similar works in the 1930s, including John Crawford Cochrane's *Trails and Tales of the North Land* (1934). First issued by trade publisher McClelland and Stewart in 1933, *They Went Forth*, written by John McNab, editor of the *Presbyterian Record* and future moderator of the Presbyterian Church in Canada, stressed the heroic adventures of famous missionaries, both overseas and in the home missions. In his foreword, theologian and Knox College principal Walter W. Bryden praised the book's 'particular value' in performing the 'increasingly perplexing task [of provoking] that enthusiasm and earnestness, especially among our young people, necessary to inspire and enlist whole-hearted life-service, on their part, in the supreme work of the Christian Church.'[30]

While history continued to be used for education and entertainment – in the 1970s, for example, the UCC emphasized Aboriginal contributions to early Canadian society in titles such as Enos T. Montour's *The Feathered U.E.L.'s: An Account of the Life and Times of Certain Canadian Native People* (1973) – religious fiction aimed at children suffered a general decline during the twentieth century. The intersection of social with literary conditions, coupled with the predominant secularism of modernist literary practice, reduced the audience for the religious earnestness enjoined in the once popular works of writers like William H. Withrow, Ralph Connor, and Norman Duncan. Religious fiction was replaced by instructive religious biography and memoirs, such as the missionary literature noted above. Often romanticized and intended to encourage devotion, individual works were targeted at children based on age and sex.

The so-called 'Protestant modernization' of the Canadian churches of the 1950s and 1960s resulted in a 'new curriculum' for youth of both the Anglican and United Churches, a phenomenon that would find its Catholic counterpoint in the Come to the Father series in the late 1960s, as Brian Hogan explains earlier in this chapter. In 1952, under general editor Peter Gordon White, the UCC began its New Curriculum publication program, issuing the first of over fifty titles in 1961.[31] The series included Sunday-school teachers' guides and texts for children and youth, providing a mostly conservative modern perspective on Christology, theology, church history, and family and youth issues. Materials for the Anglican new curriculum that appeared in 1964 were controversial because of their perceived liberal bias. Hence, church officials carefully prepared the groundwork for training teachers in the new methods.[32] However, conservative or neo-orthodox Sunday-school teachers persisted in using pedagogical materials from Britain or drew on the 1920s-vintage CEC Layman's Library of Practical Religion (1922–30). The extent to which such books supplanted the new curriculum in Canadian Sunday schools varied, but complaints abounded and Sunday-school voluntarism declined. As regular church attendance also dwindled during the 1960s and 1970s, the relationship of many young Christians to their churches became titular by 1980, with printed material of a religious nature ancillary to, or absent from, their reading lives.

chapter 11

PUBLISHING AND COMMUNITIES

Publishing and Aboriginal Communities

CHERYL SUZACK

Publishing for First Peoples up to the mid-1950s followed the familiar pattern of the production of evangelical literature by religious orders and societies for the use of missionaries. Most of these texts were Bible translations or devotional works. Of increasing importance were vocabularies and dictionaries of Aboriginal languages, intended to support the mastery of spoken languages and the preparation of Native language books. This work involved both classifying dialects according to their diachronic evolution and standardizing 'trade jargon' and oral expression to create a common language foundation for religious and educational instruction. For example, Edward Harper Thomas's *Chinook: A History and Dictionary* (1935) sought to preserve linguistic evidence of 'a vanished time and culture'[1] by recording both the utilitarian and literary features of the dominant West Coast lingua franca. Such books were usually supported financially by church or ethnological societies. The British-based Society for Promoting Christian Knowledge published John Alexander Mackay's *Psalms and Hymns in the Language of the Cree Indians*, circulating 13,000 copies between 1891 to 1932 and a further 1,500 copies in 1935; in 1949, the Church of England in Canada issued an additional 5,000 copies.[2] Leonard Bloomfield's *Plains Cree Texts* (1934) was published by the American Ethnological Society in a series edited by Franz Boas. Church-based periodicals also proliferated, such as the *Cree Monthly Guide* (Saskatoon, 1925–61). Printed in both Cree syllabics and the Roman alphabet by Reverend Canon Edward Ahenakew, it promoted Christianity with little evidence of a Cree perspective.[3]

Before the 1960s, when the intensification of writing by Aboriginal authors led to an expansion in book publishing activity, Native communities relied on newspapers and magazines as vehicles for general communication among themselves as well as sites for discussion of prominent issues of cultural loss, institutional racism, and community isolation. The founding in December 1946 of the *Native Voice* by the Native Indian Brotherhood of British Columbia established a nationwide movement of periodical publication by Aboriginal groups and organizations, which, according to Brendan F.R. Edwards, 'coincided with a growing political expression and a desire for Indian control of Indian affairs.'[4] These widely disseminated publications aligned distant communities in common social causes, shared knowledge about Native issues, and assisted in the reassertion of Aboriginal languages. Language retention was particularly visible in the Arctic, with many periodicals issued partly or entirely in Inuktitut (see illus. 11.1, p. 296). Native news magazines across the country, such as *Indian Record* (Winnipeg: Oblates of Mary Immaculate, 1938–75), *Tepatshimuwin* (Village des Hurons: Conseil attikamek-montagnais, 1976–82),[5] *Nesika* (Vancouver: Union of BC Chiefs, 1972–7), the *Micmac News* (Sydney, NS: Native Communication Society of Nova Scotia, 1965-92), and the *National Indian* (Ottawa: National Indian Brotherhood, 1977–80), formed a 'Native alternative press ... engaged in speaking out' that issued candid prose and poetry to address social and political issues.[6] The *Saskatchewan Indian* (Prince Albert: Federation of Saskatchewan Indians, 1970–) enjoyed a readership of more than 30,000 in 1971.[7]

Despite such broad circulation, periodical publishing by Aboriginal communities has always been precarious. The Native Communications Program (NCP), established by the federal government in 1974 and cancelled in 1990, provided financial support to enable Native communication societies to develop media services, mainly through newspapers but also through community radio. Fostering recruitment, media training, and Aboriginal language promotion, these publishers and broadcasters facilitated communication between reserve communities and wider Canadian society, often reminding the mainstream press that 'there was interesting news to cover in the Native world.' In addition to presenting local news of Aboriginal interest, these papers contributed to the education, economic development, cultural growth, and political awareness of reserve communities. When the NCP ended, several locally run Native communication societies disappeared, while others pressed on.[8]

The impetus behind the trend to publish books addressing community concerns has been attributed to debates surrounding the *Statement of the Government of Canada on Indian Policy* (1969), the 'controversial "White Paper" that recommended the abolition of special rights for native peoples' and sparked a burst of literary activity.[9] Maria Campbell's widely read autobiography, *Halfbreed* (1973), was the most celebrated of the many books that documented Aboriginal and Métis communities and their resistance to Canada's Indian policy. During the literary momentum of the 1960s and 1970s, Campbell's stark story matched the anti-colonial sentiments of texts such as Harold Cardinal's *The Unjust Society* (1969), Wilfred Pelletier's *No Foreign Land* (1973), and Howard Adams's *Prison of Grass* (1975). Francophone Aboriginal authors articulated similar concerns. Max Gros-Louis wrote *Le premier des Hurons* (1971; trans., *First among the Hurons*, 1973) to address the distorted versions of history that compromised present and future policies toward Aboriginal peoples. An Antane Kapesh's *Je suis une maudite sauvagesse* (1976), published in both French and Montagnais, provided a personal account of a Montagnais woman's encounters with the dominant society. Albert Connolly's *Oti-il-no Kaepe: Les Indiens Montagnais du Québec* (1972) analyzed key acts of legislation to illuminate the effect of historical policies on the Montagnais people. One of the most prolific writers of this period, Bernard Assiniwi, an Aboriginal historian, published ethnographic texts such as *Les Montagnais et Naskapi* (1979) and children's books such as *Makwa, le petit Algonquin* (1973), as well as contributing to cultural histories such as *Histoire des Indiens du Haut et du Bas Canada* (1980). In 1989, Huron scholar Georges E. Sioui issued *Pour une autohistoire amérindienne: Essai sur les fondements d'une morale sociale* (trans., *For an Amerindian Autohistory: An Essay on the Foundations of a Social Ethic*, 1992), the first of his books analyzing North American history from a First Nations perspective. According to publisher Greg Young-Ing, this surge of writing by Aboriginal authors reflected not only political activism inspired in Canada by the Red Power Movement, but also the 'fact that this was the first generation of Aboriginal people not to be subjected to residential schools, many of whom were able to learn to write by attending College and University.'[10] Authorship has also enhanced language retention, as in *Poems of Rita Joe* (1978), which presents some texts in Mi'kmaq and English in parallel columns.

Several publishing houses established during this period were devoted solely to the dissemination of literature by Aboriginal authors and to publishing culturally based materials for use in education. Iroqrafts (Ohsweken, Six Nations Reserve, Ontario), founded in 1959, produced reprints of scholarly and popular works on the culture of the Iroquois peoples. The Saskatchewan Indian Cultural Centre (Saskatoon), founded in 1972 as the first Native-controlled educational institution at the provincial level, worked with the Federation of Saskatchewan Indian Nations, the Saskatchewan Indian Cultural College, and the Saskatchewan Indian Language Institute to pursue its mission 'to strengthen and support the overall Indian education and cultural awareness of Indian people.' The Centre maintains the cultural identity

ᑕᒪᓂᓗ ᓯᑯᒥ ᐊᐅᓚᕆᑐᒥ ᓄᑲᐳ ᑕᑲᐃᓯᓗᑎᓗ. ᑕᒪᓇ ᑲᐱᐊᓇᓗᐊᑐ ᐊᑐᑎᕋᒥᐅ ᐃᓯᒪ-
ᓕᐳ ᓄᑲᑎᑕᐅᔭᓇᕈᓐᑐ ᑭᓂᓂᐊᓂᒥᓂ. ᑕᕙᓗᓂ ᑕᑲᐃᓯᐳ ᓂᑎᓗᑎᓗ. ᑕᒪᓂ ᓕᓯ ᓂᑭᓕ-
ᐅᑎᓗᒍ ᐊᐃᔅ ᐊᐃᐳ ᓕᓯᓗ ᑲᐃᔭᒥ ᑕᑯᓚᒥ ᑭᓇᐅᒪᒪᒐ ᐊᐱᑎᐳ ᑕᑐᒪ ᐃᓕᑕᓯᒥᓇᒥ. ᐊ-
ᐃᔅ ᐊᑎᒥᓂ ᐅᑲᓗᓂ ᐊᐃᐳ ᐊᐱᑎᓗᓂᓗ ᑲᓄᐃᒪᒐ. ᓕᓯ ᐅᑲᓗᓂ "ᑕᑲᐳᒐ ᐊᓯᐊᓗ".
ᐊᐃᔅ ᐅᑲᑎᐳ "ᐋᓇᒍ ᑕᒪᓇ ᐊᑐᕋᔅᐅᕆᒪ ᐊᑐᑕᐳ". ᓕᓯ ᐅᑲᑎᐳ "ᐊᒥᓯᐃᑐᓗᒐ ᑲ-
ᐱᐊᓇᑐᑯ ᐃᒥᕋᓯᒪᒐᒪ ᑕᒪᓇ ᐊᑉᑐᐃᓇᐅᐳ". ᐊᐃᔅ ᐅᑲᑎᐳ "ᑕᐅᑐᑲᑕᐳᒐ ᐊᓇᐅᒐᓗ-
ᐊᓗᑎ ᐊᒍᑎᑐ ᐱᔭᓇᕋᐱ". ᐊᒪ ᓕᓯ ᐊᐱᑎᓕᑎᐳ "ᑲᓄᓕ ᐃᓯᒪᐱ ᑕᐃᑯᐊ ᑭᓂᓂᐊᑕᐳᑦ
ᑕᑯᓂᐊᕈᑎᕆ ᑕᑯᓂᐊᕆᑯᑎᕆᓗᓂ?". ᐊᐃᔅ ᑭᐅᓗᓂ: "ᑲᐅᔾᒪᐳᒐ ᑕᑯᓂᐊᑕᐳ ᑭᓯᐊᓂ
ᑲᐅᔾᒪᕆᓕᒐ ᐃᓄᑎᓗᕆᓗᓂ ᑐᑯᒐᑎᓗᕆᓗᓂ ᑕᑯᓂᐊᒪᒐᑎᕆ". ᓕᓯ ᐊᐱᑎᓕᑎᐳ "ᑕᐃᑯᐊ

ᑐᑯᒐᓇᓯᕆᓕᐱᕆ?". ᐊᐃᔅ ᑭᐅᓗᓂ "ᑕᒪᓂ ᓄᓇᒥ ᐊᒥᓯᒪᑕ ᑲᐱᐊᓇᑐ ᐱᕆᕆᓕᐸᑲ".
ᓕᓯ ᐅᑲᑎᐳ "ᑲᐅᔾᒪᐳᒐ ᑲᐱᐊᓇᑐ ᐊᒥᓯᒪᑕ ᑕᐃᑯᓇᓂ ᐅᒪᔭᓯᐅᑐᓂ ᑭᓂᑎᐊᑕᑎᓂ ᐃ-
ᓚᑲᐱ?". ᐊᐃᔅ ᑭᐅᐳ "ᓄᑲᕋ ᐃᓚᐅᐳ ᓇᐅᓕᒥ ᐊᑎᓕ". ᐊᒪᓗ ᐊᐱᑎᓗᓂ "ᑭᓇᑯᓂᓕ
ᐃᓚᑲᐱ ᒪᓂ?". ᓕᓯ ᑭᐅᐳ "ᐊᑎᕋ ᑲᐅᔾᒪᓕᐸ ᐊᑕᑕᒐᓗ ᐊᒍᑎᒥ ᐊᑎᑲᐳ ᑕᒪᓂᓗ ᑭ
ᑭᑕᔭᐊᒥᐅᓂ ᐊᒐᔭᑲᒍᐳ, ᐋᓇᓇᒐ ᑐᑯᓚᐅᐳ ᓯᓕ ᓄᑕᕋᐅᑎᓗᒐ. ᓄᑲᑲᐳᒐ ᐊᑕᐅᓯᒥ ᐊ
ᓂᑲᓗᒐᓗ ᐊᑕᐅᓯᒥ. ᑕᐃᒪᒐ ᐊᑕᑕᓂ ᒪᓕᐸᐳᒐ ᒪᑲᐃᓕᒪ ᒪᑲᐃᑐᓗ ᐱᔮᑎᐊᓕᕆᓂ ᐊᒍ-
ᑎᐅᓗ ᐱᓇᓯᐊᒐᒐᓂ ᑲᐅᔾᒪᓯᐊᓕᐳᒐ".
ᐊᐃᔅ ᐊᐱᑎᓕᑎᐳ "ᐅᐃᑲᕆᓕᑎ ᓯᓕ?". ᓕᓯ ᑭᐅᐳ "ᐅᐃᑲᕆᓕᒐ ᓯᓕ ᐅᐃᑲᕈᒪᕆᓇᒪ".
ᐊᐃᔅ ᐅᑲᑎᐳ "ᐊᓯᐊᓗ ᐃᓂᑯᓇᕋᐱ ᓄᓕᐊᑲᕆᑯᒪ ᓄᓕᐊᑕᑎᔭᒪᒐᔫᐸᕆ".

11.1 Markoosie, *Harpoon of the Hunter* (Montreal: McGill-Queen's University Press, 1970). The first novel by a Canadian Inuk, *Harpoon of the Hunter* was initially published in the late 1960s in the indigenous-language magazine *Inuktitut*, and has been translated into more than a dozen languages. Courtesy of Inuit Tapiriit Kanatami (www.itk.ca) and McGill-Queen's University Press.

of the province's eight Aboriginal cultures: Woodland Cree, Swampy Cree, Plains Cree, Saulteaux, Dene, Dakota, Nakota, and Lakota.[11]

Incorporated in 1980 by the Manitoba Métis Federation, Pemmican Publications specializes in creative and educational texts to provide cultural and pedagogical material for the Métis people of Manitoba. Although it later expanded to encompass First Nations and Inuit authors, its initial goal was to foreground the memory of Louis Riel in Manitoba's history and culture and to provide a forum for Métis history and life stories. Today Pemmican continues as one of only two Métis book publishing houses in Canada, supported by both federal and provincial funding programs. The Gabriel Dumont Institute began publishing in Regina in 1985 as the educational arm of the Métis Nation of Saskatchewan.

Also founded in 1980 was the first publishing house in Canada to be entirely under First Nations ownership and control, Theytus Books. A division of the En'owkin Centre in Penticton, British Columbia, which also houses the En'owkin International School of Writing, Theytus has promoted creative and critical writing by Aboriginal authors with the purpose of disseminating Native cultures and world views. Staffed entirely by Aboriginals, the press has been directed by Greg Young-Ing, a staunch proponent of self-controlled Native publishing as a necessary institutional and creative response to the absence of Aboriginal people from the publishing industry and to concerns about systemic cultural racism. It prioritizes publishing by Native writers as the 'best solution' to problems of editorial discrimination, cultural sensitivity, and the promotion of 'the authentic expression of the Aboriginal Voice.' The name Theytus, a Salishan word which means 'preserving for the sake of handing down,'[12] effectively summarizes the overall motive of Aboriginal textual production in the late twentieth century.

Allophone Publishing

CATHERINE OWEN

Allophone textual production is a geographically and linguistically diverse facet of Canada's publishing landscape. To support immigrant communities as well as the writing of authors who by choice or circumstance do not publish in English or

French, allophone Canadians have established presses from the Atlantic provinces to the West Coast, in major centres like Toronto and Winnipeg, and in small communities such as Yarrow, British Columbia, and Baie du Poste, Quebec.[13] During the twentieth century, newspapers, magazines, and books, issued in languages ranging from Arabic to Ukrainian, have represented a gamut of interests, from religious traditions to political causes and personal expression. Although some language-specific bibliographies were compiled in the middle of the twentieth century, it was not until the late 1960s that Canadian archives and libraries began to collect, catalogue, and circulate allophone print materials in a systematic way, thus improving bibliographical control over their production and collection. In the 1970s, the Toronto Public Library initiated its Foreign Language Centre, and in 1973 the National Library of Canada started its Multilingual Biblioservice to disseminate print materials in twenty-seven languages to libraries across the country.[14] Even so, in 1982, Judy Young explained that it was still 'very difficult to assess the extent of this area of Canadian letters: the variety of languages involved poses insurmountable barriers to the researcher ... many of the writers have been working in isolation ... and their works, if published at all, have been printed in ethnic newspapers or published privately.'[15] The picture brightened in 1999 with the appearance of the *Encyclopedia of Canada's Peoples*, in which many entries discuss publishing.

As described in the previous volumes of this series, publishing in their original languages has been a consistent activity among immigrant communities, with wide variation in the extent, longevity, and genre preferences of each group. A group's size and cohesiveness, the social and educational background of its members, and its traditional cultural relationship with print have all made an impact. So, too, has the introduction of new immigrants into established communities. 'At a time when the first generation would have been unable to comprehend English-language instruction in Canadian farming methods or Canadian municipal politics,' Watson Kirkconnell recalled, 'the ethnic press supplied all this information in assimilable form, but wherever there was no continuing flow of new immigration the demand for the foreign language press faded away.'[16]

Funding was always a paramount concern. At the beginning of the twentieth century, publications were typically supported by churches, as was the Icelandic journal *Sameiningin* (Winnipeg, 1886–1964). Newspapers managed by political parties, such as the Ukrainian-language *Ukraïns'ki robitnychi visty* (Winnipeg, 1919–37), or by commercial enterprises, as was the case with the highly successful Finnish-language *Aika* (Nanaimo, BC, 1901–70s), were also guaranteed operational funding. For some newspapers and periodicals, government advertising proved an important source of revenue, with government departments taking advantage of these media to convey information about an array of services.

Presses producing book-length literary works were especially fragile. With the exception of the Trident Press (Winnipeg, 1939–45), which published in Ukrainian, and the tenacious Czech publishing house 68 Publishers (Toronto, 1968–80?), most allophone literary presses, whether offshoots of periodical presses or independently run endeavours, were short-lived ventures. When provincial and federal arts councils began to appear at mid-century, their emphasis on Canada's two official languages and restrictive eligibility criteria generated little funding for allophone literary publishing. In 1979–80, for instance, 7 of the 323 grants offered to writers by the Canada Council were allocated to allophone 'immigrants.'[17] Through the 1970s, the best recourse to government funding rested in the Multicultural Directorate of the Department of the Secretary of State, which provided assistance for the 'writing and/ or publication of works of fiction, drama or poetry in the non-official languages.'[18]

Historical and Geographical Overview

Although a part of Canadian print culture since the eighteenth century, allophone publishing in Canada was sparse and widely dispersed at the end of the First World War, in part because of the repression between 1914 and 1919 of languages such as German, Russian, Ukrainian, and Finnish under the War Measures Act. Through the 1920s and 1930s, allophone materials were issued with increasing regularity and linguistic diversity, only to experience a drop in production again during the Second World War, when the War Measures Act was back in force. The significant shifts in immigration policy that began after the Second World War and the subsequent fostering of multicultural values ensured that by 1980 allophone publishing would form a vibrant stratum of Canada's cultural environment – no longer Kirkconnell's prelude to assimilation, but viable on its own terms.

In 1920, five substantial communities – Finnish, Icelandic, Ukrainian, Hungarian, and Jewish (Yiddish and Hebrew) – were producing periodicals and occasional volumes of poetry. German presses would keep a low profile until the late 1920s, when several songbooks appeared. Many of these publications were inspired and supported by long-standing communities that had begun printing in their original languages shortly after their arrival in the late nineteenth century. Although Icelandic materials would continue to appear until 1980, literary production by this group, as well as by the Finns, declined over the century. Ukrainians, by contrast, would maintain an ongoing presence, while Hungarian and Jewish presses were just beginning to thrive, the latter outlined by Rebecca Margolis in the following section. By 1925, these three groups were producing newspapers, such as the long-running Ukrainian journal *Kanadyiskyi Farmer* (Winnipeg, 1903–81).[19] The Hungarians demonstrated a particular preference for poetry, perhaps because of the group's increased urbanization after the war.

At mid-century, Winnipeg was a busy centre of Icelandic and Ukrainian production.[20] Through the 1930s and 1940s, limited publishing appeared in Czech, Danish, and Japanese. The Czechs, most of whom arrived from Europe and the United States in the first fifteen years of the century to farm the Prairies, produced little in the West, but in Montreal the Czech Cultural Club issued poems and a periodical entitled *Zapad* (1930s–40s). Similarly, although immigrants from Denmark had also tended to settle in the West, a Danish paper, the *Danske Herold* (1932–40), appeared in Nova Scotia, successor to *Daneborg* (Ottawa, 1893–1932). Publication in Japanese nearly vanished during the 1940s. The community's three Vancouver-based newspapers, *Canada Shimpo* (1904–41), *Tairiku* (1907–41), and *Min Shü* (1924–41), all closed during the war, shut down by the RCMP within hours of the bombing of Pearl Harbor.[21] However, the *New Canadian* (Vancouver; Kaslo, BC; Winnipeg; Toronto, 1938–) continued in a bilingual English/Japanese format during the war years. In addition, books recounting experiences of war or internment, usually distributed under the aegis of the Anglican Church or benevolent associations, emerged during the 1940s.

Although the Second World War saw a considerable decrease in allophone publishing, there was notable activity in a few quarters. The Polish community enjoyed an upsurge in periodical publication supported by a substantial second wave of immigrants who had arrived between the wars and were collectively more literate than their predecessors, a result of Poland's introduction of compulsory education.[22] Publishing ventures were also launched in Italian and Russian. Following the success of a word list released in 1933, the Italians focused on the production of grammar texts. Speakers of Russian produced histories, issuing the earliest in Grand Forks, BC, in 1944.

The end of the war brought waves of European immigrants and refugees to Canada. Better educated than many of their predecessors and often professionally trained, they were more inclined to settle in towns and cities. The consequent resurgence in allophone publishing saw new periodicals from the Icelandic, Jewish, and Polish communities. Finnish periodicals benefited from the recruitment of agents, such as Fanny Lind, who 'sold Finnish magazines on commission.'[23] In the wake of increased Ukrainian immigration, the genres produced by this group became more diverse, with the addition of critical essays, plays, and autobiographies. The Portuguese launched their first newspaper, *Luso Canadiano* (1958–71), in Montreal.

Works in Estonian and Croatian and an Urdu collection of poetry published in Regina enhanced the range of publishing during the 1960s. The Carpatho-Rusyns initiated a periodical, *Nash holos* (Toronto, 1964–72).[24] Perhaps the most dramatic demonstration of the international significance of allophone literary publishing occurred with the founding of the Czech-language press 68 Publishers late in the decade. Operating entirely without government assistance, émigré author Josef Škvorecký and his wife, Zdena Salivarová, produced over fifty titles by 1980. Determined to combat the 'mindless persecution' of literature he had experienced in Czechoslovakia, Škvorecký issued a range of genres (with an emphasis on novels) and distributed books to Czech exile communities from North America to Nepal.[25] Among his authors was Milan Kundera, whose novel *Farewell Party* was issued in its original Czech for the first time in Toronto in 1979, three years after its appearance in English translation.

In the 1970s multilingual publishing continued to grow despite limited funds and the lack of avenues for broad dissemination. In 1977 Canada claimed 122 allophone newspapers, 6 of which were dailies (5 in Chinese and 1 in Italian). Close to one-half were published in Ontario. Quebec was the second-largest producer with 21, followed by Manitoba, British Columbia, and Alberta. The vast majority were concentrated in metropolitan areas, where there were sufficient populations and advertisers to support their survival.[26] During this decade, allophone book publication became visible in New Brunswick, with works issued in Hungarian, Romanian, and Arabic. In Nova Scotia, Gaelic enjoyed a modest revival in *Cape Breton's Magazine* (Wreck Cove, NS, 1972–), a predominantly English-language serial. Icelandic publication, however, went into hiatus throughout the country.

New appearances in print during the 1970s from the Marathi, Hispanic, and Punjabi communities further enriched Canada's multicultural ethos. At the turn of the decade, the Maharashtrians established a Toronto newsletter, *Snehabandha* (1969–), and then launched a Marathi literary magazine, *Ekata*, in 1978.[27] Because of a lack of fonts, the periodical was handwritten and mimeographed for distribution. Following the military coup of 1973 in Chile, in which President Salvador Allende was killed, many artists and intellectuals from that country sought asylum in Canada. Beginning with a group known as 'Emergent Promotions,' the Chileans came to represent Hispanic publication through the production of multiple collections of poetry. While some volumes were issued by houses such as Ediciones Cordillera and Split Quotation, the majority were self-published by Chilean writers living in

Toronto and Montreal. According to Jorge Etcheverry, self-publication was 'a permanent feature of Chilean literature [due to] the scarcity of outlets [and] to the value placed on the "alternative" in Chilean culture.'[28] After 1980, Chilean, Salvadorian, and Guatemalan writers found a receptive publisher in André Goulet's Montreal-based Les Éditions d'Orphée.[29]

Watno Dur (British Columbia, 1973–80s) heralded the debut of Punjabi on Canada's publishing stage. Begun as a leftist political magazine in 1973, it shifted to a literary focus in 1974 with the addition of poet Ajmer Rode to its board. Under playwright Sadhu Binning, who became editor in the late 1970s, the periodical served as a potent forum for poems, essays and scripts, and even spawned a reading group, Punjabi Sahit. To ensure its editorial autonomy, *Watno Dur* operated entirely on funds from its organizational board.[30]

For the majority of allophone authors and publishers in Canada, the year 1980 marked a watershed. Although the volume of literary production would not peak until 1990, when over thirty-five linguistic groups would be visible, the late 1970s and early 1980s marked the height of government funding, in terms of support for allophone publication and the production of related reports and anthologies. One of the more important studies, an update of *The Canadian Family Tree*, emerged from the Multiculturalism Directorate in 1979. Moreover, for many immigrant groups, 1980 signalled a transition from the second generation to the third, marking a point at which assimilation accelerated either the entrenchment or the erosion of many long-standing languages.

Generic Preferences

Appreciation of the history and diversity of Canada's allophone publishing is further enhanced by consideration of different groups' apparent preferences for certain literary genres. In his seminal essay 'The Origin of Genres,' Tzvetan Todorov explains that a society 'chooses and codifies the acts that correspond most closely to its ideology,' a practice that accounts for 'the existence of certain genres in one society, [and] their absence in another.'[31] With allophone publishing, ideology and practical circumstances have together shaped such choices.

The most ubiquitous literary genre is poetry. This trend can be attributed to such quotidian concerns as the fact that poetry may exist in brief formats that can often be written in less time than lengthy pieces of prose and published at a lower cost. Released in minimal print runs, volumes of poems were often distributed through churches or community clubs, or were funded and distributed by subscription. However, a more cogent reason may be poetry's unique ability to express, in condensed form, the experiences of a culture as it shifts from a stable to a diasporic identity through the upheavals of immigration. If exiled artists and intellectuals make up a large constituency, as with the Chilean community, poetry is even more likely to dominate. In contrast, for the Hungarians, a group with an established literary history in Canada, critical texts were popular. This preference suggests a desire to reflect upon and respond to their own publications, with the objective of stimulating future literary work. For the Polish community, newspapers have been the primary genre. Publications like *Czas* (Winnipeg, 1915–70s) and *Gazeta Polska* (Winnipeg, 1940–51; became *Glos Polski, Gazeta Polska*, Toronto, 1951–) enable a polyvocal dissemination of immigrant opinion that single-authored texts often fail to provide. In yet another instance, the necessity of basic language maintenance has underpinned the Ukrainian community's ongoing production of grammar guides.

Apart from ideological motivations, historical and financial factors can underlie an allophone community's tendency to express itself in one predominant genre. Groups that share a turbulent historical shift, such as the Germans and Japanese during the world wars, often produce accounts of their experience; historical texts dominated the output of both between the 1930s and the 1950s. Funding also affects genre preference. Textbook production in the Ukrainian community increased after 1980, partially through support from the Canadian Institute of Ukrainian Studies and other academic agencies. The predominance of this genre suggests that this group, along with such others as the Serbs and Croats, had to create their own resources to maintain a language threatened by assimilation. Finally, a publishing house or community dominated by a single individual can create a distinct genre preference. Novels predominated at 68 Publishers because its guiding light, Josef Škvorecký, was himself a novelist. Poetry was the genre responsible for resurrecting the use of Icelandic in Canada after the 1920s because the language's fiercest proponent was a poet, the renowned Stephan G. Stephansson.

Although allophone writers have received little attention from mainstream Canadian critics, their work is now valued as both interesting literature and a crucial record of Canadian experience. Significantly for groups such as the Punjabi, orality is now being recognized alongside the written word; in the process, it has come to be viewed as a means of allowing 'genres that are considered peripheral to literate culture (by being hybrid, unidiomatic, or vernacular)' to emerge.[32] Whether groups have focused on a particular genre or ranged broadly in their publishing habits, the

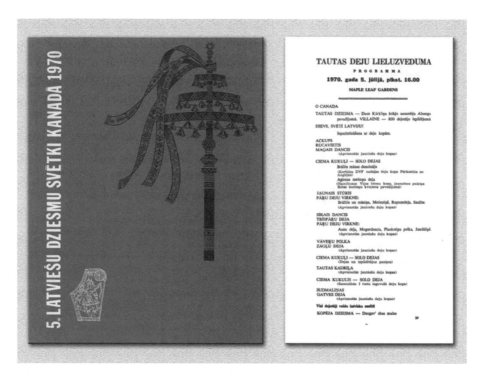

11.2 5. *Latviešu Dziesmu Svētki Kanadā 1970* (Toronto: Kanādas Rīcības komitejas izdevums, 1970). Cover and folk-dance presentation program of the Latvian Song Festival, an international cultural event held for the fifth time in Toronto. Courtesy of Arnīds Purvs; copy courtesy of Vijolīte Alksnis.

production and distribution of allophone literature in Canada has been crucial for creating channels of communication, aiding in the retention of immigrant languages, and disseminating cultural perspectives otherwise unavailable (see illus. 11.2, above). While critics differ concerning the connection between language maintenance and the preservation of culture, many concur that a viable 'ethnic tongue ensures that complete assimilation will not take place,' thereby fostering a diverse cultural demographic.[33] Furthermore, attitudes and feelings toward an adopted culture, especially as expressed in poetry or myth, cannot be effectively conveyed in a borrowed language. From an immigrant's nostalgia for the homeland, to the maintenance of a repressed literature in exile, to poetry's unique ability to express a culture as it shifts from a stable to a diasporic identity, original language production has been essential.

Jewish Print Culture

REBECCA MARGOLIS

Modern Yiddish literary culture arose in eastern Europe as a popular phenomenon after the Haskalah (Jewish Enlightenment) of the nineteenth century. Its Canadian manifestation began to emerge at the turn of the twentieth century, somewhat behind that in European and American centres, as a result of the later settlement of significant numbers of Yiddish-speaking Jews. The Jewish population, which swelled from 16,000 in 1901 to 157,000 in 1931, created a network of cultural organizations to bolster its identity nationwide. Over 95 per cent of Canadian Jews aged ten or over in 1931 claimed Yiddish as their mother tongue, a circumstance that accounts for the upsurge in Yiddish literary activity.[34]

Yiddish, a Germanic-Jewish language written in the Hebrew alphabet and spoken by most eastern European Jews before the Holocaust, was the vernacular of most Canadian Jews until English gradually supplanted it in the second half of the twentieth century. Because of its large readership, Yiddish, rather than Hebrew, served as the dominant vehicle for new Jewish literary activity. Most published works were issued from presses in the cities of Montreal, Toronto, and Winnipeg, the major hubs of Canada's Jewish population. Through literary clubs and salons, and literary evenings with local and visiting writers held in Jewish libraries and a variety of other venues, local community organizations in Montreal, Toronto, Winnipeg, and Vancouver played a key role in fostering Yiddish literary activity across the country. A network of modern secular schools promoted Yiddish literature by featuring it in their curricula and publishing literary journals to celebrate the writing of their students.

The earliest efforts at Yiddish printing in Canada began in the 1880s, and the first viable Yiddish-Hebrew press, the A.L. Kaplansky printing shop, was established in Montreal in the early 1890s.[35] The first Yiddish book published in Canada was a history of Jewish pedagogy: Elimelekh Levin's *Kinder ertsiyung bay yidn: a historishe nakhforshung* (Montreal, 1910). In the 1920s and 1930s, a maturing community of literati wrote and published in Yiddish for a growing audience. Among the most active figures were poets Yehezkel Bronshteyn, N.J. Gotlib, Ida Maze, Sh. Nepom, J.I. Segal, and Sholem Shtern, prose writer Yaacov Zipper, journalist and historian B.G. Sack, musicologist and newspaper editor Israel Rabinovitch, and community activist and critic H.M. Caiserman.[36]

For economic and socio-cultural reasons, the primary venue for the publication of Yiddish letters worldwide remained the Yiddish periodical press, rather than the publishing house. In Canada the major Yiddish dailies were all established before the First World War: the Montreal *Der keneder adler* (1907–88), the Toronto *Der idisher zhurnal* (1912–62), and the Winnipeg *Dos idishe vort* (1917–81). In addition to featuring belles lettres and scholarship in the pages of their newspapers, the presses printed or published a significant proportion of the Yiddish and Hebrew books to appear in Canada. Notably, *Der keneder adler*, under the leadership of its publisher, Hirsh Wolofsky, produced an edition of the Talmud in 1919.

Because of the country's smaller, less-developed market, the publication of Yiddish- and Hebrew-language books was never a commercial activity in Canada as it was in Europe and the United States. Literary self-publication was common, as was production through short-lived, non-commercial publishing houses. For example, in Montreal in the 1920s, Farlag 'Royerd' issued several volumes of belles lettres under the direction of J.I. Segal. Yiddish publishing often entailed communal involvement in the form of a *bukh-komitet* (book committee), whereby a group of supporters saw to the production and distribution of a work. N.Y. Gotlib's volume of poetry *Iberboy* (Montreal, 1940–1) was published by the N.Y. Gotlib-Bukh-Komitet, a group composed of some twenty writers and other members of the local Jewish community, who raised funds, promoted the work, and organized literary evenings in its support. Despite such efforts, even at the height of Yiddish publishing in the late 1920s, no more than a handful of books ever appeared in Canada in a single year.

In addition to publishing in the press and in book form, Yiddish writers founded a series of literary journals. Most of these ventures were ephemeral, but they served as a forum for the publication of innovative works of belles lettres, literary criticism, world literature in translation, and Jewish scholarship. They also provided news about literary activity throughout Canada and abroad, and acted as tribunes for diverse ideological and political movements. Between the 1920s and the 1950s, some twenty Yiddish literary journals appeared, most of them based in Montreal. The majority of these were issued in the 1920s and 1930s.[37] The only journal to appear during the Second World War was *Kanader zhurnal* (Montreal, 1940); after a lapse of fifteen years, the final serious Yiddish literary journals to emerge in Canada were *Montrealer heftn* (Montreal, 1955–8) and *Vidershtand* (Montreal, 1957–9).

The Holocaust decimated Yiddish culture in Europe and brought a significant number of literary figures to Canada. In the 1940s and 1950s, the arrival of such writers as Yehudah Elberg, Mordkhe Hosid, Rokhl Korn, Peretz Miranski, Melekh Ravitch, and Chava Rosenfarb revitalized Canada's Yiddish culture. Post-war literary output ranged from poetry to bilingual Yiddish-Hebrew interpretations of traditional Jewish texts. Notable were Symche Petrushka's six-volume Yiddish translation and interpretation of the Mishnah, *Mishnayes mit iberzetsungen un peyrush in yidish* (Montreal, 1945–9), and Shimshen Dunsky's Yiddish renditions of the biblical books of Lamentations, Ruth, Ecclesiastes, and the Song of Songs (Montreal, 1956–73). Despite this revival, Yiddish culture in Canada since 1950 has faced the attrition that has characterized it worldwide;[38] most of some three hundred Yiddish titles issued in Canada before 2000 appeared between 1920 and 1950. In the decades after 1950, this rich culture seeded a new generation of writers who published in English. Prominent among them were Irving Layton, Miriam Waddington, Adele Wiseman, Mordecai Richler, and Leonard Cohen, who added a strong Jewish dimension to English Canada's cultural environment.

CASE STUDY
The *Free Lance*
– Dorothy W. Williams

In June 1934 three Black men – Edward Packwood, William Trott, and Eric Hercules – inaugurated Montreal's first Black newspaper, the *Free Lance* (1934–41), respectively taking on the roles of editor, advertising and managing editor, and business editor.[39] Promulgating a pan-African focus and styling itself 'Canada's Greatest Negro Paper,' the *Free Lance* appeared monthly during its first year and boasted a circulation of ten thousand, reaching beyond Montreal's Black population of less than four thousand to become a national publication.[40] By September 1935 the description on the masthead, now sporting a beaver in the heart of a maple leaf, had changed to 'Afro-Canadian Weekly.' Frequent calls for contributors from across Canada and even the Caribbean gave rise to features from Manitoba, Ontario, and the Maritimes; former Montrealer Juanita de Shield became the paper's New York correspondent by the fourth issue, and additional stories were culled from the Black American press. The front page of the *Free Lance* proclaimed its philosophy: 'The People's Advocate – Inspiration for Every Home. Read from Coast to Coast. Dedicated to the Cause of Social Justice, Racial Understanding, National Progress, World Peace.'

The *Free Lance* began as a twenty-page, five-column newspaper, initially priced at three cents in Montreal and five cents outside the city. By December 1934 the paper advertised its price as '5¢ everywhere.' It was subsequently reduced in size to an eight-page tabloid. Single copies were available at various outlets around Montreal, across Canada, and overseas, while some circulation outside the city resulted from subscriptions. Despite the editors' attempts to achieve financial self-sufficiency, the paper was never debt-free. With only three national advertisers – Salada Tea, Seagrams distillery, and Molson's brewery – the *Free Lance,* like other race-based papers of the time, teetered 'on the brink of economic disaster' for lack of advertising and found itself unable 'to operate at ... full potential.'[41] Supported primarily by the households of Black railway porters, many of whom were well educated, the newspaper nonetheless failed to attract enough subscribers to become economically viable. Its two long-term editors, Trott and Packwood, supplemented their incomes with other work,[42] and, after the paper folded in 1941, Packwood paid off its debts for years.[43]

As was the case with earlier Black newspapers in Canada, discussed by Dorothy W. Williams in Volume 2 of *History of the Book in Canada*, readers bought the *Free Lance* for its stories related to social concerns, unionism, civil rights activism, and miscarriages of justice, as well as for community news and recognition of Black accomplishments. What set this newspaper apart from earlier Canadian ventures was its strong Afro-Canadianism.[44] It promoted the philosophies of Marcus Garvey, leader of the Back to Africa Movement and founder of the Universal Negro Improvement Association, and maintained an unrepentant anti-fascist and anti-imperialist viewpoint. In the city of Montreal, the *Free Lance* gave rise to the Afro-Canadian League and its auxiliary, the Self-Help Depot, which served as 'a centre for Negro publications and other progressive journals' published internationally.[45]

Small Press Publishing

DAVID MCKNIGHT

One of the most important developments in Canada's literary culture during the twentieth century was the rise of the small press. In general, the small press refers to

11.3 The Canadian Small Press / Petites maisons d'édition et revues littéraires. Concept: David McKnight; graphic artist: Jennifer Garland.

the non-commercial production of books and periodicals with a literary orientation, issued in limited runs for specialized readerships, and often dedicated to experimental writing or identity-based perspectives. In some instances, small press magazines generated publishing houses, and in others, book publishers begat magazines.

The small press derives from the artistic movements associated with international modernism and its avant-garde permutations that developed in Europe and the United States at the beginning of the twentieth century. While the first examples appeared in Canada during the 1920s, small press publication was slow to take root, largely because few writers or their advocates possessed the economic means to publish independent magazines and because the market for local modern literature was negligible, particularly during the Depression. During the early 1940s, writing communities began to form across the country, founding little magazines that opened their presses to groups with shared aesthetic perspectives and offered publishing opportunities for emerging writers. In the 1960s conditions again changed with the rapid development of literary magazines and presses, some highly political, especially in Quebec, Ontario, and British Columbia. At the beginning of the 1970s, as described in this chapter by Carole Gerson and Donald W. McLeod, Canada's neglected gender and identity-based communities developed a forceful cultural presence through the publication of little magazines and books which reflected different groups' aesthetic and political preferences. Whereas once there had been few outlets for contemporary literary and cultural expression, by the end of the 1970s, Canada's small press scene was large, amorphous, and subsidized.

The economics of small press publishing are precarious at best, with many ventures self-financed by the publisher or supported by an educational institution. Some that began in the 1960s, such as Coach House Press and Porcupine's Quill Press, were funded through profits from commercial printing operations. The Writing and Publishing Division of the Canada Council, created in 1972, has played a crucial role in the development of literary magazines and small presses. Its programs not only supported creators and publishers, but also aided in the distribution, export, and reception of literary works. Provincial arts councils have funded local publishers, thereby fostering a strong cross-country regional press network. A distinctive feature of the small press economic model is that many such publishers cannot pay their authors advances or royalties; instead, authors receive a fixed number of copies of their books to sell at readings. The founding of the Literary Press Group in 1975 united many small presses for purposes of advocacy, professional development, marketing, book distribution, and the production of a shared catalogue.

In the realm of design and material production, what distinguishes small presses from commercial publishers is the consultative relationship that often exists between publisher and author in determining layout and appearance. While aesthetics and craft feature in the production and physical appearance of little magazines and small press titles, which range from mimeographed, saddle-stitched booklets and periodicals to perfect-bound offset titles and elegant letterpress limited editions, economic concerns exert ongoing influence. To lower costs, many small press publishers perform a variety of functions, including editing, design, and production. Controlling the means of production has long been at the ideological centre of the small press movement; while not all publishers possess the inclination or skill to operate a traditional printing office, many have employed inexpensive office print technologies such as the mimeograph machine (hailed in 1960s as the 'mimeograph revolution') and, more recently, desktop publishing.

From 1918 to 1980, nearly 800 English-language little magazines and small presses – both literary and ideological – were launched in Canada. These divide into some 465 magazines and 325 small presses, with an average lifespan of two years.[46] During the same period, approximately 50 French literary presses were founded as well as a similar number of literary magazines; in both languages, the vast majority of presses and publications appeared after 1960. Montreal was a centre for both cultures until 1960, when the English scene in Toronto and Vancouver became equally significant.

English-Language Small Press Publication

Before 1940 there were efforts to establish independent literary publishing houses, such as Graphic Publishers (1925–32) of Ottawa, Louis Carrier (1924–32) of Montreal, and the ephemeral Abanaki Press in Nova Scotia, which issued the mimeographed series *The Song Fishermen's Song Sheets* (Halifax, 1928–30). Hilda Ridley's Crucible Press, founded in Toronto in 1931, produced the literary magazine *Crucible* (Toronto, 1932–43) and from 1938 to 1950 issued a regular series of volumes of conventional verse. Most enduring of these early endeavours was the Ryerson Poetry Chapbook series initiated in 1926 by Ryerson Press editor, Lorne Pierce. Reaching 184 titles by 1959, these author-financed booklets, whose contents ranged from delicate rhymes to bolder experiments, were issued in runs of several hundred copies.

Canada's commercial publishers were largely unresponsive to the generation of modernist poets who emerged in the 1920s: W.W.E. Ross, Raymond Knister, A.J.M. Smith, Leo Kennedy, Dorothy Livesay, F.R. Scott, and A.M. Klein. For modernist writers, the *Canadian Forum* (Toronto, 1920–2000) provided an important alternative outlet to the standard university quarterlies, which occasionally published poetry and fiction. In 1925, Smith and Scott helped found the landmark student literary magazine the *McGill Fortnightly Review* (Montreal, 1925–7), which promoted free verse and serious criticism, and rejected the poetry associated with the Canadian Authors Association, founded in 1921. After the *Fortnightly* expired in 1927, Scott and Kennedy, with Louis Schwartz, founded the ephemeral, H.L. Mencken–inspired *Canadian Mercury* (Montreal, 1928–9). During the 1930s the literary scene in Canada was as bleak as the economic situation, although short-lived magazines such as *Masses* (Toronto, 1932–4) and *New Frontier* (Toronto, 1936–7) provided venues for leftist politics, poetry, and opinion.

During the more prosperous 1940s and 1950s, the small press movement ignited across Canada. The most influential little magazines were *Contemporary Verse* (Victoria, 1941–52), *Fiddlehead* (Fredericton, 1945–), *Here and Now* (Toronto, 1947–8), and Montreal's *Preview* (1942–5) and *First Statement* (1942–5), which in 1945 merged into *Northern Review*. A second wave followed with *Contact* (Toronto, 1952–4), *Combustion* (Toronto, 1957–60), *CIV/n* (Montreal, 1953–5), and the *Tamarack Review* (Toronto, 1956–82). During its three decades, *Tamarack* achieved national stature as *the* literary review of record. However, all these magazines served as vehicles for debate about literary aesthetics and the nature of a Canadian literature. Editorial motives ranged from Alan Crawley's desire that *Contemporary Verse* 'play a worthy part in the building of Canadian literature' to Catherine Harmon's hope that readers of *Here and Now* 'will also see in our pages an attempt to reform the typographical manners of the country.'[47]

The twenty-eight literary magazines founded during these two decades were accompanied by few small presses. In 1945 John Sutherland, the small press pioneer associated with *First Statement* and *Northern Review,* launched the first of seven titles in the groundbreaking New Writers chapbook series. Seven years later, Sutherland's protégés Louis Dudek, Irving Layton, and Raymond Souster, who had grown impatient with their mentor's increasingly conservative editorial views, established Contact Press (1952–67) in Montreal. Drawing upon American and British models and aesthetics, Contact played a monumental role in advancing modern and experimental poetry in Canada and set the stage for the New Wave Canada poets who would burst onto the literary scene in 1967. By the end of the 1950s, younger Ontario poets were engaging in short-lived publishing experiments such as Jay Macpherson's Emblem Books and John Robert Colombo's self-publishing venture, Hawkshead Press. At the University of New Brunswick, poet and professor Fred

Cogswell, closely affiliated with the *Fiddlehead Poetry Magazine*, launched the Fiddlehead Poetry Book imprint in 1954. During the press's twenty-eight years, Cogswell published over three hundred titles, many paid for out of his own pocket.

In 1967 a special issue of *Canadian Literature* examined the recent explosion in Canadian literary publishing, noting that the number of new poetry titles had risen from twenty-four in 1959 to sixty-six in 1966. Contributors' explanations included demographic, economic, technological, social, political, and cultural factors that led to expanded university-educated audiences for Canadian art, music, and literature. This rise in cultural activity had prompted many aspiring writers and artists to found small magazines and presses, such as Toronto's iconic and iconoclastic Coach House Press, established by Stan Bevington in 1965. Through Bevington's close partnership with poet Victor Coleman, Coach House emerged as the heir to Contact Press and a publishing locus of Canada's literary avant-garde. Bevington adapted Arts and Crafts values into book production and design with a playful nod to pop art, surrealism, and dada. Coleman, on the other hand, was inspired by the work of the Beats, Charles Olson, and Robert Creeley and established important connections with the American small press community. During the late 1960s, a cluster of avantgarde presses also appeared, including Nelson Ball's Weed/Flower (Toronto), bill bissett's Blewointment Press (Vancouver), George Bowering's Imago Press (Calgary), bpNichol's Ganglia (Toronto), and Edwin Varney's Intermedia (Vancouver). Along with Coach House, they formed a loose network of small presses dedicated to literary and mixed-media experiments.

Canada's Centennial in 1967 was a banner year for small presses, with the founding of Michael Macklem's Oberon Press in Ottawa and May Cutler's Tundra Books in Montreal, the latter discussed by Suzanne Pouliot, Judith Saltman, and Gail Edwards in their account of children's publishing in chapter 7. In Toronto, Dennis Lee and Dave Godfrey, motivated by a strong social and political conscience, a commitment to literary innovation, and ardent nationalism, established the House of Anansi Press. Anansi's early publications ranged from their unexpectedly successful handbook for draft dodgers, which sold 60,000 copies between 1968 and 1971 (see illus. 11.4, p. 314), to a reprint of Margaret Atwood's *A Circle Game*, first published by Contact Press in 1966, which won a Governor General's Award. By 1969, when Dave Godfrey moved on to set up the more politically oriented New Press with James Bacque and Roy MacSkimming, Anansi was redefining its editorial stance, focusing on fiction and launching its Spiderline Fiction series to showcase youthful experiment. In the same year, David Robinson transformed his Vancouver little magazine, *talon*, into Talon Books, which emerged as the pre-eminent West Coast small press.

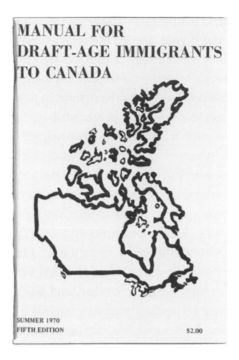

11.4 Byron Wall, ed., *Manual for Draft-Age Immigrants to Canada*, 5th ed. (Toronto: House of Anansi, 1970). Courtesy of the Thomas Fisher Rare Book Library, University of Toronto.

Like many other presses, Talon Books initially focused on poetry collections designed and printed in-house; by the mid-1970s, it had established its enduring identity as Canada's premier publisher of contemporary drama.

In the 1960s, the Vancouver literary scene was equally affected by the American poet Charles Olson and the Black Mountain school of writing promulgated in the influential mimeographed magazine *Tish* (Vancouver, 1961–9). Founded by a group of brash young poets led by Frank Davey and George Bowering, *Tish* galvanized Canadian literature and literary debate when its championing of Olson was interpreted by Canadian nationalists as a form of literary colonialism. Davey and Bowering exerted enormous influence across Canada as founding editors of such magazines as Davey's poetry newsletter *Open Letter* (Toronto, 1965–) and Bowering's little magazine *Imago*, (Vancouver, 1964–74), dedicated to the long poem genre.

Montreal experienced a rebirth in small press activity when Louis Dudek, Michael Gnarowski, and Glen Siebrasse launched the Delta imprint in 1966 to serve a new generation of Montreal writers and to counter the influence of *Tish*. The dissolution of Delta in 1972 yielded three independent imprints: DC Books and Delta Canada in Montreal, and Golden Dog Press in Ottawa. At the same time, influenced by George Bowering's presence in Montreal from 1967 to 1972, a younger generation of Montreal poets created a thriving community of diverse voices, presses, and magazines. Those affiliated with the Véhicule Gallery and Press explored a wide array of influences, including concrete, dada, and language-centred writing.

Through the 1970s, over a hundred new magazines appeared. These were increasingly affiliated with university and college departments of English or creative writing, such as Capilano College's *Capilano Review* (North Vancouver, 1972–). In addition to independent magazines, this decade saw the rise of the professional literary magazine which offered payment to authors. Some of the notable periodicals launched during this decade include *Descant* (Toronto, 1970–), *Canadian Fiction Magazine* (Vancouver, 1971–), *Exile* (Toronto, 1971–), *Grain* (Saskatoon, 1973–), *Dandelion* (Calgary, 1975–), *Matrix* (Lennoxville, QC, 1975–), *Brick* (London, ON, 1977–), *Arc* (Ottawa, 1978–), *Northward Journal* (Moonbeam, ON, 1978–90), *TickleAce* (St John's, 1977–), and *Pottersfield Portfolio* (Fredericton, 1979–). New presses also abounded, at an average of ten per year, with thirteen launched in 1976 alone. These benefited directly from two federal government programs designed to provide employment opportunities for young Canadians: the Local Initiative Program and Opportunities for Youth. At the same time, small presses began to modify their previous focus on poetry. The growing market for small press fiction was met by Oberon and Anansi. In response to the experimental theatre community, Talon Books established its commitment to Canadian drama. In 1972 the Playwrights Guild founded the Playwrights Canada Press, followed in 1974 by CTR, Canadian Theatre Review Publications.

Another trend of the 1970s was a commitment to regional publishing, often supported by provincial and municipal governments, to provide outlets for local writers and cultivate regional identities. Enduring Atlantic presses include Breakwater Books (St John's) and Ragweed Press (Charlottetown). Beyond Toronto, notable Ontario presses included Black Moss Press (Windsor) and Quarry Press (Kingston). Across the West, new presses were founded annually, such as Turnstone Press in Manitoba, Coteau Books and Thistledown Press in Saskatchewan, NeWest Press in Alberta, and Harbour Publishing in British Columbia.

In the 1970s, various ethnic and cultural groups expanded their presence in the small press. While Black writers were published widely in Canadian literary magazines across the country and in the Caribbean, their first dedicated poetry magazine was *Ebo Voice* (1965?–7), founded by Austin Clarke in Toronto. The new outlets that sprang up in the 1970s, such as *The Black i* (Montreal, 1972–) and *Black Images* (Toronto, 1972–5), illustrate the community's growing breadth of activity. In the 1980s, the emergence of presses like Williams and Wallace, and Sister Vision further transformed Black literary publishing in Canada.

The Small Press in Quebec

Commenting on the annual Salon du livre in 1952, the editors of the cultural review *Qui? Art, musique, littérature* noted enthusiastically that not only were French-Canadian writers being celebrated for the first time in the fair's history, but that French-language literary and artistic magazines were also being given a place of honour.[48] With pride, the editors catalogued more than a dozen cultural periodicals that had appeared during the previous thirty-five years. On their list were several Montreal titles recognized today as little magazines crucial to the history of Quebec's literary avant-garde, including *Le Nigog* (1918), *La Relève* and *La Nouvelle Relève* (1934–48), and *Gants du ciel* (1943–6). Absent was one notable title, Victor Barbeau's iconoclastic review, *Cahiers de Turc* (1921–7). Quebec's literary institutions and culture developed slowly during the first half of the twentieth century until the 1960s, when the full force of Quebec nationalism rippled throughout the province. The writer/artist was the *porte-parole* of the Quiet Revolution; through the medium of political, cultural, and literary reviews, the unrepentant vision of a secular, modern, independent, French-speaking Quebec was forcefully expressed and disseminated.

The birth of the monthly literary and intellectual review *La Relève* (Montreal, 1934–41) in the midst of the Depression signalled the rise of an influential generation of Quebec writers and intellectuals that included Robert Charbonneau, Paul Beaulieu, Claude Hurtubise, Robert Elie, Roger Duhamel, Hector de Saint-Denys-Garneau, and Jean Le Moyne. Heavily influenced by French-Catholic thinker Jacques Maritain, *La Relève*'s editors promoted a 'national independent Catholic group' dedicated to developing 'an art, a literature, and a line of thought, the lack of which begins to be oppressive.'[49] Issued after 1941 under the title *La Nouvelle Relève*, the periodical continued to serve as an important vehicle for Quebec writers until 1948.

With the surge in publishing activity caused by Quebec's position as a haven for French writers and publishers from the German occupation of France in 1940 until the end of the Second World War, there arose new intellectual currents influenced by a growing sense of national identity among French-Canadian writers and intellectuals. After the French authors went home at the end of the war, the condition of

Quebec's writers and the paucity of outlets for local authors were eloquently proclaimed in Robert Charbonneau's polemical *La France et nous* (1947), a rallying cry for a made-in-Quebec culture liberated from the colonial influence of France.

On the aesthetic front, a small group of Québécois avant-garde writers and artists, the Automatistes, were heavily influenced by André Breton and surrealism. Their mimeographed manifesto *Refus global* (1948) marked a turning point in Quebec's cultural history. Impatient with the conservative, Catholic, pastoral paradigm under which Quebec's writers and artists had laboured, *Refus global* voiced its authors' desire for liberty and self-expression and a vision of a secular Quebec. On the literary side, *Gants du ciel* (the title was borrowed from Jean Cocteau), edited by Guy Sylvestre and published by Fides, followed the established model of the literary and intellectual review, publishing essays, reviews, and short fiction, as well as verse by members of the next generation of Quebec poets such as Anne Hébert and Rina Lasnier. Several avant-garde literary presses emerged during the 1940s, the most important of which was Éditions de l'Arbre, launched by Robert Charbonneau and Claude Hurtubise, two members of *La Relève*. In 1944, Gilles Hénault produced two titles under his surrealist-inspired short-lived imprint, Cahiers de la file indienne. In the wake of *Refus global*, the young artist and graphic designer Roland Giguère founded Éditions Erta in 1949 to explore models of collaboration among the poet, the artist, and the designer. Giguère produced twenty-five titles, beautifully designed and hand-printed, during the 1950s.

This decade saw further initiatives that would figure in the coming Quiet Revolution. In 1953 André Goulet, a master printer and typographer, launched Éditions Orphée, closely affiliated with the avant-garde in Montreal. Greater impact was achieved with the establishment of Éditions L'Hexagone (whose name represents its six founders), also in 1953, which signalled a seismic shift among young Quebec writers who had decided to break free from Catholicism and cultural ties to France, believing that they possessed the means to create an indigenous literature that nurtured the young and protected the French language. This press launched *Liberté* (Montreal, 1959–), Quebec's most important literary review during the latter half of the twentieth century. Conceived as a nationalist organ addressing the cultural problems facing contemporary Quebec, it would play a crucial role in both the literature and politics of the Quiet Revolution. Other literary magazines of the 1950s included the institution-building *Écrits du Canada français* (Montreal, 1954–), the more narrowly focused poetry review *Emourie* (1954–65), edited and published by Gilles Vigneault in Quebec City, and *Situations* (Montreal, 1959–62), an elegantly printed monthly published by André Goulet and edited by a loose collective that included iconic nationalist Québécois writers Jacques Ferron, Michèle Lalonde, and Yves Préfontaine, and artist Guido Molinari.

Central to the fervent nationalism and cultural ferment that saw the term 'French Canadian' replaced by 'Québécois' was the politically and culturally charged review *Parti pris* (Montreal, 1963–8), home to an entire generation of Quebec's intellectuals, writers, and artists. As the separatist movement gained momentum, other little magazines were launched, such as *La Barre du jour* (Montreal, 1965–77) and *Les Herbes rouges* (Montreal, 1968–93). Different in format and editorial structure, both periodicals fostered literary experiment and debate, mirroring the growing influence of *nouvelle écriture*, which dominated literary practice in France and was eagerly embraced by Quebec's literary avant-garde. As *Parti pris* grew in importance and stature, the editors expanded to book publication, including a literary series edited by Gérald Godin, poet and future politician. Through the 1970s, new little magazines continued to appear. Several in Montreal were inspired by the model of *Les Herbes rouges,* including *Cul Q* (1973–6?), *Chroniques* (1975–8), and *Critère* (1970–86). Another trend was the growth of regional literary magazines, such as *Estuaire* (Quebec City, 1976–), and regional presses that balanced the centrality of Montreal, such as Écrits des forges, founded in Trois-Rivières in 1971 by poet Gatien Lapointe, and Éditions du Noroît, established the same year in Saint-Lambert.

In both language groups, the small press movement enabled the emergence of literary modernism, the development of nationalist cultural values, and the arrival of the avant-garde. It has now become a truism of Canadian literary history that the small press has played a major role in defining literary values and aesthetics. Independent book and magazine production mirrors the complex spectrum of forms and expression that constitutes Canadian literature, in both French and English.

Publishing by Women

CAROLE GERSON

Despite women's substantial engagement with print as authors, readers, purchasers, teachers, and librarians, their involvement in the creation of print in Canada between 1918 and 1980 resulted in proportionately few publications in which their participation was specifically identified at the level of the publisher's imprint. While women were active in the material production of print, working in printing plants as typesetters and binders, and in publishers' offices, where they were variously employed as readers, publicists, editors, and production staff, women who achieved visibility as publishers tended to do so in relation to texts on woman-specific topics or through issuing books for children.

Fairly constant throughout the period were publications emanating from women's religious organizations. The women's auxiliaries and missionary societies of the Presbyterian, Methodist, Baptist, Anglican, and United churches, as well as the Woman's Christian Temperance Union, the Ukrainian Catholic Women's League, and the many branches of the Hadassah-WIZO (Women's International Zionist Organization), produced a constant and voluminous stream of informative newsletters, reports, advocacy materials, and cookbooks. These groups were also conscious of the need to preserve their own histories. For example, in 1940 the Publications Committee of the Women's Baptist Missionary Society of Ontario West issued a title which encompasses the breadth of their concerns: *From Sea to Sea: A Study Book of Home Missions for Mission Circles, Women's Associations, Ladies' Aids and Canadian Girls in Training, Senior Missions Bands: A Story of Canadian Missions across Canada in Early Days, in the Present, and with an Outlook towards the Future*; and in the late 1950s there appeared *The Ukrainian Catholic Women's League: Its Origin and Activity.* In Quebec, two communities of nuns were prolific publishers: the Soeurs de Sainte-Anne and the Congrégation de Notre-Dame. The latter issued many editions of textbooks for the primary grades and was best known for its immensely popular cookbook, *La cuisine raisonnée*, which, through multiple editions issued between 1926 and 2003, found its way into most Quebec homes.

Until the 1960s, traces of first-wave feminism lingered in women's secular publishing. By 1919 women had acquired the right to vote nationally and in most provinces; hence, suffrage print diminished everywhere but in Quebec, where women acquired the franchise in 1940, and first executed it in 1944. The suffrage movement put its imprint on *La Sphère féminine / Women's sphere* (Montreal, 1931–45), the official organ of the Alliance canadienne pour le vote des femmes du Québec / Canadian Alliance for Women's Vote in Quebec. In both French and English Canada, women's organizations such as the National Council of Women of Canada and their provincial counterparts, which had supported women's suffrage and humanitarian causes, continued to flourish, issuing a steady flow of newsletters, yearbooks, and annual reports. Branches of national associations also took on special publication projects. For example, in 1928 the Women's Canadian Club of Victoria published *The Pioneer*

Women of Vancouver Island 1843–1866 under the epigraph 'The History of a Country is written from the lives of Men, but from the lives of Women we learn best of a Nation's soul.' A similar title, *Women of Red River*, 'A Tribute to the Women of an Earlier Day,' published by the Women's Canadian Club of Winnipeg in 1923, proved sufficiently popular to merit reissue in a Centennial edition in 1967 and a second reprint ten years later.

Second-wave feminism (women's liberation), recognized worldwide with the designation of 1975 as International Women's Year, was given a head start in Canada with the establishment in 1967 of the Royal Commission on the Status of Women. It generated a surge of research and publications, and the appearance of its liberal-minded report in 1970 coincided with the onset of a flood of print from a new generation of feminist activists whose commitment to social change extended to revision of traditional management structures. From the perspective of Myrna Kostash, writing in 1975, this new feminist press represented 'a journalism outside the commercial mainstream that has as its values that any woman can be a writer (we are all "experts" at being women alive in a sexist society), that the niceties of language and grammar are irrelevant in the campaign to propagandize, that the struggle for women's liberation is profoundly subversive (hence the impossibility, undesirability even, of counting on support from advertisers and distributors), and that a feminist newspaper should be, must be, a collective enterprise avoiding the hierarchical roles and structures of the "glossies." Not all the newspapers conform to all these principles but they all identify with some of them.'[50] Whereas only a few new women's periodicals appeared during the 1960s, the following decade saw at least fifty spring up across the country,[51] representing various regions and interest groups, a fifth of them in French. According to Eleanor Wachtel, 'A remarkable number of publications began as outgrowths of a conference, status of women meeting, or course where the participants wished to remain in contact with one another and continue to create or exchange information.'[52] The formats of these periodicals varied according to their budgets; many lasted only a few years (albeit replaced by others during the 1980s).[53] The titles from the 1970s that survived into the next century tend to fall into three categories: those with sufficient literary content to qualify for Canada Council funding; those that would receive support as scholarly journals;[54] and several titles in Quebec supported by Catholic organizations (*L'autre parole*, Rimouski, 1976–; *Femmes d'ici*, Montreal, 1977–) or the provincial government (*Gazette des femmes*, Quebec City, 1979–).

While there has been an ongoing tradition of women's organizations issuing materials relevant to their particular interests, much rarer has been the woman-

controlled publishing house. Women have sometimes taken over the family business upon the death of a publisher-husband, as when Irene Clarke became president of Clarke, Irwin in 1955. The first Canadian woman to start her own publishing
company may well have been Berthe Dulude Simpson. From 1945 to 1948, under
the imprint of B.D. Simpson, her Montreal office issued forty-five fiction and non-
fiction titles in French, only one authored by a Canadian.[55] Tundra Books, initiated
by May Cutler in 1967 to produce beautiful books for children, may have been the
second Canadian publishing house founded by a woman. Other women followed
this direction in the late 1970s with the creation of additional presses for children by
Anne Millyard (Annick) and Patsy Aldana (Groundwood Books). In general trade
publishing, Anna Porter climbed through the editorial ranks at McClelland and
Stewart, becoming president in 1977 of the company's new mass-market subsidiary,
Seal Books, and subsequently going on to found her own company, Key Porter
Books, with Michael de Pencier.

During the 1970s, second-wave feminism propelled a number of young women
not only into print but also into the entire process of production in order to issue
feminist and lesbian books for adult readers, and non-sexist books for children. As
with the management of feminist periodicals, feminist book publishers usually
operated as collectives, initially dependent upon volunteer labour and occasional
government grants from such resources as the federal Opportunities for Youth
(OFY) and Local Initiatives Program (LIP). In Vancouver, Press Gang began in 1970
as a left-wing printing co-operative and became a book publisher five years later
with its first title, *Women Look at Psychiatry*.[56] In Toronto the Canadian Women's
Educational Press (later Women's Press) assembled in 1971 in order to publish
Women Unite! (1972) and non-sexist children's books. First funded with an LIP grant,
it created the *Everywoman's Almanac* (1976–9?) to bring in a steady income.[57] A similarly enduring feminist publication has been the annual *Herstory* calendar, issued
since 1974 by the Saskatoon Women's Calendar Collective, which began as an OFY
beneficiary.[58]

The dual imprint of Ragweed/gynergy, founded in Charlottetown in 1974, illustrates both the multiple focal points of feminist publishing and the ingenuity
required to keep such a press alive. Under the Ragweed imprint, the press issued
children's books, fiction, and general titles, including saleable genres such as Atlantic tourist literature, while under the gynergy imprint, the same office produced
radical lesbian fiction and non-fiction. The desire for non-sexist children's books
inspired a number of women to start new publishing enterprises, such as the
Ontario-based Before We Are Six collective, which used a government grant to issue

several titles for preschoolers during 1971–3.[59] More enduring has been Kids Can Press, established in Toronto in 1973 by a group of students who received an OFY grant to produce non-sexist, non-racist multicultural materials.

Montreal has been an active site of feminist publishing in both official languages. Éditions de la Pleine Lune began to issue literary works by women in 1975; Éditions Remue-ménage quickly followed with children's books and translations of major American feminist authors. The two presses offer contrasting managerial practices: the first structured according to the French model of being headed by a named individual and the second following the American model of a collective undertaking.[60] In 1977, Eden Press began to produce English-language scholarly and health-related titles written from a feminist perspective. More stable than the periodicals, most of these feminist book publishers stayed afloat for many years, supported by federal and provincial grant programs, libraries, dedicated readers, and the rise of women's studies as a scholarly discipline.

Publishing against the Grain

DONALD W. MCLEOD

Beneath Canada's staid cultural exterior, throughout the twentieth century there flourished a rich panorama of publications dedicated to subverting established order or promoting unconventional values and lifestyles. Their subjects altered significantly over the decades, as Canadian society grew to accept causes and values previously deemed immoral (such as birth control and eroticism) or disruptive (such as organized labour or Quebec separatism). The collection, documentation, and study of this material reveal much about the subsequent evolution of its causes. Since the 1970s, bibliographies, archives, and scholarly studies of the once marginal print cultures of left-wing political organizations and gay communities have appeared, but other areas, such as the far right (represented by the Ku Klux Klan and neo-Nazism), have received less attention.[61]

Produced outside the mainstream channels of publication and distribution, sometimes surreptitiously, underground publications may be obscure or highly visible and are usually ephemeral. Because book and magazine publishing is expensive, underground or counterculture publishers have relied on cheaper modes of communication, such as flyers and pamphlets, to convey their messages. These publishers have also adopted new technologies – the mimeograph, the photocopier, desktop publishing, and, recently, cyberspace – to keep costs down and to experiment with formats.

One genre of underground literature that affected a particularly wide swath of Canadians was that which promoted contraception. Officially outlawed until the Canadian Criminal Code was amended in 1969, publications about birth control were distributed by hand among the urban poor of Ontario during the 1930s and reached middle-class Canadians by mail, largely through the efforts of A.H. Tyrer, whose manual *Sex, Marriage and Birth Control* (1936) 'enjoyed greater sales than any other Canadian sex education and contraception publication' during the 1930s and early 1940s. Mainstream magazines and newspapers carried advertisements for contraceptives using coded language that intimated their subject matter.[62] Despite the resistance of the Roman Catholic Church, by the 1960s family planning was so widespread that few Canadians realized that the sale and distribution of both contraceptives and information about them were still illegal. One notable mass-produced challenge to the law was the *Birth Control Handbook*, produced by the Students' Society of McGill University in 1968 and distributed to 50,000 readers in its first edition. In 1970 an equally successful French edition followed; by 1971, over three million copies of the handbook had been issued.[63]

Political causes have created one of the most important categories of contestatory print. The vast array of Canadian leftist literature devoted to progressive social or political reform includes publications issued by the Co-operative Commonwealth Federation (CCF) and its successor, the New Democratic Party (NDP), and by communist, socialist, and labour parties and organizations. Publications of trade unions and various progressive movements active in the mid and late twentieth century concern pacifism, secularism, the anti-nuclear movement, Native rights, feminism, and the co-operative movement. This material is enumerated in Peter Weinrich's bibliography *Social Protest from the Left in Canada, 1870–1970* (1982), which lists 4,395 separate imprints (more broadsides and pamphlets than books) and 800 serial titles for the period between 1918 and 1970, but excludes materials relating to Quebec. His index of authors constitutes an historical roll call of left-wing activists, such as Tim Buck, M.J. Coldwell, T.C. Douglas, Stanley Knowles, Angus MacInnis, F.R. Scott, F.H. Underhill, and J.S. Woodsworth. Prolific organizations include the Canadian Labour Congress, the Communist Party of Canada (the Labour Progressive Party from 1943 to 1958), the CCF and the NDP, the League for Social Reconstruction, One Big Union, the Socialist Party of Canada, the Trades and Labour Congress of Canada, the United Farmers of Alberta, the United Farmers of Canada, and the Young Communist League. Their materials were cheaply produced, often printed on newsprint or mimeographed, and circulated within groups or distributed at public rallies or street demonstrations. Few were sold on newsstands or entered library collections.[64] Some items were dangerous to possess, particularly those of the Communist Party of Canada during the 1920s and 1930s, and especially in Quebec after enactment of the Padlock Law (1937) enabled the police to close down the offices of publications such as the communist newspaper *Clarté* (Montreal, 1935–9; see illus. 17.1, p. 470), which nonetheless continued to appear.

In Quebec a militant, left-leaning separatist press emerged during the 1960s, reflecting the new ideological climate that accompanied the Quiet Revolution. Small activist groups such as the Front républicain pour l'indépendance (FRI), the Rassemblement pour l'indépendance nationale (RIN), and the Front de libération du Québec (FLQ) each issued many ephemeral publications. In 1964 the FRI alone launched four different short-lived serials; *Québec libre* (Montreal, 1964–5), which fought for a Quebec that was politically independent, economically free, and socially just, encountered difficulties with censorship, and many of its distributors were arrested. The press of the intellectual left was also prominent in Quebec during this decade, most notably *Parti pris* (Montreal, 1963–8). Founded by a group of university thinkers, it promoted Marxism, secularization, and independence. Other titles were issued by political parties, such as *La Gauche* (Montreal, 1965–7), a monthly from the Parti socialiste du Québec. The founding of *Québec-Presse* (1969–74) spearheaded a new political momentum, which gave rise to an abundance of serials in the 1970s.[65] Citizens' movements published *Le Droit populaire* (Montreal, 1972–4; later *Organisation populaire*, 1975–82), issued by the Association pour la défense des droits sociaux du Montréal métropolitain, and *Le Journal du FRAP* (Montreal, 1972–3), the organ of the Front d'action politique.

In contrast, literature of the far right in Canada has been meagrely documented.[66] Not that examples are lacking: numerous rightist groups – white supremacists, fascists, Nazis, and neo-Nazis – have produced leaflets, newspapers, and periodicals. The Ku Klux Klan, for example, was active in Canada by 1921 and found a particular foothold in the West in the 1920s. In Vancouver in November 1921, the Canadian Knights and Ladies of the Ku Klux Klan published pamphlets declaring that the group stood for 'Canada for Canadians, Anglo-Saxons for Anglo-Saxonism, White race for White race.'[67] In Edmonton, John James Moloney issued a Klan newspaper, the *Liberator* (ca. 1930–4), filling its pages with anti-Catholic, anti-francophone, and anti-union tirades. Moloney also circulated copies of the notorious anti-Semitic hoax *The Protocols of the Learned Elders of Zion*. In the 1920s and 1930s, the Klan had almost a hundred chapters and some forty thousand members in Saskatchewan alone. One pamphlet commonly distributed there was entitled *Why I Intend to Become a Klan Member*. Quebec also witnessed the rise of various fascist and pro-Hitler publications in the 1930s. Adrian Arcand, head of the Parti national social chrétien / National Socialist Christian Party, and Joseph Ménard were the publishers of the fascist and anti-Semitic weekly Montreal newspapers *Le Chameau* (1930–2?), *Le Goglu* (1929–33), and *Le Patriote* (1933–8). All three were bankrupt by the late 1930s, victims of an advertising boycott and arson.

The radical right in Canada collapsed by the end of the Second World War, only to revive in the 1960s. The short-lived Canadian Nazi Party, formed in 1965, distributed leaflets and sold far-right magazines and books out of its Toronto office. It was succeeded by the Edmund Burke Society, founded in 1967 and renamed the Western Guard in 1972. Its monthly magazine, *Straight Talk* (Scarborough, ON, 1967–77), published in support of a 'White Canada,' was opposed to immigration, sex education, welfare, homosexuality, abortion, big government, and Prime Minister Pierre Elliott Trudeau. In the 1970s the far right aimed its publications at a mass audience. Ernst Zundel's Samisdat Publishing in Toronto became the biggest supplier of German-language, neo-Nazi print materials in the world. *Web of Deceit* (1978), a Holocaust-denying book by schoolteacher Malcolm Ross, gained an international audience and was one of the most notorious anti-Semitic works ever produced in Canada.

More readers sought materials about sex than about politics, publications acquired through advertisements in the tabloid press. During the 1950s and 1960s, such serials offered adult publications and photographs for sale by mail order, usually from a post office box in Toronto. In *TAB Confidential* (Toronto, 195?–65), Book Import offered *The Homosexual* – 'An amazing novel of the erotic love life of the lavender boys, their habits and way of life. Read about the men in women's clothes' – as well as *Oriental Passion* – 'The strange mysterious intrigues of exotic Oriental concubines. Every nerve will vibrate to the sing song unusual sex habits of these Chinese love tales. (Illustrated).'[68] Advertisements for pin-up photos and nudist shots were also common. By the mid-1960s, tabloids such as *TAB* commonly advertised shops like Carnival Magazine Store on Queen Street West, in Toronto, which claimed the largest selection of girlie and nudist publications in Canada and offered its customers free bottles of Coca-Cola while they browsed.[69] By 1966, K.K. Books, located on Yonge Street, in Toronto, advertised a wide variety of gay books and physique magazines, as well as gay and heterosexual fetish, bondage, spanking, and whipping magazines. Kept under the watchful eye of the law, the store survived into the 1970s, even though it was raided at least once (in February 1966) and charged with possessing obscene literature for the purpose of distribution.

Despite the advertisements they carried, most tabloids attempted to incite their readers against the activities of homosexual 'perverts' – by which they meant anyone who engaged in same-sex sexual activity. But coverage of gay activities underwent a subtle transformation in some Toronto tabloids as early as 1950. Explicitly gay male (and some lesbian) material appeared in regular gossip or tidbit columns that used coded language to inform readers of local activities. One of the earliest columns, written by Masque, was published in *True News Times* (*TNT*) in 1950. Typical was 'Toronto Fairy-Go-Round,' written by Bettina for *TAB* (1956–9), which was succeeded by 'The Gay Set,' written by Lady Bessborough (1963–7) and then by Duke Gaylord (1967–75).

These columns arguably mark the beginnings of Canada's gay and lesbian press.[70] Serious articles by Jim Egan, Canada's pioneer gay activist, such as 'Homosexual Concepts' in *Justice Weekly* (December 1953–February 1954) and an untitled, fifteen-part series in the same publication (March–June 1954),[71] raised the profile of homosexuality in the Canadian tabloid press considerably and encouraged letters from readers. *Justice Weekly* also arranged to reprint foreign material, mostly from *ONE Magazine* (Los Angeles) and the *Mattachine Review* (San Francisco). Such columns and articles sowed the seeds for the eventual establishment of a Canadian gay press in 1964, with the publication in Toronto of the male-oriented periodicals *GAY* (1964–6) and *TWO* (1964–6) and in Vancouver of the *ASK Newsletter* (1964–8). In Quebec the gay press emerged in the early 1970s with publications such as *Le Tiers* (Châteauguay, 1971–2), which addressed both gay men and lesbians. The movement confirmed its strength and visibility in newspapers such as the *Body Politic* (Toronto, 1971–87) and the first Canadian lesbian publication, *Long Time Coming* (Montreal, 1973–6), and in the rise of gay male-oriented publishers such as Ian Young's Catalyst Press (Scarborough, ON, 1970–80).

The rise of youth culture during the 1960s resulted in another explosion in alternative or underground publishing, which has been described as 'exciting, revolutionary, informative, blasphemous, undisciplined, amateurish, refreshing, lively, audacious, and scatological.'[72] Characterized by hedonistic rebellion and youthful exuberance (ubiquitous sex, drugs, music), the 'hippie' press also had its serious side. It popularized non-mainstream coverage of social justice, ecology, and alternative medicine, issues that also became the backbone of New Age consciousness.

Although similar in many respects to counterculture publications that sprouted across the United States, Canada's underground newspapers could sometimes voice distinctly un-American opinions, particularly when protesting the Vietnam War, and the Americanization of Canadian industries and cultural institutions. Fortu-itously, all of this publishing enthusiasm was aided by the rise of a simple and rela-tively inexpensive technology, photo-offset printing.

Numerous underground newspapers appeared across Canada in the late 1960s. Most were sold informally through alternative bookstores and 'head shops' or were hawked at concerts or on the street. Some lasted only a few issues, a few for several years, and at least one survived into the twenty-first century. Among the first were *Satyrday* (Toronto, 1966–9) and the *Canadian Free Press* (later *Octopus*; Ottawa, 1967–70). *The Georgia Straight* (Vancouver, 1967–), founded by Dan McLeod and others, was ultimately the most successful. A high-profile battle with Vancouver mayor Tom 'Terrific' Campbell, a historic libel trial, several staff revolts, and precarious financial arrangements could not sink the *Straight*. It repositioned itself during the 1980s by focusing on local events and obtaining extensive paid advertising to become one of Canada's most successful and enduring alternative newspapers. Its peers, including *Guerilla* (Toronto, 1970–4), *Harbinger* (Toronto, 1968–72), *Logos* (Montreal, 1967–73), *New Morning* (Dartmouth, NS, 1971–3?), and *Omphalos* (Winnipeg, 1969–70), faced a litany of charges under Canadian drug, obscenity, libel, or licensing laws. By 1974 the hippie press was dead in English Canada, a victim of spiritual and financial exhaus-tion and changing values.[73] However, the 1970s witnessed a blossoming of French-language countercultural, alternative publications in Montreal, including *Mainmise* (1971–8), *Cul Q* (1973–6?), *Hobo-Québec* (1973–81), and *Le Temps fou* (1978–83, 1995–7). The ongoing patterns of Canada's underground press demonstrate that each hege-mony, however open-minded it may have appeared to be, inevitably generated countercurrents that were expressed in print.

chapter 12

SCHOLARLY AND PROFESSIONAL PUBLISHING

Scholarly and Reference Publishing

FRANCESS G. HALPENNY

'Scholarly publishing' is a term of wide application. It often suggests the books issued by university presses, learned institutes, and some trade publishers, as well as learned journals; all report the on-going results of research by largely university-based scholars writing primarily to inform their peers. But such assumptions do not take into account the research and reporting that occurred in increasing volume in Canada over the course of the twentieth century at a host of institutions and associations with research interests, such as museums and art galleries publishing research findings in exhibition catalogues. Historical societies have similarly flourished in every province, issuing accounts of people and places useful to both general and scholarly readers, while Canada's many government commissions have generated research papers often prepared by university faculty.

Antecedents to modern scholarly publishing in Canada include the proceedings of the Royal Society of Canada (est. 1882) and early university journals like the *Queen's Quarterly* (est. 1893). In the prosperous 1920s, new scholarly journals were established as graduate programs developed and scholarly inquiry deepened. The *Canadian Historical Review* (CHR) replaced its predecessor, the *Review of Historical Publications Relating to Canada*, in 1920. A revitalized Canadian Political Science Association inspired the *Canadian Journal of Economics and Political Science* in 1934. Such journals were crucial for their cross-Canada scholarly constituencies and for the study of

Canada at a time when book publication was far from the norm for Canadian academics. The arts and humanities were enhanced when University of Toronto Press (UTP), which was responsible for printing, publishing, and subsidizing these two journals, started the *University of Toronto Quarterly* in 1931. Specialist schools attached to Université de Montréal also took initiatives: École polytechnique with *Revue trimestrielle canadienne* (1915, later *L'Ingénieur*) and École des hautes études commerciales with *L'Actualité économique* (1925). Société des Dix, a society of scholars, began *Les Cahiers des Dix* in 1936. In 1947 Lionel Groulx founded the *Revue d'histoire de l'Amérique française*, a major resource for scholarly articles in French on Canadian and Quebec history.

Although the Depression and the Second World War were not propitious times for research and publication, the fortitude of individual scholars ensured that a notable amount of work found its way into print. Robert Rumilly's single-authored tour de force, *Histoire de la province de Québec* (1940–69), reached forty-one unfootnoted volumes, the last fifteen of which were published by Fides, which reprinted the whole set in the 1970s. Also of enduring value are *Glossaire du parler français au Canada* (1930; reissued 1968), a masterwork of lexicography compiled by Adjutor Rivard and Louis-Philippe Geoffrion, displaying the usages of Canadian French, and Père Louis Marie Le Jeune's *Dictionnaire général de biographie, histoire …* (1931) from Université d'Ottawa. Never completed because of lack of funds, *Notre milieu* (5 vols, 1942–6), directed by Esdras Minville, attempted a team survey of the economic development of Quebec. In 1946 Fides introduced the first collections supervised by Luc Lacourcière, *Les archives de folklore*, the major resource on folklore in French.

Anglophone scholars often sought publication abroad during these years, producing independent monographs or working in the context of large international projects. In the humanities, titles that drew international attention included Edward Togo Salmon's *History of the Roman World* (1944), issued by Macmillan in New York and Methuen in London, and Northrop Frye's *Fearful Symmetry* (1947), which appeared under Princeton's imprint. Charles Norris Cochrane's *Christianity and Classical Culture* (1940), published by Clarendon, was described by Harold A. Innis as 'the first major Canadian contribution to the intellectual history of the West.'[1] In general, Canadian publishers still lacked the resources to do such works justice. The landmark series Canadian Frontiers of Settlement (9 vols, 1934–7), published by Macmillan, had as one of its editors W.A. Mackintosh of Queen's and received data and support from an array of Canadian universities and government departments, but its leader, W.L.G. Joerg, was a member of the American Geographical Society. Similarly, for the twenty-six volumes of The Relations of Canada and the United

States (1936–45), Innis was a chief planner and editor, but the overall project was directed by James T. Shotwell, a distinguished American scholar. The series was published for a division of the Carnegie Endowment for International Peace by Ryerson in Toronto, Yale University Press in the United States, and Oxford in the United Kingdom. Included was Donald Creighton's eloquent *The Commercial Empire of the St. Lawrence, 1760–1850* (1937); when it reappeared in 1956 with Macmillan of Canada, Creighton's preface paid tribute to the initial sponsorship: 'In those days a work on Canadian history, by a Canadian, was published only with difficulty, and often, in part, at the author's expense.'[2]

During the first half of the century, the founding of national bodies such as the Association canadienne-française pour l'avancement des sciences (ACFAS, est. 1923), the Social Science Research Council (SSRC, est. 1940), and the Humanities Research Council (HRC, est. 1943) offered some hope. With assistance from the Carnegie and Rockefeller foundations, the SSRC and the HRC provided small amounts to assist research and publication through the Aid to Scholarly Publications Program (ASPP), established in 1941 and currently administered by the Canadian Federation for the Humanities and Social Sciences. 'During its first decade, the ASPP funded 33 scholarly books, including works on the history of architecture in Quebec, the aboriginal people of Bella Coola, and several volumes of the *Canadian Historical Review* ... [B]y the end of the 1970s, the ASPP was funding upwards of 140 scholarly titles each year,'[3] the majority published in Canada. Also crucial was the founding of the Canada Council for the Arts in 1957, which instituted programs of peer-reviewed research and travel grants for scholars, as well as fellowships and scholarships. While questions are sometimes raised as to whether specific kinds of grants have a steering effect on research proposals and publications, the system as a whole holds up well as a serious, vital part of the context for scholarly publishing.

In the post-war years, Canadian universities expanded dramatically in number and size. With the influx of veterans returning from the Second World War in the late 1940s, and again with the wave of baby boomers in the late 1960s, enrolment continually increased. In both French and English Canada, new institutions were founded, teaching staff grew rapidly, and graduate programs were initiated, reshaped, or strengthened. For faculty, the achievement of promotion and tenure increasingly depended on publication in recognized scholarly venues. In Quebec the dominance of clerics and civil servants before the Second World War yielded to a fresh corps of university teachers with new research interests and methods, often influenced by international trends.

As publishers' lists reflected the changing scholarly climate, university libraries –

scholarly publishing's first market – enhanced their collections. Canadian history expanded from its traditional focus on politics to social concerns, while the teaching and study of Canadian literature emerged from obscurity. In 1959 the quarterly *Canadian Literature* (CL) began at the University of British Columbia, with George Woodcock as founding editor (succeeded in 1977 by W.H. New); in its articles and comprehensive reviewing, CL would become a journal of record. A similar role was filled for French Canada by *Livres et auteurs canadiens*, founded by Adrien Thério in Montreal in 1961, replaced by *Livres et auteurs québécois* (1969–83). Equally significant were Carl F. Klinck's *Literary History of Canada* (1965) and Maurice Lemire's *Dictionnaire des oeuvres littéraires du Québec* (1978–). The overall increase in learned societies and university institutions gave rise to a new generation of scholarly journals across the spectrum of disciplines which, like their forebears, relied on subsidies from granting councils and universities and on volunteer academic labour. In 1990 these journals would come together in the Canadian Association of Learned Journals / Association canadienne des revues savantes.

An essential foundation for scholarship in Canadian and other academic studies after mid-century was bibliography. While at times assembled as part of the research study it supported, or compiled regularly for a scholarly journal to show how research in the field was moving, bibliography also emerged as a dedicated field whose importance has been underlined by the Bibliographical Society of Canada / Société bibliographique du Canada, which began publishing its *Papers/Cahiers* in 1962. The scholarship of Marie Tremaine's analytical bibliography, *A Bibliography of Canadian Imprints, 1751–1800* (1952), blazed the trail, confirming that a record of publications reveals 'something of the nature of the society which produced them.'[4] Bruce Peel travelled from library to library for years with his clutch of index cards while preparing his *Bibliography of the Prairie Provinces to 1953* (1956); vastly expanded and published in both paper and electronic formats in 2003, it would become a showcase for the progress of digitization. Another seminal contribution was R.E. Watters's *A Check List of Canadian Literature and Background Materials, 1628–1950* (1959), described in the following case study by Sandra Alston. When Canadian studies became an urgent concern in the late 1960s, the paucity of supporting bibliography was made the theme of a national conference at the University of British Columbia in 1974.[5]

In the post-war years, Canadian scholarly writing continued to follow long-established routes to receptive publishers in Britain, France, or the United States, but in Canada a few trade publishers issued scholarly titles that might appeal to a general audience. Macmillan of Canada published notable two-volume biographies of Canadian politicians Sir John A. Macdonald (1952, 1955) and George Brown (1959, 1963), which were respectively authored by Creighton and J.M.S. Careless. Three of these four volumes won Governor General's Awards for non-fiction. When Ryerson Press published the three-volume series History of the Christian Church in Canada (1966–72), it heralded a new stage in the academic study of religion in Canada. A major venture into historical publishing with a number of academic authors was made by McClelland and Stewart with the eighteen-volume Canadian Centenary series (1963–88). Oxford University Press in Canada added to scholarly as well as trade publishing with its many Oxford *Companions*. Produced under the editorial supervision of William Toye, the series began in 1967 with Norah Story's *Oxford Companion to Canadian History and Literature.*

In Quebec, three trade publishers have contributed to scholarship: Fides, Boréal, and Hurtubise HMH. Under Luc Lacourcière's direction, Fides issued the first critical literary edition in Quebec, *Poésies complètes* of Émile Nelligan (1952); many major scholarly series subsequently appeared under the firm's imprint, including the Archives des lettres canadiennes (9 vols, 1961–2002), Fleur de lys (19 vols, 1955–76), Histoire économique et sociale du Canada français (7 vols, 1966–75), and the six volumes published to date of the *Dictionnaire des oeuvres littéraires du Québec* (1978–), edited by Lemire et al. Les Éditions du Boréal Express (est. 1963, after 1987 known as Éditions du Boréal) published history, and in the 1970s specialized in new interpretations of Quebec's past and present. Hurtubise HMH issues Cahiers du Québec, a series initiated in 1971 by Robert Lahaise, which included more than 135 volumes by 2005.

These undertakings notwithstanding, after the Second World War it became increasingly evident that Canadian trade publishers were unable to handle much scholarly publication and that Canadian subject matter did not interest many foreign publishers. Yet Canada entered the post-war period with only two university presses: Les Éditions de l'Université d'Ottawa, a bilingual press, had been founded in 1936 to assist the university's faculty; and UTP, set up in 1901 to serve the printing needs of its university, still carried on that role through its own printing plant. Before the war, these presses largely focused on serving their own campuses, issuing manuals, monograph series, or journals.

The post-war progression of the university presses was an extended learning process as each press sought to develop a coherent list that would identify it to the scholarly community. Editors, by and large, learned on the job and worked at different levels. Consideration of manuscripts was paramount: determining a submission's relevance to the list, working through the assessment of its scholarly merit with outside readers, proceeding with applications for support, and reporting to the press's academic board. Senior editors developed contacts with scholarly authors to shape their publishing efforts or encourage the exploration or initiation of themes the editors sensed could be of importance. Vital to their activity was an understanding of how research and scholarly writing are conducted and how to move judiciously amid changes in subjects of inquiry and scholarly approaches. In developing their methods of soliciting and considering manuscripts and in processing of texts for publication, Canadian presses were akin to university presses in the United States, but differed from many scholarly publishers in Great Britain and France.

The post-war development of UTP, which issued its first proper catalogue in 1947, became a flagship for others. From Canadian trade and textbook publishing came new senior staff: Eleanor Harman arrived as associate editor and production manager in 1946, and Marsh Jeanneret, as director, in 1953. The editorial department expanded from journals into scholarly books, accepting manuscripts from its own campus and beyond. Francess G. Halpenny became the press's senior editor after the war and in 1957 was named Editor of the Press (following her move to the *Dictionary of Canadian Biography* in 1969, Ian Montagnes became Editor, 1972–92). UTP worked out co-publishing arrangements with other universities and institutions. Its list in the humanities and social sciences rose to some one hundred titles yearly over a range of topics and periods from the classical age to modern Canada.[6]

Over time Canada's first two university presses were joined by others. On the English side, McGill University Press was established in 1960 and merged with Queen's University in 1968 to form the enduring McGill-Queen's University Press. The University of Manitoba followed in 1967, the University of Alberta in 1969, the University of British Columbia (UBC) in 1972, Wilfrid Laurier in 1974, and Calgary and Carleton in 1981. To enable scholarly publication in French, Les Presses de l'Université Laval began in 1950 and expanded in the 1960s. Les Presses de l'Université de Montréal (PUM) was founded in 1962, followed by Les Presses de l'Université de Québec in 1969 and Les Éditions de l'Université de Sherbrooke in 1980.

With lists varying in size from twenty to one hundred titles annually, each university press has exhibited particular specializations in response to scholarly trends. McGill-Queen's has focused on aspects of Canadian studies, and Alberta on Western Canadian history, general science, and ecology. UBC has pursued interests in Native studies, the Pacific Rim, and international law. Canada's English-language university presses have published little science, a field largely served by specialized foreign publishers of scientific journals, books, and textbooks, though, as Bertrum H. MacDonald explains later in this chapter, the National Research Council of

Canada has published many notable periodicals. The French-language presses have been active in many areas, from the society of French Canada and its literature, through medieval studies and law, geography, sociology, and industrial relations, reaching out also to the physical sciences. In 1972 the presses joined to create the Association of Canadian University Presses / Association des presses universitaires canadiennes – just in time for members to find mutual support under growing financial pressures and to learn how to speak together to councils and government departments.

Because of the limited market for scholarly works, most Canadian university presses have not been economically self-sustaining. Nor have English-Canadian university presses typically competed with textbook publishers, though a few titles have entered this market. Francophone presses, however, do issue pedagogical texts, especially in science, to serve the need for material in French. To keep prices accessible, university presses in both languages have required subsidies from the granting councils, universities, or other appropriate organizations. Whereas most university presses received some support from their parent institutions, UTP was able to use net proceeds from its total operations, which include a printing plant, the university bookstore, and a distribution arm, to benefit its scholarly list. Co-publishing with foreign houses has also aided Canada's scholarly publishers.

Adaptation to technological developments has proven an ongoing concern, a leading example being the emergence of paperbacks. Tentative at first, Canada's university presses learned to use paperback formats (backed up by hardcover for libraries), often in the hope of course adoption. Changes in printing technology have been rapid. In the 1960s the advent of offset printing and then the use of camera-ready copy (from earlier printed text or new typescript) lowered production costs and also made it possible to keep more backlist titles in print. The need for subsidy did not, however, lessen. Given these growing complexities, in 1969 UTP launched the journal *Scholarly Publishing*, creating an international forum for discussion about the interactions of scholarship, scholarly publishing, technologies, and libraries.

No account of Canadian scholarly publishing between 1918 and 1980 would be complete without acknowledging the signal contribution of major reference works. Seminal were two projects directed by W. Stewart Wallace. His *Dictionary of Canadian Biography*, first issued by Macmillan in 1926 (revised and enlarged several times until 1978), provided some of the biographical data that supported *The Encyclopedia of Canada* (1935–7), a project for which Wallace himself wrote most of the articles. First published by University Associates of Canada, the encyclopedia was reissued in 1940 and 1948, with a *Supplement* for Newfoundland added in 1949.

The monumental *Dictionary of Canadian Biography / Dictionnaire biographique du Canada* (DCB/DBC), which began to appear in 1966, resulted from a bequest to the University of Toronto from a Toronto businessman, James Nicholson, for a project modelled on the British *Dictionary of National Biography*. In 1959 the DCB was founded with administration entrusted to UTP and George W. Brown, a professor of Canadian history, as editor. A crucial early decision was to organize the volumes chronologically by period, a structure that would allow sales as each was completed. Once the French edition was established at Université Laval and its press in 1961, the DCB/DBC became a fully shared editorial undertaking, a bilingual/bicultural project unusual in its time. Two of the longest-serving general editors were Francess G. Halpenny and Jean Hamelin, succeeded by Ramsay Cook and Réal Bélanger. The fifteen volumes issued to 2005 are available on CD-ROM and on-line.

Collaboration on major projects has been a distinctive feature of Canadian scholarship, evident in three national efforts from UTP: the *Literary History of Canada* (1965, 1976, 1990), the *Encyclopedia of Music in Canada* (EMC), and the *Historical Atlas of Canada* (HAC). In creating the EMC, editors Helmut Kallman, Gilles Potvin, and Kenneth Winters gathered over three thousand entries by some four hundred writers, along with bibliographies and discographies. When its first edition appeared in English in 1981 (UTP) and in French in 1983 (Fides), the EMC created a new understanding of the country's music. Innovative in a different way was the *Historical Atlas of Canada*. Although its three volumes would not appear until 1987, 1993, and 1990, with the French editions issued by PUM, research began in 1970 when a group of geographers and historians proposed 'a major Canadian historical atlas focused on social and economic themes.'[7] The infinity of precise details required by maps, as well as the countless decisions to be made among author, editor, cartographer, translator, and copy editor, ensured that this groundbreaking publication came to slow fruition.

Important initiatives that commenced at other Canadian scholarly presses during the 1970s included *The Collected Writings of Louis Riel* (5 vols, 1985), published by the University of Alberta Press and edited by George F.G. Stanley et al. Under the general editorship of Mary Jane Edwards, the Centre for Editing Early Canadian Texts was established at Carleton University in Ottawa in 1979. In the 1980s, a similar project to prepare a series of critical texts for Quebec literature began at the University of Ottawa, with the Bibliothèque du Nouveau Monde published at PUM. In addition, *La presse québécoise des origines à nos jours (1764–1975)*, which had been initiated in the 1960s and was directed by André Beaulieu and Jean Hamelin, eventually reached a final edition of ten volumes plus index (1973–90) under the imprint of Les Presses de l'Université Laval. These large Canadian projects, as well as an array of monographs and journals devoted to national and international subjects, have contributed to Canada's international reputation for scholarship and scholarly publishing.

CASE STUDY ──
R.E. Watters's *Check List of Canadian Literature*
– Sandra Alston

'Canadian literature is still largely an unknown territory, unmapped and unsurveyed, characterized by unexplored swamps and unpenetrated thickets, where the occasional blazed trails go around rather than through,' stated Reginald Watters in 1963, four years after University of Toronto Press published the first edition of his mammoth *A Check List of Canadian Literature and Background Materials, 1628–1950*.[8] When the Humanities Research Council of Canada received its first funds from the Rockefeller Foundation, its interest in facilitating comparative Commonwealth studies inspired the project that produced Watters's groundbreaking 789-page inventory of English-Canadian writing. In the absence of a bibliography of Canadian literature that paralleled one already available for Australian literature, the council invited Watters, a professor of English at the University of British Columbia, to undertake the task. A literary scholar but not a bibliographer, he decided to create a tool for readers and researchers rather than librarians or book collectors, to provide 'as complete a record as possible of the separately published works that constitute the literature of English-speaking Canada.'[9] He divided his volume into two sections: the first, a comprehensive list of all known titles of poetry, fiction, and drama; the second, a selected list of titles of history, biography, travel, and other genres that might be of value to anyone studying Canadian literature or culture.

Seven years spent searching published library catalogues, as well as bibliographical and biographical works, resulted in a list of more than 12,000 titles by 5,500 Canadian authors in the first edition of 1959. The checklist was well received, but not without criticism of Watters's methodology. For the most part, the books listed had not been examined, a circumstance that led to some misattributions and the inclusion of many bibliographical 'ghosts,' for Watters preferred to 'have the bibliography "corrected" by scoring out titles [rather] than by writing them in.'[10] As titles, rather than imprints, were important to the compiler, only one edition of each work was listed, usually the first Canadian imprint, omitting concurrent issues produced for Britain or the United States. The inclusion of library locations was somewhat arbitrary, as was the identification of 'Canadian authors.' Some writers generally considered Canadian, such as novelist Robert Barr, were excluded entirely, while others with less claim were noted. H. Pearson Gundy's assessment of the work as 'useful and often irritating' was widely shared.[11]

Despite such shortcomings, reprints in 1960 and 1966 and the 1972 publication of a revised and enlarged second edition – advancing the checklist's coverage to 1960 and its size to 1,085 pages – demonstrate that the volume met a felt need.[12] Indeed, 'Watters' has provided an essential framework for the several generations of scholars involved in Canadian literary and cultural studies since the 1960s and has yet to be superseded.

Scientific Periodicals

BERTRUM H. MACDONALD

In 1916, when the need to coordinate the scientific war effort prompted the creation of the National Research Council of Canada (NRCC), the event proved a turning point in scientific and technical research development. By 1929 'scientific papers resulting from the activities of the universities, the National Research Council and other research agencies in Canada ... [had] become so numerous as to cause difficulty in securing prompt publication,' leading the NRCC to initiate the *Canadian Journal of Research* (CJR).[13] Initially a bimonthly, the CJR was soon receiving sufficient manuscripts to become a monthly publication. While originally intended to disseminate research conducted under the auspices of NRCC, from 1931 the CJR accepted manuscripts from other sources, including non-Canadian authors. By 1935 the number of published papers had tripled, leading to the journal's division into disciplinary sections. In 1951 its sections were transformed into separate periodicals, including the *Canadian Journal of Botany*, the *Canadian Journal of Chemistry*, the *Canadian Journal of Physics*, and the *Canadian Journal of Zoology*. Later titles, such as the *Canadian Journal of Earth Sciences* (1964–), enlarged the list of NRCC periodicals. From a single journal publishing 26 papers in 1929, the NRCC's periodical list had increased by 1978 to eleven journals with bilingual titles and contents, annually carrying 2,431 papers, with a combined circulation of approximately 29,000.[14]

Professional associations, academic presses, and commercial publishers also issued scientific and technical periodicals. For example, the Quebec Society for the Protection of Plants / Société de protection des plantes du Québec published reports, monographs, and eventually a journal, *Phytoprotection* (1963–), which responded to a growing demand for more frequent publication that incorporated a refereeing process. While *Phytoprotection* soon gained a much wider readership than the Society's annual reports, the reports, notable for being issued in both English and French, met 'a great need for reliable, practical information about all aspects of plant protection, but especially about plant diseases in French.'[15] *The Canadian Mineralogist* (Ottawa, 1957–), a technical journal, also responded to a growing professional audience. Prior to 1921, mineralogical information appeared only in foreign journals or in publications issued by Canada's Department of Mines. From 1921 to 1948, *Contributions to Canadian Mineralogy* appeared as part of the *University of Toronto Studies: Geological Series* (1900–48). During the following decade, the Mineralogical Society of America devoted one of its six annual parts to *Contributions to Canadian Mineralogy*, but by the mid-1950s Canadians wanted their own journal, and *The Canadian Mineralogist* was launched.[16]

Scientific journals are read primarily by other researchers; the audience for technical periodicals, however, also includes industry practitioners. For example, a commercial publisher issues the *Canadian Chemical Journal* (Toronto, 1917–) for an industrial audience,[17] while the *Canadian Journal of Chemical Engineering* (CJCE, Ottawa, 1957–) has targeted a research readership. The *CJCE* is published by the Chemical Institute of Canada (est. 1944), which acquired its forerunner, the *Canadian Journal of Technology* (1951–7), from the NRCC when it failed to attract sufficient submissions. The new journal grew steadily: by 1990 annual volumes numbered more than 1,100 pages compared to about 200 in the late 1950s.[18]

By the mid-1970s, worldwide changes in publishing practices, costs, and technologies prompted the National Research Council to commission the Royal Society of Canada (RSC) to investigate Canada's research journals. At that time the council was publishing eleven journals and supporting forty-one others through a grants-in-aid program. The RSC's evaluation committee, composed of scientists, engineers, and librarians, recommended strengthening the NRCC publication program, in part for nationalistic reasons. 'Just as any country with pretensions to a national culture must aspire to create a literary tradition in the humanities,' the report stated, 'so there is, in the sciences and engineering, a parallel compulsion to make a national contribution to publication.'[19]

The total number of scientific journals published in Canada during the twentieth century remains uncertain. In 1978 the RSC committee cited a figure of more than 500, while qualifying that 'many of these are not primary journals but are mainly concerned with transmitting information originally published elsewhere.'[20] In 1987 Claude Bishop estimated that Canada had 170 research journals covering medicine and biomedical topics, agriculture, engineering, geosciences, life sciences, physical sciences, forest products and northern studies, and general scientific subjects. Bishop argued that Canadian research journals are necessary in order 'to maintain scientific self-respect. While science *per se* is international, nationalism still exists and as long as we are a separate country we should not use the scientific literature without contributing to it.'[21] Bishop's number did not include 34 news journals issued by societies and associations or 33 trade journals, such as the *Canadian Guernsey Breeder's Journal* (Guelph, ON, 1927–85) and *Canadian Beekeeping* (Orono, ON, 1968–). The audience for such periodicals is varied and includes both domestic and international readers, the fascinated amateur as well as the highly trained specialist.

Legal Publishing

STUART CLARKSON AND SYLVIO NORMAND

Canada's legal system follows the common-law tradition, while Quebec also retains a civil-law system of French origin. In both English Canada and Quebec, the volume of legal publishing remained relatively stable during the first half of the twentieth century. Thereafter, the total number of legal monographs in both languages rose from 39 in 1958 to 211 in 1968, and reached a high point of 381 in 1978 before declining in 1980.[22] Nonetheless, in 1980 it was evident that Canadian legal publishing was enjoying a highly productive period.[23]

Legal Publishing in Quebec

Legal publishing in Quebec has been distinguished by remarkable consistency. An examination of titles in all genres (including laws, pamphlets, and monographs) held by the Bibliothèque nationale du Québec (BNQ) shows that until the 1960s, an average of about 100 titles appeared each decade.[24] In the 1940s, production dropped to 74 titles, but subsequently rose steadily: from 145 titles in the 1960s to 311 in the 1970s.[25] Pamphlets were a significant portion of this output, representing over 15 per cent of titles published from 1918 to 1980. Laws, often accompanied by commentary, remained important in terms of the number of titles and reprints,[26] although in the 1960s their proportion began to decrease in relation to monographs.

The publication of legal periodicals continued from the previous century, with some notable changes. While the production of law reports, which had begun at the end of the nineteenth century, continued without interruption, the number of periodicals on legal doctrine grew. Lawyers in Quebec City created the *Revue du droit* (1922–39), which defined itself as a journal promoting the study of law and the defence of civil law.[27] After a vigorous start, it lost momentum and was replaced by the *Revue du Barreau* (1941–), whose goal was to advance legal scholarship.[28] A significant change occurred in the 1950s with the creation of scholarly journals, beginning with *Thémis* (1951–) at the Université de Montréal. Since the outset, these journals have largely been student initiatives, and, as is customary in North American law faculties, they include many texts written by students.

Before the Quiet Revolution, the intent of most monographs was to assist with the practice of law, and they were frequently authored by senior practitioners who taught in law faculties. Some works were impressive in their scope: Antonio Perrault published *Traité de droit commercial* in three volumes (1936–40); Gérard Trudel, with many contributors, produced the massive *Traité du droit civil du Québec* in fifteen volumes (1942–65); in 1956, Wilson et Lafleur reprinted Pierre-Basile Mignault's famous nine-volume treatise on civil law, *Le droit civil canadien [...]* (1895–1916), which remained indispensable despite its dating from the turn of the century. In the 1930s, publications in English accounted for almost 25 per cent of Quebec's output, a proportion that subsequently fell to about 10 per cent. Especially notable was Walter S. Johnson's three-volume *The Conflict of Laws with Special Reference to the Law of the Province of Quebec* (Montreal, 1932, 1933, 1937). In addition to their specific contributions to legal scholarship, these anglophone authors contributed to the development of thinking on Quebec civil law.

In the 1960s, the entry of academics into the field of legal authorship altered the nature of publication. Academic writers produced works that were more scholarly, as well as many texts, sometimes described as 'précis' or 'treatises,' related to their teaching. These changes led to the revitalization of long-neglected branches of law, with many titles in such areas as constitutional law and administrative law.

The publishing house of Wilson et Lafleur, founded in Montreal in 1909, long dominated the world of private legal publishing until the arrival of Éditions Yvon

Blais in 1978. In the 1960s, university presses strove, with some difficulty, to enter the niche of legal publishing. In 1975 the government gave the Société québécoise d'information juridique the mandate to publish and distribute legal information,[29] and it henceforth became a major participant in this field.

Publishing reveals a great deal about the evolution of legal culture in Quebec. After a lengthy dependency on foreign books, the development of local publications enabled Quebec's legal professionals to meet much of their own need.[30]

Common-Law Publishing in English Canada

Until the mid-twentieth century, the common-law provinces relied heavily upon British case law and publications, with some influence from the United States. Although some texts specific to Canada appeared in the interwar period, reliance on foreign treatises, not always well suited to Canada, remained an unfortunate necessity.[31] Beginning in the 1950s, this situation came under increasing criticism as demands grew for the establishment of a uniquely Canadian common law.[32] By the mid-1970s, a Canadian legal perspective less beholden to foreign jurisdictions had developed, fostering a sudden and important increase in legal publishing.[33] This change was encouraged by the growth of common-law schools in the country's expanding universities, which led to more funding and greater impetus for legal research, and by the creation of influential public bodies such as the Law Reform Commission of Canada, established in 1971, and the Canadian Law Information Council, established in 1973.

Canada's legal publishers were well established by 1918, with several firms dating from the Edwardian era or earlier. Principal among them were Carswell Company Limited, the British subsidiary Butterworth and Company (Canada) Limited (often called Butterworths), and Canada Law Book Company. At mid-century these companies were joined by Richard DeBoo Limited (est. 1940), a Toronto firm that initially specialized in loose-leaf services, and CCH Canadian Limited (est. 1945), a branch of CCH U.S. Beyond Toronto, some smaller companies were founded to serve particular regions, including Maritime Law Book (est. 1968) in Fredericton and Western Legal Publications (est. 1974) in Vancouver. However, the later decades of the twentieth century witnessed buy-outs and consolidation as foreign ownership became the norm. In 1987 International Thomson Organization Limited, a multinational based in Toronto, acquired both Carswell and DeBoo, leaving Canada Law Book as the only large, privately held Canadian firm specializing in legal publishing in English.

Collectively, these commercial firms published for the legal community, of which practising lawyers formed the largest part.[34] Smaller, Canadian-owned presses focused on specialties; Maritime Law Book, for example, published only law reports. Other kinds of legal publishing included texts generated by provincial law societies for the continuing education of lawyers, and legislation, reports, and monographs from various levels of government. Legal texts for readers outside the profession were typically furnished by smaller publishers such as Self-Counsel Press, founded in Vancouver by Diana Douglas and Jack James in 1970.

The increase in Canadian common-law publishing encompassed the full range of print materials, including journals, reports, monographs, and finding tools. After the *University of Toronto Law Journal* (1935–) was founded during the Depression, the expansion of academic legal research after the Second World War encouraged substantial growth in this sector, beginning with the *University of New Brunswick Law School Journal* (Fredericton, 1947–51; subsequently *University of New Brunswick Law Journal*, 1952–85) and the *McGill Law Journal* (Montreal, 1952–). As new specialities developed, new journals were launched, often by the major law publishers. For example, Canada Law Book initiated *The Canadian Business Law Journal* (Agincourt, ON, 1975–), while Carswell established the *Canadian Journal of Family Law* (Agincourt, ON, 1978–).

Law reports, which continued to appear in series such as *Supreme Court Reports* (Ottawa, 1867–) and *Western Weekly Reports* (Calgary, 1911–), were supplemented by newer titles such as the *Canadian Sales Tax Reporter* (Toronto, 1968–89) and *Reports on Family Law* (Toronto, 1971–). Criminal cases were collected by Carswell in *Criminal Reports* (Toronto, 1946–), competing with Canada Law Book's long-established *Canadian Criminal Cases* (Toronto, 1898–). The volume of law reports, many of which covered both common and civil law, increased so dramatically between 1960 and 1980 that by the 1970s duplication of information had become a concern.[35]

Canadian legal periodicals and books have been selectively included in American indexes of legal publications since 1888.[36] Seminal Canadian resources include the *Canadian Abridgement*, which began in 1935, and the *Index to Canadian Legal Literature*, the first finding tool to provide access to Canadian legal periodical literature, in which coverage begins with 1956. The *Index to Canadian Legal Periodical Literature*, initiated in Montreal by the Canadian Association of Law Libraries, began in 1965, with indexing retroactive to 1961. The initial core of Canadian legal bibliography was provided by *A Legal Bibliography of the British Commonwealth*, volume 3 (1957), produced by Sweet & Maxwell, and Boult's newer *A Bibliography of Canadian Law* (1966; 2nd ed., 1977).

In the 1960s, Canadians anticipated the importance of computer technology in legal research. Hugh Lawford's QUIC/LAW project at Queen's University mounted a groundbreaking conference in 1968 on the possible uses of computers for accessing legal information. After losing federal government support, Lawford established QL Systems Limited in 1973 to continue creating searchable databases of statutes and reasons for judgment. Assistance later came from the Canadian Law Information Council, which initiated a scheme in 1979 to increase the number and use of databases.[37] With this establishment of a computerized legal information retrieval system, legal publishing in Canada was on its way to becoming extensively digitized in the final decades of the twentieth century.

Medical Publishing

JENNIFER J. CONNOR

Building on foundations established during the late nineteenth and early twentieth centuries,[38] Canadian medical periodicals progressively acquired substantial organizational support, reflecting a global trend toward journals as the primary means of disseminating biomedical research. Many scientific journals and medical advice booklets for general readers were published by government agencies and departments. While no Canadian publisher attempted to compete with long-established foreign publishers who specialized in medical textbooks, Canadian firms increasingly issued popular books about medicine for the general trade.

Excluding newsletters produced by institutions and professional or student societies, between 1918 and 1980 approximately fifty to sixty medical journals appeared, the majority in English.[39] Most lasted for only a few years. However, some specialty and general journals did endure, notably the *Canadian Medical Association Journal* (*CMAJ*) (Toronto, 1911–60; Ottawa, 1961–) and *Union médicale du Canada* (Montreal, 1872–1995). One trade publisher, Macmillan of Canada, tried to sustain a medical journal; its *Canadian Medical Quarterly* (Toronto, 1918–20), which briefly became the *Canadian Medical Monthly* (Toronto, 1920), lasted only two years. Medical societies, however, extended an earlier practice of physician-owned stock companies by sponsoring their own journals. The *CMAJ*, the *Canadian Hospital* (Toronto, 1924–73), the *Canadian Journal of Genetics and Cytology / Journal canadien de génétique et de cytologie*

(Ottawa, 1959–86), and the *Canadian Family Physician/Médecin de famille canadien* (Toronto, est. 1954, including its two previous titles before 1967) were all society journals. Other society journals emerged from individual provinces; the *Nova Scotia Medical Bulletin* (Halifax, 1922–87), the *Saskatchewan Medical Quarterly* (Saskatoon, 1931–75), and the *Manitoba Medical Association Bulletin* (Winnipeg, 1921–33) replaced two earlier journals published for the Maritimes and Western Canada. By contrast, some new French-language journals sought readers throughout North America; *L'Indépendance médicale* (Montreal, 1920–32), for example, billed itself as a 'journal panaméricain.'

Specialty journals proliferated in this period for emerging fields such as behavioural science, medical technology, and microbiology. After the Second World War, the National Research Council of Canada published an Ottawa-based journal that would change both its name and focus several times over fifty years: the *Canadian Journal of Medical Sciences* (est. 1951), which emerged from the *Canadian Journal of Research* (est. 1929), became the *Canadian Journal of Biochemistry and Physiology* (est. 1954). In 1964 it split into the *Canadian Journal of Physiology and Pharmacology / Journal canadien de physiologie et pharmacologie* and the *Canadian Journal of Biochemistry / Journal canadien de biochimie*, the latter retitled the *Canadian Journal of Biochemistry and Cell Biology / Revue canadienne de biochimie et biologie cellulaire* in 1983. Though they remained small in number, journals also appeared for students, such as the *Queen's Medical Review* (Kingston, ON, 1953–80) and the *Dalhousie Dental Journal* (Halifax, 1960–92), and for newly professionalized allied health sciences such as nursing and dentistry – the latter had about half a dozen journals in this period. Some also presented lighter reading on medical topics: the *Calgary Associate Clinic Historical Bulletin* (1936–58) was the first journal in Canada devoted to historical subjects in medicine and also contained items of literary interest.

Following the Second World War, the publication of medical journals underwent dramatic changes. By that time, most Canadian journals had adopted a magazine format. During the 1950s their frequency increased from monthly to bimonthly, and in the 1960s they became weeklies. The medical newspaper made a successful reappearance in 1965 in the Toronto-based *Medical Post*, a publication that survives to this day. Bilingualism became formalized in 1959 in the revised title of the *Canadian Medical Association Journal / Journal de l'Association médicale canadienne*, which was followed in 1964 by the *CMAJ*'s publication of article abstracts in the second language. Peer review became the norm by the mid-1960s and more rigorous – at least in the *CMAJ* – in the late 1970s. Especially important was a 1978 meeting in Vancouver that catapulted Canadian medical journalism onto the international stage. Editors of the *CMAJ* and other prestigious English-language general medical journals developed requirements for manuscripts, including formats for bibliographic reference, which became known as the 'Vancouver system.' From this informally constituted 'Vancouver group' grew the International Committee of Medical Journal Editors, which currently publishes guidelines for biomedical authors and for the citation style used by leading medical databases and several hundred journals.

Though not intended for a professional readership, pamphlets continued to be written by physicians between 1918 and 1980, and some grew into booklets of medical advice. Their most important sponsors were governments. The Department of Health for Ontario, for instance, produced the ninety-five-page *Health Almanac for 1930*, and from 1920 the federal Department of Health issued millions of medical advice booklets, especially through its series of Little Blue Books. Patent medicine manufacturers produced annual 'advice' pamphlets containing health and medical tips, such as *Helpful Hints for Housekeepers* (1919), distributed by the Dodds Medicine Company of Toronto. A serialized pamphlet, *Healthful Living Digest*, issued by the Health Supply Centre in Winnipeg from the late 1960s, included notes on medical conditions and the promotion of health.

Some bookseller-publishers, especially in Quebec, followed an earlier tradition of producing books for local medical schools. Thus Librairie Déom published *Cours d'hygiène professé à l'Université de Montréal*, by Joseph-Albert Baudouin (1931), and *L'obstétrique des gardes-malades*, by E.-A. René de Cotret (from the fourth edition in 1936). Renouf Publishing, also in Montreal, issued *Outlines of Pathology* (1927), by McGill University author Horst Oertel, presumably for a wider audience. However, renowned medical publishers in the United States, particularly in Philadelphia, continued to attract Canadian medical authors of important texts. While at the University of Manitoba, pathologist William Boyd published *Surgical Pathology* (1925) in Philadelphia through W.B. Saunders. Following the practice of other prominent authors, including expatriate Canadian William Osler, he then signed on with the venerable Lea & Febiger, also in Philadelphia, with whom he published three more books: *The Pathology of Internal Disease* (1931), *Textbook of Pathology* (1932), and *An Introduction to Medical Science* (1937). Attention to Canada, such as reference to epidemics in Winnipeg, appears in the *Textbook*. This work had an immediate impact in the United States, with a first edition of 20,000 copies and adoption at eighteen American medical schools.[40] So successful were Boyd's books that they helped keep Lea & Febiger viable during the Depression and went through several editions to the 1990s.[41]

From the mid-twentieth century, general trade publishers issued many Canadian-authored books about medicine, favouring accounts of discoveries and heroes that helped to promote Canadian identity. Ryerson Press produced two autobiographical books by the Toronto surgeon Gordon Murray: *Medicine in the Making* (1960) and *Quest in Medicine* (1963). The first, which appeared in a modified form in Britain under the title *Surgery in the Making* (Johnson, 1964), was thought to be of special interest to readers contemplating careers in medicine.[42] Successful in both official languages was the autobiography of Hans Selye, *Le stress de ma vie* (1976) / *The Stress of My Life* (1977). From the 1940s, popular writers and trade publishers vied to celebrate Frederick Banting, co-discoverer of insulin, and Norman Bethune, communist doctor in Spain and China. J.M. Dent and Sons, Macmillan, and Ryerson Press all published books about Banting in 1946, followed by Copp Clark in 1959. The smaller New Press and Talon Books produced books on Bethune in 1973 and 1975 respectively. Some titles appeared in series of inspirational booklets for schoolchildren, such as The Canadians, published by Fitzhenry & Whiteside. Banting, Bethune, Marion Hilliard (an obstetrician at Women's College Hospital in Toronto), and Emily Stowe (Canada's first woman doctor) were all medical subjects for these heroic biographies. Popular interest in medical biography and history also stimulated a new granting agency, the Hannah Institute for the History of Medicine (est. 1976), to publish seminal works such as Charles G. Roland and Paul Potter's *Annotated Bibliography of Canadian Medical Periodicals, 1826–1975* (1979) and Roland's *Canadian Medical Journals, 1826–1910: A Microfiche Edition* (1982). By the early 1980s, medical history was a growing field among academic scholars such as historian Michael Bliss, whose *The Discovery of Insulin* (1982) and *Banting: A Biography* (1984) were issued by McClelland and Stewart.

PART FIVE

PRODUCTION

chapter 13

PRINTING AND DESIGN

The Canadian Printing Industry

ÉRIC LEROUX

Between 1921 and 1961, the printing industry ranked tenth in manufacturing production in Canada (3.7 per cent of Canadian production in 1960) and eighth in job creation, placing it just behind food, wood, iron and steel, and transportation equipment.[1] After mid-century, technological innovations significantly affected the industry, transforming the printing process. Developments within a sister industry, paper manufacturing, also came to bear on the printing industry, influencing the production quality of materials that issued from the trade's presses.

Printing

In the early 1920s, for census purposes, the Canadian government divided the printing industry into different sectors. Most important were 'printer-publishers,' a category made up of newspaper and periodical publishers which had their own presses, and 'commercial printers,'[2] a sector that primarily undertook job printing. Large-circulation newspapers represented a substantial part of the printer-publishers sector. In 1940 one-third of all documents printed in Canada were daily newspapers. Although the number of newspapers produced in Canada decreased significantly through the first half of the century, huge increases in circulation among those that did survive made up for those losses. Moreover, after the Second

World War, newspapers grew larger in terms of pages, thus contributing to the volume of production. Books were typically produced by commercial printers in Canada; in Quebec, however, until the mid-1960s it was printer-publishers who benefited from the production of textbooks and school prize books, an extremely lucrative area of the province's book trade.

Canada's commercial printing sector, second in importance in terms of volume, represented about a third of the overall industry. Since the market for new books was too marginal to support commercial printers, they had to rely on job printing, reprints, and textbooks. In 1940 books made up only 5 per cent of Canadian print production, a figure which included blank books and catalogues.[3] Job printing, which engaged most of the sector's energies, encompassed such items as envelopes, letterhead, account books, and annual reports for businesses. Lithography and specialized fields such as platemaking, wood engraving, and photogravure were the third and fourth largest sectors of the printing industry, claiming only 10 per cent and 8 per cent of the market respectively in 1950.

In 1936 the printing industry comprised 2,205 firms employing 35,445 persons, with an average of 16 workers per firm; men made up 78.5 per cent of the workforce and women 21.5 per cent. The proportion of women increased to 30 per cent in 1946, a year when the effects of the war economy were still being felt, but stabilized at about 25 per cent in the following years. The heart of the printing industry was in Ontario, which accounted for more than half of the Canadian jobs and production in this sector. Quebec took second place, followed by the Western provinces and the Atlantic region. In 1936, 943 firms in Ontario accounted for 54.5 per cent of Canadian production, while Quebec accounted for 22.5 per cent, Manitoba 7.1 per cent, British Columbia 6.5 per cent, Alberta 3.3 per cent, Saskatchewan 2.4 per cent, and the Maritime provinces 3.7 per cent.[4] Twenty years later, in 1956, the situation was the same: Ontario and Quebec dominated in terms of the number of firms, the number of jobs, and production.[5]

The 1960s witnessed the rise of small specialized shops ('quick printers') that produced cheaply. In the 1970s several small printers created chains that became very successful. The Printing House in Toronto, which opened with only three employees in 1962, had 56 franchises thirty years later. In the 1960s and 1970s, the industry split into two categories: a large number of small shops accounted for a minor percentage of the total production, while a few big firms claimed the lion's share.[6] In Quebec the printing companies Quebecor, created by Pierre Péladeau in 1965, and the Transcontinental Group, founded in 1976 by Rémi Marcoux, exemplified small firms that grew into multinationals. In 1954 Péladeau had bought the

13.1 Lionel Bisaillon, Linotypist, in the office of *L'Abeille*, Laprairie, Quebec, 1943. Courtesy of the Frères de l'Instruction chrétienne and Groupe de recherche sur l'édition littéraire au Québec.

presses of the newspaper *Le Canada* from Fides and founded the printing firm Hebdo. By the end of the 1950s, Péladeau's publications enjoyed a total circulation of 500,000 copies per week. In 1971, through the purchase of rival printers, such as the Ontario firm Graphic Web, and the construction of the Montreal-Magog printing plant, Publications Quebecor became a major player in the national market.

Technological Innovations

After the major technological innovations of the late nineteenth century, of which mechanical typesetting on Linotype and Monotype machines were the prime examples, it was not until the 1950s that the Canadian printing industry underwent another substantial technological transformation. The seeds of some of those changes had been sown as early as the 1920s, but the Depression and then the Second World War, which monopolized industrial machinery for war production, had considerably slowed technological development in the printing sector (see illus. 13.1, above).

Offset printing was without doubt the most important technological innovation. This process increased productive capacity, lowered printing costs, and achieved better quality reproduction of illustrations.[7] In Toronto, Copp Clark began to use an offset lithographic press to print its books and for some job printing in 1945.[8] In the 1950s offset printing was widely adopted by commercial printers. *Le Journal de Montréal* in 1964 and the Toronto *Sun* in 1971 were the first newspapers to follow suit. Just three years later, seventy-four dailies were using the new technology.[9] While many innovations, such as rotary presses, rendered newspaper plants more productive, the most significant invention in this field was colour presses, such as the Goss Headliner and the Hoe Streamlined Color-Convertible, both of which appeared on the market in 1945.

Other technological innovations included the automation of binding, starting in the 1950s, which reduced book production costs. Photocomposition machines, introduced in 1948, reproduced lines of type on film and gradually replaced traditional lead type. The introduction in 1950 of rubber and plastic printing blocks, obtained by stereotyping, led to the invention of new, more efficient, sheet-fed or web-fed rotary presses. Finally, the gradual introduction of the Teletypesetter in the 1950s gave rise in the 1960s and 1970s to the use of computers. Light drove out lead, with improved photocomposition machines that could typeset a thousand letters per second, far beyond the capacity of an entire shop of Linotype machines.

At the daily newspaper *Le Soleil* in Quebec City, for example, the 130 compositors in the shop finally gave up lead type in 1973 in favour of photocomposition, which had already been used for a decade to create its advertising copy. During this decade, *Le Soleil* published four editions a day, with its presses operating day and night. While the vast majority of compositors were able to adapt to the new Linotron automatic Linotype machines, twenty years later computer graphics put an end to the trades of compositor and Linotype operator. At *Le Soleil*, the printing plant finally closed in 1994, forcing some forty production workers to retrain or retire.[10]

The Paper Industry

While the First World War was a period of prosperity for Canada's pulp and paper sector, particularly in relation to newsprint,[11] the recession of the early 1920s and, even more so, the onset of the Depression in 1929 caused a major slowdown in the industry. The decline continued until the mid-1930s, with the price of a ton of newsprint dropping from $114.70 in 1921 to $40.00 in 1934. Many mergers among paper companies resulted in new firms that were important on the world market, such as the Consolidated Paper Corporation in Quebec, which was created in 1931 and could produce two thousand tons of newsprint and five hundred tons of card-board and other papers a day.[12]

During the Depression, when American daily newspapers reduced their paper consumption, the Canadian paper mills that supplied them decreased their produc-tion of newsprint by more than 30 per cent. Mills making special papers, such as fine paper or wrapping paper, weathered the crisis more easily than plants producing newsprint.[13] However, newsprint remained the industry's main product.[14] Before the 1950s, very few Canadian paper companies produced paper for books: exceptions were the Provincial Paper Company in Georgetown, Ontario, and the Howard Smith Paper Company, which had plants in Cornwall, Ontario, and Beauharnois, Quebec. Although this area of production subsequently expanded, largely as a result of tech-nological innovations that permitted Canadian paper companies to be competitive, it still remained marginal in comparison to newsprint.[15]

The largest paper producer of the period was International Paper, which con-trolled 20 per cent of the American newsprint market. In the 1920s and 1930s, in addition to plants in the United States, this American company owned newsprint plants in Trois-Rivières and Gatineau, Quebec, and Dalhousie, New Brunswick, and bleached sulphite pulp mills in Kipawa, Quebec, and Hawkesbury, Ontario.[16] By the late 1930s, Canada was the world's biggest producer of newsprint, replacing the United States. In 1940, Canadian production was three times that of the United States, and in 1950 it was five times greater. By 1938, Canada was also the world's main exporter of newsprint, accounting for 63.7 per cent of exports from the eleven main producing countries. Twenty years later, in 1957, Canada accounted for 77.3 per cent of total exports, substantially ahead of other major producing countries such as Finland (7.9 per cent), Sweden (3.7 per cent), and Norway (2.1 per cent).[17] The world paper shortage caused by the Second World War undoubtedly made it possible for Canadian paper companies to increase substantially their production and their exports. A major player internationally, the Canadian newsprint industry provided 87 per cent of the world market in 1965, and 72 per cent in 1970.[18]

Within Canada, Quebec represented the largest provincial producer of news-print from 1955 to 1976, and was home to a number of large paper companies: Rolland Paper Company, Howard Smith Paper Mills Limited, E.B. Eddy, and Kruger Pulp and Paper Limited.[19] However, the industry as a whole was spread across the country, with significant concentration in Ontario, British Columbia, and New-foundland.[20] By 1972 the pulp and paper industry was the largest of Canada's manu-facturing industries, with the newsprint sector ranking fourth in the country's exports.[21] At the end of the 1970s, Canada had 127 paper mills: 59 in Quebec, 37 in

Ontario, 11 in British Columbia, and 20 in the other provinces. Although the United States had developed this industry since the 1960s, and had 820 paper mills,[22] it remained the main export market for Canadian newsprint. Like the printing industry, paper manufacturers produced largely for the newspaper and periodical press, and the production of books represented only a very modest proportion of their market.

CASE STUDY ──────────────────────
Thérien Frères
– Éric Leroux

Thérien Frères, one of Quebec's most important book-printing firms in the mid-twentieth century, was founded on 10 May 1927 when brothers J.-Alexandre and Ernest Thérien acquired the printing firm Le Commerce ltée. Located in the Saint-Henri district of Montreal, Thérien Frères focused initially on job printing for the city, and also producing school books for religious communities and advertising materials for Dr Fernando Boisvert, owner of the well-known Lambert cough syrup. In the 1920s the firm also did printing for publisher Louis Carrier, the owner of Les Éditions du Mercure.[23]

Located on Notre-Dame Street East from 1932, the shop employed forty-five people in 1938. Its operations included a printing section with Linotype and Monotype machines, as well as an array of cylinder, platen, and offset presses, installed in 1932, which could reproduce printed matter without typesetting. In addition, the firm had a binding shop, and a lithography and photolithography department. As Rosario Bélisle, a teacher at the École technique de Montréal, explained in 1938, 'Its modern and varied equipment allows it to compete with the best firms in the field.'[24] Several of the compositors at Thérien Frères were multilingual, making it possible for the printer to produce work in many languages, including, according to Bélisle, one book in Greek; this capacity was a decided advantage in multicultural Montreal. During the Depression of the 1930s, which created hardship for all printers, Thérien Frères also had to contend with many Catholic institutions that, with the advantage of cheap labour, proved stiff competition for secular printers.

In January 1938, Thérien Frères experienced significant losses in a fire but quickly recovered. Despite the departure of one of its founders, Ernest

Thérien, in 1941, the firm benefited considerably from the publishing boom in Quebec during the Second World War and experienced its greatest prosperity in the 1940s and 1950s. The company's specialization in book printing began in the early 1940s. In 1945, J.-A. Thérien acquired Éditions Lumen (renamed Les Éditions Chantecler in 1948), which subsequently distinguished itself by publishing the scholarly Collection Humanitas from Université de Montréal's Faculté des lettres.[25]

In 1948 the company, which by then had eighty employees, moved to new premises on St Lawrence Boulevard (at the corner of Jarry Street), a location it occupied until 1979. The two-storey building, with thirty thousand square feet of space, was equipped with a modern ventilation system. In 1960 the administrative structure of the firm was broadened, and three of J.-A. Thérien's sons were appointed to the board of directors.[26] After J.-A. Thérien's death in 1977, the firm continued to advance technologically and was the first Canadian printer to acquire a two-colour offset press, which reduced printing costs and made the work of press operators easier, allowing them to do double-sided printing, perforation, and numbering of more than eight thousand copies an hour. Two years later, the firm added an Olivetti modular mini-computer and a Linoterm cathode-ray–display photocomposition machine.

Before it was sold in 1983, the company began to produce art books, printing the Collection Signatures published by former bookseller Marcel Broquet and edited by André Fortier. The first two books were devoted to the painter Jean-Paul Ladouceur and the sculptor Jean-Marc Blier. As Fortier explained, Thérien's goal was to meet 'the pressing need for high-quality books that are printed not in other countries, but right here in Quebec.'[27]

CASE STUDY ───────────────────────────────────────
From Humble Beginnings: Friesens Corporation
– Linda Bedwell

Friesens Corporation, one of Canada's most successful printing companies, has its roots in a small confectionary shop, post office, and telephone exchange purchased in 1907 by David W. Friesen in the Mennonite community of Altona, Manitoba. Operations began modestly in 1933 when the founder's son, David K. Friesen, acquired a small, hand-fed Gordon press, installed it in the shop basement, and began paying a friend $3 per week to do job printing.[28] Two years later, he purchased a second press and moved production into a new building. During these early years, printing was pains-taking: type was set by hand, and in the winter months early morning fires were needed to soften the ink so that the presses could be rolling by noon. By 1937, with funds borrowed from a retired farmer, the younger Friesen had purchased the other local printing company, enlarged the building, and acquired a Linotype.[29] In subsequent years, similar loans from the Menno-nite community aided the company's growth. Friesen responded to such local support by serving as printer for the German-language Mennonite paper, *Das Bergthaler Gemeindeblatt* (1936–72; see illus. 13.2, p. 357), beginning in 1939, and establishing a local weekly, the Altona *Echo*, in 1941. By the time David K. Friesen and his brothers, Ted and Raymond, bought out their father's share of the company and incorporated as D.W. Friesen & Sons in 1951, the business focused entirely on printing and allied activities, including publishing, binding, lithography, engraving, electrotyping, stereotyping, and the manufacture and sale of stationery supplies.[30]

Following incorporation, the Friesen brothers sought areas in which to specialize. In addition to the *Echo*, which would change hands in the mid-1990s, they issued the *Canadian Mennonite* (1953–70), which they published from 1953 to 1962 and continued to print until 1970.[31] After limited success with the production of postcards and magazines, they found their niche with school yearbooks, becoming the third largest yearbook producer in Canada by 1976.[32] Opening a new plant in 1959, they acquired offset presses and created a lithography department which enabled colour printing. Fur-ther investments in colour print technology in the 1970s paid off as sales increased from $3.4 million in 1972 to $17.7 million in 1980.[33] In tune with the commemorative impulse of small communities, accounts of local his-tory offered an additional line of specialization: Friesens attracted printing contracts by providing free 'history book workshops' – offering the services of history book representatives who not only assisted local committees with production but also helped gather material. From 1974 the firm also pre-pared their own guide, *Make History with Friesen Printers*. While most of the resulting histories were published in English, a few appeared in French and German.[34]

In the years since 1980, Friesens, now an employee-owned company, continued to expand, opening a Toronto office in 1981 followed by

Das Bergthaler Gemeindeblatt

1936

Ueber alles aber ziehet an die Liebe, die da ist das Band der Vollkommenheit. (Kol. 3, 14)

| 1. Jahrgang. | Winkler, Man., Januar 1936. | Nummer 1. |

Ein schwankend Rohr, das leicht der Sturm zerbricht.
An die Gemeinde Gottes schließ dich an,
Die halte fest mit deinem ganzen Herzen!
Denn nur auf dich gestellt, stehst du allein,

Geleitwort.

Teure Geschwister im Herrn! Gott zum Gruß!

Auf Anregung und Beschluß der allgemeinen Bruderschaft, welche im Juni 1935 tagte, tritt dieses Blättchen seine erste Reise an. Nicht ohne Absicht und Wunsch wagt es seinen Besuch und möchte jeden zweiten Monat einen freundlichen Gruß an jedes Glied der Gemeinde ausrichten. Es ist unser Gemeindeblatt und hat die Aufgabe, die Glieder der Gemeinde mehr zu verbinden und sie für den Bau des Reiches Gottes zu beleben. Sicher liegt uns das allgemeine Wohl der Menschheit und Christenheit am Herzen, aber um diesem gerecht zu werden, müssen wir daheim anfangen. Mit dem Blättchen geht mein inniger Wunsch, daß es bei jedem Gliede eine freundliche Aufnahme und ein offenes Herz finde.

Wir haben seit vielen Jahren als Gemeinde versucht, einander zu dienen. In den sonntäglichen Versammlungen haben wir viel Gemeinschaft miteinander, und sie sind ein Segen für groß und klein. Auch bei anderen Gelegenheiten, wie Hochzeiten, Begräbnisse usw. haben wir uns die Hand gereicht. Doch durch den Zuwachs an Gliedern in der Gemeinde und durch die große Zerstreuung derselben wurde das Gemeinschaftsleben sehr erschwert. Oft haben wir vor der Frage gestanden: „Wie können wir unsere Glieder mehr zusammenhalten und mehr interessieren für die Arbeit des Herrn?" Wir suchten die Lösung die er Frage, indem während den Wintermonaten auf den verschiedenen Andachtsplätzen und in Schulen verlängerte Versammlungen abgehalten wurden. In Verbindung mit diesen Versammlungen wurden auch Hausbesuche gemacht, um mehr mit den Gliedern in Fühlung zu bleiben. Diese Bestrebung kostet große Opfer, hat aber auch viel Segen gestiftet und soll, so Gott will, auch fortbestehen. Doch es bleibt noch viel zu tun übrig. Es ist noch lange nicht alles erreicht, was erreicht werden soll und kann.

Die erste Aufgabe dieses Blattes soll sein, die Glieder der Gemeinde mit den Fragen und Bestrebungen der Gemeinde auf dem Laufenden zu halten. Aus dem Grunde sollte es ein wirklicher Schatz sein, für einen jeden, der sich für den Gemeindebau im Namen Jesu interessiert.

Es ist auch sehr notwendig, daß wir uns als Gemeinde besser kennen lernen, um mehr eines Sinnes zu werden, in der Behandlung verschiedener Fragen. Auch das gegenseitige Tragen und Mithelfen, so auch die Fürbitte soll dadurch gefördert werden. Z. B.: In dieser Nummer erscheint das Programm für die Abendversammlungen. Ihr könnt dort sehen, wo eure Prediger und Arbeiter stehen, und es soll euch anspornen, für Arbeit und Arbeiter zu beten. Ihr werdet auch sehen, wann in eurer Kirche die verlängerten Versammlungen stattfinden, und könnt dann schon die nötigen Vorkehrungen treffen. Es wird noch manches andere erscheinen, daß für jedes Glied von Bedeutung ist.

13.2 *Das Bergthaler Gemeindeblatt* (Winkler, Manitoba: Rundschau Publishing House), volume 1, no. 1, January 1936, page 1. Courtesy of the Mennonite Heritage Centre, Winnipeg.

additional offices in Canada and the United States. A family business that built itself around community principles, specialization, and technological innovation has become a North American success.

Working in the Printing Trades

CHRISTINA BURR AND ÉRIC LEROUX

During the nineteenth century, workers in the Canadian printing industry were exemplars of trade union practices. As literate and articulate members of the working class, they provided leadership for the emergent labour movement. Indeed, printers were the first to organize in the early 1800s. A century later, nearly all groups associated with the printing trades (typographers, binders, pressmen, etc.) had formed unions, the majority of which were locals of 'international' organizations – American-based collectives whose centres of power were in U.S. cities, and which in turn were affiliated with an umbrella organization, the American Federation of Labor. In the twentieth century, as Canadian print workers coped with unprecedented advances in the technology that shaped their livelihoods, they witnessed tension between the local leaders and executives of their unions over policy, and jurisdictional disputes between their unions and employers over technological innovations. As well, they confronted changes in the length of their workdays, the structure of their jobs, and the gender division of labour in their industry.

The Forty-four-Hour Strike and Printing Trade Unions in Canada

In the early 1870s, workers in the print trades in Hamilton and Toronto spearheaded the struggle for the nine-hour workday. After the First World War, another drive for shorter hours, this time aimed at the establishment of the forty-four-hour week for book and job printers, occurred throughout North America. In 1919 the International Joint Conference Council of Commercial and Periodical Branches of the Printing Industry (IJCC) resolved that on 1 May 1921 the forty-four-hour week would become universal in the printing trades without any reduction in pay. This council was made up of three employers' organizations and four international labour unions: in the first group were the Printers' League of America, the closed shop branch of the United Typothetae of America (UTA), and the International Association of Employing Electrotypers and Stereotypers; in the second, the International Typographical Union (ITU), the International Brotherhood of Bookbinders, the International Printing Pressmen and Assistants' Union, and the International Stereotypers and Electrotypers' Union.

As the date for implementation of the forty-four-hour week approached, however, employers refused to recognize their commitment: Canadian members of the UTA argued that given the stagnant post-war economy, it would be 'suicidal' to accept any reduction in working hours. Underlying the UTA's concerns about wages was a desire for an open, or non-union, shop aimed at combatting what some employers called 'union tyranny.'[35] In effect, the open shop would deny workers any gains they had made with respect to the right to organize and bargain collectively. Even had Canadian locals of the ITU wished to retreat from their position, they were constrained from doing so by their union's 'overall policy for shorter hours,' and were left with 'little alternative to a strike.'[36]

The strike in Canada, which began 1 June 1921, was particularly difficult and lengthy, and concentrated in the cities of Toronto, Hamilton, Ottawa, and Montreal. At the end of December 1922, the *Typographical Journal* reported that 913 members were on strike in Ontario and 568 in Quebec.[37] After two reductions in the strike assessments levied against its membership, the ITU closed its strike rolls on 5 July 1924, thereby ending the strike.[38] The forty-four-hour week was conceded in several small Canadian book-and-job shops, but by and large the three-year battle had a devastating effect on the printing trades. It proved costly in terms of expenses for benefits, loss of union membership, and disruption in the printing business. During the strike, numerous businesses in Toronto sent work out to shops in smaller centres like Oshawa and Oakville; some continued to do so after the conflict was over. In Winnipeg the strike ended with the pressmen returning to work without a contract, and the destruction of the local bookbinders' union; Toronto ITU Local 191 was almost wiped out.[39] The ITU's failure to provide financial support to the other printing trades workers who 'downed tools' in support of the forty-four-hour movement provided ammunition for secessionists who opposed international unions.[40] The outcome of the three-year battle was the end of effective collective bargaining in most of Canada's printing trades.

Tensions between the ITU executive and Canadian locals would reignite in 1932 when a referendum calling for a five-day workweek in the newspaper sector passed and was made general policy by American union leaders without consideration of

Canadian economic conditions. The membership in Toronto split over the issue, while the locals in Winnipeg and Calgary temporarily seceded, in the interim forming the Canadian Newspapers Employees' Association (1937–44). The forty-hour workweek was eventually conceded by Canadian newspaper employers in 1937, but with an accompanying reduction in wages. In the book and job sector, the forty-four-hour week remained the norm until the mid-1940s.[41] Subsequent union action would largely focus on jurisdictional disputes raised by new technology.

The Development of Catholic Unions in Quebec's Printing Industry

In Quebec the conflict over the forty-four-hour workweek during the 1920s provided Catholic unions, which had been a part of Quebec's labour landscape since the First World War, with the opportunity to break into the printing sector.[42] In Montreal printers were divided between two ITU affiliates, the francophone Union typographique Jacques-Cartier and the anglophone Montreal Typographical Union. The strike of 1921–4 paralyzed the work of the Legislative Assembly and gave rise to virulent criticism from Alexandre Taschereau's Liberal government. In 1925 three Montreal unions, one of compositors and two of press operators, and the printers' and binders' union in Hull, joined together to form the Fédération catholique des métiers de l'imprimerie, affiliated with the Confédération des travailleurs catholiques du Canada (CTCC), which in the early 1960s became the Confédération des syndicats nationaux (CSN).[43] The following year, the Fédération began publishing a newspaper, *Le Bulletin de l'imprimerie*, to inform its members of new technology and to increase co-operation among the various unions by providing information on developments in each union.

Only Catholics were admitted to these unions, and the organization of workers on the basis of religion was a phenomenon exclusive to Quebec. The Catholic unions were created to counter the hegemony of the international unions, which they accused of subjugating Canadian workers to foreign leadership and enriching the powerful American unions with the dues of Canadian workers. They also considered social issues to be essentially questions of morality and religion, and thus under the purview of the church. In order to ensure the docility of the union membership, the church supervised the unions closely, assigning chaplains to them to monitor their activities. Catholic leaders criticized the international unions for striking too frequently and for their materialistic approach to union activity. The international unions, by contrast, favoured religious neutrality and the separation of social and religious questions.[44]

In their early years, the Catholic unions were not able to recruit many print trade workers, mainly because of their lack of zeal in defending their members' material interests. Historian Luc Desrochers estimates that the membership of the Catholic unions in this sector in the 1920s was less than 15 per cent of that of the international unions, which by 1929 claimed 1,624 workers through ten locals located in Montreal and Quebec City.[45] Between 1926 and 1934, five Catholic unions were founded in the printing sector; those in Sherbrooke and Joliette lasted only a year. In the 1930s two-thirds of Quebec unions remained affiliated with the international unions, a figure that dropped to just over 40 per cent by the 1940s and 1950s, decades during which Catholic unions represented between one-quarter and one-third of unionized Quebec print workers.[46]

Closely aligned to the clergy and the employers, Catholic unions typically preferred conciliation to confrontation, a situation that began to change during the 1950s. After Gérard Picard and Jean Marchand became its leaders in 1946 and 1947, the CTCC became more radical. For instance, when Gérard Filion, the editor of *Le Devoir*, locked out his workers on 20 April 1955 and replaced them with strikebreakers for the express purpose of saving money, Picard did not hesitate to resign from the board of directors of the newspaper and recommend that the journalists, who were members of a Catholic union, refuse to cross the picket lines even though the workers were members of international unions.[47]

The employers' counterpart to the Catholic unions was the Association des maîtres imprimeurs (AMI) of Montreal. Founded on 24 February 1934 with a membership of thirty-four master printers, the AMI's goals were to 'promote and protect the interests of the printing industry,' to improve the productivity of the Quebec industry, and to 'co-operate with the members in order to maintain selling prices that ensure legitimate profits.'[48] The AMI had only francophone members; anglophone employers in the Montreal region belonged to the Employing Printers' Association. In 1937, to defend its interests, the AMI started *Le Maître imprimeur*. Charlie Holmes was the newspaper's editor-in-chief until he left the AMI in 1946.[49] The publication is now the official organ of the Association des arts graphiques du Québec.

In 1937 seven printers in Quebec City founded their own employers' association; it quickly disappeared, to be reborn in 1938 under the name Syndicat patronal de l'imprimerie de Québec, with some thirty Quebec City printers as members.[50] More associations were created in the 1930s and 1940s, including one in the Saint-Maurice Valley in April 1938, one in Chicoutimi–Lac-Saint-Jean in 1941, and one in Ottawa-Hull, also in 1941. In 1939 the AMI and the other employers' associations in Quebec founded the Association provinciale des maîtres imprimeurs, whose purpose was to defend the interests of printers provincially. This association became dormant in the early 1950s, and the AMI joined the Conseil du patronat in 1964. Finally, on 13 November 1977, the Association des arts graphiques du Québec became the new organization representing Quebec printers.

Technology and the Gender Division of Labour

During the nineteenth century, a gender division of labour had been established in the printing and bookbinding trades with women occupying those positions defined as 'unskilled,' specifically, press feeding, and folding, collating, and stitching in the binderies. Meanwhile male workers retained higher-paying, 'skilled' jobs as compositors, pressmen, bookbinders, and lithographers. Workplace struggles over skill, technology, and trade unionism were part of the process by which men and women defined their gender identities as workers. The appropriation of technology for masculinity has been part of the process by which patriarchy is perpetuated under industrial capitalism.

After the First World War, printing trades unions were remarkably successful in their struggles with employers over mechanization and the implementation of new technologies, while protecting their masculine craft prerogatives against the onslaught of industrial capitalism. Technological advances in printing and binding raised critical issues in collective bargaining between employers and the unions, including disputes over union jurisdiction, job training, apprenticeship, job restructuring, and gender relations.

In 1944 a male worker in the printing industry earned an average of $36 a week for forty-four hours of work, while a male worker in the manufacturing sector earned $33.50 for a forty-eight-hour week. However, the average weekly wage for women in the printing industry was $15.23.[51] The analysis of leading book manufacturing centres in Canada between 1921 and 1961, presented in table 13.1, reveals that by far the largest number of women production workers in printing and publishing were found in the binderies. Consistent with the nineteenth-century gender division of labour in bookbinding, women carried out the 'forwarding' tasks in the production process: folding printed sheets, collating, and sewing collated sections onto strings or bands or stitching with wire. These specific activities required extreme dexterity, accuracy, and patience, which continued to be defined as feminine attributes by employers and male journeymen bookbinders.[52] Except for the laying of gold leaf on book covers, the ornamentation of covers or the 'finishing' component in the labour process was carried out by men. Finishing required the skills of the journeyman, who combined his facility in the craft with the 'art' of bookbinding.

In collective bargaining during the twentieth century, bindery women were classified in a separate 'female' category. In the spring of 1952, after a strike of nearly six weeks over wage rates, Toronto Local 28 of the International Brotherhood of Bookbinders and Bindery Women ratified a new collective agreement that defined four broad classifications of workers, with job descriptions and wage differentials that reinforced male gender privilege. The minimum wage rates and job classifications were as follows: journeyman bookbinder, $1.93; male bookbinder utility operator, $1.75; journeywoman bookbinder, $1.04; and female bookbinder utility operator, $0.95. Under the terms of the collective agreement, a journeyman bookbinder was a skilled artisan who had completed a four-year apprenticeship; the category included case-maker operators, paper-cutter machine operators, auto-spacer paper-cutter operators, three-knife trimmer operators, casing-in machine operators, lining and head-banding machine operators, folding machine operators, and gathering machine operators. Male bookbinder utility operators were those who had completed at least four years of apprenticeship and could perform in a 'proficient manner' the following operations: hand-indexing, edging, marbling, embossing, rounding, cornering, siding, gluing-up, lining-up, and leather-paring. Journeywomen bookbinders were those who had completed two years of apprenticeship and performed in a 'skilled manner' any of the following operations: machine indexing, page numbering, perforating, machine sewing, hand sewing, cheque binding, hand collating, wire stitching, counting, tipping, small folding machine operation, stiffening machine operation, hand folding, gang stitching, gathering-collating machine operation, and hand covering. The final category of 'female bookbinder utility operator' was a broad category intended to encompass all women bindery workers who did not fit under the category 'journeywoman bookbinder.'[53]

In the latter part of the nineteenth century, publishers and printing employers began to complain about high labour costs in the composing room. The widespread implementation of machine typesetting after Ottmar Mergenthaler patented the Linotype in 1885 resulted in a redefinition of skill, and a reassertion of masculinity among male compositors. Publishers viewed machine typesetting as analogous to the work of women typists in the clerical sector and attempted to redefine the work of composition as women's work, thereby reducing labour costs. The ITU curbed the potential threat to their domination of the craft by securing control over the operation of the machines for its mostly male membership. In doing so, the ITU

Table 13.1

Labour in the book trades: Divisions by sector, occupation, and gender in the printing trades in selected Canadian cities, 1921–1961

		Toronto					Hamilton					Vancouver					Montreal					Winnipeg				
			Male		Female			Male		Female			Male		Female			Male		Female			Male		Female	
Year	Occupation	Total	n	%	n	%	Total	n	%	n	%	Total	n	%	n	%	Total	n	%	n	%	Total	n	%	n	%
1921	Bookbinders	748	322	43	426	57	48	17	35.4	31	64.6	48	20	41.7	28	58.3	347	183	52.7	164	47.3	140	45	32.1	95	67.9
	Electrotypers & stereotypers	46	46	100	0	0	4	4	100	0	0	6	6	100	0	0	16	16	100	0	0	14	14	100	0	0
	Engravers	134	134	100	0	0	9	9	100	0	0	9	9	100	0	0	59	58	98.3	1	1.7	28	28	100	0	0
	Lithographers	252	240	95.2	12	4.8	62	58	93.5	4	6.5	16	16	100	0	0	124	124	100	0	0	22	22	100	0	0
	Pressmen & plate printers	450	411	91.3	39	8.7	73	65	89	8	11	39	31	79.5	8	20.5	298	281	94.3	17	5.7	125	115	92	10	8
	Printers, compositors & linotypers	2051	1963	95.7	88	4.3	240	234	97.5	6	2.5	253	248	98	5	2	1173	1092	93.1	81	6.9	571	546	95.6	25	4.4
	Printers & bookbinders' apprentices	548	365	66.6	183	33.4	64	53	82.8	11	17.2	33	30	90.9	3	9.1	350	291	83.1	59	16.9	192	143	74.5	49	25.5
	Printing & publishing establishment employees	146	105	71.9	41	28.1	13	8	61.5	5	38.5	9	8	88.9	1	11.1	308	137	44.5	171	55.5	42	29	69	13	31
	Owners, managers & superintendents	573	557	97.2	16	2.8	71	68	95.8	3	4.2	87	87	100	0	0	286	275	96.2	11	3.8	144	144	100	0	0
	Foremen & forewomen	41	29	70.7	12	29.3	12	11	91.6	1	8.4	4	4	100	0	0	47	39	83	8	17	12	10	83.3	2	16.7
	Agents, canvassers & collectors	210	202	96.2	8	3.8	28	28	100	0	0	29	28	96.6	1	3.4	124	124	100	0	0	47	47	100	0	0
	Office employees	1009	432	42.8	577	57.2	62	25	40.3	37	59.7	87	42	48.3	45	51.7	432	213	49.3	219	50.7	294	100	34	194	66
	Messengers & office boys	53	50	94.3	3	5.7	7	7	100	0	0	9	9	100	0	0	70	65	92.9	5	7.1	31	30	96.8	1	3.2
	Labourers	112	112	100	0	0	29	29	100	0	0	8	8	100	0	0	91	91	100	0	0	32	32	100	0	0
	TOTAL	6373	4968	77.9	1405	22.1	722	616	85.3	106	14.7	637	546	85.7	91	14.3	3725	2989	80.2	736	19.8	1694	1305	77	389	23
1931	Owners & managers	555	533	96	22	4.0	52	51	98.1	1	1.9	123	122	99.2	1	0.8	288	273	94.8	15	5.2	128	126	98.4	2	1.6
	Foremen & overseers	84	57	67.9	27	32.1	13	11	84.6	2	15.4	11	7	63.6	4	36.4	80	59	73.8	21	26.2	24	13	54.1	11	45.9
	Bookbinders	543	222	40.9	321	59.1	37	11	29.7	26	70.3	72	26	36.1	46	63.9	368	159	43.2	209	56.8	114	38	33.3	76	66.7
	Compositors & printers	2008	1982	98.7	26	1.3	264	263	99.6	1	0.4	474	471	99.4	3	0.6	1547	1467	94.9	80	5.1	658	655	99.5	3	0.5
	Electrotypers & stereotypers	108	108	100	0	0	15	15	100	0	0	19	19	100	0	0	42	42	100	0	0	25	25	100	0	0
	Lithographers	229	228	99.6	1	0.4	67	67	100	0	0	28	28	100	0	0	120	120	100	0	0	45	45	100	0	0
	Machine tenders	536	377	70.3	159	29.7	43	32	74.4	11	25.6	46	35	76.1	11	23.9	372	279	75	93	25	62	28	45.2	34	54.8
	Pressmen & plate printers	330	330	100	0	0	57	57	100	0	0	62	62	100	0	0	254	254	100	0	0	114	114	100	0	0
	Printers & bookbinders' apprentices	710	666	93.8	44	6.2	63	61	96.8	2	3.2	148	143	96.6	5	3.4	551	528	95.8	23	4.2	145	137	94.5	8	5.5
	Process engravers	314	314	100	0	0	34	33	97.1	1	2.8	40	40	100	0	0	174	174	100	0	0	49	49	100	0	0
	Proof readers	115	64	55.7	51	44.3	6	5	83.3	1	16.7	8	6	75	2	25	33	21	63.6	12	36.4	12	4	33.3	8	66.7
	TOTAL	5532	4881	88.2	651	11.8	651	606	93.1	45	6.9	1031	959	93	72	7	3829	3376	88.2	453	11.8	1376	1234	89.7	142	10.3

Table 13.1 (Concluded)

Year	Occupation	Toronto Total	Toronto Male n	Toronto Male %	Toronto Female n	Toronto Female %	Hamilton Total	Hamilton Male n	Hamilton Male %	Hamilton Female n	Hamilton Female %	Vancouver Total	Vancouver Male n	Vancouver Male %	Vancouver Female n	Vancouver Female %	Montreal Male n	Montreal Male %	Montreal Female n	Montreal Female %	Montreal Total	Winnipeg Male n	Winnipeg Male %	Winnipeg Female n	Winnipeg Female %	Winnipeg Total
1941	Bookbinders	615	211	34.3	404	65.7	21	5	23.8	16	76.2	86	32	37.2	54	62.8	149	36.3	261	63.7	410	29	30.5	66	69.5	95
	Engravers & lithographers	540	511	94.6	29	5.4	89	83	93.3	6	6.7	89	86	96.6	3	3.4	322	100	0	0	322	70	97.2	2	2.8	72
	Printers	3050	2932	96.1	118	3.9	332	326	98.2	6	1.8	667	654	98.1	13	1.9	2273	94.6	130	5.4	2403	711	97.4	19	2.6	730
	Printing & photography	356	185	51.9	171	48.1	43	28	65.1	15	34.9	56	29	51.8	27	48.2	118	49.6	120	50.7	238	42	28.9	103	71.1	145
	TOTAL	4561	3839	84.2	722	15.8	485	442	91.1	43	8.9	898	801	89.2	97	10.8	2862	84.9	511	15.1	3373	852	81.8	190	18.2	1042
1951	Bookbinders	671	243	36.2	423	63.8	36	6	16.7	30	83.3	103	27	26.2	76	73.8	173	29.8	408	70.2	581	22	22	78	78	100
	Compositors & typesetters	2086	2017	96.7	69	3.3	297	285	96	12	4	570	556	97.5	14	2.5	2045	96.2	80	3.8	2125	486	94.4	29	5.6	515
	Photoengravers & lithographers	586	569	97.1	17	2.9	84	81	96.4	3	3.6	133	122	91.7	11	8.3	381	97.7	9	2.3	390	58	100	0	0	58
	Pressmen & plate printers	1043	932	89.3	111	10.7	123	117	95.1	6	4.9	212	201	94.8	11	5.2	818	95.6	38	4.4	856	196	91.2	19	8.8	215
	Other bookbinding occupations	320	65	20.3	255	79.7	23	5	21.7	18	78.3	58	9	15.5	49	84.5	103	52.3	94	47.7	197	18	12.9	121	87.1	139
	Other printing & publishing occupations	442	348	78.7	94	21.3	34	29	85.3	5	14.7	55	51	92.7	4	7.3	229	72.9	85	27.1	314	65	87.8	9	12.2	74
	TOTAL	5148	4174	81.1	974	18.9	597	523	87.6	74	12.4	1131	966	85.4	165	14.6	3749	84	714	16	4463	845	76.7	256	23.3	1101
1961	Compositors & typesetters	1271	1212	95.4	59	4.6	256	238	93	18	7	463	432	93.3	31	6.7	1640	92.8	127	7.2	1767	393	92.7	31	7.3	424
	Pressmen	738	693	93.8	45	6.2	166	156	93	10	7	198	185	93.4	13	6.6	1194	90.1	131	9.9	1325	212	95.1	11	4.9	223
	Lithographic & offset occupations	287	276	96.2	11	3.8	99	93	93.9	6	6.1	113	105	92.9	8	7.1	385	96.3	15	3.7	400	36	83.7	7	16.3	43
	Photoengravers	139	136	97.8	3	2.2	29	27	93.1	2	6.9	16	16	100	0	0	145	99.3	1	0.7	146	14	87.5	2	12.5	16
	Bookbinders	439	148	33.7	291	66.3	34	9	26.5	25	73.5	109	38	34.9	71	65.1	193	30.6	438	69.4	631	22	24.4	68	75.6	90
	Other bookbinding occupations	269	69	25.7	200	74.3	26	4	15.4	22	84.6	59	9	15.3	50	84.7	78	59.1	54	40.9	103	13	12.6	90	87.4	103
	Printing workers	374	239	63.9	135	36.1	65	45	69.2	20	30.8	55	51	92.7	4	7.3	264	70.2	112	29.8	376	38	74.5	13	25.5	51
	TOTAL	3517	2773	78.8	744	21.2	675	572	84.7	103	15.3	1013	836	82.5	177	17.5	3899	81.6	878	18.4	4777	728	76.6	222	23.4	950

Sources: Census of Canada 1921, vol. 4, table 5; Census of Canada 1931, vol. 7, table 41; Census of Canada 1941, vol. 7, table 6; Census of Canada 1951, vol. 4, table 7; Census of Canada 1961, vol. 3, part 1, table 7. Table compiled by Christina Burr.

13.3. Albert Bisaillon, compositor, in the composing room of *L'Abeille*, Laprairie, Quebec, 1943. Courtesy of the Frères de l'Instruction chrétienne and Groupe de recherche sur l'édition littéraire au Québec.

defined the work of the machine operator as masculine by emphasizing the physical exertion required to operate the Linotype. Women compositors were unable to comply with the terms set down by the union, namely, completion of a five-year apprenticeship and employment in a union shop at wages equal to those of male compositors. Rather than join with women machine operators in the struggle with employers over composition, male unionists protected their own craft interests. By 1944 an apprenticeship in this field in Quebec usually lasted six years, with the apprentice earning half the wage of a journeyman and unable to work on a typesetting machine before having done 9,900 hours of manual typesetting.[54] He became a journeyman after 12,000 hours of apprenticeship.[55]

With the onset of the Depression of the 1930s, Canadian publishers began to investigate new technologies, particularly those that had the potential to bypass the composing room altogether. The *Canadian Printer and Publisher*, a trade journal for employers, expounded the possibilities of the Teletypesetter for reducing production costs and declared that 'the type-setting machine operator is threatened by the invention of the Teletypesetter'[56] since it was a technology that separated keyboarding from the actual casting of type. Several years earlier, the *Canadian Printer and Publisher* had also speculated that photocomposition offered 'a threat' to the Linotype

operator.[57] Previously, men who apprenticed in the compositor's craft had specialized to some extent as either Linotype operators who set type, as stone hands who
organized the type into page form (see illus. 13.3, p. 366), or as proofreaders who
checked the pages for accuracy. Once retrained in the technology of photocomposition, some of the men became keyboard operators, some paste-up hands, and some
photosetter operators. The photosetter resembled the standard Linotype machine,
except that the metal pot was replaced with camera equipment. The compositor's
skill in arranging type on the page and the artwork of layout was just as essential as
before, but hand compositors had to learn how to work with film instead of metal.
Publishers' interest in introducing phototypesetting into the production process
was stimulated by the rapid growth of offset printing.[58]

　　There was always a possibility that the ITU's jurisdiction over composition
might be challenged by the Amalgamated Lithographers or the International
Photo-Engravers' Union. Commercial artists were familiar with paste-up and strip-
ping work. On 15 December 1954 the ITU and the Photo-Engravers' Union signed a
pact covering each organization's rights on the Fotosetter. The printers were given
authority to operate the keyboard, to process film, and to prepare a corrected, positive paste-up of the film type. At the ITU convention in Boston in 1955, the delegates decided that a nationwide training program was needed if the international
union expected to maintain its numerical strength and job control in the printing
industry. The following summer, the International Photo-Engravers' Union met in
Montreal and resolved to maintain control over all photoengraving, offset platemaking, and gravure processes.[59] While compositors were deskilled in the sense of
being deprived of the power to use their original training, they were offered new
knowledge. They had influenced the way the technology was applied and managed,
and maintained their position of masculine privilege in the workplace.[60] As table
13.1 indicates, men retained control of the skilled printing jobs in composition,
photoengraving, and lithographic and offset occupations, while women workers
remained in the lower-paying, lesser-skilled jobs in the binderies.

　　'The traditional ITU approach to technological change,' according to Sally
Zerker, 'was to claim jurisdiction, but the locals nevertheless had to work this issue
out with their employers through contract negotiations.'[61] During the 1950s, the
Canadian printing industry was disrupted by jurisdictional disputes over photocomposition. As computer technology entered the field over the next two decades,
it threatened to bypass the compositor entirely and eliminate typed paper manuscript from all aspects of production. Indeed, the introduction of the first computers
and new electronic processes featured in the prolonged newspaper strike in
Toronto, which began in 1964, as well as in the conflict at Montreal's *La Presse* in 1971.

In Toronto the ITU local 'failed to extend its jurisdiction over new computers and in the process was shut out of the plants of all three Toronto dailies.' In the 1970s the ongoing dismemberment of the traditional compositor's role accelerated.[62] Even so, in 1980, microelectronics had not yet swept Canadian book publishers into a computerized age of production. Major problems, including the cost of hardware and software, the training of operators, and the communication gap between the word-processor at the publisher's office and the machines at the typesetter's, were still to be resolved.

CASE STUDY ───
Learning the Trade: The École des arts graphiques de Montréal
– Éric Leroux

Although the apprenticeship system endured as a method of training, as the twentieth century unfolded alternative forms of education slowly emerged to serve the Canadian printing industry. By 1910 the American-based International Typographical Union, with which many Canadian locals were affiliated, offered a correspondence course that covered typography, design, colour harmony, composition, layout, and imposition.[63] In the 1920s the Union typographique Jacques-Cartier exhibited a similar interest in training, a concern that became more explicit in October 1936 when it began publishing its newspaper, Le Typo. In 1942 the Catholic union in Quebec City organized graphic arts courses, which were actually given in the form of public lectures. While such events occurred in other cities, such as Sherbrooke in the summer of 1944,[64] it was the École des arts graphiques de Montréal that became the training centre for the print trade in Quebec.

In 1913 the report of the federal Royal Commission on Industrial Training and Technical Education had added impetus to a growing trend toward technical training. By the end of the following decade, graduates of Ontario vocational schools included those trained in printing and binding, Linotype operation, and lithography.[65] Similar courses were established at vocational schools in Quebec, but the most notable initiative came from the École technique de Montréal. In 1925 it established a printing section, the first training facility of its kind in Quebec.[66] Initially, it offered only manual type-setting courses, with students alternating between one week in the class-room and one week in the shop with an employer, where they put their lessons into practice.[67] The following year, the school added evening courses for press operators. In 1937 it created a binding section under the direction of Louis-Philippe Beaudoin, and in 1938 it acquired Intertype and Monotype machines so that mechanical typesetting could be taught.[68]

The printing and binding sections were merged in 1942 to form a new institution, the École des arts graphiques de Montréal. Beaudoin was appointed director of the school, which occupied the former premises of the École du meuble, itself located within the École technique.[69] Classes in drawing, layout, and engraving were added to the curriculum after engraver Albert Dumouchel was hired.[70] As the institution that trained the first Quebec layout artists and graphic artists in the 1950s, the school made it possible for Quebec publishers to transform the material form of the book, breaking with the traditional model inherited from France, as discussed by Guy de Grosbois below.

On 20 October 1956 the École des arts graphiques inaugurated new quarters on St Hubert Street north of Crémazie Boulevard and changed its name to the Institut des arts graphiques de Montréal. The new facility, which cost $4 million, including $1 million for equipment, could support 400 students in day classes and 1,500 in evening classes. It was the largest, most modern, and best-equipped school of its kind in Canada. To cover the full range of activities in the printing sector, several areas of study were added to the curriculum, a change which required the purchase of new machinery. On its premises were 'workshops for offset, photoengraving, stereotyping, electroplating, manual and mechanical typesetting (Linotype and Monotype), typography, press work, silk screening, photogravure, photography, lithography, and other work.'[71] In the early 1970s, the Institut des arts graphiques became part of CEGEP Ahuntsic, which officially took over training in the printing and graphic arts trades.

The Graphic Arts in Quebec

GUY DE GROSBOIS

The year 1918 was pivotal in the history of the graphic arts in Quebec, marked by the appearance of the twelve issues of the Montreal magazine *Le Nigog*. This avant-garde publication, whose layout was designed and executed by the great artist Ozias Leduc at the pinnacle of his career, represented everything the 'Parisianistes' stood for in their aesthetic disagreement with the 'regionalists' during the interwar period.

Until almost mid-century, the visual arts, especially book design, were marked by the European training of generations of artists. Influential in Quebec were major Paris exhibitions, such as the Exposition des arts décoratifs et industriels modernes in 1925 and the Exposition universelle of 1937. At the Exposition du livre français et canadien, held in Montreal in 1926, a good 2,500 volumes were exhibited, mostly modern illustrated books and signed fine bindings. The bookseller Cornélius Déom acquired some 600 of these works, including many from the publisher and hand bookbinder René Kieffer; these volumes later found their way into private collections. This exhibition inspired young Louis-Philippe Beaudoin to envision the development of fine bookbinding in Quebec, and he won the first Provincial Scholarship to study the subject at the École Estienne in Paris.

Throughout the 1920s and 1930s, European influence on the creation of books, periodicals, concert programs, and other printed matter was evident in art deco styles and geometric shapes inspired by cubism. The choice of typefaces and the introduction of coloured covers demonstrated fluidity, a conscious quest for novelty, and visual experimentation, particularly in *Figurines* (1918), by Édouard Chauvin, *Ateliers* (1928), by Jean Chauvin, and books illustrated with photographs, such as *Voyage autour du monde* (1923), by Charles Avila Wilson.

Alongside this European current, an indigenous aesthetic emerged, evident in books published in limited collectors' editions on fine paper, including Gonzalve Desaulniers's *Les bois qui chantent* (1930) and Claude-Henri Grignon's *Un homme et son péché* (1933 and 1935), as well as influential titles published abroad, such as the Parisian edition of Louis Hémon's *Maria Chapdelaine* (1933), illustrated by Clarence Gagnon, which today is much sought after by collectors. Children's stories and adventure novels illustrated by James McIsaac and Rodolphe Duguay, along with bindings by Marguerite Lemieux and Vianney Bélanger, were part of this trend, based on traditional design practices. Jean-Marie Gauvreau, a promoter and proponent of folk art and crafts, organized no fewer than two hundred exhibitions in the 1930s, some of which included book arts such as printing and binding.[72]

This same period saw an awakening of interest in the history of the graphic arts in Canada. In 1929 the first edition of Ægidius Fauteux's *The Introduction of Printing into Canada* was published in Montreal by the Rolland Paper Company in a high-quality format reminiscent of that of Honoré Beaugrand's *La chasse-galerie* (1900). It was followed by Louis Forest's *L'ouvrier relieur au Canada* (1933) and then Philippe Beaudoin's *Gutenberg et l'imprimerie* (1940), which contained illustrations by Louis Archambault. Articles were also published on these topics in *Le Maître imprimeur, Technique,* and *Le Livre et ses amis*, a French book collectors' journal.[73]

The École des arts graphiques, the first of its kind in North America, was established in 1942 within the École technique.[74] Before 1940 illustrators often came from the École des beaux-arts de Montréal and the École des beaux-arts de Québec. Painters such as Jean-Paul Lemieux, Alfred Pellan, and Simone Aubry illustrated many books before 1945. After the founding of the École des arts graphiques, illustrators received specialized training that was less focused on interpretation and, paradoxically, was closer to autonomous art. It is no coincidence that the first *livres d'artiste* published in Quebec date from this period. Until the 1970s this school provided theoretical and practical training in the book arts: commercial art (graphic design), illustration (engraving), printing, typography, and binding. Under the influence of Albert Dumouchel, a Quebec school of engraving emerged in the 1950s that led to increased production of *livres d'artiste*. Student journals such as *Ateliers d'arts graphiques, Impressions,* and, to some extent, *Forge* (McGill University) reflected this new trend. A number of publisher-typographers appeared in Montreal who had been educated in Quebec and had received advanced training at the École Estienne in Paris: Roland Giguère (Éditions Erta), André Goulet (Éditions Orphée), and Gaston Miron (Éditions de l'Hexagone). Other artisans, such as Pierre Guillaume and Claude Haeffely, came from Europe.

An important sign of the increasing professionalization of the graphic arts was the creation of visual identities for series. Publishers' series existed at Beauchemin and Fides before the 1960s, among them the Collection du Nénuphar (Fides, 1944–), whose cover evokes the patterns of the traditional *ceinture fléchée*. After 1960 series were increasingly distinguished by their original graphic design. Layout and cover designers played an increasingly important role in the material conception of the book, as shown, for example, in the work of the Jacques Gagnier studios, which conceived the layouts for Éditions du Jour, and that of the Gilles Robert studios, which devised the covers for Éditions HMH. In 1968 the Robert studios designed a remarkable deluxe edition of Marie-Claire Blais's *Une saison dans la vie d'Emmanuel,* issued in a slipcase. Éditions du Noroît, Art global, and Éditions La Frégate further extended the boundaries of the field.

The World's Fair in Montreal in 1967 had lasting repercussions in the areas of both graphic and industrial design, from ephemera to posters, and substantially enhanced Quebec's involvement in an international milieu.[75] In the 1970s, when graphic designers began to receive their training mainly in colleges and universities, the profession became increasingly autonomous, with a focus on either the visual arts or design. The greater visibility of Quebec publishers on the European stage and their annual participation in the Paris and Frankfurt book fairs consolidated the presence of Quebec design in the international field of print.

CASE STUDY ─────────────────────────────────
The *Livre d'artiste* in Quebec
– Claudette Hould

In Quebec the *livre d'artiste* belongs to both the arts and the book trade, and has been pursued by artists in both milieux. Distinctive works, by definition polyformic and often indeterminate, most *livres d'artiste* published in Quebec between 1900 and 1980 exemplify the characteristics of fine press books, with every step in their production carried out by hand by artist-engravers working in close collaboration with typographers.[76] Most artists have initiated, conceived, and executed their work's artistic vision, and served as their own publishers.

As early as 1931 Robert Choquette's *Metropolitan Museum*, a long poem on the history of humanity, introduced a European aesthetic of the book. Set by typographer Charles A. Bernard, it contains illustrations by painter Edwin Holgate. Holgate's thirteen woodcuts reveal the many artistic developments of the period, bearing witness to the shared aims of the young French-Canadian poet and the English-Canadian artists and artisans of the Montreal School of Fine Arts.[77]

Creative innovation in the book trades scarcely existed before the 1950s. After the Second World War, artists with an interest in poetry carried out modernist experiments, and subsequent development was rapid, with further brilliant experimentation. Poet, typographer, and engraver Roland Giguère not only founded Éditions Erta with his *Faire naître* in 1949; he also anticipated the formal development of the *livre d'artiste* with *Abécédaire* (1975), printed on an eighteen–metre strip of paper which was rolled onto two wooden spools and placed in a casket.

While activities closely related to engraving and printmaking constituted the central commitment of book artists, there were some original and forceful works by artists involved in the 'underground-overground' move-

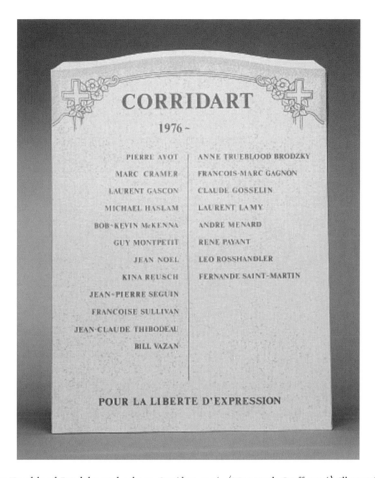

CORRIDART
1976~

PIERRE AYOT | ANNE TRUEBLOOD BRODZKY
MARC CRAMER | FRANCOIS-MARC GAGNON
LAURENT GASCON | CLAUDE GOSSELIN
MICHAEL HASLAM | LAURENT LAMY
BOB-KEVIN McKENNA | ANDRE MENARD
GUY MONTPETIT | RENE PAYANT
JEAN NOEL | LEO ROSSHANDLER
KINA REUSCH | FERNANDE SAINT-MARTIN
JEAN-PIERRE SEGUIN
FRANCOISE SULLIVAN
JEAN-CLAUDE THIBODEAU
BILL VAZAN

POUR LA LIBERTE D'EXPRESSION

13.4 Anne Trueblood Brodzky and others, *Corridart, 1976–* (Montreal: Graff, 1976). Illustrations by Pierre Ayot and others. Binding by Pierre Ouvrard. Reproduced from *Pierre Ouvrard, Master Bookbinder, Maître relieur* (Edmonton: University of Alberta Press, 2000). Courtesy of Pierre Ouvrard and the University of Alberta Libraries (Bruce Peel Special Collections).

ment of the 1970s. Many titles were published by Éditions Cul Q, and a dozen books by the artist-publisher Yrénée Bélanger were issued by Éditions de l'Oeuf. Exceptional were books that overtly expressed political or social commitment, such as the collective work for the *Corridart* project. Designed to protest the City of Montreal's censorship of outdoor art placed along the central artery of Sherbrooke Street during the Olympic Games in 1976, writers and artists contributed to an album rendered as a giant gravestone (see illus. 13.4, above). During this decade, bookbinders like Pierre

Ouvrard became increasingly involved in the creation of clever montages and ingenious constructions to stress the visual aspects of the book, transforming it into a multi-faceted work of art or, better still, an installation.

As rare as the politically committed book was the book as trace – trace of an artistic manifestation, installation, performance, or exhibition – which captured and extended the artist's creative process. Seminal in this regard was 3 *Plantations*. Unveiled in November 1973 at the Véhicule Art Gallery in Montreal, it consisted of reproductions of action photographs by Pierre Boogaerts.

In private studios and in art schools attached to universities, the book was often used as a vehicle for collective exploration and reflection on art, mixed media, and printmaking techniques, as with the innovative silk-screeners at Atelier Graff, a workshop sustained by the ongoing endeavours of Pierre Ayot. The fact that more and more artists became their own publishers to disseminate their books contributed to the expansion of the genre: the number of publications doubled between the 1970s and 1980s. The 1990s saw further increase and diversity, and even books without text, as the codex continued to explore the potential of forms and meanings.

The Private Press

RICHARD LANDON

An exact definition of the 'private press' book remains elusive, although both the creators of such works and those who collect them appreciate their distinctive qualities. In the words of Will Rueter, 'It is difficult to explain – and sometimes to justify – the fine craft of private printing. The compulsion to print texts of one's choice is the chief motivation, but there is a great responsibility and challenge in finding the appropriate visual form for a text through the careful selection of typeface, paper, and binding materials.'[78] Another Canadian printer loves 'the fact that a book creates a private space for one or two people' in which to experience a work of art.[79] In contrast to the mechanization and market orientation of commercial printing, private presses work by hand to produce limited editions that are creatively designed, often in collaboration with graphic artists. Inspired by the British Arts and Crafts movement and the work of William Morris, Canadian private presses gained visibility in the 1930s with the founding of the Golden Dog Press (Toronto). Proprietor J. Kemp Waldie produced eight titles between 1933 and 1939, including Marie Tremaine's groundbreaking study *Early Printing in Canada* (1934). His most elaborate production, *Engravings for Macbeth* (1939), featured fourteen woodcuts by Laurence Hyde.

Robert Reid, among Canada's foremost typographers and book designers, is often credited with having designed one of the most beautiful books ever printed in Canada, *The Lawrence Lande Collection of Canadiana* (Montreal: Lawrence Lande Foundation, 1965). In Vancouver in 1946, he founded the Private Press of Robert R. Reid. A particularly spectacular production resulted from his collaboration with artist George Kuthan on *Kuthan's Menagerie* (1960), issued under the imprint of Nevermore Press, which required the talents of several craftsmen to print Kuthan's multicoloured linoleum-block prints. The Honeysuckle Press, Kuthan's own imprint, created only one book, *Aphrodite's Cup* (1964), an erotically explicit tour de force of twenty-five linocuts with no text at all. British Columbia's significance as a site of private-press activity was enhanced in 1978 when Jan and Crispin Elsted founded Barbarian Press, which celebrated its twenty-fifth anniversary in 2003.

In post-war Ontario, English-speaking Canada's other significant centre of private press work, a major highlight was the establishment of Gus Rueter's Village Press in Thornhill in 1957. Before it closed in 1965, he produced ten books, including *Poems* (1961), by David Donnell, original verse by a local author, which signalled the importance of Canadian private presses in advancing creative work in multiple artistic formats. In 1959, together with Carl Dair, the designer of Canada's only original typeface of the period (described by Rod McDonald in the case study below), and Douglas Lochhead, librarian of Massey College at the University of Toronto, Rueter founded the Guild of Hand Printers, an informal association of local private printers. They occasionally issued collections of their work under the title *Wrongfount*, the most extensive being *Wrongfount Six: 'Carl Dair' in Quotes* (1968), which featured gatherings printed by some twenty printers and designers. The Toronto private-press scene of the 1960s also included the Heinrich Heine Press of Peter Dorn, active from 1963 to 1972, and Greg McDonagh's Roger Ascham Press, established in 1964, which issued five substantial books before 1980, including Douglas Lochhead's *Millwood Road Poems* (1970).

Three southern Ontario presses founded in the 1960s that remained active into the next millennium demonstrated the increasingly collaborative and innovative nature of this mode of publishing. Richard Outram and Barbara Howard started the Gauntlet Press in Toronto in 1960 to issue Outram's poetry, illustrated with Howard's wood engravings. Two years later, Will Rueter (son of Gus), an art school student who would become a well-known book designer, founded the Aliquando Press. Performing all the functions of design, typesetting, printing, and binding, he developed an innovative typographic style combining different typefaces and often published contemporary Canadian poetry. Rueter articulated his credo in his 1976 pamphlet *Order Touched with Delight* (Toronto: Aliquando), an apt general description of the books from his press. Engraver Gerard Brender à Brandis founded the Brandstead Press in Stratford in 1969 in order to present his own prints in books directly, 'with no intervening glass.'[80] By 1977 he was producing complexly integrated works such as *April Snowstorm*, by Madzy Brender à Brandis, set in Della Robbia and Kennerley types, with thirteen wood engravings. By handmaking the paper for this volume, he achieved control of almost all the material aspects of the book's production.

The 1977 exhibition of the book arts in Ontario, recorded in the catalogue *Reader, Lover of Books, Lover of Heaven* (1978), inspired the founding in 1979 of Wayzgoose, an annual festival of printing and related activities, in Grimsby, Ontario. In 1980 Marilyn Rueter could observe that 'private printing in Canada is more active today than it has been at any time since the 1950s.'[81] Canadian awareness of fine book production and design has also been exemplified in the activities of the Alcuin Society, described in the following case study.

CASE STUDY
The Alcuin Society
– Jim Rainer

The Alcuin Society was instigated in Vancouver in 1965 by Geoffrey Spencer, a sales manager, with the support of fellow founding directors Basil Stuart-Stubbs, university librarian at the University of British Columbia, Sam Black, a UBC professor of fine arts, and Bill Duthie of Duthie Books. The chief aims of the society are 'to further the interests of book collectors and to promote a wider appreciation of fine books by publishing unusual and worthwhile works in finely wrought Limited Editions.'[82] Implicit in these aims is a focus upon the physical aspects of book production, including design, typography, calligraphy, illustration, paper, printing, and binding.

The name was chosen to honour Alcuin of York (ca. 735–804), an eminent English educator, scholar, and theologian whom Charlemagne appointed abbot of St Martin of Tours, a position from which he encouraged the study and preservation of ancient texts. In honouring its namesake, the Alcuin Society has engaged in a wide range of educational activities, including lectures, workshops, exhibitions, field visits, and competitions. Since its founding, it has published a quarterly journal, *Amphora*, as well as numerous keepsakes and broadsides.

During its first eleven years, the society also pursued a publishing program guided by Stuart-Stubbs that gave rise to nine books, all but one of them reprints of previously published works that met the criteria of being rare, out of print, and intrinsically interesting Canadiana from an historical or literary perspective. The first of these, *A Theatrical Trip for a Wager! Through Canada and the United States* (1861; reprinted, 1966), by Captain Horton Rhys, was published in a letterpress and hand-bound edition of 500 copies. Designed and printed by Wil Hudson and Nick Schwabe, it was graced with an introduction by Robertson Davies and illustrations by Sam Black. The eight limited-edition titles that followed, which included Ethel Wilson's *Hetty Dorval* (1947; reprinted, 1967), Abraham S. Holmes's *Belinda; or, The Rivals: A Tale of Real Life* (1843; reprinted, 1970), and Vera Ibbett's *Flowers in Heraldry* (1977), displayed all the arts of fine book-making.[83] Each copy of *Hetty Dorval* was signed by its author. Holmes's work contained sixteen superb reproductions of watercolours painted in Upper Canada between 1827 and 1840, while Ibbett's volume, produced in Belgium, won the noted English calligrapher admission to the Society of Scribes and Illuminators. In contrast to the other titles, which were produced in print runs of 375 to 500 copies, 2,300 copies of this first edition of *Flowers in Heraldry* were issued.

In 1981 the Alcuin Society extended its commitment to quality book production by establishing its annual Book Design Award, a prize to honour Canadian designers who have successfully matched design concepts to the intellectual content of a title and realized their vision with a complementary level of production. Categories for the competition include prose fiction, prose non-fiction, poetry, pictorial works, children's books, reference works, and limited editions.

Book Design in English Canada

RANDALL SPELLER

During the first decades of the twentieth century, decisions about the structural and aesthetic requirements of a book's manufacture were largely an editorial responsibility in English Canada, as they were in Britain. Editors selected manuscripts, approved budgets, and if they had any knowledge of typography or design, attempted to draft layouts based on familiar printing practices.[84] Other details were left in the untrained hands of salesmen, secretaries, managers, and even company presidents.[85] Books were rarely contracted out to independent designers or typographers; more often than not, details of physical production were left entirely to the manufacturer. Both paper and typeface were chosen by the typesetter from an approved house selection. If the bindery was a separate company, the selection of case materials and lettering was based on availability and budgetary limitations. In Toronto, well-known firms such as T.H. Best and Hunter, Rose specialized in printing and custom binding. Among Canada's major English-language publishers, only Ryerson Press printed and bound its own books, using its own type specimen book, in-house bindery, and staff of long-serving craftsmen.

Dust jackets were a well-established feature of the English-Canadian book by 1918. Largely used to protect the cloth case and often discarded upon purchase, they were essential for eye-catching displays and sales promotions. Although many were simply text-based, jackets were often the only feature of the book sent out for illustration or graphics, a practice that continues to the present day. After the First World War, those publishers who were determined to make better-looking books began to turn to illustrators and commercial artists for help. While illustration was used cautiously in order to control costs, Group of Seven members J.E.H. MacDonald, Franz Johnston, F.H. Varley, and Lawren Harris, as well as other notable Toronto artists such as C.W. Jefferys and C.M. Manly, created a new look for the 1920s book using Canadian images and scenery.

J.E.H. MacDonald, who worked with Ryerson Press, J.M. Dent, and McClelland and Stewart in Toronto, was the most prominent illustrator of the period.[86] His work focused specifically on the illustrated elements of the book (title pages, endpapers, chapter headings, illustrations, lettering, and dust jackets) rather than on the total design package, details such as general layout and typography being decided elsewhere. MacDonald's illuminations, illustrations, and hand-lettering reflect the Arts and Crafts aesthetic of flat, patterned, and decorative forms. Enthusiastically embraced by English Canada's commercial artists, the Arts and Crafts movement directly influenced most book design and illustration up to mid-century with its 'preference for the hand over the machine.' Between 1900 and 1940, designers typically preferred illustration and hand-lettered display typography over photography and machine-set type.[87]

Although new typographic ideas were being formulated between the wars, few were embraced by publishers. Craftsmanship was bound by tradition as apprentices learned their trade from senior craftsmen. No professional trade schools existed until the establishment of the École des arts graphiques in Montreal in 1942, and art schools offered only introductory courses in typography, illustration, lettering, and design. Nonetheless, the work of Bertram Brooker (see illus. 13.5, p. 380) and J.W.G. (Jock) Macdonald demonstrated that artists were increasingly aware of international trends. Thoreau MacDonald (son of J.E.H.) practised a transitional style focusing more on typography and design, as evidenced by his work on the cover of the Canadian National Exhibition's *Catalogue of Fine, Graphic, and Applied Arts* for 1930 and 1935 (see illus. 13.6, p. 381). He took great care to craft text to image, balance page layouts, and select appropriate paper.[88] His simple illustrations were inspired by nature, while his clear, stylized lettering 'betray[ed] a more modernist hand than that of his immediate predecessors.'[89] Ottawa's Graphic Publishers (1925–32) similarly deployed typography and endpaper designs to create a distinctive look.

While the creative book designers of the 1920s continued their work into the 1930s, the Depression brought an end to many innovations. Illustration declined in part as a result of cost. Books of the period were often decorated with standard pictorial and typographic ornaments taken from stock, while publishers recycled decade-old illustrations.[90] In the words of one critic, most books were 'a sea of clumsy type, arty paper, hideous covers, and inept ornaments.'[91] Heavy 'antique book paper,' often with an untrimmed fore-edge, was fashionable. Despite a large pulp and paper industry, only a few Canadian mills produced book papers before 1945: in Ontario, the Provincial Paper Company in Georgetown and the Howard Smith Paper Company in Cornwall both made Featherweight and Antique book papers,[92] while in Quebec the Rolland Paper Company also produced fine book papers. Other papers were imported, usually from the United States.

The Second World War brought profound social, economic, and technological change. War spending stimulated the economy, while heightened nationalism spurred the market for Canadian titles. Challenged by antiquated printing equipment and shortages of binding materials, paper, and labour, some wartime

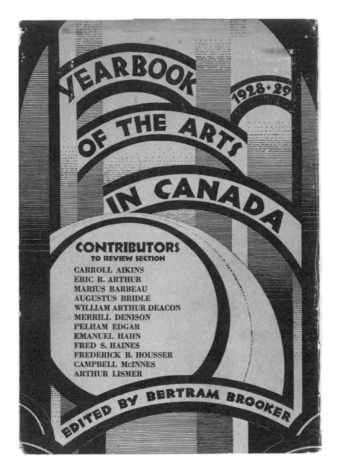

13.5 Bertram Brooker, ed. and designer, *Yearbook of the Arts in Canada, 1928–29* (Toronto: Macmillan Company of Canada, 1929). Courtesy of the Thomas Fisher Rare Book Library, University of Toronto.

publishers nonetheless found it expedient for both business and cultural reasons to produce 'well-designed, aesthetically-satisfying Canadian books.'[93] Franklin Carmichael's illustrations and typography for Grace Campbell's *Thorn-Apple Tree* (1942) and *The Higher Hill* (1944), both issued in Toronto by the Canadian subsidiary of Collins, testified to a new patriotic spirit in book production.

A post-war demand for change heralded new developments as publishers sought innovative ways of making books. British publishers led the way in the English-speaking world by hiring some of Europe's leading typographers to head up newly established book design departments. Typography began to be taught

13.6 Thoreau MacDonald (designer), *Catalogue of Fine, Graphic, and Applied Arts, and Salon of Photography. Canadian National Exhibition, August 22nd to September 6th 1930* (Toronto: Canadian National Exhibition, 1930). Courtesy of the Thomas Fisher Rare Book Library, University of Toronto.

seriously in British art schools after 1945, a move that had profound implications for Canada a decade later. As early as 1945, articles on the importance of design in book and commercial manufacturing started to appear in the professional literature. The rising cost of making books, limited selections of type, low-capacity presses, inadequate paper, and overworked binderies forced publishers to seek fresh ideas and new technologies.[94] Huge investments were required for high-speed presses and better-quality materials. Higher output and faster production raised issues of quality as traditions of craftsmanship began to disappear.[95] Illustration and decoration became increasingly expensive and old-fashioned; photography was seen as more efficient and modern. In addition, the increasing dominance of well-designed and attractive American books with their eye-catching dust jackets, which showed well in stores and libraries, challenged Canadian and British sales. Without going bankrupt, 'Canadians ... had to match American production standards with standards of equal attractiveness and sophistication.'[96]

It was to book designers that publishers turned to help them adapt to these economic realities. Book design made sound business sense as publishers realized that badly printed books using inappropriate type and paper were not cost-effective. Designers could plan better-looking and better-made books for less money using existing products and supplies. In the words of publisher John Morgan Gray, 'The solution lay in a more imaginative employment of materials and better workmanship ... [and] more professional standards.'[97] The move from commercial art to design constituted a 'fundamental shift in emphasis ... away from illustration [and] image ... toward design [and] function.'[98]

Change was evident by the end of the 1940s, for the post-war 'reappearance of good papers and book cloths [and] an abundance of metal for varied type-faces invited experiment and innovation.'[99] Canadian-born but European-trained Carl Dair became a vocal advocate of typographic design (see illus. 13.7, p. 385). Paul Arthur designed McClelland and Stewart's celebrated Indian File poetry series in 1948. Arthur Steven joined Ryerson Press in 1949 as its first full-time art director.[100] These individual circumstances coincided with the formation in 1947 of the Art Directors Club of Toronto (ADCT), an organization that did 'much to raise the creative level of editorial art.'[101] Aimed at the large commercial printing and advertising industry, ADCT exhibitions, with awards in various categories, were an annual event from 1949 to 1964. Soon publishers began to experiment with design, and company executives started to rethink issues of 'excellence' in book production. The new ideas of European modernism 'began to strike a sympathetic chord,'[102] allowing publishers to demonstrate that 'type alone, ingeniously used, can suggest many moods and messages.'[103]

Until the mid-1950s there were few trained designers or typographers at work in Canada to address industry problems. The arrival of European book designers – among others, Frank Davies in 1951, John Gibson in 1952, and Frank Newfeld, Leslie (Sam) Smart, and Antje Lingner in 1954 – transformed the industry.[104] Canadian-born Paul Arthur and Allan Fleming, who both returned from Europe in 1955, enhanced the pool of European-trained typographers and designers. All soon found jobs in Toronto firms, leading to the visual and economic dynamism of the 1955–65 period. With the creation in 1956 of the Society of Typographic Designers of Canada

(TDC), Canadian designers acquired a forum in which to share ideas, to promote and improve the quality of Canadian book design, and to bring together all those working in the field. Along with meetings and lectures, the TDC held seven annual juried exhibitions from 1958 to 1964, celebrating book, magazine, and business printing. These travelling exhibitions, and the reviews they generated, raised the profile of book design and typography to a new level, resulting in widespread debate and interest. William McConnell's Klanak Press in Vancouver (1958–74), which used typography by Takao Tanabe, was only one example of design's growing influence.

Book designers in the 1960s, recalls Frank Newfeld, 'found a veritable garden of Eden in Canada.'[105] A small group of trained professionals able to work virtually on its own terms attained international recognition for some of the most beautifully designed trade books ever produced in Canada. Newfeld's design for Roy Daniells's *The Chequered Shade* (McClelland and Stewart, 1963) won the bronze medal at the 1965 Internationale Buchkunst-Austellung in Leipzig; the following year, his design for Phyllis Gotlieb's *Within the Zodiac* (McClelland and Stewart, 1964) won the silver. Carl Dair, who in 1967 created Cartier, the first Canadian typeface, also received a 'top fifty' placement in the Fifty Books of the Year for his *Design with Type* (University of Toronto Press, 1967). Geoffrey Matthews's *Economic Atlas of Ontario* (University of Toronto Press, 1969) won 'the most beautiful book in the world' citation at Leipzig in 1969. These Canadian experts had bridged the gap between decorative illustration and functional typographic design.

The pleasures of the garden began to fade for designers by the end of the 1960s, despite the surge of nationalism inspired by the Centennial of 1967, which brought about an explosion in Canadian writing and the concomitant emergence of new and independent houses, as described by David McKnight in chapter 11. Advocates of experimental writing tended to place greater emphasis on a book's content and affordability than its design; however, some notable examples of original book design issued from these houses. Jeff and Carol Wakefield produced remarkable full-page type for the cover and title page of Robert Flanagan's *Body* (Anansi, 1970), while Victor Coleman's tire-track covers for his book *Parking Lots* (Talonbooks, 1972) demonstrated experimental creativity.[106] Established houses such as University of Toronto Press, under Allan Fleming, also produced extraordinary books. Running counter to such efforts in the late 1960s was the exponential growth of inexpensive but ill-designed paperbacks, a format in high demand as baby boomers became university students. (One exception was Frank Newfeld's original cover designs for the New Canadian Library; see illus. 7.4, p. 236). 'Perfect' (adhesive) binding became commonplace, as binderies were modernized with new equipment that allowed automated and semi-automated processes. Binding costs were significantly reduced with the elimination of sewing and hard covers.[107]

Technological innovations and dramatic changes in the general structure of the English-Canadian book trade heralded further challenges for book design in the 1970s. Every feature of the book was transformed by new technologies, from the dust jacket to the printed page. In book production, where letterpress had retained some advantages, offset printing gradually became standard. By 1972 offset book output in Canada was estimated to outnumber letterpress five to one, and by the end of the decade it seemed that 'the world of hot metal, relief printing was swept away.'[108] Photography and photocomposition became increasingly important for illustration and page layouts, as did computer typesetting. Traditional typefaces were replaced by those better adapted to new processes. 'Swiss international style,' with its 'flush-left, sans-serif typography positioned within a functional grid,' became popular,[109] especially in federal government publications. In 1966 the TDC changed its name to Graphic Designers of Canada to reflect the fact that all forms of 'visual communication' and information, not just books, were now part of the designer's mandate.

By the early 1970s, the corporate environment in publishing houses was also changing as firms grew larger and more bureaucratic, requiring more centralized controls. With a wider range and greater number of books being produced, designers had to deal with an entire season rather than individual titles.[110] Daily interaction among the editor, the designer, and the production team was no longer possible. Relationships with suppliers changed as well: production times were much shorter, and book paper was often in short supply. There was also a growing trend of having books printed outside Canada, especially for high-quality colour printing.

Nonetheless book design was not without advocates. In 1972 the Book Promotion and Editorial Club published *The Look of Books 1972*. A contest began in 1970 to encourage Canadian book designers, publishers, and printers to maintain high standards, with exhibitions from 1970 to 1973. After Design Canada, under the Department of Industry, Trade and Commerce, took over in 1974, these exhibitions continued until 1976. This tradition of awards and exhibitions was revived by the Alcuin Society in 1981.

In the 1980s the computer became an established part of book production, bringing challenges and promises to a rapidly changing industry. The new technology was both seductive and newsworthy. Nevertheless, as the novelty wore off and uniformity and lack of typographic variety became evident, producers rediscovered the economic and aesthetic necessity of design. The release in 2000 of the Cartier

13.7 Carl Dair, *Type Talks* (Hull, QC: The E.B. Eddy Co., 1948). Cover design by Dair and Henry Eveleigh. Courtesy of Domtar Inc. and the Thomas Fisher Rare Book Library, University of Toronto.

Book typeface demonstrated a renewed interest in digital typography. Automated design tools also emerged, demonstrating that as new technology becomes available, design is still of 'fundamental economic relevance to publishing.'[111]

CASE STUDY
Cartier: Canada's First Typeface
– Rod McDonald

Canada's first roman typeface was released on 1 January 1967 as a Centennial gift to the nation from its designer, Carl Dair.[112] The project was conceived

one morning in 1955 when Dair casually remarked to Allan Jarvis, director of
the National Gallery of Canada, that apart from the Cree syllabary cast by
the Reverend James Evans at Norway House in 1840,[113] no Canadian had
ever produced a typeface. Jarvis suggested that Dair apply for government
funding to study abroad, with the aim of creating a uniquely Canadian typeface. In 1956, backed by a $4,000 fellowship from the Canadian Government
Overseas Program, Dair left for Holland to study type design, punch cutting,
and casting under the renowned engraver P.H. Rädische at the Joh.
Enschedé en Zonen foundry in Haarlem. During this 'apprenticeship,' he
learned to hand-cut and cast type in a process largely unchanged from
Gutenberg's time. Dair returned to Toronto in 1957 with a deeper appreciation of how difficult it is to translate large drawings of letters into very small
characters that can be successfully combined into words.

The most noticeable feature of Cartier – named after the explorer Jacques
Cartier – is its strong calligraphic styling. An accomplished calligrapher, Dair
managed to reconcile the freedom of quickly rendered letterforms, which
often appear to 'dance' across a page, with the strict discipline of rigid forms
engraved in metal. While travelling in Europe, he had purchased two pages
from a book printed in Florence in 1482 by Antonio Miscomini. Dair was
struck by the close-fitting letterforms and heavy baseline of Miscomini's type
and incorporated these features into his roman. Cartier italic appears to have
been modelled largely on Dair's own everyday italic hand.

When it came time to cast the fonts, management at Mono Lino Typesetting in Toronto convinced Dair that Cartier should be produced for
phototypesetting rather than metal. Mergenthaler Linotype in New Jersey
manufactured the glass fonts used in its new Linofilm phototypesetters.
Mono Lino held exclusive rights to Cartier for one year, after which Linotype could market it internationally.

Cartier was greeted with polite, cautious reviews. For the most part, the
roman was praised for its originality and ease in reading. The italic fared less
well: most designers felt it was too narrow and contrasted too much with
the roman. Hampered by the lack of a suitable italic and at least one bold
weight, Cartier was eventually reduced to being a default 'Canadian content' typeface. Cartier Book, a complete reworking and expansion of Cartier
undertaken by Rod McDonald, was released in 2000. It addresses many of
the problems found in the original design and is the typeface used for
History of the Book in Canada / Histoire du livre et de l'imprimé au Canada.

PART SIX

DISTRIBUTION

chapter 14

SYSTEMS OF DISTRIBUTION

International Sources of Supply

FRÉDÉRIC BRISSON

Canada is one of the world's major importers of books. Excluding textbooks, the share of the Canadian market claimed by imported books was approximately 75 per cent in the mid-1970s.[1] Indications are that the proportion was even higher before the 1960s, with the exception of the war years. This situation has had structural effects on the entire book industry, particularly on the distribution system, which plays an important role in the financing of the country's publishers. The book market in Canada is influenced by economic and geographic realities that greatly favour imports. The close link between importing and publishing created by the distribution system was reduced somewhat when various levels of government began to subsidize the publishing industry in the 1970s.

Imports

In the 1970s, according to data from the United Nations (UN), Canada was the world's greatest importer of books and pamphlets in terms of absolute value, ahead of the United States, France, Australia, and West Germany (see chart 14.1, p. 390). With less than 1 per cent of the world's population, Canada bought between 9 and 16 per cent of the world's total book exports. Per capita, however, it was Switzerland that imported the most foreign books ($14.70 per capita in 1975), followed by New Zealand ($13.10), Canada ($9.20), Australia ($9.00), and Belgium ($8.90). Canada was

Chart 14. 1   Principal importing countries of books and pamphlets, 1970–9.

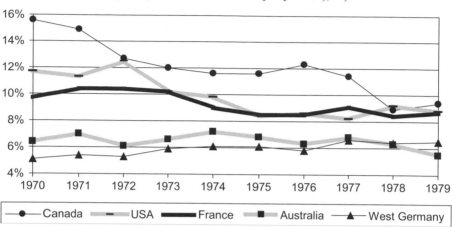

also the world's greatest importer of newspapers and magazines. Canadian purchasing in this sector was even higher: in the 1970s, 14 to 18 per cent of the world export trade in newspapers and magazines was destined for Canada.[2]

Foreign books came primarily from the United States. Before the Second World War, American books accounted for 50 to 70 per cent of imports, down from 80 per cent during the First World War,[3] while British books represented between 25 and 40 per cent of imports. Less than 10 per cent of books were imported from other countries (see chart 14.2, p. 391). Books published in languages other than English or French accounted for only 1 to 2 per cent of Canadian imports between 1939 and 1979, and these too came mainly from the United States. Germany supplied the largest numbers of imports from overseas, followed between 1950 and 1979 by the Netherlands and Italy.

During the 1930s, there was an exceptional drop in American imports and proportional rise in British imports, possibly due to the Depression, which hit the United States especially hard. However, American companies took advantage of the Second World War to strengthen their long-term position. Between 1939 and 1945, the United States was virtually the only country exporting books to Canada, and from 1949 to 1979, imports of books and pamphlets from the United States represented between 75 and 85 per cent of Canadian imports. During the same period, there was a proportional increase in the importation of French-language books from France, Belgium, and Switzerland, rising from 5 to 13 per cent. British imports never rose above 10 per cent.

The only sector in which American imports were not consistently predominant was religious books, in which category Great Britain still vied with the United States

Chart 14.2   Origin of books and pamphlets imported into Canada, 1913–79.

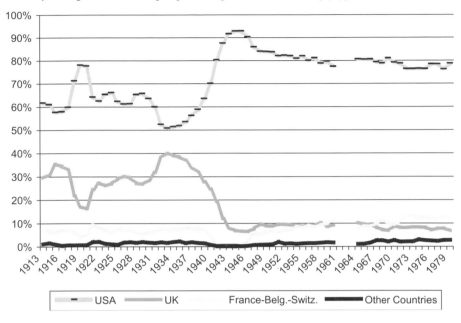

for first place before 1940. During the 1920s, 1930s, and 1950s, Belgium was the major external source of religious books in French and provided 10 to 20 per cent of all religious books imported into Canada in any language. In fact, the vast majority of imports from Belgium until 1960 consisted of religious titles. In addition, Italy and Germany carved out a niche market in this sector. Between 1913 and 1960, religious books represented from 10 to 15 per cent of all Canadian book imports; in the 1970s this figure dropped quickly to less than 5 per cent.

Like books, imported newspapers and magazines were also overwhelmingly American. From 1918 to 1943, these publications came almost exclusively from the United States,[4] other than between 1933 and 1938, when, as Mary Vipond observes in chapter 8, an increase in tariffs introduced by R.B. Bennett's Conservative government forced many American publishers to print their magazines in Canada. The data available for the years 1961 to 1975 show a slight drop in American imports in this sector, but this decrease is not very significant since the level never fell below 87 per cent.[5] The remainder came from France and Britain.

Importers

The linguistic boundary separating Canada into two distinct markets gave rise to two distribution systems. On the anglophone side, importing took place through publisher-agents, who held large numbers of exclusive distribution contracts with foreign firms, a practice described by George L. Parker in chapter 5. The importing of foreign books, the publishing of Canadian books, and the distribution system were thus all connected. With the exception of the textbook market, Canadian publishing depended in large part on profits derived from agency sales, that is, the distribution of foreign titles. Publisher Jack McClelland claimed in 1955 that only 40 per cent of his firm's revenues came from the sale of Canadian books.[6] And if imports of French-language books are also taken into account, Canada was probably one of the countries with not only the largest, but also the most varied, supply of foreign titles.

Storage and distribution costs for so many books were substantial for the small domestic market. In addition to transportation expenses, a 10 per cent tariff was applied to most American books between 1939 and 1979.[7] These costs had to be absorbed by consumers; in 1958 the price of an imported English-language book was usually 10 to 40 per cent higher in Canada than in its country of origin.[8] Consumers often reacted to high prices by purchasing directly from the nation of export. In turn, public institutions such as libraries, schools, and universities frequently ignored Canadian suppliers and sent substantial orders directly to British or American booksellers and wholesalers, even in the case of books with exclusive Canadian agents. Canadian publishers constantly complained in vain about this situation, called 'buying around,' which undermined the entire book industry. In 1975 it was estimated that this kind of parallel importing accounted for 40 per cent of the total Canadian market.[9]

In French Canada, wholesale booksellers were the main suppliers of imported books until the end of the 1960s. Some of them also published books, including textbooks; sometimes, as was the case with Librairie Beauchemin, they offered a whole range of services (printing, binding, stationery), thus maintaining a position of strength in the market. Bulk foreign purchasing permitted them to benefit from economies of scale, as well as to exercise control over prices by offering institutional discounts with which retail booksellers could not compete.[10] Because of close ties with the Quebec government and the Roman Catholic clergy before the Quiet Revolution, wholesalers sold only those books judged to be 'above suspicion.' Thus they exercised veritable control over the dissemination of books in Quebec.[11] However, the growth of the book market in the 1960s and 1970s made it possible for companies working only in distribution to establish themselves in Quebec, supplanting the wholesalers and making themselves efficient intermediaries between foreign firms and local booksellers.

Under a trade agreement between France and Canada, French-language books had been brought into Canada duty-free since 1933. Furthermore, since French publishers favoured paper bindings over hardcovers, titles from France usually cost less than English-language imports. In 1949 an English book in hardcover cost about $3.00; the equivalent French book in paper covers, cost $1.00 or $1.50.[12] Given that the federal government generated its statistics based on absolute dollar value rather than numbers of items, this difference in pricing may explain the apparent anomaly between the volume of French-language imports and the proportion of franco-phones in the Canadian population: between 1918 and 1980 French-language books accounted for between 5 and 13 per cent of Canada's total book imports, while francophones made up 25 to 30 per cent of the population. Other hypotheses could be advanced, however, such as better penetration of the Canadian market by domestic French-language publishers,[13] a lower level of book consumption among francophones,[14] or a practice among francophones outside Quebec of purchasing English-language books because few French titles were available to them locally.

The World of Bookselling

FRÉDÉRIC BRISSON

The twentieth century witnessed significant growth in Canada's retail bookselling sector. By 1980 bookstores had sprung up in all regions and represented a variety of interests. They included general, campus, antiquarian, and specialized stores, as well as chains focused on quick turnover of stock.

General Bookstores, Their Owners, and Relations with the Trade

After the First World War, the number of bookstores in Canada increased substan-tially in absolute numbers as well as in proportion to the population: from 358 book-stores in 1930 (one bookstore for every 28,600 inhabitants), the figure grew to 580 in 1951, and 1,260 in 1971 (one for every 17,200 inhabitants).[15] Predominantly an urban phenomenon, in 1951 the concentration of bookstores in major centres was approx-imately twice that of the country's average. Of Canada's three largest cities – Mont-real, Toronto, and Vancouver – the last claimed the greatest number of bookstores

14.1 Actress Juliette Béliveau chats with Aristide Pony, owner of the J.A. Pony bookstore at 554 Sainte Catherine Street East in Montreal. In her hand is a copy of *Le film*, issued by Poirier & Cie (Montreal, 1921–6?). Photograph by Conrad Poirier, 3 April 1950. Courtesy of the Bibliothèque et Archives nationales du Québec, Direction du Centre d'Archives de Montréal, Fonds Conrad Poirier, P48.S1.P23538.

per capita. Before the Second World War, relatively large book departments were also found in department stores. For example, Eaton's, through its stores, catalogues, and book club, played an important role in the dissemination of books in Canada, though its prominence gradually diminished as the number of dedicated bookstores increased.

Until mid-century the best-known bookstores were located in provincial capitals or major cities, such as The Book Room in Halifax, Garneau in Quebec City, Granger Frères, Déom, and Burton's in Montreal, Tyrrell's and Britnell's in Toronto, Russell-Lang's in Winnipeg, and Hibben's in Victoria. In the interwar period, bookstores that sold nothing but books were exceptions. Britnell's was one of the first to do so, when in 1928 it moved into its long-term quarters at 765 Yonge Street. Most bookstores also sold stationery; religious articles and toys represented other common stock. While books accorded status, stationery and other wares earned the profits. Diversity of stock was especially important to the survival of bookstores in smaller communities. In 1930 book sales accounted for only 52 per cent of the revenue of bookstores in Quebec, 31 per cent of those in Ontario, and 9 per cent of those in British Columbia.[16] In a country as large as Canada, the distance between booksellers and customers was a considerable obstacle, and some people living in rural areas purchased books by mail order. Russell-Lang's in Winnipeg and Librairie Beauchemin in Montreal, for example, handled large numbers of mail orders each year.

In English Canada in the 1920s and 1930s, some bookstores offered a lending library service. Booksellers engaged in this activity to counter the high cost of hardcover books and to increase their clientele. During the Depression, bookstores with lending libraries became very popular; for example, the Wendell Holmes Lending Libraries alone had twenty-eight branches in southwestern Ontario in 1935.[17] Lending libraries usually had between 100 and 500 subscribers, who could choose from a selection of 50 to 2,000 recent titles, paying two or three cents a day on each book borrowed.[18] From 1935 to 1943, alongside its 'Best Sellers' list, the *Bookseller & Stationer and Office Equipment Journal* dedicated a full page to 'Best Renters,' an indication of the importance of this phenomenon. The introduction of mass-market pocket books during the Second World War put an end to the rental system. With their low price, these paperbacks democratized reading and expanded the book market considerably as they were first stocked by newsstands, tobacco shops, drugstores, and other non-specialized points of sale.

From the 1950s to the 1970s, bookstores experienced successive waves of expansion. Each decade brought new stores, many owned by colourful individuals who became legends in the book world. In the mid-1950s, Wolfe Moses in Sudbury, Evelyn de Mille in Calgary, Mel Hurtig in Edmonton, Bill Duthie in Vancouver, Henri Tranquille in Montreal, and Paul Michaud in Quebec City professionalized the bookselling trade and organized readings, signings, lectures, and book launches in their stores. Booksellers played a key role in the success of such events as Young Canada's Book Week and Canada Book Week.

Even so, relations between booksellers and publishers in English Canada were often tense. The publisher-agency system of the English-language trade, which George L. Parker explains in detail in chapter 5, created particular problems. Shifting relationships between foreign publishers and Canadian agents made it difficult at times for Canadian booksellers to determine which domestic publisher supplied individual foreign titles. Not only did foreign publishers sometimes change their Canadian agents, but different series from the same publisher were sometimes distributed in Canada by different agencies, leading to wasted time and confusion when ordering. Booksellers in Western and Atlantic Canada faced additional time lags – and onerous postage costs – in fulfilling orders since most agency titles were typically routed through companies based in Toronto. In 1974, because of the time required for handling, as well as the slowness of the mail, deliveries to booksellers on the West Coast took an average of thirty days.[19] These lengthy delays, in addition to the widespread and well-founded belief that imported books were more expensive in Canada than in their country of origin, led many booksellers, as well as their customers, to bypass Canadian agents and purchase directly from abroad.[20]

Beginning in the 1920s, booksellers accused publishers of unfair competition when they offered libraries and institutions discounts that booksellers could not match,[21] effectively excluding them from this market. Worse still, booksellers felt they were being undermined when publishers sold books directly to the public, sometimes even placing order forms in books intended for sale in bookstores. Events such as McClelland and Stewart's World's Biggest Book Sale in 1969 and a similar sale organized the following year by Ryerson generated bitterness among booksellers. Publishers, for their part, had complaints about booksellers. In 1965 Sam Stewart, president of Musson, listed the problems with bookstores that hindered domestic publishing as 'the infant state of the Canadian retail book trade, ... bad buying and insufficient stocking, slow payments, poor displays and absence of initiative in going after customers and building mailing lists, ridiculous returns, petty buying around and general incompetence.'[22]

Sometimes booksellers and publishers were able to agree. For example, in 1949 a group of booksellers led by Roy Britnell convinced publishers that it was in their common interest to increase the discount to bookstores from 33 to 40 per cent.[23] The decisive argument was that if booksellers made more money selling new books than stationery, book sales would increase. The same spirit of co-operation was shown regarding the return of unsold books. Booksellers had done their purchasing on fixed account since the beginning of the century, but in 1947 Macmillan of Canada set up a plan 'under which booksellers may return up to five percent of their total trade purchases.'[24] Competing publishers soon imitated and even exceeded this policy; for example, in 1970 McClelland and Stewart accepted all returns, including paperbacks, twelve months after the date of purchase.[25] By 1980, however, the returns system had become a vicious circle from which publishers and booksellers wanted to escape.[26] A spirit of co-operation also prevailed when the first attempts were made to share advertising costs, in the Christmas season of 1960.[27] From that time on, publishers agreed to pay part of booksellers' advertising costs when their titles were featured.

The distribution system was completely different in French Canada, as was the relationship between booksellers and their suppliers. Until the end of the 1960s,

French-language bookstores obtained most of their stock from wholesalers such as Beauchemin, Granger, Fides, and Dussault in Montreal, and Garneau in Quebec City. Because of the virtual monopoly of the wholesalers, who concentrated on selling to educational institutions, small booksellers had trouble obtaining competitive prices and a good choice of titles. Only a few independent booksellers were in a position to order from foreign countries. By specializing, retail bookstores were able to get by. In Montreal in the 1920s, Wilfrid Méthot specialized in the sale of popular novels, both foreign and Canadian, and Cornélius Déom in the sale of academic books and books for collectors. In the 1950s Henri Tranquille and Paul-André Ménard served the student clientele in the Latin Quarter. Before he was bought out by Hachette in 1958, Jules Pony carved out a niche for himself as a distributor of periodicals and popular books from France (see illus. 14.1, p. 394).

Quebec publishers had to distribute their own books, which meant higher fixed costs. Until the establishment of exclusive distribution companies in the 1960s and 1970s, bookstores did not have the right to return books. The retailer's discount was around 40 per cent. In addition, starting in the early 1950s, European publishers gradually established themselves in Quebec, distributing their books themselves. It took more than twenty years for the wholesaler system to disintegrate. The arrival of distributors who were involved neither in publishing nor in retail bookselling led to improvements in supply and price structure for booksellers. Finally, in 1979, the Act Respecting the Development of Quebec Firms in the Book Industry (*RSQ*, c. D-8.1) guaranteed retail bookstores accredited by the government the exclusive right to sell to institutions, and thus ensured the development of the retail trade.

Bookstore Chains

The second half of the twentieth century was marked by the emergence and inexorable rise of bookstore chains. Their share in the book market grew quickly, increasing from 14 per cent in 1961 to 27 per cent in 1971 and 43 percent in 1981.[28] Montrealer Louis Melzack, who opened his first Classic Books in 1930 to sell used books, entered the market for new books in 1938. By 1977 he owned 56 stores, including 3 in New York.[29] Some of his early stores sold only paperbacks, a daring move at a time when their sale by drugstores, newsstands, and other outlets was seen as a threat to the survival of bookstores. When it opened its first bookstore in Canada in 1950, the seasoned British chain W.H. Smith already had 374 branches worldwide;[30] more than 40 W.H. Smith stores were operating in Canada by 1977.

Jack Cole, who began his career in Toronto in 1936, owned the largest bookstore chain in the country, with 126 branches in 1977, including 19 in the United States. Coles, which was listed on the stock exchange in 1973, made its mark with bold marketing concepts, including that of 'books by the pound.' It built a large clientele by importing American remainders and selling them at low prices. But its practice of selling cheap American editions of Canadian titles led to accusations that Coles was depriving Canadian authors and publishers of substantial revenues. In 1960 Clarke, Irwin managed to have Coles fined $200, the maximum under the copyright law, which dated from 1924. New Press in 1972 and McClelland and Stewart in 1974 also initiated legal action, but both eventually gave up because of the expense and the ridiculously innocuous penalties. In 1975 the Writers' Union of Canada, led by Pierre Berton and Margaret Atwood, organized picket lines in front of a Coles bookstore to protest this practice of dumping.[31]

The three chains, Classic, W.H. Smith, and Coles, competed fiercely through the 1970s for new locations in shopping centres being built in the suburbs. In 1980 Coles opened the World's Biggest Bookstore in Toronto as a symbol of its success; with seventy thousand square feet of space, it was indeed the biggest bookstore in Canada. Regional chains, such as Mariner Books in the Atlantic provinces (1971–4) and Julian's in British Columbia and Alberta (1972–5), failed to thrive. While western independent booksellers such as Hurtig, Duthie, and Evelyn de Mille opened a few new stores, the Woodwards department stores, with eleven autonomous bookstores in 1967, remained the biggest retailers on the West Coast in the mid-1970s. In Montreal, Fides was the first company to develop a network of bookstores, opening branches in St Boniface (Manitoba), Edmonton, and a half-dozen Quebec cities in the 1950s. The Dussault/Garneau chain became the largest book retailer in Quebec in 1977 when the seventeen stores of Librairie Garneau were merged with the nine stores of Librairie Dussault.

The spectacular rise of the bookstore chains led to strong reactions from independent booksellers, who were threatened with the loss of part of their market and even with absorption by the new giants, as occurred with the acquisition by W.H. Smith of Burton's (1954), Tyrrell's (1958), Burnill's (1963), and Evelyn de Mille's (1975) bookstores. Each side had its own strategies. The independents emphasized their passion for books, as opposed to the quest for profits, which, they claimed, was the sole raison d'être of the chains. The chains defended themselves by pointing to the need to democratize books by making them accessible to everyone. The expansion of the chains continued through the 1980s and 1990s, particularly in English Canada, where they utterly dominated the retail market, with the acquisition of Classic by W.H. Smith in 1985, followed by the merger of Coles and W.H. Smith in 1994, ultimately giving rise to Chapters.

Specialized Bookstores

Alongside the rise of chain stores, the 1970s saw the proliferation of independent bookstores specializing in such areas as religion, children's books, feminism, and sexuality. These stores offered a wide range of titles in their specialities and an expertise not available at general bookstores.

Religious bookstores were among the most stable in the country, clearly showing the advantage of specialization. Particularly long-lived were the Centre eucharistique and the Librairie dominicaine in Montreal, and the Student Christian Movement (SCM) Bookstore in Toronto. A chain was even established in this sector: in 1978 the venerable Canadian Bible Society, an affiliate of the British and Foreign Bible Society, based in London, had more than a dozen stores in Canada, with the one in Edmonton possibly the largest religious bookstore in Canada.[32]

In the 1920s booksellers identified the market for children's books, to which areas were dedicated in the stores of veteran booksellers such as William Tyrrell, Harry Burton, and A.H. Jarvis (The Bookstore, Ottawa).[33] Specialized bookstores followed: The Children's Bookshop, on the second floor of Cloke's Bookstore in Hamilton, and The Boys' & Girls' Book Shop in Montreal. The opening of Judy and Hy Sarick's Children's Bookstore in Toronto in 1974 signalled a new wave, coinciding with the growth in children's publishing discussed by Suzanne Pouliot, Judith Saltman, and Gail Edwards in chapter 7.

Prevailing nationalism in English Canada underpinned Longhouse Books, founded in Toronto in 1972 to sell only Canadian books. This example was soon followed by Oxford Canadiana (London, ON), Books Canada (Ottawa and Victoria), The Double Hook (Montreal), and A Pair of Trindles (Halifax). Similarly, the feminist movement gave rise to the Vancouver Women's Bookstore, the Toronto Women's Bookstore, and the Librairie des femmes d'ici in Montreal, which were all co-operatives staffed by volunteers. These bookstores also served as important sites for meetings and events. Glad Day in Toronto and L'Androgyne in Montreal opened in 1970 and 1973 respectively, followed by Little Sister's in Vancouver in 1983, and played a similar role for the gay community, providing books and magazines that were unavailable elsewhere. In the 1990s, with the increasing dominance of megabookstores offering a wide range of titles, some specialized bookstores closed, along with many other independent bookstores.

Campus Bookstores

The unprecedented expansion of colleges and universities in the 1960s and 1970s led to the opening of many new campus bookstores. Most were owned by the educational institutions that housed them,[34] but some were co-operatives whose profits went to the local students' association, and some belonged to private interests. With a captive student clientele, these bookstores recorded revenues averaging twice those of outlets of bookstore chains.[35] Their greatest growth occurred when the baby-boom generation reached post-secondary studies: between 1967 and 1974, their number doubled, from 104 to 210. Sales in campus bookstores during this period represented approximately one-quarter of the overall sales of all bookstores in Canada.

Used Bookstores and Antiquarian Bookstores

Many readers prefer to pay less than the cost of new books, or patronize used or antiquarian bookstores in search of out-of-print or rare books. The 1971 federal census established the average annual revenue of this type of business at $15,700, one-fifth that of regular bookstores. Owners of these bookstores, which were particularly numerous in British Columbia,[36] had to be resourceful and dedicated to maintain their business on such modest revenues after paying rent and the cost of inventory.

While used bookstores sold large numbers of books at low prices, antiquarian bookstores sought to capitalize on the value and rarity of specific books. Their main customers, who were informed of available titles through catalogues published once or twice a year, were collectors or libraries, and a large proportion of their sales took place by mail order. Gonzague Ducharme, nicknamed le père Ducharme, was without doubt Canada's best-known antiquarian bookseller during the first half of the twentieth century. He opened his bookstore in Montreal in 1914, and when he died in 1950, his stock of approximately 350,000 books occupied three storeys.[37] According to the founder of Dora Hood's Book Room in Toronto, Ducharme 'was head and shoulders above us all in his knowledge of Canadian books, both English and French ... and he willingly shared his knowledge with his clients and colleagues.'[38] Nevertheless, when Bernard Amtmann opened his bookstore in Montreal in 1951 there were too few individuals and institutions interested in Canadian books for them to be treasured as rare books, and the reputation of antiquarian bookstores still remained to be established.[39] Amtmann was one of the principal creators of Canada's antiquarian book trade, founding the Antiquarian Booksellers' Association of Canada in 1966 and, in 1967, Montreal Book Auctions, whose public auctions were sometimes spectacular. His masterful establishment of the value of Canada's print heritage illustrates the power of booksellers in influencing the success or failure of a book. As articulated by William Tyrrell, after sixty-one years in the trade: 'I sell best what I believe in.'[40]

CASE STUDY
The Book Room
– Gwendolyn Davies

Current visitors to Halifax's The Book Room might well think the name appropriate to its commercial bookstore status, but the origins of this enduring establishment lie in eighteenth-century Methodism and John Wesley's conviction that useful and devotional literature should be circulated. Thus, early itinerant Methodist ministers in the Maritime provinces wrote, disseminated, and promoted distinctively religious texts.[41] In 1839, a century after the founding of Methodism, the Wesleyan District Conference resolved 'that a Depot for the sale of our own theological literature be established in Halifax.'[42] Run in its early days from the residence of the Reverend Charles Churchill,[43] a more extensive Wesleyan Book Room had emerged by 1848. After the Book Room's overseeing body became part of the Methodist Church of Canada in 1874, printing equipment was acquired. Under the Reverend S.F. Huestis's stewardship from 1880 to 1908, substantial expansion occurred in the bookselling operation, while some shared imprints were issued with its fellow church publishing operation, the Methodist Book and Publishing House / William Briggs of Toronto.[44]

Throughout its history, The Book Room has positioned itself strategically at the heart of Halifax's downtown core. However, by the early 1920s location could not counteract the difficulties of unprepossessing premises, largely religious stock, and rampant debt. In 1923 the Ryerson Press, the trade arm of the Methodist Book and Publishing House (after 1925, the United Church Publishing House), asked Edgar J. Vickery to assume the business's management. The successful owner of Vickery's Bookstore in Yarmouth, Nova Scotia, agreed and for the next fifteen years worked tirelessly to build on Barrington Street a bookstore that was 'a joy to readers and those who like to browse around among books.' According to *The Maritime Merchant*, Vickery ensured success through open displays and book classification by subject, and by positioning the wrapping counter at the rear of the store, so that customers would view all of the stock before leaving. Upon his retirement in 1938, the Ryerson Press expressed the gratitude felt 'throughout the House, throughout the Church, and widespread throughout the Maritime Provinces' for Vickery's 'knowledge and wise counsel concerning books.'[45] Even so, the Depression had taken a toll. When the Ryerson Press decided to close the Halifax store in 1948, the Book Publishers' Branch of the Toronto Board of Trade expressed dismay, stating that the business had become an 'integral part of the cultural background of Halifax, extending its sphere of influence throughout the Maritime Provinces.'[46]

Before the official closure occurred, the store was destroyed by fire in the spring of 1949. Halifax businessmen led by Charles Jost Burchell stepped in, rebuilt the business as The Book Room, and by November of that year had it back in operation, relocated in the Chronicle Building on Granville Street. Members of the Burchell family have been associated with this independent bookstore ever since.[47] To offset the slow sale period faced each spring, by the 1950s the business had expanded into distribution and wholesaling as a sideline, and by the 1970s was also engaged in publishing, issuing such titles as Thomas H. Raddall's *A Pictorial Guide to Historic Nova Scotia* (1970), followed by other volumes of local interest. First issued in 1981, the cookbook *A Different Kettle of Fish* sold over 60,000 copies by 1993. In 1999 The Book Room celebrated its 160th anniversary, and today at its location on Barrington Street continues to serve readers as 'Canada's Oldest Trade Bookstore.'

CASE STUDY
Librairie Tranquille
– Frédéric Brisson

Henri Tranquille was a legend in Montreal bookselling. Born in 1916, he exemplified the cultivated bookseller and managed a vast inventory. A man of conviction in touch with the literary scene and the cultural movements of his time, Tranquille advocated freedom of expression, and worked to promote books of quality and to support artistic creativity.

Tranquille began his career in 1937. After associations with various Montreal booksellers, in 1948 he opened his own bookstore at 67 St Catherine Street West, where it remained until 1974. This location placed the bookstore near Gratien Gélinas's Comédie canadienne, Collège Sainte-Marie, and Place des Arts, which opened in 1963. From the outset, Tranquille was innovative, displaying art by contemporary painters on the upper walls of his store. The first of these exhibitions featured works by Prisme d'Yeux, a group established by Alfred Pellan. That same year, Tranquille became the sole agent for *Refus global* (1948), the manifesto of the Automatiste movement, which he carried in the interest of freedom of expression. In 1950 the bookseller made the news again, hosting a group of writers and artists celebrating Honoré de Balzac on the centenary of his death, an activity which had been condemned by the Comité diocésain d'action catholique de Montréal. Librairie Tranquille became a meeting place for the city's literary and artistic avant-garde.

In the 1960s and 1970s, Librairie Tranquille was known for selling all titles in Hachette's Livre de poche, a series that included the literary works controlled by France's most important publishers. In addition, Tranquille offered a collection of plays unique to Quebec, as well as the complete works of dozens of authors he particularly liked, including Paul Léautaud, Stendhal, Alphonse Allais, Blaise Cendrars, Céline, Henry Miller, and Stefan Zweig.

Up to the mid-1970s, conditions were very challenging for independent booksellers, and survival required imagination, perseverance, and conviction. Librairie Tranquille's rich collection of literary titles attracted a faithful clientele of students and other readers from a variety of backgrounds, so that the influence of the little bookstore on St Catherine Street extended far beyond its neighbourhood: 93 per cent of its customers did not live in its immediate vicinity.[48] Tranquille's renown, wit, prodigious memory, and delight in talking to people undoubtedly had a lot to do with his appeal, but despite his success, by 1974 he faced serious financial difficulties. Moving his bookstore twice in quick succession, first to Saint-Denis Street and then to Mount Royal Avenue, did not help, and the bookseller declared bankruptcy in 1975. Henri Tranquille, who was proclaimed 'Monsieur Livre' at the Salon du livre de Montréal in 1980,[49] was for generations of readers not only a bookseller but also an adviser, a mentor, and an accessible and passionate man of letters. Henri Tranquille died in 2005 soon after the publication of his biography, *Monsieur Livre, Henri Tranquille*.

Control and Content in Mass-Market Distribution

SARAH BROUILLETTE AND JACQUES MICHON

The mass-market distribution network was a mainstay for Canadian readers throughout the twentieth century, but for most consumers it was an invisible structure, facilitating the arrival of print materials into their hands without their having any knowledge of the complex processes and politics occurring behind the scenes. The network was characterized by multiple points of sale, ranging from newsstands and specialized magazine shops, to corner stores and drugstores. In Quebec, the predominance of the French language allowed greater domestic control of and access to this market than was the case in the rest of the country. By the end of the First World War, Quebec's francophone publishers already enjoyed an established foothold in the system, through which they circulated newspapers, magazines, serialized thrillers, and other popular entertainment publications. The first to do so was Montreal's Poirier, Bessette & Cie, which began with the Bibliothèque à cinq cents series (1886–94), and story magazines such as Le Samedi (1889–1963), La Revue populaire (1907–63), and La Revue moderne (1919–60).

In English Canada the situation was very different. Mass-market distribution channels were American-dominated in terms of both ownership and product. Foreign control of the system, coupled with the sheer volume of foreign publications on the market, virtually excluded Canada's English-language publishers from the field until the 1970s. Most significant in the distribution channel was the 'national' distributor, 'the dominant financial, administrative and marketing intermediary between publishers and wholesalers for periodicals, mass paperbacks and to some extent for newspapers.'[50] Typically American-owned, national distributors did not handle actual magazines and books; instead, they acted as intermediaries, allocating copies, processing orders, handling billing and returns, and granting territories to regional wholesalers. With the exception of the Alberta Book & Novelty Company, which was active by the 1930s, no significant English-Canadian ownership existed even at the wholesaler level until after the Second World War. By 1960, however, sufficient domestic ownership prevailed in this sector to have given rise to the Periodical Distributors Association of Canada, an organization of wholesalers whose members purchased from national distributors or directly from publishers, acquiring the physical stock which they then resold to retailers.[51] By the 1970s the typical distribution channel in English Canada involved transfer from the publisher (most often an American publisher or Canadian agent), to a 'national' or 'continental' distributor (again, almost exclusively American controlled and owned), to a geographic' wholesaler (typically locally owned), to one of countless retailers (until the 1970s, usually newsstands or drugstores and then increasingly chain bookstores), and finally to the reader. In the case of mass-market books, two other models of distribution are also worth noting: in one the jobber, who deals only with paperbacks, replaces the general wholesaler; in the other, books move directly from publisher to retailer, a system that was unattractive to mass-market publishers until the 1970s, when bookstore chains, which did not use wholesalers, became a lucrative part of the market.

In the decade following the First World War, Canadian magazines were scarcely visible on newsstands and in drugstores and local shops. In 1926 it was estimated that of the 25 million American magazines sold in Canada each year, 14 million were purchased from newsstands.[52] When mass-market paperbacks, popularly known as pocket books, entered the English-Canadian market in the late 1930s and early 1940s, they were integrated into the existing periodical system as a means of maximizing points of retail display through rapid turnover and almost unlimited return of unsold copies. In 1945–6 some six thousand retail mass-market paperback outlets existed in Canada, but only 3 per cent of titles they offered were 'Canadian produced.'[53] American firms such as Pocket Books and Doubleday, which held significant distribution interests, dominated the market. The notable English-Canadian experiment of the decade was Collins White Circle Pocket Editions. The undertaking of a British subsidiary, the series was launched in 1942. Most of its titles were reprints of British popular novels, but it also produced several Canadian-authored literary works. From its launch in 1949, Canadian-owned Harlequin, which also largely reprinted the works of foreign authors, had unprecedented access to English Canada's mass-market racks due to an early and fortuitous connection to Curtis Distributing, a major American player in serial distribution. McClelland and Stewart's mass-market series of the mid-1960s, the Canadian Best-seller Library, focused on reprinting the more commercial of Canadian-authored titles from its backlist; however, it was a brief and dismal venture by comparison. Its publisher halted the series after four years and forty-six titles, having 'found the economics of the mass-market distribution system prohibitive.'[54]

Between the 1940s and the 1960s, Quebec's French-language publishers fared much better in the domestic mass market. In 1944 *La Revue moderne* initiated the world's first series of French-language pocket books, Petit Format (1944–58), reprinting popular Parisian novels and translations of American mass-market fiction.[55] After the Second World War, the absence of European competition in the French-language popular market favoured the development of Canadian French-language material. While Édouard Garand had done well during the 1920s with his series Le Roman canadien, Edgar Lespérance's Imprimerie judiciaire enjoyed greater success with the series of 10–cent novels it launched in the late 1940s. The spectacular development of these novels prompted Lespérance to create his own distribution company, Agence de distribution populaire (ADP, est. 1959), an organization which in the 1970s would become the most important distributor in Quebec of mass-market print materials, including practical guidebooks and 'how to' manuals. Pierre Péladeau, who made a fortune from a broad range of print and periodical production that included regional weekly newspapers and gossip tabloids, followed Lespérance's lead by establishing in 1965 Les Messageries dynamiques, a company that would later flourish as the Quebec distributor of French-language editions of Harlequin.

By the 1970s concern in English Canada about foreign ownership in the realm of mass-market distribution prompted new initiatives by Canadian-owned publishers to have their books better represented. The Ontario Royal Commission on Book Publishing issued reports pertaining to the mass market in June 1971 and March 1972, noting that 'the Canadian aspects of book publishing' were 'poorly served by the news distribution channels'[56] and commenting on the hazards of foreign control and monopoly, which the commissioners felt ran counter to Canadian cultural interests. Few of the commission's recommendations on this subject, including that regional wholesalers carry 'reasonable inventories of all Canadian-edited and Canadian-published periodicals,'[57] found their way into policy; indeed, even in 1975 Canadian periodicals still represented 'a mere 3% of newsstand sales.'[58] However, in 1971 the provincial government did pass the Ontario Periodical Distributors Act, legislation which made Canadian ownership a requirement for new or expanding geographic wholesalers in Ontario.[59] Additionally, the Ontario Arts Council gave over half a million dollars to facilitate the development of local distribution systems.[60] Cannonbooks (est. 1975) was a partial outcome of this development: with the funding, the company placed stands stocked with Canadian paperbacks in fifty locations across central Ontario.[61] General Publishing began issuing its mass-market Paperjacks titles in 1971, and by 1978 was releasing five Canadian titles a month and acting as its own distributor.[62] The only other notable Canadian-owned national distributor in English Canada at the time was Coast to Coast Distributing Company, owned by media giant Maclean-Hunter Publications.[63]

Reflecting on this sector of the book trade in 1980, a federal government study focused on the English-language situation identified the 'recent development' among Canadian book publishers of partnering with foreign firms to develop an interest in the mass market, noting that 'in each instance their entry involves some marketing arrangement with a prominent American firm with Canadian mass paperback experience.'[64] Examples included Seal (51 per cent of which was owned by McClelland and Stewart, 49 per cent by Bantam), Signet, co-owned by New American Library (NAL) and Macmillan, and Har-Nal, a co-venture of Harlequin and NAL. The same study noted the existence of forty-one wholesalers, all but four wholly Canadian owned and most of them members of the Periodical Distributors of Canada (PDC). While this figure demonstrates the significant trend toward domestic ownership of wholesalers after mid-century, the titles they distributed remained largely foreign in origin and content. Although the PDC could claim in 1980 that 20 per cent of the mass-market paperbacks distributed by members originated in Canada,[65] this figure did not distinguish between the Canadian and foreign content of such books, a particular issue in relation to the largest of Canada's mass-market players, Harlequin, whose Canadian authors remained few.

Despite policy intervention, beyond the level of wholesaling, foreign control of the mass-market industry in English Canada continued to be the norm until 1980 and beyond. The constraints that came with a small population of widely dispersed readers had made it too challenging for a domestic English-language mass-market industry to develop and compete in a field involving large-volume quantities of product and sales, and, with much of the distribution controlled outside the country, it was especially difficult for smaller Canadian publishers to access the distribution network. After 1980, with the increasing role of major book chains as points-of-sale for mass-market titles, even Canadian-owned wholesalers would be phased out.

In Quebec, by contrast, the level of domestic control and ownership increased during the twentieth century, this pattern made possible by the differences of language and culture, as well as a much more contained geographic area in which to distribute. In the early 1980s, the printing and publishing giant Quebecor bought a subsidiary dedicated to book distribution, Québec Livres, and take over the distribution network of the French subsidiary Hachette international Canada. Hence, by 1983, 75 per cent of mass-market book distribution in French-speaking Canada was in the hands of two Quebec companies, ADP and Québec Livres,[66] while Messageries dynamiques and Benjamin News, two other Quebec companies, held substantial market shares with respect to distributing newspapers and magazines, as well as some mass-market books.

Book Clubs

ARCHANA RAMPURE AND JACQUES MICHON

Rather than turning to bookstores or mass-market racks for reading material, many Canadians, especially those residing outside urban areas, have relied on book clubs – distribution agencies that mail low-cost editions to subscribers who commit to ongoing purchases. Major American-based book clubs dominated the English-Canadian scene, whereas in Quebec such organizations were usually run by local publishers.

Although independent booksellers have traditionally conducted part of their business by mail, book clubs and large-scale mail-order sales have typically been launched by corporate entities. In the mid-1920s, two American clubs, the Book of the Month Club (BOMC) and the Literary Guild, were the first major players to enter the Canadian market; by 1930 they claimed about 4,000 Canadian readers between them.[67] Two early Canadian experiments were the Carillon Book Club of Ottawa, which was founded in 1927 and circulated only Canadian-authored titles, and Eaton's Selective Literary Service. The latter was established in 1928 to reach the same widespread population served by the store's mail-order catalogues and was managed by C.J. Eustace, former editor of *Bookseller and Stationer*. The first book featured by the Eaton's service was Frederick Philip Grove's naturalistic novel *Our Daily Bread* (1928), a selection which might suggest that Eustace and his colleagues were more concerned with inculcating a taste for serious Canadian literature than with commercial success; however, over its four-year life, during which membership peaked at 5,000, the majority of titles offered by Eaton's were British or American.[68] In 1938 Eaton's launched a second book club. Emulating a venture run by Macy's in New York, this new enterprise offered customers discount coupons after four books were purchased at full price.[69] While these early American and Canadian clubs typically featured works of general interest to middle-brow readers, privately run organizations, such as the Book Union (est. 1946), which described itself as a 'Canadian Book Club for Progressives,' and the New Catholic Readers Club (est. 1947), an organization run by clerics, soon emerged to serve more specialized audiences.[70]

From the outset, English-Canadian publishers and booksellers protested the methods adopted by corporate book clubs. Retail discounts of 15 to 40 per cent for members were based on even deeper discounts wrung from publishers, who acquiesced in the face of the sheer volume of trade. Booksellers, for their part, resented the clubs' home delivery service as well as their discounts. Throughout the period, club organizers contended that they inculcated 'the reading habit' and drew their customer base from those without access to regular bookstores.[71] Publishers and booksellers countered that the clubs' practice of packaging and selling books as commodities undermined culture as well as commerce. Some feared the ability of these organizations to shape culture through the sheer size of their print runs. In the 1970s BOMC's Canadian Alternative selections could translate into extra print runs of 15,000 to 30,000 copies – enormous volume for Canadian-authored titles.[72] In English Canada the spectre of American cultural dominance was raised since, Canadian Alternative selections notwithstanding, the BOMC, the Literary Guild, and other American organizations held the lion's share of the book-club market by mid-century, and most of the titles they offered were resolutely American.

The many French-language clubs launched by Quebec publishers in the 1940s played a significant role in the book market, expanding readers' choices by offering works that were not available in bookstores or through wholesalers. Two Montreal publishers were particularly influential: Pierre Tisseyre, owner of the Cercle du livre de France and the Cercle du livre romanesque, and Paul Michaud, owner of the Club des vedettes and the Club des livres à succès. For their memberships, which ranged from 3,000 to 10,000, Tisseyre and Michaud republished new Parisian titles, as well as books by French-Canadian writers who were already on their lists.[73] In 1952 and 1953 the Catholic publisher Fides created two additional clubs, one for adults called Club des deux livres and one for children named Club du livre des jeunes. Each had fewer than 1,000 subscribers. Distributing titles from Fides's own list as well as some foreign works, these clubs were dedicated to promoting books that upheld Catholic principles.[74] After the establishment of European distribution houses in Montreal during the 1960s, all of Quebec's French-language clubs began to lose ground as foreign publishers distributed paperback collections directly to retail bookstores, whose share of the market was rising.

The boom years for anglophone book clubs were the 1950s through the 1970s. The Canadian arm of *Reader's Digest* and its French-Canadian affiliate, *Sélection du Reader's Digest,* added 'Condensed Books' ('Le livre condensé') to their serial business in 1950. Articulating an interest in 'building a group of future readers and writers,' Scholastic began operating in Canadian classrooms by 1958; by 1973 it had placed more than 18 million books in students' hands.[75] In 1970 Canadian-owned Harlequin, which is discussed in detail in Archana Rampure's case study in chapter 5, initiated a 'reader service bureau,' a direct-mail branch of its operation that soon 'became an incredible cash cow, providing as much corporate profit as regular book distribution'; by the late 1970s, it claimed 400,000 subscribers.[76] The Book Clubs Division of American-based Doubleday also did substantial trade: in 1973 it claimed a combined Canadian membership of 200,000 in more than twenty clubs variously devoted to subjects ranging through cookbooks, military history, and science fiction.[77]

The dominance of American fare among book-club offerings encouraged Peter and Carol Martin to establish the Readers' Club of Canada (RCC) along staunchly nationalist lines in 1959.[78] Book reviewer Robert Weaver, *Saturday Night* publisher Arnold Edinborough, and *Chatelaine* editor Doris Anderson made up the RCC's first selection committee. Reading like a who's who of Canadian cultural life, this committee would later include such notables as journalist Robert Fulford and historian Ramsay Cook, as well as novelist Mordecai Richler, who later advised for the BOMC.[79] A vast difference in scale always existed between the RCC and its American competitors: by 1973 the BOMC was a $4-million operation with over 100,000 Canadian subscribers, while the RCC was struggling along with about 2,600 members. Despite moral and financial support from the Ontario Arts Council and the Canada Council in the mid-1970s, the RCC was sold in 1978 to the publishers of *Saturday Night*.[80]

Following a nationalistic impulse similar to that underlying the RCC, in 1963 Jacques Hébert created the Club du livre du Québec. Affiliated with his Éditions du Jour, a house that dealt only with books written, printed, and published in Quebec, this club had 3,000 members in 1970,[81] but it disappeared four years later, following Hébert's departure from the parent organization. Hébert's initiative was intended, in part, to counter the foreign clubs that began to infiltrate the Quebec market in the 1960s. Among these was the Lausanne-based Club des Éditions Rencontre, which issued French editions of great works of world literature and remained active in Quebec for about ten years. A more serious player was Québec Loisirs. Created in 1979 and affiliated with France Loisirs, this club was owned by the multinational Bertelsmann and soon displaced all competitors. With 320,000 members, by 1990 Québec Loisirs was aiming to increase the number of Québécois selections in a catalogue that was 80 per cent European.[82]

From readers who faithfully accepted every monthly selection of the BOMC, to the avid romance fan who put Harlequin on the map by happily buying two dozen novels by mail every month, to the small-time publisher and bookseller who simultaneously loathed and loved the clubs, the Canadian book trade was significantly changed by the presence of mail-order clubs. For fifteen-year-old future author Michel Tremblay, whose elder brother subscribed to Les Éditions Rencontre during the 1950s, the receipt of a new book from Europe, bound in leatherette and stamped in gold, provoked such a strong sensual response that he bit into the volume his brother had given him, leaving tooth marks on an edition of three Greek tragedies.[83]

Booksellers' Organizations

GEORGE L. PARKER AND PASCALE RYAN

In contrast to Quebec, where booksellers would first establish their own organization in 1960, the trade in Ontario began to organize in the 1850s. Five decades of collective activity gave rise early in the twentieth century to the Booksellers' and Stationers' Association of Ontario, which went national in 1908. As the Booksellers' and Stationers' Association of Canada (BSAC), it led the battle against the major department stores over price-cutting on trade and school books, and raised objections when publishers engaged in direct sales to the public. After its voice – predominantly anglophone – fell silent during the war years, C.H. Nelles of Guelph and A.H. Jarvis of Ottawa revived the moribund association in 1921.

Through the prosperous 1920s, the BSAC supported the Publishers' Section of the Toronto Board of Trade in mounting annual Book Weeks, while worrying that the Book of the Month Club (est. 1926) in the United States and Eaton's Selective Literary Service (est. 1928) in Canada might hurt sales. It lobbied for the removal of the new sales tax on books, and for a 40 per cent discount from publishers, but made no progress on these issues. Heated conflicts arose over 'buying around,' when retailers bypassed Canadian agency-publishers to import copyrighted works directly from foreign publishers and jobbers. The BSAC was dissolved in 1935 after failing to merge with the Stationers' Guild of Canada, even as another umbrella organization of publishers, booksellers, and authors, the Association of Canadian Bookmen (ACB), was revived with support from prominent booksellers in Montreal and Toronto. These events were reported in *Quill & Quire* (*Q&Q*), the new book-trade journal launched by Mack Seccombe and J. Rae Perigoe in April 1935 that gradually displaced *Bookseller and Stationer* (1895–1961; formerly *Books and Notions*, 1884–95) as Canada's leading English-language book-trade publication. For the remainder of the century, *Q&Q* reported the highs and lows experienced by individual Canadian booksellers and publishers, as well as the general trends of the trade.

Despite flourishing sales during the Second World War, post-war bookselling needed new blood, new outlets, and a new organization. With assistance from Roy Britnell, the Canadian Retail Booksellers' Association was founded in late 1951 with 75 members, adjusting its name to the Canadian Booksellers' Association (CBA) in 1959. With publishers the CBA discussed standardized ordering procedures, direct mailing, and in 1956 co-organized a bookselling training course. Both groups rallied around highly publicized pornography cases, such as the banning of D.H. Lawrence's *Lady Chatterley's Lover* in 1960, as discussed by Pearce Carefoote in chapter 17. Both protested the federal sales tax on books, and approved Canada's ratification of the Florence Agreement on the importation of published materials, part of which would facilitate the international free flow of books, particularly between the United States and its trading partners. The CBA also gave support to the publication of *Canadian Books in Print* (1968), which listed 6,000 English and 4,000 French titles.

Through the 1970s, the merits of new computerized ordering systems were debated within the CBA, as were the perils of competition from book chains W.H. Smith, Coles, and Louis Melzack's Classic Books. In 1973 Jim Lotz reported to the CBA that internal bickering, secrecy, and lack of statistics all hampered the way in which booksellers served their communities.[84] In 1975 the CBA appointed a full-time executive secretary and joined the umbrella organization the Book and Periodical Development Council of Canada. By 1981 CBA president G.M. Beirnes reported that the thriving retail book business accounted for annual sales of $400 million, and that membership had reached 500.[85]

From the late 1960s through the 1970s there emerged a trend to organize according to bookselling specialties and geographic location. In 1967 the Antiquarian Booksellers Association of Canada / Association de la librairie ancienne du Canada was formed, while the 1970s witnessed the creation of provincial organizations in British Columbia and Manitoba, as well as regional organizations serving Western Canada, the Atlantic provinces, and southwestern Ontario. Inspired by particular concerns, such organizations were attuned to local issues and local markets. The British Columbia Booksellers Association, for example, was established in 1974 to address the high costs related to duties, freight, and postage that were endemic to bookselling in British Columbia.

The first professional associations of booksellers and distributors in Quebec were formed in the mid-twentieth century. After a period of sustained growth that saw the number of businesses grow from 68 in 1930 to 264 in 1961, a serious crisis in the book industry threatened the network of bookstores, precipitated by the practice of wholesalers and European suppliers selling directly to the public and to teaching institutions, rather than through the province's retail booksellers.

As a result, the Société des libraires canadiens (SLC) was founded on 8 August 1960. With both retailers and wholesalers as members, the SLC's mandate was to defend the interests of professional booksellers, and to represent their collective interests to the Quebec government. As a member of the Conseil supérieur du livre, an umbrella organization representing various sectors of the Quebec book trade, in 1963 the SLC supported the Conseil's demand that the Lesage government regulate the book market. The brief submitted by the SLC to the resulting Commission d'enquête sur le commerce du livre dans la province de Québec, chaired by Maurice Bouchard, outlined the situation of retail bookstores and proposed a series of measures to revitalize the sector. The commission's recommendations supported the SLC's suggestions, but the government was slow to implement them. While the government did pursue the accreditation of bookstores through Bill 90 (SQ, 1965, 1st session, C-21), a status that would be granted only to those retailers carrying at least a specified minimum of Canadian stock, the bill did not give retailers the exclusive right of selling textbooks to schools, even though this condition had been one of the key recommendations of the Bouchard Commission.[86] Consequently, Canadian and foreign publishers continued to sell textbooks directly to institutions, to the despair of retailers.

The SLC was regularly split by the divergent interests of the wholesalers and retailers among its membership. Quebec's book distribution system was dominated by the wholesalers, who imposed their will on retailers. Organized under the Société des libraires grossistes canadiens since 1954, wholesalers still retained some power in the book industry at the end of the 1960s. Because of this, the SLC made no effort to establish an effective supply system for imported books. Retailers sought repeatedly, with little success, to free themselves from the wholesalers' grip and to advance their point of view. To this end, they created short-lived associations such as the Société des libraires de détail du Québec in 1964 and the Corporation des libraires du Québec in 1973.

In addition to representing the interests of its members, from 1965 the SLC offered one-day workshops on bookselling to remedy shortcomings in training. In 1969 the society was succeeded by the Association des libraires du Québec (ALQ), which organized yearly training seminars. During the 1970s, despite internal divisions, the ALQ continued to represent booksellers before the government. For example, as French and American companies, in particular Librairie Hachette, which had been in Quebec since the 1950s, gained increasing control of the distribution sector,[87] the ALQ pressured the government to take action. In 1972 an Order-in-Council was issued to modify Bill 90: the revised legislation obliged institutions subsidized by the government to obtain their books from bookstores in their region. However, it was not until 1979 that the Act Respecting the Development of Quebec Firms in the Book Industry (RSQ, c. D-8.1), known as Bill 51, was adopted. This law, which came into force in 1981, gave bookstores wholly owned by Canadian citizens resident in Quebec the exclusive right to sell books to institutions.[88]

The Société des libraires grossistes canadiens disbanded in 1970. In 1978 the exclusive distributors, who had finally replaced the wholesalers, created their own association, the Association des distributeurs exclusifs de livres en langue française (ADELF). Meanwhile, in 1975, following the adoption of measures by the provincial government, the Canada Council for the Arts contributed to the establishment of the Société de promotion du livre (SPL), which in its first year began publishing *Le Livre d'ici*, a weekly listing of new books published in Quebec. By 1980 it had grown to three pages and included reports on the book industry. In 1982, under the title *Livre d'ici*, the publication was transformed into the 'monthly magazine of the publishing world.' In this fifteen-page format, which was financed in part by advertising, reviews became less frequent and finally disappeared. The magazine became a vehicle for the Quebec book industry, replacing *Vient de paraître*, the 'official organ of the Conseil supérieur du livre.' In its first few years, the SPL also produced a weekly radio broadcast entitled *Livre d'ici*, which was hosted by Louise Deschâtelets and Marcel Dubé and was devoted to the promotion of Quebec literature.

By the early 1980s, after many struggles and many disappointments, the book industry in Quebec was better organized. Thanks to the work of the associations, the importance of maintaining a network of independent booksellers was recognized by the public authorities and an effective distribution system had been established. It was primarily in this decade that the positive effects of Bill 51 began to be felt throughout the entire book industry in Quebec.

PART SEVEN

REACHING READERS

chapter 15

LIBRARIES

Government Libraries

ROSS GORDON

Before 1918 most government libraries in Canada were affiliated with the country's legislative bodies. Some federal departments and institutions maintained their own libraries in Ottawa, such as the Departments of Agriculture, Defence, and Mines, along with the Dominion Archives and the Supreme Court, both of whose collections were offshoots of the Library of Parliament. In 1918 the list expanded when libraries were established at the National Gallery of Canada, the Dominion Bureau of Statistics, and the Department of Labour. The National Research Council of Canada's library dates from 1924, followed by those of Transport Canada in 1925 and the Bank of Canada in 1935.

At the provincial level, while every province had established a legislative or provincial library by 1918,[1] there were few other government libraries. In 1939 Ontario claimed a dozen, unlike the other provinces, most of which supported only one additional library, often affiliated with its department of education, archives, or provincial museum.[2] Provincial legislative libraries enhanced their official mandate for the provision of reference services to their sponsoring governments by adding varying degrees of public service. For example, in 1929 the legislative library of Prince Edward Island became by statute a legislative library, a public library, and art gallery.[3] In Quebec the library of the Legislative Assembly long served the general public and the university community as well as government administrators. In British

Columbia, the legislative library's 'open shelf collection' supplemented public access to books.[4]

The inclusion of service to the general public sometimes sparked criticism. Reflecting on the dual roles pursued by the library of the New Brunswick legislature, one commentator argued in 1930 that 'by offering a free and unsatisfactory substitute' for a public library, 'the principal result [of the legislative library was] ... to prevent the people of Fredericton from themselves organizing and supporting a good municipal library.' In contrast, Ontario's legislative librarians viewed the purpose of their institutions as specialized and accordingly confined most of their efforts to servicing the legislature and courts.[5] Similarly, the federal Library of Parliament, although recognized as one of the oldest and largest libraries in Canada with continuous legal deposit since 1841, did not act as a de facto national library with service to the general public. The country had to wait until 1953 for the establishment of its national library, as described in the following account by Paul McCormick.

The nationwide survey of Canada's libraries whose findings, published in 1933, became known as the Ridington Report identified the absence of a national library as one factor that had inhibited the development of Canada's library infrastructure and the development of government libraries, in particular. The Ridington Report placed most of the blame for the poor showing of government libraries on federal and provincial administrations that had starved the institutions of both funding and appropriately trained staff.[6] It noted that the Dominion government and the provinces possessed libraries of varying degrees of usefulness which differed widely in their physical organization, collections activities, efficiency, and service, circumstances ascribed to 'fitful government aid' and a lack of concerted policy.[7] While patronage often influenced appointments to the management of government libraries, some beneficiaries exhibited a strong commitment to their positions. Such was the case in Manitoba, British Columbia, and Saskatchewan, where the quality of collections attracted the notice of scholars from abroad.[8]

When Charles McCombs followed up on the Ridington Report in 1940, he found the overall situation of Canadian government libraries largely unchanged.[9] Except for British Columbia, all provincial libraries suffered from unhealthy political influence, under-funding, confusion of purpose, poorly trained staff, absence of standard library practices, and inadequate cataloguing. Moreover, while he estimated some 500,000 titles in the Library of Parliament, these items were so poorly arranged and catalogued that this substantial collection was almost useless.[10] More positively, Quebec's legislative library possessed an extensive collection of 170,000 volumes with strengths in history and Canadiana, and in 1937 began to send its staff for professional training. Signs of progress were also evident on the Prairies: in 1935 the government of Saskatchewan established a legal basis for the appointment of a legislative librarian, and in 1939 Manitoba passed a new Legislative Library Act, which created the Department of the Legislative Library. Nonetheless, all legislative libraries were plagued by a fundamental difficulty in obtaining documents from other provinces and from the Dominion government. Despite the establishment of the Depository Services Program in 1927, coordination was insufficient, and legal status was needed to formalize the deposit of documents.

McCombs also identified archives as an area of concern. Before the Second World War, the management of public archives was haphazard. Some legislative libraries also served as archives. The most important collections were in the Dominion Archives, and the legislative libraries of Quebec, British Columbia, and Nova Scotia. While Quebec's provincial archives were initiated in 1920, no consistent policy prevailed across the country with regard to the reception and preservation of public papers, and only British Columbia had given the archivist authority over the destruction of papers no longer wanted by government departments. In Manitoba and Saskatchewan, the legislative libraries held small collections of manuscript material, but government papers were often sent to local universities.[11] The management of federal archives improved in 1945 when a Public Records Committee, chaired by the secretary of state with the Dominion archivist as vice-chairman, was established by Privy Council Order to oversee 'the state of the public records.' The committee's duties included reviewing documents recommended by their departments for destruction or transfer to the Dominion Archives.[12]

Some of the difficulties experienced by government libraries through the 1930s and 1940s were ameliorated by the recruitment of better-trained staff and the increased organization of librarians into professional associations. The Canadian Library Association / Association canadienne des bibliothèques (CLA), which was founded in 1946, began to address the problems of legislative and government libraries through its Government Reference Libraries Committee. In 1948 it recommended that government publications be distributed and collected in an organized manner, that Canadian library education programs pay more attention to training in the area of government documents, and that uniform statutes be developed for the administration of legislative libraries.[13]

Improvements among government libraries accelerated as a result of general post-war expansion as well as the awareness of Canada's print heritage engendered by the Massey Commission. Recommendations from the Massey Report included the cataloguing of 'all government publications, federal, provincial and municipal,'[14] a responsibility assumed by *Canadiana*, a bilingual, national bibliography which has listed federal and provincial government publications since 1951. The immediate post-war years also saw the founding of the library of the federal Department of Finance and Treasury Board in 1947, and the legislative library of the new province of Newfoundland in 1949.

In 1953, when the CLA began to coordinate its efforts with the newly founded National Library, government libraries were a high priority. Funds were earmarked for expansion, collections grew, and professional librarians were hired as chief executive officers in most provinces. By 1960, although their chief librarians had no formal training in the field, British Columbia and Quebec had increased the number of professionals on staff; only Prince Edward Island and Newfoundland still lacked trained librarians.[15]

The 1950s proved a decade of significant gain for departmental libraries within federal and provincial governments. In the late 1940s, 51 such libraries existed at the federal level – the vast majority in Ottawa – while 32 functioned within provincial governments. Some of the larger libraries, such as those of the Department of Agriculture, the Dominion Bureau of Statistics, and the National Research Council, each with over 50,000 volumes, reported substantial loans. On the provincial side, a collective 960,000 volumes and 396,078 pamphlets were made available to 10,669 borrowers. Roughly one-third of the staff at both levels had formal library training.[16] By 1956 the number of departmental libraries had increased to 109 at the federal level, and more than one hundred operated provincially. Fifty-seven of the federal libraries were located in Ottawa-Hull and nine elsewhere in Ontario, while the others, spread across Canada, were for the most part branches of Agriculture Canada and the Department of Fisheries and Oceans.[17]

In 1968 the highly specialized nature of some federal department and agency libraries was recognized in a survey undertaken by National Librarian W. Kaye Lamb and Chief Librarian of the National Science Library Jack E. Brown. They designated as 'stand alone' libraries those of the Departments of Agriculture, Labour, National Health and Welfare, and National Defence, as well as those of agencies such as the Geological Survey, the National Gallery of Canada, the Dominion Bureau of Statistics, the National Museum, the Public Archives, and the Supreme Court. 'Stand alone' status acknowledged the size, professional specificity, and authority of these collections, circumstances that led Lamb and Brown to recommend that the

National Library avoid duplicating the collecting activities of these libraries. In contrast to these libraries, which clearly required highly trained staff, were the work-a-day collections held by other departments and agencies. Their contents, largely confined to 'textbooks, manuals, and handbooks,' did not require the supervision of professional librarians. Despite shifts in perception and significant gains in professionalism, in the 1960s librarians within the government service were still struggling for recognition. 'We feel that it is essential that the librarian should be in close contact with officials at the policy-making level,' Lamb and Brown remarked, for in some cases librarians reported to supervisors many levels below the real decision-makers of their departments.[18]

Libraries continued to proliferate within government in the 1970s. Newcomers included those in the offices of the Solicitor General (1969) and the Auditor General (1977). In 1974 a survey by the National Library identified many problems concerning services, staffing, and infrastructure in 193 libraries affiliated with federal departments, agencies, and Crown corporations.[19] It found the federal library service 'characterized by an uneven quality of service to users which reflects the varying degrees of interest and importance that departments and agencies attach to their libraries.'[20] Problems were attributed to small budgets, inadequate staff and space, and low status within the departmental structure. Among the exceptions were scientific research libraries, which were understood and appreciated by the departments and agencies that supported them. The report's 157 recommendations called for greater integration among government libraries, noting that the National Library had 'the statutory authority to coordinate federal library services.'[21]

This report led to the creation of the Council of Federal Libraries / Conseil des bibliothèques du gouvernement fédéral (CFL), established in 1976 by the national librarian. Subsequent sharing of resources, coordinated through the National Library, has enabled the hundreds of libraries spread across regional and departmental boundaries to function more economically and to better serve their various clients. The CFL also advises the national librarian on matters related to library services and access to information within the federal government, and promotes communication, co-operation, and professional development among federal library staff.[22]

Between the 1950s and the 1980s, Canada's government libraries stood at the forefront of introducing research aids and information technologies to elected officials, civil servants, and public users as departmental libraries branched into regions across the nation. The National Library, often through the offices of the CFL, tried to ensure some balance between libraries large and small, regional and central, by pressing for shared resources and collection development.

The Canada Institute for Scientific and Technical Information

BERTRUM H. MACDONALD

The Canada Institute for Scientific and Technical Information traces its origins to an announcement made by National Research Council of Canada (NRCC) president Henry Marshall Tory in 1924, stating the intention to develop 'a library that would serve scientific workers everywhere in Canada.'[23] Margaret Gill, who was appointed NRCC librarian four years later, assiduously guided an expansion of collections and services. In 1932, when the library moved into the new NRCC Laboratories building in Ottawa, it consisted of 12,000 volumes; when Gill retired in 1957, the collection had grown to 350,000.[24] Gill was succeeded by Jack E. Brown, the NRCC's first professionally educated librarian, whose mandate was to develop the leading science and technical library in the country. By 1970 the holdings were almost triple their 1957 total.[25]

To distinguish its position in relation to the National Library of Canada (est. 1953), the NRCC library assumed the role of National Science Library (NSL), a change confirmed in 1966 by an amendment to the legislation governing the council.[26] That year, the library also became the national library for health sciences. Through the 1960s the NSL began the first of many initiatives involving computerized products and services: the first database in 1962, the use of telex in 1964, the first national computerized selective information dissemination service (CAN/SDI) and the introduction of fax machines, both in 1969.[27] In 1972 the first real-time information tracking system in Canada (CAN/OLE) was created. These computerized systems supported a growing demand for access to scientific and technical information. By 1983 more than 200,000 copies and loans of documents were generated, 'more than any other specialized information centre in North America.'[28]

The Canada Institute for Scientific and Technical Information (CISTI), created in 1974 through the merger of the National Science Library with the Technical

Information Service, another NRCC unit, occupied a large new building in Ottawa, which was purposefully designed as a modern information centre.[29] The mandate of CISTI was 'to promote and provide for the use of scientific and technical information by the government and people of Canada for the purposes of economic, regional and social development.'[30] Among the federal government directives to the NRCC that influenced the creation and development of CISTI were two 1969 reports commissioned by the Science Council of Canada – Report no. 6, *A Policy for Scientific and Technical Information Dissemination,* and a multi-volume Special Study no. 8, *Scientific and Technical Information in Canada.* In Jack Brown's later assessment, the sixth report had the most impact since it aimed to define 'a national policy for the dissemination of scientific and technical information services which [would] be relevant to the present and future needs of the generators, processors, disseminators and users of information in Canada,'[31] and recommended the establishment of a national board to direct scientific and technical information dissemination activities.[32] In 1969 the NRCC created the Advisory Board for Scientific and Technical Information (ABSTI), with 'prominent representatives of generators, processors, and users of information.'[33]

Two years after the Science Council reports, the Organization for Economic Co-operation and Development (OECD) published its *Review of National Scientific and Information Policy, Canada*, which examined the national information policy efforts of the federal government, the National Library, the NRCC, and the NSL. While the OECD report identified some weaknesses, it gave a positive assessment of the scientific and technical information environment in Canada, finding a good foundation upon which to continue to build a national network. Another significant study resulted in *A Science Policy for Canada: Report of the Senate Special Committee on Science Policy*, issued in four volumes from 1970 to 1977 by a Senate committee chaired by Senator Maurice Lamontagne. Its many recommendations included the notion that any 'new system should recover most of its cost from its users.'[34] This view had far-reaching implications as CISTI became more entrepreneurial in subsequent decades. Through the 1980s, the private sector played an increasing role in Canada's scientific and technical information network.

Responding to international developments in science and technology and to homegrown policy initiatives, CISTI became one of the world's leading libraries in the last decades of the twentieth century. From modest beginnings, it had created collections and services that were essential for research and development in the country and had achieved both national and international stature.

National Library of Canada

PAUL MCCORMICK

'That a National Library finds no place among the federal institutions which we have been required to examine is a remarkable fact which has been the occasion of much sharp comment during our sessions,'[35] stated the Massey Report of 1951, thereby providing the final impetus for the creation of an institution that had been under discussion for almost a century. Earlier advocates included such prominent figures as Canada's first prime minister, Sir John A. Macdonald, who in 1883 had called for 'a National Library containing every book worthy of being kept on the shelves of a library.'[36] Seven decades later, in 1953, the National Library of Canada was finally established – less to enact Macdonald's lofty vision than to begin its mission of building a national collection, coordinating legal deposit and implementing bibliographic control, and providing national bibliographic services. In 2004 the library would merge with the National Archives of Canada to form Library and Archives Canada / Bibliothèque et Archives Canada.

The vehemence of the Massey Report obscures the fact that efforts to establish the National Library of Canada were already well underway by 1951. Responding to a joint submission presented in 1946 by the Royal Society of Canada, the Canadian Library Association, and several other groups, the government's appointment of Dominion Archivist W. Kaye Lamb in 1948 included special responsibilities for planning a library and chairing a National Library Advisory Committee. A recommendation that same year from the Joint Committee on the Library of Parliament gave rise in 1950 to the Canadian Bibliographic Centre, a facility that was a 'first step toward the creation of a National Library.'[37] Once established in May 1950, the centre quickly began to produce a bilingual, national bibliography, *Canadiana*. Initiated as a monthly publication in January 1951, it took over the *Canadian Catalogue of Books Published in Canada, about Canada, as Well as Those Written by Canadians*, an annual compilation produced by the Toronto Public Library from 1921 to 1949. The centre also began to collate the holdings of the country's major libraries into a national union catalogue.[38]

Passed in June 1952, the National Library Act (1 Elizabeth 2, 1952, c. 31) came into effect 1 January 1953, with Dominion Archivist Lamb additionally appointed National Librarian. The secretary of state became the federal minister responsible for the library, and established a National Library Advisory Board. The new organization absorbed the responsibilities of the Canadian Bibliographic Centre, as well as all its fourteen staff. Jean Lunn was initially editor of *Canadiana* and later director of the Cataloguing Branch; Assistant National Librarian Adèle de G. Languedoc held her position from 1964 to 1969; and Martha Shepard, director of the centre responsible for the union catalogue, later became director of the Public Services Branch.

The first *Report of the National Librarian*, issued in 1953, set the context and pattern for the new institution and described some of its critical services. Foremost was the maintenance of the national bibliography: the mission of *Canadiana* was 'to furnish as complete a record as possible of new publications of Canadian origin or authorship, together with such other publications as may, for a variety of reasons, be of special interest to Canadians.'[39] The legal deposit requirement included in the National Library Act, which obliged Canadian publishers to submit two copies of books, pamphlets, and annuals upon their issue, served two purposes: it permitted the bibliographic and subject descriptions of these materials to be created centrally and shared with libraries and the Canadian book trade through *Canadiana*; and it ensured the comprehensive collection of Canadian publications by the National Library.

Other endeavours of 1953 included checklists of Canadian fiction and theses. By 31 March 1953, almost 1.3 million catalogue cards from some fifty Canadian libraries had been microfilmed for the national union catalogue, and a book location service had been established. Also underway was a large microfilming project to capture rare titles listed in Marie Tremaine's *Bibliography of Canadian Imprints, 1751–1800*. And, at long last, planning began for a National Library building that would permit the delivery of direct services to the public and the housing of collections, including some 300,000 volumes transferred from the Library of Parliament, which had long collected Canadiana as well as non-Canadian titles that had been registered for copyright protection in Canada by Canadian and foreign publishers.

Under Lamb's leadership, the services and collections of the National Library of Canada were firmly established, with the day-to-day achievements of the institution accomplished by a small, capable staff that grew only modestly during the first few years of the library's existence. Accounts of indexes and bibliographies under development were a staple feature of his reports. In March 1967, for example, he described many services and activities. In the preceding fiscal year, *Canadiana* had listed 12,732 items in English and French, covering trade and general publications, pamphlets, theses available on microfilm, and publications issued by the federal, provincial, and territorial governments. That year, the library received some 6,100 Canadian books, pamphlets, and periodical titles on legal deposit; as well, it generated extensive book production statistics for UNESCO. *Canadian Theses* identified over 2,600 theses accepted at Canadian universities, while the library microfilmed over 700. In 1966–7 the institution responded to almost 50,000 interlibrary loan requests and completed work on a union list of serials relating to the social sciences and humanities. The initial research phase of the library's Centennial project of a comprehensive bibliography of Canadiana published between 1867 and 1900 also came to an end, some 25,000 entries having been compiled since 1953 by first Assistant National Librarian Raymond Tanghe (1953–64) and his assistant, Madeleine Pellerin. This project, which continued under Michel Thériault's supervision in the 1970s, saw fruition in 1980 with the launch on microfiche of *Canadiana 1867–1900: Monographs,* a work that would encompass over 67,000 entries. In June 1967 the opening of a purpose-built building that would house the National Library and the Public Archives in a prime location in Ottawa on Wellington Street west of the Parliament Buildings and the Supreme Court rounded out the achievements of the Centennial year and laid the groundwork for a dramatic expansion of collections, services, and staff.

National Librarian Guy Sylvestre was the second to serve in the position, from 1968 to 1983, with Associate National Librarians Lachlan F. MacRae (1970–7) and Hope E.A. Clement (1977–92). To strengthen the National Library's support for Canadian studies and for research into all aspects of the country's published heritage, he acquired major retrospective collections. In 1969 he oversaw revision of the National Library's legal deposit regulations to add sound recordings and second copies of periodicals. Three years later, legal deposit was extended still further to include educational kits of non-book materials. As well, changes in the National Library Act outlined a role for the national librarian in the coordination of library services in the federal government and allowed the National Library to enter into agreements with other libraries and with library and educational associations.

Beginning in 1970 with the creation of the Music Division under Helmut Kallmann, additional specialized collection and service areas were established, including Rare Books and Manuscripts, headed by Liana Van der Bellen; Children's Literature, under the direction of Irene E. Aubrey; Literary Manuscripts, overseen by Claude LeMoine; the Library Documentation Centre, directed by Beryl Anderson; the Multilingual Biblioservice, managed by Marie Zielinska; and the Division for the Visually and Physically Handicapped, under the supervision of Ross Hotson. Major acquisitions included the Georges-A. Daviault Collection of books, pamphlets, and brochures, and the Jacob M. Lowy Collection of Hebraica and Judaica. Other notable initiatives were Olga B. Bishop's *Publications of the Government of the Province of Canada, 1841–1867*, Dorothy E. Ryder's *Canadian Reference Sources*, and a project to add English and French subject headings to all entries in *Canadiana*. Also created were a dedicated organizational unit that specialized in the production of bibliographies on Canadian topics and housed a collection of unpublished bibliographies, and the Canadian Book Exchange Centre to redistribute surplus library materials. Public outreach included major exhibitions celebrating Canadian authors and themes, such as Manitoba Authors and Canadian Authors in Translation (1970), Notable Children's Books, Past and Present (1973), and What Is a Book? (1977).

During the 1970s the National Library of Canada flourished under the leadership of National Librarian Sylvestre. Major national and international initiatives, the development of standards, and the introduction of automation, as well as the strengthening of collections and access infrastructure for research on Canada, characterized the decade, whose many significant events included the National Conference on Cataloguing Standards in 1970, an initiative which led to the establishment of the Canadian Task Group on Cataloguing Standards. Agreements were reached with the Library of Congress to harmonize Dewey Decimal Classification, while the MARC Task Group recommended a distinctive Canadian format for cataloguing. A decentralized Cataloguing in Publication (CIP) program followed in 1976. Support for the first National Conference on the State of Canadian Bibliography (1974) coincided with the creation of the Committee on Bibliographical Services for Canada, which reported to the National Library Advisory Board. The library assumed responsibility for the assignment of International Standard Book Numbers (ISBN) to Canadian book publishers and International Standard Serial Numbers (ISSN) to Canadian periodical publishers. In addition, it established the Task Group on Library Service to the Handicapped.

By 1980 the National Library's list of accomplishments far exceeded what could have been predicted in 1953. From its roots in 1950 with the Canadian Bibliographic Centre to its multiple services and influences in 1980, the National Library of Canada achieved the goal articulated by Guy Sylvestre, soon after his appointment as national librarian in 1968, that the institution reside 'at the core of a network of libraries that extends across the country.'[40]

Bibliothèque nationale du Québec

MARCEL LAJEUNESSE

Created by the Quebec National Assembly in August 1967 (Elizabeth 2, 1966–7, c. 24), the Bibliothèque nationale du Québec (BNQ) opened in Montreal on 1 January 1968. The first provincial institution described as 'national,' its founding affirmed Quebec's culture during the Quiet Revolution. Between 1968 and 1980, the Quebec government substantially raised the BNQ's budget from $345,080 to $3.9 million, an increase of 1,148 per cent. During this period, Georges Cartier served as chief librarian from 1967 to 1973, succeeded by Jean-Rémi Brault, who held the position from 1974 to 1985.

The mandate of the BNQ, which in 2006 became the Bibliothèque et Archives nationales du Québec, is to organize and collect Laurentiana – copies of all books published in Quebec or by Quebec authors, as well as books about Quebec published elsewhere in the world, in their original form whenever possible. Private and government publications have been subject to legal deposit since the BNQ opened. These items form the basis of the *Bibliographie du Québec* (1968–), an ongoing monthly compilation. In addition, the BNQ was mandated to produce a retrospective bibliography of documents published between 1764 and 1967.[41]

When it opened, the BNQ possessed a collection of 115,000 monographs, a third of which were foreign publications, close to 10,000 rare books and documents, and tens of thousands of periodicals and government publications, as well as maps, plans, engravings, and musical scores. The core of the BNQ's original collection was drawn from the former holdings of the Bibliothèque Saint-Sulpice. Acquired by the Quebec government in 1941 (George 6, 1941, c. 8), this library had continued a long-standing Sulpician tradition of engagement with books and public access to reading, earlier evidenced in the parish library of the Œuvre des bons livres (1844), the Cabinet de lecture paroissial (1857), and the Cercle Ville-Marie (1885).[42] Its collections, developed over more than half a century, enriched the foundations of the BNQ with the personal libraries of Adolphe Chapleau, Wilfrid Sicotte, Nazaire Dubois, Louis-Joseph Papineau, Napoléon Bourassa, and Édouard-Zotique Massicotte, as well as some of John Neilson's papers.

The Rise of the Public Library in English Canada

LORNE BRUCE AND ELIZABETH HANSON

The modern public library was coming into its own in Canada when this volume takes up the story, particularly in Ontario, where the enthusiasm of citizens in conjunction with the largesse of the Carnegie Corporation yielded 111 new public library buildings between 1901 and the early 1920s.[43] The future of the public library in post-war Canada was envisioned in 1918: 'The glorious victory of the Allies ... casts a new light on the opportunities and the responsibilities that challenge every Canadian to do his duty in the building of a nobler and better Canada ... Education must play the chief part. The public library is the promoter of popular education. There is an attractive field for service for every librarian and library trustee.'[44]

In 1918 the most significant characteristic of the modern public library was that it was funded by municipal tax money, allowing all residents of a community to have access to the service at little or no charge. In 1919 the *Ontario Library Review* described the public library in post-war Canada as 'a place for collecting the best books and for making them useful.' Hence the public library 'attempts to put the right book into the hands of every reader,' ensures that 'boys and girls are helped and guided' in their reading, and always seeks new patrons.[45] For more than a decade after the war, the focus of the public library was almost exclusively local. As the century unfolded, an important development would be the broadening of the patron base in conjunction with an ever-widening notion of the communities the library should serve.

Although the concept of the public library was well established by 1918, its realization had been only selectively achieved across Canada. In 1920–1, 186 of the country's 210 free public libraries were in Ontario; these libraries held 75 per cent of the volumes in circulation.[46] At the time, Ontario's public libraries served just over half the province's 2.9 million citizens. Ontario's revised Public Libraries Act of 1920 created the framework for further library development over the four succeeding decades. Leading these changes was William O. Carson, provincial inspector of public libraries from 1916 to 1929. Carson favoured per capita funding for libraries based on community size, improved support from the provincial Department of Education (under whose purview public libraries fell), and better training of library staff. During his term, public library boards, provincial grants, expenditures on books, circulation, and the percentage of the population served all increased significantly.[47]

In addition, his office published an important practical treatise, *Reference Work and Reference Works* (1920), and offered training courses in librarianship.[48]

Although Ontario dominated in public library development, during the 1920s British Columbia also took significant steps toward improving public library service. Supported by funds from the Carnegie Corporation, in 1927 the British Columbia Public Library Commission hired an American consultant to survey library conditions throughout the province. The 'most ambitious [survey] of the sort ever attempted in the Dominion,' it led to recommendations for 'a province-wide library policy, and plans for its effective working,' including 'a scheme by which book-service may reach every citizen, from the resident of the cities to the prospector in the mountain gulch and the logger in the lumber camp.'[49] In the absence of county boundaries, the report recommended 'the recognition of library districts based upon the co-operation of the municipal and school units included within the proposed area.'[50] Funded by a further $100,000 from the Carnegie Corporation, the Fraser Valley Library Demonstration was established to test this idea, under the direction of Helen Stewart, former librarian of the Victoria Public Library. When this successful experiment ended in the middle of the Depression, voters in twenty of the original twenty-four districts supported its continuance. Subsequently adopted by other provinces and countries, the regional library concept is a unique contribution to public librarianship.

The report through which this concept became known was *Libraries in Canada: A Study of Library Conditions and Needs* (1933). Funded by the American Library Association through a Carnegie Corporation grant, this first national survey of all types of libraries was undertaken by John Ridington, librarian of the University of British Columbia, Mary Black, librarian of the Fort William Public Library in Ontario, and George Locke, chief librarian of the Toronto Public Library (TPL). Noting that 'too often the library is the Cinderella of the municipal family,' falling well behind fire protection, policing, and schools in its claims for financing, the commission made three general recommendations for Canada as a whole.[51] First, it proposed 'the creation of larger administrative library units, based on the county, or a co-operative combination of urban and rural municipalities into a Regional Library District [like those in British Columbia].' The second recommendation favoured 'extension of library service, by branch libraries, library trucks, etc., until it is as nearly universal as the postal system.' Finally, the commissioners recommended 'competent professional supervision of library activities as a direct responsibility of provincial government.'[52]

The Ridington Report provides a snapshot of public library service in the early 1930s. In the commissioners' estimation, about four-fifths of Canada's 10.5 million citizens were 'utterly without library service of any kind.' Worse still, only three of nine provincial governments (Newfoundland would not enter Confederation until 1949) gave 'more than a pious, theoretical approval to the principle that the library is an integral part of a people's welfare and education programme, or that, as such, it deserves and demands attention, direction and support, as a governmental policy, responsibility and duty.' In addition, Canada's regional structure was evident in its library service, with responsibilities in 'the hands of nine different authorities,' because libraries fell under provincial rather than federal purview.[53]

The commissioners noted that in 1931 only five provinces – Ontario, British Columbia, Manitoba, Saskatchewan, and Alberta – had general public library legislation in place, and even the best – Ontario's – needed revision, while some of the others 'might well be entirely rewritten ... A majority ... do nothing more than permit the formation of libraries. Only four have supervising agencies ... None provides for an adequate income.' In making their point, the commissioners set out four 'qualifications for a good Library Act': (1) 'A definite statement of the purpose of a public library, basing its claim for public recognition and financial support on the same grounds of service as other educational institutions'; (2) 'A central supervising and energizing agency'; (3) 'Representative and responsible management'; and (4) 'A sure and adequate income.'[54]

As library advocates and officials identified services in need of improvement, the Depression provided an opportunity to demonstrate the value of public libraries. While funding was cut, usage of libraries dramatically increased.[55] As George Locke explained, the TPL had 'gone after the man without a job, and has, by means of a series of carefully selected and attractive books, said ... "If you would make yourself more efficient in your trade or profession, or if you would seek what you think may be a more attractive trade or profession, the Public Library will provide the books which are recognized as being the best authorities and make them accessible to you."'[56] Kathleen Jenkins, chief librarian of the Westmount Public Library in Quebec, remembered both the practical and compassionate aspects of serving the public during these years. 'There were so few of us to cope with the crowds, many of them individuals unfamiliar with a library of any sort,' she recalled, yet the library staff 'never stopped running – up and down stairs, across the reference room, searching for books which might help some poor soul learn new skills, and less tangible but terribly important, just listening and talking.'[57]

While the importance of public libraries became more apparent during the Depression, many Canadians still lacked library service. To serve rural residents more effectively, Ontario communities began to experiment with co-operative libraries based on county jurisdictions despite the absence of enabling legislation.[58] Prince Edward Island followed British Columbia's lead, initiating a second regional library demonstration funded by the Carnegie Corporation. In Quebec, however, where the influence of the Catholic Church in social and cultural matters was strong among the francophone population, public libraries remained virtually absent in the 1930s, a situation explained by Marcel Lajeunesse in the following article. Until 1959 public libraries in Quebec would continue to be actively discouraged, except in locations where an anglophone enclave held sway over a municipal government. Enduring libraries for specific communities include the Fraser-Hickson Library, a subscription library founded in Montreal in 1885; the Westmount Public Library, founded in 1897; and Montreal's Jewish Public Library, founded in 1914.

Despite a tradition of social and mechanics' institutes, Nova Scotia lacked much public library activity in the 1930s. Most service was centred in towns and cities, such as Yarmouth, Truro, Sydney, and Halifax, though Ridington and his colleagues reported that the Halifax library had 'scandalously inadequate' financing, ill-trained staff, poor administration, and atrocious housing.[59] On a more positive note, the province's superintendent of education expressed a modern outlook on public library development. In the spring of 1937, as a result of interest in a regional library for Cape Breton, the government passed an Act to Provide for the Support of Regional Libraries (SNS, 1937, c. 11). Later that year, Nora Bateson, formerly of the Fraser Valley Regional Library and the Prince Edward Island Library Demonstration, was hired to conduct a survey of libraries in Nova Scotia.

Bateson's activities went far beyond ascertaining present library conditions: she identified the need 'for a province-wide system of county libraries'; in addition, she laid out a plan for provincial library service whose recommendations included the creation of a public library commission, the hiring of a director of libraries, and sound library legislation.[60] The first two recommendations were speedily enacted, and in the spring of 1938 the legislature amended the act of 1937 to incorporate the new commission and director of libraries (SNS, 1938, c. 57). Bateson's plan also gar-nered financial support from the Carnegie Corporation, which granted $50,000 for new books. Bateson continued to work for the library cause in Nova Scotia, endeav-ouring to establish a regional library in Cape Breton, whose residents unfortunately proved unable to support the system through tax dollars.

Despite such notable accomplishments during the 1930s, access to public librar-ies in Canada as a whole still remained sparse at the end of the decade. By 1938 more than 90 per cent of urban inhabitants had access to libraries, but 58 per cent of those in small towns and villages, and 95 per cent of rural residents, remained without

service.[61] In the Prairie provinces the number of public libraries had increased significantly after the passage of legislation early in the century. Nonetheless, through the
1930s and into the 1940s many Prairie residents, particularly in rural areas, depended
on provincial travelling libraries as well as libraries established by co-operative
groups, such as the Homemaker's Club of Saskatchewan, the United Farm Women
of Alberta, the Women's Institute, and the provincial wheat pools, the last two of
which are discussed in chapter 18 in case studies by Jean Cogswell and Elise Moore.
These organizations, which linked libraries to education, community betterment,
and equal rights, encouraged the transformation of institute collections into public
libraries. Of the three provinces, Manitoba was the slowest to do so: in 1930 only 5
public libraries were in existence compared to 40 institute libraries. Saskatchewan,
in comparison, established 73 public libraries by 1933, when fewer than 20 mechanics' and literary institute collections remained in that province.[62]

While the Depression and the Second World War inhibited the overall growth of
public libraries, the 1930s and 1940s were important decades for librarians and their
organizations. The Ridington Report made Ontario's librarians more conscious of
the need for systematic planning, and for provincial and national alliances. To that
end, the Ontario Library Association (OLA) presented a brief to the Royal Commission on Dominion-Provincial Relations in 1938 and organized joint conferences with
Quebec and Maritime librarians in Ottawa in 1937 and Montreal in 1939. At the second conference, the Canadian Association of Children's Librarians was formed with
the goal of promoting reading on a national scale, a topic further developed by
Lorna Knight in chapter 17. After the war, the OLA lobbied for improved legislation
and an expanded provincial library service, while the Canadian Library Council
(CLC) published *Libraries in the Life of the Canadian Nation*, presenting the results of a
new survey of public libraries.[63] According to the CLC, public library service still varied widely in 1946 and remained 'almost non-existent' in some provinces. Identifying 'gaps in urban service,' it noted that 'Fredericton and Quebec [City] have no
public libraries' and that in 'Manitoba there are only two tax-supported libraries –
Winnipeg and Brandon.'[64]

After the end of the war, public libraries moved into a new phase of development, particularly with regard to regional library systems. In the immediate post-
war period, Ontario's plans revolved around larger administrative units, such as the
co-operative county libraries that developed in the southwestern region and provided bookmobile services to rural populations, a phenomenon addressed in Eric
Bungay's case study in chapter 18. New county library legislation replaced these co-
operatives in 1957, followed two years later by regional co-operative legislation

supported by a revamped Provincial Library System. By contrast, public library activity in Nova Scotia stumbled in the immediate post-war period under an unsympathetic provincial administration. However, the situation dramatically altered in 1948 when Peter Grossman of the Fraser Valley Regional Library in British Columbia became Nova Scotia's director of libraries, and Alberta Letts, who had worked in county library service in Ontario and Ohio, became assistant director. In January 1949 the Annapolis Valley Regional Library was established, and two years later the long-desired library in Cape Breton finally became a reality. Regional libraries followed in Colchester–East Hants and Pictou County. By the late 1940s, regional libraries had been established on the Prairies, supported by new legislation in Saskatchewan (1946), Manitoba (1948), and Alberta (1956). A federal survey undertaken in 1958 determined that 77.7 per cent of the Canadian population had access to public libraries, 'with 95.1 per cent of the population in centres over 10,000 served.' Those residing in communities under 10,000 and rural areas had access to regional and provincial public library services, to the extent of 65.1 per cent.[65] In 1959 Quebec passed its first public libraries act, legislation that created the Service des bibliothèques du Québec.

Between 1960 and 1980, public libraries experienced rapid growth and shifts in policy. Across the country more than one hundred library buildings were either built or remodelled as Centennial projects in 1967, including fifteen in communities in Newfoundland that had never before enjoyed a public library. By the end of the Centennial year, 'every province and the two Territories had at least partial coverage by regional libraries.'[66]

Ontario's new public libraries act of 1966, which removed some traditional funding clauses, formed the basis for rapid, sometimes conflicting, developments in service up to the mid-1980s. With differing resources and financial bases, the fourteen library regions were successful in instituting better communication patterns, introducing technology such as the telex, which aided interlibrary loans. Metropolitan Toronto, which assumed TPL's reference collection, opened a new reference library in the heart of the city in 1977. Across Ontario, newly created regional film 'pools' and union catalogues of audiovisual resources provided local libraries and individuals with a broad range of popular materials.[67] By 1980, 99 per cent of Ontarians had direct access to public library service. Multilingual collections, which had been available mainly in urban libraries in earlier decades, were now being offered in smaller libraries. Outreach services, such as book deliveries to homebound readers, a topic developed at greater length by Lorna Knight in chapter 18, had also appeared by 1970.[68]

At the national level, 1980 marked completion of a new cross-country survey of Canada's libraries. Sponsored by the Canadian Library Association, *Project Progress* focused on the market orientation of libraries, shifting demographic patterns, and the provision of information to the private sector. The report also identified the importance of technological advances that were beginning to transform reference and information services, and the need for ongoing training of management and staff.[69] Few of the report's recommendations, however, were enacted. In some parts of Canada, librarians remained preoccupied with the provision of basic service. Notable were new efforts in the North: in 1980 the Yukon spent more than $31 per capita in extending library service, about $13 more per resident than Ontario.[70] Reflecting on the situation in the territory just a few years earlier, one librarian noted that 'an aspect of working in the Yukon which is difficult to convey is the relationship between the small population, 23,000, and the size of the area, 207,203 square miles ... There are so few people ... that almost every individual can be dealt with on a personal basis.'[71]

Between the First World War and the 1980s, the goals of improving service for a broadening reading public, developing bibliographic systems, and linking citizens with information remained constant in Canada's public library community. Ever increasing emphasis on co-operation facilitated those efforts. Progressive refinements in service to communities, the introduction of the regional library service model, advances in technology, the growth of the liberal welfare state in the public services sector, bilingualism, and multiculturalism provided the framework for library promoters' innovations. By 1980, as libraries united in co-operative efforts to share resources and apply automation to daily operations, the old relationships with printed resources were in transition: an electronic future was offering challenges that in the succeeding decades would require further study and action.

The Public Library in Quebec

MARCEL LAJEUNESSE

In 1924 Quebec's Bureau of Statistics noted fifteen public, municipal, or association libraries – six in Montreal, seven in Quebec City, one in Sherbrooke, and one in

Shawinigan – holding a total of 556,374 publications.[72] From the 1920s through the 1940s, among francophones the primary source of public reading material was parish libraries, 80 per cent of which had been founded in the nineteenth century. In 1925 there were 225 parish libraries holding 155,650 publications; one-third of these belonged to four institutions,[73] and only the libraries run by religious orders (Jesuits, Oblates, Redemptorists, and Sulpicians) possessed collections of any size.[74]

In 1930, during the Quebec hearings of the Ridington Commission, Premier Taschereau stated, 'A public library is not without its perils to our modern generation, and specially to the younger ones.'[75] The commission noted that the Montreal City Library, in the middle of the Depression, demanded a deposit of $3 to $6 to borrow books, and regarded the Westmount Public Library as exemplary for its building, collection, and staff. The commission cited 175 parish libraries, many of them moribund, which spent an average of $50 a year on book purchases. Its members were puzzled by the singularly dismal situation of public libraries in Quebec, so very different from that of the rest of Canada and the United States. Their correspondence during their deliberations reveals they did not know what to make of these 'so-called libraries.'[76] Their report nonetheless recommended the development of parish libraries, even though they had little faith in them. It noted that there were more radios per inhabitant in Quebec than anywhere else in Canada or the United States and that the newspaper with the largest circulation in Canada was *La Presse*, the Montreal French-language daily.[77]

The 1940s were a favourable period for the development of public libraries in Quebec. In November 1944, the library school of the Université de Montréal, which was founded in 1937, published a manifesto titled *Les bibliothèques dans la province de Québec: La formule des progrès futurs*, which was circulated widely by *Le Devoir*, *L'Action catholique*, *Le Droit*, *Relations*, the Société Saint-Jean-Baptiste, and the Quebec Assembly of Archbishops and Bishops. It called for the establishment of a provincial library commission attached to the Catholic Committee of the Department of Public Instruction, but no such body was ever created.[78] The first French-language professional association, the Association canadienne des bibliothèques d'institution, was founded in 1943. During the war, when Montreal became a world hub of French-language publishing, new houses, a surge of publications (including reprints), and the introduction of literary supplements in newspapers stimulated interest in reading and encouraged the development of libraries. The Montreal City Library abolished the cash deposit demanded of subscribers, which had discouraged library use, and opened new branches in various neighbourhoods.

After the Second World War, Quebec's librarians found it difficult to define their role, hesitating between the model of the North American public library and that of the parish library. In *Plaidoyer pour les bibliothèques publiques,* which envisioned the American model, the librarian of the provincial legislature, Georges-Émile Marquis, stated that 'our directives should no longer come from Europe, since the centre of the world today from every point of view is no longer on that side of the Atlantic.'[79] Edmond Desrochers, another proponent of American methods, wrote a pamphlet titled *Le rôle social des bibliothèques publiques,* which saw libraries playing a role in popular education similar to that in place across the border.[80] Raymond Tanghe, however, felt that parish libraries were more likely to reinstate the sense of social solidarity that had dwindled in urban centres.[81] During the 1940s and 1950s, several Quebec municipalities founded public libraries; among the 24 libraries counted in 1956 were those of Drummondville, Ville Mont-Royal, Richmond, Rock Island, St-Jérôme, Sorel, Trois-Rivières, Val d'Or, Valleyfield, Verdun, and Victoriaville.

While the Massey Report of 1951 simply noted that libraries should take an essential place among local educational and cultural institutions, it was Quebec's Royal Commission of Inquiry on Constitutional Problems (Tremblay Commission, 1953–6) that paved the way for the development of policy in this area.[82] Its report stated that only thirteen of forty-two towns with more than 10,000 inhabitants had public libraries, that just 35 per cent of the urban population and 5 per cent of the rural population had access to a library, and that the contribution of the provincial and municipal governments was insufficient. For the commission, a meaningful policy on public libraries had to be based on appropriate legislation and adequate funding.

In December 1959 the Paul Sauvé government passed the first law on public libraries in Quebec (*RSQ*, c. B-3, law 35), which was based in large part on the joint brief of the Association des bibliothèques du Québec / Quebec Library Association and the Association canadienne des bibliothécaires de langue française, submitted to the government earlier that year. This law led to the creation of two new bodies, one advisory – the Commission des bibliothèques publiques – and the other administrative – the Service des bibliothèques publiques. Both were under the Direction des bibliothèques publiques. In 1960 the two came under the jurisdiction of the Department of the Provincial Secretary, and as of 1 April 1961, under the new ministère des Affaires culturelles.

Soon after its inception, the Service des bibliothèques publiques, headed by Gérard Martin, surveyed the 1,672 municipalities of Quebec. It found a state of chronic underdevelopment: most of the approximately seventy public libraries examined operated without qualified personnel and with so little funding that they had to rely on volunteers. At this time, the total budget for public libraries was barely over a million dollars. The challenge was colossal: a library network had to be built almost from scratch, and the provincial and municipal governments had to be convinced to invest resources. In the regulations adopted in 1964, the calculation of provincial subsidies was based on the municipal contribution and the size of the population served; in the modifications adopted in 1975–6, the principle of per-capita funding was dropped in favour of a method based on taxable property assessments.[83]

The 1959 law contained no provisions for the establishment of regional libraries to serve people in rural areas or municipalities of fewer than 5,000. A survey by the ministère des Affaires culturelles in 1962 revealed that 94 per cent of the rural population had virtually no library service. In response to this finding, in the 1960s the first two central lending libraries were created in the Mauricie (1962) and in the Outaouais (1964). In the 1970s the remainder of Quebec acquired service: Saguenay–Lac-Saint-Jean (1970), Bas-Saint-Laurent-Gaspésie (1975), Abitibi-Témiscamingue (1976), Estrie (1977), Montérégie (1978), Québec-Appalaches (1978), and the Côte-Nord (1979). A regional co-operation initiative, the West Island Regional Library Council, was also encouraged west of Montreal.

Over these years, considerable effort was made in the media to promote libraries and to stimulate reading in Quebec, while the government increased the subsidies to public libraries, whose numbers expanded accordingly. At the end of the 1970s, in spite of the creation of new central lending libraries and reinforcement of the municipal library network, 20 per cent of libraries still had no full-time employees and 60 per cent lacked a professional librarian. Decisive measures were once again required.

In 1978 Denis Vaugeois, the new minister of cultural affairs, presented a five-year plan for the development of public libraries which further increased support for the construction and renovation of municipal libraries. In addition, the government increased the operating funding to these institutions and subsidized collections whose costs had increased after the adoption of Bill 51 (RSQ, c. D-8.1), which forced libraries to purchase their books at retail prices from ministry-accredited bookstores. In order to be eligible for the entire program, municipalities had to provide free services to all their residents, and those with more than 10,000 inhabitants had to employ at least one full-time professional librarian. This initiative brought tangible results in just a few years.[84] The Vaugeois plan thus contributed to the rapid expansion of the province's libraries and became a benchmark in the development of a reading culture in Quebec.

Academic Libraries

MARCEL LAJEUNESSE AND PETER F. MCNALLY

'If I were founding a university,' wrote Stephen Leacock in 1922, 'I would found first a smoking room; then when I had a little more money in hand I would found a dormitory; then after that, or more probably with it, a decent reading room and a library. After that, if I still had money over that I couldn't use, I would hire a professor and get some textbooks.'[85] The priorities of Canada's leading humorist, who was also an economics professor at McGill University, were seldom shared by those who controlled the purse strings. At McMaster (Hamilton, ON), for example, the Mills Memorial Library was built in 1950 only because the university was able to persuade the trustees of the Davella Mills Foundation that a library would be of greater service than a chapel.[86] At the University of Alberta in Edmonton, more than two decades intervened between the president's request for a new library building in 1928 and the opening of the Rutherford Library in 1951.[87]

The story of Canada's university libraries is largely an account of ongoing struggles to attain sufficient resources to handle ever-expanding enrolments, growing faculty research specialization, surging rates of publication, and challenging technological innovations. The development of graduate programs created additional pressure, based on the estimate that 'graduate students, especially in the Humanities and Social Sciences, require about eight times the resources needed by undergraduates.'[88] In 1921, with a population of nearly 9 million, Canada had nearly 30,000 undergraduates and exactly 344 graduate students. By 1981 the country's population had nearly tripled, the number of full-time undergraduates had increased more than tenfold to nearly 338,000, and full-time graduate students had swelled more than one-hundred–fold, to more than 38,000.[89]

After the First World War, Canada's universities and colleges, along with their libraries, enjoyed considerable growth, but few new institutions would be founded before the middle of the century. Wide variations existed among the country's twenty-three universities: most focused on teaching, with McGill (Montreal), the University of Toronto, Queen's University (Kingston, ON), and Dalhousie (Halifax) the most prominent in research. While Ontario and the western provinces provided some support for their institutions, the National Conference of Canadian Universities noted in 1920 that the majority were 'almost wholly dependent for their maintenance and development on gifts from private citizens.'[90] American philanthropy supported specific projects within institutions; for example, in 1933 the University of New Brunswick (Fredericton) received $4,500 over three years from the Carnegie Foundation to purchase needed books, on the condition that the university hire an 'assistant librarian,' and in 1943 a further $3,000 from the Rockefeller Foundation for research into New Brunswick history.[91]

The relative prosperity of the 1920s prompted English-language academic libraries to improve facilities, or fill gaps in their collections caused by interruption of the book trade during the First World War. Dedicated library buildings were constructed at the University of British Columbia (Vancouver) and Queen's University in 1924, Mount Allison University (Sackville, NB) in 1927, and the University of New Brunswick in 1929. However, only one library opened during the Great Depression of the 1930s, the Lawson Memorial Library at the University of Western Ontario (London, ON) in 1934.

The province of Quebec housed Canada's two major French-language Catholic universities, both of which later became non-denominational. In Quebec City, Université Laval, whose origins trace back to the Séminaire de Québec, founded in 1663, possessed a collection of 180,000 volumes in 1930.[92] Université de Montréal, which was founded in 1878 as a branch of Laval and became independent in 1920, experienced a serious fire in November 1919. As a result, the Bibliothèque Saint-Sulpice became the library for the university, enabling its director, Ægidius Fauteux, to claim the title of librarian of Université de Montréal.[93] When Saint-Sulpice closed in 1931 because of the Sulpician order's financial problems, the university found itself practically without a library until it opened a new building on Mount Royal in 1942. At that time, it hired its first official librarian, Raymond Tanghe. Quebec's two English-language universities were McGill, more than a century old and with a growing reputation, and the small Bishop's University in Lennoxville in the Eastern Townships. In 1930, McGill possessed Canada's largest academic collection, totalling 411,000 volumes, followed by Toronto with more than 252,000.[94]

The Depression slowed the development of university collections considerably. In 1936 financial problems forced McGill to transfer to Princeton University the Gest Chinese Collection, which it had acquired ten years earlier.[95] In 1941 the McCombs Report, funded by the Rockefeller Foundation, showed that university libraries throughout the country suffered problems in administration, facilities, budgets, and staff. For example, contributions from the Carnegie Foundation to assist thirty-two Canadian colleges with such essentials as staffing and book purchases had totalled $213,300 in 1938.[96] Some libraries managed better than others: McCombs noted that Acadia University (Wolfville, NS) had developed 'by all odds the best library in the Maritime Provinces' and commended its librarian, Mary Ingraham, as 'a woman of unusual ability.'[97] However, the total spending of Canadian university libraries on books and periodicals in 1939 was $184,108, a year when the budget for the same category at the library of Columbia University in New York was $144,818.[98] In 1947 the new library at Université de Montréal was still in a sorry state. 'If we did not have the library of the city of Montreal and, especially, that of McGill University, which welcomes our students with a friendliness for which I am very grateful, we might as well close our doors,' admitted the dean of the Faculty of Literature, Canon Arthur Sideleau. 'The value of a faculty of literature lies as much in its library as its professors, and I almost want to add that it could more easily do without the professors than the library.'[99] That same year, Professors Watson Kirkconnell and A.S.P. Woodhouse stressed the general poverty of the humanities collections of Canadian universities, stating that 'libraries are to the humanities what laboratories are to the sciences.'[100]

Post-secondary registration increased moderately during the Second World War and dramatically after 1945. The causes were many: the opening up of educational institutions to returning veterans, the expansion of continuing education, greater access to university for women, increased registration in graduate studies, the creation of new professional programs, and greater numbers of foreign students. Libraries benefited from post-war economic prosperity and increased support from governments. Federal assistance, recommended by the Massey Commission, encouraged the provinces to increase their financial participation. New libraries were built at the University of Alberta and McMaster University in 1951, the University of Saskatchewan (Saskatoon) in 1956, and Bishop's in 1959. McGill University, in 1953, and the University of Toronto, in 1954, substantially expanded facilities which dated from the 1890s.

The 1960s were a golden age for Canada's university libraries. Four major studies encouraged the development of collections in specific academic areas: Edwin E. Williams assessed the humanities and social sciences (1962), Beatrice V. Simon surveyed resources on medical education and research (1964), G.S. Bonn did the same for science and technology (1966), and Robert B. Downs reported on the overall resources of academic and research libraries (1967).[101] Budget increases enabled improvements in acquisitions, staff, and services such that Canada's academic libraries began to compare favourably with those in the United States.[102]

During the 1950s, and especially the 1960s, there were also radical alterations in the way university libraries operated. Increases in student numbers, graduate programs, and research activity highlighted the core role of the library in the mission of the university. Inquiries into the structure and management of post-secondary libraries prompted university administrations to review and reform their library systems. For example, in 1962 the Williams-Filion Report, after a very negative assessment of the libraries of Université Laval, proposed substantial changes: hiring of large numbers of professional librarians, centralization of the libraries and their administration, development of the collections, and construction of a central library – in short, the creation of a research library.[103] At McGill and Université de Montréal, external review committees recommended the appointment of a single director to oversee the integration of services and the construction of a research library; McGill's McLennan Library opened in 1969, the same year as the new library at Laval. Such actions responded to the challenge of establishing more effective structures and setting new priorities in order to create 'authentic university libraries.'[104]

However, the increasing demand for trained librarians created new pressures on library administrators. For example, a low salary scale at the University of Toronto made it difficult for Chief Librarian Robert H. Blackburn to recruit top graduates from his own university's library school. Staff needs were exacerbated by the sudden doubling of his book budget in 1963, a year when 'we lost 70 people from a support staff of 115, and made 159 new appointments ... The rate of turnover reached a peak of 68 percent in 1965–66.'[105] In their continuing need for more staff, space, and resources, academic libraries were victims of their own success in demonstrating to students, administrators, and the public at large that 'the library is the heart of the university.'[106]

The Conference of Rectors and Principals of Quebec Universities (CREPUQ), created in 1967, placed priority on the coordination of the libraries. From the outset, its members expressed a firm desire to intensify co-operation and joint initiatives among the libraries. In the following ten years, the universities of Quebec set up an interlibrary loan service, worked on planning and rationalizing the development of collections, and experimented with co-operation in automated information processing.[107] With the founding of Université de Moncton in New Brunswick in 1963 and Université du Québec in 1968, the latter with sites in different regions of the province, Canada's network of French-language universities also expanded. Quebec's education reform in the 1960s led to the creation of collèges d'enseignement général et professionnel (colleges of general and vocational education), known as CEGEPs, the vast majority of them descendants of the classical colleges. From 1967 to 1980, forty-five CEGEPs set up libraries to support their teaching programs. In 1980 these libraries possessed more than 2.5 million volumes, employed nearly a hundred librarians, had total budgets of 12.5 million dollars, and served 128,500 users, both teachers and students.[108]

During the same era, expanding college systems in other provinces, particularly Ontario and British Columbia, likewise led to the construction of many new libraries and services to meet the needs of teachers and students. In 1968 Ontario established its Colleges of Applied Arts and Technology Bibliographical Centre, known as the College Bibliocentre, which emerged from the 'McMaster Project,' directed by Professor William Ready in 1967. This was 'designed to speed the opening of the colleges and eliminate costly duplication of expenditures ([for such things as] book selection, acquisition and cataloguing) for courses which were to be taught at multiple colleges.'[109]

To house exponentially growing collections and users, new library buildings opened across the country in the 1960s and 1970s. Some sites were newer universities, such as Simon Fraser University, east of Vancouver, which opened in 1964, and York University, which moved to its new campus northwest of Toronto in 1965. Older universities that constructed new library quarters included Memorial University of Newfoundland (1961, with a further annex in 1968), Dalhousie University (1970), the University of Western Ontario (1971), and the University of Alberta (1973). Most spectacular was the Robarts Library at the University of Toronto, one of the world's largest academic library buildings, which opened in 1972 to house the humanities and social science collections, with separate wings for the Thomas Fisher Rare Book Library (see illus. 15.1, p. 444) and the university's library school. Its construction was finally approved in 1968 following a cliff-hanging sequence of negotiations between the university and various levels of government. Robert H. Blackburn described his library's construction as 'a miracle of timing: if any of our proposals made during the previous 10 years had been realized we should have had a much smaller building,' he explained, 'and if the final stages of our planning had taken just eight weeks longer we could not have built anything at all,'[110] referring to the provincial government's subsequent imposition of a space formula followed by a general freeze on construction in Ontario universities.

Alongside the expansion of buildings and enrolments, two other trends marked the early 1970s – co-operation and spending cuts. Ontario led the way with co-operative ventures, its Ontario New University Libraries Project spurred by the need to create libraries for five new provincial universities established in the 1960s. Other successful co-operative programs included improved interlibrary loan systems and personal borrowing procedures. In order to facilitate these developments, an unsuccessful project was launched to create a provincial union catalogue, with the assistance of nascent information technology: the UTLAS bibliographic utility, created by the University of Toronto, and the UNICAT user network. Other provinces experimented with co-operative projects, computerized or not, with varying results.[111] Across Canada, university libraries were at the forefront of introducing electronic systems to manage large bodies of information. As electronic catalogues

15.1 Interior of the Thomas Fisher Rare Book Library. Courtesy of the Thomas Fisher Rare Book Library, University of Toronto.

and user systems gradually replaced card catalogues and manual circulation procedures, methods of serving individuals and communicating between institutions also changed, marking the first steps toward the highly technological information environment that students and faculty now take for granted on campuses all across Canada. In 1976 the libraries at the larger research universities (those with doctoral programs in both the arts and sciences) joined with several major federal government libraries to form the Canadian Association of Research Libraries / Association des bibliothèques de recherche du Canada (CARL/ABRC) to work together regarding national policies, programs, and sharing of information and resources.

During the 1970s the stagflation of the Western world played out in Canada in government reduction of public spending, leading to lower budgets for all government institutions, including universities and their libraries. As staff, services, and collections coped with smaller budgets and reduced plans for expansion, it was feared that the hard fought battles for adequate Canadian academic libraries would be reversed. Symptomatic was Robert H. Blackburn's decision to retire early from his position at Toronto, stating, 'I did not wish to go on negotiating annual budgets that built down what I had helped to build up.' Nonetheless, Blackburn remained optimistic, noting that 'the brief Golden Age that our University experienced in the 1960s was not the first, and I trust it will not be the last.'[112]

Despite funding and staffing problems, by 1980 Canada's academic libraries had achieved a level of size and quality undreamed of in 1918. Alongside the long-established research universities, younger institutions were creating new fields of study and new graduate programs, and institutions of higher education were becoming key players in Canada's developing information and knowledge society. Their libraries now possessed rich teaching and research collections and had become a respected and significant presence upon the world stage.

Special Libraries

ELAINE BOONE

In 1918 only a handful of special libraries – collections of books or materials addressing a particular subject, assembled for a specific purpose, and provided for a designated group – existed in Canada. Several dated back to the mid-nineteenth century,[113] and most were concentrated in Montreal, then the heartland of Canadian business, with a few others located in Ontario and the West.[114] By 1932 special libraries in Canada were sufficiently numerous to justify a section of the American-based Special Libraries Association (est. 1909). With an office in Montreal, it attracted a national membership; in 1940, other regional sections were founded.[115] After the Second World War, economic growth led to an expansion in the number of special libraries. It became increasingly evident to businesses, as well as to certain cultural and professional communities, that they benefited from ready access to relevant information managed by a well-trained staff. By 1980 special libraries were found throughout Canada in all types of enterprises and sectors.[116]

Within Canada's business community, the growth of commerce and industry that began during the First World War created a demand for specialized information that was first felt by the major banks. The Bank of Montreal (est. 1817), whose library had been established more than half a century before the war, functioned much like a public library for its employees. During the early decades of the twentieth century, at a time when few public libraries existed in Quebec, the library of the Bank of Montreal circulated a wide variety of books throughout its branches. However, by 1958 this library had narrowed its focus to banking and business.[117] The library of the Toronto-Dominion Bank, established in 1960, reflected twentieth-century realities: staffed by a professional librarian from the outset, it was initiated by the bank's Economic Research Department to generate reports on the economy and industry, but by 1980 it served the business needs of the organization as a whole.

Canada's oldest business, the Hudson's Bay Company (HBC), established as fur traders in 1670, assembled library and archival collections in a very distinct way. Much more than a corporate record, the HBC's collections have preserved the history of the country itself. To support the work of its archive department, the company founded its main corporate library in London, England, in the 1920s; in 1974 this library was transferred to Winnipeg, where it joined a secondary library previously created at Hudson's Bay House around 1933 to assist with research relating to *The Beaver* (1920–), the company's popular historical magazine. This smaller library resided in the editor's office until 1956. Containing titles about exploration, history, geography, the fur trade, and western Canadian and Arctic travel, as well as books about the HBC itself, this collection supported the company's Canadian headquarters and provided reference services for those seeking information about HBC history. When *The Beaver*'s offices moved to the HBC's downtown Winnipeg store, the library moved with it. After the main corporate library was transferred from England to Canada, the smaller Canadian collection ceased its query function and limited its services to the magazine's staff and members of the company's History Society. All holdings dealing with HBC history were transferred to the Archives of Manitoba in 1999–2000.

Sectors of the economy reliant on ongoing research and development have been leaders in the creation of special libraries. For companies needing ready access to information, the ability to manage sensitive corporate data, and the capacity to monitor the activities of competitors, a professional librarian is a vital asset. Organizations with their own libraries range from pharmaceutical companies, such as Geigy Pharmaceuticals, which established a medical library in Montreal in 1959, to producers of alcoholic beverages, such as the Labatt brewing company, which in the 1950s created a collection stocked with titles on biochemistry, microbiology, biotechnology, engineering, and food and brewing science at its headquarters in London, Ontario. Open to all employees, the Labatt library is primarily used by research and development staff; public access is rarer, most often granted to local university students.

Seagram distilleries took the internal research library a step further in 1970 when it opened an Information Centre in La Salle, Quebec, with a mandate to acquire, arrange, and make available to employees all historical and contemporary records pertaining to the alcoholic beverage industry in general and the Seagram Company in particular. The collection grew to include significant and rare books on early Canada, and became one of the world's finest collections on beverage alcohol. In 1982 the library moved to Waterloo, Ontario, where it joined the Seagram Museum. When the museum closed in 1997, three nearby universities became beneficiaries: Wilfrid Laurier received prints, paintings, lithographs, and works on paper; Waterloo acquired the nine-hundred-volume rare book and early archival collection; and Brock in St Catharines, close to the vineyards of the Niagara Peninsula, became home to the wine-related library, as well as historic wine bottles and other artifacts.

Libraries within cultural institutions differ significantly from most business libraries in that they are not concerned with maintaining secrets or limiting access. As long as they have adequate staffing and space, such institutions prefer to share their library materials. Canada's museums and galleries, both public and private, have a long history of creating special libraries, many of which began in a modest fashion with varying levels of access. Materials in the libraries of the Provincial Museum of Newfoundland and Labrador in St John's and the Royal British Columbia Museum in Victoria, for example, were managed within individual departments and not under the purview of specially trained librarians; consequently, they were closed to the public. The library collection of the Royal Ontario Museum (ROM) in

Toronto, which evolved gradually after the museum opened its doors in 1914, was neither centralized nor managed by professional staff until 1961; however, in addition to serving museum employees, the ROM library eventually functioned as a reference library open to the public. The outstanding library collection of the Montreal Museum of Fine Arts originated in 1882 as the 'Art reading room' for members of the Art Association of Montreal. At the federal level, the library at the National Gallery of Canada (est. 1880), a collection that took root only in 1910 when Eric Brown became the first full-time curator, consolidated its activities after a formally trained librarian was hired in 1956. The gallery adopted a leadership role, and by 1980 it held Canada's most comprehensive library collection on Canadian art.[118] Smaller museums also develop specialized collections accessible to the public, such as the Stewart Museum, created in 1955 in the old fort on St Helen's Island outside Montreal, whose library began with its patron's collection of historic books and maps.

Music and media libraries may be grouped with museum and art libraries in fulfilling a cultural role. While often closely associated with university departments or faculties of music, music libraries have emerged in other contexts as well. At the Toronto headquarters of the Canadian Broadcasting Corporation (CBC), an extensive music library has been closely allied with the organization's museum and archives. By 2005 it included several hundred thousand audio recordings as well as musical scores for original CBC commissions. The CBC's reference library, in turn, holds a 20,000–volume collection on Canadian radio and television broadcasting. The CBC libraries serve the needs of the corporation's personnel across the country.[119]

Newspaper libraries fall between cultural and business libraries. With size and staffing tied to circulation figures, these collections vary widely. A paper with a circulation of over 50,000 is more likely to maintain a large library and value the expertise of professional librarians. The *Winnipeg Free Press* (est. 1872), which has always had a library, holds a complete run of the newspaper, a substantial photo collection, and other relevant research materials, much of which dates from the 1920s. However, it is not open to the public, unlike the large, full-service library of the *Toronto Star*. Newspapers in smaller communities, such as the Saint John *Telegraph-Journal* in New Brunswick, have more limited collections, designed primarily for internal use. In the past, small urban newspapers had librarians on staff, but since the 1980s many positions have disappeared as a result of budget cuts, leaving libraries to function on a self-serve basis.

Professionals and their associations frequently rely on special libraries for research materials. For the benefit of its members the Canadian Professional

Engineers' Association has long maintained a small, internal library without professional staff at its Ottawa office. In 1960 the Canadian Medical Association created a dedicated library in Toronto for its members, and hired librarians. Perhaps more than any other profession, lawyers have required customized libraries, and law librarianship has become highly specialized. Because the citing of case law is integral to the profession, librarians in this sector must collect material in the legal areas specific to the practice or organization that employs them and maintain a collection that includes the most recent court decisions. In Canada most large law firms have maintained their own libraries, while smaller firms and law students have turned to the collections held by various law schools or legal associations, such as that of the Law Society of Upper Canada, which was established in Toronto in 1826. Serving the professional, cultural, and business sectors, special libraries increased in number and influence in the twentieth century, demonstrating a growing awareness that access to information facilitates prosperity and cultural enrichment across divergent spheres of Canadian society.

The Profession of Librarianship

MARTIN DOWDING

The education of Canada's librarians underwent major evolution in the twentieth century, from summer school courses to advanced graduate degrees, and from a perspective of custodianship of library collections to a commitment to providing and promoting access to information. With the enhancement of librarians' accreditation and intellectual status came professional organizations as well as publications and public outreach. As the century unfolded, librarianship fostered champions of intellectual freedom who defended the right to read, acted as lobbyists, and advocated the use of technology to facilitate access to information.

At the end of the First World War, Canada had two library schools. Increased literacy, coupled with Andrew Carnegie's philanthropy, had created a demand for trained library staff, particularly in urban centres. McGill University, which first offered a summer school in Montreal in 1904, developed a one-year diploma in 1927 and Canada's first bachelor of library science (BLS) degree in 1930, both programs accredited by the American Library Association (ALA). In Toronto, the Ontario Department of Education launched a series of courses that by 1919 had developed into a three-month program. In 1928 the University of Toronto initiated a one-year diploma program, followed by a BLS program in 1936, which was accredited by the ALA the next year.[120] Following a French-language summer course offered through McGill in 1932, Montreal's first francophone program began in 1937 at École des bibliothécaires, a private institution affiliated with Université de Montréal. From 1945 this school offered a bachelor's degree in librarianship and bibliography. By the end of the Second World War, the university-based American accreditation model was well established at Canada's English and French library schools, in contrast to the apprenticeship model followed in Britian and France.

Beginning in the 1930s, the establishment of additional educational programs represented one of the most significant influences on Canadian librarianship. Halifax's Mount Saint Vincent University began a BLS program in 1936, while the University of Ottawa initiated a part-time program in 1938. Insufficient funding and absence of ALA accreditation brought an end to these two programs in 1956 and the early 1970s respectively. Ottawa subsequently benefited from an off-site program maintained by the University of Western Ontario (London, ON), whose own master's program began in 1967. After 1960, librarianship programs developed in regions where the demand for trained professionals had increased as a result of population growth. In Vancouver, the University of British Columbia established a school in 1961, the same year that École de bibliothéconomie opened at Université de Montréal. The University of Alberta followed suit in Edmonton in 1968, as did Dalhousie University in Halifax in 1969. In the year of its founding, the Dalhousie school initiated an important series of 'Occasional Papers' (twenty-five of which had appeared by 1979), which addressed such topics as Canadian publishing, Canadian government publications, and public libraries located in schools.

While the BLS, a program that required at least an undergraduate degree in some other field, remained the basic degree for librarians in Canada considerably longer than in the United States, diversification in library education began in the 1950s. In 1951 and 1956 respectively, Toronto and McGill established ALA-accredited master's degrees; ten years later, McGill pioneered a two-year master of library science (MLS), which soon became 'the Canadian norm.'[121] By 1980 all the master's programs of Canada's seven schools of information studies were accredited by the ALA. Designed originally to augment the established bachelor's degree, the MLS became increasingly directed toward research, professional administration, and new technologies in a field that was in the process of being renamed 'library and information science.' This shift was not without controversy: '"Information Science" became a ubiquitous, if ambiguous, rallying cry as curricula were revamped to facilitate the application of automated systems to libraries, and the principles of librarianship to environments other than traditional libraries. Computer-literate faculty were hired, and equipment purchased, in a largely successful attempt to remain abreast of a rapidly changing world. In the process, however, some schools eliminated the historical and cultural dimensions of librarianship from their curricula.'[122]

The 1970s saw the establishment of Canada's first doctoral programs at the University of Toronto (1971) and the University of Western Ontario (1973), a move that recognized the growing need for research faculty in all areas of library studies and raised the academic and social status of librarians at a time when women were taking on leadership roles in both library education and the ranks of the country's senior librarians and information specialists. Alongside this increasing academic specialization, in the 1960s various library technician programs were established, largely in community colleges and CEGEPs, the first appearing in Winnipeg in 1962 at the Manitoba Institute of Technology (later Red River Community College) and in Quebec at Collège de Jonquière in 1966. Focused on technical applications, these programs were designed to standardize the skills and training of non-professional library employees.

As formal education advanced the status of individual library personnel, the increasing political and social influence of library associations enhanced the significance and visibility of the profession as a whole. While the Ontario Library Association (est. 1901) and the British Columbia Library Association (est. 1911) pre-dated the First World War, it was not until the mid-1930s that provincial or regional associations spanned the country from coast to coast.[123] Several associations served the profession in Quebec, where distinctions of language and culture required particular regional attention. These included the bilingual Association des bibliothèques du Québec / Quebec Library Association (est. 1932) and the Association canadienne des bibliothécaires de langue française (ACBLF, 1943–74).[124] In 1974 the ACBLF was replaced by the Association pour l'avancement des sciences et des techniques de la documentation (ASTED). At the national level, the Canadian Library Association / Association canadienne des bibliothèques (CLA) was founded in 1946. Originally bilingual, it reduced its mandate to English-speaking Canada in 1971. The period after 1960 witnessed the proliferation of specialized organizations, such as the Canadian Association for Information Science (CAIS, est. 1970), designed for professors of librarianship and information science, and professionals undertaking research in the access, retrieval, organization, management, and dissemination of information.

By 1980 almost 150 local, provincial, and national library associations existed in Canada, representing the material and political interests of public libraries, school, college, and university libraries, and special libraries, as well as the concerns of specific user groups, including ethnic communities, the disabled, and trustees.

Among the most significant activities of associations has been the publication of research tools and materials relevant to professional development. These run the gamut from newsletters, annual reports, and bulletins to professional journals, monographs, bibliographies, indexes, and association and local histories. In Quebec, ACBLF published a quarterly known as the *Bulletin de l'ACBLF* (1955–72), followed in 1973 by *Documentation et Bibliothèques,* while its successor, ASTED, issued many books and reports, including the two volumes dedicated to Edmond Desrochers under the title *Livre, bibliothèque et culture québécoise* (1977). The Corporation of Professional Librarians of Quebec, created in 1969 by a law of the National Assembly of Quebec, publishes the journal *Argus* (1971–). In 1976 CAIS initiated the bilingual peer-reviewed *Canadian Journal of Information Science / Revue canadienne des sciences de l'information* to provide a forum for the highly specialized research of its members. Between 1946 and 1980 the CLA published well over one hundred titles, covering such professional topics as cataloguing, copyright, freedom of information, interlibrary loan, information technology, and children's services. Representative titles include *Canadian Public Library Laws* (1946, 1966) and *Basic Book List for Canadian Schools* (1968–9). The CLA has also issued research tools, such as the *Canadian Periodical Index,* that have been invaluable to scholars in many fields, as well as the *Canadian Library Journal* (1944–92).

In addition to providing forums for professional discussion and publication, library organizations have entered cultural debates and wielded influence in the public sphere. In the 1940s and early 1950s, the CLA, along with provincial and local library associations, was instrumental in the creation of the National Library of Canada. In the following decades, the CLA and its provincial counterparts regularly submitted briefs to government investigations on issues of broad social and cultural interest, such as copyright and censorship. Over the course of the twentieth century, the image of Canadian librarians shifted from meek custodians of books to champions of the freedom to read, and indispensable experts in information technology and the intricacies of copyright.

chapter 16

READING HABITS

Measuring Literacy

MICHEL VERRETTE

If literacy was difficult to define in earlier periods, in the twentieth century the concept became even more problematic. Literacy could no longer be assessed according to criteria employed before the First World War. At the turn of the twentieth century, a signature was still considered a valid indication of literacy, although by then a grasp of basic reading and writing already prevailed as the functional understanding of the term. In 1911 the proportion of the Canadian population over the age of five who knew how to read and write was reported at 89 per cent; those who only knew how to read made up just 0.5 per cent, a statistically insignificant figure.

By 1921, Canada as a whole had nearly achieved full literacy. If the measured rate reached a plateau of 90 per cent, this was partly the result of an immigration policy open to individuals who could speak neither English nor French. As literacy was measured in the census by ability in one of these two languages, these statistics do not account for immigrants who could read and write in their mother tongues.[1] Also excluded was the population of Newfoundland (where literacy was known to be lower) as the province did not enter Confederation until 1949.

In 1931, the last year when literacy figured in the census, attention was focused on people ten years of age or older, in order to ensure that the population surveyed had attended school long enough to learn to read and write.[2] According to this census, which excluded Native peoples, just 3.4 per cent of the population could be considered illiterate. Subsequent censuses only asked about school attendance and level of schooling. The low rate of illiteracy in 1931 was undoubtedly considered residual and impossible to reduce further.

Nonetheless, the general picture of literacy before the Second World War bears further examination. For example, in Quebec, among farmers in the Saguenay region, full literacy was not achieved until mid-century.[3] In the Trois-Rivières region, according to the signatures on marriage certificates, full literacy was reached in the 1920s,[4] that is, a decade later than in the country as a whole. Other exceptional cases might also be found among other distinct populations, in particular the Métis and First Nations, people in newly settled areas in the West, and immigrants who arrived after the First World War.

In Ontario, which recorded almost full literacy by the end of the nineteenth century, there had been early initiatives designed to reach populations in remote regions. In 1899, Alfred Fitzpatrick, a Protestant minister, established the Canadian Reading Camp Association, which in 1919 became Frontier College. The college created the concept of the teacher-farmer, an idea that soon spread to the rest of Canada, with its focus no longer only on farmers in newly settled regions, but also on miners and railway workers.[5]

After the Second World War, and especially in the 1960s with the initial passage of baby boomers into adulthood and the growing bureaucratization of government and the economy, national and international organizations, led by UNESCO, developed the concept of functional literacy: people were considered illiterate if they had not completed five years of schooling, and functionally illiterate if they had not completed nine years. The definition of a literate person thus rose from the level of elementary school to secondary school,[6] since it was considered that a person could not function adequately in an increasingly bureaucratic society dominated by written documents without having finished grade nine. To stress the importance of literacy, 8 September was established as World Literacy Day in 1967.

The new concept of functional literacy swept aside Canada's high literacy statistics of previous decades. The functional illiteracy rate of the Canadian population was assessed at 30 per cent in 1971,[7] 28.4 per cent in 1976,[8] and still 20 per cent in 1981.[9] In 1976 most provinces had functional illiteracy rates approaching one-third of the population. Ontario stood at 25 per cent, while British Columbia, Alberta, and Yukon were close to 20 per cent.[10]

These rather alarming figures gave rise to heated debate. First, the relevance of linking the literacy rate and the level of schooling was disputed. Was the fact that someone had completed grade nine the best measure of his or her chance of economic success or capacity to function in society? To answer this question, one would have to be able to measure the effectiveness of the education received; hence, experts felt cautious about statistics based solely on years of schooling. In addition, these statistics did not take into account regional economic differences that required varying levels of education of their populations.

Nonetheless, measures were undertaken to correct what appeared to be an important social problem. Community action groups specializing in literacy sprang up throughout Canada. Provincial and national associations were created to coordinate the work and to manage the grants allocated to them by governments that had assessed the social and economic costs associated with functional illiteracy. The target populations of these action groups were diverse. First, there were immigrants who entered Canada without being able to speak either of the country's two official languages. Then there were illiterate adults who had never learned to read and write effectively but who found they needed to improve these skills because of changes in the job market. Finally, there were school dropouts, whom the literacy groups strove to reclaim before it was too late. On the whole, as the country passed from the 1970s to the 1980s, 10 to 15 per cent of the Canadian population needed these services.

A level of literacy long considered sufficient for life in Canadian society, one that did not constitute an insurmountable obstacle for new immigrants, came to be recognized as insufficient in the second half of the century. By century's end, the newer concept of technological or computer illiteracy also arose as a factor in defining functional literacy, raising additional questions of adaptation and education.

Surveying the Habit of Reading

HEATHER MURRAY AND ANDREA ROTUNDO

Surveys of readers undertaken between the First World War and 1980 are surprisingly numerous. While of unequal evidentiary value, all illuminate Canadian social history: what was their purpose? how did surveyors conceptualize reading? and what questions did – or did they not – deem important enough to ask their respondents? While 'survey' could denote any collation of readerly demographics and tastes, such as detailed library circulation figures or book sales, the term is restricted here to the direct polling of readers about their tastes and habits, through census, questionnaire, interview, or focus group.[11] An exception is made for Dominion Bureau of Statistics / Statistics Canada data on libraries, which, while indirect, are the primary source of national readership information before 1978.

Readership surveys have a variety of purposes. Some assess a newspaper's or magazine's own readers in order to recruit new audiences or markets, or to better match contents to tastes.[12] Most famously, beginning in 1940, *Maclean's Magazine* annually used door-to-door 'gumshoe men' to take its readers' temperatures, and then, in editorials, informed them of their expectations for the magazine and the steps *Maclean's* would take to meet them.[13] Trade organizations commissioned more general studies: a first independent audit of magazine circulation in 1949, for the newly formed Magazine Research Group of Canada, characterized the readers of eleven periodicals in both English and French.[14] A 1962 poll for the Canadian Daily Newspaper Publishers Association involved more than three thousand face-to-face interviews (almost one-third with children and teenagers) on the 'where, how, and when' of newspaper reading.[15] The emergence of 'youth' as a separate readerly demographic is apparent in the 1967 survey for *The Canadian* magazine, which attempted to gauge, among other questions, whether the magazine could 'get through' to teenagers.[16]

Inquiries by commercial organizations or trade journals were not necessarily narrow. In the early 1920s, the *Canadian Bookman* agonized over whether Canada was a 'bookish' nation and attempted to provide some specifics. One article titled 'What Do Canadians Read?' speculated that the first Book Week of the Canadian Authors Association had raised awareness of homegrown materials, while another on 'What Moose Jaw Reads' showed novels representing fully 85 per cent of adult library borrowing according to one Saturday's figures.[17] The need for more definitive information was answered, at least in part, by the commencement in 1921 of the Dominion Bureau of Statistics' regular *Survey of Libraries*, which collected national and provincial circulation data, as well as figures from individual libraries in the early years.[18] Certain significant trends emerge: the decline of adult circulation with the increase in employment after the Depression, for example, and the steady rise of juvenile borrowing, which achieved its 'majority' of more than 50 per cent of national circulation at mid-century.[19] Some figures call for further study: did the 25 per cent decline in fiction borrowing during and after the Second World War[20] reflect changing tastes, reduced leisure, the popularity of magazine serial fiction, the appeal of cheap pocket books, or the efforts of librarians to steer readers away from light fiction? The statistical road not taken is shown by the anomalous survey of 1936–8, which included sections entitled 'Who Uses the Libraries' and 'What They Read.' Here we see breakdowns for men and women borrowers; find commentary on the differences between urban and rural reading tastes; and learn that Prince Edward Island led the nation in its taste for sociology due to the strength of the study-group movement in that province, a phenomenon discussed by DeNel Rehberg Sedo in chapter 18.

Some individual libraries and systems, needing more inflected data, surveyed their own constituencies. In 1960 the Toronto Public Library report *Toronto Speaks* extensively assessed literacy levels, language preferences, and recreational reading patterns in the adult post-war immigrant population,[21] while the detailed Lake Erie Regional Library survey of 1972 examined language adherences and reading tastes of the many 'newcomer' groups to the area.[22] In that same year, Vancouver Public Library surveyed users of the different divisions at the Central Library[23] to prepare for a more ambitious survey designed to determine 'What People Want in a Library.'[24] Readers clearly did judge books by their covers, as demonstrated by an ingenious Toronto Public Library survey in 1944, showing that books with dust jackets had significantly greater appeal.[25] Such library surveys, great and small, are to be found in annual reports, library association journals, and libraries' own files.

While reports from the *Survey of Libraries* constitute the most sustained readership data, government bodies surveyed readers intermittently for other purposes. In 1972 the Ontario Royal Commission on Book Publishing distributed some 2,500 questionnaires to members of the Readers' Club of Canada.[26] The failure in 1980 of two respected dailies occasioned a Royal Commission on Newspapers, which conducted a pilot study in December 1980 prefatory to a fuller 'National Readership Study' of 3,500 adults. Its report documented interesting regional divergences, such as less reading of newspapers in the Atlantic and Prairie provinces, and correlated newspaper reading to book, magazine, radio, and television use.[27] In what must be the most extensive Canadian readership survey ever undertaken, the Secretary of State attached a 'Survey of Selected Leisure Activities: Reading Habits' to its monthly *Labour Force Survey* of February 1978. Approximately 17,000 respondents were asked about the place of reading in their lives, their tastes and attitudes, and sources of materials. The thorough data analysis is especially interesting for breakdowns by genre and subject matter, bicultural contrasts, and statistical comparisons with other countries; although the survey made some inquiries about the countries of origin of reading materials, as well as the languages in which they were printed, no analysis of this information was undertaken. Based on its comprehensive picture of adult leisure-time reading, the report queried the supposed 'gender gap' in book readership, found alarming discrepancies in book access and adult reading levels nationwide, and challenged earlier surveys which correlated readership to an equally active involvement in other leisure pursuits.[28] This survey continues to be used as a comparator for later readership studies. In Quebec, similar work was performed in 1976 by CROP (Centre de recherche sur l'opinion publique) in assessing leisure time-use and cultural activities in the province, where the surprisingly low levels of discretionary adult reading created a call for action on the part of educators and publishers.[29]

One noteworthy outcome of the 1978 national survey was the monumental report of 1980 by James Lorimer, with the raw leisure-activities data reworked by Susan Shaw. *Book Reading in Canada* (1983), commissioned by the Association of Canadian Publishers, provided a comprehensive portrait of the book-reading populace with more focus on the awareness of Canadian materials than in the original report. That Canadian publishers needed to know Canadian readers was a premise shared by the innovative CANLIT action-research team.[30] In 1975 a pilot project, *Something for Nothing*, recorded the reactions of north Toronto residents when given (and asked to read) a free paperback book, chosen from a miscellany of a hundred titles donated by Canadian publishers;[31] this was followed in 1978 by a thorough study of several hundred Peterborough-area residents and a nationwide audit of sixteen high-school Canadian literature classes.[32] Evidently 1978 was a landmark year for readership surveys: in addition to those already mentioned, the *Ontario Reading Survey*[33] tested the impact of the 'Half Back' program, which allowed use of unsuccesful provincial lottery tickets toward purchase of Canadian books, and *Weekend Magazine* commissioned a telephone survey of more than one thousand urbanites, including specific queries about favourite genres and authors.[34]

Quebec sociologists, cultural analysts, and members of the book trade had sensed the need for more specialized studies as early as 1944 when publisher Albert Lévesque undertook his landmark survey of 2,239 French-speaking households. Taking its name from a colloquial threshold greeting, *Entrez Donc*, it included francophones outside of Quebec. It offered interesting breakdowns of book and newspaper reading by region and occupational grouping, and considered the impact of other media (radio, in this case) on reading, a theme that remains characteristic of Quebec readership surveys. Persistent figures showing an abnormally low provincial book readership rate continued to demand either correction or explanation. Alain Bergeron's survey of one hundred respondents in Quebec City in 1973 focused on the familial and educational factors affecting a predisposition to read and concluded that the cultural level of these urban readers was the same as the rest of 'the western world.'[35] Jean Mirucki's two-volume study *Le marché du livre au Canada* (1986) is a francophone counterpart to the Lorimer report, with Mirucki returning as well to selected 1978 StatsCan data.[36] He provides extensive socio-demographic information and tables showing book availability, patterns of book acquisition, book club membership, and other information linking 'Les lecteurs et la demande de livres,' to cite the title of one chapter. The urban bias of many surveys also generated rural or regional readership studies, such as one undertaken in 1970 with the co-operation of Quebec's ministère des Affaires culturelles.[37] Surveys and studies of Quebec readers so proliferated throughout the 1970s that they became a topic in their own right: Marc Alain analyzed psycho-sociological studies of reading habits in 1972 for both English Canada and Quebec, while Lise Brunet's synopsis of 1980 provides a critical overview of the dominant tendencies and methodological assumptions of the field.[38]

Although many readership surveys were narrowly or commercially focused, most attempted to grasp broader issues which emerged over the course of the twentieth century. Between the wars, they were engaged with questioning whether Canada was a culturally literate nation and whether public libraries reached and adequately served the population; in the 1960s and 1970s, they asked if there was a constituency who would 'read Canadian' and support a domestic publishing sector, and whether provinces, regions, or cultural or ethnic groups were truly represented in national audits.

Best-Sellers

KLAY DYER, DENIS SAINT-JACQUES, AND CLAUDE MARTIN

Debate over the aesthetics and politics of popular writing, and by extension over the influence of books that attain best-seller status, has a long history. To many critics, such works are little more than exemplars of a degraded and intensely commodified mass culture. To others, 'bestselling novels are particularly important cultural artifacts because they are primarily a social rather than a literary phenomenon. Although they are books, their status as "bestsellers" is socially constituted,'[39] and they provide valuable insights into the social and cultural dynamics of reading as a real-world activity. To peruse a best-seller list is to engage with 'a kind of corrective reality,' to recognize what a literate culture is actually buying – and presumably reading – as distinct from the dictates of cultural gatekeepers: 'Like stepping on the scales, [the best-seller] tells us the truth, however unflattering, and is therefore ... a pretty good way of assessing our culture ...'[40]

The impetus to document and compare sales figures accompanied the commodification of bookselling in the United States: '... with its first issue in February, 1895, the American *Bookman* began publishing lists of books "in order of demand," based on information gathered from bookstores across the United States.'[41] This inaugural list was eclipsed in 1911 when *Publisher's Weekly* began to issue what became the most influential rating list of the day.

Best-Sellers in English

In 1901 the Canadian *Bookseller and Stationer* adopted the *Bookman* model and produced 'a "Canadian summary" of the six best sellers nationwide each month.'[42] Canadian writers were prominent, led by the successes of Sir Gilbert Parker, whose penchant for feeding contemporary appetites for historical romance kept his name on best-seller lists well into the years of the First World War. Also visible were Ralph Connor, L.M. Montgomery, Stephen Leacock, and Norman Duncan; Parker, Connor, and the now-forgotten Basil King figured prominently on American lists.

Not surprisingly, the outbreak of the First World War altered the tone and focus of Canadian-authored best-sellers. Robert Service's *Rhymes of a Red Cross Man* hit number one on the American non-fiction list for both 1917 and 1918, outpacing the popularity of John McCrae's *In Flanders Fields and Other Poems*, which rose to fifth the next year. On the international fiction list, Connor continued his best-seller run with *The Major* (ranked seventh in 1918) and *The Sky Pilot in No Man's Land*, which reached number one on the Canadian list the following year. Although Canadian lists were still driven by familiar genres such as historical romance, war stories, biography, and self-improvement, a handful of works regarded as more literary, including Martha Ostenso's *Wild Geese* (1925) and Ernest Thompson Seton's *Wild Animals I Have Known* (1926; a new edition of his 1898 volume), found their way into the rankings, effectively problematizing critics' tendency to demonize popular titles.

As in the pre-war era, the post-war years saw British and American writers dominate Canadian best-seller lists, with such names as Zane Grey, W.J. Locke, and Mary Roberts Rinehart figuring prominently. As Mary Vipond details: 'Overall during the 1920s, about 17% of the best-selling novels in Canada were by Canadian authors, 37% by American, 45% by British and 3% by authors of other nationalities. This compares with proportions of 20%, 44%, 36% and zero for the period from 1899 to 1918.' As the 1920s progressed, the Canadian presence on local best-seller lists dropped significantly, from 20 per cent in the first half of the decade to 14 per cent in the second.[43] Ironically, it was during this period of decline that Mazo de la Roche's *Jalna* (1927) signalled the breakthrough of Canada's next international best-selling author: 'During her lifetime, the chronicles of the Whiteoak family of Jalna ... sold more than eleven million copies in one hundred and ninety-three English editions and ninety-two foreign editions.'[44]

Following the Second World War, a few well-established trends persisted: American influence on Canadian best-seller lists continued to expand, and corporate reshapings allowed a few large publishing companies to dominate the market for best-sellers, a concentration of power that contributed to the development of a kind of literary star system. The impact of book clubs became more visible with two large American-based book clubs – the Book of the Month Club and the Literary Guild – providing the biggest influence on Canadian best-seller markets. Book clubs proved advantageous for at least one Canadian writer, Thomas B. Costain, whose *The Black Rose* climbed to third place on the *Publisher's Weekly* list for 1945 on the strength of 2.1 million copies sold.[45] A subsequent novel, *High Towers*, ranked seventh for 1949 and sold more than one million copies, including a Dollar Book Club sale of over 800,000 copies,[46] virtually guaranteeing Costain an audience that would sustain his best-seller status well into the 1950s.

The successes of expatriate Costain, like those of Arthur Hailey, the international best-selling novelist who moved to Canada from England in 1947 but relocated to the Bahamas after he achieved international popularity with such novels as *Airport* (first in 1968) and *Wheels* (first in 1971), also raise questions about the relationship between literature (popular or otherwise) and the shaping of a distinctly Canadian imagination. The only Canadian literary novel to achieve American best-seller status during the middle decades of the century was Gwethalyn Graham's *Earth and High Heaven*, which ranked ninth in 1945.

From the mid-twentieth century through the end of the 1970s, best-seller status in English Canada became increasingly difficult to measure, in part because of the proliferation of designations and the absence of reliable data. National and local lists, compiled from reports from bookstores, began to appear in newspapers. For about a year (1969–70), *Quill & Quire* printed lists from different bookstores across the country which showed that despite regional variations, American books vastly predominated. That year's favourite Canadian titles included politician Judy LaMarsh's *Memoirs of a Bird in a Gilded Cage* and Leonard Cohen's *Selected Poems*. Lists also became specialized, separating Canadian from international authors, paperbacks from hardcover editions, and making broad distinctions based on genre or content. Though the 1960s and 1970s saw a surge in both paperback publishing and the number of English-Canadian books in print, no single Canadian book ranked in the top fifteen titles of the international list. This situation would not improve before the end of the millennium, despite the ability of Canadian authors to win major international prizes.

Best-Sellers in French

Regular best-seller lists did not appear in Quebec newspapers until the 1970s. Before 1954, the number of reprints was the measure of a book's success, each printing normally representing 1,000 copies. From 1954 to 1970, the lists that appeared sporadically revealed a growing awareness of the phenomenon of the best-seller.

Before the 1950s, the most famous and successful novels – *Un homme et son péché* (1933) by Claude-Henri Grignon, *Menaud, maître draveur* (1937) by Félix-Antoine Savard, and *Le survenant* (1945) by Germaine Guèvremont – each enjoyed many printings.[47] The first two were helped by radio and television adaptations, but the success of *Menaud* was in part the result of an enthusiastic reception by nationalist critics and distribution of the book in schools. Gabrielle Roy's *Bonheur d'occasion* (1945) was remarkably successful beyond the borders of Canada: the novel was awarded the Prix Femina; the 1947 translation (*The Tin Flute*) was a selection of the Book of the Month Club in New York; and by 1978 the novel in French had gone into six editions in Quebec, one in France, and one in Switzerland.

From 1954 to 1958, *Le Petit Journal* published a weekly column entitled 'Livres en vedette,' in which some fifteen titles were selected, with no ranking. Publications from France made up an enviable proportion of these (57 per cent), followed by Quebec titles (30 per cent). From 1959 to 1962, the column was replaced by a best-seller list, with five titles ranked in order of importance. The biggest successes of that period – *Les insolences du frère Untel*, the call to arms of the Quiet Revolution; *Le dernier des justes,* by André Schwarz-Bart, winner of the Prix Goncourt; *Mémoires intérieurs,* by François Mauriac; *La saison des pluies* (translation of *A Burnt-Out Case*), by Graham Greene; and *Le docteur Jivago,* by Boris Pasternak, awarded the Nobel Prize in 1958, which the Russian government forbade him to accept – show the Quebec market's openness to successful foreign works and its penetration by certain Parisian publishers, such as Gàllimard and Robert Laffont, the latter of which distributed a series titled 'Best-sellers.'[48] From 1962 to 1969, the number of reprints was still the best indicator of the top sellers. *Une saison dans la vie d'Emmanuel* (1965), by Marie-

Claire Blais, with eight printings, a Prix Médicis, and ten translations, was the clear leader among Quebec's best-sellers of this decade.

Starting in January 1970, the Montreal daily *La Presse* published a weekly best-seller list of ten titles. It included everything from *Papillon*, by Henri Charrière, to *Le parrain* (translation of *The Godfather*), by Mario Puzo, and *Le petit manuel d'histoire du Québec,* by Léandre Bergeron. During this decade, the two titles that appeared most frequently were *Le choc du futur* (translation of *Future Shock*), by Alvin Toffler (ninety times), and *Kamouraska*, by Anne Hébert (sixty-two times).[49] The proportion of Quebec books among the twenty-five most popular titles of the year hovered around 60 per cent in the early 1970s, and 40 per cent in 1980. France's publishers vied with those in Quebec for the largest market share, although 40 per cent of their best-selling titles were translations of American books. Short fiction, novels, and comic books occupied an increasingly important place on the annual best-seller lists of the 1970s, representing about a third of the titles. Biographies followed at 20 per cent, while other forms of non-fiction and how-to books appeared to lose ground, dropping from 45 per cent to 30 per cent.

Data from surveys on cultural practices in Quebec show that the proportion of readers of best-sellers increased with the level of education. The most important segment, representing two-thirds of readers, was employed women with a college education. They read books written for both women and men, regardless of the sex of the author, whereas male readers avoided literature intended for a female audience. In general, readers confirmed that what they sought in a best-seller was a protagonist who was exemplary in overcoming adversity and a story that was helpful to them in their own lives. The development of the market for best-sellers in the 1970s led Quebec authors such as Yves Beauchemin, Arlette Cousture, and Marie Laberge to write for this readership in the following decades.

Fan Mail from Readers

CLARENCE KARR

Images of obsessed fans were one of the more salient features of mass culture in the twentieth century; extremes of the phenomenon were exemplified in the distinctive costumes and even languages adopted by *Star Trek* devotees. Literary counterparts often become important symbols of their age: for example, in the early twentieth century, the earthy American poet Walt Whitman inspired admirers to form Whitman clubs and cults, including two in the Toronto region.[50] More enduring has been veneration of the eighteenth-century Scottish populist poet Robert Burns, whose birthday is still celebrated across Canada with haggis suppers on 25 January. However, such public displays of literary appreciation have been relatively rare among Canadian fans of books and authors, whose behaviour has generally been more individualistic, more internalized, more private, and of shorter duration: the fan letter prevailed as the vital means of communicating their responses, involving readers in private relationships with living authors. Many collections of authors' papers retain such correspondence; Mazo de la Roche, for example, 'received thousands of letters from all over the world, in countless languages, from individuals with varying levels of education.'[51]

Apart from mere autograph seekers, readers who write fan letters to authors tend to have experienced a significant interaction with a text. Because such letters are personal responses, they provide crucial insight into the reception of print culture. Although many letter writers seem bewildered by their actions, often apologizing for bothering authors, they nonetheless feel compelled to share intimacies in a confessional tone that demonstrates a significant level of trust. Such readers filter the text through the fabric of their own lives, and experience a deep emotional and even intellectual connection with the person they envision the author to be. Many correspondents speak of being under the spell of the text and having a soul-to-soul experience. For example, in the mid-1930s a nineteen-year-old reader found that Ralph Connor's *The Man from Glengarry* struck a responsive chord: 'It seems to penetrate your inner self,' he wrote. 'Its exquisite theme haunts you.'[52] For some fans, books provided comfort and consolation. Others gained new perspectives on their own lives. 'Oh! it is such a comfort,' a reader told Arthur Stringer, 'to read thoughts which you have often felt but could not express.'[53] Generations of female readers have identified with the independent spirit of L.M. Montgomery's Anne Shirley (of Green Gables). Readers also inform authors of the support their books have provided in confronting life with greater confidence and fortitude. A Swedish immigrant to the Canadian prairies who identified strongly with Chaddie, the heroine of Stringer's 'Prairie Trilogy,' felt the shock of the immigrant experience softened by her reading and discovered within herself the strength and courage to persevere.[54] Many children, such as the son of an Edmonton fan of Mazo de la Roche, have been named after authors or characters.[55]

Some readers claim that books have significantly changed the course of their lives. In 1931 a man who was contemplating suicide after the tragic death of his only son told Ralph Connor: 'If I come through it will be by the help of your works.'[56] Several clergymen credited their career choice to reading Connor's fiction. Sometimes an enduring spiritual bond connects a reader with a text or author – creating a sense of what the fictional Anne Shirley described as meeting a 'kindred spirit.' On other occasions, it is the similarity of textual circumstances, characters, or events to those of the reader's life that prompts both the intense interaction and the fan mail.

Books eliciting such responses tend to be those which express a deep faith in human nature. Readers are struck not so much by the presence of an authorial voice as by the absence of a negative or cynical attitude toward the human condition. A consistent theme among fans of Margaret Laurence was her breadth of characterization and non-judgmental portrayal of people, qualities that touched readers deeply and prompted both laughter and tears. 'I love your novels,' wrote one admirer in 1975, 'because you do care honestly and intelligently about life – the livingness of things – and about people.'[57]

By the late twentieth century, fan response to the printed page was less likely to be transmitted through the postal system than to be centred in Internet chat rooms or other on-line formats, such as the 'Kindred Spirits' listserv hosted by the L.M. Montgomery Institute at the University of Prince Edward Island. Such communal structures, however, generally bypass the author and reveal much less about individuals' interaction with the texts than do personal heartfelt letters from a reader to a writer.

Autobiographies of Reading: L.M. Montgomery and Marcel Lavallé

CLARENCE KARR

Motivated by the desire to be well read, serious book lovers choose an eclectic range of texts. In the first half of the twentieth century, these readers were inspired by broadly conceived school readers, publishers' series of the world's best books, and bountiful cheap reprints. Ignoring academic boundaries, such reading reflected self-images and aspirations of individuals. The private journals of L.M. Montgomery

(1874–1942), the celebrated daughter of Prince Edward Island who achieved international success as the author of *Anne of Green Gables* (1908), and of Marcel Lavallé (1922–63), the son of a poor rural Quebec family who passed much of his adult life in prison, present comparable autobiographies of reading.

Separated by gender, education, religion, language, social class, and two generations, these individuals led very different lives, read few of the same books, and displayed markedly disparate responses to modernism. Montgomery documented her reading over the course of her entire adult life, while Lavallé described the books in both French and English that he devoured while imprisoned during the 1950s. Nonetheless, the commonalities of their experience suggest some patterns of reading behaviour that may be further generalized.[58] Each read prodigiously for both enlightenment and entertainment, ranging widely and randomly through poetry, novels, the Bible, biography, history, drama, essays, and the classics. Self-confessed addicts who often spoke of the desire to read as an unquenchable thirst, they sometimes read quickly, sometimes slowly and intensely. For example, from the collection in the prison library and occasional trades with fellow inmates, Lavallé consumed in rapid succession a critical study of Victor Hugo, followed by translations of a John Steinbeck novel, Adolph Hitler's *Mein Kampf*, and Plato's *Dialogues*. In contrast, he savoured *Propos sur le bonheur*, by Alain (Émile-Auguste Chartier), over several days in an effort to absorb its wisdom; similarly, Montgomery found that Ralph Waldo Emerson's *Essays* demanded her complete attention. Other common traits were the rereading of favourites, memorization of passages, and compilation of maxims for both guidance and reaffirmation. Neither reader valued books as objects; only the text was important.

Although Montgomery was a liberal Christian who questioned certain doctrines and Lavallé was a self-professed atheist, both were shaped by childhood experiences of home and church. Each systematically read and reread the Bible for its wisdom, stories, and imagery, favouring the prophet Job. Neither liked moralizing texts. Alongside serious works, they devoured detective fiction: Montgomery read all of Agatha Christie, while Lavallé adored Georges Simenon. They also read for distraction and comfort: Lavallé chose contemporary popular fiction as well as passages from J.S. Mill's *On Liberty*, while Montgomery in her later years returned to childhood favourites by Sir Walter Scott, Anthony Trollope, and Ian Maclaren.

To increase their knowledge, both readers tackled difficult volumes in history, philosophy, and science. With less formal schooling than Montgomery, Lavallé possessed a greater desire for self-education and studied dictionaries to enlarge his vocabulary. Intellectual nourishment came from different sources. Poetry by Robert

Browning, essays by Bliss Carman, and the fiction and biography of George Eliot provided Montgomery with insights and inspiration. Lavallé esteemed André Gide for his passion for grand adventure and for encouraging his readers to be themselves.

Books also provided companionship and consolation. Immersing himself in George Bernanos's *Journal d'un curé de campagne* eased the despair and depression Lavallé suffered in his prison cell, while he found comfort in La Fontaine's poetry. Montgomery, chafing against the constraints of an unhappy marriage and public life as a Presbyterian minister's wife, credited books with restoring her spirits. After one hectic play rehearsal, she sought relief in Edward Gibbon's *Decline and Fall of the Roman Empire*; on another occasion, reading George Grote's *History of Greece* helped minimize her grief during a time of personal crisis.

However absorbing or entertaining the material, both readers rarely suspended critical judgment. Even when profoundly connected with a book, they remained conscious of the reading process and filtered texts through their personal experiences. Montgomery and Lavallé each exhibited the Calvinistic trait of introspection and used their reading for self-discovery, especially in their younger years. In her last decades, Montgomery, who lived longer than Lavallé, was more given to retrospection.

Each reader, however, is inevitably informed by personal contexts. Typical of her generation, Montgomery abhorred tell-all realism and preferred the idealistic humanism of the great writers of the nineteenth century. Yet she enjoyed contemporary histories and biographies: among her favourites were Lytton Strachey's *Queen Victoria* and Margo (Asquith) Tennant's *Reminiscences*. More attuned to modernism, Lavallé loved the terse, brutal style of his favourite authors, including Roger Martin du Gard, André Malraux, and François Mauriac, and the honest portrayals of homosexuality provided by Gide and Gore Vidal. He also appreciated the writings of cutting-edge Americans such as Norman Mailer, Truman Capote, and Thomas Wolfe. For Lavallé, Erskine Caldwell's account of rural American poverty in *Tragic Ground* and *God's Little Acre* seemed more real than the traditional Quebec village portrayed in Ringuet's *Trente arpents*. In his estimation, Quebec literature was self-censored and failed to capture the spoken language of the people. In his taste, critical outlook, and negative assessment of the church and small-town Quebec society, Lavallé was remarkably progressive for a young man of his day.

Despite their many differences, both readers celebrated a liberal humanism that shaped and was shaped by their compulsive reading. For Montgomery and Lavallé, books provided anchors as well as wings.

chapter 17

CONTROLLING AND ADVISING READERS

Government Censorship of Print

PEARCE CAREFOOTE

The regulation of print in Canada has its roots in the Customs Act of 1847, legislation originated by the Province of Canada which prohibited the importation of 'books and drawings of an immoral or indecent character.'[1] Since then jurisprudence has evolved to take into account new situations and technologies with a view to combatting sedition as well. Controls tightened during wartime and periods of political tension. The difficulty for Canadians, however, has been to agree upon definitions of 'obscenity' or 'sedition' that reflect the changing mores of society.

Since Confederation in 1867 customs agents have been the front line in the control of literature entering the country, while the Criminal Code and the Canadian judicial system have regulated domestic publications. A 'Customs Tariff' initiated in the early 1930s, for example, prohibited 'books, printed paper, drawings, painting, prints, photographs or representations of any kind of a treasonable or seditious nature, or of an immoral or indecent character.'[2] Until 1958 officials could refer to a list of proscribed publications to supplement their own discretion when refusing to admit a book into the country. The first list, issued in 1895, named forty-seven American serials; by 1957 over one thousand 'indecent' books were prohibited, reflecting the growth of the paperback book trade.[3] At the end of the twentieth century, customs agents still operated in accord with the spirit of these earliest tariff laws, to which gay bookstores like Little Sister's in Vancouver, Glad Day in Toronto, and

Androgyne in Montreal can well attest. Except in times of political or social crisis, when they actively pursued a policy of censorship, Canada's federal and provincial governments have been less vigilant in controlling domestic print materials, choosing instead to play a supporting role, propping up often vague notions of 'community standards' at large in Canadian society.[4]

The First World War provoked unprecedented levels of censorship at home as well as on the battlefield.[5] The War Measures Act of 1914 provided for the 'censorship and control and suppression of publications, writings, maps, plans, photographs, communication and means of communication.'[6] After the armistice of 1918, with labour unrest at home and the Russian Revolution a recent memory, fear of socialism pervaded the corridors of power. At the suggestion of Lieutenant-Colonel Ernest J. Chambers, chief censor, the federal government extended the War Measures Act to the end of 1919, ostensibly to allow for reconstruction of the faltering Canadian economy. As a result, numerous leftist books and journals were banned from importation. While some Canadian journals were also suppressed in 1918 and 1919, Vancouver's *Western Clarion* and *The Red Flag* among them, Chambers was less successful in prosecuting organizations willing to print forbidden materials inside the country. In 1919, for example, the Socialist Party of Canada issued an edition of Karl Marx's *The Communist Manifesto* (see illus. 5.2, p. 189).

In the inter-war period, bureaucrats focused their attentions on print materials that threatened the social and political order within their jurisdictions. The Winnipeg General Strike of May 1919, coupled with general labour discontent throughout the Dominion, provoked the addition of Section 98 to the Criminal Code, a text that established a twenty-year prison term for anyone involved in the production or distribution of printed materials that advocated or defended the use of force or terrorism to achieve political or economic change.[7]

In Quebec the government of Maurice Duplessis passed the 'Padlock Law' in 1937, making it illegal to print communist materials and giving prosecutors the right to close printing houses and imprison persons suspected of disseminating communist ideas (see illus. 17.1, p. 470). In this violation of freedom of expression, the Quebec government was supported by the Catholic Church, which traditionally had served as censor in the province. As is often the case in censorship, the Padlock Law did not define 'propagation,' and, given the perceived threat to Canadian society coming from the emerging socialist movement, the federal government did not challenge the provincial government's action. The law remained in force for twenty years.[8]

Less successful were the efforts of Premier William Aberhart's Social Credit government in Alberta, which attempted to restrict freedom of the press through a

17.1 *Clarté, journal d'opinions et d'action populaire*, 17 April 1937. Published from 1935 to 1939 in Montreal, this communist newspaper defied efforts to close it down. The caption for S. Field's editorial cartoon translates: 'The Padlock Law of 1937 threatens the freedom gained by the Canadian people in 1837.' The heading 'L'ombre du fascisme' links the Duplessis era in Quebec with the rise of fascism. Courtesy of Bibliothèque de l'Assemblée nationale, Quebec City.

series of increasingly draconian actions between 1935 and 1937. In 1937 the government passed the Alberta Press Act, requiring newspapers to publish, free of charge, statements furnished by the Social Credit Board chairman related to government policies. If demanded by the party, editors had to print up to one full page of text every day a newspaper was published. The act also required newspapers to divulge the names of anyone involved in the writing of editorials. Penalties included suspension of publication and bans against journalists. The *Edmonton Journal* challenged the act before the Supreme Court of Canada, which unanimously agreed in March 1938 that it was unconstitutional. For their defence of press freedom, the paper's editors received a special Pulitzer Prize.[9]

The revival of hostilities in Europe in 1939 saw a return to more stringent censorship in Canada. Domestic censorship was voluntary, meaning that editors acted as censors within their own domains, in accordance with the articles of the War Measures Act and the Defence of Canada Regulations, which came into effect in September 1939.[10] As with the First World War, censorship focused on the protection of military secrets, national safety, the prosecution of the war abroad, and the maintenance of morale at home. Contrary to common law tradition, the burden of proof fell on the person who was charged with any violation of the regulations. Although the chief censor was empowered to say what did *not* infringe the regulations, he was never authorized to state positively that the publication of a story *was* a violation, leading to some confusion among journalists, especially with reference to reporting troop deployment and logistical information. Fear of transgression caused editor Hugh S. Eayrs at Macmillan of Canada to insist that Irene Baird make some minor modifications to her protest novel, *Waste Heritage* (1939).[11] As the war progressed, the censor's office became more specific in its instructions, and writers were generally compliant. At the war's peak, some six hundred publications were banned by Ottawa.[12]

The October Crisis of 1970 was the last time in the twentieth century that freedom of expression was curtailed in response to a national emergency. When Prime Minister Pierre Elliott Trudeau invoked the War Measures Act to deal with the perceived threat from the Front de libération du Québec to peace in Canada in general and Quebec in particular, the act's power to censor and suppress print immediately came into play. The limitations imposed on coverage by newspapers and magazines received surprisingly little disapproval at the time.[13] Once the crisis had passed, however, the government was criticized for exercising such sweeping control of print media. As a result, the War Measures Act was replaced by the Emergencies Act of 1988, legislation which makes no mention of censorship.

Although the federal and provincial governments were the driving force behind censorship during times of real or imagined danger to the country, at other times they used agencies, such as Canada Customs, to support the community standards of the day, especially with reference to allegedly obscene materials. James Joyce's *Ulysses*, for example, was banned from 1923 until 1949, when *Maclean's Magazine* questioned the continued detention of a recognized classic.[14] When the uncensored text of D.H. Lawrence's *Lady Chatterley's Lover* appeared in 1960, it was immediately banned. Judge T.A. Fontaine of Montreal pronounced the work obscene and set aside the testimony of noted Canadian authors Hugh MacLennan and Morley Callaghan, declaring their interventions to be 'purely personal opinion.'[15] The following year, Customs even held up the importation of the transcript from the book's British trial because it contained explicit details. In 1962 the Supreme Court of Canada ruled in the book's favour, allowing for its sale.

In 1949, of the 126 titles excluded from Canada, only 29 were considered seditious; the rest were categorized as 'obscene,' including Norman Mailer's *The Naked and the Dead* (1948), a book that the *Globe and Mail* described as 'pure pornography.'[16] After ten weeks on the best-seller list of the *New York Times*, in February 1949 Mailer's work was banned by the minister of national revenue, J.J. McCann. Like many other censors, McCann admitted that he had never read the book. Instead, he based his judgment on highlights supplied by his staff, condemned the work as 'disgusting,' and removed it from the shelves.[17] A similar fate had befallen Henry Miller's *Tropic of Cancer* (1934), which was banned in Canada until the University of Toronto Library successfully appealed to the minister of national revenue in 1962.

It could be argued that the problem with Canadian law is not so much with the definition of obscenity as with its interpretation. In 1954 the government defined 'obscenity' in the Criminal Code, amending the definition five years later to its present-day formulation that 'any publication a dominant characteristic of which is the undue exploitation of sex, or of sex and any one or more of the following subjects, namely, crime, horror, cruelty and violence, shall be deemed to be obscene.'[18] Under the Criminal Code, proof-texting – highlighting specific passages in a work, without regard to their literary context, to support the argument of obscenity – remains the legal means for prosecuting books and those associated with them.[19] This method has proven equally popular among parent groups who, especially in the 1970s, sought greater control over students' reading. In 1976 a group of parents in Lakefield, Ontario, the town where Margaret Laurence resided, united under the banner of the 'Citizens in Defence of Decency' to demand that Laurence's *The Diviners* (1974) be removed from schools on the grounds that it was 'unsavory pornography' that promoted 'degradation, indecency and immorality.' Although this organization's demands were ultimately rejected, another group challenged the book in 1985, even though its members acknowledged that they had not read it in its entirety.[20] Similar complaints have been raised by parent councils across the country against such classics as Morley Callaghan's *Such Is My Beloved* (1934), W.O. Mitchell's *Who Has Seen the Wind* (1947), and Alice Munro's *Lives of Girls and Women* (1971).

As the 1980s approached, it was clear that the motives for censorship were shifting from concerns over 'national security' to the protection of 'family values,' partisan views, and/or religious and minority rights. It is also noteworthy that challenges to literary freedom were no longer coming exclusively from the political spectrum, although Canada Customs did not diminish its role as a protector of community standards. With the entrenchment of the Charter of Rights and Freedoms in the Constitution of Canada (1982), however, limitations on literary expression would become far more difficult, though not impossible, to justify.

Religious Censorship in English Canada

DANIEL O'LEARY

Bruce Ryder uses the term 'undercover censorship' to describe tacit or covert editorial suppression of objectionable print, and points out that censorship of this kind is 'an inevitable feature of social organization.'[21] Church influence at major publishing houses such as the United Church–owned Ryerson Press meant that editors like Lorne Pierce, himself an ordained minister, occasionally acted as censors on religious or moral grounds, but the line between censorship and simple editorial bias, or inclination, is often difficult to draw. Lorne Pierce admitted using his power to refuse publication to uncongenial works: 'I thought of my publishing house as a great organ in a cathedral, upon the console of which I could bring out whatever music I desired ... therefore, I would, as long as I held my chair, not allow publication of anything unbeautiful, untrue or unsympathetic.'[22] He rejected E.J. Pratt's long poem *The Witches' Brew* on moral grounds in 1924,[23] yet the following year he published Frederick Philip Grove's controversial realistic novel *Settlers of the Marsh*.

Self-censorship by educators intent on conforming to the conventions of their religious communities has been inevitable, limiting the need for open or explicit control of printed matter. In his memoirs, publisher Marsh Jeanneret offered an illuminating example of this phenomenon, recalling that during the interwar period Copp Clark published a complete series of Shakespeare's plays. Edited by O.J. Stevenson of the Ontario Agricultural College, the texts were 'so thoroughly bowdlerized ... that they were more than fit for classroom study anywhere, even Sunday schools if necessary.'[24] In fact, the presence of devout persons in key positions in all sectors of the communications circuit made aggressive public censorship unnecessary. However, following the Second World War, the decline of religious influence in public life and the emergence of more liberal publishing standards stimulated evangelical and conservative religious activism.

Always vigilant, prior to 1939 the Roman Catholic Church devoted considerable energy to discussion of the negative effects of inappropriate or corrupt reading materials and to the production of alternatives. For example, *The Raphaelite*, published three times a year in the 1930s by the women of the Mount Carmel Academy in Saint John, New Brunswick, announced in one issue: 'Secular reading matter rarely urges us to better Christian civilization. Usually its spirit and its teachings are directly opposed to the spirit of Christ and His teachings. The reading of good Catholic literature,' it affirmed, 'is an indispensable means for the preparation necessary for Catholic Action and for the Christianizing of our country.'[25] Since the 1950s, the Catholic Women's League (CWL), in turn, has acted as a pressure group for the regulation of Canadian reading by lobbying federal and provincial governments to censor publications deemed immoral. In Alberta in 1954, the CWL joined farm women's unions and the University Women's League on Alberta's Advisory Board on Objectionable Publications, which operated until 1973. This body 'maintained a list of objectionable publications that it forwarded to distributors' with the tacit understanding 'that the attorney general would not institute or encourage obscenity prosecutions in return for their adherence to the board's recommendations.'[26] In 1955, under archdiocesan council president Evelyn Markle, the CWL launched a 'Decency Crusade,' publishing the *National Organization for Decent Literature's List of 300 Objectionable Publications*. In 1956 the Ontario attorney general responded to this pressure, forming an eight-member committee, known between 1960 and 1972 as the Obscene Literature Committee, which operated so as to moderate the activism of religious pressure groups.[27]

Law professor Joel Bakan has studied the importance of schools as sites of ideological, political, and sexual coercion in relation to free speech, noting the influence of 'conservative and far-right religious organizations' on legislation affecting school curricula in North America.[28] Although the influence of such groups is often subtle and unrecorded, the banning of books in the classroom attracts attention and has been identified as a notable feature of Canadian educational history. A discussion guide to school-book censorship issued by the Canadian Library Association (CLA) in 1982 listed 117 English-language magazine and newspaper articles on the topic, most published between 1976 and 1979.[29] While objections often came from individual parents, whose grounds for criticism included political bias, violence, or stereotyping, the CLA named Renaissance International as a 'fundamentalist Christian organization ... active across Canada [which] crops up frequently in reports of school book controversies.'[30] But such interventions often backfire. In 1978, when the school board of Richmond, BC, decided to remove the anonymously written *Go Ask Alice* from secondary school libraries and send it to the public library, 'students were outraged and presented a petition to the school board ... One seventeen-year-old Richmond student pointed out that banning the book encouraged people to read it. This proved to be true: Richmond bookstores quickly sold out of this title.'[31]

From Censoring Print to Advising Readers in Quebec

PIERRE HÉBERT

From 1840, when Mgr Bourget became head of the Roman Catholic Church's Diocese of Montreal, until the Quiet Revolution, by tacit agreement the clergy exercised control over printed materials in Quebec. Throughout the nineteenth century, repressive censorship was the method of choice, the limited amount of print in circulation and the absence of independent publishers facilitating a control based on prohibition.[32] However, in the twentieth century, the clergy gradually lost its grip on the dissemination of publications. Up to mid-century, existing or newly created periodicals reflecting clerical views competed with an increasing number of literary and commercial publications expressing secular values; after 1960, the voices heard by readers were almost entirely secular and professional. General circulation newspapers, such as *La Presse* and *La Patrie*, which were financially independent, similarly paid less and less attention to church directives, while new publishers, such as Albert Lévesque and Albert Pelletier, took risks in their choice of publications. In addition, beginning in the 1940s, the rise of popular literature and crime comics raised the issue of obscenity.

The Decline of Clerical Censorship

By the First World War, the Roman Catholic clergy had abandoned their repressive nineteenth-century practice of overt censorship and adopted a prescriptive approach to print in Quebec. Recognizing the impossibility of suppressing publications that deviated from the church's standards, the clergy instead inculcated its particular ideas through its own print materials and other means. It was in this context that the clerical intelligentsia in Quebec took on the vast enterprise of nationalizing French-Canadian literature, placing an emphasis on the qualities of Catholicism, language, and the pastoral when assessing its worth.[33] Abbés Camille Roy and Lionel Groulx led the way. Roy engaged in literary criticism, while Groulx exerted his influence through writing and publishing activities, as well as his directorship of the Bibliothèque de l'Action française. During the first third of the twentieth century, an 'orgy of the soil,' to use Jean-Charles Harvey's description, dominated French-Canadian literature.[34] That no significant clerical prohibitions occurred between 1913, when the newspaper *Le Pays* was suspected of freemasonry, and 1934, when Jean-Charles Harvey's novel *Les demi-civilisés* was condemned by the archbishop of Quebec for its deliberate transgression of the moral standards of the time, should not be seen as a relaxation of censorship but, on the contrary, as the successful imposition of orthodoxy before publication, and thus upon thought itself.

Significant challenges to clerical control did occur in the early 1930s. Although ultimately he was forced to back down under clerical pressure, in 1931 and 1932 Montreal publisher Albert Lévesque, who tried to maintain a certain distance from a readership that was still steeped in the principles of Action française, issued four novels in the series Romans de la jeune génération that were not entirely in keeping with religious morality: Éva Senécal's *Dans les ombres,* Jovette Bernier's *La chaire décevante,* Claude Robillard's *Le dilettante,* and Rex Desmarchais's *L'initiatrice.* Equally important was Groulx's decision to leave Lévesque's publishing house for Librairie Granger Frères, a company whose politics were closer to those of the clergy. Then, in 1934, Albert Pelletier, the publisher of Éditions du Totem, issued Medjé Vézina's *Chaque heure a son visage,* a collection of poems whose rebellion broke through the surface, as well as Harvey's aforementioned *Les demi-civilisés.* The following year,

Pelletier launched *Les Idées* (Montreal, 1935–9), a magazine which consistently attacked clericalism, especially in education. During these two years, Olivar Asselin founded *L'Ordre* (Montreal, 1934–5), a liberal newspaper immediately condemned by Cardinal Villeneuve,[35] and soon replaced by *La Renaissance* (Montreal, 1935).

This opposition to clericalism proved to be, in Alfred DesRochers apt phrase, a 'fireworks display ... above our twilight.'[36] With the election of Maurice Duplessis as premier of Quebec in 1936 and the onset of the Second World War, opposition diminished, and a wave of conservatism engulfed the province. The Padlock Law (1937) and, later, the Roncarelli Affair (1946)[37] demonstrated the repressive nature of the government, and the clergy saw a chance to strengthen its ties with the authorities. In addition, the war brought a climate of censorship which diminished freedom of expression. Indeed, the Roman Catholic Church in Quebec used the war for its own purposes, interpreting it as God's punishment for moral and religious decadence. During this period, the church rarely used its power of censorship, other than in 1942, when the *Semaine religieuse de Québec* condemned Jean-Charles Harvey's *Le Jour* for republishng an article from *Life* magazine which presented an unflattering picture of Quebec's clergy.[38] Instead, it persisted in its efforts to control printed matter. With the blessing of Cardinal Villeneuve, Éditions Fides began publishing *Lectures* (1946–65), a magazine which monitored new publications and guided reading practices by rating the morality of individual titles. Such ratings were designed to exert increased control over those who influenced reading, including critics, teachers, and librarians.

Appearances were deceiving, however. During the war, many works that did not comply with the church's morality were nonetheless published as a result of the Patents, Designs, Copyright and Trade Marks (Emergency) Order (1939), a federal decree adopted under the War Measures Act that allowed Quebec to function as a centre of French-language publishing while France was occupied by Germany. Consequently, new ideas circulated, laying the groundwork for change in the 1960s. Other events during this period further undermined the power of the clergy. Jean-Paul Sartre presented a lecture in Montreal in 1946, showing the ineffectiveness, indeed the futility, of censorship. Painter Paul-Émile Borduas responded to the fear of change with *Refus global* (1948), a text discussed in greater detail by A.B. McKillop in chapter 1. Psychological novels, exhibiting an array of values that would previously have been unthinkable, appeared on the market. By the following decade, the clergy was losing the power to control reading and printed matter.

Throughout the 1950s, however, the Roman Catholic Church in Quebec was marked by increasing doctrinal rigidity. In 1950 Mgr Valois, director of the Comité diocésain d'action catholique, prohibited any commemoration of the centenary of Honoré de Balzac's death, forcing the Société des écrivains canadiens, which had initiated the event, to drop its plans. The remainder of the decade witnessed a proliferation of campaigns for public morality and leagues against undesirable reading as the Catholic hierarchy seemed to be returning to the strategies of the nineteenth century. Popular publications and crime comics, mass-market literature completely beyond the clergy's control, caused the greatest fuss, and the church had to appeal to secular authorities to contain the new threat. Thus, in 1959, after a great deal of pressure from churches throughout Canada, but in particular from the Catholic clergy in Quebec, the legal definition of obscenity in the Criminal Code was amended, as Pearce Carefoote explains earlier in this chapter. After this major victory, the clergy halted its public interventions into books and printed matter. On the one hand, it recognized the state's authority over censorship. On the other, the Roman Catholic Church as a whole had realized that its censorship was ineffective, and, in keeping with a broad movement throughout the West, in 1966 it abolished the *Index*, the list of prohibited titles the church had maintained since the sixteenth century.

The Quiet Revolution of the 1960s radically changed the nature of book censorship in Quebec. Judicial authorities now acted as censors, protecting morals generally, as shown in the legal action taken in 1969 against André Loiselet's *Le mal des anges*, a work accused of being pornographic.[39] Through the 1960s and 1970s, clerical censorship occurred very rarely outside the church's immediate sphere. One exception was the reaction to Denise Boucher's *Les fées ont soif* (1978), a play that attacked the image of the Virgin Mary. However, the events surrounding this work provide a good illustration of the division of powers and the manner in which censorship had come to operate. In this borderline case that involved morality as much as religion, the courts had to respond to an application for an injunction to prevent its performance. While the desire for censorship came from marginal groups, indicating the fragmentation of power, the legal system represented the main means of censorship in a society governed by the rule of law. Having left the religious sphere, censorship now lurked in more secular sites, such as libraries and schools, where it particularly affected books for children.

The Rise of Secular Advice

Throughout the twentieth century, magazines and newspapers in Quebec played a key role in providing guidelines for reading. During the interwar period, magazines such as *L'Action française* (Montreal, 1917–28) and *Le Terroir* (Quebec City, 1918–40) recommended reading that was in keeping with the clerical program of language, faith, and nation. Books outside this category had little chance of breaking through and were criticized in light of traditional values. Nonetheless, existing alongside Catholic publications that called for the distribution of 'good books' were a number of periodicals whose intellectual and financial independence allowed them to promote a critical point of view based on secular values. The first of these, the short-lived *Le Nigog* (Montreal, 1918), advocated an art for art's sake philosophy and favoured an autonomous literature. *La Revue moderne*, a general-circulation magazine, published articles by Louis Dantin, the most influential and innovative literary critic of the interwar period. In the magazine world of the 1930s and 1940s, a few dissident voices were heard even among Catholics. *La Relève* (Montreal, 1934–41) and *La Nouvelle relève* (1941–8), for example, took part in the debate on a Catholicism open to modern, secular values, one based on Jacques Maritain's integral humanism and Emmanuel Mounier's personalism.

A decisive change in the discourse on reading occurred in the literary pages of *Le Devoir* at the end of the 1940s, after Gérard Filion and André Laurendeau took over the running of the Montreal daily. Criticism that rejected clericalism began to appear, leading to a discussion of books that brought *Le Devoir* into direct conflict with the clerical magazine *Lectures*, whose editors lashed out against the newspaper.[40] The late 1940s also witnessed a changing of the guard among critics. Those who spoke for the clergy, such as Henri d'Arles, Maurice Hébert, Camille Roy, and Carmel Brouillard, gave way to representatives of a modern, liberal view of French-Canadian literature, such as Alfred DesRochers, Jean Le Moyne, Maurice Blain, and Ernest Gagnon. Others of this new generation included Pierre Baillargeon, co-founder of *Amérique française* (Montreal, 1941–55); Gilles Marcotte, who during the 1950s revitalized the book pages of *Le Devoir*; Guy Sylvestre, the founder of *Gants du ciel* (Montreal, 1943–6); and Pierre de Grandpré, who in the 1960s published *Histoire de la littérature française du Québec* (Montreal, 1967–9), praised for its scope and rigour as well as its presentation of a multiplicity of voices.

Professional critics regularly contributed to magazines such as *Cité libre* (Montreal, 1950–66) and *Écrits du Canada français* (Montreal, 1954–), as well as to university publications. Journalists and teachers formed a new intelligentsia who would make an impact on the critical discourse of this era and would help promote Quebec literature to the general public. Even *Lectures*, when it dropped its moral ratings in 1965, recognized that 'the problem of reading material primarily concerns readers.'[41]

With the Quiet Revolution, a new era began: readers needed to be informed rather than educated. New publications like *Livres et auteurs canadiens* (Montreal,

Quebec City, 1961–82; in 1969 retitled *Livres et auteurs québécois*) and *Lettres québécoises* (Montreal, 1975–) met this need and broadened the readership for Quebec's national literature. Intellectual magazines such as *Parti pris* (Montreal, 1963–8), *Liberté* (Montreal, 1959–), and *La Barre du jour* (Montreal, 1965–77) reflected a more radical change and a definitive transition to modernity. Starting in the 1970s, little magazines of criticism and literature exhibiting various schools of thought were founded in Montreal, such as the Marxist *Chroniques* (1975–8) and the feminist *Nouvelle Barre du jour* (1977–90), *Herbes rouges* (1968–93), and *Stratégie* (1972–7). Many new scholarly journals were also created in Montreal – *Études françaises* (1965–), *Voix et images du pays* (1967–74; subsequently *Voix et images*, 1975–), and *Études littéraires* (1968–) – and in Sherbrooke, *Présence francophone* (1970–98). Newspapers continued to expand their book pages, with such features as weekly best-seller lists. Information and advertising were now part of the 'book industry,' and the strategy was to diversify and even segment the market. The Latin word *legere* means to read, but also to choose. In the middle of the twentieth century, a radical shift took place in Quebec: from publications requiring clerical censorship and intervention, newspapers, magazines, and books became sources of information and commercial commodities, and readers could make their own choices rather than having their reading selected for them.

'Read Canadian'

W.H. NEW

Reviewers and critics sort through published writings, evaluate worth, describe patterns, elucidate significance, trace trends, and distinguish among different kinds of books for differing circumstances, such as lists for summer reading or Christmas giving. By encouraging or discouraging readers, reviews can powerfully affect writers' reputations. Yet reviewers' comments are only superficially objective. Whether openly idiosyncratic or claiming adherence to a 'universal standard,' they are, like the texts at which they look and the venues in which they publish, shaped by training, experience, politics, and personal bias. Over the twentieth century, reading guides, critical commentaries, and reviews of Canadian books appeared in whatever media were current: from newspaper and periodical notices to radio and television programs, documentary films, literary journalism, and book-length argument and analysis. While scholarly criticism affected general readers indirectly, by influencing teaching practices and the construction of curricular canons, reviews in newspapers, magazines, and broadcast media spoke directly to the book-buying public.

In popular magazines and newspapers, columnists could have substantial impact, both locally and across the nation. From 1907 until his death in 1933, Professor Archibald MacMechan sent his regular column, 'The Dean's Window,' from Halifax to the *Montreal Standard*, where he advocated books that brought joy to readers.[42] One of the strongest such personalities was William Arthur Deacon, literary editor of *Saturday Night* from 1922 to 1928 and the *Globe and Mail* from 1936 to 1960, who dismissed anything hinting of romance, whether by Arthur Stringer or L.M. Montgomery. While his reviews seem not to have affected these writers' sales, Deacon, like his colleague Hector Charlesworth, feuded with some authors but established the careers of many others.[43] On the West Coast, Jack Scott, writing in the *Vancouver Sun* in March 1961, recuperated the career and later writings of Malcolm Lowry, turning *Under the Volcano* into a strong seller. Some influential reviewers, such as Robert Fulford, published in a variety of venues, from *Maclean's* to the *Financial Post*, as well as airing their views on radio. Others remained within one or two venues, such as Robertson Davies, whose columns in the *Peterborough Examiner* through the 1940s and 1950s extolled fine writing and decried small-mindedness, and Doris Giller, who wrote for the *Montreal Star* before moving in 1979 to the *Montreal Gazette*, where she created the paper's first book review section. Commentary in wide-circulation periodicals often came to be associated with specific individuals: *Saturday Night* with B.K. Sandwell (editor from 1932 to 1951) and Arnold Edinborough (editor from 1958 to 1962; owner and publisher from 1963 to 1970); the *Globe* with William French (literary editor from 1960 to 1990).

The increasing number of review journals after 1918 suggests the changing state of literary awareness in Canada. Book reviews appeared not only in wide-circulation periodicals such as the *Canadian Magazine of Politics, Science, Art and Literature* (Toronto, 1893–1939), but also in specialized publications such as the *Canadian National Railways Magazine* (Montreal, 1915–57; 'Railways' was dropped from its title in 1937), aimed at railway employees, which included reviews and short fiction alongside recipes, staff activities, and travel writing. During the interwar period, the reviewing policies of a wave of new journals (popular, political, trade, professional, and academic) deliberately fostered national cultural enthusiasms. The commitment of the *Canadian Forum* (Toronto, 1920–2000), which grew out of the three-year-old *Rebel*, was to promote 'informed discussion of public questions and, behind the strife of parties, to trace and value those developments of art and letters which are distinctly Canadian.'[44] Other new journals influenced Canadian reading by addressing those who selected titles on behalf of buyers and borrowers, such as the book trade's *Quill & Quire* (Toronto, 1935–), whose reviews targeted booksellers' stocking practices, and the various publications issued by the Canadian Library Association, which addressed librarians' selections. The university-based journals, the *Queen's Quarterly* (Kingston, ON, 1893–) and the *Dalhousie Review* (Halifax, 1921–), broadly based guides to intellectual inquiry, included non-specialist survey reviews of histories, biographies, and commentaries on culture. In 1935 the *University of Toronto Quarterly* (UTQ) began its annual 'Letters in Canada,' which reviewed the year's work in Canadian literature, reflected current critical debates, and shaped the modernist tone of Canadian canonical judgment into the 1960s. Among other contributors, Watson Kirkconnell summarized allophone publications, and Northrop Frye reviewed Canadian poetry between 1951 and 1960. As in his other critical writings, including *The Bush Garden* (1971), Frye read Canadian and international writing mythopoeically, an approach that profoundly influenced the teaching and classroom reading of Canadian literature during the 1960s and 1970s, and reached the informed public through such works as *The Educated Imagination* (1963), frequently reprinted after its initial broadcast in the CBC's Massey Lectures series.

As the majority of the magazines and periodicals read by anglophone Canadians have been imported from Britain and the United States, these have provided ample guidance regarding foreign books. However, advice about Canadian titles has been found primarily in Canadian sources. These began to proliferate when the cultural nationalism of the 1920s saw a spate of books whose goal was to educate the reading public about Canadian writers; hence information-gathering models, both historical and biographical, informed works like MacMechan's *Headwaters of Canadian Literature* (1924; based on his articles in the *Montreal Standard*) and Lorne Pierce's *Outline of Canadian Literature (French and English)* (1927), as well as the Makers of Canadian Literature series that Pierce commissioned for Ryerson Press beginning in 1923.[45] After 1960, as Canadian literature became a topic of scholarly concern, anchored by Carl F. Klinck's monumental *Literary History of Canada* (1965), criticism became more specialized and voluminous as academic discussion gathered momentum, abroad as well as at home. W.H. New's annual survey of Canadian literary publications began in 1970 in the *Journal of Commonwealth Literature* (University of Leeds), moving later to *Canadian Literature*, then ceasing in 2003. Outside the university, readers' desire for guidance was met most effectively (in terms of sales) by Margaret Atwood's sprightly *Survival* (1972), a best-selling general thematic survey that was originally conceived as an advertising campaign for books published by House of Anansi Press. Atwood's book satisfied both a hunger for cultural celebration and the illusion of a clear definition of Canadian identity. Widely consulted for the next two decades, it also helped establish her name in the popular imagination.

Yet the divide between academic practice and public access remained wide. In the 1950s the combined circulation for the three university quarterlies was less than 4,000, with UTQ at some points in its history having fewer than 100 subscribers. For comparison, in November 1957, Toronto's *Star Weekly* magazine (1910–68) boasted 885,000 subscribers, inevitably influencing literary reputations, through biographical profiles more than through formal reviews. To address this imbalance, the editors of *Canadian Historical Review* (Toronto, 1920–) devoted approximately twenty pages of each issue to 'recent publications relating to Canadian history,' eager to give reviewers 'the latitude they require'[46] to make discriminating judgments. Despite this hope for greater detail, many reviews remained perfunctory. The same held true with literary reception, although when *Canadian Literature* was founded in Vancouver in 1959, the first editor, George Woodcock, took *Scrutiny* and *Sewanee Review* as his models, seeking discursive essays from practising writers as well as academics. During its first years, the quarterly reviewed all significant Canadian literary works, but despite its own growth in size and distribution, the radical increase in the number of published works by 1980 made this practice no longer possible. Other journals, founded to focus on more specialized subjects, such as *Canadian Theatre Review* (Toronto, 1974), *Canadian Children's Literature / Littérature canadienne pour la jeunesse* (Guelph, 1975–), and journals in geography, political science, and law, reviewed books for their distinct readerships. *Canadian Dimension* (Winnipeg, 1963–) addressed books through a socially engaged approach to society and mass media, as did *This Magazine* (Toronto, 1966–) in its attention to writings on educational policy and practice.

Facing an increasing number of publications, readers turned to still other guides: announcements of national and local prizewinners, weekly lists of best-sellers, weekend entertainment sections of major newspapers, and media interviews. In the 1950s, for example, in programs such as *Critically Speaking* and *Fighting Words*, the CBC brought several commentators to nationwide audiences, including Nathan Cohen, the acerbic reviewer for the *Toronto Star*. The Readers' Club of Canada published the *Canadian Reader* (Toronto, 1959–81), a pamphlet that each month promoted a particular Canadian work, beginning with Mordecai Richler's *The Apprenticeship of Duddy Kravitz*, reviewed by Robert Weaver, and continuing in 1960 with praise for Malcolm Ross's stewardship of the newly established New Canadian

Library (club members received a 20 per cent discount). Another enterprise aimed at the general reading public, *Books in Canada* (Toronto, 1971–), was initially distributed free, supported almost entirely by advertising. Under Val Clery's editorship, this periodical began as a self-declared 'biased' magazine, in favour of breaking the 'virtual monopoly' of American publications in the Canadian market. Its popularity indicates that Canadian readers in the 1970s were keen to find out about their own writers. Yet, according to David Staines, such opportunities diminished substantially between 1959 and 1986, with a decline in book sections and original reviews in Canadian newspapers, and a greater reliance on commentary received from American wire services.[47] Other than occasional star turns in international venues, such as Edmund Wilson's laudatory 'Morley Callaghan of Toronto' in *The New Yorker* in 1960, and the international attention that accrues to winners of international awards, it remained necessary in the 1970s to turn to Canadian resources to guide those desiring to 'read Canadian.'[48]

Encouraging Children to Read

LORNA KNIGHT

As a distinct group of readers, children have always been subject to the intervention of adults. In Sheila Egoff's words, 'Every book that a child reads comes to him only after a decision about it has been made by an adult, or, more exactly, by many adults: writer, publisher, bookseller, librarian, parent and/or teacher.'[49] Through the twentieth century, adults developed strategies to both foster and control children's reading. Public libraries, long the champions of reading for pleasure, also addressed literacy. Schools, given primary responsibility for teaching children to read, realized the need for effective school libraries and parental involvement. In the 1960s recognition of the importance of preschool readiness-to-read programming brought more players into the field. By 1980 teachers, and public and school librarians, were joined by education theorists, parents, publishers, writers, and illustrators as recognized participants.

Before the First World War, several urban libraries pioneered services for children by hiring specialists in children's literature who created separate children's areas (a requirement of Carnegie-funded libraries) and initiated the hallmark of children's programming, the story hour.[50] In 1922, following more than a decade of growing services for young readers, the Toronto Public Library (TPL) established Boys and Girls House, the first library in the British Empire devoted exclusively to children. Its director, Lillian H. Smith, firmly believed that children should enjoy reading: 'No force in the world can compel children to read, for long, what they do not want ... They may not know why they reject one book and cling to another, for their judgment is seldom analytical. It is based on something genuine – pleasure' (see illus. 17.2, p. 486).[51] The Montreal City Library followed suit in 1941 by creating a children's room with open shelves. Weekly programs included a story hour, as well as occasional films, art classes, and discussions of favourite children's authors.[52]

In the 1930s and 1940s, the TPL collected data about children's preferences and was concerned about directing them toward its own definition of 'the best.' Excluded were series, comics, and, for some unaccountable reason, Frances Hodgson Burnett's classic novel, *The Secret Garden*. Its recommendations, published with frequent updates as *Books for Boys and Girls* (1927, 1928, 1940, 1954), sold around the world.[53] In Quebec, children's literature was also a frequent topic of discussion. One of the best known publications was Guy Boulizon's *Livres roses et séries noires* (1957), described in its subtitle as a 'psychological and bibliographical guide.' His moralistic recommendations condemned comic books and what he called the '"pink" danger' of sentimental stories for girls, which, he believed, created a world of false illusion.[54]

In November 1949 the Canadian Association of Children's Librarians (est. 1939) and the Canadian Library Association (est. 1946) initiated Young Canada's Book Week (see illus. 17.3, p. 487). The event offered an opportunity for children's librarians to engage more fully with the larger community while promoting children's reading. With the advent of television in the 1960s, children's departments, worried about competition, further extended their efforts to attract school-aged children to summer reading programs, arts and crafts, and other activities to augment previously established story hours, reading clubs, and drama and puppetry groups. In the same decade, in addition to addressing children of reading age, libraries added 'books for babies' programs, using 'finger plays, chants and songs to introduce infants under two to books.'[55] Children's reading was actively promoted in Quebec in the 1970s, through the programming of Communication-jeunesse, described in chapter 4 by Françoise Lepage, Judith Saltman, and Gail Edwards.

In Canada, schools traditionally assumed responsibility for the teaching of reading, with basal readers as the primary tool. However, criticism of these texts and their pedagogical approach quickly followed Rudolf Flesch's best-seller, *Why Johnny*

17.2 Pegi Nicol MacLeod, *Jane Reading* (ca. 1948). Courtesy of the J.M. Barnicke Art Gallery, Hart House, University of Toronto.

Can't Read: And What You Can Do about It (1955). Concerns about television usurping the role of the book in children's entertainment spurred teachers and educationists to study language acquisition and reading trends. Flesch's condemnation of the failure of schools to teach reading became a household issue and helped unite the disparate groups for whom childhood reading was a paramount concern. The year 1955 also marked the first Canadian Conference on Reading organized by the Federation

17.3 Barbara Cooney (illustrator), promotional brochure for Young Canada's Book Week / La semaine du livre pour la jeunesse canadienne, 1959. Courtesy of The Children's Book Council, Inc. (New York) and the Barbara Cooney Porter Royalty Trust.

of Women's Teachers Associations of Ontario, an event that brought together various interest groups. In her introduction to the published proceedings, Florence Irvine remarked that reading instruction now involved paying attention to 'the place of reading in the elementary curriculum, developmental reading programmes, the retarded reader ... teaching new citizens to read, developing independence in reading ... and teaching reading to the gifted child.'[56]

From the late 1950s and into the 1960s, in both English and French Canada, school libraries were stocked with resources to assist them with their expanding role in children's reading, and teacher-librarians were trained to staff them. Provincial governments, responsible for education, had long recognized the need for both school and public libraries to complement the teaching of reading in the schools. In Newfoundland, for example, the Department of Education established a travelling library service for schools in 1926, followed by Nova Scotia's Department of Education in 1929. Not surprisingly, the evolution of school library service was shaped by evolving philosophies of education and changes in pedagogical thinking. New child-centred learning concepts brought with them resource-based learning and some-times controversial approaches to teaching children how to read. The Canadian School Library Association published their *Standard of Library Service for Canadian Schools* in 1967 (translated as *Normes de service de bibliothèque pour les écoles canadiennes* in 1968) to guide schools in providing programs and facilities to encourage a love of reading and to teach students to find information independently. In addition to serving avid young readers and teaching them to use the public library, the school librarian was responsible for providing varied experiences for the entire school pop-ulation, including exceptional students. Optimistic curriculum guides such as Ontario's *Partners in Action: The Library Resource Centre in the School Curriculum* codified the new role that schools assumed in 1982.

The emergence of other media affected approaches to reading. While school radio broadcasts began in 1939, the first one to air in Canada with a distinctive liter-ary component was *Tales from Far and Near*, imported in 1942–3 from the School of the Air of the Americas in New York. In 1944, CBC Radio began to broadcast readings by TPL librarians, who also selected titles for the program *Stories for You*, which ran from 1945 to 1957. Also popular was a series of dramatizations from children's books whose aim was 'to instill in children a love for fine tales, good books, and a habit of turning to them for joy and refreshment.'[57]

From the late 1950s through to the early 1970s, the CBC continued its national school radio broadcasts, emphasizing literary appreciation rather than reading. Tele-vision proved an effective medium for reaching preschoolers; *The Friendly Giant*, CBC's signature children's program for twenty-six years, was a fifteen-minute show during which Friendly, Jerome the Giraffe, and Rusty the Rooster chatted, read sto-rybooks, played music, and sang. Its low-key, entertaining, and educational style appealed to the preschooler who was getting ready to learn to read. For French-speaking toddlers, *Bobino* (1957–85) and *Passe-partout* (1977–87) likewise valorized books as sources of both knowledge and pleasure. From 1958 to 1964, three times a week, preschool children and their parents could also watch *Nursery School Time*, a program combining entertainment and education for small children. CBC produc-ers assisted parents by publishing programs in advance and by providing lists of recommended children's books. In the late 1950s, the Vancouver office of the CBC produced *Hidden Pages*, a weekly half-hour program that dramatized books for pre-adolescents.

The role of parents gained more prominence with the advent of television. As the nature of families altered in the post-war period, schools responded to criticism by outlining the importance of the parent as the child's first instructor. In 1956 the New Brunswick Federation of Home and School Associations' thirty-nine-page *Primer for Parents* stated, 'Too much has been said by too many people who know too little about the teaching of this, the most important subject in the elementary curriculum.' Reading was now taught 'in a different order,' the primer explained, and admonished parents not to shirk responsibility: 'Reading aloud, sharing, understanding, guiding – these are the things wise parents ... can do to help their children discover books.'[58] With the spread of early childhood education, nursery schools, and daycare centres, parental involvement in the reading process was now seen to begin in the child's first years.

During the 1970s, when questions about the quality of children's reading inspired numerous surveys, debates about what constituted 'good' and 'bad' books for children revived once more, this time focusing on the notion that television was the root of all reading evils. Sarah Landy's survey was among those to pinpoint some of the reasons why children do not read. She found that 'the nonreader tends to associate reading almost exclusively with seeking information and for school-related assignments. Nonreaders have seldom experienced any pleasurable associations with reading.'[59] Her conclusion – that children need to be provided with a wide range of reading materials including comic books, magazines, joke books, and sport-oriented material – met with some opposition but influenced the acquisition policies of many public and school libraries.

The involvement of Canadian writers and publishers in this debate stems from the concerns raised by a decade of exhaustive surveying and the popularity of the term 'reluctant reader,' derived from Lillian H. Smith's earlier study of children's books, *The Unreluctant Years* (1953). As an alternative to comic books and other discredited reading material, high-interest, low-vocabulary books for Canada's reluctant readers first made their appearance in the late 1970s. Plunging into the middle of the action, with scant character development and cliff-hanging chapter-endings, these stories imitate the narrative style of television as a strategy for captivating non-readers. They are now a staple of classrooms and a genre favoured by several Canadian writers and publishers.

Children themselves were invited directly into the debate when the Ottawa-area parent group, the Citizens' Committee on Children, initiated *Children's Choices* in 1979. Acknowledging that 'children's tastes are not always in accord with adult good judgment,' the group aimed to advise parents regarding the kinds of material children like to read. As the project developed, 'countless teachers and librarians found the material in *Children's Choices* invaluable in their work. By using the extensive indexes, teachers could now find supplementary reading for topics being covered in social studies or language units in their classrooms. Librarians could quickly answer the queries of parents seeking books for reluctant readers, or children looking for good books incorporating their major interests.'[60] By 1980 encouraging children to read had become the combined responsibility of parents, caregivers, librarians, teachers, booksellers, publishers, writers, illustrators, and, occasionally, Canadian children themselves.

chapter 18

SPECIAL COMMUNITIES OF READERS

Reaching Out to Isolated Readers

LORNA KNIGHT

The nature of isolation and therefore of isolated readers changed markedly during the twentieth century. From a predominantly rural population with limited access to reading materials, Canadians became largely urban, with outlying communities served by provincially sponsored regional library systems and foreign and domestic book clubs. For those living beyond these networks and for groups and individuals who were truly isolated by geography, circumstance, or disability, innovative solutions were devised to bring books and people together.

Isolated workers living in mining and lumber camps and in fishing communities were often not readers at all, so that literacy instruction was as much a concern as providing reading materials. Continuing a tradition pioneered by Bible and tract societies earlier in the nineteenth century, the Reading Camp Association, funded by J.R. Booth, began in the 1890s to deliver books to 'reading cabins' in Ontario's lumber camps. Similarly in Quebec, the Catholic Church encouraged loggers to read particular kinds of print. The Montreal publisher Fides initiated one such venture in August 1946 when it launched a circulating library service that travelled to the lumber camps of Quebec's North Shore Paper Company at Baie-Comeau, Franklin, and Shelter Bay.[1] Frontier College, which sent teachers to remote work sites to teach English, arithmetic, and citizenship, primarily addressed immigrant workers. In the early 1950s, at the request of the International Woodworkers of America, British

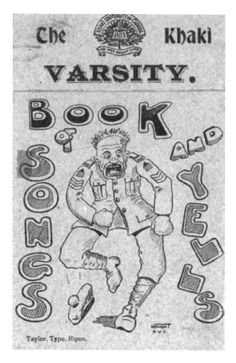

18.1 *The Khaki Varsity Book of Songs and Yells* (Ripon, England: Taylor/Khaki University of Canada, 1918?). Courtesy of YMCA Canada and LAC/BAC, e003895015.

Columbia's loggers received labour-related reading materials through the University of British Columbia's Extension Department.

War created a different kind of isolated reader. During the First World War, the Canadian military allowed study groups based on the Canadian YMCA model to be established in some of its British army camps. To formalize these initiatives, Henry Marshall Tory was brought in as a consultant by the Canadian YMCA, and by 1917 nineteen centres of education, known as the Khaki College (and later the Khaki University), had been organized in the camps in England with about 50,000 men taking courses. The university offered undergraduate courses with textbooks and set up libraries to support the educational services of the Canadian forces overseas (see illus. 18.1, above). It remained in operation until the early summer of 1919 to allow those enrolled to complete a full year of study.[2] Although the Khaki University itself would not be revived until late in the Second World War, the Canadian Legion, through its Educational Services (est. 1939) and with the sanction of the federal government, undertook a similar program. Formalizing educational efforts already

underway, in 1941 the legion instituted a series of classroom-based and correspondence courses for troops stationed at home and abroad, and oversaw the creation
and dissemination of textbooks. During the course of the war, the legion established nearly 800 classroom-based courses in Britain and 1,300 in Canada, with
cumulative enrolments of 23,000 and 60,000 respectively. As the war progressed,
this program, which offered both high-school and university courses, was extended
to other branches of military and domestic service, including the Royal Air Force,
the Newfoundland Forces, the Merchant Navy, the Royal Canadian Mounted Police,
and Canadian firefighters. An arrangement with the International Red Cross facilitated the exchange of almost 60,000 textbooks and enabled almost 2,000 Canadian
prisoners of war to continue their studies.[3]

While the Canadian Legion focused on education, during the Second World War
the Imperial Order Daughters of the Empire (IODE) was the voluntary agency primarily concerned with general library services. At its Central Book and Magazine
Depot in Montreal, the organization received, sorted, and distributed reading materials throughout Canada, as well as to Newfoundland and points abroad where
Canadian troops were stationed. The IODE's efforts included the creation of a Provincial Travelling Library Service in New Brunswick. Begun in 1941, this service jour-
neyed through the camps of 'the army, navy, air force, merchant marine, and the
home guard regardless of place or period of encampment.'[4] In its fiscal year 1942–3,
the IODE claimed a distribution of 516,255 magazines and 27,100 books.[5] The Canadian Home Reading Union (est. 1890), which initiated its own war effort, provided
recreation rooms for troops, and similarly supplied them with magazines and
books.

According to Angus Mowat, the Ontario inspector of public libraries who undertook a tour of fifty-two Canadian-based army camp libraries in 1943, many camp collections were dated in content and badly managed by military personnel devoid of
any library training.[6] On the other hand, by that year, the Montreal publisher Fides
was making current literature in French available at cost to individuals or organizations purchasing reading material for free distribution among military personnel,
and had founded its own Service des lectures pour les soldats, for which it collected
books and periodicals which it then forwarded to the armed forces.[7] All across Canada, service personnel benefited from the outreach activities of regional and other
provincially or municipally based library services (see illus. 18.2, p. 494). Typical
efforts were the program of the Calgary Coordinating Council, which worked out of
the Calgary Public Library to distribute 'books and magazines to the army, air force,
navy, and internment camps' near the city, while in Ontario 'the Newmarket Camp

18.2 Molly Lamb Bobak, *CWAC [Canadian Women's Army Corps] Reading a Book* [1943?]. Courtesy of LAC/BAC, Acc. No. 1990-255-58. Gift of Molly Lamb Bobak, NAC 135738.

library was organized and operated by the alumni of the Library School at the University of Toronto.'[8]

Until well after the war, challenges of geography and climate rendered Canada's North a frontier where access to reading materials remained difficult. In the Yukon, until 1961, when the territorial government established the Yukon Regional Library system, residents outside Dawson received miscellaneous services sponsored by a variety of voluntary organizations such as the Home and School Association, community recreation clubs, the IODE, the Women's Institute, and churches. Among the community initiatives was a small library established in 1954 in the silver mining company town of Elsa. The Northwest Territories waited until the mid-1960s to organize a regional library system. From its head office at Hay River, by 1986 it was facilitating the work of twenty community libraries scattered from the Mackenzie Delta to Baffin Island.

By the 1960s, with much of Canada's population located in urban areas, other kinds of isolated readers began to receive attention. Though not physically remote, these potential readers lacked access to public libraries for a variety of reasons. During the 1960s and 1970s, the Canadian Library Association (CLA) coordinated the nation's recognition of the needs and rights of the urban isolated. A Greater Victoria Public Library study of 1974 summed up contemporary thinking. 'Within the context of operating a modern library in an urban centre, there has been a trend in recent years toward reaching out to serve the needs of a larger clientele,' the report explained. 'The view that the public library is "that smug, impressive edifice that houses a multitude of books for the scholar, the researcher, the middle-class, average reader" is regarded as a thing of the past.'⁹ The report targeted seven categories of persons in the community – the physically handicapped, the economically disadvantaged, senior citizens, hospital patients, those incarcerated in correctional institutions, Native citizens, and those addicted to alcohol or drugs. This study, along with others undertaken coast to coast, proposed decentralization of public library service; instead of expecting people to come to the library, the modern urban library would travel to isolated patrons, and co-operate closely with various community groups and service organizations. For example, following formal surveys of library services for the infirm and the elderly in the mid-1960s, library shut-in services, books-on-wheels, and the establishment of libraries in nursing and seniors' homes made library headlines. Anne Dean's published account of story time in a local retirement home illustrates a commitment to reaching all citizens. Her moving description of visits to a Pickering seniors' home concludes: 'There is nothing gained in terms of new memberships or increased circulation. The patrons I visit here neither know nor care where I am from, indeed they have forgotten me almost before I'm out of the room. As part of the community, however, they have a right to as much library service as they can use.'¹⁰

Prison libraries have been a particular challenge. Changes in thinking about the role of prisons date from the early 1960s, when the solicitor general of Canada, Warren Allmand, recommended that library services be updated and expanded for the benefit of the inmates and 'geared to all aspects of institutional programming – vocational, academic, industrial, and recreational.' In 1973 most libraries within the federal penal system were 'nothing more than rectangular rooms with antiquated book stacks, virtually no storage space, work rooms, conference rooms, offices, out-side telephone lines, or adequate study and reading areas.'[11] Such conditions con-textualize the reading of prisoner Marcel Lavallé, described by Clarence Karr in chapter 16. A federal survey of Canada's prison libraries undertaken in 1977 resulted, by 1981, in two types of libraries: those maintained from within the prison system, as in the federal penitentiaries, and those served by deposit collections from outside libraries.[12] Provincial correctional facilities faced similar challenges in their deten-tion centres, industrial farms, reformatories, clinics, training schools for juvenile offenders, and district jails.

In 1982 the Ontario Public Library Association's Visiting Library Services Com-mittee summarized the trend toward inclusiveness when it recommended 'that public libraries intensify their efforts to reassess their community's need for alterna-tive service delivery systems, re-evaluate their current level of response to those needs and investigate new approaches to serving persons unable to use established traditional library facilities.'[13] Over the course of the twentieth century, librarians and numerous voluntary organizations did much pioneering in this field, making print materials available to a range of isolated individuals – from lumber workers in the forests to urban shut-ins – in order to overcome their lack of access to conven-tional library services.

CASE STUDY
Libraries on the Move
– Eric Bungay

Bookmobile service came to Canada in 1930 in a summertime venture in the Atlantic region and, on the West Coast, in an experimental 'book truck' out-fitted to provide library services to the 44,000 people living along an eighty-mile stretch of the Fraser Valley just east of Vancouver. The latter endeavour allowed users to browse several hundred titles from stacks located on both sides of the truck, an enterprise larger in scale than circulating travelling libraries and more mobile than the British 'perambulating library' hand-carts of the 1850s or Mary Titcomb's Maryland-based, horse-drawn 'book wagon' of the early 1900s.[14] The Fraser Valley experiment proved a success, encouraging parallel services in the Okanagan Valley (1935) and Vancouver (1936) and attracting the interest of the National Film Board of Canada, whose film, *Library on Wheels* (1945), inspired the launch of similar vehicles

18.3 Prince Edward Island's demonstration bookmobile service, directed by Nora Bateson from 1933 to 1936 with support from the Carnegie Foundation, may have been inspired by the successful summertime mobile service to the Maritimes run by Acadia University in 1930 and 1931. Courtesy of Public Archives and Records Office of Prince Edward Island, RG10-P-4.

throughout the Pacific region. Characterizing the bookmobile as a 'mobilized front line of learning,' the film concluded, 'Books are like people: they can become good friends, and you get to know them quicker when they come halfway to meet you'[15] (see illus. 18.3, above).

Between the 1940s and the 1960s, bookmobiles were adopted in every province in Canada, although formal services never reached the Arctic. While initially conceived in order to reach rural residents, the bookmobile was also deployed in urban centres and suburbs to meet the needs of their burgeoning populations. In Ontario, following a 'book train' established in 1931 for northern students, Middlesex County organized the province's first formal, rural bookmobile service in 1940.[16] In the 1950s the county added a public address system to its bookmobiles, an effective attention-getter that on one occasion – much to the hilarity of the librarians present – sparked the interest of a herd of cows.[17] Alberta was the first province to use the bookmobile model in an urban setting, launching its 'book streetcar' in Edmonton in 1941, an innovation soon copied by Calgary.[18] Newfoundland's six official regional bookmobile services (est. 1968) were preceded in 1947 by a 'boatmobile' established in St Kyran's Roman Catholic parish, which ministered to several outport communities, an operation overseen throughout the 1950s and 1960s by the supervisor of regional libraries, Jessie Mifflen.[19] 'Peace River Parnassus,' a bookmobile affectionately named after Christopher Morley's novel *Parnassus on Wheels* (1917), began to serve British Columbia's northern communities in 1964;[20] it represented the province's enduring commitment to this form of library service, unbroken despite a brief curtailment during the 1940s as a result of wartime gas and tire rationing.[21] In 1965, Montreal initiated its enduring bibliobus service to outlying sectors of the city.[22]

In the 1970s funding cuts, stabilized populations, the construction of branch libraries, improvements in transportation, and other forms of alternative library service, such as books by mail, brought about the decline of bookmobile service throughout Canada. By 2000 fewer than twenty bookmobiles plied the country's rural roads and urban streets, remnants of a movement whose ingenuity in reaching readers had involved cars, trucks, trains, boats, buses, and streetcars.[23]

CASE STUDY ──
Women's Institute Libraries
– Jean Cogswell

From their creation of the first anglophone public library in Lachute, Quebec, in the 1930s to their present-day donations of time and money to the rural libraries of Alberta, members of the Federated Women's Institutes of Canada have made a significant contribution to the development of rural library service. This commitment has been a natural outgrowth of an organization which, from the founding of the first Women's Institute in Stoney Creek, Ontario, in 1897, has considered itself, first and foremost, an educational organization for rural women.

Following the educational model of Farmers' Institutes, Women's Institutes provided courses and lectures on domestic economy, health, sanitation, scientific housekeeping, education, Canadian legislation, and international affairs. When institutes were first organized, speakers came from the extension departments of universities or agricultural colleges, but local members soon took over the preparation of their own programs. With few printed resource materials available to them locally, rural women in Ontario and the Prairies turned to these extension departments for educational material. Assistance was provided in the form of 'loan papers,' topical pamphlets and papers that were sent to local Women's Institutes. Collections of these loan papers, designated exclusively for the use of members, formed the first rudimentary institute libraries.

By the 1920s, providing their members and the larger community with better access to printed materials had become one of the institutes' concerns. From early in their existence, Women's Institutes organized and/or lobbied for school and community libraries or oversaw the distribution of books from travelling libraries. In 1929, at the request of the Manitoba Women's Institutes, the Manitoba Agricultural College offered two-week courses that included lectures on books, reading, and book selection for home and community libraries; by 1933 the Manitoba Women's Institutes owned and operated forty-three libraries, and eighty-two institutes in the province handled books from 'various traveling libraries.'[24] Prairie libraries such as these were sometimes run out of institute 'rest rooms,' places where rural women were welcome to take tea and rest with their children during visits to town, while others functioned as storefront operations located in available and affordable spaces such as general stores, rural schools, railroad stations, and even a converted streetcar.

Institute libraries benefited substantially from donations of books. In response to the increasing demand, Lady Tweedsmuir, a long-time supporter of the Women's Institute movement and wife of the governor general, inaugurated in 1936 the Lady Tweedsmuir W.I. Rural Library Scheme, a venture that provided boxes of books to be rotated among institute libraries in Prairie communities.[25] Ten years later, the Alberta Women's Institute launched an appeal for books in the *Edmonton Journal*; it brought in approximately a thousand books from the public, the Edmonton and Calgary public libraries, the T. Eaton Company, and military camps.[26] Such donations left local institutes ready and eager to continue their independent development of rural library service. However, by the middle decades of the century it had become clear that the Prairies would benefit more from regionally or provincially organized library systems. To that end, the Women's Institutes lobbied extensively to bring about revised provincial library acts in Saskatchewan (1946), Manitoba (1948), and Alberta (1956) that would support such reorganization of library service.

Wheat Pool Libraries
– Elise Moore

Farmers in the Prairie provinces formed wheat pools in the 1920s and 1930s to protect themselves from the vagaries of the free market by taking control over the sale of their grain. To educate members in the co-operative theory on which the pools were based, each association in Manitoba, Saskatchewan, and Alberta established its own reference library. The pools' education and publicity departments viewed these libraries as a means of both enlightening the rural community and empowering it to challenge the status quo, for co-operation was seen not simply as a socio-economic theory, but as a way of life. This belief, combined with a general commitment to education and concern over limited library service on the Prairies, encouraged the pool libraries in Manitoba (1926–49) and Saskatchewan (1930–69) to expand their mandates and become free circulating collections distributing educational books through the mail.[27]

Unlike the Manitoba Wheat Pool, which closed its library after provincial legislation created municipal libraries in 1948, the Saskatchewan Wheat Pool library continued for more than twenty years after the Saskatchewan government passed a revised library act. Despite both libraries' commitment to co-operative and educational literature, borrowers showed keen interest in other types of material. Before it became a free circulating collection in 1935, statistics for the Manitoba Wheat Pool library indicate a marked discrepancy between its organizers' expectations and readers' preferences: during the years 1928–30 the categories registering the lowest circulations were co-operation and education. Education, however, seems to have been narrowly defined: science, sociology, history, economics, and agriculture appeared as separate categories. Throughout the period, science registered the highest circulation figures. Co-operation remained 'consistently at the bottom, or near there,'[28] even though works with a co-operative or socialist theme were promoted in the library column of the *Manitoba Co-operator* (Winnipeg, 1943–2000), the pool's official publication. Highlighted titles included *How to Teach Consumers' Cooperation* (1942), by C.M. Wieting, the Winnipeg-published *An International Treasury of Leftwing Humour* (1945), histories of the labour movement in England and socialist experiments in the Soviet Union and China, and a co-operative retelling of 'The Three Little Pigs' titled *Porky, Rorky Goes Co-op*.[29]

Mother Goose notwithstanding, the directors of the Manitoba library resisted including fiction in its collection, believing it served no educational purpose.[30] However, they might have felt that literary works were already well represented in the province's travelling libraries, whose distribution the Manitoba Wheat Pool also oversaw. The Saskatchewan Wheat Pool library also expressed misgivings about fiction but adopted a more conciliatory attitude. 'The policy of purchasing books of good quality is being maintained,' declared its annual report of 1940. 'Fiction purchases are made sparingly, although a classics section is being built up in response to a steady demand for old favourites.'[31] By 1955 the library's catalogue included a 'Fiction' section subdivided into two standard categories – 'General' and 'Historical' – as well as two ideological ones – 'The Soil and Nature' and 'Social.' The latter categories included such Canadian-authored titles as Mazo de la Roche's *Whiteoaks of Jalna* (1929), W.O. Mitchell's *Who Has Seen the Wind* (1947), and Hugh MacLennan's *Two Solitudes* (1945).[32]

Although its borrowers were doubtless denied some of the fiction they would have liked to read, the Saskatchewan Wheat Pool library, like its Manitoba counterpart, supplemented the meagre library services available to Prairie residents during the first half of the twentieth century. 'It is hard to express the pleasure and interest we have found in the library,' wrote Fred and Eva Levins to the Manitoba Wheat Pool in 1947, just two years before its closure. 'We know of no other source of education and enjoyment.'[33]

Reading on the 'Rez'

BRENDAN FREDERICK R. EDWARDS

In October 2001 thirteen-year-old Skawenniio Barnes from the Kahnawake Mohawk reserve in Quebec wrote a passionate letter to her chief and council requesting the establishment of a public library in her community. 'We do not have any place to go to obtain books, both for leisure reading and for research,' she explained.[34] Barnes's efforts attracted international attention after the American teen magazine *Cosmo Girl* and the *Montreal Gazette* ran features on her request; subsequently, donations of books and other reading materials poured in from around the globe. Thanks to Barnes's plea, Kahnawake now has a community library.

This positive story contrasts sharply with the neglect of library services in Native communities and schools during the nineteenth century and well into the twentieth. The federal Department of Indian Affairs (DIA), which was given responsibility for the education of status Indians after Confederation, had repeatedly refused requests for community libraries before the First World War.[35] Moreover, while some missionaries and teachers endeavoured to establish day-school libraries on reserves, these efforts were not widespread and depended entirely on donated books. In the half century following the war, the Aboriginal relationship with print continued to be characterized by haphazard initiatives. Although the desire to read was often evident, reading material was not readily accessible.

Literacy among Aboriginal peoples in Canada was historically associated with Christianity. Catholic and Protestant missions had used reading, often in indigenous languages, as a tool of conversion and Christian indoctrination since the seventeenth century. This linkage continued after the First World War, as the federal government typically funded church- or missionary-run residential and day schools rather than establishing secular educational institutions. However, literacy in Aboriginal languages was no longer favoured. Since the 1870s, the implicit goal and effective result of federal Indian education was to promote assimilation and eliminate Aboriginal languages.

First Peoples had their own reasons for embracing Western print culture. Many Aboriginal peoples recognized that the ability to read and write in English or French was critical to their cultural and economic relations with the ever-growing and powerful non-Aboriginal population. However, the Indian schools achieved poor academic results, most of them offering a limited curriculum that emphasized religious and vocational instruction. As a result, the schools were slow to foster effective skills in English or French and discouraged literacy in Aboriginal languages, many of which very nearly disappeared. Nonetheless, teachers and missionaries noted that outside the classroom, reading was a preferred pastime among some Aboriginal children, particularly in winter. They, as well as the government-appointed Indian agents who managed the reserves, offered accounts of children reading for recreational purposes as proof of the progressive and lasting effects of a school system whose purpose was assimilation. As tools of Western knowledge, history, communication, and religion, books and other printed materials were considered central agents in assimilating and converting Native children.

By the 1930s the federal government began to promote reading and libraries in Indian schools. The DIA surveyed the state of Indian school libraries and drafted lists of recommended reading materials,[36] finding that libraries were chronically underfunded and their collections unsuited to the needs and interests of Aboriginal children. The literary holdings, almost entirely based on provincial education curricula, included selections such as Louisa May Alcott's *Little Women*, James Cahill's *Flying with the Mounties*, and Jean De Brunhoff's *Babar the King*, as well as titles from the Blackie's Bible Stories series. Such works were intended for non-Aboriginal children who attended properly financed schools and came from dramatically different cultural and linguistic backgrounds.[37] Schoolteachers who wrote to the department in the 1940s often cited what they characterized as distinctive reading preferences held by Aboriginal children. Many indicated that their students preferred books with pictures. 'These children can read but the story has to be very simple,' one teacher explained, adding that 'A few nursery rhyme books with pictures and a number of *National Geographics* (Second Hand) are very advisable.'[38] Despite the DIA's greater interest in libraries and reading after 1930, little meaningful change would occur within the schools until well into the 1950s.

At the community level, Indian agents appealed to the DIA on behalf of Aboriginal peoples, requesting libraries for both adults and children. In making a case for establishing a department-run travelling library for British Columbia, one agent wrote revealingly in 1944: 'The reading material of most villages consists almost entirely of the type of magazines found on the coast steamer newsstands, generally speaking a far from appetizing type of reading material for Indians.' In a subsequent letter, the agent argued that, unless more reading material was made available, 'our Indians will come to the conclusion that the white man's literary tastes run largely to the present pulp type of magazine ... I am noticing more and more a desire among them for some worth while type of literature.'[39] Similar requests for travelling library services came from Indian agents on behalf of communities in Bella Bella and Kitamaat in British Columbia, and in Rama, Mud Lake, and Alnwick in Ontario. Despite repeated pleas from across the country for community library service, the DIA limited its mandate to skeleton libraries for the Indian day schools. It was thanks to Angus Mowat, Ontario's director of provincial library services, that Aboriginal communities in his province gained library service in the late 1950s. His tireless efforts finally resulted in a public library for the Ojibwa and Cree at Moose

Factory and the expansion of travelling library services to Shoal Lake, Whitefish Bay, Alnwick, Curve Lake, Gibson, Golden Lake, Mississauga, Muncey, Parry Island, Rice Lake, Tyendinega, and Craigleith.[40] In the northern territories, libraries for Inuit, Dene, and Métis communities similarly began to appear in the 1960s and 1970s, with the Northwest Territories Public Library Service commencing in the mid-1960s.

Local initiatives also improved access to appealing and relevant reading material. For example, United Church minister Reverend F.G. Stevens at the Norway House Mission in Manitoba edited *Spiritual Light* (1932–46), a quarterly for students and their families that was printed entirely in Cree syllabics. Its pages combined religious content with articles on Aboriginal health, selections of poetry, and translated stories by popular authors such as Charles Dickens. In 1954 the Fort St James Indian Homemakers' Club established a library for its members and neighbouring families on the Nak'azdli Reserve in British Columbia.[41] Created primarily to serve Aboriginal women whose interests were rooted in homemaking, child care, and health issues, the library operated with little or no DIA assistance or supervision. In the mid-1970s the Dene-Métis Negotiations Secretariat joined with the Métis Nation to organize the Dene Nation Library in Yellowknife, the only Aboriginal-run library in the territory.[42]

Throughout the 1960s and 1970s, Native communities across the country established libraries, and Aboriginal writers began to find a growing audience. Nonetheless, high dropout rates and low literacy among Aboriginal students persisted, despite some federal efforts to reorganize the education system after the Second World War. In response, the National Indian Brotherhood presented a policy paper on Indian education to the DIA in 1972. *Indian Control of Indian Education* argued that radical changes were needed to render Indian education relevant to the philosophy and needs of First Peoples. Among the recommendations were calls to provide reading materials appropriate to the experiences of Native children, as well as to foster literacy in Aboriginal languages, encourage literary expression, and adapt traditional oral languages to written forms.[43] The government adopted the recommendations, and by 1983 more than two hundred schools were being managed in whole or in part by band councils.[44]

These changes were part of a general improvement in Aboriginal cultural and communication activities. Throughout the 1970s federal funding was increased for the development of Native friendship centres, whose activities often included literacy instruction and the publication of magazines and newspapers. The cultural renaissance of First Peoples during this decade (also discussed in this volume by

Blanca Schorcht and by Cheryl Suzack) and an increasing awareness among the non-Aboriginal Canadian public helped to foster an environment in which Aboriginal journalism thrived, coinciding with an unprecedented output of poetry, fiction, history, and children's literature by Aboriginal writers, work that would be enjoyed by Aboriginals and non-Aboriginals alike in the years to come.

In February 2003, Ontario's First Nations Libraries launched their own community reading program in response to CBC Radio's *Canada Reads*. During First Nations Public Library Week, initiated in 2000 by the First Nations Libraries' Advisory Committees of northern and southern Ontario, readers of all ages were urged to read *Dragonfly Kites*, a bilingual (English and Cree) picture book by acclaimed Aboriginal writer Tomson Highway. This effort demonstrated the growing strength and recognition of the collective importance of libraries and reading within Aboriginal communities in Canada.

Reading in Alternative Formats

JANET B. FRISKNEY

Print flourished in Canadian society during the twentieth century, but it was never a medium equally shared by the country's blind and visually impaired. For this community, the reading of standard print was a mediated process that relied upon the transformation of texts into alternative formats, as well as the existence of institutions able to provide the means for their purchase and circulation; these specially produced formats were prohibitively expensive for individuals to buy and unavailable through regular distribution networks. Limited domestic production ensured that the bulk of what circulated was imported from the United States, Britain, and France. Canadiana, in particular, remained scarce until the 1960s, when advances in production technology facilitated an increase in the domestic manufacture of reading materials.

Reading among this community dates back to the latter half of the nineteenth century, when newly established Canadian schools for the blind began to teach various forms of embossed print. By 1918 several schools offered circulating libraries, while the Toronto-based Canadian Free Library for the Blind (CFLB) had been active for over a decade. Circulation by these libraries was facilitated by Canada's 1898 postal regulation allowing free domestic carriage of embossed materials for the blind. The first country in the world to adopt such a regulation, Canada extended the practice further in 1916, when it entered a reciprocal arrangement with New-foundland, and again in 1926, when it commenced a quadrilateral agreement with Newfoundland, the United States, and Mexico.

Following the First World War, public awareness of blindness was particularly high because of eye injuries sustained by soldiers and by victims of the Halifax Explosion (1917). That awareness supported the founding in 1918 of the Canadian National Institute for the Blind (CNIB), an organization spearheaded by a number of individuals affiliated with the CFLB. In early 1919 the CNIB absorbed the CFLB as its library and publishing department. Contemporaneously with these events, the United States adopted a standard embossed type, grade 1½ Braille. The new Ameri-can system, a compromise between grades 1 and 2 British Braille, severely restricted the use of contractions.[45] While the English-language schools at Halifax and Vancou-ver, as well as the home teaching department of the CNIB, continued to teach Brit-ish Braille, the Ontario School for the Blind (OSB, est. 1872), traditionally a follower of American reading and writing practice, adopted grade 1½.[46] This change repre-sented a significant advance in literacy among the Canadian blind, for grade 1½ was the first American system to represent the roman alphabet using the same dot con-figurations as those found in British and French Braille. No matter where blind Canadians were schooled in the country in the future, they would have at least a basic communication system in common. Moreover, by the mid-1920s many OSB students were opting to learn the additional contractions of grade 2 British Braille in order to read books produced in that system.[47] In 1932 the Americans and the Brit-ish finally reached an accommodation over the issue of contractions, at which time a standard English-language Braille code was adopted internationally.

Even as differences over embossed print were being resolved, new reading for-mats were introduced. By the early 1930s, Canada's provincial educational authori-ties had established 'sight saving' classes to serve low-vision students, who were then schooled using large print reading materials. Of greater impact were radios and talking books, which appeared in the 1920s and mid-1930s respectively. These innovations proved a great boon to the majority of blind and visually impaired Canadians, most of whom had suffered loss of sight in adulthood and had been unable to learn either Braille or Moon type, the latter being a simpler tactile reading system sometimes favoured by adults. Even those who mastered Braille as children could lose their tactile reading ability as adults if their hands were exposed to manual labour. The CNIB's provision of discounted reception equipment and free radio licences gave its clients access to daily news and a broad range of programming on par with the sighted. By 1947 at least two radio stations in Western Canada were providing specialized programs for the blind.[48] Talking books, which were introduced in the form of records in 1935, gained immediate popularity. These publications, revealed one isolated western reader, 'opened such vast fields of enjoyment that it almost took my breath away.'[49] Of the 223 individuals who borrowed from the CNIB Library in 1938–9, 155 (70 per cent) requested talking books only.[50] Although the post office adopted a special low postage rate in the first year that talking books were circulated, it was not until 1942 that the existing postal act was amended to include them.

In his long career as CNIB librarian, Sherman Swift often stated that the reading preferences of the blind paralleled those of the sighted; accordingly, works of fiction, history, and travel found particular favour.[51] He was pleased to report in the mid-1920s that the major English-language presses of the National Institute for the Blind (NIB; London, England) and the American Printing House for the Blind (Louisville, Kentucky) were producing substantially more contemporary and popular fiction, for he firmly believed that his library's 'continuing growth and expansion' was assured 'so long as we give material of a popular nature.'[52] In the mid-1930s he railed at the near cessation of stereotyped production of embossed works in France, since the decision undermined his ability to purchase or replace French-language works for which there was a demand. Although Canada's francophone readers had access to the circulating library of the Institut Nazareth (est. 1861) in Montreal, the school's Catholic affiliation translated into an emphasis on religious works. Those wishing to sample literature 'of a thoroughly modern character …, even when such material [was] found on the Index,' turned to the CNIB Library.[53] During the Second World War, anglophone and francophone readers alike experienced restrictions on reading as paper shortages, the bombing of the NIB talking-book laboratory, and the fall of France slowed the flow of books from overseas to a trickle. One well-received venture that did cross the ocean during these years was the Panda series, a cheaply produced collection of light Braille reading that was the NIB's answer to the successful Penguin paperback imprint.

Before the 1960s, Canada's blind and visually impaired had limited access to Canadiana. With the exception of popular authors such as Stephen Leacock and L.M. Montgomery, foreign presses produced few Canadian-authored titles. In

Canada the use of a stereotyper and press was largely confined to the printing of school materials or magazines, such as the CNIB's *Braille Courier* (Toronto, est. 1919) and the Société amicale des aveugles's *L'Action typhlophile canadienne* (Montreal, est. 1951); these were the only publications commanding large enough print runs to justify such a production method. Educational materials were not necessarily Canadian in content, but in the 1920s and 1930s the Halifax School for the Blind did produce in-house Braille editions of the Nova Scotia Readers, while the OSB turned to the CNIB for classroom sets of the Ontario Readers. Over the years, the Institut Louis-Braille (est. 1953) and the Institut Nazareth similarly generated school materials on in-house presses, but many of the volumes in the latter's library were transcriptions produced on Braillers by sighted volunteers or blind individuals to whom the printed texts were dictated. Between 1911 and 1963, dedicated Nazareth volunteer Pauline David transcribed 1,373 volumes of Braille, running the gamut from Latin texts to the novels of Gabrielle Roy.[54]

The CNIB did not seriously undertake Braille and audio transcription until the 1950s, when increased post-secondary enrolment among its clients created a demand for the service (see illus. 18.4, p. 509). By 1960 the CNIB began directing a portion of its volunteer transcribers toward the production of Canadiana for its circulating library. The introduction of audio transcription onto tape and thermal vacuum forming technology made this small-scale, in-house production of talking and Braille books viable. Even so, while Canadian materials dominated the institute's production for students, in 1971 Canadian-authored titles still constituted only 1 per cent of the talking book and 3 per cent of the Braille holdings of the CNIB Library's general collection.[55] Over the next decade, the CNIB expanded its production efforts, while the Institut Nazareth, the fledgling Crane Library (est. 1968) at the University of British Columbia, and the BC Library Development Commission (BCLDC) joined the field as serious players in talking-book production in Canada. Provisioning post-secondary students was Crane's primary mandate, but by the mid-1970s part of its publishing program was devoted to Canadian literature and non-fiction.[56] Canadiana also figured on the BCLDC's list. In general, the BCLDC's production activities indicated a growing concern among the country's public libraries to provide access to all print-disabled Canadians, whether their handicap was visual, physical, or perceptual. During the final two decades of the century, facilitating access to conventional print became an increasing preoccupation for a variety of government agencies, rather than the exclusive province of educational authorities and dedicated non-profit organizations as it had been in the past.

18.4 Braille being stereotyped at the CNIB Library by Michael Bocian, supervisor of Braille production. *CNIB National Report, Year Ended March 31st, 1959* (Toronto: CNIB, 1959). Courtesy of the Canadian National Institute for the Blind / L'Institut national canadien pour les aveugles.

Reading and Study Clubs

DENEL REHBERG SEDO

Reading and study groups can be broadly categorized according to their structures and practices as formal (institutional), semi-formal, or informal. While many Canadian reading clubs that began before 1918 continued to meet well into the twentieth century, some of their names and mandates altered to reflect a changing society. Liberal education and socialization through reading and dialogue have constituted the core of these clubs, with the texts acting as catalysts for conversation, learning, and community formation.

Throughout Canada, formal study groups established by universities, government agencies, or religious institutions in the early part of the twentieth century reflected the growing momentum of the adult education movement that began in the late 1870s. These groups were sometimes inspired by progressive ideologies that saw education as a means of social change, and at other times by a more conservative perspective that valued education for social stability. Of particular significance because of its ongoing influence both within and outside Canada was the Antigonish Movement of Nova Scotia, which was especially active from 1929 to 1959. With the goal of fostering social and economic transformation through alternative models of education, Roman Catholic priests J.J. (Father Jimmy) Tompkins and Moses Coady of St Francis Xavier University created educational co-operatives, study clubs, and communal learning forums open to both men and women. Meeting once a week, participants discussed a wide range of topics from farm management to the prevention of tuberculosis. University staff wrote pamphlets and articles for the study clubs, the first titled *How We Came to Be What We Are*, and travelling and permanent libraries were eventually established throughout Nova Scotia and Prince Edward Island to support members' reading.[57] The discussion groups of the federally sponsored Farmers' Institutes pursued topics similar to those of the Antigonish Movement, exhibiting a particular concern for scientific methods and innovations in farm management. The educational forums and study circles of the Women's Institutes, in contrast, encouraged improvements to home, health, and community through lectures, discussions, and benevolent activities, including the establishment of rural libraries, a topic previously discussed in Jean Cogswell's case study. In Quebec the most prominent formal organization was the Société d'étude et de conférences, founded in Montreal in 1933 to further the education of women, as described below by Fanie St-Laurent.

In addition to providing practical education, many formal reading circles disseminated ideological, philosophical, and political messages. For example, with 'Canadianization' as an objective, Saskatchewan's Masonic Scholarship Project placed 'Anglo-Saxon' teachers in isolated central and eastern European immigrant communities, encouraging them to visit local picnics, sewing circles, and literary societies.[58] Common across Canada were religious groups that consolidated community identities through the study of selected texts. The records of St Mark's Hall in Vancouver reveal connections to the Society for the Promotion of Christian Knowledge, whose philosophy partly informed the Students' Literary Society.[59] In Winnipeg, All Peoples' Sutherland Avenue United Church (1925–70), in which the early sermons were given in Polish, hosted a Tuesday Evening Social and Literary Program;[60] Robertson Memorial United Church hosted a Women's Group / Study Club and the Minnie Houston Study Group from 1930 to 1959.[61] Between the wars,

Calgary had a Jewish Literary Club, while a Jewish 'Reading Circle' that began in Ottawa in 1922 is still active.[62] The Mennonite Literary Society of Winnipeg, which began in 1971, is loosely modelled on pre-1950s literary societies of Mennonite churches and Amish Mennonite communities in Ontario.[63]

In addition to the network of education clubs supported by formal institutions, English-speaking communities across Canada spawned numerous semi-formal reading groups, which typically adopted distinct policies regarding their membership and programs, and kept records of their meetings. Many women's groups that began before the First World War lasted for most of the twentieth century, such as the Women's Literary Club of St Catharines, Ontario, the Searchlight Book Club of Winnipeg, the Women's Literary Club of Medicine Hat, Alberta, and the Calgary Women's Literary Club. The name of the Canadian Literature Club of Toronto, which included both men and women, indicated its specific focus. Other semi-formal groups in Canada were affiliated with influential American and British organizations, such as the Chautauqua Literary and Scientific Circles and the National Home Reading Union (NHRU). Members of these affiliates created their own reading lists and interpretive practices to fit their specific needs, while maintaining the ideology of education and socialization through prescribed reading and dialogue.[64] One specific example is the Victoria Literary Society (VLS, 1899–1946) in British Columbia, which began as an NHRU reading circle. Two years after its inception, this mixed-gender group, which met biweekly, diverged from the prescribed reading lists, but still restricted discussion to the works of Shakespeare and other English and Scottish authors. By the mid-1920s, the twenty-five–member society was also reading North American titles, with one evening in 1924 partially devoted to Canadian authors.

The exclusively female Once-in-a-While Club (est. 1913) of Sackville, New Brunswick, represents another semi-formal club that began with an institutional affiliation. Established under the guidance of Professor Dewight of Mount Allison University, the club followed the lyceum model of some nineteenth-century literary societies, in which a member researches, prepares, and delivers a speech or presentation on a self- or group-selected topic. Like the VLS, the members of the Once-in-a-While Club soon took control of their own programs. The club's written records and oral histories reflect the intellectual, literary, and political currents of Canadian society throughout the century. An historical account of the club presented in 1977 by Clementina Godfrey, a member of forty-five years, highlighted the pride the women felt in educating themselves through participation in literary evenings, plays, musical performances, and business meetings. 'We have prepared our own pages, taken all the parts in the plays, many times sung our songs and played our own piano selections,' wrote Godfrey. 'We have had the minimum of outside assistance except with the musical evenings. In all the 64 years only five men have had a part in our evenings.'[65] Members who joined the group in the 1960s noted that they still valued the original mandate to 'intellectually stimulate' themselves through presentations researched and written by the members.[66]

Once-in-a-While Club member Margaret Dixon also belonged to the Canadian Reading Club (1922–44). This group was formally affiliated with the Sackville Women's Civic Council and resembled an amalgamation of subscription libraries of the nineteenth century, in which each member paid a portion of the cost for a shared text, and contemporary book clubs, in which a single text is discussed at each meeting. The club's reports in the local newspaper provide insight into the reading sensibilities of the time. Maude W. McCready, who in a 1934 memoir recounted her responses to some of the club's self-selected titles, declared that while '*Marriage by Capture*, by Arthur Stringer does not sound assuring, ... he who would find any real wrong in the book must get it out of his own brain.' Hiram A. Cody's *The Girl at Bullet Lake* was similarly deemed a 'clean' book that could 'be left within reach of the youth of the household.' After reading L.M. Montgomery's *Pat of Silver Bush,* McCready reflected: 'Too ideal are her girls – Yes, we may reply, but so refreshing, in its contrast to to-day's utter lack of ideals ...'[67]

By the 1960s formal study clubs had largely disappeared in Canada. In turn, the semi-formal groups prevalent in English-speaking Canada were giving way to informal groups. The memberships of informal groups drew on loose social affiliations, such as neighbourhoods, parent-teacher associations, and activist circles. For example, Toronto's Holly Street book club began in 1955 when seventeen University of Toronto graduates sought to retain the intellectual stimulation of student life after they became young mothers.[68] The private meetings and records of book clubs like this one illustrate a changing Canadian print culture and help us understand the role of the book in the social fabric of daily life. Political and cultural complexities are especially evident in the oral histories of the private women's reading clubs that emerged in the 1960s and 1970s.

The distance from formal institutions and the gendered composition of these groups often provided members with an intellectual and social respite from work and family.[69] '[O]ur lives were bouncing off of walls with kids and jobs and one thing and another,' recalled one woman whose Vancouver club formed in the early 1970s, 'but we wanted the rigour, the intellectual stimulation of actually talking about the book and dealing with it.'[70] Typical was Marie Coulter's Newmarket, Ontario, group.

Launched in 1974 with six members of the local chapter of the University Women's Club, it brought together women with similar socio-economic backgrounds and educational experiences, who were living in the same neighbourhood and were at the same stage of life. 'We were all readers but wanted to read and discuss "more literary" books than we would on our own,' reflected Coulter. This club, which still includes its original members, has traditionally concentrated on Canadian-authored titles. '[W]e just tended to pick them and still do,' explained Coulter. 'Our first book was Margaret Laurence's *Stone Angel*. We revisited this book on our 25th anniversary and our reaction to Hagar was very different than our first meeting.'[71] Such comments reveal the importance of books in people's everyday lives: for education, enlightenment, entertainment, distraction, and validation of experience and identity, as individuals and as Canadians.

CASE STUDY ─────────────────────────────────────
Société d'étude et de conférences
– Fanie St-Laurent

Founded in Montreal in 1933, the Société d'étude et de conférences, whose membership is exclusively female, organizes lectures on literary and scholarly topics to improve its members' general knowledge. Over the years, the Société has founded over two hundred clubs throughout Quebec, mostly in cities and larger towns. Each club, with an average of ten members, places a strong emphasis on members' presentations of their work.

The Société was initially affiliated with the philosophy faculty of the Université de Montréal and headed by Father Marie-Ceslas Forest, o.p. While invited lecturers did not receive large fees, they found an audience of attentive, interested women readers. Among the better-known foreign speakers were Jacques Maritain (1944), Georges Simenon (1946), Jean-Paul Sartre (1946), Pierre Emmanuel (1952), and Claude Mauriac (1955); Canadian speakers included Philippe Panneton (1934), Lionel Groulx (1936), Paul-Émile Borduas (1942), and René Lévesque (1955). Between 1933 and 1980, more than six hundred lecturers, both women and men, spoke to the Montreal section alone. These activities usually took place at the Windsor Hotel or at tea meetings, which quickly became fashionable get-togethers.

From time to time, the Société involved itself in the cultural debates and projects of the day: in 1949 it submitted a brief to the Royal Commission on

National Development in the Arts, Letters and Sciences in Canada; in the 1950s it participated in the organization of the early Montreal book fairs; and in 1965 it made a submission to the Royal Commission on Bilingualism and Biculturalism. The Société also published a regular newsletter, *Bulletin – Société d'étude et de conférences* (Montreal, 1951–67) and *Bulletin d'information de la Société d'étude et de conférences* (1974–), and organized literary competitions in which collections of winning texts were published. To the present day, the Société remains faithful to its main objective: to enable women to improve their education and acquire knowledge through discussion and reading.

CODA

CAROLE GERSON AND JACQUES MICHON

'Literary history used to be impossible to write; lately it has become much harder,' quipped an American critic in 1995.[1] Book history, covering an even broader spectrum of activity, likewise becomes ever more elusive as we come closer to the present. What summaries and analyses can be made of issues whose outcomes are not yet known? False prophecies have always accompanied cultural history. In the 1920s some devotees of silent films predicted that no one would be interested in 'talkies'; in the 1940s publishers and booksellers wedded to the iconic format of the hardcover volume closed their eyes to the paperback revolution; in the 1990s advocates of new media erroneously predicted the 'end of the book.' In the first decade of the new millennium, we see that print and the codex continue to maintain their foothold, even as new on-line and Web-based formats are being tested as means of delivering texts to readers, and electronic publishing has become the norm in some specialized areas. Although fewer people receive their news from the daily press, printed newspapers, serials, and periodicals have diversified to new audiences, and many imprints have been driven by changing technologies: for example, entire bookstores are dedicated to publications about computers. The printed page – portable, accessible, and adaptable, however stapled, glued, or bound into magazines or books – remains a dominant cultural medium, precisely because of its material stability and enduring cultural capital.

While the twentieth century was a period of continual change, the rate of transformation accelerated dramatically during the final decades, with the adoption of new technologies in all fields of book activity – from the author composing at the computer keyboard, to the publisher typesetting in-house, to the bookstore owner competing with on-line sales formats. Libraries have been dramatically altered by changes in technology, as manifested in the transition from card files to electronic catalogues, with databases and digital resources replacing or enhancing print formats. In a country as geographically vast as Canada, these new media enhance communications and resource sharing, but they also lead to new problems arising from the speed of technological obsolescence and the challenge of preserving electronic records. Writers' and publishers' archives are no longer only paper collections of letters and manuscripts, while digital formats render copyright ever more complicated. The ease of Internet access to political, sexual, and racist material raises new issues of censorship and control. Michel Tremblay's account of the local librarian's refusal to loan him a forbidden book in the 1950s now seems quaint.[2] No longer gatekeepers, librarians now promote freedom of access, and recognize both the practical and moral difficulties of attempting to police the Web.

Events in the post-1980 period demonstrate that a number of important facets of Canadian book history saw very different trajectories in English Canada and Quebec. Canada's English-language booksellers constitute another book community drastically affected by new technologies. In the 1990s two factors combined to alter irrevocably the once stable business of the independent bookstore. Big bookstore chains such as Chapters and Indigo constructed attractive outlets, replete with cappuccino bars, on strategic downtown sites in direct competition with local bookstores. Their sheer size created economies of scale that permitted them to offer substantial discounts on best-selling titles, thereby undercutting the economic base that had enabled independent bookstores to develop their distinct identities. Further competition arose from electronic sales, which bypass the bookstore entirely. Ironically, the strategy perfected by Amazon.com and Chapters.Indigo.ca depends upon a combination of one of the oldest communication systems – the standard post office – with the revolutionary medium of the Internet. The subsequent demise of independent bookstores, including most of Duthie's outlets in Vancouver and Britnell's in Toronto, has been mourned in the trade as the end of an era of individualistic, dedicated booksellers. The shift also affected publishers: '... by 2000, Chapters had killed off so many of the independents, whose aggregate market share had shrunk from 60 percent a decade earlier to about 35 percent, that Canadian literary, children's and regional publishers had lost market share also.'[3] Feisty establishments in smaller communities, such as Munro's Books in Victoria and the Bookshelf in Guelph, Ontario, have remained afloat due to canny planning and the smaller scale of local commercial activity. While general booksellers have declined, specialized bookstores which became a locus for a specific community have often flourished. These range from shops featuring books for children, or women, or cooks, or gardeners, to Little Sister's Bookstore in Vancouver, which has led the battle to overcome Canada Customs' interference with the importation of gay publications. Notable is the success of Abebooks, the on-line company founded in 1995 in Victoria, which now claims to be 'the world's largest market for new, used, rare, and out-of-print books.'[4]

The story in Quebec, however, has been quite different. The Act Respecting the Development of Quebec Firms in the Book Industry (Bill 51), passed in 1979 and put into effect in 1981, has protected independent bookstores, leading to expansion and prosperity despite the general North American trend toward concentration of the book trade in the hands of the big chains. Quebec's flourishing bookstores represent a different overall model of the book industries. Recognizing the importance of print for the maintenance of the French language and the fostering of cultural identity, Quebec's policy has been to protect and regulate its book trades, rather than leave them vulnerable to the forces of the free market, where smaller businesses tend to be swallowed by bigger, and often foreign, enterprises.

Power relationships have also shifted in the processes of publishing. With desktop technology, anyone can become a publisher. It has long been possible for writers to pay to have their work printed and bound at their local printing or newspaper office, but without the distribution system of established publishing houses, few were able to reach readers beyond their local communities. Since the late 1990s, however, enterprises such as Granville Island Publishing in Vancouver specialize in providing 'full services for clients (individual, corporate, institutional) who finance, and therefore control, the publication of their own books.'[5] The Web also facilitates enterprises such as Whitlands Publishing of Victoria, which exists solely to produce and market books by its two owners, J. Robert Whittle and Joyce Sandilands.[6] Increasing numbers of poets and other authors have established individual small imprints, with their own ISBNs, specifically to issue their own work. Books from such companies can be purchased on-line directly or through Internet agencies, and are occasionally stocked in local bookstores. Such enterprises, while enabling more writers to get their work into print, have created little competition with Canada's established publishers.

The post-1980 era saw some sectors flourish, notably children's literature, an area in which Canadian authors, illustrators, and publishers in both English and French have achieved international recognition. Feminist publishing – and women's bookstores – enjoyed a period of dynamism extending from the 1970s into the mid-1990s. Practical genres such as self-help and travel books also proved viable. The training of publishing personnel became more professionalized, with the introduction of new programs in Banff, Alberta, and at Ryerson University in Toronto, along with the establishment of a master of publishing degree at Simon Fraser University in Vancouver.

Canada's English-language literary, scholarly, and reference publishers, however, continued to struggle. Illustrative is an anecdote from Roy MacSkimming: 'As they prepared to launch Annick Press in 1975, Anne Millyard and Rick Wilks asked Bill Clarke, "How do you start a small publishing house in Canada?" "Oh, it's easy," Clarke replied. "You just start a large one and wait."'[7] As MacSkimming documents, the history of English-Canadian publishing is a narrative of dedicated individuals such as Bill Clarke and Jack McClelland deciding to take business risks out of an ideological commitment to Canadian cultural identity; their Quebec counterparts included Pierre Tisseyre, Jacques Hébert, and Gaston Miron. In the 1980s and 1990s, this pattern of strong-minded individualism continued in Quebec with people like Jacques Fortin (Québec Amérique), Bertrand Gauthier (Courte échelle), and Alain Stanké, and with Malcolm Lester and Mel Hurtig in English Canada. Like their predecessors, the latter two learned the hard way that government and market support was often fickle. Hurtig's downfall was his *Junior Encyclopedia* (1990), while the 1995 snap decision of Ontario's Conservative government to cancel the province's long-standing loan guarantee program for publishers contributed to Lester Publishing's demise.

But the most important impact across Canada came from federal policies. The Federal Cultural Policy Review Committee (Applebaum-Hébert, 1980–2) recommended stronger support for Canadian book and magazine publishing. The establishment of what became known as the 'Baie-Comeau policy' (1985), which seemed a commitment to protect the Canadian book industry from foreign control, conflicted with the general policy of encouraging foreign investment in Canada that was confirmed with the Canada-U.S. Free Trade Agreement (FTA) of 1988. Although culture was officially excluded from the FTA, takeovers continued of Canadian publishers, distributors, and agencies.[8] The Canadian Book Publishing Development Program, initiated in 1979, was reformulated in 1992 as the Book Publishing Industry Development Program. While its promise of more stable support kept many Canadian-owned publishers afloat, its sudden reduction in 1995 and subsequent restoration disconcerted publishers' confidence and finances.

The picture at the turn of the millennium showed the previous strength of mid-sized Canadian publishers, such as McClelland and Stewart, and Douglas & McIntyre, yielding to the dominance of widespread foreign ownership, notably by the German-owned Bertelsmann, which in 1998, under the name of Random House of Canada, controlled 25 per cent of Canada's English-language trade market.

In 2000, the conglomerate made further inroads into the Canadian market, acquiring 25 per cent of McClelland and Stewart's shares, two seats on the board, and responsibility for the company's sales, distribution, accounting, and financial management. At the same time, to survive the discounts demanded by Chapters, Canadian publishers set out to penetrate American markets. To do so has often required changes that range from adopting American spelling in Canadian children's books to developing a list designed to appeal to the popular American market, as has been done by ECW Press.[9] Another casualty of Chapters was Jack Stoddart's General Publishing, which had formed a distribution service that handled sixty-two Canadian publishers. All suffered when General, unable to deal with Chapters' practice of over-orders and returns, filed for bankruptcy in 2002. In *The Perilous Trade* (2003), an invaluable account of the tribulations of English-Canadian publishing, Roy MacSkimming tried valiantly to end on a positive note, only to conclude with an epilogue relating the demise of the very publisher who had initially contracted to issue his book.

With publishing as with bookselling, the situation in Quebec has been quite different over the past twenty-five years. The protective systems for distribution and bookstores established at the end of the 1970s remained stable, and bore fruit in the prosperity of the province's publishers during the 1980s and 1990s. Despite some stagnation of sales at the end of the 1990s, the number of active publishers and the number of titles grew consistently. The major question to be faced by Quebec's publishers at the end of the twentieth century was in fact produced by this pattern of growth. Victims of their own success, many small publishing houses established during the 1970s confronted a problem of succession several decades later, as their founders reached the age of retirement. Some of these independent publishers have been taken over by large distribution organizations. Hence the 1990s saw an industry concentration as small, independent publishers fell into the hands of communication conglomerates such as Quebecor and Sogides which, nonetheless, remain under Québécois ownership and are thus eligible for government grants from both federal and provincial sources.

Although Canada's English-language book publishers existed in a continual state of crisis in the 1980–2005 period, many authors, writing in both official languages, enjoyed quite a different trajectory. The country's growing multiculturalism suffused its literary production, with celebrated immigrant writers like Rohinton Mistry and Dany Laferrière vastly expanding the range of subjects and audiences for writing of all sorts, especially fiction. Writing and publishing in allophone communities also flourished as immigrants were encouraged to retain their original languages. In the 1980s, French-language publishers arose in the Maritimes, Ontario, and the West in sufficient numbers to found their own association, the Regroupement des éditeurs canadiens-français (est. 1989). This sense of globalization at home was accompanied by enhanced recognition abroad, with Canadians winning such prominent awards as the Prix Goncourt (Antonine Maillet in 1979), the Prix Femina (Anne Hébert in 1982), the Man Booker Prize (Michael Ondaatje in 1992, Margaret Atwood in 2000, and Yann Martel in 2002), the Pulitzer Prize (Carol Shields in 1995), the Orange Prize (Ann Michaels in 1997 and Carol Shields in 1998), and the IMPAC Dublin Literary Award (Alistair MacLeod in 2001). Further publicity and earnings for authors accrued with the establishment of big Canadian prizes, beginning with the creation of the Prix Gilles-Corbeil in 1990, which every three years awards $100,000 to a francophone writer. The Giller Prize was founded in 1994 to award $25,000 annually to the author of the best Canadian novel or short story collection published in English, and the Griffin Poetry Prize, established in 2001, awards $40,000 for a collection published in English by a living Canadian poet. Between the global hegemony of the English language, the literary hegemony of the novel, the rise of Canadian literary agents, and the international cultural networks of a postcolonial world, some established Canadian novelists have been able to enjoy viable international careers.

On average, however, authors can expect to earn about $7,000 a year.[10] Roy MacSkimming points out that the 'blockbuster syndrome' does little to nourish the seedbed of Canadian authorship, which is Canadian-owned publishing. In the year 2000, 87 per cent of the 'new Canadian trade titles listed that year in *Quill & Quire*'s spring and fall announcements ... came from indigenous firms.'[11] The most successful of authors nurtured by these firms typically move on to larger companies – often the multinationals – for the promise of greater distribution and better royalties. The complex interrelations among Canada's publishers, authors, booksellers, and governments are still a story *in medias res*, whose narrative rests in the hands of Canada's next generation of book historians.

These future scholars will find it much easier to discern the history of reading during the post-1980 period than has been the case for authors and editors of earlier volumes. Leah Price points out that within literary criticism, the rise of reader-response theories and reception studies in the 1970s 'shifted the making of meaning from authors to readers.'[12] In Canadian book history, this change resulted in an abundance of surveys for the final decades of the twentieth century, in contrast with the paucity of data for most of the period covered by this volume. While attention to authors dominated Canadian cultural nationalism through the twentieth century, the twenty-first opened with attention to readers with the establishment of CBC Radio's annual *Canada Reads* competition in 2002. This national program reflects the growth of annual literary events that began at the local level in the 1970s with public sessions like Toronto's Harbourfront Reading Series, and expanded in the 1980s and 1990s with such activities as Word on the Street. Established in Toronto in 1989, this public fair soon spread to other cities, along with the expansion of annual writers' and readers' festivals across the country. Likewise on the French side, annual *salons du livre*, initiated in Montreal in 1978 and in Quebec City in 1993, have expanded, with provincial government support, across the entire province, including Abitibi-Témiscamingue, Bas-Saint-Laurent, Côte-Nord, Estrie, Mauricie, Outaouais, and Saguenay-Lac-St-Jean.

Should a subsequent volume in this series be written to cover the decades after 1980, many of the narrative threads that comprise the Canadian and Quebec versions of Darnton's communication circuit may be spinning into directions unforeseeable today. Canada's authors, publishers, booksellers, distributors, libraries, and readers are living through an era of great change – technological, ideological, cultural, political, and economic – in which the only remaining constant might prove to be the elemental relation between the creators of print and their readers, maintained through the enduring medium of the material book.

NOTES

Editors' Introduction

1 F. Barbier, *Histoire du livre*, 241.
2 W. Templeton, *Architects of Culture*.
3 R. Darnton, 'What Is the History of Books?'
4 T.R. Adams and N. Barker, 'A New Model for the Study of the Book.'

1. The Book and the Nation

1 See J.O. Miller, ed., *New Era in Canada*.
2 W.L. Morton, 'The 1920s,' 205.
3 Goldwin Smith, a liberal rationalist, argued in *Canada and the Canadian Question* (1891) that
   the country's fate was determined by its north-south geographical orientation and that its
   future rested in a continental integration determined more by economic law than political
   act. George Parkin, an apostle of empire, postulated in *Imperial Federation: The Problem of
   National Unity* (1892) that by preserving imperial sentiment a Canadian polity could with-
   stand American influence and the arid logic of Reason. In *Christianity and Idealism* (1897),
   John Watson, an idealist philosopher, favoured revitalizing Christianity in an increasingly
   materialistic civilization by championing a new form of identity drawn from Hegel and
   Kant, one in which the true freedom of individuals came through commitment to the public good.
4 See C. Berger, *Sense of Power.*
5 C. Berger, *Writing of Canadian History*, 14.
6 D. Creighton, 'Preface to the Re-Issue,' in *Empire of the St Lawrence*, [iii].
7 T. Crowley, *Marriage of Minds*, 124–5, 149–50.
8 A.R.M. Lower, *My First Seventy-five Years*, 265, 296, 294; and Lower quoted in C. Berger, *Writing of
   Canadian History*, 121. While Lower emphasized environmental factors, he recognized the
   intangible role played by monarchy in preserving 'the loyalties of the average man.' See
   A.R.M. Lower, 'King and the Crown,' 140.

9 K. McNaught, *Conscience and History*, 98.

10 J. Watson, *State in Peace and War*, viii.

11 D. Owram, *Government Generation*; B. Ferguson and D. Owram, 'Social Scientists and Public Policy.' See also T.A. Keenleyside, 'Lament for a Foreign Service.'

12 Groulx quoted in R. Rudin, *Making History*, 23–4.

13 R. Rudin, *Making History*, 50, 62–3.

14 D. Foisy-Geoffroy, 'Esdras Minville, le catholicisme social et le nationalisme économique.'

15 G.B. Kines, 'Chief Man-of-Many-Sides: John Murray Gibbon.'

16 J.R. Smallwood, 'Letter to the Editor,' *Daily News* (St John's), 2 March 1946, p. 5.

17 A.B. McKillop, *Matters of Mind*, 453–71.

18 G. Grant, *Technology and Empire*, 88. Grant's thought on this subject was profoundly influenced by that of philosopher Leo Strauss. See also G. Grant, *Technology and Justice*; A. Davis, ed., *George Grant and the Subversion of Modernity.*

19 Canada, Royal Commission on Bilingualism and Biculturalism, *Report*, 1:173.

20 D. Monière, 'André Laurendeau et la vision québécoise du Canada,' 194.

21 H. Troper, 'Multiculturalism,' 417.

22 Ramsay Cook quoted in J.M.S. Careless, '"Limited Identities" in Canada,' 1.

23 N. Kattan, 'In Praise of Imprecision,' 18.

24 R.J.F. Day, *Multiculturalism and the History of Canadian Diversity*, 178.

25 H. Troper, 'Multiculturalism,' in *ECP*, 1001.

26 Canada, *Statutes*, 1914, 5 George 5, c. 2, 'War Measures Act.'

27 P. Hjartarson, 'Print Culture, Ethnicity, and Identity,' 44–6.

28 Canada, Parliament, House of Commons, *Debates*, 2nd Session, 16th Parliament, vol. 3 (7 June 1928): 3926.

29 I. Abella and H. Troper, *None Is Too Many*, ix.

30 N. Kelley and M. Trebilcock, *Making of the Mosaic*, 274.

31 W.L.M. King cited in R. Perin and H. Troper, 'Immigration Policy,' in *ECP*, 706.

32 N. Kelley and M. Trebilcock, *Making of the Mosaic*, 313.

33 Ibid., 329.

34 R. Perin and H. Troper, 'Immigration Policy,' in *ECP*, 709–10.

35 Canada, Parliament, House of Commons, *Debates*, 3rd Session, 28th Parliament, vol. 8 (8 October 1971), 8545.

36 H. Troper, 'Multiculturalism,' in *ECP*, 1005.

37 R. McGrath, *Canadian Inuit Literature*, 3, 7; 'A Greenland Ode,' *Gentleman's Magazine* 15 (July 1745): 376–7.

38 See C.J. Jaenen, 'Aboriginal Communities.'

39 Emily Pauline Johnson, 'The Cattle Thief,' in *E. Pauline Johnson (Tekahionwake): Collected Poems and Selected Prose*, ed. Carole Gerson and Veronica Strong-Boag (Toronto: University of Toronto Press, 2002), 99.

40 See H. Mortimer with Chief Dan George, *You Call Me Chief.*

41 See J. Harjo and G. Bird, eds, *Reinventing the Enemy's Language.*

42 P. Rutherford, *Making of the Canadian Media*, 55.

43 M. Tippett, *Making Culture: English-Canadian Institutions and the Arts*, 70–7.

44 Ibid., 175.

45 B. Ostry, *Cultural Connection*, 73.

46 Canada, Royal Commission on National Development in the Arts, Letters and Sciences, *Report*, 223, 222; see also P. Litt, *The Muses, the Masses, and the Massey Commission.*

47 In 1967–8, for example, it granted $595,559 to the performing arts, while literature received not a penny. The Ontario Arts Council did not hire a literary officer until 1969.

48 McLuhan cited by Mavor Moore in 'You Can't Toot Your Own Horn If You Have No Horn to Toot,' *Globe and Mail*, 28 December 1985, p. D1.

49 M. Vipond, *Mass Media in Canada*, 62–4.

50 Department of Communications (DOC), *News Release*, 18 June 1986, p. 3, cited in R. Lorimer, 'Book Publishing,' 21.

51 R. Ellenwood, 'Government Funding'; P. Aldana, *Canadian Publishing*, 36.

52 P. Audley, *Canada's Cultural Industries*, 91, 124; R. Lorimer, 'Book Publishing,' 21.

53 P. Aldana, *Canadian Publishing*, 38–42.

54 Between 1908 and 1960, the council convened fewer than ten times. See L.-P. Audet, *Histoire du Conseil de l'instruction publique de la province de Québec*, 166.

55 P. Aubin, *Les communautés religieuses et l'édition du manuel scolaire*, 23.

56 F. Landry, *Beauchemin et l'édition au Québec (1840–1940)*, 177–8.

57 P.-É. Farley, *Livres d'enfants*, 8–9.

58 BNQ, MSS-061, fonds Société des écrivains canadiens (SÉC), 'Memoire de la Société des écrivains canadiens à la Commission royale pour l'avancement des arts, des lettres et des sciences au Canada,' 20 October 1949.

59 S. Bernier, 'Prix littéraires et champ du pouvoir: Le prix David, 1923–1970.'

60 J. Vincent, 'Le Conseil supérieur du livre, du rapport Bouchard à la loi 51.'

61 P. Tisseyre, *Lorsque notre littérature était jeune*, 156–8. Relevant documents in the archives of the CSL include memos and papers regarding this law, many of which appear to be the work of Tisseyre. See ANQM, fonds Conseil supérieur du livre.

62 J. Vincent, *Les tribulations du livre québécois en France (1959–1985).*

63 'Les difficultés de l'édition,' *Le Devoir*, 13 November 1954, p. 23.

64 P. de Bellefeuille, A. Pontaut et al., *La bataille du livre au Québec.*

65 K. Mezei et al., *Bibliography of Criticism on English and French Literary Translations*, 3.

66 F. Méléka, 'Le bureau des traductions, 1934–1977' *Meta* 22.1 (March 1977): 59–60.

67 Canada, Archives of the House of Commons, Mr Hocken, *Return to an Order of the House of the 19th April, 1920*, Sessional Paper no. 154, Ottawa, 1920.

68 J. Delisle, *Bridging the Language Solitudes*, 17–28.

69 J. Delisle, 'Serving Official Bilingualism for Half a Century,' 7.

70 P. Cardinal, 'Regard critique sur la traduction au Canada,' *Meta* 23.2 (June 1978): 143.

71 M. Robins, 'Service de la traduction,' 54.

72 C. Romney, 'Enquête sur la traduction en 1972,' *Meta* 19.2 (June 1974): 118.

73 G. Jourdain, 'La législation bilingue au Manitoba,' *Meta* 47.2 (June 2002): 255–6.

74 P. Stratford, ed., *Bibliography of Canadian Books in Translation*, ii.

75 R. Giguère, 'Translations: English to French: To 1981,' in *OCCL*, 1124.

76 J.J. O'Connor, 'Translations: French to English,' in *OCCL*, 1128–32.

77 See R. Giguère, 'Translations: English to French: To 1981,' in *OCCL*, 1123–5.

78 J.J. O'Connor, 'Translations: French to English,' in *OCCL*, 1127.

79 Ibid.

80 P. Stratford, 'A Bridge between Two Solitudes,' 10.

81 Ibid., 12.

82 T.H.B. Symons, *To Know Ourselves*, 1:12.

83 S. Campbell, 'Nationalism, Morality, and Gender,' 142.

84 L. Groulx, *Correspondance, 1894–1967*, 3:471; 488; 509, note 12; 521.

85 Canada, Royal Commission on National Development in the Arts, Letters and Sciences, *Report*, 15–16.

86 S. Djwa, *Professing English*, 311; and F.R. Scott, 'Introduction,' 8–9.

87 R. McDougall, 'Reprinting of Canadian Books' and J. McClelland, 'Reprinting of Canadian Books,' *Ontario Library Review* 41.3 (August 1957): 183–92.

88 J. Wadland, 'Voices in Search of a Conversation,' 58.

89 J. Melançon, 'L'enseignement littéraire et ses effets de marché,' 122.

90 Canada, Royal Commission on Bilingualism and Biculturalism, *Report*, 2:281–2. See also M. Trudel and G. Jain, *Canadian History Textbooks: A Comparative Study*.

91 Canada, Royal Commission on Bilingualism and Biculturalism, *Report*, 2:283.

92 A.B. Hodgetts, *What Culture? What Heritage?* 1, 44, 5–6, 43, 103.

93 A.B. Hodgetts and P. Gallagher, *Teaching Canada for the '80s*, 1–2.

94 Ibid., 2.

95 LAC, MG 31, D 190, Robin Mathews, 'Research, Curriculum, Scholarship, and Endowment in the Study of Canadian Literature,' 4. This paper was presented at the Association of Canadian University Teachers of English in May 1972.

96 T.H.B. Symons, *To Know Ourselves*, 1:1.

97 M. McCormack, 'Preserving and Providing Access to Canada's Printed Heritage,' 7, 9.

98 J.E. Page, *Reflections on the Symons Report*, 5–6, 190, 14.

99 T.H.B. Symons and J.E. Page, *Some Questions of Balance*, 2.

100 See M. Cambron, 'Présence de la littérature nationale dans l'enseignement primaire au Québec.'

101 Ladies Auxiliary of the Lunenburg Hospital Society, *Dutch Oven: A Cook Book of Coveted Traditional Recipes* (Lunenburg, NS: Progress-Enterprise Company, 1953), 6.

102 E. Fowke, 'Personal Odyssey,' 46.

103 F.M. Mealing, Review of *Sbornik: Dukhoborcheskikh Psalmov, Stikhov i Pesen* (*A Collection: Doukhobor Psalms, Hymns and Songs*) and *Book of Life of Doukhobors*, *Canadian Folklore canadien* 3.1 (1981): 89.

104 E. Fowke and C.H. Carpenter, *Bibliography of Canadian Folklore*, ix.

105 See J.-N. De Surmont, *La bonne chanson*.

106 H. Creighton, *Life in Folklore*, 63, 80.

107 E. Fowke, 'Personal Odyssey,' 41.

108 The National Museum of Canada became the Museum of Man in 1968, and the Museum of Civilization in 1986.

109 N.V. Rosenberg, 'Gerald S. Doyle Songsters,' 46.

110 J.J. Connor, 'Legend of Joseph Montferrand.'

111 B. Powell, 'Saskatchewan Community Histories.'

112 See E. Driver, 'Cookbooks.'

113 Donald J.C. Phillipson, 'John Murray Gibbon,' in CE (2000), 976.

114 [M. Waddington], *Canadian Souvenir View Albums*.

115 M. Langford, 'Introduction.' See also P. Couvrette, 'National Film Board Stills Division'; and A. Thomas, 'Canadian Nationalism and Canadian Imagery.'

116 [E. Brown], Foreword to *Portfolio of Pictures*, [4].

117 J. Zemans, 'Establishing the Canon.'

118 N. MacTavish, *Fine Arts in Canada*, v.

119 F.B. Housser, *Canadian Art Movement*, 24.

120 B. Brooker, 'When We Awake!'; A. Lismer, 'Art Appreciation,' 64.

121 A.H. Robson, *Canadian Landscape Painters*, 12.

122 J. Zemans, 'Envisioning Nation' and 'Sampson-Matthews and the NGC.'

2. Symbolic Value of Books

1 See P.L. Fleming, 'Picturing Readers'; Y. Lamonde, 'Representation of Reading.'

2 Ozias Leduc, *Portrait of Frederick Bindoff* (1935, oil on canvas), in O. Leduc, *Ozias Leduc*, 246, plate 195; Glenbow Archives, NA-3957–3, Rosettis Studio, *Doctor Earle P. Scarlett in His Study, Calgary, Alberta*.

3 Adrien Hébert, *Portrait de Marcel Dugas* (ca. 1923), in J.-R. Ostiguy, *Adrien Hébert: Premier inteprète*, 25, fig. 6; LAC, Yousuf Karsh Collection, Acc. 1987–054, PA-164279, Yousuf Karsh, *Marshall McLuhan, University of Toronto* (photograph, 1974); and Yousuf Karsh, *Marshall McLuhan* (photograph, 1974), in Y. Karsh, *Yousuf Karsh*, 112, fig. 93.

4 See Adrien Hébert's *L'atelier, Place Christin* (1927) and *Le dîner à l'atelier* (ca. 1928), in J.-R. Ostiguy, *Adrien Hébert: Thirty Years of His Art / Trente ans de son oeuvre, 1923–1953*, 42, plate 11, and 45, plate 14.

5 See Adrien Hébert's *Portrait d'Hélène Charbonneau* (oil on canvas, ca. 1926), in J.-R. Ostiguy, *Adrien Hébert: Premier interprète*, 57, plate 33; and Jacques de Tonnancour's *Portrait of Madame Gagnon* (painting, 1943), in F.-M. Gagnon, *Paul-Émile Borduas*, 162, fig. 35.

6 Y. Lamonde, 'La représentation de l'imprimé,' 84.

7 LAC, MG 30, D 399, Marian Scott, *F.R. Scott Reading in Bed*.

8 Edwin Holgate, *Portrait of Jean Chauvin* (oil on canvas, 1933), in E. Holgate, *Edwin Holgate*, 129; Adrien Hébert, *Henri Hébert lisant* (oil on canvas, ca. 1938), in J.-R. Ostiguy, *Adrien Hébert: Premier interprète*, 62, plate 53; John Lyman, *The Artist's Father* (1922), in J. Lyman, *John Lyman [Catalogue of an Exhibition]*, n.pag., fig. 26.

9 See Musée national des beaux-arts du Québec, Ernst Neumann, *Le parc* (1931); McCord Museum, Ernst Neumann, *Man Reading Book with Boots Off* (1933); and Musée national des beaux-arts du Québec, Robert Mayerovitch, *Voyageurs dans un tramway* (1934). A rare female newspaper reader appears in Nathan Petroff's *Modern Times* (watercolour, 1937), in B. Lord, *History of Painting in Canada*, 183, fig. 166.

10 See Paul Goranson, *Posted to Newfie* (watercolour on art board, 1942), T.R. MacDonald, *Night Travellers* (oil on canvas, ca. 1943), and Austin Taylor, *Off-Hours* (egg tempera on cardboard, 1945), in D.F. Oliver and L. Brandon, *Canvas of War*, 78, 81, 115.

11 See Charles Hepburn Scott's *Alfresco* (1932) and *Reading on the Beach* (ca. 1932), in C.H. Scott, *Charles Hepburn Scott*, cover image and page 22.

12 Jeanne Rhéaume, *Portrait of a Woman* (oil on canvas, 1947), in J.-R. Ostiguy, *Modernism in Quebec Art*, 101, fig. 69.

13 In addition to this Holgate painting (15), J. de Roussan's *Le nu dans l'art au Québec* includes nudes with books by Ozias Leduc (42), James Wilson Morrice (43), Marc-Aurèle de Foy Suzor-Coté (44), and Allan Harrison (110).

14 John Lyman, *The Serial Novel* (oil on canvas, ca. 1935), in J.-R. Ostiguy, *Modernism in Quebec Art*, 75, fig. 43.

15 Christiane Pflug, *Self Portrait in a Window Pane* (pencil, 1962), in A. Davis, *Somewhere Waiting*, 192; Betty Goodwin, *Self-Portrait Three* (etching and aquatint, ca. 1954–5), in R.L. Tovell et al., *Prints of Betty Goodwin*, 72–3, plate 5.

16 See G. Roberts, *Goodridge Roberts: A Retrospective Exhibition / Une exposition rétrospective*, 128, plate 105; 134, plate 115; 135, plate 116; 136, plate 118; 143, plate 127; and 151, plate 139.

17 Paul-Émile Borduas, *Still Life (Table and Writing Materials)* (charcoal and graphite on paper, 1923) and *Composition in Blue, White and Red* (1944), in F.-M. Gagnon, *Paul-Émile Borduas*, 61, plate 8; 117, fig. 15.

18 M. Butor, *Les mots dans la peinture*, 140–58.

19 Ozias Leduc, *Still Life (with Books and Magnifying Glass)* (oil on fibreboard, after 1924) and *Still Life (with Book, Inkwell and Eyeglasses)* (oil and graphite on canvas, 1948), in O. Leduc, *Ozias Leduc*, 237, plate 185; 275, plate 236.

20 Alfred Pellan, *La table verte* (ca. 1934), in M. Martin and S. Grant Marchand, *Alfred Pellan*, 50, plate 15.

21 LAC, MG 30, D 399, Norman Bethune, *Norman Bethune Sick in Bed* (watercolour, 1935).

22 Maxwell Bates, *Modern Olympia* (oil on canvas, 1969) and *Reception #4* (oil on canvas, 1971), in K.M. Snow, *Maxwell Bates: Biography of an Artist*, 180, 271.

23 S. Godfrey, 'Eight Young Romantics Take Vancouver by Storm,' *Globe and Mail*, 12 August 1985, p. 11.

24 R. Johnston, *Selling Themselves*, chapter 5.

25 R. Robidoux, 'Fortune et infortunes de l'abbé Casgrain,' 157.

26 F. Landry, 'La Bibliothèque religieuse et nationale, 1882–1912 (Cadieux & Derome).'

27 J. Michon, ed., *HÉLQ*, 1:154–62.

28 F. Landry, *Beauchemin et l'édition au Québec (1840–1940)*, 331–7.

29 H.J. Chaytor, *From Script to Print*; D. Diringer, *Alphabet*; L. Febvre and H.-J. Martin, *L'apparition du livre*; H.A. Innis, *Empire and Communications* and *Bias of Communication*.

30 R. Williams, 'Structure of Insights.'

31 W.T. Gordon, *Marshall McLuhan: Escape into Understanding*, 267.

32 E.L. Eisenstein, *Printing Press as an Agent of Change*, 17, 40–1.

33 M. McLuhan, Review of Elizabeth L. Eisenstein's *The Printing Press as an Agent of Change*.

34 As noted by R.B. Mason, 'Report on the Carl Dair Symposium.'

35 E. Lupton and J.A. Miller, *Design Writing Research*.

3. Authors' Careers

1 Jacques Poulin, *Volkswagen Blues*, trans. Sheila Fischman (Toronto: McClelland and Stewart, 1988), 19.

2 C.S. Ross, *Alice Munro: A Double Life*, 65.

3 N. Heinich, *Être écrivain: Création et identité*, 12.

4 M. Vessillier-Ressi, *Le métier d'auteur*.

5 J. Vincent, 'Les professionnels du livre,' 143–4.

6 See G. Ripley and A.V. Mercer, *Who's Who in Canadian Literature, 1983–1984*, which lists 950 authors, 204 francophones and 746 anglophones, of whom only 201 were members of the WUC (27%), and omits 128 other authors who belonged to the WUC in 1980.

7 B.R. Harrison, *Canadian Freelance Writers*, 97. In addition to the national organizations discussed here, this survey includes a selection of regional organizations and associations dedicated to specific genres such as poetry, drama, periodical writing, and children's literature.

8 Using available membership lists, the chosen years are 1936, 1944, 1954, 1963, and 1978.

9 J. Godbout, quoted by J. Vincent, 'Les professionnels du livre,' 156.

10 B.R. Harrison, *Cunadian Freelance Writers*, 23.

11 L. Robert, quoted by J. Vincent, 'Les professionnels du livre,' 145.

12 Data compiled by Maude Dénommée-Beaudoin and Josée Vincent from the following sources: ANQM, fonds Société des écrivains canadiens; V. Barbeau, *La Société des écrivains canadiens*; *Répertoire bio-bibliographique de la Société des écrivains canadiens, 1954*; *Annuaire des membres de l'UNÉQ* (1978).

13 *New Provinces: Poems of Several Authors* (Toronto: Macmillan, 1936), 55.

14 C. Gerson, 'Anthologies and the Canon of Early Canadian Women Writers,' 58–9.

15 B.R. Harrison, *Canadian Freelance Writers*, 21.

16 *Canadian Bookman* 3 (September 1921): 56–8; *The Authors' Bulletin* 7 (December 1929): 27–35.

17 C. Templeton, *Charles Templeton: An Anecdotal Memoir*, 319–20.

18 L. Robert, *L'institution du littéraire au Québec*, 83–4.

19 B.R. Harrison, *Canadian Freelance Writers*, 25.

20 D. Chartier, *Dictionnaire des écrivains émigrés au Québec*, 323.

21 We lack specific details about the place of residence of members of the UNÉQ in 1978.

22 B.R. Harrison, *Canadian Freelance Writers*, 19. His inclusion of periodical writers and scriptwriters likely accounts for the low representation of British Columbia in his sample.

23 These observations derive from the biographical notes in *Writers' Union of Canada: A Directory of Members*.

24 B.R. Harrison, *Canadian Freelance Writers*, 34–6.

25 W. Kirkconnell, *Slice of Canada: Memoirs*, chapter 7.

26 L. Zeller cited in A. Machalski, *Hispanic Writers in Canada*, 22.

27 P. Hjartarson, 'Icelandic Authorship in Canada.'

28 A. Machalski, *Hispanic Writers in Canada*, 11.

29 A. Wallace cited in C. Fagan, 'New Voices, New Presses,' 26.

30 L. Kos-Rabcewicz-Zubkowski, *Poles in Canada*, 144.

31 J. Young, 'Canadian Literature in the Non-Official Languages,' 145.

32 M. Ziniak, 'Belarusans,' in *ECP*, 255.

33 S. Miezitis and J. Dreifelds, 'Latvians,' in *ECP*, 914.

34 D. Chartier, *Dictionnaire des écrivains émigrés au Québec*, 271.

35 J. Miska, *Ethnic and Native Canadian Literature*, 369–70.

36 C.S. Hale, 'Danes,' in *ECP*, 411.

37 J. Hesse, ed., *Voices of Change*, 63.

38 See B. Czaykowski's discussion of critics of 'ethnic literature' in *Polish Writing in Canada*, 17.

39 E.N. Herberg, *Ethnic Groups in Canada*, 301.

40 A. Machalski, *Hispanic Writers in Canada*, 10–11.

41 See W. Kirkconnell, *Slice of Canada: Memoirs*, chapter 6 and 374–5.

42 J.C. Adams, *Sir Charles God Damn*, 130, 138, 146, 172–3.

43 L.K. MacKendrick, 'Al Purdy,' 161–2.

44 M.S. Greenwald, *Secret of the Hardy Boys*, 263.

45 Canada, Statistics Canada, Education, Science and Culture Division, 'Preliminary Statistics on Writers in Canada.'

46 A study by the Ministère des affaires culturelles du Québec shows that in 1983, of 428 authors questioned, more than 60 per cent earned less than $5,000 per annum, approximately 27 per cent earned between $5,000 and $25,000, and only 6.5 per cent declared an income above $25,000. The average income from writing was $7,500, and the median income was $2,000 (S. Provost and R. Garon, 'Auteur: Pleinement ou à demi?' 8–9).

47 E.K. Brown, 'Contemporary Situation in Canadian Literature,' 10.

48 J.M. Gray, 'Book Publishing,' 61–2.

49 E. Cameron, *Hugh MacLennan: A Writer's Life*, 193.

50 F. Ricard, *Gabrielle Roy: A Life*, 264–8.

51 Canada, Statistics Canada, Education, Science and Culture Division, *Literary and Journalistic Awards, 1923–1973*, 7.

52 H.R. Percy, 'The Canada Council and the Writer,' *Canadian Author and Bookman* 39.3 (1964): 7.

53 L. Robert, 'Les écrivains et leurs études,' 534.

54 E. Cameron, *Earle Birney: A Life*, 391, 389.

55 C. Karr, *Authors and Audiences*, 77–8.

56 J. King, *Farley: The Life of Farley Mowat*, 109–11.

57 E. Cameron, *Hugh MacLennan: A Writer's Life*, 161; and J. McCaig, 'Alice Munro's Agency,' 92–3.

58 R. Bernatchez, 'John Goodwin, le monde des arts, en deuil,' *La Presse*, 25 November 1985, p. C1.

59 L. Harrington, *Syllables of Recorded Time*, 221–4.

60 K.M. Glazier, 'Preface,' 1.

61 McGill University Libraries' Rare Books and Special Collections Division had previously acquired a substantial collection of MacLennan's papers.

62 K.M. Glazier, 'Preface,' 2.

63 N. Levine, 'Thin Ice.'

64 University of Toronto Archives, A85–0021/002, file 'Writer-in-Residence 1980–81,' M. Engel to J.R. Ham, 11 July 1979.

65 Canada Council for the Arts, *13th Annual Report, 1969–70*, 86.

66 G. Huggan, 'Prizing "Otherness,"' 413.

67 K. Lippold, A. Lonardo, and S. Sexty, 'Canadian Literary Awards, 1900–2000,' database. We would like to thank Suzanne Sexty, director of this project, for generously assisting with our compilation of data.

68 'Three Canadian Writers Win CAA '76 Literary Awards,' *Canadian Author and Bookman* 51.4 (Summer 1976): 9–10.

69 A.Wiseman, *Old Woman at Play* (Toronto: Clarke, Irwin, 1978), 39.

70 Information from K. Lippold, A. Lonardo, and S. Sexty, 'Canadian Literary Awards, 1900–2000,' database.

71 Ibid.; R.G. Siemens, 'Awards and Literary Prizes.'

72 K. Lippold, A. Lonardo, and S. Sexty, 'Canadian Literary Awards, 1900–2000,' database.

73 Y. Thériault, interview with J. Royer, 'Les prix du Québec,' *Le Devoir*, 20 October 1979, p. 21.

74 See R. Lapierre, 'La politique des bas prix (les prix littéraires),' *Liberté* 134 (March-April 1981): 53–6; and A. Thério, 'Lettre aux organismes qui décernent des prix,' *Lettres québécoises* 19 (September 1980): 79.

75 G. Laroque cited in P.-A. Bourque, *Les prix bi-nationaux*, 11–12.

76 G.L. Parker, *Beginnings of the Book Trade*, 253–4.

77 L. Harrington, *Syllables of Recorded Time*, 86.

78 See LAC, MG 28, I 2, vol. 6, file 11, 'Draft: Application for Funding Assistance from the Canada Council,' 2; and vol. 27, file 40, 'Clippings, 1930,' 'Authors' Foundation Is Initiated by Citizens.'

79 LAC, MG 28, I 2, vol. 27, files 5–6; Thomas Fisher Rare Book Library, University of Toronto, MS coll. 119, box 3B, file 30, and microfilm 110.

80 'Ottawa Branch of the Authors' Assn.,' Citizen (Ottawa), 21 April 1921, p. 5.

81 G. Davies, 'Song Fishermen.'

82 D. Stouck, As for Sinclair Ross, 72, 102; D. Stouck, Ethel Wilson: A Critical Biography, 162.

83 Thanks to Patricia Belier for information on the Bliss Carman Society.

84 J. Michon, ed., HÉLQ, 1:406–9.

85 Despite many efforts, regional chapters outside of Quebec and Ottawa proved short-lived, especially before the 1970s.

86 The Rencontre des poètes canadiens (1957–8) became the Rencontre des écrivains canadiens from 1959 to 1961. It was succeeded by the Rencontre des écrivains, under the auspices of Liberté, from 1968 to 1971, and finally by the Rencontre québécoise internationale des écrivains from 1972 to 1992.

87 J.W. Pickersgill, Mackenzie King Record, 1:31.

88 P. Buitenhuis, Great War of Words, 98–100.

89 L. Harrington, Syllables of Recorded Time, 209.

90 Cited in ibid., 211.

91 Ibid., 211–12.

92 W. Kirkconnell cited in ibid., 213.

93 R.W. Button, 'Wartime Information Board,' 47.

94 LAC, RG 36, series 31, vol. 6, Grierson's speech to the American Informational Association Meeting, 3 June 1943.

95 Cited in L. Harrington, Syllables of Recorded Time, 214.

4. The Author and the Market

1 Dan Ross cited in J. Rogers, 'He Writes Fast!' Atlantic Advocate 62.6 (February 1972): 34.

2 C. Karr, Authors and Audiences, 62.

3 H. Napier Moore, cited in 'A Magazine Editor's Views,' The Authors' Bulletin 7.1 (December 1929): 18.

4 Margaret Lawrence, 'Umph,' Canadian Author 15.3 (April 1938): 28.

5 F. Landry, 'Les Éditions Édouard Garand et les années 20,' 52–3.

6 Robert Choquette, 'The Decade in French Canada,' The Authors' Bulletin 9.1 (September 1931): 29.

7 M. Greenstein, 'Robert Choquette,' 72–3.

8 J. Michon, ed., HÉLQ, 1:319.

9 S. Stewart, From Coast to Coast, 86.

10 M. Callaghan, 'Plight of Canadian Fiction,' 156, 158–9.

11 M. Laurence cited in R. Sullivan, 'Interview with Margaret Laurence,' 61.

12 J.M. Gray, 'Book Publishing,' 58.

13 Book Publishers' Association of Canada, Brief to the Royal Commission on Publications, 2.

14 Queen's University Archives, Lorne Pierce fonds, 'The Ryerson Fiction Award: Seventh Year' [1957 brochure].

15 H. MacLennan, 'Fiction in Canada 1930–1980,' 37.

16 J.M. Gray, 'Book Publishing,' 58.
17 J. Gerols, *Le roman québécois en France*, 162.
18 J. Vincent, *Les tribulations du livre québécois en France (1959–1985)*, 123–4.
19 S. Young, *A Writer's Life*, 151–5.
20 W. Weintraub, *Getting Started: A Memoir of the 1950s*, 34.
21 H. MacLennan to M. Engel, 26 February 1968, in C. Verduyn and K. Garay, eds, *Marian Engel: Life in Letters*, 68.
22 D. Ross, 'Pay Dirt in Paperbacks,' *Canadian Author and Bookman* 46.3 (Spring 1971): 1.
23 H. Lafrance, *Yves Thériault et l'institution littéraire québécoise*, 29; A. de Fabry, 'Yves Thériault,' 314.
24 P. Webb, 'The Poet and the Publisher,' 506.
25 J. Metcalf, *Aesthetic Underground: A Literary Memoir*, 286–7.
26 R. Lecker et al., eds, *English-Canadian Literary Anthologies*. The 1980s saw only a slight further increase.
27 J. Coldwell, 'Walking the Tightrope with Anne Wilkinson,' 8.
28 M. Laurence cited in J. King, *Life of Margaret Laurence*, 359–60.
29 Writers Club Toronto, *Canadian Writer's Market Survey*, 23–75, 123–65.
30 D. French, 'The Writer's Corner,' *Canadian Bookman* 6 (October 1924): 217.
31 C. Thomas and J. Lennox, *William Arthur Deacon*, 93, 96.
32 A.R.M. Lower, *My First Seventy-five Years*, 293; and M. Trudel, *Memoirs of a Less Travelled Road*, chapter 11.
33 S. Stewart, *From Coast to Coast*, 40.
34 M. Lang, *Women Who Made the News*, 186.
35 Peter Gzowski cited in M. Hurtig, *At Twilight in the Country*, 169.
36 R. Allen, 'The Magazine,' 68–9, 72.
37 R. Woodbridge, 'Why Not Try Writing for the Trade Journals,' *Canadian Author and Bookman* 35 (Summer 1959): 12; and Business Newspapers Association of Canada, *Submission to the Royal Commission on Publications*, 1, 10.
38 Book Publishers' Association of Canada, *Brief to the Royal Commission on Publications*, 4.
39 J. King, *Farley: The Life of Farley Mowat*, 337.
40 V[alerie] T[hompson], 'Charting the Country's Bestsellers,' *Quill & Quire* 42 (February 1976): 1; and J. King, *Jack: A Life with Writers*, 309.
41 M. Hurtig, *At Twilight in the Country*, 187.
42 B. Kidd, 'Sports in Print.'
43 S. Young, *A Writer's Life*, 147–9.
44 M. Lang, *Women Who Made the News*, 256.
45 D. Broten and P. Birdsall, *The Canadian Reader I*, 45–8.
46 F. Lepage, *Histoire de la littérature pour la jeunesse*, 110–12.
47 Ibid., 113–18.
48 M. Poulin, 'Eugène Achard éditeur.'
49 F. Lepage, *Histoire de la littérature pour la jeunesse*, 217–45.
50 Ibid., 229–33.
51 N. Sorin, 'Historique des prix littéraires du Québec,' 79–80.
52 F. Lepage, *Paule Daveluy ou la passion des mots*, 179.
53 N. Sorin, 'Historique des prix littéraires du Québec,' 80–3.
54 'Radio for Bookmen,' *Quill & Quire* 13 (June 1947): 32.

55 Jean Little, telephone interview with J. Saltman, April 2004.

56 S. Young, *A Writer's Life*, 151.

57 Sue Ann Alderson, interview with J. Saltman, April 2004.

58 C. Davies, 'Bridge between Two Realities,' 8.

59 Janet Lunn, telephone interview with J. Saltman, April 2004.

60 Sue Ann Alderson, interview with J. Saltman, April 2004.

61 Norma Charles and Claire Mackay, telephone interviews with J. Saltman, April 2004.

62 Claire Mackay, telephone interview with J. Saltman, April 2004.

63 Sue Ann Alderson, interview with J. Saltman, April 2004.

64 Norma Charles, Ann Blades, Sandy Frances Duncan, and Janet Lunn, telephone interviews with J. Saltman, April 2004.

65 Claire Mackay, telephone interview with J. Saltman, April 2004.

66 Ian Wallace, telephone interview with J. Saltman, April 2004.

67 H. Sarick and J. Sarick, 'Children's Book Store in Toronto.'

68 F.W. Dixon [Leslie McFarlane], *The Sinister Sign Post* (New York, 1936), 57.

69 L. McFarlane, *Ghost of the Hardy Boys*, 62, 72, 191, 196.

70 M.S. Greenwald, *Secret of the Hardy Boys,* provides a full biography of McFarlane. See also McMaster University Library, William Ready Division of Archives and Research Collections, Leslie McFarlane fonds.

71 L. McFarlane, *Ghost of the Hardy Boys*, 39, 46.

72 Ibid., 63–4, 67–70, 179, 182–6.

73 C. Kismaric and M. Heiferman, *Mysterious Case*, 20; L. McFarlane, *Ghost of the Hardy Boys*, 207.

74 Canada, Royal Commission on Radio Broadcasting, *Report*, 6.

75 A. Allan, *Andrew Allan: A Self-Portrait*, 109.

76 A. Munro, 'Foreword,' ix.

77 CBC Reference Library, Geraldine Sherman, 'Literature and CBC Radio,' internal report, CBC, 1984, p. 8.

78 W.H. New, *Dreams of Speech and Violence*, 80–1.

79 Mavis Gallant, quoted in W.H. New, *Dreams of Speech and Violence*, 81.

80 LAC, MG 31, D 162, vol. 1, file 3, Milton Acorn to Robert Weaver, 15 August 1968.

81 N. Frye, *Divisions on a Ground*, 65.

82 Don Domanski, quoted by R. Weaver in LAC, MG 31, D 162, vol. 7, file 22, Robert Weaver to Robert Patchell, 12 September 1980.

83 P. Morris, *Embattled Shadows*, 110.

84 L.M. Montgomery, *Selected Journals*, 2:358 and 4:260; B. Lefebvre, 'Stand by Your Man,' 152–3.

85 See P. Berton, *Hollywood's Canada*, 19–20.

86 J. Leach, *Claude Jutra*, 145.

87 See M. Richler, 'Making a Movie.'

88 J. King, *Life of Margaret Laurence*, 236, 259.

5. Trade and Regional Book Publishing in English

1 C.H. Dickinson, 'Book Publishing in Toronto,' *Canadian Library Association Bulletin* 7 (March 1951): 161.

2 D. McGill, 'Marketing of Trade Books,' 176.

3 G.J. McLeod, 'Books,' *Bookseller and Stationer* 36 (February 1920): 48.

4 S.B. Watson, 'Competing for the Public's Spare Time,' *Bookseller and Stationer* 41 (July 1925): 48.

5 H.S. Eayrs, 'Past and Future of Canadian Publishing,' *Publishers' Weekly,* 23 June 1928, p. 2514.

6 Canadian Book Publishers' Council papers, Book Publishers' Branch, *Importation of Books for Educational Institutions*; 'Extract from Minutes of the Meeting 5 May 1939: Vancouver Public Library Purchases for School Libraries in Vancouver'; and 'Extract from the Minutes of the Meeting 19 May 1939: Importation of Books to Detriment of Canadian Publishers.'

7 Advertisement, *Bookseller and Stationer* 46 (March 1930): 70.

8 S.J.R. Saunders, 'Arm in Arm: The Publisher and Bookseller in Canada,' *Quill & Quire* 11 (June 1945): 44.

9 J.M. Gray, 'English Language Publishing in Canada 1945–1955,' *Canadian Library Association Bulletin* 11 (June 1955): 294.

10 J.N. Wolfe, 'Market for Books in Canada,' 542–3, 546.

11 N.D. Lewis, 'Editorial: The Prospect of Improvement,' *Quill & Quire* 33 (October 1967): 15.

12 Kildare Dobbs, 'Independent Publisher Urges More Control of Distribution,' *Toronto Star*, 30 March 1972, p. 38.

13 Paul Audley, 'Book Publishers' [letter], *Globe and Mail*, 28 January 1975, p. 7.

14 W. Roberts cited in D. Westell, 'Canadian Book Trade Facing New Challenge,' *Globe and Mail*, 10 May 1979, p. B1.

15 John McClelland cited in John Murray Gibbon, 'Where Is Canadian Literature?' *Canadian Magazine* 50 (February 1918): 338.

16 [H.S. Eayrs], *Canadian Publishing House*, 18–19.

17 L. Pierce, *Editor's Creed*, 6, 3.

18 W.S. Wallace, Foreword to *Ryerson Imprint*, 5.

19 See M. Fee, 'Lorne Pierce, Ryerson Press, and The Makers of Canadian Literature Series.'

20 S. Campbell, 'From Romantic History to Communications Theory,' 95.

21 D. Young, 'Macmillan Company of Canada in the 1930s,' 120–2.

22 H.S. Eayrs, *It Isn't Good Enough*, 6.

23 G. Campbell, 'William Collins during World War II'; and 'Margaret Paull: 42 Years with Collins,' *Quill & Quire* 51 (May 1985): 20.

24 'Perspective: The Book Business Comes of Age,' *Quill & Quire* 22 (January 1956): 4.

25 J.M. Gray, 'English Language Publishing in Canada 1945–1955,' *Canadian Library Association Bulletin* 11 (June 1955): 293, 294.

26 B. Whiteman, C. Stewart, and C. Funnell, *Bibliography of Macmillan of Canada*, xii-xiii.

27 McMaster University Library, William Ready Division of Archives and Research Collections, Macmillan Company of Canada fonds, box 173, file 15, J.M. Gray to F. Whitehead, 16 December 1968; box 173, file 15, J.M. Gray to F. Whitehead, 14 April 1969, and J.M. Gray to F. Whitehead, 1 August 1969; and box 177, file 18, H. Kane to F. Whitehead, 26 June 1970.

28 J. McClelland cited in S. Carson, 'Jack McClelland: Valet, Wet Nurse and Publisher,' *Vancouver Sun Weekend Magazine* 23 (10 March 1973): 8.

29 G.L. Parker, 'History of a Canadian Publishing House,' 287.

30 J.G. McClelland, 'Book Publishing in Canada,' *Business Quarterly* 18.4 (Winter 1954): 205.

31 M. Laurence cited in S. Solecki, ed., *Imagining Canadian Literature*, 282.

32 J. McClelland cited in J. Strong, 'Publishing Is "a Terrible Business,"' *Globe and Mail*, 9 February 1984, p. 13.

33 See J. King, *Jack: A Life with Writers.*

34 'Ernst & Ernst Report: Findings – a Summary,' *Quill & Quire* 37 (15 January 1971): 1.

35 Canada, Statistics Canada, Education, Culture, and Tourism Division, *Culture Statistics: Book Publishing Industry, 1983*, 6.

36 W. French, 'Books and Bookmen,' *The Globe Magazine*, 27 June 1970, p. 15.

37 See S. Ferré, *L'édition au Canada atlantique*; H. Melanson, comp., *Literary Presses in Canada*; and G. Tratt, comp., *Check List of Canadian Small Presses: English Language*.

38 T.H. Raddall, *In My Time: A Memoir*, 242.

39 G. Kennedy, 'Memories of a Pensioner,' 27.

40 I.J. Isaacs, comp., *City of Halifax*, 61.

41 The archives of WPPB are held at the University of Regina Archives.

42 P. Sanders, 'Mary Scorer: An Appreciation.'

43 G. Brydon, 'Publishing in Manitoba,' *Manitoba Library Association Bulletin* 17.2 (1987): 5.

44 P.G. Boultbee, 'Vain Dream to Mainstream,' 51.

45 L. Daniels, 'Prairie Publishing,' 31–2.

46 Pemmican Publications, home page, http://www.pemmican.mb.ca (accessed 5 August 2006).

47 P. Voisey, 'Rural Local History and the Prairie West.'

48 See M. Hurtig, *At Twilight in the Country*.

49 K.H. Siegler, *Avoiding the False Dialectic, Culture versus Commerce*, 67.

50 K. Opre, 'West Looks East and South,' 26.

51 Spreadsheets of quantitative data about Prairie publishing were created for this project. The longest run of consistent data is for the 1960s and 1970s and comes from Statistics Canada's *Printing, Publishing and Allied Industries* in the Annual Census of Manufactures series. In the early 1960s, the federal government redefined the Standard Industrial Classification code for publishing, thus making it unwise to offer direct comparisons with earlier periods.

52 Other numerical comparisons are difficult to make since data for Manitoba and Saskatchewan are restricted for various years as a result of the non-identifying requirements of the Statistics Act.

53 E. Hemmungs Wirtén, *Global Infatuation*, 183–4. The quotation in the title comes from Sheila Holland, cited in J. McAleer, *Passion's Fortune*, 285.

54 P. Grescoe, *Merchants of Venus*, 38–40.

55 Ibid., 110–12.

56 Ibid., 251.

57 Ibid., 170. Grescoe's estimate includes a consideration of lost revenues suffered by Harlequin between 1981 and 1984, an outright purchase price of $10 million in 1984, and the 'variable amount not to exceed $25 million' that it agreed to pay Simon & Schuster over the following seven years.

58 J. McAleer, *Passion's Fortune*, 290.

59 See E. Hemmungs Wirtén, *Global Infatuation*.

60 Canada, Bureau of Management Consulting, *Publishing Industry in Canada*, 297. The comments of J.J. Douglas provided useful guidance during the writing of this paper.

61 N. Varnay, *Gyakorlati angol nyelvkönyv, bevándorló magyaroknak: A Practical English Language Course for Hungarian Immigrants* (1957); W. Dawson, *Coastal Cruising: An Authoritative Guide to British Columbian and Puget Sound–San Juan Islands Waters* (1959).

62 SFU Library, Special Collections, J.J. Douglas fonds, J.J. Douglas, 'Autobiographical Narrative to Douglas & McIntyre Archives.'

63 R. MacSkimming, *Perilous Trade*, 221.

64 SFU Library, Special Collections, J.J. Douglas fonds, J.J. Douglas, 'Autobiographical Narrative to Douglas & McIntyre Archives.'

65 J.J. Douglas, personal communication with the author, 5 January 2004.

66 R. Bringhurst, comp., *Ocean Paper Stone*, 26.

67 M. Hayward, 'Talonbooks,' part 6.

68 University of British Columbia Library, Rare Books and Special Collections, Association of Book Publishers of British Columbia fonds, box 1, folder 7, Jack James to members of BC Publishers Group, 21 May 1974; minutes, 11 June 1974.

69 Ibid., box 3, folder 34.

70 Ibid., box 2, file 16, Linda Turnbull, executive director's report, January 1980; box 3, folder 34, 'Association Registration Statistics,' 24 August 1977.

71 R. Lorimer, 'Book Publishing [in BC],' 85.

72 Ronne Heming, e-mail communication with author, 29 September 2003.

73 *Daily News* (Dawson), 21 July 1909.

74 For the correct dating of this book, see C. Gerson, '"Only a Working Girl,"' 149.

75 P.J. Mitham, 'History of the Book in Yukon,' 64–5.

76 Angela Sidney, Kitty Smith, and Rachel Dawson, *My Stories Are My Wealth*, comp. Julie Cruikshank (Whitehorse, 1977).

77 *The Lost Whole Moose Catalogue: A Yukon Way of Knowledge* (Whitehorse: Rock & Roll Moose Meat Collective, 1979); *Another Lost Whole Moose Catalogue* (Whitehorse: Lost Moose Publishing, 1991); Max Fraser, telephone communication with the author, 21 October 2003. In 2004, Lost Moose was sold to Harbour Publishing in Madeira Park, BC.

78 M.J. McCahill, 'Canadian Book Publishers' Council: The Early Years, 1919–1921,' unpublished essay, April 1972, p. 5.

79 General statements about the CBPC's activities are based on a study of its archives, which are held privately by the organization in Toronto.

80 Canadian Book Publishers' Council papers, Book Publishers' Section of the Board of Trade of the City of Toronto, *Annual Report*, 19 December 1928.

81 Ibid., box C1–B1–D1, 'Association of Canadian Bookmen' file. Although on paper the association survived into the 1950s, it appears to have lapsed into inactivity sometime before that.

82 D. Hood, *Side Door*, 228–9.

83 See G.L. Parker, 'Growing Pains in World War II.'

84 'Trade Committee Presents Brief,' *Quill & Quire* 15 (March 1949): 31, 34.

85 Board of Trade of the City of Toronto, Book Publishers' Branch, *Brief Submitted to the Royal Commission on National Development in the Arts, Letters and Sciences*, 2 March 1950, p. 17.

86 Canadian Book Publishers' Council papers, 'Review of Activities for 1951,' 27 December 1951.

87 R. MacSkimming, *Perilous Trade*, 205.

88 SFU Archives, ACP fonds, F-57–1–0–1, Constitution of the Independent Publishers' Association, 1971.

89 F[iona] M[ee], 'Seven Canadian Firms Leave CBPC,' *Quill & Quire* 42 (February 1976): 1, 26, 32.

90 R. MacSkimming, *Perilous Trade*, 112–13.

91 'New Association of Canadian University Presses,' *Quill & Quire* 38 (August 1972): 6.

92 'The Alphabet Jungle,' *Saturday Night*, April 1978, p. 3.

93 The Conference on English-Language Publishing in Canada hosted by Trent University in Jan-

uary 1975 was a catalyst for the creation of the BPDC. See 'State of English Language Publishing in Canada.'

94 Canadian Book Publishers' Council papers, 'Course in Commerce and Finance, Lectures in Business Administration, Spring Term – 1928, The Printing and Publishing Industries.'

95 J.G. McClelland, 'Book Publishing in Canada,' *Quill & Quire* 22 (April 1956): 16–18, 24–6, 28, 30–2.

96 See Centennial College's calendars for the years 1972 to 1980; Craig Barrett, interview with N. Earle and J.B. Friskney, Toronto, 20 March 2003.

97 See L.A. Coser, C. Kadushin, and W.W. Powell, *Books*, chapter 6. This study of women in the American publishing industry is also relevant to the Canadian context.

98 Francess G. Halpenny, personal communication, December 2004. See also R. MacSkimming, *Perilous Trade*, 51.

99 SFU Archives, ACP fonds, F-57-5-6-10, Barbara Byam cited in BPPA press release, 23 September 1977.

100 'Publicity and Editorial Types Form Club,' *Quill & Quire* 17 (July 1951): 21.

101 Book Promotion and Editorial Club, *Look of Books 1972*.

102 'What's in a Name?' *Quill & Quire* 40 (May 1974): 11.

103 'New Award Honours Bookseller,' *Quill & Quire* 40 (May 1974): 29.

104 SFU Archives, ACP fonds, F-57-5-6-10, undated BPPA press release [1977].

6. Publishing Books in French

1 J. Michon, ed., *HÉLQ*, 1:281.

2 L. Bergeron, 'Catalogue de la Librairie d'Action canadienne-française et des Éditions Albert Lévesque,' 203.

3 B. Whiteman, *Lasting Impressions*, 61–4.

4 J. Michon, ed., *HÉLQ*, 1:299–305.

5 Ibid., 291.

6 The source for this information is *Notices en langue française du 'Canadian Catalogue of Books,' 1921–1949*, known to be incomplete.

7 J. Vincent, 'Les professionnels du livre,' 342.

8 J. Hébert, 'Hébert: "Pour moi, publier un livre, c'est une fête,"' *La Presse*, 10 May 1969, p. 35.

9 See J. Michon, 'Jacques Hébert, First Editor of the Quiet Revolution.'

10 J. Michon, 'L'édition du roman québécois, 1961–1974,' 299–316.

11 On the circumstances of this rupture, see V.-L. Beaulieu, *Les mots des autres*; and J. Hébert, *Écrire en 13 points Garamond*.

12 J. Michon, *Fides*, 121–50.

13 Gaston Miron, cited in J. Michon, 'L'édition littéraire saisie par le marché,' 31–2. See M.-H. Marcoux, 'Collections et image de marque aux Éditions de l'Hexagone.'

14 P. de Bellefeuille, A. Pontaut et al., *La bataille du livre au Québec*, 32.

15 With a preface by André Laurendeau. See A. Fournier, *Un best-seller de la Révolution tranquille: 'Les insolences du frère Untel.'*

16 J.-P. Desbiens, *The Impertinences of Brother Anonymous*, 29. This book established the term 'joual' to designate the popular form of French spoken in Quebec.

17 J.-P. Desbiens, *Les insolences du frère Untel*, annotated by the author, preface by Jacques Hébert (Montreal: Éditions de l'Homme, 1988), 191.

18 English translation by Miriam Chapin (Montreal: Harvest House, 1962).

19 F. Paré, quoted by Robert Yergeau, 'Prémisses à une histoire de l'édition franco-ontarienne,' *Liaison* 96 (15 March 1998): 13.

20 Adrien Thério, 'Entrevue: Léopold Lanctôt, directeur des Éditions de l'Université d'Ottawa,' *Lettres québécoises* 13 (February 1979): 60–3.

21 The titles of the anthologies, compiled by Yolande Grisé, were *Parli, parlo, parlons!*, *Les yeux en fête*, *Des mots pour se connaître*, and *Pour se faire un nom*. The two guides issued by CFORP were *Guide pédagogique pour 'Les yeux en fête'* and *Guide pédagogique pour 'Des mots pour se connaître.'*

22 M. Maillet, *Bibliographie des publications de l'Acadie des provinces maritimes*, 62–6.

23 S. Ferré-Rode, *L'édition au Canada atlantique*, 243–51.

24 Daniel Lonergan, 'Un cri de terre en Acadie,' *L'Acadie nouvelle*, 30 April 1997, p. 32.

25 P. Brault, 'La presse francophone dans l'Ouest.'

26 Université de Sherbrooke, Archives du GRÉLQ, A. Bélanger, 'Les maisons d'édition franco-phones – Manitoba, Saskatchewan, Alberta et Colombie-Britannique,' unpublished paper.

27 J. Michon, ed., *HÉLQ*, 1:325–7.

28 Information from Guy Poirier, director of Le Centre d'études francophones Québec-Pacifique. This centre collects French-language publications issued in British Columbia.

29 J. Vincent, 'Les professionnels du livre,' 248–98.

30 J. Vincent, *Les tribulations du livre québécois en France (1959–1985)*.

7. Publishing for Children and Students

1 P.-É. Farley, *Livres d'enfants*, 8.

2 J. Michon, *Fides*, 168.

3 '[F]ive children's novels were published in 1921–2, five in 1923, and none at all in 1935' (S. Egoff, 'Writing and Publishing of Canadian Children's Books,' 250).

4 These included Dent; Longmans; Little, Brown; Ryerson; Clarke, Irwin; Nelson; Musson; and McGraw-Hill.

5 S. Egoff, 'Writing and Publishing of Canadian Children's Books,' 250.

6 I. McDonough, 'Foreword,' *In Review* 4.3 (Summer 1970): 4.

7 S. Egoff, 'Writing and Publishing of Canadian Children's Books,' 258–60.

8 William Toye, interview with J. Saltman, Toronto, June 2003.

9 'Publishers Answer,' *Canadian Author and Bookman* 47.2 (1971): 1.

10 I. McDonough, 'Foreword,' *In Review* 7.3 (Summer 1973): 4; 8.3 (Summer 1974): 4; and 9.4 (Autumn 1975): 4.

11 R. MacSkimming, *Perilous Trade*, 275.

12 Janet Lunn, telephone interview with J. Saltman, April 2004.

13 R. MacSkimming, *Perilous Trade*, 278.

14 May Cutler, interview with G. Edwards, Montreal, April 2003.

15 McGill University Libraries, Rare Books and Special Collections Division, MS 925, box 1, file 1, Tundra History.

16 Ibid., box 2, file 2, May Cutler and Ann Blades correspondence.

17 I. McDonough, 'Foreword,' *In Review* 13.5 (October 1979): 4.

18 Ontario, Royal Commission on Book Publishing, *Canadian Publishers and Canadian Publishing*, 168.

19 Provincial Archives of Newfoundland and Labrador, GN 7711/B, box E17, Lewis H. Wellon to the secretary for education, 15 November 1945.
20 N. Sutherland, '"Triumph of Formalism."'
21 P. Clark, 'Publishing of School Books in English.'
22 W.H. Clarke, 'An Art, a Craft, and a Business,' 7.
23 R. MacSkimming, *Perilous Trade*, 33.
24 J.M. Gray, *Fun Tomorrow*, 157.
25 S.J. Totton, 'Marketing of Educational Books in Canada,' 277.
26 Ontario, Royal Commission on Book Publishing, *Canadian Publishers and Canadian Publishing*, 130.
27 Ibid., 28.
28 J.M. Gray, *Fun Tomorrow*, 176.
29 D. Young, 'Macmillan Company of Canada in the 1930s,' 125.
30 V.E. Parvin, *Authorization of Textbooks*, 106.
31 Canada, Royal Commission on National Development in the Arts, Letters and Sciences, *Report*, 15–16.
32 R. MacSkimming, *Perilous Trade*, 33.
33 Ibid., 74.
34 J.M. Gray, *Fun Tomorrow*, 176.
35 S. Cheda and P. Yaffe. 'Needed: Canadian Textbooks,' *Chatelaine*, November 1975, p. 49.
36 Ontario, Royal Commission on Book Publishing, *Canadian Publishers and Canadian Publishing*, 33.
37 F.L. Barrett, 'Textbook Selection,' 338.
38 D. Broten and P. Birdsall, *Paper Phoenix*, 31.
39 The Hall-Dennis Report of 1968 in Ontario and the Worth Report of 1972 in Alberta are two examples.
40 R. Lorimer, 'Publishers, Governments, and Learning Materials,' 291.
41 P. Robinson, 'Atlantic Canada Buys American,' *Quill & Quire* 45 (February 1979): 4.
42 R. MacSkimming, *Perilous Trade*, 401.
43 Ruth Martin, 'Jack Cole,' *Trade News*, 31 January 1970, pp. 40–2 (unverified clipping).
44 S. Alston and P. Fleming, *Toronto in Print*, 94.
45 See J.B. Friskney, 'Many Aspects of a General Editorship.' For a list of NCL and Carleton Library titles, see C. Spadoni and J. Donnelly, *Bibliography of McClelland and Stewart Imprints*, 775–7, 770–2.
46 Calculations of sales are based on a spreadsheet of NCL sales, 1958–79 (McMaster University Library, William Ready Division of Archives and Research Collections, McClelland and Stewart fonds, series A, box 93, file 14).
47 McMaster University Library, William Ready Division of Archives and Research Collections, McClelland and Stewart fonds, box 17, file 18, memo from Robert McDougall re: meeting of editorial board, 13 February 1970.
48 S.F. Wise (and Naomi Griffiths) to J.B. Friskney, 2 October 2004.
49 P. Aubin, 'Les manuels scolaires québécois.'
50 Quebec, Royal Commission of Inquiry on Education in the Province of Quebec, *Report*.
51 P. Aubin, 'School-Book Publishing in Quebec.'
52 P. Aubin, *Les communautés religieuses et l'édition du manuel scolaire*, 112.
53 Paul Riverin, 'Est-ce une concurrence déloyale?' *Le Jour*, 29 October 1938, p. 8; and 'Les imprimeries des maisons religieuses,' *Le Jour*, 5 November 1938, p. 5.

54 Québec, Commission d'enquête sur le commerce du livre dans la province de Québec, *Rapport*, 62.

55 Ibid., 109–21.

56 Claude Hurtubise, cited by J. Michon, *Fides*, 215–19.

57 P. Aubin, 'La pénétration des manuels scolaires de France au Québec,' 16.

58 This figure does not refer to the purchase of books produced abroad, but to the Quebec publication of foreign textbooks, including translations, adaptations, and complete reprintings.

59 Y. St-Arnaud, 'L'enseignement de l'histoire dans l'Ouest,' 89; P. Aubin, *Les communautés religieuses et l'édition du manuel scolaire*, 48–9.

60 R. Beaudry, 'L'enseignement de l'histoire dans les Maritimes,' 27–8.

61 According to the ongoing compilation of a catalogue of Quebec textbooks, nearly 3,000 titles were published during the 1980s.

62 J. Michon, *Fides*, 135.

63 From the Archives de la Corporation des Éditions Fides.

8. The Serial Press

1 Canada, Royal Commission on Newspapers, *Report*, 53.

2 Ibid.; P. Audley, *Canada's Cultural Industries*, 75.

3 Canada, Royal Commission on Newspapers, *Report*, 55; P. Audley, *Canada's Cultural Industries*, 75.

4 P. Audley, *Canada's Cultural Industries*, 37–40.

5 L. Kubas, *Newspapers and Their Readers*, 96.

6 This figure was calculated after the closure of the Winnipeg *Tribune* and the Ottawa *Journal*.

7 Canada, Royal Commission on Newspapers, *Report*, xi.

8 Ibid., 101–2.

9 See S.E. Houston, '"A Little Steam, a Little Sizzle and a Little Sleaze."'

10 L. Kubas, *Newspapers and Their Readers*, 99.

11 P. Desbarats, *Newspapers and Computers*, 1.

12 I.A. Litvak and C.J. Maule, *Cultural Sovereignty*, 30, 31.

13 Canada, Parliament, Senate, Special Committee on Mass Media, *Uncertain Mirror*, 164.

14 P. Audley, *Canada's Cultural Industries*, 68.

15 Ibid., 57.

16 Ibid., 75–7.

17 Ibid., 66.

18 Canada, Royal Commission on Newspapers, *Report*, 33.

19 Ibid., 35.

20 F.J. Fletcher, *The Newspaper and Public Affairs*, 40.

21 See D.W. Smythe, *Dependency Road*.

22 P. Audley, *Canada's Cultural Industries*, 63.

23 Québec, Comité de travail sur la concentration de la presse écrite, *De la précarité de la presse ou le citoyen menacé*.

24 *The Canadian Newspaper Directory*; *McKim's Directory of Canadian Publications*, 1924–42.

25 See D. Saint-Jacques and M.-J. des Rivières, 'Le magazine en France, aux États-Unis et au Québec.'

26 See M.-J. des Rivières, *Châtelaine et la littérature (1960–1975)*.

27 F. Sutherland, *Monthly Epic*, 158.

28 V.J. Korinek, *Roughing It in the Suburbs*, 33–5.

29 D. Anderson, 'Chatelaine,' in *CE* (1988), 1:399.

30 V.J. Korinek, *Roughing It in the Suburbs*, 35.

31 S. Fraser, ed., *Woman's Place*, 180.

32 V.J. Korinek, *Roughing It in the Suburbs*, 15.

33 D. Anderson, *Rebel Daughter*, 154.

34 Ibid., 152.

35 Ibid., 174.

36 Ibid., 164.

37 Ibid., 150–1.

38 V.J. Korinek, *Roughing It in the Suburbs*, 66–9.

39 R. Maynard, 'Introduction,' 7.

40 J. Donnelly and H.-J. Lüsebrink, 'Almanacs,' 381–2.

41 J. Michon, 'L'almanach comme vecteur des stratégies éditoriales au Québec,' 233.

42 See F. Landry, *Beauchemin et l'édition au Québec (1840–1940)*, 274–80.

43 Guy Frenette to F. Brisson, e-mail correspondence, 29 October 2003. Frenette was Beauchemin's director of publications from 1970 to 1977.

44 Collections are available at the Bibliothèque et Archives nationales du Québec. For a complete list of the series documented to date, see J. Michon, ed., *HÉLQ*, 2:298–301.

45 G. Bouchard et al., *Le phénomène IXE-13*.

46 Ibid., 39–40.

47 Substantial holdings of these magazines can be found in Library and Archives Canada's Pulp Art and Fiction Collection. For a longer discussion, see C. Strange and T. Loo, *True Crime, True North*.

48 Canada, Parliament, House of Commons, *Debates*, 2nd Session, 21st Parliament, vol. 3 (5 December 1949): 2690 (emphasis added).

9. Government and Corporate Publishing

1 Canada, Parliament, House of Commons, *Debates*, 2nd Session, 20th Parliament, vol. 3 (5 July 1946): 3187.

2 Ibid., 1st Session, 26th Parliament, vol. 6 (29 November 1963): 5299–300.

3 Ibid., 5th Session, 20th Parliament, vol. 2 (23 March 1949): 1879.

4 Ibid., 4th Session, 21st Parliament, vol. 5 (29 June 1951): 4972, 4974.

5 Québec, Législature, Assemblée législative, *Débats de l'Assemblée législative*, 4th session, 16th legislature, 1927, p. 315.

6 O.B. Bishop, *Canadian Official Publications*, 188.

7 P. Tripp, 'On the Tracks of Municipal Government Publications in Canada,' 464.

8 In 1907 Toronto and Montreal cited infant mortality rates – deaths of children under the age of one year – at one in five and one in three respectively (K. Arnup, *Education for Motherhood*, 14–15). Not all births were registered.

9 K. Arnup, *Education for Motherhood*, 52.

10 Canada, Parliament, *Annual Departmental Reports*, 1941–2, vol. 3, 'Division of Child and Maternal Hygiene,' 144, and 'Publicity and Health Education Service,' 151.

11 Canada, Parliament, *Annual Departmental Reports*, 1948–9, 'Child and Maternal Health Division,' 21.
12 D. Dodd, 'Advice to Parents,' 211.
13 K. Arnup, *Education for Motherhood*, 85–7.
14 A. Canuel, 'Les avatars de la radio publique d'expression française au Canada, 1932–1939.'
15 M.A. Hume, '*Just Mary*,' 127; LAC, RG 41, series A-V-2, vol. 867, file PG4–Just Mary Pt. 1, 1938–1947, CBC internal memo, 18 March 1942, S.W. Griffiths to W.O. Findlay.
16 M.A. Hume, '*Just Mary*,' chapters 7 and 8.
17 G. Potvin, 'CBC Recordings,' 232.
18 'C.B.C. Publishing – 10,000 Copies Not Unusual,' *Quill & Quire* 35 (9 May 1969): 1, 5. Thanks to Sheila Latham for her research contribution regarding the Massey Lectures.
19 F. Seguin, 'Avertissement,' 13.
20 I. Stevenson, 'Books for Improvement,' 33–4.
21 Ibid., 35.
22 M.H. Choko and D.L. Jones, *Posters of the Canadian Pacific*, 13.
23 The CPR Archives, housed at Windsor Station in Montreal, contain a large collection of printed and manuscript material, as does the Wallace B. Chung and Madeline H. Chung Collection at the University of British Columbia Library.
24 University of British Columbia Library, Chung Collection, folder 0041/31.
25 Canadian Pacific Railway, *British Columbia: Canada's Most Westerly Province ... A Handbook of Trustworthy Information* (no printer or place of publication), various editions from 1905.
26 E.J. Hart, *Selling of Canada*, 141.
27 CPR *Staff Bulletin*, October 1937, p. 5.
28 I. Stevenson, 'Books for Improvement,' 37.

10. Organized Religion and Print

1 *Il fermo proposito*, encyclical of Pius X, Rome, 11 June 1905.
2 Sources for the data are A. Beaulieu, J. Hamelin et al., *La presse québécoise des origines à nos jours*, and the catalogue of the BNQ in 2003.
3 *Annales de la Bonne Sainte-Anne* (1873–1967) became *Sainte-Anne de Beaupré* (1968–84), and *La Revue Sainte-Anne* in 1985.
4 'Bref pontifical de S.S. Pie X à notre vénérable Frère Louis-Nazaire, archevêque de Québec,' 26.
5 D. Marquis, *Un quotidien pour l'Église*.
6 From an analysis of titles in the BNQ catalogue in 2003.
7 See J. Michon, ed., *HÉLQ*, 1:337–51.
8 In 1930, *Le Messager canadien du Sacré-Cœur* had a subscription list of 90,000, and the *Annales de Saint-Joseph* had a print run of 100,000 copies.
9 Y. Cloutier, 'L'activité éditoriale des dominicains,' 82; J. Michon, ed., *HÉLQ*, 1:353–7 and 2:164–72.
10 J. Michon, *Fides*.
11 L'Imprimerie du Messager nonetheless published 3,375 titles between 1942 and 1959, of which 10 per cent were religious works.
12 J. Marcoux, *Littérature jeunesse au Québec*. L'Apostolat de la presse became Éditions Paulines in 1971, then Médiaspaul in 1994.

13 G. Raymond, *Journal de Gérard Raymond*, 115 and passim.

14 R. Lemelin, *The Town Below*, trans. Samuel Putnam (New York: Reynal & Hitchcock, 1948), 100.

15 J. Lemieux, 'Gérard Raymond: Un étudiant ardent et généreux.'

16 Formal interviews and informal conversations with the following colleagues and archivists proved invaluable to the writing of this text: Phyllis Airhart (Emmanuel College, Toronto, 24 July 2003), Alan Hayes (Wycliffe College, Toronto, 6 November 2003), John S. Moir (Port Dover, 26 March 2004), Joseph O'Connell (St Michael's College, Toronto, 12 January 2005), James K. Farge, Terence Fay, Ronald Griffin, Kevin Kirley, Margaret Sanche, and Colleen Shantz.

17 Melly Safari, production manager, CBS, telephone interview with B. Hogan, 24 February 2005.

18 Transcript of a video interview with Professor John W. Grant, Emmanuel College, Toronto. Courtesy of Phyllis Airhart.

19 Baptist Hymnary Committee of Canada, *Hymnary for Use in Baptist Churches*, iii–iv.

20 Kevin Kirley, CSB, archivist, General Archives of the Basilian Fathers of Toronto, April 2004.

21 J.S. Moir, 'Canadian Religious Historiography – an Overview,' 138–9.

22 Church of England in Canada, General Synod, *Journal of Proceedings of the Tenth Session*, 232–3.

23 B.F. Hogan, 'Salted with Fire,' 40.

24 D. Polachic, 'End of Road for *Our Family*,' *Star Phoenix* (Saskatoon, SK), 2 February 2002, p. F8.

25 A.W. Harrison, *Check-List of United Church of Canada Publications*, 2:69–73, 108–10, 183–5.

26 Presbyterian Church in Canada, Board of Sabbath Schools and Young People's Societies, *Forward Movement and Christian Education*, 11.

27 Church of England in Canada, Council on Girls' Work, *Fourfold Programme for Canadian Girls*, 14–16.

28 Church of England in Canada, General Synod, *Journal of Proceedings of the Tenth Session*, 232–3.

29 Marion Pardy cited in J. Bird, 'Minding Our "Holy Manners": New Moderator Rt. Rev. Marion Pardy Is an Educator, Learner and Pastor,' *United Church Observer*, October 2000, p. 17.

30 W.W. Bryden, 'Foreword,' vii.

31 United Church of Canada, Board of Christian Education and the Board of Publication, *Prospectus*; and D.M. Mathers, *Word and the Way*.

32 M. Creal, *Opportunities Implied in the Introduction of a New Curriculum*.

11. Publishing and Communities

1 E.H. Thomas, *Chinook: A History and Dictionary*, xi.

2 J.M Banks, comp., *Books in Native Languages*, 54–5; J.A. Mackay, *Psalms and Hymns in the Language of the Cree Indians* (1949), verso of title page.

3 B.F.R. Edwards, *Paper Talk*, 138.

4 Ibid., 142.

5 The newspaper was founded by the Conseil atikamekw-montagnais and published in three languages: French, Montagnais, and Attikamek (D. Boudreau, *Histoire de la littérature amérindienne*, 106–7).

6 J.C. Armstrong, 'Four Decades,' xvii–xviii.

7 B.F.R. Edwards, *Paper Talk*, 158.

8 J. Demay, 'Persistence and Creativity,' 91, 89.

9 P. Petrone, *Native Literature in Canada*, 112.

10 G. Young-Ing, 'Aboriginal Peoples' Estrangement,' 183.

11 Saskatchewan Indian Culture Centre, 'About the Centre.'

12 G. Young-Ing, 'Aboriginal Peoples' Estrangement,' 187, 186.

13 J.W. Berry and J.A. LaPonce, *Ethnicity and Culture in Canada*, 27.

14 The latter initiative ceased in 1995; individual libraries have long maintained their own collections of allophone materials, shaping them to suit the needs of their communities.

15 J. Young, 'Unheard Voices,' 104.

16 W. Kirkconnell, *Slice of Canada*, 261.

17 Canada Council for the Arts, *Trends in Support to Artists*, 31.

18 P. Aldana, *Canadian Publishing*, 36.

19 See P. Hjartarson, 'Print Culture, Ethnicity, and Identity,' 49.

20 A.F. Jamieson, ed., *Selective Bibliography of Canadiana*.

21 M.M. Ayukawa and P.E. Roy, 'Japanese,' in *ECP*, 851.

22 J.R. Burnet with H. Palmer, '*Coming Canadians*,' 35.

23 Henry Lahti, interview with the author, 30 July 2001.

24 P.R. Magocsi, 'Carpatho-Rusyns,' in *ECP*, 341.

25 P. Stuewe, 'Mark of the Exile,' 5.

26 Canada, Statistics Canada, Education, Culture, and Tourism Division, *Culture Statistics: Newspapers and Periodicals, 1976–77*, 17–18, 26.

27 N.K. Wagle, 'Maharashtrians,' in *ECP*, 948.

28 J. Etcheverry, 'Chilean Literature in Canada,' 54–5.

29 A. Marquis, 'Conscience politique et ouverture culturelle,' 104.

30 Ajmer Rode, interview with the author, 25 July 2001.

31 T. Todorov, 'Origin of Genres,' 200.

32 M. Dalbello-Lovrić, 'Croatian Diaspora Almanacs,' 297.

33 K.G. O'Bryan, J.G. Reitz, and O.M. Kuplowska, *Non-Official Languages*, 2.

34 L. Rosenberg, *Canada's Jews*, 4, 257.

35 See Jewish Public Library Archives, Montreal, Eiran Harris, 'Hebrew and Yiddish Printing in Canada, 1844–1915'; M. Ravitch, 'Yiddish Culture in Canada,' 76; D. Rome, comp., *First Jewish Literary School*, 13.

36 For biographies of these and other Canadian-Yiddish authors, see K.L. Fuks, ed., *Hundert yor yidishe un hebreyishe literatur in kanade*.

37 The journals to appear during these years were *Nyuansn* (Montreal, 1921), *Epokhe* (Montreal, 1922), *Royerd* (Montreal, 1922), *Der kval* (Montreal, 1922), *Kanade* (Montreal, 1925), *Royerd* (Montreal, 1927, 1929), *Heftn* (Montreal and Toronto, 1929), *Di yidishe velt* (Vancouver, 1928, 1935), *Basheydn*, *In gevirbl* (Toronto, 1930), *Ba undz* (Toronto, 1931), *Montreol* (Montreal, 1932–5), *Prolit* (Montreal, 1935), and *Heftn* (Montreal-Detroit, 1936–7).

38 I. Vaisman, 'Yiddish Publishing in Eastern Europe.'

39 The *Free Lance* is not available at any library or archives in Canada, but copies are held by the family of one of the original editors, Edward Packwood.

40 See the masthead of the *Free Lance*, September 1934, p. 1.

41 C.B. Goodlett, 'Challenges Still Confront Black Press,' 14.

42 By December 1934, editor Eric E.L. Hercules was no longer listed, Packwood apparently having taken over his responsibilities. Despite a search through the issues on hand, I could find no other references to Hercules after September 1934.

43 The debt load was a constant concern for the editors (Lucille Cuevas, interview with the author, Ottawa, 2 February 2000).

44 R.W. Winks, *Blacks in Canada*, 404.

45 'Four Eventful Years,' *Free Lance*, 11 June 1938, p. 2.

46 Sources include G. Tratt, comp., *Check List of Canadian Small Presses*; H. Melanson, comp., *Literary Presses in Canada*; and D. McKnight, 'Annotated Bibliography of English Canadian Little Magazines.'

47 A. Crawley, 'Foreword,' *Contemporary Verse* 1 (1941): 2; C. Harmon, 'Editorial,' *Here and Now* 1.1 (1947): 6.

48 'Les revues québécoises au Salon du livre 1952,' *Qui? Art, musique, littérature* 4.2 (1952): iii.

49 'Positions,' *La Relève* 1.1 (March 1934): 1.

50 M. Kostash, 'The Feminist Press – Is Anyone Out There Listening?' *Chatelaine*, March 1975, p. 24.

51 In the absence of a reliable inventory of Canada's feminist press, I have compiled a list of some fifty publications founded before 1980, drawn from numerous sources and all subsequently verified through AMICUS, Library and Archives Canada's on-line national catalogue. Most were produced in the major cities of Toronto, Montreal, and Vancouver, and a few in smaller cities such as Edmonton (*On Our Way*, 1972–4; *Branching Out*, 1974–80), Whitehorse (*OptiMSt*, 1974?–95?), Windsor, ON (*Windsor Woman*, 1972–3?), Ottawa (*Upstream*, 1976–80), and Saskatoon (*Prairie Woman*, 1979–81).

52 E. Wachtel, *Feminist Print Media*, 23.

53 E. Wachtel, *Update on Feminist Periodicals*, 14, 21. A 1991 survey lists forty-four extant periodicals, more than half founded after 1980 (P. Masters, 'Word from the Press,' 34–5).

54 The first category includes: *La Barre du jour* (Montreal, 1965–77), which continued as *La Nouvelle Barre du jour* (Montreal, 1977–); *Room of One's Own* (Victoria, 1975–); and *Fireweed* (Toronto, 1978–). In the second category there are: *Canadian Newsletter of Research on Women* (Waterloo, ON, 1972–8), which became *Resources for Feminist Research / Documentation sur la recherche féministe (RFR/DRF)* (Toronto, 1978–); *Atlantis* (Wolfville, NS, 1975–); *Canadian Woman Studies / Les Cahiers de la femme* (Toronto, 1978–); and *International Journal of Women's Studies* (Montreal, 1978–).

55 J. Michon, 'Mme B.D. Simpson,' 169.

56 Press Gang's archives are held by Simon Fraser University Library, Special Collections.

57 K. Govier, 'Coach House and Women's Press,' *Quill & Quire* 45 (July 1979): 14–16.

58 M. Holmlund and G. Youngberg, *Inspiring Women*, iii–iv. Funding from the Women's Program of the Secretary of State seems to have been limited to special issues and promotion campaigns until 1983, when feminist publications became eligible for operational funding (E. Wachtel, *Update on Feminist Periodicals*, 33).

59 N. Naglin, 'Consciousness Raising for Kids,' *Quill & Quire* 39 (December 1973): 5.

60 I. Boisclair, 'Édition féministe, édition spécialisée.'

61 For example, substantial archives of lesbian and gay materials have been established in Toronto (the Canadian Lesbian and Gay Archives, 1973) and Montreal (Archives gaies du Québec, 1983).

62 A. McLaren and A.T. McLaren, *Bedroom and the State*, 93, 20–3.

63 Ibid., 132, 178. The *Birth Control Handbook* was soon taken over by Montreal Health Press and remains in print in both official languages (D. Cherniak and A. Feingold, 'Birth Control Handbook,' 110–11).

64 An exception is the Robert S. Kenny Collection at the Thomas Fisher Rare Book Library, University of Toronto.

65 M. Raboy, *Movements and Messages*, 156.
66 Exceptions are W. Kinsella, *Web of Hate*, and L.-R. Betcherman, *Swastika and the Maple Leaf*.
67 W. Kinsella, *Web of Hate*, 14.
68 *TAB Confidential*, 4 April 1959, p. 4.
69 Carnival Magazine Store advertisement, *TAB*, 12 June 1965, p. 8.
70 D.S. Churchill, 'Mother Goose's Map.'
71 J. Egan, *Challenging the Conspiracy of Silence*, 44–57.
72 A. Leibl, 'Canada's Underground Press,' 16.
73 R. Verzuh, *Underground Times*, chapter 10.

12. Scholarly and Professional Publishing

1 H.A. Innis, 'Charles Norris Cochrane, 1889–1945,' 96.
2 D. Creighton, 'Preface to the Re-Issue,' in *Empire of the St Lawrence*, [iii].
3 Canadian Federation for the Humanities and Social Sciences, 'About ASPP.'
4 M. Tremaine, *Bibliography of Canadian Imprints, 1751–1800*, v.
5 See A.B. Piternick et al., eds, *National Conference on the State of Canadian Bibliography*.
6 F.G. Halpenny, '100 Books for 100 Years.'
7 W.G. Dean, 'Foreword.'
8 Queen's University Archives, 2058a, box 2, file 'Speeches,' R.E. Watters, 'Where Every Prospect Teases,' dated in MS 'March 1963,' 3–4.
9 Ibid., R.E. Watters, Untitled address to the Bibliographical Society of Canada, 14 June 1957, 1–2; and R.E. Watters, *Check List of Canadian Literature* (1st ed.), vii.
10 Queen's University Archives, 2058a, box 2, file 'Speeches,' 'Canadian bibliography,' dated in MS 'Toronto, 1952,' 1.
11 H.P. Gundy, Review, *Queen's Quarterly* 66 (Summer 1959): 326–8.
12 R.E. Watters, *Checklist of Canadian Literature* (2nd ed.).
13 H.M. Tory, 'Foreword,' 3.
14 N.T. Gridgeman, 'Semicentennial: The NRCC Research Journals, 1929–1979,' v, xiii–xv.
15 R.H. Estey, 'History of the Quebec Society for the Protection of Plants,' 21, 13.
16 I.G. Berry, 'Presidential Reminiscences,' 433, 435.
17 This journal, like many others, changed title several times: *Canadian Chemistry and Metallurgy* in 1921, *Canadian Chemistry and Process Industries* in 1938, *Canadian Chemical Processing* in 1961, and *Process Industries* in 1984.
18 L.W. Shemilt and T.H.G. Michael, 'Privatization of a Journal,' 79, 91.
19 Royal Society of Canada, Committee on Publication Policies and Practices for Research Journals and Other Periodicals in Science and Engineering in Canada, *Press of Knowledge*, 1.
20 Ibid., 13.
21 C.T. Bishop, 'Overview of Canadian Scientific Publications,' 28, 20.
22 A. Janisch, *Profile of Published Legal Research*, 5. Thanks to Balfour Halévy and Philip Girard for advice with this text.
23 N. Campbell, 'Canadian Legal Bibliography,' 247.
24 R.A. Macdonald, 'Understanding Civil Law Scholarship in Quebec'; S. Normand, 'Une analyse quantitative de la doctrine en droit civil québécois.'
25 According to the bibliography compiled for this project by the BNQ in 2003, which does not include titles in French published outside Quebec.

26 Information gathered from an inventory of the stocks of Wilson et Lafleur Inc., whose archives are held privately by Claude Wilson in Montreal.

27 S. Normand, 'Un thème dominant de la pensée juridique traditionnelle au Québec.'

28 A. Perrault, 'Aux lecteurs,' *La Revue du Barreau de la province de Québec* 1.1 (January 1941): 2.

29 *Loi sur la Société québécoise d'information juridique*, (LRQ, c. S-20).

30 P.-G. Jobin, 'L'influence de la doctrine française sur le droit civil québécois.'

31 *Law and Learning*, 124.

32 H.E. Read, 'Judicial Process in Canada.'

33 G.L. Starr, 'Subject Bibliography – Law,' in A.B. Piternick et al., eds, *National Conference on the State of Canadian Bibliography*, 332–4.

34 V.K. Denton, 'Canadian Legal Publishers,' 41.

35 Ibid., 38.

36 *Index to Legal Periodical Literature* (Boston, 1888–1939); *Index to Legal Periodicals and Books* (New York, 1908–94).

37 D.S. Marshall, 'History of Computer-Assisted Legal Research,' 103–5; J.N. Davis, 'Digital Storage, Retrieval and Transmission,' 142–50.

38 See J.J. Connor, 'Medicine and Health.'

39 D.S. Crawford, *Bibliography of Canadian Health Sciences Periodicals*.

40 I. Carr, *William Boyd*, 118–23.

41 R.K. Bussy, *Two Hundred Years of Publishing*, 115.

42 'Publisher's Introduction,' in G. Murray, *Medicine in the Making* (Toronto: Ryerson Press, 1960), xi.

13. Printing and Design

1 B. Dewalt, *Technology and Canadian Printing*, 86.

2 Ibid., 87–8.

3 Ibid., 87–8.

4 Canada, Dominion Bureau of Statistics, Forestry Section, *Report on the Printing Trades in Canada*, 1936, p. 1; table 2, pp. 6–7; 1946, pp. 1–2.

5 *Canadian Printer and Publisher*, January 1959, pp. 72–3.

6 B. Dewalt, *Technology and Canadian Printing*, 114.

7 Technological details are taken from B. Dewalt, *Technology and Canadian Printing*, 90–108, 119–34; A. Devost, *L'imprimerie au Québec*, 207–25; and R. Lechêne, *L'imprimerie, de Gutenberg à l'électron*, 139–50.

8 C.J. Eustace, 'Developments in Canadian Book Production and Design,' 48.

9 B. Dewalt, *Technology and Canadian Printing*, 123.

10 L.-G. Lemieux, *Le roman du 'Soleil*,' 235–42.

11 G. Piédalue, 'Les groupes financiers et la guerre du papier au Canada 1920–1930,' 224.

12 J.-P. Charland, *Les pâtes et papiers au Québec 1880–1980*, 135.

13 Ibid., 135–7.

14 R. Létourneau, 'Analyse conjoncturelle des expéditions de l'industrie canadienne du papier journal,' 10.

15 C.J. Eustace, 'Developments in Canadian Book Production and Design,' 48.

16 J.-P. Charland, *Les pâtes et papiers au Québec 1880–1980*, 136.

17 Ibid., 141.

18 R. Létourneau, 'Analyse conjoncturelle des expéditions de l'industrie canadienne du papier journal,' 6.

19 Canadian Pulp and Paper Association / Association canadienne des producteurs de pâtes et papiers, in Association des industries forestières du Québec, *L'évolution de l'industrie québécoise des pâtes et papiers*, 1–8.

20 *Historical Atlas of Canada*, 3: plate 50.

21 According to the Canadian Pulp and Paper Association / Association canadienne des producteurs de pâtes et papiers, *Tables de statistiques 1975*, 31, cited in R. Létourneau, 'Analyse conjoncturelle des expéditions de l'industrie canadienne du papier journal,' 8–9.

22 J.-P. Charland, *Les pâtes et papiers au Québec 1880–1980*, 159.

23 *Le Maître imprimeur*, June 1977, p. 3; May 1979, p. 19; June-July 2001, p. 17; J.-A. Fortin, ed., *Biographies canadiennes-françaises*, 1063; J. Michon, ed., *HÉLQ*, 1:21.

24 R. Bélisle, 'Visite à la Maison Thérien Frères limitée,' *Technique*, January 1938, pp. 9–12, 25.

25 *Le Maître imprimeur*, July 1951, p. 9; J. Michon, ed., *HÉLQ*, 1:13.

26 *Le Maître imprimeur*, May 1947, p. 3; June 1977, p. 3; May 1979, p. 19.

27 Ibid., May 1979, p. 22.

28 D.K. Friesen, 'Executive Message,' [iv].

29 J. Thiessen, 'Friesens Corporation,' 21, 22.

30 Ibid., 26.

31 Curwin Friesen to the author, 12 April 2005; and J. Thiessen, 'Friesens Corporation,' 36–7.

32 J. Thiessen, 'Friesens Corporation,' 30.

33 Ibid., 116.

34 Friesen Printers, *Make History with Friesen Printers*, 9, 27–44.

35 E.F. Baker, *Printers and Technology*, 301–2; S.F. Zerker, *Rise and Fall of the Toronto Typographical Union*, 178.

36 S.F. Zerker, *Rise and Fall of the Toronto Typographical Union*, 203.

37 *Typographical Journal*, February 1923, p. 150.

38 Ibid., June 1921, pp. 670–1; April 1924, pp. 490–1; July 1924, p. 2.

39 Communications, Energy and Paperworkers Union, 'Local 191 – an ITU Local, 1900 to 1930.'

40 H.A. Logan, *Trade Unions in Canada*, 110.

41 Ibid., 111.

42 Y. Belzile, 'La grève des typographes de Montréal (1921–1924).' On the forty-four–hour movement, see S.F. Zerker, *Rise and Fall of the Toronto Typographical Union*, 178–204.

43 B. Dansereau, 'Le mouvement ouvrier montréalais, 1918–1929,' 233.

44 J. Rouillard, *Les syndicats nationaux au Québec de 1900 à 1930*, 222–31.

45 L. Desrochers, 'Les facteurs d'apparition du syndicalisme catholique dans l'imprimerie, 1921–1945,' 253–5; and Canada, Department of Labour, *Labour Organization in Canada*, 204.

46 J. Rouillard, *Histoire du syndicalisme au Québec*, 131–210.

47 *Le Devoir*, 23, 25, and 26 April 1955.

48 Association des arts graphiques du Québec, fonds AMI, 'Règlements de l'Association des maîtres imprimeurs de Montréal (section française)' (1934), 6.

49 *Le Maître imprimeur*, January 1946, p. 3.

50 Ibid., November 1938, p. 1.

51 F.-A. Angers and R. Parenteau, *Statistiques manufacturières du Québec 1665–1948*, 148–52.

52 E.F. Baker, *Technology and Woman's Work*, 181–2; J.R. MacDonald, ed., *Women in the Printing Trades*, 3–5; M. Van Kleeck, *Women in the Bookbinding Trade*, 38.

53 *Canadian Printer and Publisher*, April 1952, p. 68; August 1953, pp. 27, 42–3.

54 A.H. Barker, *Apprentice of Tomorrow*, 3.

55 J. Delorme, 'L'imprimerie,' *Technique*, January 1944, p. 21.

56 *Canadian Printer and Publisher*, September 1931, p. 43.

57 Ibid., February 1928, pp. 52–3.

58 Ibid., July 1945, pp. 19–20.

59 Ibid., September 1956, pp. 86, 88.

60 C. Cockburn, *Brothers: Male Dominance and Technological Change*, 114–15, 120.

61 S.F. Zerker, *Rise and Fall of the Toronto Typographical Union*, 250.

62 B. Dewalt, *Technology and Canadian Printing*, 139.

63 'Section 2: Correspondence Course of the International Typographical Union,' in Canada, Royal Commission on Industrial Training and Technical Education, *Report*, 4:2052.

64 *Le Maître imprimeur*, October 1942, p. 8; August 1944, p. 1.

65 F.S. Rutherford, 'What Technical Schools Have Done to Meet the Recommendations of the Royal Commission on Technical Education,' 17.

66 A. Frigon, 'Notre nouvelle école d'imprimerie, *Technique*, February 1926, p. 5.

67 *Prospectus de l'École technique de Montréal* (Montreal: [1930?]), 13.

68 'L'École des arts graphiques de la province de Québec,' *Technique pour tous*, October 1956, p. 46.

69 *Le Maître imprimeur*, August 1942, p. 1.

70 'L'École des arts graphiques de la province de Québec,' *Technique pour tous*, October 1956, p. 46.

71 Ibid., 47.

72 A.-A. de Sève, *Hommage à Jean-Marie Gauvreau*.

73 Marcel Dugas, 'Louis Forest, relieur canadien,' *Le Livre et ses amis* 8 (June 1946): 56–7; and G. de Grosbois, 'Towards a History of Québec Bookbinding.'

74 S. Beaudoin-Dumouchel, *La première école d'arts graphiques en Amérique*.

75 See M.H. Choko, P. Bourassa, and G. Baril, *Le design au Québec*.

76 C. Hould and S. Laramée, *Répertoire des livres d'artistes au Québec, 1900–1980*.

77 S. Bernier, *Du texte à l'image*, 187–224.

78 W. Rueter, 'Introduction,' [3].

79 G. Brender à Brandis cited in A.J. Horne et al., *Fine Printing*, 24.

80 G. Brender à Brandis cited in *Reader, Lover of Books*, 26.

81 M. Rueter, 'Private Press in Canada,' 113.

82 University of British Columbia Library, Rare Books and Special Collections, Alcuin Society Papers, box 1, file 2, 'Announcing the Establishment of the Alcuin Society' [1965].

83 Full bibliographic details are provided in Alcuin Society, *The Alcuin Society: A Compilation of Its Publications*.

84 W. Toye, 'Book Design in Canada,' 53.

85 J.M. Gray, *Fun Tomorrow*, 175.

86 See R. Stacey with H. Bishop, *J.E.H. MacDonald, Designer*.

87 W. Novosedlik, 'Our Modernist Heritage,' [Part 1], 31.

88 T. MacDonald, *Notebooks*, 100, 102–3.

89 W. Novosedlik, 'Our Modernist Heritage,' [Part 1], 31.

90 S. Pantazzi, 'Book Illustration and Design,' 24.

91 M.E. Edison, *Thoreau MacDonald*, 22.

92 C.J. Eustace, 'Developments in Canadian Book Production,' 48.

93 G. Campbell, 'William Collins during World War II,' 64.

94 C.J. Eustace, 'Developments in Canadian Book Production,' 47–8.

95 W.H. Clarke, 'An Art, a Craft, and a Business,' 22–4.

96 G. Campbell, 'William Collins during World War II,' 57.

97 J.M. Gray, 'English Language Publishing in Canada 1945–1955,' *Canadian Library Association Bulletin* 11 (June 1955): 295.

98 B. Donnelly, 'Mass Modernism,' 6.

99 J.M. Gray, 'English Language Publishing in Canada 1945–1955,' *Canadian Library Association Bulletin* 11 (June 1955): 295.

100 See R. Speller, 'Arthur Steven at the Ryerson Press.'

101 P. Duval, 'Word and Picture,' [20].

102 W. Novosedlik, 'Our Modernist Heritage,' [Part 1], 32.

103 'Blurbism,' *Saturday Night*, 13 December 1949, p. 24.

104 See R. Speller, 'Frank Newfeld'; and M. Biagioli, 'Humble Servant.'

105 F. Newfeld, 'Book Design and Production,' 34.

106 K. Scherf, 'Legacy of Canadian Cultural Tradition,' 135–6.

107 C.J. Eustace, 'Developments in Canadian Book Production,' 49.

108 B. Dewalt, *Technology and Canadian Printing*, 119.

109 W. Novosedlik, 'Our Modernist Heritage,' [Part 2], 82.

110 F. Newfeld, 'Book Design and Production,' 26.

111 D. Williamson, 'Book Design,' 48.

112 See D. McLeod, ed., 'Carl Dair Special Issue.'

113 See J.M. Banks, '"And not hearers only,"' 1:288–9.

14. Systems of Distribution

1 Data for 1975 and 1976 are drawn from Canada, Statistics Canada, Education, Science and Culture Division, *Culture Statistics: Book Publishing: An Industry Analysis* (no. 87-601), and *Culture Statistics, Book Publishing, Textbooks* (no. 87-603), 1975–6.

2 United Nations, *Yearbook of International Trade Statistics*, 1976–86.

3 Canada, Dominion Bureau of Statistics, *Trade of Canada (Imports for Consumption and Exports)*, 65-D-22 (1913–25), 65-D-23 (1926–38); Canada, Dominion Bureau of Statistics (Statistics Canada), External Trade Division, *Trade of Canada, vol. 3: Imports*, 65-203 (1939–79).

4 According to available data from 1918 to 1943 and from 1961 to 1975, in Canada, Dominion Bureau of Statistics (Statistics Canada), *Canada Year Book*.

5 About 90 per cent of other printed matter (such as notices, pamphlets, brochures, printed forms, postcards, sheet music) came from the United States.

6 W.K. Lamb, 'Copyright and the Canadian Book Market,' *Canadian Library Association Bulletin* 12.2 (October 1955): 73.

7 During this period, school texts, religious books, books for public libraries, books in foreign languages, and most books from Britain were exempted.

8 J.N. Wolfe, 'Market for Books in Canada,' 544.

9 P. Audley, *Canada's Cultural Industries*, 88.

10 I. Cau, *L'édition au Québec de 1960 à 1977*, 22.

11 J. Michon and J. Vincent, 'La librairie française à Montréal au tournant du siècle.'

12 R.J. Cooke, 'Lure of the Pocket-Book Ladies,' *Canadian Business* 22 (November 1949): 26–7.

13 In 1979 original titles from French-Canadian publishers took 43.1 per cent of the market, whereas the figure for English-Canadian publishers was 23.6 per cent, according to P. Audley, *Canada's Cultural Industries*, 90.

14 See the Statistics Canada study on household comsumption in 1974, cited in Y. Ferland, 'Les Canadiens s'intéressent-ils au livre?' *Le Devoir*, 18 May 1976, p. 2.

15 Compiled from federal census data for 1931, 1951, and 1971. Figures for 1971 are confirmed in J. Lorimer and S.M. Shaw, *Book Reading in Canada*, 255. Thanks to Valerie Frith for her contributions to this article.

16 Canada, *Seventh Census of Canada, 1931. Volume X: Merchandising and Service Establishments*.

17 'Wendell Holmes' Business Certainly Has an Interesting Background,' *Bookseller and Stationer* 51 (15 December 1935): 27.

18 'Lending Library Survey Reveals Wide Variations in Methods,' *Bookseller and Stationer* 45 (July 1929): 41–4. Forty-six lending libraries pariticipated in the survey.

19 G. Matheson, 'Deliveries West Take 30 Days,' *Quill & Quire* 40 (April 1974): 12.

20 G. Graham, 'Why Books Cost Too Much,' *Maclean's Magazine*, 15 September 1947, pp. 22, 39–43; J.A. Davidson, 'The Crazy World of Book Publishing,' *Saturday Night*, 24 October 1959, p. 70.

21 'Canadian Retail Book Trade Invaded by Unfair Practices, Say Booksellers,' *Bookseller and Stationer* 45 (July 1929): 1.

22 S. Stewart, 'Speaking for Myself ... Joint Committees Are Only Effective If All Members Show Goodwill Instead of Bellyaching,' *Quill & Quire* 31 (May/June 1965): 28.

23 R. Britnell, 'Mr. Publisher ... What Now?' *Quill & Quire* 15 (June 1949): 6–7.

24 'Letters to the Editor: The Macmillan Protection Plan,' *Quill & Quire* 13 (September 1947): 69.

25 'New Trade Discount and Returns Policy,' *Quill & Quire* 36 (19 June 1970): 3.

26 V. Frith, 'Coming Back for Less: Returns Reform at Hand?' *Quill & Quire* 46 (December 1980): 9.

27 'Co-operative Christmas Advertising,' *Quill & Quire* 26 (June–July 1960): 10.

28 Canada, Statistics Canada, Merchandising and Services Division, *Retail Chain and Department Stores* (1981). These numbers exclude campus bookstores.

29 V. Thompson, 'Battle of the Bookstore Chains,' *Quill & Quire* 43 (April 1977): 4–5, 14.

30 J. Whitteker, 'Trade Bookstores in Canada,' 206.

31 'What the Act Says,' *Quill & Quire* 41 (February 1975): 7; 'What Has Happened,' *Quill & Quire* 41 (February 1975): 7; E. Staton, 'WUC Stages Picket of Coles in Ottawa,' *Quill & Quire* 41 (1 December 1975): 1.

32 'Selling to All Denominations,' *Quill & Quire* 44 (November 1978): 6.

33 A.H. Jarvis, 'Confessions of a Bookseller,' *Quill & Quire* 3 (November 1937): 19.

34 F.B. Moore, 'College Bookstores,' 221.

35 This calcuation is based on figures for 1981 drawn from Canada, Statistics Canada, Merchandising and Services Division, *Campus Book Stores, Retail Chain and Department Stores*, and *Retail Trade*.

36 One-third of the used bookstores (54 out of 164) enumerated in the federal census of 1971 were in British Columbia, a province with 10 per cent of Canada's population.

37 J. Michon, ed., *HÉLQ*, 2:369.

38 D. Hood, *Side Door*, 52–3.

39 W.F.E. Morley, 'Preface,' [5].

40 William Tyrrell cited in R.K. Bythell, 'Wm. Tyrrell Looks Back,' *Bookseller & Stationer and Office Equipment Journal* 54 (15 October 1938): 22.

41 D.W. Johnson, *History of Methodism in Eastern British America*, 143.

42 *The Wesleyan* (15 July 1839) quoted in The Book Room, 'News Release,' October 1985, p. 1. See also D.W. Johnson, *History of Methodism in Eastern British America*, 391.

43 Advertisement, *The Wesleyan* 2.23 (16 December 1839): 365.

44 L. Pierce, *Chronicle of a Century*, 123.

45 'Sixty-three Years in the Book and Stationery Business,' *The Maritime Merchant*, 10 March 1938, p. 36.

46 Canadian Book Publishers' Council papers (privately held), box 167, file 'Book Publishers Branch – General 1948,' Victor Knight to C.H. Dickinson, 27 October 1948.

47 Charles P. Burchell, president and manager of The Book Room, personal interview with the author, 26 September 2005; and S. Payne, '150 Years at The Book Room,' *Canadian Bookseller*, October 1989, pp. 16–17.

48 According to the special order register maintained by the Librairie Tranquille, 1963–5 (Service des archives de l'Université de Sherbrooke).

49 Y. Gauthier, *Monsieur livre: Henri Tranquille*, 260.

50 I.A. Litvak and C.J. Maule, *Development in the Distribution Systems*, 47.

51 Periodical Distributors Association of Canada, *Brief to the Royal Commission on Publications*, 1, 4.

52 C.S. Stokes, 'Our Americanized News-stands,' *Saturday Night*, 27 February 1926, p. 2.

53 D. Broten and P. Birdsall, *Paper Phoenix*, 23.

54 R. MacSkimming, *Perilous Trade*, 157.

55 J. Michon, ed., *HÉLQ*, 2:288–92; R. Saint-Germain et al., *Littérature en poche*.

56 Ontario, Royal Commission on Book Publishing, 'Second Interim Report,' 291.

57 Ontario, Royal Commission on Book Publishing, 'Final Report on the Distribution of Paperbacks and Periodicals,' 318.

58 S. Craig, 'Magazines in 1975: The Year of Change,' *Marketing*, 20 July 1975, p. 13.

59 Ontario, Royal Commission on Book Publishing, 'Final Report on the Distribution of Paperbacks and Periodicals,' 303.

60 See P. Martin, 'Access to Books,' *Canadian Reader* 15.4 (1974): 7.

61 See P. Martin, 'Will Cannon Boom?' *Canadian Reader* 16.6 (1975): 8; and D. Broten and P. Birdsall, *Paper Phoenix*, 38.

62 D. Broten and P. Birdsall, *Paper Phoenix*, 72.

63 I.A. Litvak and C.J. Maule, *Development in the Distribution Systems*, 47.

64 Ibid., 70.

65 Ibid., 53, 56.

66 Joan Blouin, 'Les super-camelots de l'édition,' *Livre d'ici* 9.3 (November 1983): 21; Bruno Dostie, 'Le boom de l'édition au Québec,' *La Presse*, 18 November 1989, p. K2.

67 M. Vipond, 'Best Sellers in English Canada: 1919–1928,' 74–5.

68 Ibid., 75; 'Canada's First Book Club,' *Quill & Quire* 39 (January 1973): 1.

69 'Eaton's Announce a Book Club,' *Quill & Quire* 4 (March 1938): 1A.

70 'Canadian Book Club for Progressives,' *Quill & Quire* 12 (January 1946): 46; 'New Catholic Readers Club,' *Quill & Quire* 13 (January 1947): 40–1.

71 'Book Club Reaches Readers in Book-Scarce Rural Areas,' *Financial Post*, 2 April 1960, p. 24.

72 'BOMC,' *Quill & Quire* 39 (January 1973): 7.

73 J. Michon, ed., *HÉLQ*, 2:326–52.

74 J. Michon, *Fides*, 243–4.
75 'Other Clubs,' *Quill & Quire* 39 (January 1973): 2.
76 P. Grescoe, *Merchants of Venus*, 91–3.
77 'Literary Guild and Doubleday Book Clubs,' *Quill & Quire* 39 (January 1973): 2.
78 'Canadians Buy Books ... If They Are Sold,' *Quill & Quire* 30 (March/April 1964): 24, 26, 28.
79 'Readers Club of Canada,' *Quill & Quire* 39 (January 1973): 3.
80 D. Broten and P. Birdsall, *Paper Phoenix*, 41; 'Readers' Club Receives Financial Assistance,' *Canadian Reader* 15.1 (1974): 7.
81 J. Hébert, 'Problèmes de diffusion,' *Liberté* 12 (May–June 1970): 93–107.
82 M.-N. Delatte, 'Québec Loisirs: Une décennie,' *Livre d'ici* 16.4 (December 1990): 16–17.
83 M. Tremblay, *Birth of a Bookworm*, 132–42.
84 William French, 'Poor Service,' *Globe and Mail*, 1 May 1973, p. 17.
85 Albert Sigurdson, 'CBA Reports Book Trade Is Thriving, Expects Fall Titles to Generate Sales,' *Globe and Mail*, 22 July 1981, p. B1.
86 J. Vincent, 'Le Conseil supérieur du livre, du rapport Bouchard à la loi 51,' 176.
87 See P. de Bellefeuille, A. Pontaut et al., *La bataille du livre au Québec*.
88 M. Ménard, *Les chiffres des mots*, 35, 105–6 ; and D. Vaugeois, *L'amour du livre*, 42–57.

15. Libraries

1 The history of all these libraries appears in G. Bernier, G. Gallichan, and R. Gordon, eds, *Les bibliothèques et les institutions parlementaires du XVIIIe siècle à nos jours*.
2 Canada, Dominion Bureau of Statistics, Education Branch, *Libraries in Canada, 1938–1940*.
3 Prince Edward Island, *Statutes*, 1929, c. 2.
4 Carnegie Corporation of New York, Commission of Enquiry, *Libraries in Canada*, 100.
5 Ibid., 115–16.
6 Ibid., 105–7.
7 John Hosie, provincial librarian and archivist for British Columbia, quoted in ibid., 113.
8 Carnegie Corporation of New York, Commission of Enquiry, *Libraries in Canada*, 106.
9 C.F. McCombs, 'Report on Canadian Libraries,' 5.
10 Ibid., 48–9.
11 Ibid., 44.
12 Canada, Royal Commission on National Development in the Arts, Letters and Sciences, *Report*, 113.
13 J.R. Beard, *Canadian Provincial Libraries*, 61, 83.
14 Canada, Royal Commission on National Development in the Arts, Letters and Sciences, *Report*, 330.
15 J.R. Beard, *Canadian Provincial Libraries*, 66.
16 Canada, Dominion Bureau of Statistics, Education Division, *Survey of Libraries, 1946–48*, 21–8.
17 Canada, Dominion Bureau of Statistics, Education Division, *Survey of Libraries, 1954–56*, 29–30.
18 W.K. Lamb and J.E. Brown, *Report of the National Librarian*, 31.
19 National Library of Canada, *Summary of the Federal Government Library Survey Report*, 1.
20 Ibid., 4.
21 Ibid., 22.
22 Library and Archives Canada, Council of Federal Libraries, 'About CFL.'

23 H.M. Tory cited in S. Robillard, 'From Books to Bytes,' 3.

24 Ibid., 3.

25 B.R. Steeves,'Visionary Leadership at the Canada Institute for Scientific and Technical Information: Its role in the Evolution of a National Scientific and Technical Information Policy and
Network for Canada,' paper presented at the 8th Kingston Conference of the Canadian Science and Technology Historical Association, Kingston, ON, October 1993, Appendix.

26 'National Science Library Experiences Phenomenal Growth,' 24. Earlier, in 1959, the National
Library and the National Science Library signed a formal agreement regarding the subject
area responsibilities of each institution.

27 G. Ember, 'Dissemination of Scientific and Technological Information,' 5.

28 S. Robillard, 'From Books to Bytes,' 4–5.

29 The term 'Institute' was used in order to distinguish it from the National Library of Canada
and to prevent jurisdictional disputes.

30 B. Hurst, 'CISTI: Meeting the Needs of the Canadian Scientific and Technical Community,'
Serials Librarian 19.4 (1991): 19.

31 Science Council of Canada, *Policy for Scientific and Technical Information Dissemination*, Report
no. 6, 1.

32 J.E. Brown, personal interview with B.R. Steeves, 23 February 1993.

33 G. Ember, 'Dissemination of Scientific and Technological Information,' 6.

34 Canada, Parliament, Senate, Special Committee on Science Policy, *Science Policy for Canada*, 2:
413.

35 Canada, Royal Commission on National Development in the Arts, Letters and Sciences, *Report*,
101.

36 J.A. Macdonald cited in F.D. Donnelly, *National Library of Canada*, 19.

37 W.K. Lamb, 'Canada's National Library,' 166.

38 C. Robertson, *Canadian Bibliographic Centre.*

39 National Library of Canada, *Report of the National Librarian, 1953*, 4.

40 G. Sylvestre cited in B. Stuart-Stubbs, 'Guy Sylvestre and the Development of the National
Library of Canada,' 23, note.

41 The twenty-six volumes of this retrospective bibliography appeared between 1980 and 1995
and are listed on 'Iris,' the on-line catalogue of the BAnQ.

42 M. Lajeunesse, *Les sulpiciens et la vie culturelle à Montréal au XIXe siècle*, and J.-R. Lassonde, *La Bibliothèque Saint-Sulpice, 1910–1931.*

43 Y. Lamonde, P.F. McNally, and A. Rotundo, 'Public Libraries and the Emergence of a Public
Culture.'

44 H.J. Cody, 'Dawn of a New Era,' *Ontario Library Review* 3.2 (November 1918): 25.

45 'The Modern Public Library,' *Ontario Library Review* 3.3 (February 1919): 1.

46 Canada, Dominion Bureau of Statistics, Education Branch, *Library Statistics of Canada, 1920–21.*

47 For an overview of Carson's opinions, see W.O. Carson, 'Canadian Public Library as a Social
Force.'

48 E.A. Boone, '"Holding the Key to the Hall of Democracy."'

49 Carnegie Corporation of New York, Commission of Enquiry, *Libraries in Canada*, 96.

50 British Columbia, *British Columbia Library Survey, 1927–28*, 20.

51 Carnegie Corporation of New York, Commission of Enquiry, *Libraries in Canada*, 141.

52 Ibid., 14.

53 Ibid., 139, 137.

54 Ibid., 133, 134.

55 M. Penman, *Century of Service*, 41–5.

56 Annual report of the Toronto Public Library as quoted in E. Hanson, 'Architecture and Public Librarianship,' 195.

57 Ibid., 195–6.

58 D. Carlisle, 'Lambton County Library Project,' *American Library Association Bulletin* 28 (September 1934): 632–3.

59 Carnegie Corporation of New York, Commission of Enquiry, *Libraries in Canada*, 29.

60 N. Bateson, *Library Survey of Nova Scotia*, 36–9.

61 Canada, Dominion Bureau of Statistics, Education Branch, *Survey of Libraries in Canada, 1936–38*, 6.

62 Many thanks to Ernie Ingles for providing these insights on public library development in the Prairies.

63 Ontario Library Association, Reconstruction Committee, *Library Needs of the Province of Ontario*.

64 Canadian Library Council, *Libraries in the Life of the Canadian Nation*, 1.

65 Canada, Dominion Bureau of Statistics, Education Division, *Survey of Libraries. Part I: Public Libraries, 1958*, 21.

66 M. Gilroy, 'Regional Libraries in Retrospect,' 68.

67 E.C. Bow, *Ontario Regional Library System Specialized Union Products*.

68 See, for example, North York Public Library, *Public Library Service to the Shut-In*.

69 Urban Dimensions Group, *Project Progress: A Study of Canadian Public Libraries*.

70 Canada, Statistics Canada, Education, Culture and Tourism Division, *Culture Statistics: Public Libraries in Canada, 1979–1981*, tables 15 and 16.

71 P.L. Smith and G. Graham, 'Library Service North of the Sixtieth Parallel,' 118–19.

72 G.-É. Marquis, *Nos bibliothèques publiques*, 12.

73 Quebec, Bureau of Statistics, *Statistical Year Book*, 1925, p. 152.

74 M. Lajeunesse, 'Les bibliothèques paroissiales, précurseurs des bibliothèques publiques au Québec?' 55.

75 Carnegie Corporation of New York, Commission of Enquiry, *Libraries in Canada*, 35.

76 Ridington Papers cited in M. Lajeunesse, 'La lecture publique au Québec au XXe siècle,' 194–5, and 204, note 20.

77 Carnegie Corporation of New York, Commission of Enquiry, *Libraries in Canada*, 39.

78 'Les bibliothèques de la province de Québec,' *Revue trimestrielle canadienne* 30 (December 1944): 427–9.

79 G.-É. Marquis, *Plaidoyer pour les bibliothèques publiques*, 16.

80 E. Desrochers, *Le rôle social des bibliothèques publiques*.

81 R. Tanghe, *Pour un système cohérent de bibliothèques au Canada français*, 14.

82 Quebec, Royal Commission of Inquiry on Constitutional Problems, *Report*, 3:231–41.

83 G. Martin, 'La direction des bibliothèques publiques du Québec.'

84 Québec, Commission d'étude sur les bibliothèques publiques du Québec, *Les bibliothèques publiques*.

85 S. Leacock, *My Discovery of England* (New York: Dodd Mead, 1923), 113–14.

86 N. Russell, 'McMaster's Mills Memorial Library, 1950–1963–1970,' 196.

87 B. Peel, *History of the University of Alberta Library*, 6, 11.

88   H.P. Gundy, quoted in P.-É. Filion, 'University Libraries before and after Williams,' 76.

89   Canada, Dominion Bureau of Statistics, *Canada Year Book*, 1921, p. 157; and *Canada Year Book*, 1985, p. 139. In 1921 there were more than 5,000 additional students categorized as 'other.' In 1981 there were also some 213,000 part-time undergraduates and 32,000 part-time graduate students; community college students numbered over 260,000.

90   R.S. Harris, *History of Higher Education in Canada*, 210.

91   L.S. Hansen, '"In the Room Known as the Library,"' 120–1.

92   Carnegie Corporation of New York, Commission of Enquiry, *Libraries in Canada*, 131.

93   J.-R. Lassonde, *La Bibliothèque Saint-Sulpice, 1910–1931*, 124.

94   Carnegie Corporation of New York, Commission of Enquiry, *Libraries in Canada*, 127.

95   P.F. McNally, 'McGill University Libraries.'

96   C.F. McCombs, 'Report on Canadian Libraries,' 7a.

97   Ibid., 18.

98   Ibid., 38.

99   *La Presse*, 28 October 1947, cited in H.-A. Bizier, *L'Université de Montréal*, 175.

100 W. Kirkconnell and A.S.P. Woodhouse, *Humanities in Canada*, 154.

101 E.E. Williams, *Resources of Canadian University Libraries for Research in the Humanities and Social Sciences*; B.V. Simon, *Library Support of Medical Education and Research in Canada*; G.S. Bonn, *Science-Technology Literature Resources in Canada*; R.B. Downs, *Resources of Canadian Academic and Research Libraries*.

102 K. Stubbs and D. Buxton, comp., *Cumulated ARL University Library Statistics, 1962–63 through 1978–79*.

103 E.E. Williams and P.-É. Filion, *Vers une bibliothèque digne de Laval* and *Les objectifs à poursuivre*.

104 Edmond Desrochers, 'Aurons-nous d'authentiques bibliothèques universitaires?' *Relations* 298 (October 1965): 295–7.

105 R.H. Blackburn, *Evolution of the Heart*, 300–1, 303.

106 Ibid., [ix], citing the report of the Spinks Commission to Study the Development of Graduate Programmes in Ontario Universities, 1966.

107 O. Dupuis, 'Dix ans de coopération entre les bibliothèques universitaires du Québec'; J.-R. Brault, 'Les bibliothèques universitaires du Québec.'

108 M. Lajeunesse and D. Morin, 'Les bibliothèques des collèges d'enseignement général et professionnel du Québec.'

109 Bibliocentre, 'About Bibliocentre.'

110 R.H. Blackburn, *Evolution of the Heart*, 220.

111 B. Peel and W.J. Kurmey, *Cooperation among Ontario University Libraries*, 62.

112 R.H. Blackburn, *Evolution of the Heart*, 317, 315.

113 Y. Lamonde, *Les bibliothèques de collectivités à Montréal*.

114 S. Normand, 'Les bibliothèques d'entreprises au Québec,' 115; P.F. McNally, 'Fifty Years of Special Libraries'; and C.A. Pearce, 'Development of Special Libraries in Montreal and Toronto.'

115 S. Normand, 'Les bibliothèques d'entreprises au Québec,' 106–7, 112.

116 Much of my research was carried out through e-mail. I am indebted to the following for details about special libraries that appear in this study: Phil Andrews, deputy managing editor, Saint John *Telegraph-Journal*; Marc Bourgeois, director of communications and public affairs, CCPE Ottawa; Danielle Brosseau, head reference librarian, Borden Ladner Gervais LLP, Toronto; Lyn Crothers, *Winnipeg Free Press* Library; Heather Dansereau, pharmaceutical

librarian (retired); Patricia Domaine, manager, Knowledge Centre, TD Bank; Ryan Filson, associate, Weir and Foulds LLP, Toronto; Stephen Francom, Royal Bank History; Sheila Hathorn, administrative coordinator, Toronto Association of Law Libraries; Penny Holden, chief curator, Provincial Museum of Newfoundland and Labrador; Lorraine Leff, librarian, Labatt Canada; Julia Matthews, head librarian, Royal Ontario Museum; Michelle McCart, librarian, Canadian Medical Association, Ottawa; Mark Mietkiewicz, project manager, CBC Web site, Toronto; Joan Murray, outreach librarian, Hudson's Bay Company Heritage Services; Del Rosario, archives librarian, Royal British Columbia Museum; and Judith Silverstone, executive director, Saskatchewan Library Association.

117 Y. Lamonde, *Les bibliothèques de collectivités à Montréal*, 79–80; and S. Normand, 'Les bibliothèques d'entreprises au Québec,' 109.
118 Canadian Centre for the Visual Arts, *Library and Archives: Collection Development Policy*, 11–12.
119 Canadian Broadcasting Corporation (CBC) Archives, 'Other Libraries.'
120 P.F. McNally, 'Fanfares and Celebrations,' 43.
121 Ibid., 47.
122 P.F. McNally, 'One Hundred Years of Canadian Graduate Education for Library and Information Studies,' *Feliciter* 50.5 (2004): 210–11.
123 While most were province-based associations, in 1935 New Brunswick, Prince Edward Island, and Nova Scotia joined in the Maritime Library Association (MLA), which became the Atlantic Provinces Library Association (APLA) with the addition of Newfoundland in 1957. In 1973 library workers in Nova Scotia established an independent provincial body, the Nova Scotia Library Association.
124 Best known as the ACBLF, the organization changed its name several times during its history.

16. Reading Habits

1 W. Clark, 'Cent ans d'éducation scolaire,' 23.
2 Canada, Census, *Seventh Census of Canada, 1931*, 269.
3 G. Bouchard, *Quelques arpents d'Amérique*, 446.
4 C. Lessard, 'L'alphabétisation à Trois-Rivières, 1634–1939,' 87.
5 J.H. Morrison, '"Black Flies, Hard Work, Low Pay."'
6 A.M. Thomas, *Adult Illiteracy in Canada*, 16.
7 W. Clark, 'Cent ans d'éducation scolaire,' 23.
8 A.M. Thomas, *Adult Illiteracy in Canada*, 63.
9 J.J. Tuinman, 'Literacy,' in CE (1985), 2:1012.
10 A.M. Thomas, *Adult Illiteracy in Canada*, 63.
11 The many surveys of adult literacy, and of children's reading levels, are excluded here.
12 See, for example, the *Marketing 'Profile' Survey*, undertaken for the trade journal of that name in 1978; and United Church of Canada Victoria University Archives, *Survey of Readers of the 'United Church Observer'* (Toronto: Gruneau Research Ltd, 1961) and *Continuing Study of Publication Audiences: C.S.P.A. Report on 'United Church Observer,' July 1964* (Toronto: Gruneau Research Ltd, 1964) aimed at potential advertisers in the *United Church Observer*.
13 See, for example, 'In the Editor's Confidence,' *Maclean's Magazine*, 15 May 1947, p. 4; and 'Canada's Newsmagazine Enters Year Two: A Progress Report to *Maclean's* Readers,' *Maclean's Magazine*, 4 October 1976, p. 14.

14 'Test 11 Magazines' Audience in Biggest Reader Survey,' *Financial Post*, 15 January 1949, p. 9.

15 Canadian Facts Ltd., *Report of a Study of the Daily Newspaper.*

16 'Series of Surveys Include Teenage Readership Details,' *Marketing*, 21 April 1967, p. 6.

17 G.H.L., 'What Do Canadians Read?' *Canadian Bookman* 5 (November 1923): 318; A.H. Gibbard, 'What Moose Jaw Reads,' *Canadian Bookman* 4 (April 1922): 121–2.

18 Library statistics were initially classified with 'education' but shifted to the 'cultural' envelope in 1975. The published information for this period first focuses on book accessibility, then on librarian training and credentials, and finally on funding and infrastructure.

19 Canada, Dominion Bureau of Statistics, Education Division, *Survey of Libraries in Canada, 1952–54*, 26.

20 Ibid., *1946–48*, 5.

21 A. Kapos, *Toronto Speaks.*

22 J. Talbot and M. Liversage, *Lake Erie Regional Library System.*

23 R. Stanton, *Vancouver Public Library: Users Survey at the Central Library, July 1972.*

24 G. Soules, *What People Want in a Library.*

25 Toronto Public Library, *Reading in Toronto*, 20.

26 'Survey of Canadian Book Buyers,' *Quill & Quire* 38 (April 1972): 1.

27 L. Kubas, *Newspapers and Their Readers.*

28 K.F. Watson et al., *Leisure Reading Habits*, 120–1.

29 See C. Delude-Clift, *Le comportement des Québécois.* 'One out of three Quebeckers does not read newspapers, and 56 per cent admit to never having read a book in their life,' began a report of the survey in *Le Devoir*, 7 January 1978, p. 28.

30 The University of Calgary Library, Special Collections, houses the records of the CANLIT group, including original survey returns.

31 L. Wheatcroft, *Something for Nothing.*

32 D. Broten and P. Birdsall, *Canadian Reader I*; and D. Broten, P. Birdsall, and G. Donald, *Canadian Reader II.*

33 M. Ben-Gera, *Ontario Reading Survey.*

34 'Weekend Poll: Reading Habits,' *Vancouver Sun Weekend Magazine*, 24 June 1978, p. 3.

35 A. Bergeron, *Les habitudes de lecture des Québécois*, 63.

36 J. Mirucki, *Le marché du livre au Canada*, 1:1.

37 G. Gagnon, *Habitudes et comportements des lecteurs.*

38 M. Alain, 'Recherches psycho-sociologiques sur les habitudes de lecture au Canada'; L. Brunet, 'Les tendances de la recherche sur les habitudes de lecture au Québec.'

39 E. Long, *American Dream and the Popular Novel*, 5.

40 M. Korda, *Making the List*, x–xi.

41 M. Vipond, 'Best Sellers in English Canada, 1899–1918,' 99.

42 Ibid., 99.

43 M. Vipond, 'Best Sellers in English Canada, 1919–1928,' 88–9, 99.

44 D.M. Daymond, 'Mazo de la Roche,' 108.

45 Costain would return to the list again in 1947 (*The Moneyman*, #2); 1949 (*High Towers*, #7); 1952–3 (*The Silver Chalice*, #1); 1955 (*The Tontine*, #9); and 1957 (*Below the Salt*, #9).

46 A.P. Hackett and J.H. Burke, *80 Years of Best Sellers: 1895–1975*, 150.

47 According to the database of Quebec literary reprints compiled by Max Roy, archives of the Centre de recherche interuniversitaire sur la littérature et la culture québécoises (CRILCQ),

Université du Québec à Montréal.

48 For the period 1954–8, the data were drawn from an analysis of each year's top 25 titles (150 out of 4,007). For 1959–62, 774 titles were analyzed. Data were compiled by Claude Martin with the collaboration of Caroline Bergeron and Gaëlle Jeannesson.

49 D. Saint-Jacques et al., *Ces livres que vous avez aimés.*

50 S.E. McMullin, 'Walt Whitman's Influence in Canada.'

51 R. Panofsky, 'At Odds: Reviewers and Readers of the *Jalna* Novels,' 65. De la Roche's papers are held at the University of Toronto's Thomas Fisher Rare Book Library.

52 University of Manitoba Archives and Special Collections, MSS 56, box 49, file 2, John B. Merchant to R. Connor, 18 November 1934.

53 University of Western Ontario Archives, Arthur Stringer Papers, box 3, file 3, Meredith Floris Waite to A. Stringer, 18 September 1921.

54 Ibid., Lisa Elliot to A. Stringer, 7 January 1922.

55 R. Panofsky, 'At Odds: Reviewers and Readers of the *Jalna* Novels,' 67–8.

56 University of Manitoba Archives and Special Collections, MSS 56, box 49, file 1, Roy Wilkinson to R. Connor, 6 July 1931.

57 York University Archives and Special Collections, Margaret Laurence Fonds, 1980–001/007 (07), [David Glassco?] to M. Laurence, 21 June 1975.

58 All references are to L.M. Montgomery, *Selected Journals*, and M. Lavallé, *Journal d'un prisonnier.* For more on Montgomery's reading activities, see C. Karr, 'Addicted to Reading.'

17. Controlling and Advising Readers

1 Canada, *Statutes*, 1847, 10 & 11 Victoria, c. 31, 'An Act for Repealing and Consolidating the Present Duties of Customs in This Province.'

2 'Banned Books – 1938,' *Quill & Quire* 5 (April 1939): 37.

3 B. Ryder, 'Undercover Censorship,' 134–5.

4 R. Whitaker, 'Chameleon on a Changing Background,' 20.

5 J. Keshen, 'First World War in Print.'

6 Canada, *Statutes*, 1914, 5 George 5, c. 2, 'War Measures Act.'

7 J. Keshen, *Propaganda and Censorship during Canada's Great War*, 93.

8 R. Whitaker, 'Chameleon on a Changing Background,' 26.

9 H.D. Fischer, *Struggle for Press Freedom in Canada*, 53–64.

10 G. Purcell, 'Wartime Press Censorship in Canada,' 10.

11 McMaster University Library, William Ready Division of Archives and Research Collections, Macmillan Company of Canada fonds, first accrual, authors' series, part 1, box 47, H.S. Eayrs to I. Baird, 6 November 1939 and 13 November 1939.

12 G. Purcell, 'Wartime Press Censorship in Canada,' 80.

13 R. Whitaker, 'Chameleon on a Changing Background,' 31.

14 B. Fraser, 'Our Hush-Hush Censorship: How Books Are Banned,' *Maclean's Magazine*, 15 December 1949, p. 25; 'Ulysses Comes Out of Hiding,' *Vancouver Sun*, 13 April 1950, p. 12.

15 'The Case of Lady Chatterley,' *Vancouver Sun*, 20 June 1960, p. 4.

16 J.V. McAree, 'Failing as Artists They Turn to Dirt,' *Globe and Mail*, 3 February 1949, p. 6.

17 J. Clydesdale, '*The Naked and the Dead* by Norman Mailer – Under the Hood,' *This Magazine* 36.2 (September–October 2002): 2.

18 Canada, *Criminal Code of Canada* (2006), sect. 163 (8).

19 Ibid., sect. 587 (1)(d).

20 M. Czarnecki, 'Margaret Laurence and the Book Banners,' *Chatelaine*, October 1985, pp. 55, 190.

21 B. Ryder, 'Undercover Censorship,' 129.

22 Quoted in A.W. Harrison, *Check-List of United Church of Canada Publications*, vol. 1, epigraph.

23 Queen's University Archives, Lorne Pierce fonds, Lorne Pierce to E.J. Pratt, 16 December 1924.

24 M. Jeanneret, *God and Mammon*, 1–2.

25 *The Raphaelite* [Saint John, Mount Carmel Academy] 3 (1937): 36.

26 B. Ryder, 'Undercover Censorship,' 139.

27 Ibid., 138–45.

28 J. Bakan, 'Beyond Censorship,' 84–8.

29 J. Dick, *Not in Our Schools?!!! School Book Censorship in Canada*, 88–93.

30 Ibid., 39.

31 Ibid., 9–10.

32 P. Hébert with P. Nicol, *Censure et littérature au Québec ... (1625–1919)*.

33 P. Hébert, 'Une censure totale?'

34 J.-C. Harvey, *Pages de critique*, 94.

35 *Semaine religieuse de Québec*, 4 April 1935, 489.

36 A. DesRochers, 'Les "individualistes" de 1925,' *Le Devoir*, 25 November 1951, p. 9.

37 In December 1946, Maurice Duplessis, the premier and attorney general of Quebec, engineered the revocation of the liquor licence of Montreal restaurant owner Frank Roncarelli, thereby ruining his business, after Roncarelli had stood bail for four hundred Jehovah's Witnesses. The ensuing legal battle ended in Roncarelli's favour in September 1959, when the Supreme Court of Canada ruled that the premier had committed a civil wrong and ordered him personally to pay substantial damages.

38 P. Hébert with É. Salaün, *Censure et littérature au Québec ... (1920–1959)*, 125–6.

39 Ibid., 228.

40 T. Bertrand, '*Le Devoir* et la littérature: Une page littéraire décevante,' *Lectures* 5.10 (June 1949): 577–86.

41 R.-M. Charland, 'L'état adulte,' *Lectures* 12.1 (September 1965): 2.

42 J.E. Baker, *Archibald MacMechan*, 126.

43 For Deacon's lively correspondence, see W.A. Deacon, *Dear Bill*.

44 *Canadian Forum* 1.1 (October 1920): 3.

45 See M. Fee, 'Lorne Pierce, Ryerson Press, and The Makers of Canadian Literature Series.'

46 *Canadian Historical Review* 1 (1920): 1.

47 D. Staines, 'Reviewing Practices in English Canada,' 63–4.

48 R. Fulford, D. Godfrey, and A. Rotstein, eds, *Read Canadian*.

49 S. Egoff, *Republic of Childhood*, 13.

50 Y. Lamonde, P.F. McNally, and A. Rotundo, 'Public Libraries and the Emergence of a Public Culture,' 2:270; and L.A. McGrath, 'Service to Children in the Toronto Public Library,' 192.

51 L.H. Smith, *Unreluctant Years*, 13.

52 J. Chabot, *Montréal et le rayonnement des bibliothèques publiques*, 41–2.

53 L.A. McGrath, 'Service to Children in the Toronto Public Library,' 104–5, 87, 123, 111.

54 G. Boulizon, *Livres roses et séries noires*, 166–8.

55 L.A. McGrath, 'Service to Children in the Toronto Public Library,' 331.

56 F. Irvine, 'Introduction,' in *Current Problems in Reading Instruction*, iii.

57 *Young Canada Listens: School Broadcasts, 1942–1943*, 27.

58 New Brunswick Federation of Home and School Associations, *Primer for Parents*, 4.

59 S. Landy, 'Why Johnny Can Read ... but Doesn't,' *Canadian Library Journal* 34 (October 1977): 387.

60 L. Nilson, comp., *Best of Children's Choices*, 102.

18. Special Communities of Readers

1 Paul-Aimé Martin, 'La bibliothèque circulante en forêt de Baie-Comeau,' *Lectures* 5.1 (September 1948): 58–9.

2 E.A. Corbett, *Henry Marshall Tory*, chapter 13. We are grateful for the input of the Canadian YMCA.

3 J. Hale, *Branching Out*, 67.

4 T.B. Richards, 'Books for the Troops,' 6, 7.

5 Ibid., 10.

6 Ibid., 14–16.

7 Université de Sherbrooke, Archives du GRÉLQ, documents 1–28, 1993–7, Paul-Aimé Martin, 'Notes sur ma vie, mes activités, et les principales réalisations des Éditions Fides,' 44.

8 T.B. Richards, 'Books for the Troops,' 8–9, 10.

9 A.L. Watson, *Exploratory Study of Library Services for the Disadvantaged in Greater Victoria*, 1.

10 A. Dean, 'Story-Time for the Elderly,' *Comment* [Central Ontario Regional Library System], May–June 1981, p. 19.

11 J. Rhodes, 'New Life for a Tired System – the Prison Library,' 248.

12 C.M. Nason, *Report on Institutional Library Service*.

13 'OPLA Visiting Library Services Committee,' *Focus* 8.3 (June 1982): 5.

14 R.T. Jordan, *Tomorrow's Library*, 17–18; and E.F. Brown, *Bookmobiles and Bookmobile Service*, 14.

15 *Library on Wheels*.

16 C.W. MacDonald, *Report on a Survey of Mobile Library Service*, 8.

17 H. Overend, *Book Guy*, 21–4.

18 H.J. Medd, 'Yes, We Have Them, Too: Some Notes on Mobile Libraries in Canada,' *The Public Library Reporter* 14 (1969): 11–12.

19 P.A. Lotz, 'History of Library Development in the Atlantic Provinces,' 19.

20 H. Overend, *Book Guy*, 215–20, 239–45.

21 A. Woodland and E. Heaney, eds, *British Columbia Libraries: Historical Profiles*, 76.

22 Ville de Montréal, Divison de la gestion de documents et des archives, 4th series, reel 356, file 1682.16/1.

23 L. Mackey, 'Mobile Library Service in Canada.'

24 Manitoba Women's Institute, *Great Human Heart*, 109.

25 Ibid., 110.

26 C.C. Cole and J. Larmour, *Many and Remarkable*, 72–3.

27 G.L. Fairbairn, *From Prairie Roots*, 131; and F.W. Hamilton, *Service at Cost*, 110. I have not found any record of the Alberta Wheat Pool library having become a circulating library.

28 J. Blanchard, 'Manitoba Pool Library,' 9.

29 Brandon University, John E. Robbins Library, S.J. McKee Archives, RG 4, library columns of the *Manitoba Co-operator*, 1943–9.

30 Although the Manitoba pool's self-published histories repeatedly emphasize that no fiction was held in the library collection, F.W. Hamilton includes 'popular novels of the day' in his description of the collection (*Service at Cost*, 72).

31 Saskatchewan Co-operative Wheat Producers, *16th Annual Report* (Regina, 1940), 21.

32 Saskatchewan Archives Board, R-1523:1, file II.7, *Catalogue of Books in the Saskatchewan Wheat Pool Library as at January 1, 1955* (Regina: Saskatchewan Wheat Pool, 1955), 85–9.

33 *Manitoba Co-operator*, 6 November 1947, p. 4.

34 S. Barnes, 'We Need a Library,' *Eastern Door* 11.5 (2002): 1.

35 B.F.R. Edwards, '"To put the talk upon paper"'; and B.F.R. Edwards, *Paper Talk*.

36 LAC, RG 10, vol. 6032, file 150–41, part 1, Headquarters – Supplementary Reading Books for Indian Schools, 1931–42.

37 See ibid., vol. 6035, file 150–83, part 1, Headquarters – Day Schools – Listings of Library Books, 1943.

38 Ibid., vol. 6035, file 150–83, part 1, J. Swibb to R.A. Hoey, 13 May 1943.

39 Ibid., vol. 3251, file 600, 533, F. Earl Anfield to Major D.M. MacKay, British Columbia Indian commissioner, 24 February 1944 and 6 April 1944.

40 B.F.R. Edwards, *Paper Talk*, 149–53.

41 Ibid., 145–7.

42 See G.H. Hills, *Native Libraries*, 122–3.

43 National Indian Brotherhood, *Indian Control of Indian Education*, 10, 16.

44 H. McCue, 'Native People – Education,' in CE (2000), 1582.

45 Grade 1 British Braille, designed for fledgling readers, was uncontracted, while grade 2, intended for the average reader, utilized about two hundred contractions and abbreviations. British Braille also had a third grade, largely used for stenography, that included a further thousand contractions and abbreviations.

46 M.R. Chandler, *Century of Challenge*, chapter 4.

47 Archives of Ontario, RG 2–204, box 2, file 55, Supt. [W.B. Race] to K. Maxfield, 31 March 1926.

48 CNIB, Western Division, *Annual Report, 1946–47* (Victoria), 5, 9.

49 CNIB, Western Division, *Annual Report, 1936–37* (Victoria), 17.

50 CNIB, *Annual Report, 1938–39* (Toronto), 26.

51 LAC, MG 28, I 233, vol. 11, file 16, S. Swift to E.M. Lindholm, 3 June 1924.

52 Ibid., vol. 11, file 16, S. Swift to E.A. Baker, 3 April 1925.

53 Ibid., vol. 14, file 'NIB 1928–39,' S. Swift to W.M. Eagar, 27 November 1935.

54 S. Commend, *Les Instituts Nazareth et Louis-Braille*, 95.

55 CNIB, 'Submission to the Ontario Royal Commission on Book Publishing (May 1971),' 5.

56 *Crane Library News* 5.2 (January 1975): 5.

57 R. Fast, 'Impact of Sponsorship,' 62–5.

58 S.E. Wurtele, 'Nation-Building from the Ground Up.'

59 Anglican Provincial Synod of British Columbia Archives, St Mark's Hall, 1909–25; 1943–8.

60 United Church of Canada, Conference of Manitoba and Northwestern Ontario Archives, Ex-35; 80-15; 83-9, All Peoples' Sutherland Avenue United Church, 1925–58.

61 Ibid., Ex-11; Ex-37; Ex-54; 81-28; 98-1; 98-11, Robertson Memorial United Church, 1917–97.

62 The Ottawa Jewish Reading Circle papers are held by the Ottawa Jewish Historical Society.

Ephemeral and printed material related to the Calgary Jewish Literary Club is held in the Jewish Archives and Historical Society of Edmonton and Northern Alberta, Abraham Shnitka, SHN.02.1, 1915–35.

63 Mennonite Historical Society of Canada, 'Literary Societies' in 'Canadian Mennonite Encyclopedia Online'; and Mennonite Literary Society, *Rhubarb* home page.

64 See H. Murray, 'Literary Societies'; and R. Snape, *Leisure and the Rise of the Public Library.*

65 Mount Allison University Archives, 7303/8, 25 January 1977.

66 Once-in-a-While Club, personal communication, 18 November 2003.

67 Mount Allison University Archives, 7203, 4.

68 J. Stoffman, 'Literature for a Lifetime,' *Toronto Star*, 21 May 2005, p. H13.

69 D. Rehberg Sedo, 'Badges of Wisdom.'

70 Name withheld for privacy, personal communication, 8 January 2000.

71 Marie Coulter, personal communication, 11 June 2003.

Coda

1 L. Lipking, 'Trout in the Milk,' 1.

2 M. Tremblay, *Birth of a Bookworm*, 157–61.

3 R. MacSkimming, *Perilous Trade*, 365.

4 Abebooks, home page, http://www.abebooks.com (accessed 2 March 2006).

5 Granville Island Publishing, 'About Us,' http://www.granvilleislandpublishing.com (accessed 16 September 2005).

6 Whitlands Publishing, home page, http://www.whitlands.com (accessed 15 September 2005).

7 R. MacSkimming, *Perilous Trade*, 297.

8 Ibid., 330.

9 Ibid., 368, 374–5, 358–60.

10 J. Traves, 'Author's Note: Don't Quit Your Day Job,' *Toronto Star*, 3 January 2004, p. J12.

11 R. MacSkimming, *Perilous Trade*, 372, 393.

12 L. Price, 'Reading: The State of the Discipline,' 311.

SOURCES CITED

Archival Sources

Anglican Provincial Synod of British Columbia Archives
St Mark's Hall, 1909–25; 1943–8

Archives de la Corporation des Éditions Fides, Montreal

Archives gaies du Québec, Montreal

Archives nationales du Québec à Montréal (ANQM)
Conseil supérieur du livre fonds
Société des écrivains canadiens fonds

Archives of Ontario (AO)
RG 2-204, Ministry of Education, Ontario School for the Blind fonds

Archives of the House of Commons, Canada

Association des arts graphiques du Québec, Montreal
Association des maîtres imprimeurs (AMI) fonds

Bibliothèque nationale du Québec (BNQ)
MSS-061, Société des écrivains canadiens fonds

Brandon University, John E. Robbins Library, S.J. McKee Archives
RG 4, Manitoba Pool Elevators fonds

Canadian Book Publishers' Council papers (held privately by the organization), Toronto

Canadian Broadcasting Corporation (CBC) Reference Library, Toronto

Canadian Lesbian and Gay Archives, Toronto

Canadian Pacific Railway (CPR) Archives, Montreal

City of Montreal, Division de la gestion de documents et des archives

Jewish Archives and Historical Society of Edmonton and Northern Alberta
Abraham Shnitka, SHN.02.1, 1915–35

Jewish Public Library Archives, Montreal

Library and Archives Canada / Bibliothèque et Archives Canada (LAC / BAC)
MG 28, I 2 [new number: R2799-0-3-E], Canadian Authors Association fonds
MG 28, I 233 [new number R3647-0-9-E], Canadian National Institute for the Blind fonds
MG 30, D 399 [new number R2437-0-2-E], Marion Scott fonds
MG 31, D 162 [new number R5318-0-4-E], Robert Weaver fonds
MG 31, D 190 [new number R4403-0-9-E], Robin Mathews fonds
RG 10 [new number R216-0-0-E], Department of Indian Affairs and Northern Development fonds
RG 36–31, Government of Canada: Boards, Offices and Commissions, Broadcasts – Wartime Information Board Reports
RG 41 [new number R1190-0-3-E], Canadian Broadcasting Corporation fonds
Pulp Art and Fiction Collection
Yousuf Karsh Collection

McGill University Libraries, Rare Books and Special Collections Division
MS 925, Tundra Books archives

McMaster University Library, William Ready Division of Archives and Research Collections
Leslie McFarlane fonds
Macmillan Company of Canada fonds
McClelland and Stewart fonds
Writers' Union of Canada fonds

Mount Allison University Archives
No. 7203, Sackville Women's Civic Council fonds
No. 7303, Once-in-a-While Club fonds

Ottawa Jewish Historical Society

Provincial Archives of Newfoundland and Labrador
GN 7711/B, Government of Newfoundland, Department of Education

Queen's University Archives
2058a, Reginald Eyre Watters fonds
Lorne Pierce fonds

Saskatchewan Archives Board
R-1523, Saskatchewan Wheat Pool fonds

Simon Fraser University (SFU) Archives
F-57, Association of Canadian Publishers (ACP) fonds

Simon Fraser University (SFU) Library, Special Collections
J.J. Douglas fonds
Press Gang archives

Thomas Fisher Rare Book Library, University of Toronto
MS collection 119, James Mavor Papers
MS collection 120, Mazo de la Roche Papers
Robert S. Kenny Collection

United Church of Canada, Conference of Manitoba and Northwestern Ontario Archives, Winnipeg

Université de Sherbrooke
Archives du GRÉLQ
Service des archives de l'Université de Sherbrooke

University of British Columbia Library, Rare Books and Special Collections
Alcuin Society Papers, 1965–79
Association of Book Publishers of British Columbia fonds, 1972–2000
Wallace B. Chung and Madeline H. Chung Collection

University of Calgary Library, Special Collections
CANLIT

University of Manitoba Archives and Special Collections
MSS 56, Charles W. Gordon (Ralph Connor) Papers

University of Regina Archives
Western Producer Prairie Books

University of Toronto Archives
A85–0021/002, Office of the President

University of Western Ontario Archives
Arthur Stringer Papers

York University Archives and Special Collections
Margaret Laurence fonds

Published Sources

Abella, Irving, and Harold Troper. *None Is Too Many: Canada and the Jews of Europe, 1933–1948.* Toronto: Lester & Orpen Dennys, 1982.

Adams, John Coldwell. *Sir Charles God Damn: The Life of Sir Charles G.D. Roberts.* Toronto: University of Toronto Press, 1986.

Adams, Thomas R., and Nicolas Barker. 'A New Model for the Study of the Book.' In *The Potencie of Life: Books in Society: The Clark Lectures, 1986–1987,* ed. Nicolas Barker, 5–43. London: The British Library, 1993.

Alain, Marc. 'Recherches psycho-sociologiques sur les habitudes de lecture au Canada.' *Bulletin de l'Association canadienne des bibliothécaires de langue française* 18.3 (September 1972): 191–7.

Alcuin Society. *The Alcuin Society: A Compilation of Its Publications from 1965 to 1998.* Vancouver: Alcuin Society, 1999.

Aldana, Patricia. *Canadian Publishing: An Industrial Strategy for Its Preservation and Development in the Eighties.* Toronto: Association of Canadian Publishers, 1980.

Allan, Andrew. *Andrew Allan: A Self-Portrait.* Toronto: Macmillan Company of Canada, 1974.

Allen, Ralph. 'The Magazine.' In *Writing in Canada: Proceedings of the Canadian Writers' Conference, Queen's University, 28–31 July 1955,* ed. George Whalley, 65–73. Toronto: Macmillan Company of Canada, 1956.

Alston, Sandra, and Patricia Fleming. *Toronto in Print: A Celebration of 200 Years of the Printing Press in Toronto, 1798–1998.* Toronto: University of Toronto Library, 1998.

Anderson, Doris. *Rebel Daughter: An Autobiography.* Toronto: Key Porter Books, 1996.

Angers, François-Albert, and Roland Parenteau. *Statistiques manufacturières du Québec 1665–1948 (avec quelques données comparatives pour le Canada et les autres provinces).* Montreal: Institut d'économie appliquée, École des hautes études commerciales, 1966.

Armstrong, Jeannette C. 'Four Decades: An Anthology of Canadian Native Poetry from 1960 to 2000.' In *Native Poetry in Canada: A Contemporary Anthology,* ed. Jeannette C. Armstrong and Lally Grauer, xv–xx. Peterborough, ON: Broadview Press, 2001.

Arnup, Katherine. *Education for Motherhood: Advice for Mothers in Twentieth-Century Canada.* Toronto: University of Toronto Press, 1994.

Association des industries forestières du Québec. *L'évolution de l'industrie québécoise des pâtes et papiers: Mémoire présenté à la Commission parlementaire des richesses naturelles et des terres et forêts.* [Montreal]: Association des industries forestières du Québec, 1977.

Aubin, Paul. *Les communautés religieuses et l'édition du manuel scolaire au Québec, 1765–1964.* Sherbrooke: Éditions Ex Libris, 2001.

– 'Les manuels scolaires québécois.' http://www.bibl.ulaval.ca/ress/manscol/ (accessed 31 December 2005).

– 'La pénétration des manuels scolaires de France au Québec: Un cas-type: Les Frères des écoles chrétiennes, XIXe–XXe siècles.' *Histoire de l'éducation* 85 (January 2000): 3–24.

– 'School-Book Publishing in Quebec.' In *History of the Book in Canada,* ed. Yvan Lamonde, Patricia Lockhart Fleming, and Fiona A. Black, 2:340–2. Toronto: University of Toronto Press, 2005.

Audet, Louis-Philippe. *Histoire du Conseil de l'instruction publique de la province de Québec, 1856–1964.* Montreal: Éditions Leméac, 1964.

Audley, Paul. *Canada's Cultural Industries: Broadcasting, Publishing, Records and Film.* Toronto: James Lorimer & Company, in association with the Canadian Institute for Economic Policy, 1983.

Bakan, Joel. 'Beyond Censorship: An Essay on Free Speech and Law.' In *Interpreting Censorship in Canada*, ed. Klaus Petersen and Allan C. Hutchinson, 80–100. Toronto: University of Toronto Press, 1999.

Baker, Elizabeth Faulkner. *Printers and Technology: A History of the International Printing Pressmen and Assistants' Union.* New York: Columbia University Press, 1957.

– *Technology and Woman's Work.* New York: Columbia University Press, 1964.

Baker, Janet E. *Archibald MacMechan: Canadian Man of Letters.* Lockeport, NS: Roseway, 2000.

Banks, Joyce M. '"And not hearers only": Books in Native Languages.' In *History of the Book in Canada*, ed. Patricia Lockhart Fleming, Gilles Gallichan, and Yvan Lamonde, 1:278–89. Toronto: University of Toronto Press, 2004.

– comp. *Books in Native Languages in the Rare Book Collections of the National Library of Canada.* Ottawa: National Library of Canada, 1985.

Baptist Hymnary Committee of Canada. *The Hymnary for Use in Baptist Churches.* Toronto: Ryerson Press, 1936.

Barbeau, Victor. *La Société des écrivains canadiens: Ses règlements, son action, biobibliographie de ses membres.* Montreal: Éditions de la Société des écrivains canadiens, 1944.

Barbier, Frédéric. *Histoire du livre.* Paris: A. Colin, 2000.

Barker, A.H. *The Apprentice of Tomorrow.* A talk by A.H. Barker given at the annual meeting of the National Council of Employing Printers and Lithographers, 15 to 18 September 1945, Quebec City. Quebec: s.n., 1945.

Barrett, F.L. 'Textbook Selection in the Other Canadian Provinces.' In *Ontario Royal Commission on Book Publishing: Background Papers*, 331–43. Toronto: Queen's Printer and Publisher, 1972.

Bateson, Nora. *Library Survey of Nova Scotia.* Halifax: Department of Education, 1938.

Beard, John Robert. *Canadian Provincial Libraries.* Ottawa: Canadian Library Association, 1967.

Beaudoin-Dumouchel, Suzanne. *La première école d'arts graphiques en Amérique, fondée par Louis-Philippe Beaudoin (1900–1967).* [Montreal]: s.n., [1979?].

Beaudry, René. 'L'enseignement de l'histoire dans les Maritimes.' In *Compte rendu du septième congrès tenu à Edmundston, N.B., les 6, 7, 8 et 9 août 1955*, by the Association canadienne des éducateurs de langue française, 24–33. Quebec: Éditions de l'ACÉLF, 1956.

Beaulieu, André, Jean Hamelin, et al. *La presse québécoise des origines à nos jours (1764–1975).* 2nd ed. 10 vols and cumulative index to vols 1–7 (1764–1944). Quebec (later Sainte-Foy): Les Presses de l'Université Laval, 1973–90.

Beaulieu, Victor-Lévy. *Les mots des autres: La passion d'éditer.* Montreal: VLB éditeur, 2001.

Bellefeuille, Pierre de, Alain Pontaut, et al. *La bataille du livre au Québec: Oui à la culture française, non au colonialisme culturel.* [Montreal]: Leméac, 1972.

Belzile, Yves. 'La grève des typographes de Montréal (1921–1924).' *Cahiers d'histoire* 11.2 (August 1990): 47–71.

Ben-Gera, Michal. *Ontario Reading Survey: Executive Summary / Enquête sur les habitudes de la lecture en Ontario: Résumé.* Ottawa: ABT Associates, 1978.

Benson, Eugene, and Wiliam Toye, eds. *The Oxford Companion to Canadian Literature.* 2nd ed. Toronto: Oxford University Press, 1997.

Berger, Carl. *The Sense of Power: Studies in the Ideas of Canadian Imperialism, 1867–1914.* Toronto: University of Toronto Press, 1970.

– *The Writing of Canadian History: Aspects of English-Canadian Historical Writing, 1900 to 1970.* Toronto: Oxford University Press, 1976.

Bergeron, Alain. *Les habitudes de lecture des Québécois: Rapport de recherche.* Quebec: Université Laval, Institut supérieur des sciences humaines, 1973.

Bergeron, Liette. 'Catalogue de la Librairie d'Action canadienne-française et des Éditions Albert Lévesque.' In *L'édition littéraire en quête d'autonomie: Albert Lévesque et son temps,* ed. Jacques Michon, 165–203. Sainte-Foy: Les Presses de l'Université Laval, 1994.

Bernier, Gaston, Gilles Gallichan, and Ross Gordon, eds. *Les bibliothèques et les institutions parlementaires du XVIIIe siècle à nos jours: Actes du colloque tenu à l'occasion du deuxième centenaire de la Bibliothèque de l'Assemblée nationale du Québec, 24 septembre 2002.* Quebec: Bibliothèque de l'Assemblée nationale, 2003.

Bernier, Silvie. *Du texte à l'image: Le livre illustré au Québec.* Sainte-Foy: Les Presses de l'Université Laval, 1990.

– 'Prix littéraires et champ du pouvoir: Le prix David, 1923–1970.' Master's thesis, Université de Sherbrooke, 1983.

Berry, I.G. 'Presidential Reminiscences.' *Canadian Mineralogist* 15, part 4 (1977): 433–6.

Berry, J.W., and J.A. LaPonce. *Ethnicity and Culture in Canada: The Research Landscape.* Toronto: University of Toronto Press, 1994.

Berton, Pierre. *Hollywood's Canada: The Americanization of Our National Image.* Toronto: McClelland and Stewart, 1975.

Betcherman, Lita-Rose. *The Swastika and the Maple Leaf: Fascist Movements in Canada in the Thirties.* Toronto: Fitzhenry & Whiteside, 1975.

Biagioli, Monica. 'Humble Servant of the Printed Word: Antje Lingner.' *DA: A Journal of the Printing Arts* 47 (2000): 4–16.

Bibliocentre. 'About Bibliocentre.' http://www.bibliocentre.ca/acccF.html (accessed 21 September 2005).

Bishop, Claude T. 'An Overview of Canadian Scientific Publications.' *Canadian Journal of Information Science* 12.1 (1987): 20–34.

Bishop, Olga B. *Canadian Official Publications.* Toronto/Oxford: Pergamon Press, 1980.

Bizier, Hélène-Andrée. *L'Université de Montréal: La quête du savoir.* Montreal: Libre Expression, 1993.

Blackburn, Robert H. *Evolution of the Heart: A History of the University of Toronto Library up to 1981.* Toronto: University of Toronto Library, 1989.

Blanchard, Jim. 'Manitoba Pool Library 1928 [*sic*] to 1949.' *Manitoba Library Association Bulletin* 12.4 (1982): 7–11.

Board of Trade of the City of Toronto, Book Publishers' Branch. *Brief Submitted to the Royal Commission on National Development in the Arts, Letters and Sciences.* Toronto: s.n., 1950.

Boisclair, Isabelle. 'Édition féministe, édition spécialisée: Ouvrir le champ.' In *Les mutations du livre et de l'édition dans le monde du XVIIIe siècle à l'an 2000: Actes du colloque international, Sherbrooke, 2000,* ed. Jacques Michon and Jean-Yves Mollier, 496–503. [Sainte-Foy]: Presses de l'Université Laval, 2001.

Bonn, George Schlegel. *Science-Technology Literature Resources in Canada: Report of a Survey for the Associate Committee on Scientific Information.* Ottawa: Associate Committee on Scientific Information, National Research Council, 1966.

Book Promotion and Editorial Club. *The Look of Books 1972: The Twenty-eight Books Chosen as the Outstanding Examples of Canadian Book Design and Production.* Toronto: s.n., 1972.

Book Publishers' Association of Canada. *Brief to the Royal Commission on Publications.* Toronto: s.n., 1960.

Boone, Elaine A. '"Holding the Key to the Hall of Democracy": Professional Education for Librarianship in Toronto, 1882–1936.' Ph.D. diss., University of Toronto, 1997.

Bouchard, Gérard. *Quelques arpents d'Amérique: Population, économie, famille au Saguenay, 1838–1971.* [Montreal]: Boréal, 1996.

Bouchard, Guy, et al. *Le phénomène IXE-13.* Quebec: Les Presses de l'Université Laval, 1984.

Boudreau, Diane. *Histoire de la littérature amérindienne au Québec: Oralité et écriture: essai.* Montreal: L'Hexagone, 1993.

Boulizon, Guy. *Livres roses et séries noires: Guide psychologique et bibliographique de la littérature de jeunesse.* Montreal: Éditions Beauchemin, 1957.

Boultbee, Paul G. 'Vain Dream to Mainstream: The Growth of Red Deer College Press.' *PBSC/CSBC* 33.1 (Spring 1995): 51–66.

Bourque, Paul-André. *Les prix bi-nationaux.* Ed. André Corriveau. Les prix littéraires, no. 5. Montreal: Service des transcriptions et dérivés de la radio, Maison de Radio-Canada, 1983.

Bow, Eric C. *Ontario Regional Library System Specialized Union Products: A Study.* Toronto: Network Development Office, Libraries and Community Information Branch, 1982.

Brault, Jean-Rémi. 'Les bibliothèques universitaires du Québec: 25 ans de coopération.' *Documentation et bibliothèques* 39 (July–September 1993): 141–52.

Brault, Pierre. 'La presse francophone dans l'Ouest, son histoire, son influence.' In *Médias francophones hors Québec et identité*, ed. Fernand Harvey, 281–95. Quebec: Institut québécois de recherche sur la culture, 1992.

'Bref pontifical de S.S. Pie X à notre vénérable Frère Louis-Nazaire, archevêque de Québec.' In *L'Action sociale catholique et l'oeuvre de la presse catholique: Motifs, programme, organisation, ressources*, 25–8. Quebec: Imprimerie Édouard Marcotte, 1907.

Bringhurst, Robert, comp. *Ocean Paper Stone: The Catalogue of an Exhibition of Printed Objects Which Chronicle More than a Century of Literary Publishing in British Columbia.* Vancouver: William Hoffer, 1984.

British Columbia. *British Columbia Library Survey, 1927–28.* Victoria: Charles F. Banfield, 1929.

Brooker, Bertram. 'When We Awake! A General Introduction.' In *Yearbook of the Arts in Canada 1928–1929*, ed. Bertram Brooker, 3–17. Toronto: Macmillan Company of Canada, 1929.

Broten, Delores, and Peter Birdsall. *The Canadian Reader I: Peterborough and Area.* Peterborough, ON: CANLIT, 1977.

– *Paper Phoenix: A History of Book Publishing in English Canada.* Victoria: CANLIT, 1980.

Broten, Delores, Peter Birdsall, and Gail Donald. *The Canadian Reader II: High School Canadian Literature Students.* Peterborough, ON: CANLIT, 1978.

Brown, E.K. 'The Contemporary Situation in Canadian Literature.' In *Canadian Literature Today: A Series of Broadcasts Sponsored by the Canadian Broadcasting Corporation*, 9–16. Toronto: University of Toronto Press, 1938.

Brown, Eléanor Frances. *Bookmobiles and Bookmobile Service.* Metuchen, NJ: Scarecrow Press, 1967.

[Brown, Eric]. 'Foreword.' In *A Portfolio of Pictures from the Canadian Section of Fine Arts*, [3–4]. London: British Empire Exhibition, 1924.

Brunet, Lise. 'Les tendances de la recherche sur les habitudes de lecture au Québec.' *Documentation et bibliothèques* 26.3 (September 1980): 161–7.

Bryden, Walter W. 'Foreword.' In *They Went Forth*, by John McNab, vii-viii. Toronto: McClelland and Stewart, 1953.

Buitenhuis, Peter. *The Great War of Words: British, American, and Canadian Propaganda and Fiction, 1914–1933*. Vancouver: University of British Columbia Press, 1987.

Burnet, Jean R., with Howard Palmer. *'Coming Canadians': An Introduction to a History of Canada's Peoples*. Toronto: McClelland and Stewart and the Multiculturalism Directorate, 1988.

Business Newspapers Association of Canada. *Submission to the Royal Commission on Publications*. s.l.: s.n., November 1960.

Bussy, R. Kenneth. *Two Hundred Years of Publishing: A History of the Oldest Publishing Company in the United States, Lea & Febiger, 1785–1985*. Philadelphia: Lea & Febiger, 1985.

Butor, Michel. *Les mots dans la peinture*. Geneva: Éditions d'Art Albert Skira, 1969.

Button, Roger W. 'Wartime Information Board and the Development of Canadian Government Information Policy during World War Two.' Master's research essay, Carleton University, 1972.

Callaghan, Morley. 'The Plight of Canadian Fiction.' *University of Toronto Quarterly* 7.2 (1938): 152–61.

Cambron, Micheline. 'Présence de la littérature nationale dans l'enseignement primaire au Québec.' In *Deux littératures francophones en dialogue: Du Québec et de la Suisse romande*, ed. Martin Doré and Doris Jakubec, 245–58. Quebec: Les Presses de l'Université Laval, 2004.

Cameron, Elspeth. *Earle Birney: A Life*. Toronto: Viking, 1994.

– *Hugh MacLennan: A Writer's Life*. Toronto: University of Toronto Press, 1981.

Campbell, Grant. 'William Collins during World War II: Nationalism Meets a Wartime Economy in Canadian Publishing.' *PBSC/CSBC* 39.1 (Spring 2001): 45–65.

Campbell, Neil. 'Canadian Legal Bibliography.' *Canadian Law Libraries / Bibliothèques de droit canadiennes* 21.1 (Spring 1996): 241–54.

Campbell, Sandra. 'From Romantic History to Communications Theory: Lorne Pierce as Publisher of C.W. Jefferys and Harold Innis.' *Journal of Canadian Studies* 30.3 (Fall 1995): 91–116.

– 'Nationalism, Morality, and Gender: Lorne Pierce and the Canadian Literary Canon, 1920–60.' *PBSC/CSBC* 32.2 (Fall 1994): 135–60.

Canada. *Statutes of Canada*. Ottawa: Queen's/King's Printer, 1847–1940.

Canada. Bureau of Management Consulting. *The Publishing Industry in Canada: A Report*. Ottawa: Arts and Culture Branch, Department of the Secretary of State, 1977.

Canada. Census. *Seventh Census of Canada, 1931*. Ottawa: Dominion Bureau of Statistics, 1932–4.

– *Seventh Census of Canada, 1931. Volume X: Merchandising and Service Establishments. Part I, Retail Merchandise Trade*. Ottawa: Dominion Bureau of Statistics, 1934.

– *Ninth Census of Canada, 1951. Volume VII: Distribution, Retail Trade*. Ottawa: Dominion Bureau of Statistics, 1954.

– *1971 Census of Canada: Retail Trade*. Bulletin nos. 97–701 to 97–707. [Ottawa]: Statistics Canada, 1976–77.

Canada. Department of Labour. *Labour Organization in Canada (for the Calendar Year 1929)*. Ottawa: The Department, 1930.

Canada. Dominion Bureau of Statistics (later Statistics Canada). *The Canada Year Book*. Ottawa: Census and Statistics Office, 1918–85.

– *Printing, Publishing, and Allied Industries*. Annual Census of Manufactures Series. Ottawa: Dominion Bureau of Statistics, Industry Division, 1966–80.

– *Trade of Canada (Imports for Consumption and Exports)*. Catalogue nos. 65–D-22 (1913–25), 65-D-23 (1926–38). Ottawa: The Bureau, 1926–38.

Canada. Dominion Bureau of Statistics (later Statistics Canada). Education Branch. *Library Statistics of Canada, 1920–21.* Ottawa: The Bureau, 1923.

– *Survey of Libraries in Canada, 1936–38.* Ottawa: The Bureau, [1939].

– *Libraries in Canada, 1938–40: Being Part III of the Biennial Survey of Education in Canada.* Ottawa: The Bureau, 1941.

Canada. Dominion Bureau of Statistics (later Statistics Canada). Education Division. *Survey of Libraries, 1946–48 [– 1954–56].* Ottawa: The Bureau, 1950–9.

– *Survey of Libraries. Part I: Public Libraries, 1958.* Ottawa: The Bureau, 1960.

Canada. Dominion Bureau of Statistics (later Statistics Canada). External Trade Division. *Trade of Canada, Vol. 3: Imports.* Catalogue nos. 65-203 (1939–79). [Ottawa]: The Bureau, 1939–79.

Canada. Dominion Bureau of Statistics (later Statistics Canada). Forestry Section. *Report on the Printing Trades in Canada.* Ottawa: Queen's Printer, 1936, 1946.

Canada. Dominion Bureau of Statistics (later Statistics Canada). Merchandising and Services Division. *Campus Book Stores.* [Ottawa]: The Bureau, 1970–81.

Canada. Parliament. *Annual Departmental Reports.* Ottawa: King's/Queen's Printer, [1925–55].

Canada. Parliament. House of Commons. *Debates.* King's/Queen's Printer, 1918–80.

Canada. Parliament. Senate. Special Committee on Mass Media. *The Uncertain Mirror: Report of the Special Senate Committee on Mass Media.* Vol. 1. Ottawa: Queen's Printer, 1970.

– Special Committee on Science Policy. *A Science Policy for Canada: Report of the Senate Special Committee on Science Policy.* 4 vols. Ottawa: Queen's Printer, 1970–2.

Canada. Royal Commission on Bilingualism and Biculturalism. *Report.* 4 vols. Ottawa: Queen's Printer, 1967–70.

Canada. Royal Commission on Industrial Training and Technical Education. *Report.* 4 vols. Ottawa: King's Printer, 1913.

Canada. Royal Commission on National Development in the Arts, Letters and Sciences. *Report.* Ottawa: King's Printer, 1951.

Canada. Royal Commission on Newspapers. *Report.* Ottawa: The Commission, 981.

Canada. Royal Commission on Radio Broadcasting. *Report.* Ottawa: King's Printer, 1929.

Canada. Statistics Canada. Education, Culture, and Tourism Division. *Culture Statistics: Book Publishing Industry, 1983.* Ottawa: Statistics Canada, 1985.

– *Culture Statistics: Newspapers and Periodicals, 1976–77: First Issue.* Ottawa: Statistics Canada, February 1979.

– *Culture Statistics: Public Libraries in Canada, 1979–1981.* Ottawa: Statistics Canada, 1983.

Canada. Statistics Canada. Education, Science and Culture Division. *Culture Statistics: Book Publishing: An Industry Analysis.* Catalogue no. 87-601. Ottawa: Statistics Canada, 1975–9.

– *Culture Statistics, Book Publishing, Textbooks.* Catalogue no. 87–603. 2 vols. Ottawa: Statistics Canada, 1975–6.

– *Literary and Journalistic Awards in Canada, 1923–1973.* Ottawa: Statistics Canada, 1976.

– 'Preliminary Statistics on Writers in Canada.' *Service Bulletin* 3.8 (December 1980).

Canada. Statistics Canada. Merchandising and Services Division. *Retail Chain and Department Stores.* Ottawa: Statistics Canada, 1981.

– *Retail Trade.* Catalogue no. 63–005. 1981.

Canada Council for the Arts. *Trends in Support to Artists by Sex, Language, Citizenship, and Program: Technical Tables.* 2nd ed. [Ottawa]: Research and Evaluation, The Council, 1987.

Canadian Broadcasting Corporation (CBC) Archives. 'Other Libraries.' http://archives.cbc.ca/info/281g_en26.shtml (accessed 12 December 2005).

Canadian Centre for the Visual Arts. *Library and Archives: Collection Development Policy.* Library and
    Archives Occasional Paper, no. 1. [Ottawa]: National Gallery of Canada, 1997.
The Canadian Encyclopedia. Ed. James H. Marsh. 3 vols. Edmonton: Hurtig Publishers, 1985.
The Canadian Encyclopedia. Ed. James H. Marsh. 2nd ed. 4 vols. Edmonton: Hurtig Publishers, 1988.
The Canadian Encyclopedia. Ed. James H. Marsh. Year 2000 ed. Toronto: McClelland and Stewart,
    1999. http://www.thecanadianencyclopedia.com/.
Canadian Facts Ltd. *Report of a Study of the Daily Newspaper in Canada and Its Reading Public: September-
    October, 1962.* Conducted for the Canadian Daily Newspaper Publishers Association, in
    consultation with the Canadian Advertising Research Foundation. Toronto, 1963?
Canadian Federation for the Humanities and Social Sciences. 'About ASPP.' http://www.fedcan.ca/
    english/aspp/about/ (accessed 15 September 2005).
Canadian Library Council. *Libraries in the Life of the Canadian Nation.* Ottawa: s.n., 1946.
Canadian National Institute for the Blind (CNIB). 'Submission to the Ontario Royal Commission
    on Book Publishing (May 1971).' In *Briefs to the Ontario Royal Commission on Book Publishing.*
    [Toronto]: The Commission, 1971–197?
The Canadian Newspaper Directory. 16 vols. Montreal: A. McKim, 1892–1923.
Canuel, Alain. 'Les avatars de la radio publique d'expression française au Canada, 1932–1939.' *RHAF*
    51.3 (Winter 1998): 327–56.
Careless, J.M.S. '"Limited Identities" in Canada.' *Canadian Historical Review* 50 (March 1969): 1–10.
Carnegie Corporation of New York. Commission of Enquiry. *Libraries in Canada: A Study of Library
    Conditions and Needs.* Toronto: Ryerson Press, 1933.
Carr, Ian. *William Boyd: Silver Tongue and Golden Pen.* Canadian Medical Lives, no. 15. Markham, ON:
    Associated Medical Services and Fitzhenry & Whiteside, 1993.
Carson, W.O. 'The Canadian Public Library as a Social Force.' In *The Proceedings of the Ontario Library
    Association: Annual Meeting,* 36–42. Toronto: L.K. Cameron, 1915.
Cau, Ignace. *L'édition au Québec de 1960 à 1977.* Quebec: Ministère des Affaires culturelles, 1981.
Chabot, Juliette. *Montréal et le rayonnement des bibliothèques publiques.* Montreal: Éditions Fides, 1963.
Chandler, Margaret Ross. *A Century of Challenge: The History of the Ontario School for the Blind.* Belleville,
    ON: Mika Publishing Company, 1980.
Charland, Jean-Pierre. *Les pâtes et papiers au Québec 1880–1980: Technologies, travail et travailleurs.*
    Quebec: Institut québécois de recherche sur la culture, 1990.
Chartier, Daniel. *Dictionnaire des écrivains émigrés au Québec, 1800–1999.* Quebec: Éditions Nota bene,
    2003.
Chaytor, H.J. *From Script to Print: An Introduction to Medieval Vernacular Literature.* Cambridge: The
    University Press, 1945.
Cherniak, Donna, and Allan Feingold. 'Birth Control Handbook.' In *Women Unite! An Anthology of the
    Canadian Women's Movement,* 109–13. Toronto: Canadian Women's Educational Press, 1972.
Choko, Marc H., Paul Bourassa, and Gérald Baril. *Le design au Québec.* Montreal: Éditions de
    l'Homme, 2003.
Choko, Marc H., and David L. Jones. *Posters of the Canadian Pacific.* Richmond Hill, ON: Firefly Books,
    2004.
Churchill, David S. 'Mother Goose's Map: Tabloid Geographies and Gay Male Experience in 1950s
    Toronto.' *Journal of Urban History* 30.6 (2004): 826–52.
Church of England in Canada. Council on Girls' Work. *A Fourfold Programme for Canadian Girls: A
    Suggested Programme of Mid-Week Activities for the Use of Older Girls.* Prepared by the Council on

Girls' Work of the General Board of Religious Education, in consultation with representatives of the Dominion Board of the W.A. 3 vols. Toronto: The Church, ca. 1920.

Church of England in Canada. General Synod. *Journal of Proceedings of the Tenth Session: Held in the City of London from September 24th to October 2nd, Inclusive, in the Year of Our Lord 1924: With Appendices.* Kingston, ON: Hanson and Edgar, 1924.

Clark, Penney. 'The Publishing of School Books in English.' In *History of the Book in Canada*, ed. Yvan Lamonde, Patricia Lockhart Fleming, and Fiona A. Black, 2:335–40. Toronto: University of Toronto Press, 2005.

Clark, Warren. 'Cent ans d'éducation scolaire.' *Revue trimestrielle de l'éducation* 7.3 (2001): 20–6.

Clarke, William Henry. 'An Art, a Craft, and a Business.' In *William Henry Clarke, 1902–1955: A Memorial Volume*, 1–32. Toronto: Clarke, Irwin, 1955?

Cloutier, Yvan. 'L'activité éditoriale des dominicains: Les Éditions du Lévrier (1937–1975).' In *L'édition littéraire en quête d'autonomie: Albert Lévesque et son temps*, ed. Jacques Michon, 77–97. Sainte-Foy: Les Presses de l'Université Laval, 1994.

Cockburn, Cynthia. *Brothers: Male Dominance and Technological Change.* London: Pluto Press, 1991.

Coldwell, Joan. 'Walking the Tightrope with Anne Wilkinson.' In *Editing Women: Papers Given at the Thirty-First Annual Conference on Editorial Problems, University of Toronto, 3–4 November 1995*, ed. Ann M. Hutchison, 3–25. Toronto: University of Toronto Press, 1998.

Cole, Catherine C., and Judy Larmour. *Many and Remarkable: The Story of the Alberta Women's Institutes.* Edmonton: Alberta Women's Institutes, 1997.

Commend, Susanne. *Les Instituts Nazareth et Louis-Braille, 1861–2001: Une histoire de coeur et de vision.* Sillery, QC: Septentrion, 2001.

Communications, Energy and Paperworkers Union. 'Local 191 – an ITU Local, 1900 to 1930.' http://www.cep191.ca/history/hist2.html, (accessed 28 November 2005).

Connor, Jennifer J. 'The Legend of Joseph Montferrand and Its Scientific Context in the 1880s.' *Canadian Folklore canadien* 8 (1986): 7–20.

– 'Medicine and Health.' In *History of the Book in Canada*, ed. Yvan Lamonde, Patricia Lockhart Fleming, and Fiona A. Black, 2:419–23. Toronto: University of Toronto Press, 2005.

Corbett, E.A. *Henry Marshall Tory: Beloved Canadian.* Toronto: Ryerson Press, 1954.

Coser, Lewis A., Charles Kadushin, and Walter W. Powell. *Books: The Culture and Commerce of Publishing.* Chicago and London: University of Chicago Press, 1982.

Couvrette, Paul. 'National Film Board Stills Division, Past and Present.' In *Canadian Perspectives: A National Conference on Canadian Photography, March 1–4, 1979*, 254–84. Toronto: Ryerson Polytechnic Institute, 1979.

Crawford, David S. *Bibliography of Canadian Health Sciences Periodicals.* http://www.health.library.mcgill.ca/osler/canjournals/conten ts.htm.

Creal, Michael. *Opportunities Implied in the Introduction of a New Curriculum.* Parish Education Papers, no. 2. Toronto: Department of Religious Education, Anglican Church of Canada, 1963.

Creighton, Donald. *The Empire of the St Lawrence.* Toronto: Macmillan Company of Canada, 1956.

Creighton, Helen. *A Life in Folklore: Helen Creighton.* Toronto: McGraw-Hill Ryerson, 1975.

Crowley, Terry. *Marriage of Minds: Isabel and Oscar Skelton Reinventing Canada.* Toronto: University of Toronto Press, 2003.

Czaykowski, Bogdan. *Polish Writing in Canada: A Preliminary Study.* Ed. Michael S. Batts. [Ottawa]: Department of the Secretary of State of Canada, 1988.

Dalbello-Lovrić, Marija. 'Croatian Diaspora Almanacs: A Historical and Cultural Analysis.' Ph.D. diss., University of Toronto, 1999.

Daniels, Lorne. 'Prairie Publishing: A Community Grows.' *Canadian Forum* 58 (October–November 1978): 31–2.

Dansereau, Bernard. 'Le mouvement ouvrier montréalais, 1918–1929: Structure et conjoncture.' Ph.D. diss., Université de Montréal, 2000.

Darnton, Robert. 'What Is the History of Books?' In *The Kiss of Lamourette: Reflections in Cultural History*, 107–35. New York: W.W. Norton & Company, 1990.

Davies, Cory. 'Bridge between Two Realities: An Interview with Christie Harris.' *Canadian Children's Literature* 51 (1988): 6–24.

Davies, Gwendolyn. 'The Song Fishermen: A Regional Poetry Celebration.' In *Studies in Maritime Literary History 1760–1930*, 163–73. Fredericton: Acadiensis Press, 1991.

Davis, Ann. *Somewhere Waiting: The Life and Art of Christiane Pflug.* Toronto: Oxford University Press, 1991.

Davis, Arthur, ed. *George Grant and the Subversion of Modernity: Art, Philosophy, Politics, Religion, and Education.* Toronto: University of Toronto Press, 1996.

Davis, John N. 'The Digital Storage, Retrieval and Transmission of Case Reports in Canada: A Brief History.' In *Law Reporting and Legal Publishing in Canada: A History*, ed. Martha L. Foote, 139–86. Kingston, ON: Canadian Association of Law Libraries, 1997.

Day, Richard J.F. *Multiculturalism and the History of Canadian Diversity.* Toronto: University of Toronto Press, 2000.

Daymond, D.M. 'Mazo de la Roche.' In *Dictionary of Literary Biography, Vol. 68: Canadian Writers, 1920–1959, First Series*, ed. W.H. New, 106–12. Detroit, MI: Gale Research Company, 1988.

Deacon, William Arthur. *Dear Bill: The Correspondence of William Arthur Deacon.* Ed. John Lennox and Michèle Lacombe. Toronto: University of Toronto Press, 1988.

Dean, W.G. 'Foreword.' In *Historical Atlas of Canada*, cartographer/designer, Geoffrey J. Matthews, ed. R. Cole Harris, 1:I. Toronto: University of Toronto Press, 1987.

Delisle, Jean. *Bridging the Language Solitudes: Growth and Development of the Translation Bureau of the Government of Canada, 1934–84 / Au coeur du trialogue canadien: Croissance et évolution du Bureau des traductions du gouvernement canadien, 1934–1984.* Ottawa: Secretary of State, 1984.

– 'Serving Official Bilingualism for Half a Century.' *Language and Society* 15 (Winter 1985): 4–9.

Delude-Clift, Camille. *Le comportement des Québécois en matière d'activités culturelles de loisir.* Montreal: CROP, 1976.

Demay, Joël. 'The Persistence and Creativity of Canadian Aboriginal Newspapers.' *Canadian Journal of Communication* 18.1 (1993): 89–100.

Denton, Vivienne K. 'Canadian Legal Publishers: A Look at the Development of the Legal Publishing Industry in Canada.' In *Law Reporting and Legal Publishing in Canada: A History*, ed. Martha L. Foote, 16–42. Kingston, ON: Canadian Association of Law Libraries, 1997.

Desbarats, Peter. *Newspapers and Computers: An Industry in Transition.* Canada, Royal Commission on Newspapers, Research Publications, no. 8. Ottawa: Minister of Supply and Services Canada, 1981.

Desbiens, Jean-Paul. *The Impertinences of Brother Anonymous.* Trans. Miriam Chapin. Montreal: Harvest House, 1962.

– *Les insolences du frère Untel.* Preface by Jacques Hébert. Montreal: Éditions de l'Homme, 1988.

Des Rivières, Marie-José. *Châtelaine et la littérature (1960–1975).* Montreal: L'Hexagone, 1992.

Desrochers, Edmond. *Le rôle social des bibliothèques publiques.* Montreal: Éditions Bellarmin / Institut social populaire, 1952.

Desrochers, Luc. 'Les facteurs d'apparition du syndicalisme catholique dans l'imprimerie, 1921–1945.' *RHAF* 37.2 (September 1983): 241–69.

De Surmont, Jean-Nicolas. *La bonne chanson: Le commerce de la tradition en France et au Québec dans la première moitié du XXe siècle.* Montreal: Triptyque, 2001.

Devost, Alain. *L'imprimerie au Québec: Son historique, ses aspects socio-économiques, ses techniques, les risques pour la santé et la sécurité, la prévention de ces risques.* [Quebec]: Gouvernement du Québec, Commission de la santé et de la sécurité du travail, 1982.

Dewalt, Bryan. *Technology and Canadian Printing: A History from Lead Type to Lasers.* Transformation Series, no. 3. Ottawa: National Museum of Science and Technology, 1995.

Dick, Judith. *Not in Our Schools?!!! School Book Censorship in Canada: A Discussion Guide.* Ottawa: Canadian Library Association, 1982.

Diringer, David. *The Alphabet: A Key to the History of Mankind.* London: Hutchinson's Scientific and Technical Publications, [1948].

Djwa, Sandra. *Professing English: A Life of Roy Daniells.* Toronto: University of Toronto Press, 2002.

Dodd, Dianne. 'Advice to Parents: The Blue Books, Helen MacMurchy, MD, and the Federal Department of Health, 1920–34.' *Canadian Bulletin of Medical History / Bulletin canadien d'histoire de la médecine* 8.2 (1991): 203–30.

Donnelly, Brian. 'Mass Modernism: Graphic Design in Central Canada, 1955–1965, and the Changing Definition of Modernism.' Master's thesis, Carleton University, 1997.

Donnelly, F. Dolores. *The National Library of Canada: A Historical Analysis of the Forces Which Contributed to Its Establishment and to the Identification of Its Role and Responsibilities.* Ottawa: Canadian Library Association, 1973.

Donnelly, Judy, and Hans-Jürgen Lüsebrink. 'Almanacs.' In *History of the Book in Canada*, ed. Yvan Lamonde, Patricia Lockhart Fleming, and Fiona A. Black, 2:375–84. Toronto: University of Toronto Press, 2005.

Downs, Robert B. *Resources of Canadian Academic and Research Libraries.* Ottawa: Association of Universities and Colleges of Canada, 1967.

Driver, Elizabeth. 'Cookbooks.' In *History of the Book in Canada*, ed. Yvan Lamonde, Patricia Lockhart Fleming, and Fiona A. Black, 2:408–12. Toronto: University of Toronto Press, 2005.

Dupuis, Onil. 'Dix ans de coopération entre les bibliothèques universitaires du Québec: Un bilan.' *Documentation et bibliothèques* 23 (September 1977): 143–50.

Duval, Paul. 'Word and Picture: The Story of Illustration in Canada.' *Provincial's Paper* 26.2 (1961).

Eayrs, Hugh S. *It Isn't Good Enough: An Address Delivered to the Annual Meeting of the Canadian Authors Association, July 3rd, 1939.* Toronto: Macmillan Company of Canada, 1939.

[Eayrs, Hugh S.]. *A Canadian Publishing House.* Toronto: Macmillan Company of Canada, 1923.

Edison, Margaret E. *Thoreau MacDonald: A Catalogue of Design and Illustration.* Toronto: University of Toronto Press, 1973.

Edwards, Brendan Frederick R. *Paper Talk: A History of Libraries, Print Culture, and Aboriginal Peoples in Canada before 1960.* Lanham, MD: Scarecrow Press, 2005.

– '"To put the talk upon paper": Aboriginal Communities.' *History of the Book in Canada*, ed. Yvan Lamonde, Patricia Lockhart Fleming, and Fiona A. Black, 2:481–8. Toronto: University of Toronto Press, 2005.

Egan, Jim. *Challenging the Conspiracy of Silence: My Life as a Canadian Gay Activist.* Comp. and ed. Donald W. McLeod. Toronto: The Canadian Lesbian and Gay Archives / Homewood Books, 1998.

Egoff, Sheila. *The Republic of Childhood: A Critical Guide to Canadian Children's Literature in English.* Toronto: Oxford University Press, 1967.

– 'The Writing and Publishing of Canadian Children's Books in English.' In *Ontario Royal Commission on Book Publishing: Background Papers*, 245–69. Toronto: Queen's Printer and Publisher, 1972.

Eisenstein, Elizabeth L. *The Printing Press as an Agent of Change: Communications and Cultural Transformations in Early-Modern Europe.* Cambridge: Cambridge University Press, 1979.

Ellenwood, Ray. 'Government Funding: Writers, Translators, and Their Associations.' In *Questions of Funding, Publishing, and Distribution: Proceedings of a Conference, Towards a History of the Literary Institution in Canada 2 / Questions d'édition et de diffusion: Vers une histoire de l'institution littéraire au Canada 2*, ed. I.S. MacLaren and C. Potvin, 77–84. Edmonton: Research Institute for Comparative Literature at the University of Alberta, 1989.

Ember, George. 'Dissemination of Scientific and Technological Information in Canada.' *Journal of Chemical Documentation* 13.1 (1973): 4–7.

Encyclopedia of Canada's Peoples. Ed. Paul Robert Magocsi. Toronto: University of Toronto Press, 1999.

Estey, Ralph H. 'A History of the Quebec Society for the Protection of Plants.' *Phytoprotection* 64 (1983): 1–22.

Etcheverry, Jorge. 'Chilean Literature in Canada between the Coup and the Plebiscite.' *Canadian Ethnic Studies* 21.2 (1989): 53–67.

Eustace, C.J. 'Developments in Canadian Book Production and Design.' In *Ontario Royal Commission on Book Publishing: Background Papers*, 38–60. Toronto: Queen's Printer and Publisher, 1972.

Fabry, Ann de. 'Yves Thériault.' In *Dictionary of Literary Biography, Vol. 88: Canadian Writers, 1920–1959, Second Series*, ed. W.H. New, 311–16. Detroit, MI: Gale Research Company, 1989.

Fagan, Cary. 'New Voices, New Presses.' *Books in Canada* 20.6 (September 1991): 26–8.

Fairbairn, Garry Lawrence. *From Prairie Roots: The Remarkable Story of Saskatchewan Wheat Pool.* Saskatoon: Western Producer Prairie Books, 1984.

Farley, Paul-Émile. *Livres d'enfants.* Montreal: Clercs de Saint-Viateur, 1929.

Fast, Rosabel. 'The Impact of Sponsorship: The University of Manitoba's Rural Adult Education Program, 1936–1945.' Master's thesis, University of Alberta, 1991.

Febvre, Lucien, and Henri-Jean Martin. *L'apparition du livre.* Paris: A. Michel, 1958.

Fee, Margery. 'Lorne Pierce, Ryerson Press, and The Makers of Canadian Literature Series.' *PBSC/CSBC* 24 (1985): 51–71.

Ferguson, Barry, and Doug Owram. 'Social Scientists and Public Policy from the 1920s through World War II.' *Journal of Canadian Studies* 15.4 (1980–1): 3–17.

Ferré, Sandrine. *L'édition au Canada atlantique: Le défi de publier une région.* Collection des Thèses, no. 5. Paris: Centre d'Études Canadiennes de L'Université de Paris III – Sorbonne Nouvelle, 1999.

Filion, Paul-Émile. 'University Libraries before and after Williams.' In *Librarianship in Canada, 1946–1967: Essays in Honour of Elizabeth Homer Morton / Le bibliothécariat au Canada de 1946 à 1967: Hommages à Elizabeth Homer Morton*, ed. Bruce Peel, 73–86. Victoria: Canadian Library Association, 1968.

Fischer, Heinz Dietrich. *Struggle for Press Freedom in Canada: A Case Study from the Province of Alberta and the Key Role Played by the 'Edmonton Journal' in 1938: Based on a Pulitzer Prize Winning Exhibit.* Bochum, Germany: Universitätsverlag Dr. N. Brockmeyer, 1992.

Fleming, Patricia Lockhart. 'Picturing Readers.' In *History of the Book in Canada*, ed. Patricia Lockhart Fleming, Gilles Gallichan, and Yvan Lamonde, 1:194–202. Toronto: University of Toronto Press, 2004.

Fletcher, Frederick J. *The Newspaper and Public Affairs.* Canada, Royal Commission on Newspapers, Research Publications, no. 7. Ottawa: Minister of Supply and Services Canada, 1981.

Foisy-Geoffroy, Dominique. 'Esdras Minville, le catholicisme social et le nationalisme économique, 1923–1939.' *Mens* 1.1 (Fall 2000): 51–68.

Fortin, J.-Alphonse, ed. *Biographies canadiennes-françaises, 1965.* Montreal: J.-A. Fortin, 1965.

Fournier, Alain. *Un best-seller de la Révolution tranquille: 'Les insolences du frère Untel.'* Quebec: CRELIQ, Université Laval / Nuit blanche éditeur, 1988.

Fowke, Edith. 'A Personal Odyssey and Personal Prejudices.' In *Undisciplined Women: Tradition and Culture in Canada*, ed. Pauline Greenhill and Diane Tye, 39–48. Montreal and Kingston: McGill-Queen's University Press, 1997.

Fowke, Edith, and Carole Henderson Carpenter. *A Bibliography of Canadian Folklore in English.* Toronto: University of Toronto Press, 1981.

Fraser, Sylvia, ed. *A Woman's Place: Seventy Years in the Lives of Canadian Women.* Toronto: Key Porter Books, 1997.

Friesen, D.K. 'Executive Message.' In *D.W. Friesen & Sons, Ltd.: 75, 1907–1982*, [ii-vii]. Altona, MB: D.W. Friesen & Sons, 1982.

Friesen Printers. *Make History with Friesen Printers.* Rev. ed. Altona, MB: Friesen Printers, 1978.

Friskney, Janet B. 'The Many Aspects of a General Editorship: Malcolm Ross and the NCL.' *Canadian Poetry* 52 (Spring/Summer 2003): 26–53.

Frye, Northrop. *Divisions on a Ground: Essays on Canadian Culture.* Toronto: House of Anansi Press, 1982.

Fuks, Khayim Leyb, ed. *Hundert yor yidishe un hebreyishe literatur in kanade.* Montreal: KH. L. Fuks Bukh Fund Komitet, 1982.

Fulford, Robert, David Godfrey, and Abraham Rotstein, eds. *Read Canadian: A Book about Canadian Books.* Toronto: James Lewis & Samuel, 1972.

Gagnon, François-Marc. *Paul-Émile Borduas.* Trans. Jill Corner, Susan Le Pan, and Helena Scheffer. Montreal: Montreal Museum of Fine Arts, 1988.

Gagnon, Gilbert. *Habitudes et comportements des lecteurs: Région de la Mauricie.* Quebec: Ministère des Affaires culturelles, 1970.

Gauthier, Yves. *Monsieur livre: Henri Tranquille.* Quebec: Septentrion, 2005.

Gerols, Jacqueline. *Le roman québécois en France.* Ville laSalle, QC: Hurtubise, HMH, 1984.

Gerson, Carole. 'Anthologies and the Canon of Early Canadian Women Writers.' In *Re(dis)covering Our Foremothers: Nineteenth-Century Canadian Women Writers*, ed. Lorraine McMullen, 55–76. Ottawa: University of Ottawa Press, 1990.

–   '"Only a Working Girl": The Story of Marie Joussaye Fotheringham.' *Northern Review* 19 (Winter 1998): 141–60.

Gilroy, Marion. 'Regional Libraries in Retrospect, 1927–1967.' In *Librarianship in Canada, 1946–1967: Essays in Honour of Elizabeth Homer Morton / Le bibliothécariat au Canada de 1946 à 1967: Hommages à Elizabeth Homer Morton*, ed. Bruce Peel, 58–72. Victoria: Canadian Library Association, 1968.

Glazier, Kenneth M. 'Preface.' In *Canadian Authors Manuscripts: A Guide to the Collections*, 1–3. Calgary: University of Calgary Library, Department of Rare Books and Special Collections, 1978.

Goodlett, Carlton B. 'Challenges Still Confront Black Press.' In *Black Press Handbook 1977: Sesquicentennial 1827–1977*, by The National Newspaper Publishers Association, 12–24. Washington, DC: The Association, 1977.

Gordon, W. Terrence. *Marshall McLuhan: Escape into Understanding.* Toronto: Stoddart, 1997.

Grant, George. *Technology and Empire: Perspectives on North America.* Toronto: House of Anansi Press, 1969.

– *Technology and Justice.* Toronto: House of Anansi Press, 1986.

Gray, John Morgan. 'Book Publishing.' In *Writing in Canada: Proceedings of the Canadian Writers' Conference, Queen's University, 28–31 July 1955*, ed. George Whalley, 53–65. Toronto: Macmillan Company of Canada, 1956.

– *Fun Tomorrow: Learning to Be a Publisher and Much Else.* Toronto: Macmillan Company of Canada, 1978.

Greenstein, Michael. 'Robert Choquette.' In *Dictionary of Literary Biography, Vol. 68: Canadian Writers, 1920–1959, First Series*, ed. W.H. New, 70–3. Detroit, MI: Gale Research Company, 1988.

Greenwald, Marilyn S. *The Secret of the Hardy Boys: Leslie McFarlane and the Stratemeyer Syndicate.* Athens, OH: Ohio University Press, 2004.

Grescoe, Paul. *The Merchants of Venus: Inside Harlequin and the Empire of Romance.* Vancouver: Raincoast Books, 1996.

Gridgeman, N.T. 'A Semicentennial: The NRCC Research Journals, 1929–1979 / Un Cinquantenaire: Les journaux de la recherche du CNRC, 1929–1979.' *Canadian Journal of Physics* 57.7 (July 1979): iii–xvi.

Grosbois, Guy de. 'Towards a History of Québec Bookbinding Materials and Research Prospects.' In *Cinquième forum international de la reliure d'art*, 33–9. Montreal: Les Amis de la reliure d'art, ARA Canada, 1996.

Groulx, Lionel. *Correspondance, 1894–1967, Vol. 3: L'intellectuel et l'historien novices, 1909–1915.* Ed. Giselle Huot, Juliette Lalonde-Rémillard, and Pierre Trépanier. [Montreal]: Éditions Fides, 2003.

Hackett, Alice Payne, and James Henry Burke. *80 Years of Best Sellers: 1895–1975.* New York: R.R. Bowker Co., 1977.

Hale, James. *Branching Out: The Story of the Royal Canadian Legion.* Ottawa: Royal Canadian Legion, 1995.

Halpenny, Francess G. '100 Books for 100 Years.' *PBSC/CSBC* 40.2 (Fall 2002): 57–93.

Hamilton, F.W. *Service at Cost: A History of Manitoba Pool Elevators.* s.l.: Manitoba Pool Elevators, 1976?

Hansen, Linda Squiers. '"In the Room Known as the Library": A Brief History of the Library of the University of New Brunswick.' In *Hardiness, Perseverance and Faith: New Brunswick Library History*, ed. Eric L. Swanick, 101–29. Halifax: Dalhousie University, School of Library and Information Studies, 1991.

Hanson, Elizabeth. 'Architecture and Public Librarianship in the Early Twentieth Century: The Westmount Public Library, 1899–1939.' *Libraries & Culture* 23.2 (1988): 172–203.

Harjo, Joy, and Gloria Bird, eds. *Reinventing the Enemy's Language: Contemporary Native Women's Writings of North America.* Ed. Joy Harjo and Gloria Bird with Patricia Blanco, Beth Cuthand, and Valerie Martínez. New York: W.W. Norton & Company, 1997.

Harrington, Lyn. *Syllables of Recorded Time: The Story of the Canadian Authors Association 1921–1981.* Toronto: Simon & Pierre Publishing, 1981.

Harris, Robin S. *A History of Higher Education in Canada, 1663–1960.* Toronto: University of Toronto Press, 1976.

Harrison, Alice W. *Check-List of United Church of Canada Publications, 1925–1986: Sixty-one Years: A Union List of Catalogued Holdings in Nine Libraries.* 2 vols. Halifax: Atlantic School of Theology Library, 1987.

Harrison, Brian R. *Canadian Freelance Writers: Characteristics and Issues.* Ottawa: Government of Canada, Department of Communications, Arts and Culture Sector, Research and Statistics Directorate, 1982.

Hart, E.J. *The Selling of Canada: The CPR and the Beginnings of Canadian Tourism.* Banff, AB: Altitude Publishing, 1983.

Harvey, Jean-Charles. *Pages de critique: Sur quelques aspects de la littérature française au Canada.* Quebec: Compagnie d'imprimerie Le Soleil ltée, 1926.

Hayward, Michael. 'Talonbooks: Publishing from the Margins.' April 1991. http://www.harbour.sfu.ca/~hayward/talon/part6.html (accessed 24 February 2005).

Hébert, Jacques. *Écrire en 13 points Garamond.* Notre-Dame-des-Neiges, QC: Éditions Trois-Pistoles, 2002.

Hébert, Pierre. 'Une censure totale? L'Église québécoise et la nationalisation de l'imaginaire littéraire (1920–1929).' *Études d'histoire religieuse* 67 (2001): 293–300.

Hébert, Pierre, with Patrick Nicol. *Censure et littérature au Québec: Le livre crucifié (1625–1919).* [Saint-Laurent, QC]: Éditions Fides, 1997.

Hébert, Pierre, with Élise Salaün. *Censure et littérature au Québec: Des vieux couvents au plaisir de vivre (1920–1959).* [Montreal]: Éditions Fides, 2004.

Heinich, Nathalie. *Être écrivain: Création et identité.* Paris: Éditions de la Découverte, 2000.

Hemmungs Wirtén, Eva. *Global Infatuation: Explorations in Transnational Publishing and Texts: The Case of Harlequin Enterprises and Sweden.* Publications from the Section for Sociology of Literature at the Department of Literature, Uppsala University, no. 38. Uppsala: Uppsala University, 1998.

Herberg, Edward N. *Ethnic Groups in Canada: Adaptations and Transitions.* Scarborough, ON: Nelson Canada, 1989.

Hesse, Jurgen, ed. *Voices of Change: Immigrant Writers Speak Out.* Vancouver: Pulp Press, 1990.

Hills, Gordon H. *Native Libraries: Cross-cultural Conditions in the Circumpolar Countries.* Lanham, MD: Scarecrow Press, 1997.

Historical Atlas of Canada, Volume III: Addressing the Twentieth Century, 1891–1961. Cartographer/designer, Geoffrey J. Matthews. Ed. Donald Kerr and Deryk W. Holdsworth, with Susan L. Laskin. Toronto: University of Toronto Press, 1990.

Hjartarson, Paul. 'Icelandic Authorship in Canada.' In *History of the Book in Canada*, ed. Yvan Lamonde, Patricia Lockhart Fleming, and Fiona A. Black, 2:136–9. Toronto: University of Toronto Press, 2005.

– 'Print Culture, Ethnicity, and Identity.' In *History of the Book in Canada*, ed. Yvan Lamonde, Patricia Lockhart Fleming, and Fiona A. Black, 2:43–54. Toronto: University of Toronto Press, 2005.

Hodgetts, A.B. *What Culture? What Heritage? A Study of Civic Education in Canada.* Toronto: Ontario Institute for Studies in Education, 1968.

Hodgetts, A.B., and Paul Gallagher. *Teaching Canada for the '80s.* Toronto: Ontario Institute for Studies in Education, 1978.

Hogan, Brian F. 'Salted with Fire: Studies in Catholic Social Thought and Action in Ontario, 1931–1961.' Ph.D. diss., University of Toronto, 1986.

Holgate, Edwin. *Edwin Holgate.* Chief curator of the exhibition, Rosalind Pepall; guest curator, Brian Foss; essays by Laura Brandon et al. Trans. Judith Terry. Montreal: Montreal Museum of Fine Arts, 2005.

Holmlund, Mona, and Gail Youngberg. *Inspiring Women: A Celebration of Herstory.* Regina: Coteau Books, 2003.

Hood, Dora. *The Side Door: Twenty-six Years in My Book Room.* Toronto: Ryerson Press, 1958.

Horne, Alan J., and Guy Upjohn for the Canadian Bookbinders and Book Artists Guild, and the Friends of the Thomas Fisher Rare Book Library. *Fine Printing: The Private Press in Canada.* Toronto: Canadian Bookbinders and Book Artists Guild, 1995.

Hould, Claudette, and Sylvie Laramée. *Répertoire des livres d'artistes au Québec, 1900–1980.* Montreal: Bibliothèque nationale du Québec, 1982.

Housser, F.B. *A Canadian Art Movement: The Story of the Group of Seven.* Toronto: Macmillan Company of Canada, 1926.

Houston, Susan E. '"A Little Steam, a Little Sizzle and a Little Sleaze": English-Language Tabloids in the Interwar Period.' *PBSC/CSBC* 40.1 (Spring 2002): 37–60.

Huggan, Graham. 'Prizing "Otherness": A Short History of the Booker.' *Studies in the Novel* 29.3 (1997): 412–33.

Hume, Margaret Anne. *'Just Mary': The Life of Mary Evelyn Grannan.* Toronto: Dundurn Group, 2006.

Hurtig, Mel. *At Twilight in the Country: Memoirs of a Canadian Nationalist.* Toronto: Stoddart, 1996.

Il fermo proposito. Encyclical of Pius X. 11 June 1905. http://www.vatican.va/holy_father/pius_x/encyclicals/index.htm.

Innis, Harold A. *The Bias of Communication.* Toronto: University of Toronto Press, 1951.

– 'Charles Norris Cochrane, 1889–1945.' *Canadian Journal of Economics and Political Science* 12 (February 1946): 95–6.

– *Empire and Communications.* Oxford: Clarendon Press, 1950.

Irvine, Florence. 'Introduction.' In *Current Problems in Reading Instruction: Proceedings of the First Canadian Conference on Reading, 1955,* iii-iv. Toronto: Federation of Women Teachers' Associations of Ontario, 1956.

Isaacs, I.J., comp. *The City of Halifax: The Capital of Nova Scotia, Canada, Its Advantages and Facilities.* Compiled under approval of the Board of Trade. Halifax: McNab & Son, 1909.

Jaenen, Cornelius J. 'Aboriginal Communities.' In *History of the Book in Canada,* ed. Yvan Lamonde, Patricia Lockhart Fleming, and Fiona A. Black, 2:33–40. Toronto: University of Toronto Press, 2005.

Jamieson, A.F., ed. *A Selective Bibliography of Canadiana of the Prairie Provinces: Publications Relating to Western Canada by English, French, Icelandic, Mennonite, and Ukrainian Authors.* Comp. Edna Greer et al. Winnipeg: Winnipeg Public Library, 1949.

Janisch, Alice. *Profile of Published Legal Research: A Report to the Consultative Group on Research and Education in Law Based on a Survey of Canadian Legal Publications.* Ottawa: Social Sciences and Humanities Research Council of Canada, 1982.

Jeanneret, Marsh. *God and Mammon: Universities as Publishers.* Toronto: Macmillan of Canada, 1989.

Jobin, Pierre-Gabriel. 'L'influence de la doctrine française sur le droit civil québécois: Le rapprochement et l'éloignement de deux continents.' In *Droit québécois et droit français: Communauté, autonomie, concordance,* ed. H. Patrick Glenn, 91–117. Cowansville, QC: Les Éditions Yvon Blais, 1993.

Johnson, D.W. *History of Methodism in Eastern British America*. Sackville, NB: The Tribune Printing Co.,
    n.d.

Johnston, Russell. *Selling Themselves: The Emergence of Canadian Advertising*. Toronto: University of
    Toronto Press, 2001.

Jordan, Robert T. *Tomorrow's Library: Direct Access and Delivery*. New York: Bowker, 1970.

Kapos, Andrew. *Toronto Speaks: A Survey of the Educational Adjustment and Leisure Time Activities of Adult
    Residents in the West and Central Areas of the City of Toronto*. Toronto: Toronto Public Libraries, [1960].

Karr, Clarence. 'Addicted to Reading: L.M. Montgomery and the Value of Reading.' *Canadian
    Children's Literature / Littérature canadienne pour la jeunesse* 113–14 (Spring–Summer 2004): 17–33.

– *Authors and Audiences: Popular Canadian Fiction in the Early Twentieth Century*. Montreal and
    Kingston: McGill-Queen's University Press, 2000.

Karsh, Yousuf. *Yousuf Karsh: Heroes of Light and Shadow*. Ed. Dieter Vorsteher and Janet Yates. Toronto:
    Stoddart, 2001.

Kattan, Naïm. 'In Praise of Imprecision.' Trans. William J. Guthrie. In *Divided We Stand*, ed. Gary
    Geddes, 17–19. Toronto: Peter Martin Associates Ltd, 1977.

Keenleyside, T.A. 'Lament for a Foreign Service: The Decline of Canadian Idealism.' *Journal of
    Canadian Studies* 15.4 (1980–1): 75–84.

Kelley, Ninette, and Michael Trebilcock. *The Making of the Mosaic: A History of Canadian Immigration
    Policy*. Toronto: University of Toronto Press, 1998.

Kennedy, George. 'Memories of a Pensioner.' In *A Century of Progress, 1869–1969: Commemorating the
    100th Anniversary of the Halifax Typographical Union, Local 130 of the International Typographical Union*,
    27–9. Halifax: Kentville Publishing Co., 1969.

Keshen, Jeff. 'The First World War in Print.' In *History of the Book in Canada*, ed. Yvan Lamonde,
    Patricia Lockhart Fleming, and Fiona A. Black, 2:352–4. Toronto: University of Toronto Press,
    2005.

– *Propaganda and Censorship during Canada's Great War*. Edmonton: University of Alberta Press,
    1996.

Kidd, Bruce. 'Sports in Print.' In *History of the Book in Canada*, ed. Yvan Lamonde, Patricia Lockhart
    Fleming, and Fiona A. Black, 2:442–7. Toronto: University of Toronto Press, 2005.

Kines, Gary Bret. 'Chief Man-of-Many-Sides: John Murray Gibbon and His Contribution to the
    Development of Tourism and the Arts in Canada.' Master's thesis, Carleton University, 1988.

King, James. *Farley: The Life of Farley Mowat*. Toronto: HarperFlamingoCanada, 2002.

– *Jack: A Life with Writers: The Story of Jack McClelland*. Toronto: Alfred A. Knopf Canada, 1999.

– *The Life of Margaret Laurence*. Toronto: Vintage Canada, 1997.

Kinsella, Warren. *Web of Hate: Inside Canada's Far Right Network*. Toronto: HarperCollins Publishers,
    1994.

Kirkconnell, Watson. *A Slice of Canada: Memoirs*. Toronto: University of Toronto Press, 1967.

Kirkconnell, Watson, and A.S.P. Woodhouse. *The Humanities in Canada*. Ottawa: Humanities
    Research Council of Canada, 1947.

Kismaric, Carole, and Marvin Heiferman. *The Mysterious Case of Nancy Drew & the Hardy Boys*. New
    York: Simon & Schuster, 1998.

Korda, Michael. *Making the List: A Cultural History of the American Bestseller, 1900–1999*. New York:
    Barnes & Noble Books, 2001.

Korinek, Valerie J. *Roughing It in the Suburbs: Reading Chatelaine Magazine in the Fifties and Sixties*.
    Toronto: University of Toronto Press, 2000.

Kos-Rabcewicz-Zubkowski, Ludwik. *The Poles in Canada*. Canada Ethnica, no. 7. Toronto: Polish Alliance Press, 1968.

Kubas, Leonard, with the Communications Research Center. *Newspapers and Their Readers*. Canada, Royal Commission on Newspapers, Research Publications, no. 1. Ottawa: Minister of Supply and Services Canada, 1981.

Lafrance, Hélène. *Yves Thériault et l'institution littéraire québécoise*. Quebec: Institut québécois de recherche sur la culture, 1984.

Lajeunesse, Marcel. 'Les bibliothèques paroissiales, précurseurs des bibliothèques publiques au Québec?' In *Les bibliothèques québécoises d'hier à aujourd'hui: Actes du colloque de l'ASTED et de l'AQÉI, Trois-Rivières, 27 octobre 1997*, [ed.] Gilles Gallichan, 189–205. Montreal: Association pour l'avancement des sciences et techniques de la documentation (ASTED), 1998.

– 'La lecture publique au Québec au XXe siècle: L'ambivalence des solutions.' In *L'imprimé au Québec, aspects historiques (18e-20e siècle)*, ed. Yvan Lamonde, 189–205. Quebec: Institut québécois de recherche sur la culture, 1983.

– *Les sulpiciens et la vie culturelle à Montréal au XIXe siècle*. Montreal: Éditions Fides, 1982.

Lajeunesse, Marcel, and Daniel Morin. 'Les bibliothèques des collèges d'enseignement général et professionnel du Québec (1969–1983): Services pédagogiques ou comptoirs de prêt?' *Argus* 15.2 (June 1986): 33–47.

Lamb, W. Kaye. 'Canada's National Library.' In *Encyclopedia of Library and Information Science*, ed. Allen Kent and Harold Lancour, with William Z. Nasri, 4:165–9. New York: Marcel Dekker, 1970.

Lamb, W. Kaye, and Jack E. Brown. *Report of the National Librarian for the Fiscal Year Ending March 31, 1968*. Ottawa: Queen's Printer, 1968.

Lamonde, Yvan. *Les bibliothèques de collectivités à Montréal (17e–19e siècle): Sources et problèmes*. Montreal: Bibliothèque nationale du Québec, 1979.

– 'La représentation de l'imprimé dans la peinture et la gravure québécoises (1760–1840).' In *Portrait des arts, des lettres et de l'éloquence au Québec (1760–1840)*, ed. Bernard Andrès and Marc André Bernier, 73–98. Quebec: Les Presses de l'Université Laval, 2002.

– 'The Representation of Reading.' In *History of the Book in Canada*, ed. Yvan Lamonde, Patricia Lockhart Fleming, and Fiona A. Black, 2:465–72. Toronto: University of Toronto Press, 2005.

Lamonde, Yvan, Peter F. McNally, and Andrea Rotundo. 'Public Libraries and the Emergence of a Public Culture.' In *History of the Book in Canada*, ed. Yvan Lamonde, Patricia Lockhart Fleming, and Fiona A. Black, 2:250–71. Toronto: University of Toronto Press, 2005.

Landry, François. *Beauchemin et l'édition au Québec (1840–1940): Une culture modèle*. [Saint-Laurent, QC]: Éditions Fides, 1997.

– 'La Bibliothèque religieuse et nationale, 1882–1912 (Cadieux & Derome).' *Documentation et bibliothèques* 36.3 (July–September 1990): 99–104.

– 'Les Éditions Édouard Garand et les années 20.' In *L'édition du livre populaire: Études sur les éditions Édouard Garand, de l'Étoile, Marquis, Granger frères*, ed. Jacques Michon, 35–76. Sherbrooke: Éditions Ex Libris, 1988.

Lang, Marjory. *Women Who Made the News: Female Journalists in Canada, 1880–1945*. Montreal and Kingston: McGill-Queen's University Press, 1999.

Langford, Martha. 'Introduction.' In *Contemporary Canadian Photography from the Collection of the National Film Board / Photographie canadienne contemporaine de la collection de l'Office national du film*, by The National Film Board of Canada, Still Photography Division / L'Office national du film du Canada, Service de la photographie, 7–16. Edmonton: Hurtig Publishers, 1984.

Lassonde, Jean-René. *La Bibliothèque Saint-Sulpice, 1910–1931.* 3rd ed. Montreal: Bibliothèque nationale du Québec, 2001.

Lavallé, Marcel. *Journal d'un prisonnier.* Montreal: Éditions de l'Aurore, 1978.

Law and Learning: Report to the Social Sciences and Humanities Research Council of Canada by the Consultative Group on Research and Education in Law. Ottawa: Social Sciences and Humanities Research Council of Canada, 1983.

Leach, Jim. *Claude Jutra: Filmmaker.* Montreal and Kingston: McGill-Queen's University Press, 1999.

Lechêne, Robert. *L'imprimerie, de Gutenberg à l'électron.* Paris: Éditions La Farandole, 1972.

Lecker, Robert, with Colin Hill and Peter Lipert, eds. *English-Canadian Literary Anthologies: An Enumerative Bibliography.* Teeswater, ON: Reference Press, 1997.

Leduc, Ozias. *Ozias Leduc: An Art of Love and Reverie.* Ed. Laurier Lacroix. [Quebec and Montreal]: Musée du Québec and Montreal Museum of Fine Arts, 1996.

Lefebvre, Benjamin. 'Stand by Your Man: Adapting L.M. Montgomery's *Anne of Green Gables*.' *Essays on Canadian Writing* 76 (2002): 149–69.

Leibl, Anne. 'Canada's Underground Press.' *Canadian Library Journal* 27.1 (1970): 16–23.

Lemieux, Jacques. 'Gérard Raymond: Un étudiant ardent et généreux.' http://www.diocese-edmundston.ca/les-saints-de-chez-nous/gerard.raymond.htm (accessed 7 October 2004).

Lemieux, Louis-Guy. *Le roman du 'Soleil': Un journal dans son siècle.* Sillery, QC: Septentrion, 1997.

Lepage, Françoise. *Histoire de la littérature pour la jeunesse (Québec et francophonies du Canada), suivie d'un Dictionnaire des auteurs et des illustrateurs.* Orléans: Éditions David, 2000.

– *Paule Daveluy ou la passion des mots.* Montreal: Pierre Tisseyre, 2003.

Lessard, Claude. 'L'alphabétisation à Trois-Rivières, 1634–1939.' *Cahiers nicoletains* 12.3 (1990): 83–117.

Létourneau, Raynald. 'Analyse conjoncturelle des expéditions de l'industrie canadienne du papier journal (1950–1973).' Master's thesis, Université de Montréal, 1977.

Lévesque, Albert. *'Entrez donc': Analyse du comportement familial de la population de langue française au Canada.* Montreal: Informations A. Lévesque Enrg, [1944].

Levine, Norman. 'Thin Ice.' In *Thin Ice*, 114–24. Ottawa: Deneau and Greenberg, 1979.

Library and Archives Canada. Council of Federal Libraries. 'About CFL.' http://www.collections canada.ca/cfl-cbgf/s37-1120-e.html (accessed 24 September 2005).

Library on Wheels. Film. National Film Board of Canada, 1945.

Lipking, Lawrence. 'A Trout in the Milk.' In *The Uses of Literary History*, ed. Marshall Brown, 1–12. Durham, NC: Duke University Press, 1995.

Lippold, Karen, Angela Lonardo, and Suzanne Sexty. 'Canadian Literary Awards, 1900–2000 / Prix de Littérature au Canada, 1900–2000.' Database. Memorial University of Newfoundland, Queen Elizabeth II Library. http://info.library.mun.ca:81/index13.html.

Lismer, Arthur. 'Art Appreciation.' In *Yearbook of the Arts in Canada 1928–1929*, ed. Bertram Brooker, 57–71. Toronto: Macmillan Company of Canada, 1929.

Litt, Paul. *The Muses, the Masses, and the Massey Commission.* Toronto: University of Toronto Press, 1992.

Litvak, Isaiah A., and Christopher J. Maule. *Cultural Sovereignty: The 'Time' and 'Reader's Digest' Case in Canada.* New York: Praeger Publishers, 1974.

– *Development in the Distribution Systems for Canadian Periodical, Book and Newspaper Publishers.* A Report Prepared for the Research and Statistics Directorate, Arts and Culture Branch. Ottawa: Government of Canada, Department of Communications, 1980.

Logan, H.A. *Trade Unions in Canada: Their Development and Functioning*. Toronto: Macmillan Company of Canada, 1948.

Long, Elizabeth. *The American Dream and the Popular Novel*. Boston: Routledge and K. Paul, 1984.

Lord, Barry. *The History of Painting in Canada: Toward a People's Art*. Toronto: NC Press, 1974.

Lorimer, James, and Susan M. Shaw. *Book Reading in Canada: The Audience, the Marketplace, and the Distribution System for Trade Books in English Canada*. Toronto: Association of Canadian Publishers, 1983.

Lorimer, Rowland. 'Book Publishing.' In *The Cultural Industries in Canada: Problems, Policies, and Prospects*, ed. Michael Dorland, 3–34. Toronto: James Lorimer & Company, 1996.

– 'Book Publishing [in BC].' In *Encyclopedia of British Columbia*, ed. Daniel Francis, 84–5. Madeira Park, BC: Harbour Publishing, 2000.

– 'Publishers, Governments, and Learning Materials: The Canadian Context.' *Curriculum Inquiry* 14.3 (1984): 287–99.

Lotz, Patricia A. 'The History of Library Development in the Atlantic Provinces.' In *Canadian Libraries in Their Changing Environment*, ed. Loraine Spencer Garry and Carl Garry, 3–23. Toronto: York University, Centre for Continuing Education, 1977.

Lower, A.R.M. 'The King and the Crown.' In *Manitoba Essays: Written in Commemoration of the Sixtieth Anniversary of the University of Manitoba*, ed. R.C. Lodge, 122–41. Toronto: Macmillan Company of Canada, 1937.

– *My First Seventy-five Years*. Toronto: Macmillan Company of Canada, 1967.

Lupton, Ellen, and J. Abbott Miller. *Design Writing Research: Writing on Graphic Design*. New York: Kiosk, 1996.

Lyman, John. *John Lyman: [Catalogue of an Exhibition Held at] the Montreal Museum of Fine Arts / le Musée des beaux-arts de Montréal, 5 septembre–29 septembre, 1963; the National Gallery of Canada / la Galerie nationale du Canada, 4 October–27 October, 1963; [and] the Art Gallery of Hamilton / la Galerie d'art de Hamilton, 8 November–1 December, 1963*. [Montreal: The Museum, 1963.]

MacDonald, Charles W. *Report on a Survey of Mobile Library Service, October 1964*. Occasional Paper, no. 49. Ottawa: Canadian Library Association, 1965.

MacDonald, J. Ramsay, ed. *Women in the Printing Trades: A Sociological Study*. 1904. New York: Garland, 1980.

Macdonald, Roderick A. 'Understanding Civil Law Scholarship in Quebec.' *Osgoode Law Journal* 23 (1985): 573–608.

MacDonald, Thoreau. *Notebooks*. Moonbeam, ON: Penumbra Press, 1980.

Machalski, Andrew. *Hispanic Writers in Canada: A Preliminary Survey of the Activities of Spanish and Latin-American Writers in Canada*. Ed. Michael S. Batts. [Ottawa]: Department of the Secretary of State of Canada, Multiculturalism, 1988.

MacKendrick, Louis K. 'Al Purdy.' In *ECW's Biographical Guide to Canadian Poets*, 160–3. Toronto: ECW Press, 1993.

Mackey, Laurette. 'Mobile Library Service in Canada: Bookmobiles at the Crossroads.' Paper presented at the 66th IFLA Council and General Conference, 13–18 August 2000, Jerusalem. www.ifla.org/IV/ifla66/papers/161–116e.htm.

MacLennan, Hugh. 'Fiction in Canada 1930–1980.' In *The Arts in Canada: The Last Fifty Years*, ed. W.J. Keith and B.-Z. Shek, 29–42. Toronto: University of Toronto Press, 1980.

MacSkimming, Roy. *The Perilous Trade: Publishing Canada's Writers*. Toronto: McClelland and Stewart, 2003.

MacTavish, Newton. *The Fine Arts in Canada.* Toronto: Macmillan Company of Canada, 1925.

Maillet, Marguerite. *Bibliographie des publications de l'Acadie des provinces maritimes: Livres et brochures, 1609–1995.* Moncton: Éditions d'Acadie, 1997.

Manitoba Women's Institute. *The Great Human Heart: A History of the Manitoba Women's Institute, 1910–1980.* Winnipeg: Manitoba Women's Institute, 1980.

Marcoux, Josée. *Littérature jeunesse au Québec: Médiaspaul (Éditions Paulines 1947–1995).* Montreal: Médiaspaul, 2000.

Marcoux, Marie-Hélène. 'Collections et image de marque aux Éditions de l'Hexagone, 1953–1983.' *Présence francophone* 49 (1996): 155–75.

Marketing 'Profile' Survey. [Toronto]: MacLean-Hunter Research Bureau, 1978.

Marquis, André. 'Conscience politique et ouverture culturelle: Les Éditions d'Orphée.' In *L'édition de poésie: Les éditions Erta, Orphée, Nocturne, Quartz, Atys et l'Hexagone*, ed. Richard Giguère and André Marquis, 87–120. Sherbrooke: Éditions Ex Libris, 1989.

Marquis, Dominique. *Un quotidien pour l'Église: 'L'Action catholique,' 1910–1940.* Montreal: Leméac, 2004.

Marquis, Georges-Émile. *Nos bibliothèques publiques.* Quebec: Imprimerie du Soleil / Éditions du Terroir, 1925.

– *Plaidoyer pour les bibliothèques publiques.* Montreal: École sociale populaire / Oeuvre des tracts, 1946.

Marshall, Denis S. 'The History of Computer-Assisted Legal Research in Canada.' In *Law Libraries in Canada: Essays to Honour Diana M. Priestly*, ed. Joan N. Fraser, 103–15. Toronto: Carswell, 1988.

Martin, Gérard. 'La direction des bibliothèques publiques du Québec.' In *Livre, bibliothèque et culture québécoise: Mélanges offerts à Edmond Desrochers, s.j.*, ed. Georges-A. Chartrand, 651–64. Montreal: ASTED, 1977.

Martin, Michel, and Sandra Grant Marchand. *Alfred Pellan.* With contributions by Marie Carani and Germain Lefebvre. Quebec: Musée du Québec, 1993.

Mason, R.B. 'Report on the Carl Dair Symposium.' *DA: A Journal of the Printing Arts* 36 (1995): 10–12.

Masters, Phillinda. 'A Word from the Press: A Brief Survey of Feminist Publishing.' *Resources for Feminist Research / Documentation sur la recherche féministe* 20.1/2 (1991): 27–35.

Mathers, Donald M. *The Word and the Way: Personal Christian Faith for Today.* Toronto: United Church Publishing House, 1962.

Maynard, Rona. 'Introduction.' In *A Woman's Place: Seventy Years in the Lives of Canadian Women*, ed. Sylvia Fraser, 7–10. Toronto: Key Porter Books, 1997.

McAleer, Joseph. *Passion's Fortune: The Story of Mills & Boon.* Oxford: Oxford University Press, 1999.

McCaig, JoAnn. 'Alice Munro's Agency: The Virginia Barber Correspondence, 1976–83.' *Essays on Canadian Writing* 66 (Winter 1998): 81–102.

McCombs, Charles F. '"Report on Canadian Libraries," [as] Submitted to the Rockefeller Foundation in 1941.' In *American Philanthropy and Canadian Libraries: The Politics of Knowledge and Information*, by William J. Buxton and Charles R. Acland. Montreal: Graduate School of Library and Information Studies and the Centre for Research on Canadian Cultural Industries and Institutions, McGill University, 1998.

McCormack, Myriam. 'Preserving and Providing Access to Canada's Printed Heritage: The Canadian Institute for Historical Microreproductions at 25 Years.' *PBSC/CSBC* 41.1 (Spring 2003): 7–41.

McFarlane, Leslie. *Ghost of the Hardy Boys: An Autobiography.* Toronto: Methuen / Two Continents, 1976.

McGill, David. 'The Marketing of Trade Books in Canada.' In *Ontario Royal Commission on Book Publishing: Background Papers*, 173–94. Toronto: Queen's Printer and Publisher, 1972.

McGrath, Leslie Anne. 'Service to Children in the Toronto Public Library: A Case Study, 1912–1949.' Ph.D. diss., University of Toronto, 2005.

McGrath, Robin. *Canadian Inuit Literature: The Development of a Tradition.* National Museum of Man Mercury Series. Canadian Ethnology Service Paper, no. 94. Ottawa: National Museums of Canada / Musées nationaux du Canada, 1984.

McKillop, A.B. *Matters of Mind: The University in Ontario, 1791–1951.* Ontario Historical Studies Series. Toronto: University of Toronto Press, 1994.

McKim's Directory of Canadian Publications. 19 vols. 17th ed.–35th ed. Montreal: A. McKim, 1924–42.

McKnight, David. 'An Annotated Bibliography of English Canadian Little Magazines, 1940–1980.' Master's thesis, Concordia University, 1992.

McLaren, Angus, and Arlene Tigar McLaren. *The Bedroom and the State: The Changing Practices and Politics of Contraception and Abortion in Canada, 1880–1980.* Toronto: McClelland and Stewart, 1986.

McLeod, Don, ed. 'Carl Dair Special Issue.' *DA: A Journal of the Printing Arts* 48 (Spring/Summer 2001).

McLuhan, Marshall. Review of *The Printing Press as an Agent of Change*, by Elizabeth Eisenstein. *Renaissance and Reformation* 5.2 (1981): 98–104.

McMullin, Stanley E. 'Walt Whitman's Influence in Canada.' *Dalhousie Review* 49 (1969): 361–8.

McNally, Peter F. 'Fanfares and Celebrations: Anniversaries in Canadian Graduate Education for Library and Information Studies.' In *Readings in Canadian Library History* 2, ed. Peter F. McNally, 39–56. Ottawa: Canadian Library Association, 1996.

– 'Fifty Years of Special Libraries in Montreal and Eastern Canada, 1932–1982.' *Bulletin – Special Libraries Association, Eastern Canada Chapter* 47.4 (March 1982): 26–9.

– 'McGill University Libraries.' In *International Dictionary of Library Histories*, ed. David H. Stam, 1:437. Chicago: Fitzroy Dearborn Publishers, 2001.

McNaught, Kenneth. *Conscience and History: A Memoir.* Toronto: University of Toronto Press, 1999.

Melançon, Joseph. 'L'enseignement littéraire et ses effets de marché.' In *Le poids des politiques: Livres, lecture et littérature*, ed. Maurice Lemire with Pierrette Dionne and Michel Lord, 105–25. Quebec: Institut québécois de recherche sur la culture, 1987.

Melanson, Holly, comp. *Literary Presses in Canada, 1975–1985: A Checklist and Bibliography.* Halifax: Dalhousie University, School of Library and Information Studies, 1988.

Ménard, Marc. *Les chiffres des mots: Portrait économique du livre au Québec.* Montreal: Société de développement des entreprises culturelles (SODEC), 2001.

Mennonite Historical Society of Canada. 'Canadian Mennonite Encyclopedia Online.' http://www.mhsc.ca (accessed 12 October 2003).

Mennonite Literary Society. *Rhubarb* home page. www.mennolit.com (accessed 23 October 2003).

Metcalf, John. *An Aesthetic Underground: A Literary Memoir.* Toronto: Thomas Allen Publishers, 2003.

Mezei, Kathy, with Patricia Matson and Maureen Hole. *Bibliography of Criticism on English and French Literary Translations in Canada, 1950–1986: Annotated / Bibliographie de la critique des traductions littéraires anglaises et françaises au Canada, de 1950 à 1986, avec commentaires.* Cahiers de traductologie, no. 7. Ottawa: University of Ottawa Press and Canadian Federation for the Humanities, 1988.

Michon, Jacques. 'L'almanach comme vecteur des stratégies éditoriales au Québec au temps de la naissance d'une littérature nationale (1880–1939).' In *Les lectures du peuple en Europe et dans les*

Amériques (XVIIe-XXe siècle), ed. Hans-Jürgen Lüsebrink et al., 233–40. Bruxelles: Éditions Complexe, 2003.

– 'L'édition du roman québécois, 1961–1974: Les Éditions du Jour et Le Cercle du livre de France.' In *Le roman québécois depuis 1960: Méthodes et analyses*, ed. Louise Milot and Jaap Lintvelt, 299–316. Sainte-Foy: Les Presses de l'Université Laval, 1992.

– 'L'édition littéraire saisie par le marché.' *Communication* 12.1 (1991): 29–47.

– *Fides: La grande aventure éditoriale du père Paul-Aimé Martin.* [Saint-Laurent, QC]: Éditions Fides, 1998.

– 'Jacques Hébert, Foremost Publisher of the Quiet Revolution.' In *Literary Cultures and the Material Book*, ed. Simon Eliot, 297–306. London: British Library, 2007.

– 'Mme B.D. Simpson, éditrice (1945–1948).' In *Éditeurs transatlantiques*, ed. Jacques Michon, 161–83. Sherbrooke: Éditions Ex Libris; Montreal: Éditions Triptyque, 1991.

– ed. *Histoire de l'édition littéraire au Québec au XXe siècle.* 2 vols. Saint-Laurent, QC (later Montreal): Éditions Fides, 1999–2004.

Michon, Jacques, and Josée Vincent. 'La librairie française à Montréal au tournant du siècle.' In *Le commerce de la librairie en France au XIXe siècle, 1789–1914*, ed. Jean-Yves Mollier, 359–72. Paris: IMEC éditions / Éditions de la Maison des sciences de l'homme, 1997.

Miller, J.O., ed. *The New Era in Canada: Essays Dealing with the Upbuilding of the Canadian Commonwealth.* London: Dent, 1917.

Mirucki, Jean. *Le marché du livre au Canada: Les lecteurs, les composantes du marché et les réseaux de distribution du livre francophone au Canada.* 2 vols. [Montreal]: Université du Québec à Montréal, Département des sciences economiques, 1986.

Miska, John. *Ethnic and Native Canadian Literature: A Bibliography.* Toronto: University of Toronto Press, 1990.

Mitham, Peter J. 'History of the Book in Yukon: A Discussion Paper.' *Northern Review* 21 (Summer 2000): 57–71.

Moir, John S. 'Canadian Religious Historiography – an Overview.' In *Christianity in Canada: Historical Essays by John S. Moir*, ed. Paul Laverdure, 136–50. Yorkton, SK: Redeemer's Voice Press and Laverdure & Associates, 2002.

Monière, Denis. 'André Laurendeau et la vision québécoise du Canada.' In *André Laurendeau: Un intellectuel d'ici*, ed. Robert Comeau and Lucille Beaudry, 191–200. Sillery, QC: Presses de l'Université du Québec, 1990.

Montgomery, L.M. *The Selected Journals of L.M. Montgomery.* Ed. Mary Rubio and Elizabeth Waterston. 5 vols. Toronto: Oxford University Press, 1985–2004.

Moore, F. Beverley. 'College Bookstores.' In *Ontario Royal Commission on Book Publishing: Background Papers*, 211–22. Toronto: Queen's Printer and Publisher, 1972.

Morley, William F.E. 'Preface.' In *Bernard Amtmann, 1907–1979: A Personal Memoir*, by John Mappin and John Archer, [5]. [Toronto]: Amtmann Circle, 1987.

Morris, Peter. *Embattled Shadows: A History of Canadian Cinema, 1895–1939.* Montreal: McGill-Queen's University Press, 1978.

Morrison, James H. '"Black Flies, Hard Work, Low Pay": A Century of Frontier College.' *The Beaver* 79.5 (October/November 1999): 33–8.

Mortimer, Hilda, with Chief Dan George. *You Call Me Chief: Impressions of the Life of Chief Dan George.* Toronto: Doubleday Canada, 1981.

Morton, W.L. 'The 1920s.' In *The Canadians, 1867–1967*, ed. J.M.S. Careless and R. Craig Brown, 205–35. Toronto: Macmillan Company of Canada, 1967.

Munro, Alice. 'Foreword.' In *The Anthology Anthology: A Selection from 30 Years of CBC Radio's 'Anthology,'* ed. Robert Weaver, ix–x. Toronto: Macmillan of Canada / CBC Enterprises, 1984.

Murray, Heather. 'Literary Societies.' In *History of the Book in Canada*, ed. Yvan Lamonde, Patricia Lockhart Fleming, and Fiona A. Black, 2:473–8. Toronto: University of Toronto Press, 2005.

Nason, C.M. *Report on Institutional Library Service.* Ottawa: Correctional Service of Canada, 1981.

National Indian Brotherhood. *Indian Control of Indian Education: Policy Paper Presented to the Minister of Indian Affairs and Northern Development.* Ottawa: National Indian Brotherhood, 1972.

National Library of Canada. *Report of the National Librarian, 1953.* Ottawa: Queen's Printer, 1953.

– *Summary of the Federal Government Library Survey Report.* Ottawa: National Library of Canada, 1974.

'National Science Library Experiences Phenomenal Growth.' *Science Dimension* 1.4 (October 1969): 24–30.

New, W.H. *Dreams of Speech and Violence: The Art of the Short Story in Canada and New Zealand.* Toronto: University of Toronto Press, 1987.

New Brunswick Federation of Home and School Associations. *Primer for Parents.* Fredericton?: New Brunswick Federation of Home and School Associations, 1956?

Newfeld, Frank. 'Book Design and Production.' In *Publishing in Canada: Proceedings of the Institute on Publishing in Canada, June 27–30, 1971,* ed. G. Pomahac and M. Richeson, 26–35. Edmonton: University of Alberta, School of Library Science, 1972.

Nilson, Lenore, comp. *The Best of Children's Choices.* Ed. Jane Charlton. Ottawa: Citizens' Committee on Children, 1988.

Normand, Sylvio. 'Une analyse quantitative de la doctrine en droit civil québécois.' *Les Cahiers de droit* 23 (1982): 1009–28.

– 'Les bibliothèques d'entreprises au Québec.' In *Les bibliothèques québécoises d'hier à aujourd'hui: Actes du colloque de l'ASTED et de l'AQÉI, Trois-Rivières, 27 octobre 1997,* 101–19. Montreal: Éditions ASTED, 1998.

– 'Un thème dominant de la pensée juridique traditionnelle au Québec: La sauvegarde de l'intégrité du droit civil.' *McGill Law Journal / Revue de droit de McGill* 32 (1986–7): 559–601.

North York Public Library. *Public Library Service to the Shut-in in Institutions and Community: A Survey.* North York, ON: North York Public Library, 1968.

Notices en langue française du 'Canadian Catalogue of Books,' 1921–1949. Index by Henri-Bernard Boivin. Montreal: Bibliothèque nationale du Québec, 1975.

Novosedlik, Will. 'Our Modernist Heritage.' *Applied Arts Magazine* 11.1/2 (March/April–May/June 1996): 30–5, 81–8.

O'Bryan, K.G., J.G. Reitz, and O.M. Kuplowska. *Non-official Languages: A Study in Canadian Multiculturalism.* Ottawa: Supply and Services Canada, 1976.

Oliver, Dean F., and Laura Brandon. *Canvas of War: Painting the Canadian Experience, 1914 to 1945.* Vancouver: Douglas & McIntyre, 2000.

Ontario. Royal Commission on Book Publishing. *Canadian Publishers and Canadian Publishing.* Toronto: Queen's Printer for Ontario, 1973.

– 'Final Report on the Distribution of Paperbacks and Periodicals in Ontario, March 27, 1972.' In *Canadian Publishers and Canadian Publishing,* 302–26. Toronto: Queen's Printer for Ontario, 1973.

– 'Second Interim Report, June 8, 1971.' In *Canadian Publishers and Canadian Publishing,* 290–4. Toronto: Queen's Printer for Ontario, 1973.

Ontario Library Association. Reconstruction Committee. *Library Needs of the Province of Ontario: A Brief Submitted to the Minister of Education, Province of Ontario, March 30, 1944.* Toronto?: s.n., 1944?

Opre, Kal. 'West Looks East and South.' In *Publishing in Canada II: 'East Looks West,'* ed. John R.T. Ettlinger, 25–36. Halifax: Dalhousie University, School of Library Service, 1973.

Ostiguy, Jean-René. *Adrien Hébert: Premier interprète de la modernité québécoise.* Saint-Laurent, QC: Éditions du Trécarré, 1986.

– *Adrien Hébert: Thirty Years of His Art / Trente ans de son oeuvre, 1923–1953.* Ottawa: National Gallery of Canada, 1971.

– *Modernism in Quebec Art, 1916–1946.* Ottawa: National Gallery of Canada, 1982.

Ostry, Bernard. *The Cultural Connection: An Essay on Culture and Government Policy in Canada.* Toronto: McClelland and Stewart, 1978.

Overend, Howard. *Book Guy: A Librarian in the Peace.* Victoria: TouchWood Editions, 2001.

Owram, Doug. *The Government Generation: Canadian Intellectuals and the State, 1900–1945.* Toronto: University of Toronto Press, 1986.

Page, James E. *Reflections on the Symons Report: The State of Canadian Studies in 1980.* A report prepared for the Department of the Secretary of State of Canada. Ottawa: Minister of Supply and Services Canada, 1981.

Panofsky, Ruth. 'At Odds: Reviewers and Readers of the *Jalna* Novels.' *Studies in Canadian Literature / Études en littérature canadienne* 25.1 (2000): 57–72.

Pantazzi, Sybille. 'Book Illustration and Design by Canadian Artists, 1890–1940, with a List of Books Illustrated by Members of the Group of Seven.' *National Gallery of Canada Bulletin* 4.1 (1966): 6–24.

Parker, George L. *The Beginnings of the Book Trade in Canada.* Toronto: University of Toronto Press, 1985.

– 'Growing Pains in World War II: The Struggle to Build a Real Publishing Trade in Canada, with a Little Help from the British.' *English Studies in Canada* 25.3/4 (September/December 1999): 369–406.

– 'A History of a Canadian Publishing House: A Study of the Relation between Publishing and the Profession of Writing 1890–1940.' Ph.D. diss., University of Toronto, 1969.

Parkin, George R. *Imperial Federation: The Problem of National Unity.* London: Macmillan, 1892.

Parvin, Viola E. *Authorization of Textbooks for the Schools of Ontario, 1846–1950.* Toronto: University of Toronto Press, 1965.

Pearce, Catherine Anne. 'The Development of Special Libraries in Montreal and Toronto.' Master's thesis, University of Illinois, 1947.

Peel, Bruce. *History of the University of Alberta Library, 1909–1979.* Edmonton: s.n., 1979.

Peel, Bruce, and William J. Kurmey. *Cooperation among Ontario University Libraries.* Toronto: Council of Ontario Universities / Conseil des universités de l'Ontario, 1983.

Penman, Margaret. *A Century of Service: Toronto Public Library, 1883–1983.* Toronto: Toronto Public Library, 1983.

Periodical Distributors Association of Canada. *Brief to the Royal Commission on Publications.* Toronto: s.n., 1960.

Petrone, Penny. *Native Literature in Canada: From the Oral Tradition to the Present.* Toronto: Oxford University Press, 1990.

Pickersgill, J.W. *The Mackenzie King Record.* Vol. 1. Chicago and Toronto: University of Chicago Press and University of Toronto Press, 1960.

Piédalue, Gilles. 'Les groupes financiers et la guerre du papier au Canada 1920–1930.' *RHAF* 30.2 (September 1976): 223–53.

Pierce, Lorne. *The Chronicle of a Century: 1829–1929: The Record of One Hundred Years of Progress in the Publishing Concerns of the Methodist, Presbyterian and Congregational Churches in Canada.* Toronto: United Church Publishing House, Ryerson Press, [1929].

– *An Editor's Creed.* Toronto: Ryerson Press, 1960.

Piternick, Anne B., et al., eds. *National Conference on the State of Canadian Bibliography, Vancouver, Canada, May 22–24, 1974: Proceedings.* Ottawa: National Library of Canada, 1977.

Potvin, Gilles. 'CBC Recordings.' In *Encyclopedia of Music in Canada*, 2nd ed., ed. Helmut Kallmann, Gilles Potvin et al., 231–2. Toronto: University of Toronto Press, 1992.

Poulin, Manon. 'Eugène Achard éditeur: L'émergence d'une édition pour la jeunesse.' Ph.D. diss., Université de Sherbrooke, 1994.

Powell, Barbara. 'Saskatchewan Community Histories.' Abstract for the Prairie Print Culture Colloquium, Regina, March 2001. http://www.hbic.library.utoronto.ca/abstractspr_en.htm (accessed 17 September 2005).

Presbyterian Church in Canada. Board of Sabbath Schools and Young People's Societies. *The Forward Movement and Christian Education: A Survey of the Work of Christian Education and Its Requirements for the Next Five Years.* [Toronto]: Committee of the Forward Movement of the Presbyterian Church in Canada, [1918].

Price, Leah. 'Reading: The State of the Discipline.' *Book History* 7 (2004): 303–20.

Provost, Sylvie, and Rosaire Garon. 'Auteur: Pleinement ou à demi?' Special issue of *Chiffres à l'appui: Bulletin de service de la planification, des politiques et de la recherche*, no. 3. Quebec: Ministère des Affaires culturelles du Québec, May 1986.

Purcell, Gillis. 'Wartime Press Censorship in Canada.' Master's thesis, University of Toronto, 1946.

Quebec. Bureau of Statistics. *Statistical Year Book.* Quebec: L.A. Proulx, King's Printer, 1925.

Québec. Comité de travail sur la concentration de la presse écrite. *De la précarité de la presse ou le citoyen menacé: Rapport du Comité de travail sur la concentration de la presse écrite.* Quebec: Service des communications, 1977.

Québec. Commission d'enquête sur le commerce du livre dans la province de Québec. *Rapport.* Montreal: s.n., 1963.

Québec. Commission d'étude sur les bibliothèques publiques du Québec. *Les bibliothèques publiques, une responsabilité à partager: Rapport de la Commission d'étude sur les bibliothèques publiques du Québec.* [Quebec]: La Commission, 1987.

Québec. Législature. Assemblée législative. *Débats de l'Assemblée législative.* Quebec: Assemblée législative, 1927.

Quebec. Royal Commission of Inquiry on Constitutional Problems. *Report.* 4 vols. Quebec: s.n., 1956.

Quebec. Royal Commission of Inquiry on Education in the Province of Quebec. *Report.* 5 vols. Quebec: Pierre Des Marais, 1963–6.

Raboy, Marc. *Movements and Messages: Media and Radical Politics in Quebec.* Trans. David Homel. Toronto: Between the Lines, 1984.

Raddall, Thomas H. *In My Time: A Memoir.* Toronto: McClelland and Stewart, 1976.

Ravitch, Melech. 'Yiddish Culture in Canada.' In *Canadian Jewish Reference Book and Directory*, ed. Eli Gottesman, 75–80. Montreal: Mortimer, 1963.

Raymond, Gérard. *Journal de Gérard Raymond.* Quebec: s.n., 1937.

Read, Horace E. 'The Judicial Process in Canada.' *Canadian Bar Review* 37.2 (May 1959): 265–93.

Reader, Lover of Books, Lover of Heaven: A Catalogue Based on an Exhibition of the Book Arts in Ontario.

Compiled by David B. Kotin with a checklist of Ontario private presses by Marilyn Rueter and an introduction by Douglas Lochhead. Canadiana Collection Publication, no. 1. Willowdale, ON: North York Public Library, 1978.

Rehberg Sedo, DeNel. 'Badges of Wisdom, Spaces for Being: A Study of Contemporary Women's Book Clubs.' Ph.D. diss., Simon Fraser University, 2004.

Répertoire bio-bibliographique de la Société des écrivains canadiens, 1954. Montreal: Société des écrivains canadiens, 1955.

Rhodes, J. 'New Life for a Tired System – the Prison Library.' *Canadian Library Journal* 30.3 (May–June 1973): 246–9.

Ricard, François. *Gabrielle Roy: A Life.* Trans. Patricia Claxton. Toronto: McClelland and Stewart, 1999.

Richards, Trevor B. 'Books for the Troops: The Role of Volunteer Organizations in the Provision of Library Services for the Canadian Military during the World Wars.' *Épilogue* 13/14 (1992): 1–17.

Richler, Mordecai. 'Making a Movie.' In *Home Sweet Home: My Canadian Album*, 118–41. New York: Alfred A. Knopf, 1984.

Ripley, Gordon, and Anne V. Mercer. *Who's Who in Canadian Literature, 1983–1984.* Toronto: Reference Press, 1983.

Robert, Lucie. 'Les écrivains et leurs études: Comment on fabrique les génies.' *Études littéraires* 14.3 (December 1981): 527–39.

– *L'institution du littéraire au Québec.* Quebec: Les Presses de l'Université Laval, 1989.

Roberts, Goodridge. *Goodridge Roberts: A Retrospective Exhibition / Une exposition rétrospective.* Introduction and catalogue by James Borcoman. Ottawa: Published by the National Gallery of Canada for the Queen's Printer, 1969.

Robertson, Carolynn. *The Canadian Bibliographic Centre: Preparing the Way for the National Library of Canada.* Ottawa: National Library of Canada, 1999.

Robidoux, Réjean. 'Fortune et infortunes de l'abbé Casgrain.' In *Fonder une littérature nationale: Notes d'histoire littéraire*, 147–80. Ottawa: Éditions David, 1994.

Robillard, Sylvain. 'From Books to Bytes: Pioneers of the Scientific Information Highway.' *CISTI News* 16.5 (June 1999): 1–8.

Robins, Marion. 'Service de la traduction.' In *Rapport annuel du Secrétariat de la province, 1964–1965*, 54–5. Quebec: Queen's Printer, 1965.

Robson, Albert H. *Canadian Landscape Painters.* Toronto: Ryerson Press, 1932.

Rome, David, comp. *The First Jewish Literary School.* Canadian Jewish Archives, new series, no. 41. Montreal: National Archives, Canadian Jewish Congress, 1988.

Rosenberg, Louis. *Canada's Jews: A Social and Economic Study of Jews in Canada in the 1930s.* 1939. Reprint edited by Morton Weinfeld. Montreal and Kingston: McGill-Queen's University Press, 1993.

Rosenberg, Neil V. 'The Gerald S. Doyle Songsters and the Politics of Newfoundland Folksong.' *Canadian Folklore canadien* 13.1 (1991): 45–57.

Ross, Catherine Sheldrick. *Alice Munro: A Double Life.* Toronto: ECW Press, 1992.

Rouillard, Jacques. *Histoire du syndicalisme au Québec: Des origines à nos jours.* Montreal: Boréal, 1989.

– *Les syndicats nationaux au Québec de 1900 à 1930.* Quebec: Presses de l'Université Laval, 1979.

Roussan, Jacques de. *Le nu dans l'art au Québec.* La Prairie, QC: Éditions Marcel Broquet, 1982.

Royal Society of Canada. The Committee on Publication Policies and Practices for Research Journals and Other Periodicals in Science and Engineering in Canada. *The Press of Knowledge: A Report.* s.l.: The Royal Society of Canada, June 1978.

Rudin, Ronald. *Making History in Twentieth-Century Quebec*. Toronto: University of Toronto Press, 1997.

Rueter, Marilyn. 'The Private Press in Canada: A Brief Survey.' In *Sticks and Stones: Some Aspects of Canadian Printing History*, ed. and comp. John Gibson and Laurie Lewis, 93–114. Toronto: Toronto Typographic Association, 1980.

Rueter, William. 'Introduction.' In *The Aliquando Press: Three Decades of Private Printing: An Exhibition of Letterpress Books, Broadsides, and Ephemera from Will Rueter's Private Press*, [3–4]. Toronto: The Aliquando Press, 1993.

Russell, Norman. 'McMaster's Mills Memorial Library, 1950–1963–1970.' *Canadian Library Journal* 27 (1970): 196–8.

Rutherford, F.S. 'What Technical Schools Have Done to Meet the Recommendations of the Royal Commission on Technical Education.' In *Three of the Papers Read at the Third Annual Convention of the Technical Section of the Ontario Education Association, 1928*. Vocational Education Series. Bulletin no. 29. Ottawa: Technical Education Branch, Department of Labour, 1929.

Rutherford, Paul. *The Making of the Canadian Media*. Toronto: McGraw-Hill Ryerson, 1978.

Ryder, Bruce. 'Undercover Censorship: Exploring the History of the Regulation of Publications in Canada.' In *Interpreting Censorship in Canada*, ed. Klaus Petersen and Allan C. Hutchinson, 129–56. Toronto: University of Toronto Press, 1999.

Saint-Germain, Richard, Julia Bettinotti, and Paul Bleton. *Littérature en poche: Collection 'Petit format,' 1944–1958: Répertoire bibliographique*. Sherbrooke: Éditions Ex Libris, 1992.

Saint-Jacques, Denis, and Marie-José des Rivières. 'Le magazine en France, aux États-Unis et au Québec.' In *Production(s) du populaire: Colloque international de Limoges (2002)*, ed. Jacques Migozzi and Philippe Le Gern, 29–37. Limoges: Presses de l'Université de Limoges, 2005.

Saint-Jacques, Denis, et al. *Ces livres que vous avez aimés: Les best-sellers au Québec de 1970 à aujourd'hui*. 2nd ed. Quebec: Nuit blanche éditeur, 1997.

Sanders, Pat. 'Mary Scorer: An Appreciation.' *Border Crossings* 7.2 (Spring 1988): 44–5.

Sarick, Hy, and Judy Sarick. 'The Children's Book Store in Toronto.' *The Horn Book Magazine* 53.2 (1977): 202–5.

Saskatchewan Indian Cultural Centre. 'About the Centre.' http://www.sicc.sk.ca/aboutus.html (accessed 21 February 2006).

Scherf, Kathleen. 'A Legacy of Canadian Cultural Tradition and the Small Press: The Case of Talonbooks.' *Studies in Canadian Literature* 25.1 (2000): 131–49.

Science Council of Canada. *A Policy for Scientific and Technical Information Dissemination*. Report no. 6. Ottawa: Queen's Printer, 1969.

Scott, Charles Hepburn. *Charles Hepburn Scott: Vancouver Art Gallery, June 14 to August 7, 1989*. Text about the artist written by Ian M. Thom. Vancouver: Vancouver Art Gallery, 1989.

Scott, F.R. 'Introduction.' In *Writing in Canada: Proceedings of the Canadian Writers' Conference, Queen's University, 28–31 July 1955*, ed. George Whalley, 1–10. Toronto: Macmillan Company of Canada, 1956.

Seguin, Fernand. 'Avertissement.' In *Fernand Seguin rencontre Han Suyin*, 13–14. Montreal: Éditions de l'Homme / Éditions Ici Radio-Canada, 1969.

Sève, Andrée-Anne de. *Hommage à Jean-Marie Gauvreau: Étude ethno-historique*. Montreal: Conseil des métiers d'arts du Québec, 1995.

Shemilt, L.W., and T.H.G. Michael. 'Privatization of a Journal: A History of the *Canadian Journal of Chemical Engineering*.' In *Chemical Engineering in Canada: An Historical Perspective*, ed. L.W. Shemilt, 77–98. Ottawa: Canadian Society for Chemical Engineering, 1991.

Siegler, Karl H. *Avoiding the False Dialectic, Culture versus Commerce: A Report on Manitoba Publishers of Culturally Significant Books and Periodicals and Recommendations for Government Action.* Prepared for Manitoba Culture, Heritage and Recreation. Winnipeg: The Department, 1984.

Siemens, R.G. 'Awards and Literary Prizes.' In *Encyclopedia of Literature in Canada*, ed. W.H. New, 55–86. Toronto: University of Toronto Press, 2002.

Simon, Beatrice V. *Library Support of Medical Education and Research in Canada: A Report of a Survey of Medical College Libraries of Canada, together with Suggestions for Improving and Extending Medical Library Service at Local, Regional, and National Levels.* Montreal: s.n., 1964.

Smith, Goldwin. *Canada and the Canadian Question.* London: Macmillan, 1891.

Smith, Lillian H. *The Unreluctant Years: A Critical Approach to Children's Literature.* Chicago: American Library Association, 1953.

Smith, Patricia L., and Garth Graham. 'Library Service North of the Sixtieth Parallel: The Yukon and Northwest Territories.' In *Canadian Libraries in Their Changing Environment*, ed. Loraine S. Garry and Carl Garry, 118–43. Downsview, ON: York University, 1977.

Smythe, Dallas W. *Dependency Road: Communications, Capitalism, Consciousness, and Canada.* Norwood, NJ: Ablex Publishing Corporation, 1981.

Snape, Robert. *Leisure and the Rise of the Public Library.* London: Library Association Publishing, 1995.

Snow, Kathleen M. *Maxwell Bates: Biography of an Artist.* Calgary: University of Calgary Press, [1993].

Solecki, Sam, ed. *Imagining Canadian Literature: The Selected Letters of Jack McClelland.* Toronto: Key Porter Books, 1998.

Sorin, Noëlle. 'Historique des prix littéraires du Québec attribués à la littérature de jeunesse.' *Canadian Children's Literature / Littérature canadienne pour la jeunesse* 100/101 (2000–1): 69–93.

Soules, Gordon. *What People Want in a Library: The Kind of Information Every Library Needs to Provide the Best Possible Service to Its Community.* Vancouver: G. Soules Economic and Marketing Research, 1975.

Spadoni, Carl, and Judy Donnelly. *A Bibliography of McClelland and Stewart Imprints, 1909–1985: A Publisher's Legacy.* Toronto: ECW Press, 1994.

Speller, Randall. 'Arthur Steven at the Ryerson Press: Designing the Post-War Years (1949–1969).' *PBSC/CSBC* 41.2 (Fall 2003): 7–44.

– 'Frank Newfeld and the Visual Awakening of the Canadian Book.' *DA: A Journal of the Printing Arts* 45 (Fall/Winter 1999): 3–31.

Stacey, Robert, with Hunter Bishop. *J.E.H. MacDonald, Designer: An Anthology of Graphic Design, Illustration and Lettering.* Ottawa: Archives of Canadian Art, 1996.

Staines, David. 'Reviewing Practices in English Canada.' In *Problems of Literary Reception / Problèmes de réception littéraire*, ed. E.D. Blodgett and A.G. Purdy, 61–8. Edmonton: Research Institute for Comparative Literature, 1988.

Stanton, Ralph. *Vancouver Public Library: Users Survey at the Central Library, July 1972.* Vancouver: Vancouver Public Library Board, 1972.

St-Arnaud, Yves. 'L'enseignement de l'histoire dans l'Ouest, A: Rapport sur l'enseignement de l'histoire au cours primaire.' In Association canadienne des éducateurs de langue française, *Compte rendu du septième congrès tenu à Edmundston, N.B., les 6, 7, 8 et 9 août 1955*, 79–95. Quebec: Éditions de l'ACÉLF, 1956.

'The State of English Language Publishing in Canada.' Special issue of *Journal of Canadian Studies / Revue d'études canadiennes* 10.2 (May 1975).

Stevenson, Iain. 'Books for Improvement: The Canadian Pacific Foundation Library.' *PBSC/CSBC* 43.1 (Spring 2005): 33–44.

Stewart, Sandy. *From Coast to Coast: A Personal History of Radio in Canada.* Montreal, Toronto, New York, London: CBC Enterprises / Les Entreprises Radio-Canada, 1985.

Stouck, David. *As for Sinclair Ross.* Toronto: University of Toronto Press, 2005.

– *Ethel Wilson: A Critical Biography.* Toronto: University of Toronto Press, 2003.

Strange, Carolyn, and Tina Loo. *True Crime, True North: The Golden Age of Canadian Pulp Magazines.* Vancouver: Raincoast Books, 2004.

Stratford, Philip. 'A Bridge between Two Solitudes.' *Language and Society* 11 (1983): 8–13.

– ed. *Bibliography of Canadian Books in Translation: French to English and English to French / Bibliographie de livres canadiens traduits de l'anglais au français et du français à l'anglais.* 2nd ed. Ottawa: Humanities Research Council of Canada / Conseil canadien de recherches sur les humanités, 1977.

Stuart-Stubbs, Basil. 'Guy Sylvestre and the Development of the National Library of Canada.' In *The National Library of Canada and Canadian Libraries: Essays in Honour of Guy Sylvestre / La Bibliothèque nationale du Canada et les bibliothèques canadiennes: Essais en l'honneur de Guy Sylvestre*, ed. Jean-Rémi Brault, Gwynneth Evans, and Richard Paré, 21–32. Ottawa and Montreal: Canadian Library Association and Association pour l'avancement des sciences et des techniques de la documentation, 1996.

Stubbs, Kendon, and David Buxton, comp. *Cumulated ARL University Library Statistics, 1962–63 through 1978–79.* Washington, DC: Association of Research Libraries, 1981.

Stuewe, Paul. 'The Mark of the Exile: A Profile of Josef Škvorecký.' *Books in Canada* 10.8 (October 1981): 4–5.

Sullivan, Rosemary. 'An Interview with Margaret Laurence.' In *A Place to Stand On: Essays by and about Margaret Laurence*, ed. George Woodcock, 61–79. Edmonton: NeWest Press, 1983.

Sutherland, Fraser. *The Monthly Epic: A History of Canadian Magazines 1789–1989.* Markham, ON: Fitzhenry & Whiteside, 1989.

Sutherland, Neil. '"The Triumph of Formalism": Elementary Schooling in Vancouver from the 1920s to the 1960s.' In *Children, Teachers and Schools in the History of British Columbia*, 2nd ed., ed. Jean Barman and Mona Gleason, 319–42. Calgary: Detselig, 2003.

Sylvestre, Guy, Brandon Conron, and Carl F. Klink. *Écrivains canadiens: Un dictionnaire biographique / Canadian Writers: A Biographical Dictionary.* Montreal: Éditions HMH, 1964.

Symons, T.H.B. *To Know Ourselves: The Report of the Commission on Canadian Studies.* Vols 1 and 2. Ottawa: Association of Universities and Colleges of Canada, 1975.

Symons, T.H.B., and James E. Page. *Some Questions of Balance: Human Resources, Higher Education and Canadian Studies.* Vol. 3 of *To Know Ourselves: The Report of the Commission on Canadian Studies.* Ottawa: Association of Universities and Colleges of Canada, 1984.

Talbot, Joan, and Mel Liversage. *Lake Erie Regional Library System (Counties of Elgin, Middlesex, Norfolk, and Oxford) Regional Cultural Survey.* s.l.: s.n., 1972.

Tanghe, Raymond. *Pour un système cohérent de bibliothèques au Canada français.* Montreal: Éditions Fides, 1952.

Templeton, Charles. *Charles Templeton: An Anecdotal Memoir.* Toronto: McClelland and Stewart, 1983.

Templeton, Wayne. *Architects of Culture: A Preliminary Analysis of the History and Structure of Publishing in English Canada.* Burnaby, BC: s.n., 1977.

Thiessen, Janis. 'Friesens Corporation: Printers in Mennonite Manitoba, 1951–1995.' Master's thesis, University of Manitoba, 1997.

Thomas, Ann. 'Canadian Nationalism and Canadian Imagery.' In *Canadian Perspectives: A National Conference on Canadian Photography, March 1–4, 1979*, 68–77. Toronto: Ryerson Polytechnical Institute, 1979.

Thomas, Audrey M. *Adult Illiteracy in Canada: A Challenge.* Occasional Paper, no. 42. Ottawa: Canadian Commission for UNESCO, 1983.

Thomas, Clara, and John Lennox. *William Arthur Deacon: A Canadian Literary Life.* Toronto: University of Toronto Press, 1982.

Thomas, Edward Harper. *Chinook: A History and Dictionary of the Northwest Coast Trade Jargon.* Portland, OR: Binfords & Mort, 1935.

Tippett, Maria. *Making Culture: English-Canadian Institutions and the Arts before the Massey Commission.* Toronto: University of Toronto Press, 1990.

Tisseyre, Pierre. *Lorsque notre littérature était jeune.* Propos recueillis et présentés par Jean-Pierre Guay. Montreal: Le Cercle du livre de France / Pierre Tisseyre, 1983.

Todorov, Tzvetan. 'The Origin of Genres.' In *Modern Genre Theory*, ed. David Duff, 193–209. [London]: Longman; New York: Pearson Education, 2000.

Toronto Public Library. *Reading in Toronto: Annual Report of the Toronto Public Library, 1944.* Toronto: Ryerson Press, 1944.

Tory, Henry Marshall. 'Foreword.' *Canadian Journal of Research* 1.1 (1929): 3.

Totton, S.J. 'The Marketing of Educational Books in Canada.' In *Ontario Royal Commission on Book Publishing: Background Papers*, 270–310. Toronto: Queen's Printer and Publisher, 1972.

Tovell, Rosemarie L., et al. *The Prints of Betty Goodwin.* With the assistance of Scott McMorran and Anne-Marie Ninacs; technical essay by Anne F. Maheux. Ottawa: National Gallery of Canada in association with Douglas & McIntyre, 2002.

Toye, William. 'Book Design in Canada.' *Canadian Literature* 15 (Winter 1963): 52–63.

Tratt, Grace, comp. *Check List of Canadian Small Presses: English Language.* Occasional Paper, no. 7. Halifax: Dalhousie University, University Libraries and School of Library Service, 1974.

Tremaine, Marie. *A Bibliography of Canadian Imprints, 1751–1800.* Toronto: University of Toronto Press, 1952.

Tremblay, Michel. *Birth of a Bookworm.* Trans. Sheila Fischman. Vancouver: Talonbooks, 2003.

Tripp, Pat. 'On the Tracks of Municipal Government Publications in Canada.' *Canadian Library Journal* 28.6 (1971): 464–7.

Troper, Harold. 'Multiculturalism.' In *The Oxford Companion to Canadian History*, ed. Gerald Hallowell, 417. Toronto: Oxford University Press, 2004.

Trudel, Marcel. *Memoirs of a Less Travelled Road: A Historian's Life.* Trans. Jane Brierley. Montreal: Véhicule, 2002.

Trudel, Marcel, and Geneviève Jain. *Canadian History Textbooks: A Comparative Study.* Studies of the Royal Commission on Bilingualism and Biculturalism, no. 5. Ottawa: Queen's Printer, 1970.

United Church of Canada. Board of Christian Education and the Board of Publication. *Prospectus: A Look at the New Curriculum, Including the Presuppositions on Which It Is Based, the Principle by Which It Is Organized, and Some of Its Distinctive Features.* Toronto: United Church of Canada, 1961.

United Nations. *Yearbook of International Trade Statistics.* New York: United Nations, 1976–86.

Urban Dimensions Group. *Project Progress: A Study of Canadian Public Libraries.* Ottawa: Canadian Library Association, 1981.

Vaisman, Iosif. 'Yiddish Publishing in Eastern Europe.' *Mendele: Yiddish Literature and Language*, vol. 10.045. http://shakti.   trincoll.edu/~mendele/vol10/vol10045.txt (accessed 30 January 2001).

Van Kleeck, Mary. *Women in the Bookbinding Trade.* New York: Survey Associates, 1913.

Vaugeois, Denis. *L'amour du livre: L'édition au Québec, ses petits secrets et ses mystères.* Sillery, QC: Septentrion, 2005.

Verduyn, Christl, and Kathleen Garay, eds. *Marian Engel: Life in Letters.* Toronto: University of Toronto Press, 2004.

Verzuh, Ron. *Underground Times: Canada's Flower-Child Revolutionaries.* Toronto: Deneau Publishers, 1989.

Vessillier-Ressi, Michèle. *Le métier d'auteur: Comment vivent-ils?* Paris: Dunod, 1982.

Vincent, Josée. 'Le Conseil supérieur du livre, du rapport Bouchard à la loi 51: Pour une politique du livre au Québec.' *Présence francophone* 45 (1994): 173–91.

– 'Les professionnels du livre à la conquête de leur marché: Les associations professionnelles dans le champ littéraire au Québec (1921–1960).' Ph.D. diss., Université de Sherbrooke, 2002.

– *Les tribulations du livre québécois en France (1959–1985).* [Quebec]: Nuit blanche éditeur, 1997.

Vipond, Mary. 'Best Sellers in English Canada, 1899–1918: An Overview.' *Journal of Canadian Fiction* 24 (1978): 96–119.

– 'Best Sellers in English Canada: 1919–1928.' *Journal of Canadian Fiction* 35/36 (1986): 73–105.

– *The Mass Media in Canada.* 2nd ed. Toronto: J. Lorimer, 1992.

Voisey, Paul. 'Rural Local History and the Prairie West.' In *The Prairie West: Historical Readings*, ed. R. Douglas Francis and Howard Palmer, 497–509. Edmonton: Pica Pica Press, 1992.

Wachtel, Eleanor. *Feminist Print Media.* Contracted research paper submitted to the Women's Program, Secretary of State, 20 May 1982.

– *Update on Feminist Periodicals.* Contracted research paper submitted to the Women's Program, Secretary of State, 31 July 1985.

[Waddington, Murray]. *Canadian Souvenir View Albums.* Library and Archives Exhibition, no. 9. Ottawa: National Gallery of Canada Library and Archives, 2001.

Wadland, John. 'Voices in Search of a Conversation: An Unfinished Project.' *Journal of Canadian Studies* 35.1 (Spring 2000): 52–75.

Wallace, W. Stewart. *The Ryerson Imprint: A Check-List of the Books and Pamphlets Published by the Ryerson Press since the Foundation of the House in 1829.* Toronto: Ryerson Press, 1954.

Watson, Alfred L. *Exploratory Study of Library Services for the Disadvantaged in Greater Victoria.* Victoria: [Greater Victoria Public Library], 1974.

Watson, John. *Christianity and Idealism: The Christian Ideal of Life in Its Relations to the Greek and Jewish Ideals and to Modern Philosophy.* London: Macmillan, 1897.

– *The State in Peace and War.* Glasgow: James Maclehose and Sons, 1919.

Watson, Kenneth F., and ABT Associates. *Leisure Reading Habits: A Survey of the Leisure Reading Habits of Canadian Adults with Some International Comparisons.* Ottawa: Infoscan, 1980.

Watters, Reginald Eyre. *A Check List of Canadian Literature and Background Materials, 1628–1950.* Toronto: University of Toronto Press, 1959.

– *A Checklist of Canadian Literature and Background Materials, 1628–1960.* 2nd ed., rev. and enl. Toronto: University of Toronto Press, 1972.

Webb, Phyllis. 'The Poet and the Publisher.' *Queen's Quarterly* 61 (Winter 1954–5): 498–512.

Weintraub, William. *Getting Started: A Memoir of the 1950s.* Toronto: McClelland and Stewart, 2001.

Wheatcroft, Les. *Something for Nothing: An Experimental Book Exposure Programme.* Peterborough, ON: CANLIT, 1975.

Whitaker, Reg. 'Chameleon on a Changing Background: The Politics of Censorship in Canada.' In *Interpreting Censorship in Canada*, ed. Klaus Petersen and Allan C. Hutchinson, 19–39. Toronto: University of Toronto Press, 1999.

Whiteman, Bruce. *Lasting Impressions: A Short History of English Publishing in Quebec.* Montreal: Véhicule Press, 1994.

Whiteman, Bruce, Charlotte Stewart, and Catherine Funnell. *A Bibliography of Macmillan of Canada Imprints 1906–1980.* London, ON: Dundurn Press, 1985.

Whitteker, June. 'Trade Bookstores in Canada.' In *Ontario Royal Commission on Book Publishing: Background Papers*, 195–210. Toronto: Queen's Printer and Publisher, 1972.

Williams, Edwin E. *Resources of Canadian University Libraries for Research in the Humanities and Social Sciences: Report of a Survey for the National Conference of Canadian Universities and Colleges.* Ottawa: National Conference of Canadian Universities and Colleges, 1962.

Williams, Edwin E., and Paul-Émile Filion. *Les objectifs à poursuivre: 1966–1971: Supplément à l'enquête (1962) sur la Bibliothèque de l'Université Laval.* Quebec: s.n., 1965.

– *Vers une bibliothèque digne de Laval: Rapport d'une enquête sur la Bibliothèque de l'Université Laval.* s.l.: s.n., 1962.

Williams, Raymond. 'A Structure of Insights.' *University of Toronto Quarterly* (April 1964). Rpt. in *McLuhan: Hot and Cool*, ed. Gerald Emanuel Stearn, 186–9. New York: Dial Press, 1967.

Williamson, Douglas. 'Book Design: More than Meets the Eye.' *Logos* 5.1 (1994): 42–8.

Winks, Robin W. *The Blacks in Canada: A History.* 2nd ed. Montreal and Kingston: McGill-Queen's University Press, 1997.

Wolfe, J.N. 'The Market for Books in Canada.' *Canadian Journal of Economics and Political Science* 24.4 (1958): 541–53.

Woodland, Alan, and Ellen Heaney, eds. *British Columbia Libraries: Historical Profiles.* Vancouver: British Columbia Library Association, 1986.

Writers Club Toronto. *Canadian Writer's Market Survey.* Ottawa: Graphic Publishers, 1931.

Writers' Union of Canada. *The Writers' Union of Canada: A Directory of Members.* Ed. Ted Whittaker. Toronto: The Union, 1981.

Wurtele, Susan E. 'Nation-Building from the Ground Up: Assimilation through Domestic and Community Transformation in Inter-war Saskatchewan.' Ph.D. diss., Queen's University, 1993.

Young, David. 'The Macmillan Company of Canada in the 1930s.' *Journal of Canadian Studies* 30.3 (Fall 1995): 117–33.

Young, Judy. 'Canadian Literature in the Non-official Languages: A Review of Recent Publications and Work in Progress.' *Canadian Ethnic Studies* 14.1 (1982): 138–49.

– 'The Unheard Voices: Ideological or Literary Identification of Canada's Ethnic Writers.' In *Identifications: Ethnicity and the Writer in Canada*, ed. Jars Balan, 104–15. Edmonton: Canadian Institute of Ukrainian Studies, University of Alberta, 1982.

Young, Scott. *A Writer's Life.* Toronto: Doubleday Canada, 1994.

Young Canada Listens: School Broadcasts, 1942–1943. Toronto: Canadian Broadcasting Corporation, 1943.

Young-Ing, Greg. 'Aboriginal Peoples' Estrangement: Marginalization in the Publishing Industry.' In *Looking at the Words of Our People: First Nations Analysis of Literature*, ed. Jeannette Armstrong, 177–88. Penticton, BC: Theytus Books, 1993.

Zemans, Joyce. 'Envisioning Nation: Nationhood, Identity and the Sampson-Matthews Silkscreen Project: The Wartime Prints.' *Journal of Canadian Art History / Annales d'histoire de l'art canadien* 19.1 (1998): 6–51.

– 'Establishing the Canon: Nationhood, Identity and the National Gallery's First Reproduction Program of Canadian Art.' *Journal of Canadian Art History / Annales d'histoire de l'art canadien* 16.2 (1995): 6–35.

– 'Sampson-Matthews and the NGC: The Post-War Years.' *Journal of Canadian Art History / Annales d'histoire de l'art canadien* 21.1/2 (2000): 96–139.

Zerker, Sally F. *The Rise and Fall of the Toronto Typographical Union 1832–1972: A Case Study of Foreign Domination.* Toronto: University of Toronto Press, 1982.

CONTRIBUTORS

Sandra Alston, Canadiana specialist at the University of Toronto Library, has published the Second Supplement to the Toronto Public Library's *A Bibliography of Canadiana* (1985–9), and with Patricia Lockhart Fleming, *Toronto in Print* (1998) and *Early Canadian Printing: A Supplement to Marie Tremaine's 'A Bibliography of Canadian Imprints, 1751–1800'* (1999).

Katherine Arnup is a historian and associate professor in the School of Canadian Studies at Carleton University. Author of a book on the history of motherhood in Canada and numerous articles on the Canadian family, she is director of Carleton's Institute of Interdisciplinary Studies.

Paul Aubin, an independent researcher affiliated with the Centre interuniversitaire d'études québécoises at Université Laval and Université du Québec à Trois-Rivières, has concentrated his research on the history of textbooks in Quebec and Canada for more than ten years.

Linda Bedwell is a reference and instruction librarian at Dalhousie University's Killam Library. She recently received her MLIS from Dalhousie's School of Information Management, where she worked as a graduate research assistant on Volume 2 of HBiC/HLIC.

Jo Nordley Beglo is bibliographer at the library of the National Gallery of Canada and the Canadian contributor to the *Bibliography of the History of Art*. Her current research focuses on the history of art librarianship in Canada.

Fiona A. Black is director of the School of Information Management at Dalhousie University and an editor of Volume 2 of HBiC/HLIC. Her research areas are Scottish contributions to Canadian print culture and applications of geographic information systems for print culture research.

Elaine Boone is an independent scholar living in Belleville, Ontario. Professional education, women in higher education, library history, tourism, and biblical studies are among her research interests.

Frédéric Brisson, a doctoral candidate at Université de Sherbrooke, holds a fellowship from the Social Sciences and Humanities Research Council of Canada. A graduate research assistant with Volume 3 of HBiC/HLIC, he studies bookstores and book distribution.

Ian Brockie taught courses in English literature and education for Memorial University of Newfoundland for nine years and currently teaches communication for professionals at the College of the North Atlantic–Qatar in Doha. He is interested in the informal and alternative discourses by which students come to acquire literary understanding.

Sarah Brouillette, assistant professor in the literature program at MIT, works on the colonial and postcolonial history of the book, and contemporary literature. She is currently completing a monograph about postcolonial authors and the literary marketplace.

Lorne Bruce currently serves as head, Archival and Special Collections, University of Guelph Library. He has published widely on a variety of library and book history topics ranging from ancient Rome to the public library system in Ontario.

Peter Buitenhuis was professor emeritus in the Department of English at Simon Fraser University at the time of his death in December 2004. He published extensively on Canadian literature and on wartime propaganda.

Eric Bungay is Web development librarian at the University of Guelph. His main areas of interest are Web-site design, information architecture, and usability.

Christina Burr, associate professor of history at the University of Windsor, is completing a monograph on Petrolia, Ontario, and beginning a project on the cultural meaning of women's exercising bodies.

Pearce Carefoote, the medieval manuscript and early books librarian at the Thomas Fisher Rare Book Library, University of Toronto, holds a doctorate in sacred theology from the Katholieke Universiteit Leuven, Belgium. He is interested in theological history and the history of censorship.

Richard Cavell is professor of English and founding director of the International Canadian Studies Centre at the University of British Columbia. His research explores spatial mediation within a broad cultural studies context.

Penney Clark, assistant professor in the Department of Curriculum Studies at the University of British Columbia, works on curriculum in historical and political contexts and on students' historical consciousness.

Stuart Clarkson recently graduated from Dalhousie University's School of Information Management with an MLIS degree, and is doing research on William Letson, a Nova Scotia bookseller, printer, and publisher.

Yvan Cloutier retired as professor of philosophy at Collège de Sherbrooke and is associate professor in the Faculté des lettres et sciences humaines and the Faculté de théologie, d'éthique et de philosophie at Université de Sherbrooke. He researches Quebec intellectual history, the publishing activity of religious congregations, and the Quebec reception of Maritain, Mounier, and Sartre.

Jean Cogswell holds an honours BA from Concordia University and an MLIS from McGill University. A member of the Women's Institute for over thirty years, she is also active in the Bibliographical Society of Canada and the Quebec Library Association.

Jennifer J. Connor is associate professor in the Departments of Community Health and History at Memorial University of Newfoundland. Her research on medical literature in Canada has appeared in many North American journals.

Frank Davey retired in 2005 from the Carl F. Klinck Chair in Canadian Literature at the University of Western Ontario. He is editor of the journal *Open Letter* and author of more than thirty books of poetry and literary and cultural criticism.

Gwendolyn Davies is dean of graduate studies and associate vice-president for research at the University of New Brunswick. Professor in the Department of English, she has published extensively on Atlantic literature from 1749 to 1930.

Jean Delisle is director of the School of Translation and Interpretation at the University of Ottawa. A specialist in the history and teaching of translation, he is the author of a dozen works on translation and translators.

Marie-José des Rivières is research adviser in the Faculté des sciences de l'éducation at Université Laval, associate professor in the Département des littératures, and member of the Centre de recherche interuniversitaire sur la littérature et la culture québécoises (CRILCQ). With Denis Saint-Jacques, she is preparing a history of magazines in Quebec.

Peter Dickinson, assistant professor in the Department of English at Simon Fraser University, is the author of *Here Is Queer: Nationalisms, Sexualities, and the Literatures of Canada* (1999), and numerous articles on comparative Canadian literature, modern drama, film studies, and gender studies.

Martin Dowding is assistant professor in the Department of Communication Studies at Wilfrid Laurier University. His main research interests are the history of information transfer, and communication and information policy in Latin America.

Klay Dyer is an independent scholar with a long-standing interest in readers and reading in early and modern Canada. Currently editing a critical edition of Duncan Campbell Scott's *In the Village of Viger*, he is also working on a study of the aesthetics and ideologies surrounding itinerant booksellers in Canadian history.

Nancy Earle is completing her doctorate in the English Department at Simon Fraser University with a dissertation on writer-in-residence programs in Canada. She worked extensively with Volume 3 of HBiC/HLIC as a senior graduate researcher and text editor.

Brendan Frederick R. Edwards holds an MA from Trent University and an MLIS degree from McGill University. Currently a doctoral candidate in history at the University of Saskatchewan, he has published *Paper Talk: A History of Libraries, Print Culture, and Aboriginal Peoples in Canada before 1960* (2005).

Gail Edwards teaches Canadian, British Columbian, and Aboriginal history at Douglas College, and the history of children's illustrated books at the University of British Columbia. Her current research examines intersections between Aboriginal history, missionary history, and the history of print culture in British Columbia.

Sandrine Ferré-Rode is maître de conférences at Université de Versailles à Saint-Quentin-en-Yvelines, where she teaches North American civilization. Pursuant to her disssertation on publishing in Atlantic Canada (published as *L'édition au Canada atlantique: Le défi de publier une région*), she is examining questions of regionalism and multiculturalism in North America.

Janet B. Friskney is associate editor with Volume 3 of HBiC/HLIC. Her research specialty is publishing history, with specific interests in the Methodist Book and Publishing House, McClelland and Stewart's New Canadian Library series, and the history of library and publishing services for the blind in Canada.

Gilles Gallichan is librarian and historian at the library of the Assemblée nationale du Québec. He holds a degree in library science from Université de Montréal and a doctorate in history from Université Laval. An editor of Volume 1 of HBiC/HLIC, he is currently working on projects relating to the parliamentary history of Quebec.

Carole Gerson is professor in the English Department at Simon Fraser University, and an editor of Volume 3 of HBiC/HLIC. Her next research project will return to her previous focus on Canada's early women writers.

Ross Gordon, Director of the Library, Canadian Police College in Ottawa, holds an MA in history and an MLIS. He is completing a doctoral dissertation at McGill University on the history of the Library of Parliament to 1886.

Guy de Grosbois is an antiquarian bookseller in Montreal. He holds graduate degrees in art history from Université de Montréal and in history from EHESS-Paris, and is currently preparing a study of the material history of books.

Francess G. Halpenny C.C. is professor emerita at the Faculty of Information Studies at the University of Toronto, which she joined in 1972 after many years as managing editor of University of Toronto Press. General editor of the *DCB/DBC* from 1969 to 1989, she has often written on authors and publishing.

Elizabeth Hanson is gifts librarian at Indiana University, Bloomington. She received her PhD from Indiana University's School of Library and Information Science in 1994 with a dissertation published in 1997 as *A Jewel in a Park: Westmount Public Library, 1897–1918*. The development of public libraries in Canada continues to be her primary research interest.

Pierre Hébert, professor in the Département des lettres et communications at Université de Sherbrooke, has been researching literary censorship in Quebec for many years. He has published two books on this topic, in 1997 and 2004.

Paul Hjartarson is professor of English and film studies at the University of Alberta. His writing and teaching focus on Canadian literature and culture, book history, and creative non-fiction. His most recent book, with Tracy Kulba, is *The Politics of Cultural Mediation* (2003).

Brian Hogan taught in the history departments of the University of Saskatchewan and St Michael's College in the Toronto School of Theology. His research addresses religious and social issues in the modern period, and he has issued a bibliography of publications in Canadian religious history, 1964–2005, on CD-ROM.

Claudette Hould retired in 2003 from her position as professor in the Département d'histoire de l'art at Université du Québec à Montréal, where she is now adjunct professor. Specialist in the history of the *livre d'artiste* in Quebec, she is currently researching iconography during the French Revolution and recently published *La révolution par l'écriture: Les tableaux historiques de la révolution française, une histoire éditoriale d'information (1791–1817)* (Paris, 2005).

Russell Johnston, an associate professor of communications at Brock University, is the author of *Selling Themselves: The Emergence of Canadian Advertising* (2001). His research examines the history of print media, broadcasting, and marketing.

Clarence Karr has retired from his position as professor of history at Malaspina University College in Nanaimo, British Columbia. Author of *Authors and Audiences: Popular Canadian Fiction in the Early Twentieth Century* (2000), he is currently researching popular fiction, fan mail, and L.M. Montgomery as reader.

Peggy Lynn Kelly teaches English at the University of Ottawa and works on Canadian women writers and the roles played by cultural institutions in canon construction.

Lorna Knight is currently archivist for Kingston General Hospital. Her research interests include Canadian writers and publishing, nineteenth-century printed ephemera, life writing, and Canadian medical history.

Marcel Lajeunesse has served as professor and director at the École de bibliothéconomie et des sciences de l'information at Université de Montréal since 1970, and as vice-dean of the Faculté des lettres et des sciences from 1994 to 2002. Quebec publishing and the history of the book, libraries, and information studies are his research interests.

Yvan Lamonde is professor of Quebec history and literature at McGill University and is a general editor of HBiC/HLIC and an editor of Volumes 1 and 2. He is the author of *Histoire sociale des idées au Québec*, volumes 1 (1760–1896) and 2 (1896–1929), and editor, with Sophie Montreuil, of *Lire au Québec au XIXe siècle* (2003).

Richard Landon is director of the Thomas Fisher Rare Book Library and professor of English at the University of Toronto. His areas of research include book history and bibliography, and he has published *Literary Forgeries and Mystifications* (2003).

François Landry teaches French and Quebec literature at Université de Sherbrooke and has long been associated with the Groupe de recherche sur l'édition littéraire au Québec (GRÉLQ). Author of several articles on publishing as well as *Beauchemin et l'édition au Québec (1840–1940)* (1997), he is currently working on his second novel.

Sheila Latham, librarian at George Brown College, Toronto, is co-editor of *Magic Lies: The Art of W.O. Mitchell* (1997) and editor of the *Papers of the Bibliographical Society of Canada / Cahiers de la Société bibliographique du Canada*.

Françoise Lepage taught children's literature in the Département des lettres françaises at Université d'Ottawa. She has published widely on the history of children's literature and book illustration, including *Histoire de la littérature pour la jeunesse (Québec et francophonies du Canada)* (2000), and has written books for young readers.

Éric Leroux is assistant professor in the École de bibliothéconomie et des sciences de l'information at Université de Montréal. His primary research interests are the history of printing in Quebec and the history of book-trade workers in Canada.

Paul Litt is associate professor in the Department of History and the School of Canadian Studies at Carleton University. His research addresses Canadian cultural nationalism and cultural policy, and public history and memory.

Tina Loo teaches in the Department of History at the University of British Columbia, where she holds a Canada Research Chair in environmental history. She has written on Canadian legal and cultural history, and is currently working on various studies in environmental history.

Marie-Pier Luneau is assistant professor in the Département des lettres et communications at Université de Sherbrooke and co-director, with Josée Vincent, of the Groupe de recherche sur l'édition littéraire au Québec (GRÉLQ). Author of *Lionel Groulx, le mythe du berger* (2003), she is currently researching authorial strategies, the construction of the author, and popular literature.

Bertrum H. MacDonald, associate dean (research), Faculty of Management, Dalhousie University, is editor of electronic resources for HBiC/HLIC. His primary research interest is the diffusion of scientific information, particularly among Canadian scientists, from the nineteenth century to the present.

Rebecca Margolis holds a PhD in Yiddish studies from Columbia University. She teaches in the Vered Jewish Canadian Program at the University of Ottawa, where she is an assistant professor in the Department of Modern Languages and Literatures. Her research interests include Yiddish culture and broader issues relating to ethnicity.

Dominique Marquis is assistant professor in the Département d'histoire at Université du Québec à Montréal. An expert on the history of the Quebec press, she has published *Un quotidien pour l'Église: 'L'Action catholique,' 1910–1940* (2004) and continues to research twentieth-century Quebec cultural history.

Claude Martin is an economist and professor in the Département des communications at Université de Montréal. His research focuses on culture and communications statistics, the development of cultural industries in Quebec, best-selling books in Quebec, and television programming.

Paul McCormick is a consultant in Ottawa. Until 2006 he was director general, Published Heritage Branch, at Library and Archives Canada. He previously served as director general for strategic policy and planning and for information resource management at the former National Library of Canada.

Rod McDonald is a typographer and type designer whose work includes typefaces for *Maclean's* and *Chatelaine* magazines. His Cartier Book, based on Canada's first roman typeface, Cartier, is used for HBiC/HLIC. He has taught typography at Sheridan College, the Ontario College of Art and Design, and NSCAD University.

A.B. McKillop is Chancellor's Professor and chair of the Department of History at Carleton University. Author of several books on Canadian cultural and intellectual history, he is currently completing a biography of journalist and historian Pierre Berton.

David McKnight is director of the Schoenberg Center for Electronic Text and Image at the University of Pennsylvania. He previously occupied a similar position at McGill University, where he was also part-time lecturer in the McGill Institute for the Study of Canada.

Donald W. McLeod, a librarian at the John P. Robarts Library, University of Toronto, is editor of *DA: A Journal of the Printing Arts* and author of several books on Canadian gay history.

Peter F. McNally is professor at McGill University's Graduate School of Library and Information Studies and director of the History of McGill Project. He is a past president of the Bibliographical Society of Canada and convenor of the Library History Interest Group of the Canadian Library Association.

Jacques Michon is professor at Université de Sherbrooke, where he holds the Canada Research Chair in Book and Publishing History and until 2006 directed the Groupe de recherche sur l'édition littéraire au Québec (GRÉLQ). He has published extensively on book history and is an editor of Volume 3 of HBiC/HLIC.

Peter J. Mitham is a writer based in Vancouver. He contributed to the founding conference for the History of the Book in Canada Project (1997) and published *Robert W. Service: A Bibliography* (2000).

Elise Moore pursued graduate studies in English literature at McGill University before entering the three-year play-writing program at the National Theatre School of Canada in Montreal. Her first play was produced in Winnipeg when she was eighteen.

Heather Murray is professor of English at the University of Toronto and author of *Come, Bright Improvement! The Literary Societies of Nineteenth-Century Ontario* (2002). She is now researching the rhetoric of early Canadian reform movements.

W.H. New is Killam University Professor Emeritus at the University of British Columbia. He has published many volumes of poetry, criticism, and children's literature, and edited the *Encyclopedia of Literature in Canada* (2002) and six Canadian volumes of the *Dictionary of Literary Biography*.

Sylvio Normand is professor in the Faculté de droit at Université Laval, where his research focuses primarily on the history of Quebec legal culture. He has published many studies on the role of print in the practice of law, and the influence it has exerted on legal doctrine.

Lyndsey Nowakowski-Dailey studied at Brock University.

Daniel O'Leary is assistant professor of Canadian literature at Concordia University in Montreal. Interested in book history, Canadian nationalism, and memoirs by Canadians, he is completing *Britons in the New Dominion*, a study of Victorian-Canadian nationalist literature.

Catherine Owen earned her MA in English from Simon Fraser University, where she worked as a research assistant with Volume 3 of HBiC/HLIC. She has published eight collections of poetry, including *The Wrecks of Eden* (2001), nominated for a BC Book Prize.

Ruth Panofsky, associate professor in the Department of English at Ryerson University in Toronto, specializes in Canadian literature, publishing history, and textual studies. Her latest book is *'The Force of Vocation': The Literary Career of Adele Wiseman* (2006).

George L. Parker taught Canadian and American literature at the Royal Military College of Canada, Kingston, and now resides in Halifax. He has authored numerous publications on Canadian publishing history, copyright, and Canadian literary history.

Michael A. Peterman teaches English and Canadian studies at Trent University, where he is principal of Catharine Parr Traill College. He has published extensively on nineteenth-century Canadian literary culture and is currently at work on Irish-Canadian writers James McCarroll and Isabella Valancy Crawford.

Suzanne Pouliot is professor at Université de Sherbrooke and a reseacher with the Groupe de recherche sur l'édition littéraire au Québec (GRÉLQ). She is interested in the history of children's literature, the teaching of French, and publishing for children and youth.

Michelle Preston studied at Brock University.

Jim Rainer completed a thirty-seven-year career in the forest industry and retired in 1992 as senior vice-president of Fletcher Challenge Canada. A director of the Alcuin Society since 1991, he served as its chairman from 1993 to 2004.

Archana Rampure recently completed her doctorate at the University of Toronto and is currently assistant professor in the English Department at Dalhousie University. She works in the area of global literatures in English and is interested in discourses of travel, romance, and history, as well as in cultural theory and academic labour.

DeNel Rehberg Sedo teaches at Mount Saint Vincent University in Halifax, and is a co-researcher with Danielle Fuller (University of Birmingham, UK) on an international project titled 'Beyond the Book: Mass Reading Events and Contemporary Cultures of Reading in the UK, USA and Canada.' Historical and contemporary reading communities are at the centre of her research.

Lucie Robert is professor in the Département d'études littéraires at Université du Québec à Montréal. Member of the Centre de recherche interuniversitaire sur la littérature et la culture québécoises (CRILCQ) and of the editorial teams of the *Dictionnaire des oeuvres littéraires du Québec* (1978–87) and *La vie littéraire au Québec*, she has published extensively on Quebec literature and theatre.

Andrea Rotundo is a doctoral student in the Faculty of Information Studies and the Collaborative Program in Book History and Print Culture at the University of Toronto. Her area of research is Toronto's literary culture in the late nineteenth century.

Pascale Ryan is research attaché to the secretary general of the Bibliothèque et archives nationales du Québec (BANQ). She holds a doctorate in Quebec intellectual history and worked as a post-doctoral fellow with Volume 3 of HBiC/HLIC. Her dissertation on *L'Action nationale* is soon to be published by Éditions Leméac.

Denis Saint-Jacques, professor of French and Quebec literature in the Département des littératures at Université Laval and a member of the Centre de recherche interuniversitaire sur la littérature et la culture québécoises (CRILCQ), directs the multi-volume project, *La vie littéraire au Québec.*

Judith Saltman is associate professor in the School of Library, Archival and Information Studies, and chair of the multidisciplinary Master of Arts in Children's Literature Program at the University of British Columbia. She works on children's literature and publishing, and illustrated children's books.

Blanca Schorcht is on faculty in the English Department and serves as chair for the South-Central Region of the University of Northern British Columbia. Her book, *Storied Voices in Native American Texts*, was published in 2003.

Randall Speller is a librarian at the Art Gallery of Ontario in Toronto. He is interested in twentieth-century Canadian book illustration and design, especially the period after the Second World War.

Apollonia Steele is special collections librarian at the University of Calgary, where she has been involved in the development of archival resources in areas of Canadian creativity. She has co-edited numerous published archival inventories.

Iain Stevenson is professor of publishing studies at University College London. A graduate of Glasgow, Simon Fraser, and London universities, he was an academic publisher for a quarter of a century before turning to teaching and research in publishing and book history, with a special interest in the book in English and French Canada.

Fanie St-Laurent is a doctoral candidate at Université de Sherbrooke and a graduate research assistant with Volume 3 of HBiC/HLIC. She holds a fellowship from the Social Sciences and Humanities Research Council to support her research on the social and cultural history of the Société d'étude et de conférences.

Carolyn Strange is currently director of graduate studies at the Centre for Cross-Cultural Research, Australian National University, and also adjunct professor of criminology and history at the University of Toronto. She has published extensively on the history of crime and punishment in Canada, the United States, and Australia.

Cheryl Suzack is assistant professor in the Department of English at the University of Victoria. Her research and teaching focus is on Aboriginal and Indigenous literatures, colonial law, postcolonial theory, and feminist theory.

Jaime Sweeting holds an Honours BA in business communications from Brock University. Her research interests include feminist cultural analysis, symbolism in advertising, and film and television analysis, particularly film noir.

Simone Vannucci is a member of the Groupe de recherche sur l'édition littéraire au Québec (GRÉLQ) at Université de Sherbrooke. She completed a doctoral dissertation on the publishing activity of the Jesuits and continues to research the role of religious communities in shaping literature and literary publishing in Quebec.

Christl Verduyn is professor of English and Canadian studies at Mount Allison University in Sackville, NB. She has published extensively on Canadian and Québécois literatures with a focus on women's writing, multicultural writing, and life writing.

Michel Verrette is associate professor at Collège universitaire de Saint-Boniface and author of *L'alphabétisation au Québec, 1660–1900: En marche vers la modernité culturelle* (2002). His research interests include socio-cultural history, focusing on education and literacy.

Josée Vincent is associate professor in the Département des lettres et communications at Université de Sherbrooke, where she teaches book and publishing history and is co-director, with Marie-Pier Luneau, of the Groupe de recherche sur l'édition littéraire au Québec (GRÉLQ). She works on book policy, professional associations, and relations between France and Quebec in the field of books and publishing.

Mary Vipond is professor of history at Concordia University, Montreal. She studies the history of the Canadian media, with a particular interest in early broadcasting.

Dorothy W. Williams recently received her doctorate from the Graduate School of Library and Information Studies at McGill University. She is currently researching the history of Black periodical culture in Montreal, and she continues to develop reference tools on the Black experience in Canada.

Robert Yergeau is professor in the Département des lettres françaises at Université d'Ottawa. In 1988 he founded les Éditions du Nordir. Author of several collections of poems, he has also published two critical studies, the second of which is *Art, argent, arrangement: Le mécénat d'État* (2004).

INDEX

Page references to illustrations are in *italic*.

Abanaki Press, 179, 311

Abebooks, 517

Abeille, L' (Laprairie, QC), 216–17, *351*, *366*

Aboriginal peoples: authors, 29–34, 150, 183, 191, 224, 293–7, 504–5; autobiographies, 30, 32–4, 183, 295; and Canadian art, 71, 79; education, 293, 295–6, 501–5; En'owkin International School of Writing, 224, 297; languages, 293–7; libraries, 495, 501–5; literacy, 29, 502, 504; oral traditions, 29–34; publishing, 32, 224, 294–7; reading, 29, 501–5; religion, 290–1, 293–4; stories for children, 32, 150, 222; works about, 188, 190, 224, 290–1, 294–6, 333. *See also* individual Aboriginal peoples; individual languages; syllabics; translation

Acadia: French-language publishing in, 210–11; textbooks from Quebec, 239

Acadia University, 440, 497

Acadiensis (Fredericton), 180

Achard, Eugène (1884–76), 147, 200, 217

Act Respecting the Development of Quebec Firms in the Book Industry (Bill 51), 51, 205, 397, 414, 517

Action canadienne française, L' (Montreal), 200; *See also Action française, L'*

Action catholique, L' (Quebec City), 264, 277, 278, 436

Action française, L' (Montreal), 18, 200, 478–9. *See also* Bibliothèque de l'Action française

Action populaire, L' (Joliette, QC), 278

Action sociale, L' (Quebec City), 277

Actualité, L' (Montreal), 245. *See also Magazine Maclean, Le*

advertising: in feminist publications, 320; in the *Free Lance*, 308; government, 253, 261–2, 263, 298–9; patent medicine, 345; reading and books depicted in, 80–2, 83–5

Afro-Canadian League, 308

Agence de distribution populaire (ADP), 255, 406, 407

agency system and branch-plant publishing, 163–8, 171, 173, 190, 192, 227, 230, 391–2, 395–6, 411

agriculture, 139, 183, 248–9, 252, 265, 266, 277, 324, 339, 500–1

Alberta: censorship, 469, 471, 474; education, 26, 44, 61, 182; government support of the arts, 37, 44, 114; libraries, 113–14, 431, 433, 434, 439, 441, 497–8, 500; literacy, 454; mass-market distribution, 404; publishing, 124, 182, 184, 194, 212–13, 263

Alcuin Society, 376–7

Aldana, Patsy (1946–), 223, 224, 321

Alderson, Sue Ann (1940–), 150, 151; *Hurry Up, Bonnie!* 151

Allen, Ralph (1913–66), 134, 140, 143

allophones: archives, 298; authors, 23, 96–7, 100–3, 305–7, 519–20; autobiographies, 300–1; as critics, 23, 101–2, 300, 303; culture, 28–9; defined, 24, 43, 100; education, 26; folklore collections, 67, 68; genres of publication, 101–2, 302–4, 305–7; government policy toward, 24–9; government support of culture, 43; imported books, 390; language retention, 26, 28–9, 303–4; literacy, 453; literary journals, 306; materials in libraries, 298, 544n14; publishing, 177, 297–304; reviews of publications, 100, 482; study of, 102; translated works, 101, 103, 301. *See also* individual languages; Kirkconnell, Watson

almanacs, 67, 179; French-language, 200, 251–3

Amelia Frances Howard-Gibbon Award, 145, 223

American culture. *See* United States

Amérique française, L' (Montreal), 479

Amtmann, Bernard (1907–79), 400–1

Anansi. *See* House of Anansi Press

Anderson, Doris (1921–), 250–1, 410

Androgyne, L' (bookstore, Montreal), 399, 469

Anglican Church of Canada (formerly Church of England in Canada), 284, 285, 287, 289, 290, 291, 293, 300, 319

Annick Press, 224, 321, 518

anthologies: based on identity, 97; literary, 124, 137, 210; non-fiction, 141; as textbooks, 137

antiquarian books, 393, 400–1, 412

Apostolat de la presse, 217, 218, 281

Applebaum-Hébert. *See* Federal Cultural Policy Review Committee

Aquin, Hubert (1929–77), 109, 121, 135, 158, 204; *Le jour est noir,* 203

archives, 113–14, 265, 298, 322, 417, 419, 424, 426, 428, 446–7, 447, 516, 545n61

Arctic. *See* North

art: books about, 70–4, 190, 355; depictions of books and readers, 75–9. *See also* artists

art galleries, 70, 71, 328, 417, 447

artists: as designers, 18, 72, 72, 172, 224, 251, 370; as illustrators, 218–22, 274, 371, 372, 375, 377, 378–81

Association of Canadian Publishers (formerly Independent Publishers' Association), 155, 167, 175, 194, 195, 458

Atlantic Advocate (Fredericton), 178, 179

Atlantic Canada: bookselling, 395–6, 398, 401–2, 412; folklore, 66–8; government publishing, 265; government support of the arts, 37; libraries, 432, 440–1, 496, 497, 557n123; periodicals, 178–80; publishers in, 31, 178–81, 194, 230, 231, 311, 341, 342, 344; tourism, 321. *See also* Acadia; individual provinces

Atlantic Insight (Halifax), 180

atlases and maps, 60, 230, 273, 335, 383, 428, 448

Atwood, Margaret (1939–), 54, 108, 125, 138, 174, 233, 482–3, 520; *The Circle Game,* 119, 313; *Survival,* 482–3

authors and authorship, 93–112; Aboriginal peoples, 30, 32–4, 150, 183, 191, 224, 294–6, 297, 305–7, 504–5; allophones, 23, 96–7, 100–3, 519–20; associations and networks, 122–30, 147, 152, 180, 529n7, 531n86; Black, 97, 315–16; contracts, 107, 111, 112–13, 125, 151, 164; demographics, 93–100; economics, 99, 103–13, 115, 122, 127, 131–3, 136, 138–9, 149, 153, 170, 178, 311, 315, 330, 520, 530n46; fan mail to, 463–5; free-lance, 98, 105, 140; genres, 99–100; identity, 93–4, 100; lobbying for state support, 37, 46; other careers, 95–6, 105, 108–10, 133, 148, 149; papers of, 107–8, 113–14, 464, 516; professionalization, 128–9, 132, 133; pseudonymous, 95, 97, 136, 153–4; religious, 95–6, 139, 147, 466–7. *See also* Canada Council for the Arts; individual associations; individual authors; individual genres of writing; prizes; self-publishing

autobiographies and biographies: Aboriginal peoples, 30, 32–4, 183, 291, 295; allophone, 96, 102, 300–1; dictionaries of, 140, 329, 334–5; religious figures, 95, 96, 290–1;

sports figures, 143, 144; travellers, 191, 290–1; war, 189; writers, 33, 152, 170, 272

avant-garde, 203, 310, 313, 317, 318, 369–70, 403

awards. *See* individual prizes; prizes

Baie-Comeau policy, 518

Bailey, A.G. (Alfred Goldsworthy; 1905–97), 109, 127, 179

Baird, Irene (1901–81), 109, 471; *Waste Heritage*, 471

Baptist Church of Canada, 285, 289, 290, 319

Barbeau, Marius (1883–1969), 30, 31, 54, 65–6, 73, 170; *The Downfall of Temlaham*, 30; *Tsimsyan Myths*, 30

Barbeau, Victor (1884–1994), 128, 139, 316; *Pour nous grandir*, 139

Barre du jour, La (Montreal), 318, 480

Beaudoin, Louis-Philippe (1900–67), 369, 371

Beaulieu, Victor-Lévy (1945–), 105, 121, 203, 283; *Manuel de la petite littérature au Québec*, 283

Belaney, Archibald Stansfeld (pseud. Grey Owl; 1888–1938), 53, 97, 141, 170, 172

Belgium: books produced in, 280, 377; imports from, 59, 238, 390–1; promotion of books in, 49, 214–15

Bergeron, Léandre (1933–), 141, 463; *Petit manuel d'histoire du Québec*, 141, 463

Bernier, Jovette (1900–81), 105, 200, 476

Bertelsmann, 518–19

Berton, Pierre (1920–2004), 103–4, 105, 119, 140, 141, 150, 158, 174; *The Dionne Quintuplets*, 158; *The Dionne Years*, 158; *The Golden Trail: The Story of the Klondike Rush*, 222; *The Great Railway Illustrated*, 176; *The Impossible Railway*, 158; *The Last Spike*, 23, 141, 158, 174; *The Mysterious North*, 21; *The National Dream*, 23, 158

best-sellers, 21, 105, 271, 395, 459–63, 472, 480, 483; children's literature, 154, 174, 190, 220, 224; cookbooks, 319, 402; international, 105, 141, 142, 143, 169, 170, 224; non-fiction, 33, 87, 95, 103–4, 141, 207, 313; poetry, 174, 203, 204, 211, 239, 241, 460, 461; religious, 96, 282–3, 293

Bible, 96, 281, 282, 284, 289, 290, 293, 307, 466

bibliographies, 55, 62, 74, 298, 323, 335, 342, 345, 346, 427, 443, 452; Canadiana, 55, 128, 331, 424, 425, 426, 427, 428

Bibliothèque à cinq cents (series), 404

Bibliothèque canadienne (series), 86–8, 87

Bibliothèque canadienne-française (series), 239–41

Bibliothèque de l'Action française, 88, 200, 476

Bibliothèque nationale du Québec, 339, 428

Bibliothèque religieuse et nationale (series), 86

Bibliothèque Saint-Sulpice, 428, 440

Bien public, Le (Trois-Rivières), 47

bilingual publishing, 28–9, 170, 201; Aboriginal languages, 29, 295, 505; allophone, 300, 307; children's, 224; government documents, 52–3, 268–9; scholarly, 332, 335, 344; textbooks, 26; timetables, 273

Bill 51. *See* Act Respecting the Development of Quebec Firms in the Book Industry

Birney, Earle (1904–95), 109–10, 127, 170

birth control, 323, 545n63

Bishop's University, 116, 440, 441

Black authors and publishers, 97, 307–8, 315–16

Blais, Marie-Claire (1939–), 112, 122; *La belle bête*, 135; *Une saison dans la vie d'Emmanuel*, 203, 371, 462–3

blind and visually impaired readers, 505–8, 509; *Braille Courier*, 507

Boas, Franz (1858–1942), 30, 31, 293

Bonne chanson, La (series), 66

Book and Periodical Development Council of Canada, 195, 412

book bindings and bookbinders, 82, 154, 172, 264, 352, 377, 383–4, 384, 410; fine, 118, 370, 377; prize books, 86–8; women, 362–3, 364, 365. *See also* paperbacks

book clubs (commercial), 105, 136, 171, 202, 408–11, 459, 460, 461

book design. *See* design.

book fairs, 49, 135, 193, 214, 224, 372, 514

Book Publishers' Professional Association / Book Promotion Editorial Club, 196–8, 384

Book Publishing Industry Development Program, 43, 205, 518. *See also* government

book reviewing and criticism, 152–3, 221, 223, 279, 317, 328, 460, 478–84

Book Room (bookstore, Halifax), 394, 401–2

book trade and review journals: *Atlantic Provinces Book Review* (Halifax), 180; *Books in Canada* (Toronto), 483; *Bookseller and Stationer* (Toronto), 395, 460; *Le Bulletin de l'imprimerie*, (Montreal), 360; *Canadian Author and Bookman* (Toronto), 112, 123; *Canadian Bookman* (Toronto), 456; *Canadian Books in Print* (Toronto), 412; *Canadian Printer and Publisher* (Toronto), 366; *Children's Book News* (Toronto), 152; *CM: Canadian Materials* (Ottawa), 223; *In Review: Canadian Books for Canadian Children* (Toronto), 223; *Livre d'ici* (Montreal), 214, 414; *Livres et auteurs canadiens* (Montreal), 331, 479–80; *Livres et auteurs québécois* (Montreal), 331, 470; *Le Maître imprimeur* (Montreal), 361; *Quill & Quire* (Toronto), 411, 461, 482; *Le Typo* (Montreal), 368; *Vient de paraître* (Montreal), 214, 414; *The Writer's Studio* (Toronto), 132

book weeks: Canada Book Week, 46, 123, 127, 395, 456; Young Canada's Book Week, 395, 485, 487

bookmobiles, 495, 496–8

Books for Boys and Girls, 485

booksellers and bookstores: accredited in Quebec, 50–1, 205, 397, 413, 438, 519; antiquarian and used, 393, 400–1, 412, 517; campus, 137, 334, 393, 400; chains, 393, 397–9, 405, 407, 412, 516, 517; children's, 152, 223, 399; commercial lending libraries, 136, 395; cooperative, 399, 400; department stores, 171, 394, 398, 408, 411; distribution systems, 167; gay and lesbian, 399, 468–9, 517; government, 262; independent, 398–403, 516–17; on-line, 515, 517; organizations, 123, 195, 400–1, 411–14; prizes for, 198; as publishers, 179, 202, 208, 232–3, 345, 355, 402; in small communities, 208, 394–5; specialized, 327, 399, 412, 515, 516–17; trade journals, 214, 411; training, 195, 412, 413. *See also* book trade and review journals; Chapters; distribution; individual booksellers; wholesalers

Bookshelf (bookstore, Guelph, ON), 516

Borduas, Paul-Émile (1905–60), 18, 73, 78, 477, 513

Bouchard, Maurice (1924–2000), 50, 205, 238, 413

Boucher, Denise (1935–): *Les fées ont soif*, 478

Boulizon, Guy (1906–2003), 146–7, 217, 485

Bourassa, Henri (1868–1953), 14, 16, 18, 58, 278

branch-plant publishing. *See* agency system and branch-plant publishing

Breakwater Books, 67–8, 181, 315

Britain: branch publishing operations in Canada, 164, 167–8, 405; Canadians published in, 105; imports from, 164–5, 166, 390; literary agents in, 111; promotion of Canadian works in, 71, 193

British Book Service, 166

British Columbia: Aboriginal peoples, 30–1, 71, 114, 294, 297, 503, 504; allophone publishing, 298, 300, 301, 302; booksellers, 396, 398, 400, 412, 516, 517; government publishing, 263; government support of the arts, 37; libraries, 43, 420, 430, 431, 442, 447, 451, 457, 495, 496–7, 504, 508; literacy, 454; paper industry, 353–4; publishing, 188–92, 194, 213, 224, 297, 313, 315, 327, 375, 376–7; works about, 273–4, 319–20. *See also* Vancouver

Britnell, Roy, 394, 396, 412; Britnell's (bookstore, Toronto), 394, 516; Roy Britnell Award, 198

broadcasters, 144, 147

broadcasting, 154–6, 270–2; and Aboriginal peoples, 294; and authors, 104, 105–6, 108–10, 133, 140, 154–60, 462; for the blind, 506, 507; and children, 147, 148–9, 271, 272, 488; government intervention, 35, 36, 38, 39, 40; and publishing, 140, 270–3, 462, 482; and reading, 245, 247, 278, 414, 436, 458, 486, 488, 489; works adapted for, 110, 157–60, 193, 462. *See also* Canadian Broadcasting Corporation (CBC) / Société Radio-Canada (SRC); scriptwriters

Brock University, 447

Brooker, Bertram (1888–1955), 379, 380

Bruchési, Jean (1901–79), 47, 128

buying around, 165, 166, 167, 193, 392, 411. *See also* agency system and branch-plant publishing

Cahiers des Dix, Les (Montreal), 329

Cahiers du Québec (series), 332

Cailloux, André (pseud. Grand-père Cailloux; 1920–2002), 106, 147

Calgary, 313, 315, 344, 493, 498, 511

Callaghan, Morley (1903–90), 56, 98, 109, 133–5, 170, 171–2, 233, 472, 484; *Such Is My Beloved*, 236, 473

Campbell, Maria (1940–): *Halfbreed*, 33, 295

Canada Books of Prose and Verse (series), 57

Canada Council for the Arts: Book Promotion and Distribution Program, 42, 414; Book Purchase Program, 42, 43, 414; children's literature, 145, 148, 152, 223; creation of, 39–40, 106, 173; grants for publishers, 42, 49, 62, 107, 173, 175, 180, 202, 211, 212, 225, 235, 310, 320; grants for scholars, 330; grants for translation, 55–6; grants for writers, 40, 107, 115, 138, 173, 299; prizes, 119, 145, 148; Public Readings Program, 107; Writer-in-Residence Program, 40, 107, 115–16; Writing and Publication Section, 109, 310. *See also* Governor General's Literary Awards

Canada Customs, 472, 473, 517

Canada Institute for Scientific and Technical Information (CISTI), 422–3

Canada Year Book, 265

Canadian Art (series), 73

Canadian Arts Council, 37, 128

Canadian Authors Association: 35, 37, 46, 94, 123, 125, 127, 456; advice on contracts, 113; advice on markets, 131–2; and poetry, 312; prizes given by, 117; publishers' support of, 169; wartime propaganda, 129–30

Canadian Best-seller Library (series), 405

Canadian Bibliographic Centre, 424–5

Canadian Book Publishers' Council (also known as the Book Publishers' Branch /

Book Publishers' Section / Book Publishers' Association of Canada [Toronto Board of Trade]), 165, 192, 193–4, 195, 402

Canadian Broadcasting Corporation (CBC) / Société Radio-Canada (SRC), 36, 38, 39, 154–6, 270–2; authors employed by, 103, 106, 109; awards, 117, 155; children's programming, 148–9, 488–9; developing reading audiences, 134, 148, 482, 483, 505; library and archives, 448

Canadian Broadcasting Corporation (CBC) / Société Radio-Canada (SRC), radio and television programs by title: *Anthology*, 155, 156; *Bobino*, 272, 488; *Canada Reads*, 505; *CBC University of the Air*, 271; *CBC Wednesday Night*, 155; *Citizens' Forum*, 109; *Critically Speaking*, 483; *Femina*, 140; *Fighting Words*, 109, 483; *Friendly Giant*, 488; *Hidden Pages*, 489; *Hockey Night in Canada*, 144; *Ideas*, 155–6, 271; *Just Mary*, 148–9, 271; *Massey Lectures*, 21, 156, 271, 482; *Morningside*, 155; *Nic et Pic*, 272; *Now I Ask You*, 109; *Nursery School Time*, 488; *Passe-partout*, 488; *Stories for You*, 488; *Tales from Far and Near*, 488; *This Country in the Morning*, 140

Canadian Centenary Series, 332

Canadian Centennial History Series, 174

Canadian Forum (Toronto), 15, 134, 312, 481–2

Canadian Frontiers of Settlement (series), 329

Canadian Historical Review (Toronto), 328, 330, 483

Canadian History Readers (series), 57

Canadian Home Journal (Toronto), 132, 250

Canadian Home Reading Union, 493

Canadian Homes and Gardens (Toronto), 139

Canadian Illustrated Library (series), 174

Canadian Library Association, 195, 223, 419, 420, 424, 435, 452, 475, 482, 485, 495

Canadian Literature (Vancouver), 313, 331, 482, 483

Canadian Pacific Railway (CPR), 19, 23, 70, 139, 140, 158, 272–5

Canadian Periodical Publishers' Association, 195

Canadian Poetry Magazine (Toronto), 124

Canadian Press (news service), 35, 243

Canadian studies, 39, 40, 57, 59, 60, 61, 62–3, 67, 331, 482–3

Canadian Theatre Review (North York, ON), 315, 483

Canadian Treasury Readers, 230

Canadiana, reprints of, 169, 173, 235, 265, 377

Canadiana (Ottawa), 420, 424, 425–6, 427

Carleton Library (series), 59, 235–7

Carman, Bliss (1861–1929), 123, 170, 467; Bliss Carman Society, 127

Carmichael, Franklin (1890–1945), 172, 380

Carnegie funding, 429, 430, 432, 440, 485, 497

Carpatho-Rusyn (language), 301

Carr, Emily (1871–1945), 56, 70–1, 74; *Klee Wyck*, 56

Carrier, Louis (1898–1961), 73, 170, 171, 200, 201, 311, 354

Carrier, Roch (1937–), 112, 144, 145, 203; *The Hockey Sweater*, 144, 145

Cartier (typeface), 383, 384–6

catalogues: exhibition, 70, 72, 74, 79, 152, 328, 376, 379; promotional, 135, 152, 193, 194, 200, 214–15, 310, 381

Catholic Church: book clubs, 408; censorship, 469, 474, 475–80, 507; and education, 45, 206–7, 211–12, 237–9; labour unions, 360–2, 368; and libraries, 428, 432, 440, 491, 507; and publishing, 63, 96, 146, 210, 217, 218, 237–9, 276–83, 289, 316, 319, 320, 476. *See also* Quiet Revolution; *Refus global*

CBC Radio. *See* Canadian Broadcasting Corporation (CBC) / Société Radio-Canada (SRC)

CEGEPs, 59–60, 64, 369, 442, 451

censorship, 258, 322–7, 373, 412, 468–73; pre-publication censorship, 467, 474; religious, 473–5, 475–8. *See also* War Measures Act

Centennial of Canadian Confederation, 8, 23, 40, 71, 113, 173, 174, 180, 313, 320, 332, 383, 385, 426, 434. *See also* Expo 67

Centre de psychologie et de pédagogie, 50, 214, 220, 238

Cercle du livre de France, 121–2, 202, 204, 409

Chapters (bookstore), 120, 232, 398, 516, 519

Charbonneau, Robert (1911–67), 18, 109, 316, 317

Charlesworth, Hector (1872–1945), 139, 481

Chartier, Alain-Émile-Auguste, 58, 466

Chatelaine / Châtelaine, 84, 245, 248–51. *See also* Anderson, Doris; Saint-Martin, Fernande

Chauvin, Jean (1895–1958), 73, 76, 370

children: bookstores, 152, 223, 399; broadcasting, 147, 148–9, 271, 272, 488; depicted with books, 76, 77, 81, 486, 487; health, 267–70; reading, 433, 456, 484–90. *See also* textbooks

children's literature: associations, 128, 147, 152; authors, 95, 100, 102, 106, 109, 145–54, 217, 218, 295, 505; illustrations, 145, 149, 150, 152, 181, 218, 219, 221, 222, 370, 517; libraries, 153, 426, 433, 452, 484–5, 487, 488; magazines, 151, 216–18, 225, 280; non-fiction, 144, 146, 150–1, 219, 222, 295; non-sexist, 321–2; picture books, 150, 200, 218, 220–1, 224, 503, 505; poetry, 150, 174, 222; prizes for, 118, 145–6, 147–8, 223, 224, 337, 517; promotion, 152, 195, 218; publishing, 173, 177, 181, 211, 216–26, 281, 319, 321; religion, 96, 146, 217–18, 288–92; in school books, 64; sciences, 146, 217, 225; series, 56, 217; sports, 144; study of, 152–3, 223, 483; translated, 56. *See also* book trade and review journals; comics; Communication-Jeunesse; textbooks

Chileans in Canada, 97, 101, 301–2, 303

Chinese (language), 29, 301

Choquette, Robert (1905–91), 133, 201, 372; *Le curé du village*, 133

Church of England in Canada. *See* Anglican Church of Canada

Cité libre (Montreal), 22, 204, 479

Clarke, Austin (1934–), 97, 115, 315

Clarke, Irwin, 171, 175, 191, 194, 223, 227, 234, 321

Clarté (Montreal), 324, 470

Classic Books (bookstore, Montreal), 397–9, 412. *See also* Melzack, Louis

Classiques canadiens (series), 239–41

clubs. *See* book clubs; reading

Coach House Press, 56, 118, 310, 313

Cogswell, Fred (1917–2004), 179, 180, 181, 312–13

Cohen, Leonard (1934–), 54, 97, 138, 174, 307, 461

Cole, Jack, 232–3, 398; book enterprises, 68, 398–9, 412

Coleman, Victor (1944–), 313, 383

Coles Notes, 232–3

Collection art vivant (series), 73

Collection canadienne (series), 217

Collection des deux solitudes (series), 55–6, 204, 218

Collection du Nénuphar (series), 239–41, 371

Collection pour la jeunesse canadienne (series), 217

Collection Signatures (series), 355

Collins White Circle Pocket Editions, 172, 186, 405

Colombo, John Robert (1936–), 54, 90, 312

comics, 217, 218, 219, 220, 255–6, 256, 463, 489

Commission d'enquête sur le commerce du livre dans la Province de Québec, 8, 46, 50, 205, 238, 413

Commission on Canadian Studies (Symons Commission), 61, 62, 74, 231

Communication-Jeunesse, 126, 148, 217, 218, 485

Communist Party of Canada, 27, 124–5, 188, 189, 323, 324

computers, 127, 167, 244, 267, 515, 516; information technology, 74, 342–3, 422, 435, 443, 445, 451, 516; in printing and publishing, 311, 323, 352, 367–8, 384–5

Connor, Ralph (Charles W. Gordon; 1860–1937), 95, 157, 158, 164, 291, 465; *The Major,* 460; *The Man from Glengarry,* 157, 464; *The Sky Pilot in No Man's Land,* 169, 460

Conseil supérieur du livre (Quebec), 48, 50, 128, 205, 214–15, 413, 414

Contes historiques (series), 146

Cook, Ramsay (1931–), 23, 335, 410

cookbooks and recipes, 64–5, 67, 68–9, 95, 102, 183, 190, 203, 211, 249, 266, 271, 319, 402, 410

Copithorne, Judith (1939–), 79, *80*

Copp Clark, 172, 227, 346, 352, 474

copyright, 110–11, 123, 127, 133, 169; Canadian Copyright Edition, 164–5; foreign, 163–4; legislation, 27, 35, 110–11, 164, 165, 169. *See also* buying around; rights

Corridart (Montreal), 373

counterculture, 322–7

Couture, Ernest (b. 1891), 268–9; *The Canadian Mother and Child / La mère canadienne et son enfant,* 269

CPR. *See* Canadian Pacific Railway

Cree (language), 293–4, 504, 505; syllabics, 30, 293–4, 386, 504

Cree Monthly Guide (Saskatoon), 293–4

Cree peoples, 297

Creighton, Donald (1902–79), 15, 119, 330, 332

Croatian (language), 301, 303

Cul Q (Montreal), 318, 327, 373

Cutler, May (1923–), 224, 313, 321

Czech (language), 67, 299, 300, 301

Dafoe, John W. (1866–1944): *Laurier: A Study in Canadian Politics,* 15; *The Voice of Dafoe: A Selection of Editorials on Collective Security, 1931–1944,* 141

Daily News (Dawson, YT), 191

Daily News (St John's), 140

Dair, Carl (1912–67), 375, 382, 383, 385, 385–6

D'Alfonso, Antonio (1953–), 177

Dalhousie Review (Halifax), 179, 482

Dalhousie University, 439, 443, 450

Danish (language), 102, 300

Danske Herold (Kentville, NS), 300

Dantin, Louis (1865–1945), 200, 201, 217, 241, 479

Daveluy, Marie-Claire (1880–1968), 109, 146, 217; *Les aventures de Perrine et Charlot,* 146

Daveluy, Paule (1919–), 56, 147, 148

Davey Committee. *See* Special Senate Committee on the Mass Media

Davies, Robertson (1913–95), 54, 56, 109, 119, 138, 174, 377, 481

de la Roche, Mazo (1879–1961), 54, 103, 117, 120, 157–8, 170, 172, 464; *Jalna,* 117, 157–8,

461; *Whiteoaks*, 158; *Whiteoaks of Jalna*, 157–8, 170, 501

de Mille, Evelyn (1919–), 395, 398

Deacon, William Arthur (1890–1977), 139, 481; *Pens and Pirates*, 139

Delta press, 314–15

Dene peoples, 297

Department of Education (Quebec), 63, 87, 148, 207, 238, 239

Department of the Provincial Secretary (Quebec), 45, 46–8, 53, 128, 201, 437

Department of Public Instruction (Quebec), 21, 45–6, 86–7, 206–7, 238, 436

Depression, Great, 76, 153, 312, 379; bookselling and publishing, 73, 124, 134, 165, 168, 171, 201, 221, 329, 345, 390, 395, 402; libraries, 430, 431–2, 433, 436, 440–1; paper and printing industries, 351, 352, 366

Desbiens, Jean-Paul (frère Pierre-Jérôme, frère Untel; 1927–2006), 206–7; *Les insolences du frère Untel*, 21, 203, 206–7, 462, 537n16

design, 197, 236, 273–5, 369–72, 378–85, 385–6; by artists, 71, 72, 73, 172, 370, 378–81; children's literature, 222, 224. *See also* Alcuin Society; *livres d'artiste*; private press; small press publishing

Desparois, Lucille (pseud. Tante Lucille; 1910–), 105–6, 147, 217

DesRochers, Alfred (1910–78), 200, 479; *À l'ombre de l'Orford*, 239

Desrosiers, Léo-Paul (1896–1967): *Les engagés du grand portage*, 135, 239

Devoir, Le (Montreal), 17, 22, 141, 207, 245, 278, 361, 436, 479

dictionaries, 293, 331, 334–5

Dictionary of Canadian Biography / Dictionnaire biographique du Canada, 139, 334, 335

Dictionnaire des oeuvres littéraires du Québec, 94, 331, 332

distribution, 191, 389–414; allophone publications, 302–4; foreign ownership, 406–7; government documents, 262, 268–9; government support, 9, 42, 43–4, 59; on-line, 516, 517; religious publications, 280–8; surreptitious, 322–7. *See also* agency system and branch-plant publishing; post office

Dodd, Mead, 117, 165, 170, 189

domestic advice, 67, 69, 251–2, 268, 270, 345, 498, 504, 510

Dominicans, 18, 279, 280, 399

Doubleday, 106, 166, 171, 227, 405, 410

Douglas, Tommy (Thomas Clement; 1904–86), 182, 323

Douglas & McIntyre, 189, 190, 232, 518

Doukhobor people, 67

drama and dramatists, 30, 60, 98–9, 105–6, 118, 119–20, 133, 140, 155, 209, 300, 314. *See also* broadcasting; film

Droit, Le (Montreal), 208, 436

Droit populaire, Le (Montreal), 324

Dubé, Marcel (1930–), 106, 414

Ducharme, Gonzague (1875–1950), 400

Dudek, Louis (1918–2001), 109, 312, 314

Duplessis, Maurice (1890–1959), 18, 142, 206, 477, 560n37

Duthie Books (Vancouver), 376, 395, 398, 516

Eaton's (department store), 394, 408, 411

Eayrs, Hugh S. (1894–1940), 165, 169, 170, 192, 195, 471

École des arts graphiques de Montréal, 368–9, 371, 379

Écrits du Canada français, 317

Edinborough, Arnold (1922–), 410, 481

Éditions Albert Lévesque, 88, 200. *See also* Lévesque, Albert

Éditions Anne Sigier, 282

Éditions Bellarmin, 281

Éditions Bernard Valiquette, 202

Éditions Chantecler, 355

Éditions d'Acadie, 211

Éditions de la Courte Échelle, 148, 218, 518

Éditions de la Francophonie, 211

Éditions de la Nouvelle Plume, 213

Éditions de la Pleine Lune, 322

Éditions de l'Arbre, Les, 73, 202, 204, 217, 317

Éditions de l'Églantier, 212

Éditions de l'Hexagone, 128, 202, 204, 317, 371

Éditions de l'Homme, 144, 202–3, 206, 255, 272, 282

Éditions des Aboiteaux, 210–11

Éditions des Plaines, 212

Éditions d'Orphée, 202, 302, 317, 371

Éditions du Blé, 212

Éditions du Boréal, 332

Éditions du Boréal Express, Les, 332

Éditions du Jour, 203, 204, 282, 371, 410

Éditions du Mercure / Mercury Press, 201, 354

Éditions du Noroît, 318, 371

Éditions du Pélican, 218

Éditions du Phare Ouest, 213

Éditions du Totem, 201, 476

Éditions Édouard Garand, 200–1. *See also* Garand, Édouard

Éditions Erta, 317, 371, 372

Éditions Fides, 48, 50, 87, 137, 141, 202, 204, 210, 217, 219, 239–41, 281, 282, 317, 329, 332, 335, 371, 397, 398, 409, 477, 491, 493

Éditions Héritage, 56, 218, 272

Éditions Hurtubise HMH, 56, 202, 204, 218, 272, 332, 371

Éditions jeunesse, 217, 218

Éditions Le Tamanoir, 148

Éditions Leméac, 144, 202, 203, 218, 272

Éditions Louis Riel, 213

Éditions Lumen, 355

Éditions Marabout, 218, 255

Éditions Ovale, 219

Éditions Parti pris, 202, 204. *See also Parti pris*

Éditions Paulines, 218. *See also* Médiaspaul

Éditions Perce-Neige, 211

Éditions Police Journal, 255

Éditions Prise de parole, 208, 209

Éditions Quinze, 203

Éditions Remue-ménage, 322

Éditions Stanké, 203, 282, 518

Éditions Variétés, 87, 202, 217

Éditions Yvon Blais, 340–1

editors, 61, 95, 109, 169, 196, 198, 223, 249, 250, 319, 333, 335

Edmonton, 124, 184, 212–13, 324–5, 399, 498

Edmonton Journal, 471

education: adult, 274, 275, 466, 491–3, 509–14; Canadian content, 56–64, 153; curricula, 226–7, 229, 231, 239, 291, 305, 502; and libraries, 429, 433, 437; publishers, 181, 193–4, 205, 209–10, 226–32; reform in Quebec, 206–7. *See also* Canadian studies; children; literacy; post-secondary education; textbooks; universities

Egoff, Sheila (1918–2005), 484; *The Republic of Childhood: A Critical Guide to Canadian Children's Literature in English*, 152

Encyclopedia of Canada, 334

Encyclopedia of Canada's Peoples, 298

Encyclopedia of Music in Canada, 335

encyclopedias, 180, 184, 298, 334, 335, 518

Engel, Marian (1933–1985), 108, 115, 125

ephemera, 68, 266, 322–3, 324, 371

Estonian (language), 301

ethnicity. *See* allophones; multiculturalism

Eustace, C.J., 229, 408

Évangéline, L' (Digby, NS, and Moncton, NB), 210

exhibitions: book design, 197, 370, 376, 379, 381, 382, 383, 384; catalogues, 70–1, 72, 74, 79, 152, 328, 376, 379, 381; literary, 128, 152, 370, 427

Expo 67, 23, 49, 371

export of Canadian publications, 39, 42, 46, 49, 62, 135–6, 168, 175, 187–8, 193, 201, 215, 301, 519

fan mail, 463–5

Federal Cultural Policy Review Committee (Applebaum-Hébert), 43, 518

feminism, 54, 79, 249–51, 399, 480, 517, 545n51, 545n58; and publishing, 318–22

Fennario, David (1947–), 54, 120

Ferron, Jacques (1921–85), 109, 318; *Dr. Cotnoir: A Novel*, 56

fiction, 131–8; allophone, 303; crime fiction, 137, 243–5, 253–4, 255–8; prizes, 106, 117–22; pulp fiction, 132, 136, 253–5, 255–8, 405, 406; on radio, 105–6, 154–5; religious, 289, 290–1; romances, 137, 185–8, 248, 253–6; serialized, 132, 140, 146; translated, 54–5. *See also* authors and authorship; children's literature; Governor General's Literary Awards

Fiddlehead (press and journal, Fredericton), 127, 179, 180, 312, 313

Fides. *See* Éditions Fides

Filion, Gérard (1909–2005), 206, 361, 479

film, 35–6, 104, 105, 109, 110, 130, 144–5, 157–60, 394. *See also* National Film Board of Canada; scriptwriters

Findley, Timothy (1930–2002), 156, 158; *The Newcomers*, 158

fine press books. *See livres d'artiste*; private press

Finnish (language), 25, 298, 299, 300

First Nations. *See* Aboriginal peoples

First World War, 24–5, 164, 169, 268, 460, 469, 492, 506

Floyd S. Chalmers Canadian Play Awards, 119–20

folklore and folk songs, 30, 58, 64–9, 73, 102, 179, 181, 211, 221, 274, 304, 329

Foreign Investment Review Agency, 42, 175

foyer, Le (Montreal), 248

France: branch-plant publishing in Canada, 50, 205; Canadians published in, 51–2, 53–4, 135–6, 462; exports to, 49, 135–6; French works published in Canada, 133, 136, 201–2, 238, 405; imports from, 59, 331, 390, 392, 393, 403, 409, 462, 505, 507; literary prizes, 122, 135; Paris book fair, 372; promotion of Canadian books in, 49, 193. *See also* Librairie Hachette; Second World War

Franco, Le (Edmonton), 212

Franco-albertain, Le (Edmonton), 212

Franco-Ontarian publishing, 208–10

Fraser Valley Library Demonstration, 430

Free Lance, The (Montreal), 307–8

Free Trade Agreement: Canada-United States, 44, 175, 518

French, David (1939–), 106, 120; *Leaving Home*, 120; *Of the Fields, Lately*, 120

Frère Untel. *See* Desbiens, Jean-Paul

Friesens Corporation, 68, 183, 355–8

Frontier College, 454, 491

Frye, Northrop (1912–91), 54, 95, 109, 156, 271,

482; *The Bush Garden*, 482; *The Educated Imagination*, 482; *Fearful Symmetry*, 329

Fulford, Robert (1932–), 410, 481

Gaelic (language), 66, 301

Gagnon, Maurice (1912–99), 147, 218

Gallimard, 135, 462

Gants du ciel (Montreal), 316, 479

Garand, Édouard (1901–65), 45, 133, 200, 213, 406

gay and lesbian literature, 325–6, 399, 468–9, 517, 545n61

Gélinas, Gratien (1909–99): *Bousille et les justes*, 133; *Tit-coq*, 133, 159

gender: and authors, 93, 94–5, 96, 108, 110, 143; and children's literature, 146, 147, 148; and magazines, 248–51; in the printing trades, 358–60, 362–8; and prizes, 117, 119; and publishing, 172, 196–8, 224, 249, 251, 310, 318–22; and reading habits, 75–7, 82, 83–5, 143, 249, 457–8, 463; in textbooks, 231. *See also* feminism; gay and lesbian literature; women

General (publishing and distributing), 172, 173, 406, 519

Gérin-Lajoie, Paul (1920–), 207

German (language), 25, 30, 288, 299, 303, 325, 356, 357, 390

Gibbon, John Murray (1875–1952), 70, 123, 130; *Canadian Mosaic*, 13, 19

Giguère, Roland (1929–2003), 121, 317, 371; *L'âge de la parole*, 204; *Faire naître*, 372

Globe and Mail (Toronto), 143, 481

Godbout, Jacques (1933–), 94, 109, 129, 135, 158

Goulet, André (1933–2001), 302, 317, 371

government: and Aboriginal peoples, 30–1, 294–5, 502–4; advertising, 253, 261–2, 263, 298–9; and allophones, 24–9, 100–1, 102, 298–9, 302; as author and publisher, 182, 259–70, 343, 345; federal intervention into arts and culture, 34–44, 106, 107, 108, 111, 125, 135–6, 156, 158, 159, 167, 174–5, 184, 190, 193, 194, 223–4, 297, 518, 519, 545n58; libraries, 417–28; provincial intervention into arts and culture, 40, 41, 43–4, 46–51, 61–2, 86, 106–7, 120, 125, 128–9, 167, 174–5, 185, 201, 231, 297, 310, 315, 406, 410, 518, 519, 521. *See also* Canada Council for the Arts; Canadian Broadcasting Corporation; censorship; individual provinces; individual royal commissions

Governor General's Literary Awards, 39–40, 87, 93, 96, 106, 116–22, 124, 125, 141, 145–6, 313, 332

Graham, Gwethalyn (1913–65), 106; *Earth and High Heaven*, 461

Grandbois, Alain (1900–75), 204, 241

Granger Frères, 88, 217, 238, 280, 394, 397, 476

Grannan, Mary ('Just Mary'; 1900–75), 148–9, 271

Graphic Publishers, 171, 311, 379

Gray, John Morgan (1907–78), 105, 134, 135, 173–4, 227, 382

Great Depression. *See* Depression, Great

Grey Owl. *See* Belaney, Archibald Stansfeld (pseud. Grey Owl)

Grignon, Claude-Henri (1894–1976), 133; *Un homme et son péché*, 105, 201, 370, 462

Groulx, Lionel (1878–1967), 16, 17, 58, 139, 200, 217, 329, 476, 513; *Si Dollard revient*, 17, 139

Groundwood Books, 224, 321

Group of Seven, 71–2, 74, 378. *See also* Carmichael, Franklin; Lismer, Arthur; Mac-Donald, J.E.H.

Grove, Frederick Philip (1879–1948), 97, 108–9, 170, 408, 473; *Over Prairie Trails*, 236; *Settlers of the Marsh*, 473

Guèvremont, Germaine (1893–1968), 128; *Le survenant*, 239, 241, 462

Gustafson, Ralph (1909–55), 109, 116

Gzowski, Peter (1934–2002), 140, 155

Hachette. *See* Librairie Hachette

Haig-Brown, Roderick (1908–76), 144, 150, 188, 222

Halifax, 178–9, 180, 399, 401–2, 506, 508

Hardy Boys series, 103, 153–4

Harlequin Enterprises, 136, 185–8, 405, 406, 407, 409, 535n57

Harris, Christie (1907–2002), 114, 150, 222

Harvest House, 56, 177

Harvey, Jean-Charles (1891–1967), 201, 476, 477; *Les demi-civilisés*, 201, 476

health. *See* medicine and health

Hébert, Anne (1916–2000), 54, 98, 109, 122, 138, 158, 317, 520; *La canne à pêche*, 158; *Kamouraska*, 135, 158–9, 463; *The Torrent: Novellas and Short Stories*, 56

Hébert, Jacques (1923–), 141, 202–3, 204, 206–7, 214, 255, 410, 518; *Scandales à Bordeaux*, 206; *Two Innocents in Red China*, 141

Hébert, Maurice (1888–1960), 201, 479

Hebrew (language), 102, 299, 305–7

Hémon, Louis (1880–1913), 54; *Maria Chapdelaine*, 155, 157, 169, 370

Herald (Halifax), 178, 179

Herald (Oxbow, SK), 246

Herbes rouges, Les (Montreal), 318, 480

Historical Atlas of Canada / L'Atlas historique du Canada, 335

historical societies, 68, 213, 328, 356, 447

history, 14–16, 99, 100, 139–40, 141, 158, 174, 179–80, 181, 182, 200–1, 328–30, 332–4, 446; allophone, 101, 102, 300, 303; children's literature and textbooks, 15, 58, 60, 62, 86, 146, 147, 150–1, 201, 217, 219, 222, 227, 230, 238–9, 295; local, 67–70, 179–83, 210, 213, 319–20, 356, 452; prizes for, 119, 141; religious, 95–6, 210, 290–1, 319, 332. *See also* archives

hockey, 143–4, 145, 149, 252. *See also* sports

Hodgetts, A.B. (Alfred Birnie, b. 1911): *What Culture? What Heritage?* 60, 61

Holgate, Edwin (1892–1977), 75, 76, 77, 124, 372

Hollywood, 98, 157, 158, 159–60

Hood, Hugh (1928–2000), 144, 173, 177

House of Anansi Press, 194, 313, 314, 315, 383, 483

how-to books, 99, 191, 203, 406, 463, 517

Hudson's Bay Company, 446–7; *The Beaver*, 446

Humanities Research Council, 330, 336

humour and satire, 34, 95, 98, 100, 119, 124, 139, 141, 501

Hungarian (language), 28, 67, 188, 299–300

Huron peoples, 30

Hurtig, Mel (1932–), 184, 395, 398, 518; *Canadian Encyclopedia*, 184

Hurtubise, Claude (1914–99), 204, 214, 316, 317

Hutchison, Bruce (1901–92), 15, 114, 119; *Canada: Tomorrow's Giant*, 141; *The Unknown Country*, 15, 141

hymnals, 284–5, 293

Icelandic Canadians, 96, 101

Icelandic (language), 101, 298, 299, 300, 301, 303

Idées, Les (Montreal), 201, 477

illustration, 70–4, 183–4, 201, 252, 253, 258, 263, 265, 375–6, 378–82; children's literature, 26, 118, 145–6, 150, 152, 181, 184, 218–26, 370, 517; techniques, 71, 219–20, 350, 351–2, 356, 362, 367, 368–9, 372, 375. *See also* design; photography; private press

immigration. *See* allophones; multiculturalism

Imperial Order Daughters of the Empire (IODE), 106, 117, 493, 494

imports, 255, 389–93, 397. *See also* agency system and branch-plant publishing; distribution; taxes and tariffs

Independent Publishers' Association. *See* Association of Canadian Publishers

Innis, Harold A. (1894–1952), 87, 329–30; *The Fur Trade in Canada*, 14–15

intellectual property. *See* copyright

Inuit peoples and Inuktitut, 29, 31, 32, 34, 291, 294, 296; Inuktitut syllabics, 30, 33, 296

Iroquois peoples, 295

Italian (language), 300, 301

Japanese (language), 27, 300, 303

Jasmin, Claude (1930–), 121, 135, 204; *Ethel and the Terrorist*, 56

Jeanneret, Marsh (b. 1917), 172, 195, 333, 474

Jesuits. *See* Society of Jesus

Jeunesse-pop series, 218, 281

Jewish Literary Club (Calgary), 511

Jewish people, 23–4, 27, 97, 284, 290, 299–300,
305–7, 319, 427, 432, 511; anti-Semitism, 325. *See also* Yiddish (language)

J.J. Douglas Limited. *See* Douglas & McIntyre

J.M. Dent (publishing house), 66, 165, 171, 225, 227, 230, 346, 378

Journal (Ottawa), 243

Journal de Montréal, Le, 243, 352

journalists and journalism, 21–3, 101, 104, 105, 132, 138–9, 140, 141, 142–4, 144, 146, 154, 305, 361

journals. *See* magazines

Just Mary. *See* Grannan, Mary

Kallman, Helmut (1922–), 335, 426

Kent Commission. *See* Royal Commission on Newspapers

Key Porter Books, 177, 321

Khaki University, 492

Kids Can Press, 224, 322

King's Printer. *See* Queen's/King's Printer

Kirkconnell, Watson (1895–1977), 27, 100, 101, 103, 130, 170, 441, 482

Klanak Press, 190, 383

Klein, A.M. (Abraham Moses, 1909–72), 97, 109, 311

Klinck, Carl F. (1908–90), 131; *Literary History of Canada*, 331, 335, 482

Knister, Raymond (1899–1932), 170, 311

Ku Klux Klan, 324–5

Kundera, Milan (1929–): *Farewell Party*, 301

Kurelek, William (1927–77): *A Prairie Boy's Summer*, 184; *A Prairie Boy's Winter*, 184, 224

La Palme, Robert (1908–97), 219, 220

labour. *See* printers and printing

Lacerte, Emma-Adèle (1870–1935), 146, 209

Lacombe, Patrice, (1807–63): *La terre paternelle*, 86

Lacourcière, Luc (1910–89), 66, 239, 329, 332

Laffont, Robert (1917–), 135, 462

L'Allier, Jean-Paul (1938–), 51

LaMarsh, Judy (1924–80): *Memoirs of a Bird in a Gilded Cage*, 142, 461

Lamb, W. Kaye (1904–99), 420–1, 424

Lamy, Pauline (1918–97), 219, 220

Langevin, André (1927–), 109, 114, 121, 135, 204; *Poussière sur la ville*, 159

languages. *See* Aboriginal peoples; allophones; individual languages; Official Languages Act

Lapalme, Georges-Émile (1907–85), 48, 50

Lapointe, Gatien (1931–83), 318; *Ode au Saint-Laurent*, 203; *Le premier mot*, 203

Lapointe, Paul-Marie (1929–), 109, 204; *Le réel absolu*, 204

Lasnier, Rina (1915–97), 241, 317

Latvian (language), 304

Laurence, Margaret (1926–87), 54, 56, 98, 108, 119, 125, 134, 138, 160, 174, 175, 465, 472; *The Diviners*, 472–3; *A Jest of God*, 160; *Rachel, Rachel*, 160; *The Stone Angel*, 233, 513; *This Side Jordan*, 134

Laurendeau, André (1912–68), 18, 22, 140, 141, 479; *Ces choses qui nous arrivent: Chronique des années 1961–1966*, 22

Laurentian Library (series), 137, 234–5

Lavallé, Marcel (1922–63), 465–7, 496

law books and legal publishing, 263, 264, 267, 339–43

law libraries, 342, 449

Lawrence, D.H.: *Lady Chatterly's Lover*, 412, 472. *See also* censorship

Layton, Irving (1912–2006), 97, 174, 307, 312

Le Moyne, Jean (1913–96), 204, 316, 479

Leacock, Stephen (1869–1944), 54, 75, 123, 124, 169, 439, 460, 507; *Literary Lapses*, 236; Stephen Leacock Memorial Medal, 98, 119; *Sunshine Sketches of a Little Town*, 155, 159

League of Canadian Poets, 107, 125, 126

Leblanc, Raoul, 209

Leclerc, Félix (1914–88), 217, 241

Lectures (Montreal), 477, 479

Leduc, Alec (1917–2000), 219, 220

Leduc, Ozias (1864–1955), 75, 78, 369–70

Lee, Dennis (1939–), 54, 174, 224–5, 313; *Alligator Pie*, 150, 174, 224–5

leftist publication and distribution, 25, 177, 188–9, 302, 312, 321, 322, 323–5, 501. *See also* Communist Party of Canada; Padlock Law

(Quebec); printers and printing; Socialist Party of Canada; wheat pools

legal deposit, 424, 425, 426, 428

legislative libraries, 417–20

Leméac. *See* Éditions Leméac

Lemelin, Roger (1919–92), 54, 105, 133, 159, 283; *Au pied de la pente douce*, 283; *La famille Plouffe*, 159; *Les Plouffe*, 105

Lemieux, Jean-Paul (1904–90), 219, 371

lesbian publications, 321, 325–6, 399, 468, 545n61. *See also* gay and lesbian literature

Lespérance, Edgar (1909–64), 137, 203, 255, 406

Lester, Orpen and Dennys, 177

Lester Publishing, 518

Lettres québécoises (Montreal), 480

Lévesque, Albert (1900–79), 45, 200, 213, 217, 458. *See also* Éditions Albert Lévesque

Lévesque, René (1922–87), 22, 513; *Option Québec*, 22

Levine, Norman (1923–2005), 98, 115

Liberté (Montreal), 129, 317, 480

Librairie Beauchemin, 45, 86, 87, 147, 202, 238, 253, 280, 371, 392, 395, 397

Librairie Dussault, 397, 398

Librairie Garneau, 205, 394, 397, 398

Librairie générale canadienne, 88, 147, 201, 217

Librairie Hachette, 50, 205, 238, 255, 407, 413

Librairie J.-A. Pony, 394, 397. *See also* Pony, Aristide

Librairie Tranquille, 395, 397, 402–3. *See also* Tranquille, Henri

librarians: organizations and training, 195, 419, 420, 421, 433, 436, 437, 438, 442, 446, 449–52, 484–5, 487, 488, 495, 557n123

libraries, 417–49; Aboriginal, 495, 501–5; academic, 107, 113–14, 330–1, 439–45; accessibility, 426, 427, 491–508, 509; buildings, 425, 429, 434, 438, 440–3, 444; children's services, 153, 426, 433, 452, 484–5, 487, 488; deposit collections, 262, 419; government, 417–28, 445; Jewish, 305, 432; law, 342; multilingual materials, 298, 426, 434; in museums, 447–8; parish, 428, 436; prison, 466, 493, 495–6; public, English Canada, 429–35;

public, Quebec, 435–8; rare books, 114, 425, 426, 428, 443, 444, 447; readership, 456–7; in schools, 153, 484–8, 499, 502, 505–6, 508; special, 445–9; studies and surveys of, 334, 430–1, 432, 433, 435, 438, 440, 441, 442, 456; subscription, 43, 512; and technologies, 515–16; travelling, 433, 491, 493–9, 503–4, 510; voluntary organizations, 437, 493–5, 498–501. *See also* Bibliothèque nationale du Québec; legal deposit; librarians; National Library of Canada; Public Lending Right

Libraries in Canada: A Study of Library Conditions and Needs (Ridington Report), 418, 430–1, 433, 436

Library and Archives Canada / Bibliothèque et Archives Canada, 424

Library of Parliament, 417, 418, 424, 425

Library on Wheels (film), 496–7

Lidec-Aventures series, 218

Lismer, Arthur (1885–1969), 66, 72–3

literacy, 453–5, 491–2; Aboriginal peoples, 29, 502, 504; children, 484–90

literary agents, 111–12, 132, 149, 150, 215

Literary Press Group, 194, 310. *See also* small press publishing and little magazines

Literary Translators' Association of Canada, 55

Little, Jean (1932–), 149, 222

Little Blue Books (series), 268–9, 345. *See also* medicine and health

Little Sister's (bookstore, Vancouver), 399, 468, 517

Livesay, Dorothy (1909–96), 115, 125, 170, 171–2, 311

livres d'artiste, 371, 372–4

Local Initiatives Program (LIP), 107, 223–4, 315, 321

Lorne Pierce Medal, 66, 117, 121

Lunenburg, NS, 64, 65, 68

Lunn, Janet (1928–), 109, 150, 222

Lyman, John (1886–1967), 73, 76

MacDonald, J.E.H. (1873–1932), 71, 72, 73, 378–9

MacDonald, Thoreau (1901–89), 73, 221, 379, 381

MacEwan, Grant (1902–2000), 114, 182

Macklem, Michael, 177, 313

Maclean-Hunter Publications, 166, 167, 174, 245, 249, 406

Maclean's Magazine, 85, 106, 132, 140, 143, 244, 245, 246, 456, 481. *See also Magazine Maclean, Le*

MacLennan, Hugh (1907–90), 21, 112, 114, 119, 134–5, 136, 174, 179, 233, 472; *Barometer Rising*, 105; *Each Man's Son*, 135, 158; *Two Solitudes*, 21, 51–2, 119, 155, 501

MacMechan, Archibald (1862–1933), 481, 482

Macmillan Company of Canada, 134, 137, 140, 164, 165, 167, 169, 171–4, 221, 222, 224–5, 227, 230, 234–5, 271, 330, 331–2, 343, 346, 380, 407. *See also* Eayrs, Hugh S.; Gray, John Morgan

MacMurchy, Helen (1862–1953), 267–70; *The Canadian Mother's Book*, 268–9; Little Blue Books, 268–9, 345

Magazine de la Canadienne, Le (Montreal), 249

Magazine Maclean, Le (Montreal), 22, 83, 143, 245; *See also Actualité, L'*; Maclean-Hunter Publications; *Maclean's Magazine*

magazines, 35, 69, 132, 138–9, 244–7, 250–1, 273, 294, 370, 404–6, 446, 456, 477, 518; advertising, 244, 247; allophone, 297–304; associations, 195, 404, 407, 456; children's, 146, 151, 216–18, 225, 281, 290; fiction, 132–4, 136, 250; government assessment of industry, 40–1, 44, 242–3, 244–5; imported, 60, 132, 390, 391, 405; literary (*see* small press publishing and little magazines); pulp, 132, 139, 201, 253–8, 503; religious, 277, 278–9, 281, 287–8, 290; 'slicks,' 132, 139; split-run, 244; women's, 248–51; writers, 104, 105, 106, 117, 140, 143. *See also* individual magazines; journalists and journalism

Maillet, Andrée (1921–96): *Ristontac*, 220

Maillet, Antonine (1929–), 203, 210, 520; *Pélagie-la-Charette*, 122

Mainmise (Montreal), 327

Major, Henriette (1933–), 106, 220; *Un drôle de petit cheval*, 220

Makers of Canadian Literature (series), 170, 482

Mandel, Eli (1922–92), 109, 233

Manitoba: Aboriginal people, 297; authors, 126–7; government support and publishing, 53, 106, 185, 263, 265–6; libraries, 418, 419, 431, 433, 434, 446, 448, 451, 499, 500, 562n30; printing and publishing, 21, 26, 62, 182–5, 185–8, 194, 297, 301, 315

manuscripts, literary, 107–8, 113–14, 117, 426

maps. *See* atlases and maps

Maracle, Lee (1950–), 34

Marathi (language), 301

Marchand, Jean (1918–88), 19, 361

Marcotte, Gilles (1925–), 204, 479

Maritimes. *See* Atlantic Canada

marketing. *See* promotion

Markoosie (1941–): *Harpoon of the Hunter*, 32, 296

Marquis, G.-E.: *Plaidoyer pour les bibliothèques publiques*, 437

Martin, Claire (1914–), 115, 135, 204

Martin, Gérard, 437

Martin, Paul-Aimé (1917–2001), 204, 280

Martin, Peter, 194, 223, 410

Marx, Karl (1818–83), 188, *189*, 469; *The Communist Manifesto*, 188, *189*

Marxism, 324, 480

mass media, 35, 36, 40–1, 167, 242–7, 483. *See also* magazines; newspapers

Massey Commission. *See* Royal Commission on National Development in the Arts, Letters and Sciences

McClelland, Jack (John Gordon, 1922–2004), 41, 59, 120, 172–5, *176*, 195, 518

McClelland, John (1877–1968), 169, 170–1, 192

McClelland and Stewart, 34, 56, 172–3, 227, 321, 396; as agent, 16–17, 164, 165, 174, 392, 398; Canadian authors, 134, 143, 169–70, 174, 181, 291, 346; children's literature, 221, 225; design, 372, 382, 383; financial problems, 167, 171, 175; foreign ownership of, 518–19; paperback reprints, 59, 137, 151, 233–4, *236*, 405; series, 174, 332, 405, 407. *See also* Seal Books

McClung, Nellie (1873–1951), 95, 123, 250

McCombs, Charles (1887–1947), 418–19, 440; *Report on Canadian Libraries*, 440

McCrae, John (1872–1918): *In Flanders Fields and Other Poems*, 460

McFarlane, Leslie (1902–77), 103, 109, 153–4; as Hardy Boys author, 153–4

McGill Fortnightly Review (Montreal), 312

McGill University, 97, 323, 439, 440, 441, 442, 449–50

McGraw-Hill Company of Canada, 50, 166, 167, 173, 227

McLuhan, Marshall (1911–80), 40, 54, 75, 88–90, 119, 203; *The Gutenberg Galaxy*, 88–90, 119; *The Medium Is the Massage*, 90; *Verbi-Voco-Visual Explorations*, 90

McMaster University, 439, 441; Mills Memorial Library, 439

medals. *See* prizes

Médiaspaul, 523n12. *See also* Éditions Paulines

medicine and health, 82, 249, 250, 252, 267–70, 279, 322, 323, 326, 339, 422, 504, 510; authors, 95, 99, 100, 268, 345; libraries, 421, 441

medical publishing, 343–6

Melzack, Louis (1914–2002), 397. *See also* Classic Books

Memorial University of Newfoundland, 180, 443

Mennonites, 67, 97, 183, 356, 357, 511

Methodist Church of Canada. *See* United Church of Canada

Métis people, 295, 297, 504

Michaud, Paul (1915–2000), 214, 395, 409

microforms, 62, 346, 425, 426

Mi'kmaq (language), 295

Millyard, Anne W. (1929–), 224, 321, 518

mimeographs, 18, 232, 266, 301, 310, 314, 317, 323, 324

ministère des Affaires culturelles (Quebec), 48–9, 51, 109, 202, 437, 459

Minville, Esdras (1896–1975), 16, 18, 329

Miron, Gaston (1928–96), 116, 371, 518

Mitchell, W.O. (William Ormond, 1914–98), 56, 114, 155, 156; *Black Bonspiel of Wullie MacCrimmon*, 185; *Who Has Seen the Wind*, 185, 473, 501

Mitchell Press, 188–9, 191

modernism, 123, 133–4, 310, 311–12, 318

Mohawk peoples, 33, 188, 501

Molinaro, Matie, 112

Molson Prize, 119, 122

Montagnais (language), 295

Montgomery, L.M. (1874–1942), 95, 103, 150, 158, 169, 460, 464–7, 481, 507; *Anne of Green Gables*, 157, 159, 464, 465, 466; *Anne of Windy Poplars*, 157; *Pat of Silver Bush*, 512

Montreal: archives in, 545n61; associations based in, 127–8, 300, 324; authors in, 97, 109, 123, 142, 314–15; book fairs, 49, 521; booksellers, 50, 394, 399, 400–1, 402–3; branch-plant publishers in, 50, 205; distributors, 404; Grand Prix littéraire, 49, 117; libraries, 432, 435–6, 441, 446, 447, 448, 485, 498; magazines and newspapers, 143, 243, 245, 251–3, 278, 279, 305, 306, 307, 316, 324, 327, 348–9, 470, 477, 480; publishing in, 55, 56, 170, 172, 177, 199–205, 213, 224, 280, 288, 302, 305; small presses, 311, 314–18, 321, 322

Montreal Gazette, 481

Montreal Standard, 481, 482

Montreal Star, 481

Moore, Brian (1921–99), 56, 114, 132, 136

Mount Allison University, 440

Mount Saint Vincent University, 450

movies. *See* films

Mowat, Angus (1892–1977), 493, 503–4

Mowat, Farley (1921–), 103–4, 112, 141, 150, 174, 222; *Never Cry Wolf*, 141; *People of the Deer*, 141

multiculturalism: children's literature, 224, 322; government policy and programs, 23, 28–9, 43, 97, 101, 299, 301; libraries and archives, 298, 426, 434, 452; printing and publishing, 97, 231, 290, 315–16, 354. *See also* allophones

multi-volume works, 18, 23, 265–6, 329, 331–2, 335, 340

Munro, Alice (1931–), 93, 108, 114, 115, 119, 155, 173; *Lives of Girls and Women*, 473; *The Newcomers*, 158

Murray, Gordon (1894–1976), 346

museums, 70, 74, 180, 328, 447–8

music, 69, 99, 100, 101, 159, 209, 271, 305, 335, 426, 428, 448; songs, 30, 66–7, 130, 274, 290, 293, 299, 304, 492

National Archives of Canada (formerly Public Archives of Canada), 420, 424, 426

National Film Board of Canada, 71, 103, 109, 130, 144, 158, 496

National Gallery of Canada, 70, 71–2, 73–4, 420, 448

National Home Monthly (Toronto), 249

National Library Act, 424, 426

National Library of Canada, 39, 62, 108, 152, 298, 420, 421, 423, 424–7

National Museum of Canada, 65–6, 67, 71, 420, 526n108

National Printing Bureau, 262–3

National Research Council of Canada, 333–4, 337–9, 344, 422–3

National Science Library, 420, 422

nationalism: articulated through books and print, 13–24, 34–44, 45–51, 89, 117, 128, 134, 141, 285, 338, 379, 406, 410, 476; Canadian iconography, 71–3; cultural, 36, 38–9, 51, 123, 125, 167, 223, 247, 480–3, 517, 520–1; education, 56–64, 86–8; French-Canadian, 16–19, 22, 45, 52–3, 58–9, 63, 86, 128, 141, 146, 200, 201, 204, 217, 316, 476, 517; publishers, 36, 169–71, 175, 194, 201, 310, 313, 481, 518. *See also* Quiet Revolution; Royal Commission on National Development in the Arts, Letters and Sciences

Neatby, Hilda (1904–75): *So Little for the Mind*, 20

Nelligan, Émile (1874–1941), 239, 240, 332; *Poésies complètes (1896–1899)*, 239, 332

New, W.H. (William Herbert, 1938–), 156, 331, 482

New Brunswick, 3, 52–3, 301, 353, 448, 489, 511–12; bilingualism, 52, 53; libraries, 418, 433, 442, 493; publishing, 178–81. *See also* Acadia; Atlantic Canada

New Canadian Library (series), 59, 137, 173, 234–5, 236, 383, 483–4

New Press, 313, 346, 398

NeWest Press, 183, 315

Newfeld, Frank (1928–), 222, 234, 236, 382, 383

Newfoundland and Labrador, 19, 20, 67, 95, 140, 180, 181, 334, 353–4; government publishing, 263, 265; libraries, 420, 434, 443, 447, 488, 557n123; paper industry, 353–4; publishing, 67–8, 69, 180, 181. *See also* Smallwood, Joseph R.

Newman, Peter C. (1929–), 54, 97, 141–2, 174; *The Canadian Establishment*, 141

newspapers, 242–7; Aboriginal, 294–7; allophone, 27, 301, 303; Black, 307–8; as book publishers, 208, 210; book reviews, 480–1; community and regional, 212, 243, 308, 356, 406; gay and lesbian, 326; government assessment of industry, 40–1, 244–5, 247; imported, 390, 391; job printing, 178, 191, 208; libraries, 448; medical, 344; Mennonite, 356, 357; news services, 35, 243; printers' strikes, 359–60, 367–8; readership, 457, 458; religious, 212, 277–8, 287–8; and sports, 142; tabloids, 243–4, 245, 247, 257, 278, 308, 325, 406; underground, 327; weekend supplements, 142; Yiddish, 305–7. *See also* individual newspapers; journalists and journalism; printers and printing

Nichol, bp (Barry Philip, 1944–88), 90, 313

Nigog, Le (Montreal), 316, 369–70, 479

non-fiction, 58, 60, 67, 102, 114, 116, 118, 119, 138–42, 158, 317. *See also* autobiographies and biographies

North: Aboriginal culture and languages, 29, 31, 294, *296*; accounts of missions, 95, 290–1; libraries, 434, 435, 446, 494–5, 504; literacy, 454; publishing, 191–2

Northwest Territories, 191, 495, 504

Nouvelle Relève, La (Montreal), 316, 479. *See also Relève, La*

Nova Scotia: authors, 126, 178; booksellers, 394, 398, 399, 401–2; government publishing, 263; government support of the arts, 37; libraries, 432, 434, 488, 510; publishing and newspapers, 178–81, 300, 327, 508. *See also* Acadia; Atlantic Canada; Halifax

Novalis, 209, 287

Oberon Press, 56, 175, 181, 313, 315

Oblates of Mary Immaculate, 208–9, 287, 288; Missionary Oblates of Mary Immaculate, 211–12, 280, 294

obscenity. *See* censorship

October Crisis (1970), 121, 203, 471

Official Languages Act, 22, 53

Oiseau bleu, L' (Montreal), 216–17

Ojibwa stories, 31, 32

O'Leary Commission. *See* Royal Commission on Publications

Ondaatje, Michael (1943–), 116, 520; *Coming through Slaughter*, 120; *The English Patient*, 120

one-dollar books, 202–3, 206, 255

Ontario: booksellers, 393, 401, 411; education, 52, 62, 208, 209–10, 227, 265, 368, 429, 450, 486–8, 506; ethnology and folklore, 66–8; French-language publishing, 208–10, 520; government support of the arts and publishing, 37, 40, 41, 42, 44, 106, 119, 173, 174–5, 195, 222, 230, 406, 410, 457, 458, 518; government translation and publishing, 53, 265, 508; libraries, 43, 417–18, 429, 431, 433–4, 442–3, 446, 447, 449, 496, 497, 499, 503–4, 505; literacy, 454; printing and paper industries, 350, 353; publishing, 102, 163–8, 168–78, 208–10, 301, 375. *See also* Ontario Royal Commission on Book Publishing; Ottawa; Toronto

Ontario Arts Council, 40, 119, 406, 410, 525n47

Ontario Library Association, 59, 433, 451

Ontario Royal Commission on Book Publishing, 41, 44, 195, 222, 230, 406, 457

Opportunities for Youth (OFY), 107, 223–4, 315, 321, 322

oral culture: Aboriginal, 29–34; allophone, 102, 303; folklore collections, 66–8, 211; and print, 34, 65, 88–9; publishers, 209

Ordre, L' (Montreal), 477

Ostenso, Martha (1900–63), 120; *Wild Geese*, 117, 170, 460

Ottawa: authors, 97, 123, 128; book clubs, 408; booksellers, 198, 399, 410; libraries, 417,

420–2; publishing, 171, 175, 208–9, 243, 280, 300, 315, 327, 337–9

Ottawa Citizen, 102

Ouvrard, Pierre (1929–), *118*, 373–4

Oxford University Press (Canada), 164, 171, 172–3, 221, 222, 225, 227, 230, 332

Padlock Law (Quebec), 324, 469, 470, 477

Panneton, Philippe. *See* Ringuet

paper, 352–4, 370, 376, 379, 382, 384

paperbacks, 136–8, 140, 171, *176*, 219, 234, 241, 258, 383–4, 395, 397, 404–7; Harlequin, 185–8; imported, 392–3, 405, 409; quality, 59, 137, 234–6; and reading, 395, 456; reprints, 59, 68, 137, 141, 186, 234–6; scholarly, 334

Parent, Louis, 220

Parent Report. *See* Royal Commission of Inquiry on Education in the Province of Quebec

Paris. *See* France

Parti pris, 318, 324, 480. *See also* Éditions Partis pris

Patrie, La (Montreal), 141, 475

Patriote, Le (Montreal), 325

Péladeau, Pierre (1925–97), 243, 350–1, 406

Pellan, Alfred (1906–88), 78, 371, 403

Pelletier, Albert (1896–1971), 200, 201, 476–7

Pemmican Publications, 183, 224, 297

PEN International, 123, 125

periodicals. *See* individual periodicals; magazines; newspapers

Peterborough Examiner, 481

photography, 370, 381–2, 384; souvenir view books, 71, 183. *See also* illustration

Pierce, Lorne (1890–1961), 57, 73, 95, 169, 201, 311, 473; *Outline of Canadian Literature (French and English)*, 482. *See also* Lorne Pierce Medal; Ryerson Press

playwrights. *See* drama and dramatists

Pocket Books, 171, 186, 187, 405

poetry and poets: Aboriginal, 29, 33, 294, 295; allophone, 101–3, 299, 302–3, 305–6; anthologies, 124, 127; best-sellers, 138, 174; chapbooks, 134, 180, 190, 312; income, 103, 105, 109–10, 137; organizations, 107, 125–7; prizes

for, 118, 119, 124, 520; publication, 54, 124, 170, 171–2, 173, 177, 181, 188, 203, 204, 209, 211, 212, 308–18, 375–6; religious, 95, 289, 290; reviews of, 482; textbooks, 57, 60, 230; translations, 54, 55, 101, 103. *See also* small presses and little magazines

Polish (language), 101, 300, 303, 510

Pony, Aristide, 394. *See also* Librairie J.-A. Pony

Porcupine's Quill, 310

pornography, 412, 472–3

Porter, Anna, 177, 321

Portuguese (language), 301

post office: distribution by mail, 323, 325, 395, 396, 400, 408, 409, 412, 516; rates and subsidies, 37, 38, 242–3, 245, 506; stamps, 52, 71

post-secondary education: Canadian content, 57, 61, 67; growth in, 328, 330, 400, 439, 441, 556n89; textbooks, 137, 227–8, 234. *See also* booksellers and bookstores, campus; scholarly publishing; universities

Poulin, Jacques (1937–), 100, 203; *Volkswagen Blues*, 93

Prairies, 182–5, 211–13; folklore, 67; libraries, 419, 433, 434, 499–501; publishing, 26, 139, 182–8, 211–13, 287–8, 331; study groups, 510–11. *See also* individual cities and provinces; Ukrainian (language)

Pratt, E.J. (Edwin John, 1882–1964), 95, 109, 119, 170, 473; *The Witches' Brew*, 473

Prentice-Hall, 50, 166, 230, 232

Presbyterian Church of Canada, 288, 289, 291, 319

Press Gang, 190, 321

Presse, La (Montreal), 367, 436, 463, 475

Presse québécoise des origines à nos jours, La, 335

Prince Edward Island: libraries, 417, 420, 432, 497, 510; publishing, 180, 181; reading habits, 457

printers and printing, 349–86; foreign ownership, 353; gender, 362–8; industry and technology, 334, 349–52, 354–8, 362–8, 384, 386, 427; labour and unions, 358–68; outside Canada, 225, 384; printer-publishers, 178–9, 183, 188–9, 208, 210, 350; training, 363, 366, 368–9, 379, 386. *See also* book trade and review journals; illustration; *livres d'artiste*; private press

prisons, 224, 284, 466–7, 493, 495–6

private press, 18, 374–8

Prix Alvine-Bélisle, 148

Prix d'Action intellectuelle, 121

Prix David, 47–8, 66, 117, 121

Prix de la province de Québec, 147–8

Prix des Librairies de France, 122

Prix du Cercle du livre de France, 106

Prix Femina, 122, 135, 462, 520

Prix France-Acadie, 211

Prix Gilles-Corbeil, 122, 520

Prix Goncourt, 122, 462, 520

Prix Ludger Duvernay, 121

Prix Marie-Claire-Daveluy, 148

Prix Maxine, 147

Prix Medicis, 122, 203, 463

Prix Robert-Cliche, 121–2

prize books, 45–6, 58, 64, 86–8, 87, 146, 148, 217, 218, 350

prizes: for authors, 47–8, 49, 106, 116–22, 147, 155, 203, 211, 520; for bookselling, 198; for children's books, 147–8, 223, 224, 377, 517; for design, 377, 382, 383, 384; international, 117, 121, 122, 135, 159, 170, 203, 462, 463, 517, 520; for translation, 55. *See also* individual prizes

promotion: by authors, 123, 127–8, 191, 193, 214–15; by booksellers and publishers, 112, 134, 152, 170, 176, 192–5, 214–15, 411–14; by government, 42, 43, 49–50, 414. *See also* book weeks; catalogues; prizes

propaganda, 125, 129–30, 325

Public Lending Right, 107, 125

public libraries acts, 429, 431, 432, 434, 437, 500

publishers and publishing: Aboriginal, 293–7; allophone, 297–304; books in English, 163–98; books in French, 199–215; for children, 216–26; fine press, 372–4; foreign, 205, 518; by government, 261–5, 267–70; religious, 276–92; scholarly, 328–37; small press and little magazines, 308–18; training, 195–8. *See also* bilingual publishing; book trade and

review journals; magazines; newspapers; 'publishing' under genres, languages, places, professions, etc.

Publishers Loss Insurance Act (Quebec), 48–9

Publisher's Weekly, 460, 461

Punjabi (language), 102, 301, 302, 303

Purdy, Al (1918–2000), 103, 107, 174

Quebec: Act Respecting the Development of Quebec Firms in the Book Industry, 51, 205, 397, 414, 517; best-sellers, 462–3; book clubs, 409, 410; book publishing, 199–207, 213–15; broadcasting, 105–6, 272; censorship, 469–71, 475–8; Department of Education, 63, 87, 148, 207, 238, 239; Department of the Provincial Secretary, 45, 46–8, 53, 128, 201, 437; Department of Public Instruction, 21, 45–6, 86–8, 206–7, 238, 436; education and textbooks, 20, 56, 58, 59–60, 62–4, 237–41, 345, 392–3; films, 157–60; government book policies, 45–51; government publishing, 52–3, 263–5, 266; graphic arts in, 369–72; libraries, 417, 418–19, 420, 428, 431, 432, 433, 435–8, 451, 452; literacy, 454; mass market publishing and distribution, 136, 253–5, 405–6; ministère des Affaires culturelles (Department of Cultural Affairs), 48–9, 51, 109, 202, 437, 459; printing and paper industries, 350, 352, 354–5; prize books, 86–8; prizes in, 47–8, 49, 117, 121–2; publishing, 199–207, 519; reading, 458–9, 465–7; Second World War publishing, 201–2, 253, 281, 316, 355, 406, 436, 477; small presses, 316–18, 519; study groups, 510, 513–14; wholesale and retail bookselling, 391–403, 412–14. *See also* authors and authorship; Catholic Church; magazines; Montreal; newspapers; Quiet Revolution; religious publications

Quebec Chronicle Telegraph (Quebec City), 264

Quebec City, 49, 128, 435; publishing in, 213, 243, 263–4, 277, 278, 282–3, 340, 478

Québec Livres, 407

Quebec Official Publisher, 264–5

Québec-Presse (Montreal), 324

Quebecor, 243, 350–1, 407, 519

Queen's/King's Printer, 261–2

Queen's Quarterly (Kingston, ON), 328, 482

Queen's University, 59, 333, 343, 344, 439, 440

Quiet Revolution (Quebec), 18–19, 20, 21, 28, 238, 281–2, 475–8; writers and publishers, 135, 202–4, 206, 214, 316–18, 324

Quill & Quire (Toronto), 411, 461, 482, 520. *See also* book trade and review journals

Quran, 284

Raddall, Thomas H. (1903–94), 178, 179, 402

radio. *See* broadcasting; Canadian Broadcasting Corporation (CBC) / Société Radio-Canada (SRC); drama and dramatists

Ragweed Press, 181, 315, 321; Ragweed/gynergy, 321

rare books: antiquarian booksellers, 400–1, 517; library collections, 114, 425, 426, 428, 443, 444, 447

Raymond, Gérard (1912–32), 282–3

Readers' Club of Canada, 410, 457, 483

Readers' Digest, 409

readers (school). *See* textbooks

reading, 453–514, Aboriginal peoples, 29, 501–5; advice on, 289, 474, 475–80, 480–4, 484–90, 503; children, 147, 148, 289, 409, 429, 433, 484–90, 502; depicted, 75–9, 486, 487, 494; experience of, 463–7; and gender, 75–7, 82, 83–5, 143, 457–8, 463; popular, 185–8, 248–58, 459–63; promotion of, 134, 193, 438; reader-response theories, 520–1; reading and study clubs, 509–14; remote and isolated readers, 409, 454, 491–505; surveys of, 455–9, 520–1; and television, 278, 486, 489. *See also* censorship; literacy

Reading Camp Association, 491

Reaney, James (1926–), 109, 119, 120, 174

Red Deer College Press, 183

Redemptorists, 277, 436

Refus global, 13, 18, 317, 403, 477

Regina Public Library, 115

Relations (Montreal), 278–9, 436

Relations of Canada and the United States (series), 15, 329–30

Relève, La (Montreal), 316, 479. *See also Nouvelle Relève, La*

religion: Aboriginal peoples, 290–1, 293; autobiographies, 95; bookstores, 399, 400; Catholic unions based on, 360–2; and censorship, 473–8; history, 210, 290–1, 319, 332; religious authors, 95–6, 99, 100, 109. *See also* individual religions; religious publishing

religious publishing, 276–92; for allophone communities, 298, 306; children's literature and textbooks, 146, 217–18, 237, 288–92, 474; English-language, 283–92; French-language, 208–12, 276–83; hymnals, 284–5, 293; imported, 390–1, 550n7; magazines, 278–9, 281, 287–8, 290; newsletters, 277–8, 280, 287, 319; by women's groups, 319. *See also* individual religions

Rencontre des poètes / écrivains, 126, 129, 531n86

reprints: Canadiana, 68, 169, 173, 235, 265, 377; and the paperback revolution, 136, 173, 185–8, 233–4, 405. *See also* anthologies; textbooks

Revue dominicaine, La (St Hyacinthe, QC), 279

Revue moderne, La (Montreal), 143, 248, 404, 405, 479; Petit Format, 405–6

Revue populaire, La (Montreal), 143, 249, 404

Richard, Maurice ('Rocket Richard'; 1921–2000), 144, 207

Richards, David Adams (1950–), 177, 181

Richardson, Evelyn (1902–76), 179; *Desired Haven*, 134

Richler, Mordecai (1931–2001), 54, 98, 114, 134, 144, 159, 174, 233, 307, 410; *The Apprenticeship of Duddy Kravitz*, 159, 483; *Jacob Two-Two Meets the Hooded Fang*, 56

Ridington Report. *See Libraries in Canada: A Study of Library Conditions and Needs*

Riel, Louis (1844–85), 297, 335

rights: authors' and creators', 111, 132–3, 152, 164; film and other subsidiary rights, 105, 110–12, 157, 160, 164

Ringuet (Panneton, Philippe; 1895–1960), 109, 135, 239; *Trente arpents*, 135, 239

Roberts, Charles G.D. (1860–1943), 103, 123, 124

Robinson, David, 190, 313

Rockefeller Foundation, 330, 336, 440

Rode, Ajmer (1940–), 102, 302

Rolland Paper Company, 353, 370, 379

Roman canadien (series), 133, 200–1, 406

Roman Catholic Church. *See* Catholic Church

Romans de la jeune génération (series), 476

Romans missionnaires (series), 218

Roncarelli Affair, 477, 560n37

Ross, Dan (W.E. Dan; 1912–95), 131, 136

Ross, Malcolm (neo-Nazi; 1946–), 325

Ross, Malcolm (professor/editor; 1911–2002), 59, 234, 483–4

Ross, Sinclair (1908–96), 109, 127, 134; *As for Me and My House,* 236

Roy, Camille (1870–1943), 58, 63, 201, 476, 479; *Tableau de l'histoire de la littérature canadienne-française,* 58, 63

Roy, Gabrielle (1909–83), 54, 103, 105, 108, 112, 119, 122, 135, 174, 462, 508; *Bonheur d'occasion / The Tin Flute,* 135, 462; *L'été enchanté,* 147; fonds Gabrielle Roy, 108

Royal Commission of Inquiry on Education in the Province of Quebec, 56, 59, 237

Royal Commission on Bilingualism and Biculturalism, 21, 22, 23, 28, 53, 60, 101, 514

Royal Commission on National Development in the Arts, Letters and Sciences, 19–20, 38, 39, 46, 58, 74, 106, 125, 128, 159, 173, 193, 420, 513–14; on education, 229, 234; on libraries, 420, 424, 437, 441; on writing and publishing, 38

Royal Commission on Newspapers, 243, 245, 247, 457

Royal Commission on Patents, Copyright, Trade Marks, and Industrial Design, 111

Royal Commission on Publications, 40, 244

Royal Commission on the Status of Women, 320

royal commissions, 40, 41, 265–6. *See also* individual royal commissions

Royal Society of Canada, 66, 117, 119, 121, 328, 338, 424

royalties, 103, 105, 106, 110, 112, 136, 137–8, 164. *See also* authors and authorship; rights

Rueter, Gus, 375

Rueter, Will (1940–), 374, 376; *Order Touched with Delight,* 376

Rumilly, Robert (1897–1983), 329

Russell-Lang's (bookstore, Winnipeg), 394, 395

Russian (language), 25, 300

Ruthenian (language), 26

Ryan, Claude (1925–2004), 22. *See also Devoir, Le*

Ryerson Poetry Chapbooks, 170, 311

Ryerson Press, 73, 134, 139, 171, 173, 234, 271, 330; agency arrangements, 165; bookselling, 396, 401–2; Canadian Copyright Editions, 165; Canadian nationalism, 57, 139, 169, 170, 201, 346, 482; censorship, 473; contests, 106, 120; design, 172, 173, 378, 382; sale to McGraw-Hill, 41, 167, 173, 194, 223, 230; scholarly publishing, 330, 332; textbooks, 57, 140, 170, 227, 230. *See also* Pierce, Lorne; United Church Publishing House

Ryerson University, 196, 518

Saint-Martin, Fernande (1927–), 249, 250

Saint Paul University, 209, 287

Salishan (language), 297

salons du livre: Montreal, 49, 214, 403, 514, 521; Quebec, 49, 521. *See also* book fairs

Salvation Army, 287; *The War Cry,* 287

Salverson, Laura Goodman (1890–1970): *Confessions of an Immigrant's Daughter,* 96, 119

Samedi, Le (Montreal), 249, 404

Sandwell, B.K. (Bernard Keble, 1876–1954), 123, 481

Sarick, Judy, 152, 399

Saskatchewan: Aboriginal peoples, 294–7; authors, 125; government support of the arts, 37; libraries, 418, 419, 431, 433, 434, 441, 500; newspapers, 246, 294; publishing in, 182–3, 194, 212, 213, 263, 287–8, 315, 321. *See also* Prairies

Saskatchewan Indian (Prince Albert, SK), 294

Saskatchewan Wheat Pool, 182, 500

Saturday Night (Toronto), 481

Saulteaux peoples, 297

Saurel, Pierre (Pierre Daignault, 1925–2003), 253, 254

Savard, Félix-Antoine (1896–1982), 239, 240, 462; *Menaud maître draveur*, 238–41, 462

scholarly publishing, 328–37; anthropological and folk collections, 29–32, 65–7. *See also* law books and legal publishing; medical publishing; scientific publishing; university presses

Scholarly Publishing (Toronto), 334

schools. *See* censorship; children; education; libraries; reading; textbooks

scientific publishing, 337–9. *See also* medical publishing

Scott, F.R. (Francis Reginald, 1899–1985), 54, 76, 95, 109, 119, 125, 133, 311, 312, 323

scriptwriters, 98, 158, 159

Seal Books, 106, 120, 138, 141, 321, 407

Second World War: allophone publishing, 27, 300, 303, 306; authors, 125, 129–30; censorship, 471, 477; government publishing, 27, 262; imports, 165–6, 253–8, 507; paper and printing, 351, 353; publishing in Quebec, 201–2, 253, 281, 316, 355, 406, 436, 477; pulp magazines, 253–8; trade and scholarly publishing, 172, 329, 379–80

Séguin, Fernand (1922–88), 140

Self-Counsel Press, 191, 342

self-publishing, 103, 177, 180, 210, 306, 517; poetry, 134, 170, 311, 312–13, 517

Selye, Hans (1907–82): *The Stress of My Life*, 346

Serbian (language), 303

Service, Robert (1874–1958), 123, 157, 158; *Rhymes of a Red Cross Man*, 460

sexually explicit material, 31, 322, 325–6, 375, 399, 412, 472–3

Sherbrooke, QC, 49, 54, 128, 139, 278, 281, 435, 480

Shuswap peoples, 33

Siegler, Karl (1948–), 190

Simard, Jean (1916–2005), 56, 219

Simon Fraser University, 196, 443, 518

Simpson, Berthe Dulude (1896–1971), 321

Sinclair, Lister (1921–2006), 140, 156

Sioui, Georges (1948–): *Pour une autohistoire amérindienne: Essai sur les fondements d'une morale sociale*, 295; *Le premier des Hurons*, 295

Škvorecký, Josef (1924–), 301, 303; 68 Publishers, 299, 301, 303

small press publishing and little magazines, 54, 134, 155, 180, 194, 301, 308–18

Smallwood, Joseph R. (1900–91), 19, 140, 180

Smith, A.J.M. (Albert James Marshall, 1902–80), 109, 133, 170, 311, 312

Smith, Lillian H. (1887–1983), 485; *The Unreluctant Years*, 489

Smucker, Barbara (1915–2003): *Underground to Canada*, 56, 151

Socialist Party of Canada, 188, *189*, 324, 469

Société des écrivains canadiens (SÉC), 46, 94, 97, 98, 128, 130, 478

Société des éditeurs canadiens du livre français, 193, 202, 213

Société d'étude et de conférences, 510, 513–14

Société Radio-Canada (SRC). *See* Canadian Broadcasting Corporation (CBC) / Société Radio-Canada (SRC)

Société Saint-Jean-Baptiste, 121, 146, 217, 436

Société Saint-Paul, 218, 280, 281

Society of Jesus (Jesuits), 279, 280, 281, 436

Soleil, Le (Quebec City), 264, 352

Soleil de Colombie, Le (Vancouver), 213

Soleil de Vancouver, Le, 213

Song Fishermen of Nova Scotia, 126, 179, 311

Souster, Raymond (1921–), 109, 312

Spanish (language), 101, 301–2

Special Senate Committee on the Mass Media, 40–1, 244

Sphère feminine, La / Women's Sphere (Montreal), 319

sports writing, 142–4, 188, 253, 489

St Francis Xavier University, 510

St Hyacinthe, QC, 66, 279

Staines, David (1946–), 235, 484

Star Weekly Magazine (Toronto), 483

Stephansson, Stephan G. (1853–1927), 101, 303

Stephen Leacock Memorial Medal, 98, 119

Steven, Arthur (1920–), 382

Stringer, Arthur (1874–1950), 112, 132, 169, 464, 469, 481, 512

Sudbury, ON, 209

Sulpicians, 428, 436, 440

Survey of Libraries, 456

Switzerland, 390, 410, 462; Canada-Switzerland literary prize, 122

syllabics: Cree, 30, 293–4, 386, 504; Inuktitut, 30, 33, 296

Sylvestre, Guy (1918–), 317, 426, 427, 479

TAB Confidential (Toronto), 325, 326

Takashima, Shizuye (1928–): *A Child in a Prison Camp*, 224

Talmud, 306

Talon Books, 56, 190, 313–14, 315, 346, 383

Tamarack Review (Toronto), 53, 155, 312

Tanghe, Raymond (1898–1969), 426, 440

taxes and tariffs: on authors' incomes, 105, 125; on book imports, 35, 164, 165, 166, 171, 392, 468; lobbying by publishers and booksellers, 192, 193, 244, 411; on magazines, 243, 244–5, 291; sales tax on books, 38, 171, 193, 243, 411, 412

technologies. *See* computers; printers and printing

téléromans, 133, 159

télétéâtre, 133

television. *See* broadcasting; Canadian Broadcasting Corporation (CBC) / Société Radio-Canada (SRC)

Templeton, Charles (1915–2001), 96

textbooks, 63–4, 226–32, 236, 237–9; allophone, 26, 303; Braille, 508; Canadian content, 42, 50, 57, 63–4, 140, 229–31, 238; distribution of, 59, 411, 413–14; English-language, 182, 226–32; French-language, 45–6, 209–10, 236, 237–41, 319, 334, 392–3, 413–14; ministries of education, 45–6, 226–7, 230–1; publishers' associations, 193–4, 214; studies of, 231, 238, 485–6. *See also* children; reading

theatre. *See* drama and dramatists

Thériault, Yves (1915–83), 103, 120–1, 136–7, 147, 218

Thérien Frères, 354–5

Theytus Books, 191, 224, 297. *See also* Young-Ing, Greg

This Magazine (Toronto), 483

TickleAce (St John's), 180, 315

Tiers, Le (Montreal), 326

Time Magazine, 244, 245

Tish (Vancouver), 314

Tisseyre, Pierre (1909–95), 48, 50, 55, 120, 121, 204, 214, 218, 409, 518

To Know Ourselves, 56–7, 61, 62, 231. *See also* Commission on Canadian Studies

Torah, 284

Toronto: allophone publishing, 101, 102, 298, 299, 300, 301, 303, 304, 305, 306; booksellers, 152, 398, 399, 400, 516; City of Toronto Book Award, 117; libraries, 443, 447–8, 505; newspapers and magazines, 132, 243–4, 248, 249, 301, 312, 327, 338, 483; printing industry, 350, 356, 378; publishing, 163–75, 187–8, 223–5, 227, 230, 256, 267, 284, 288, 299, 311–13, 322, 341, 375. *See also* Toronto Public Library

Toronto Public Library, 298, 434, 457, 485, 488; *Books for Boys and Girls*, 485; *Canadian Catalogue of Books ...*, 424

Toronto Star, 187, 448, 483

Toronto Sun, 243, 244, 352

Tory, Henry Marshall (1864–1947), 422, 492

tourism, 52, 71, 188, 265, 321, 402

Toye, William (1926–), 172–3, 222, 332

Tranquille, Henri (1916–2005), 395, 397, 402–3. *See also* Librairie Tranquille

translation, 51–6, 66, 186, 262, 283, 322; and Aboriginal languages, 3, 29–33, 284, 293, 296; allophone, 101, 103, 301. *See also* translators

Translation Bureau, 52

translators: government, 52, 53; literary, 51, 101, 102; prizes for, 118–19

travel guides, 102, 273; view books, 71, 183

Tree Frog Press, 151

Tremaine, Marie (1902–84), 331, 375, 425

Tremblay, Gaston (1924–1998), 209

Tremblay, Jules (1879–1927), 209

Tremblay, Michel (1942–), 54, 106, 112, 203,

410–11; *Les belles soeurs*, 133, 159; *Il était une fois dans l'est*, 159

Tribune (Sackville, NB), 178

Tribune, La (Sherbrooke, QC), 139

Tribune (Winnipeg), 243

Trois-Rivières, QC, 47, 49, 128, 277, 318, 353, 454

Trudeau, Pierre Elliott (1919–2000), 22, 28–9, 40, 140, 203, 204, 471; *The Asbestos Strike*, 141; *Federalism and the French Canadians*, 22; *Two Innocents in Red China*, 141

Tsimshian peoples, 30, 31

Tundra Books, 184, 224, 313, 321

typography and typographers. *See* printers and printing

Tyrell's (bookstore, Toronto), 394, 398, 399

Ukrainian (language), 25, 26, 67, 102, 298, 299, 303

Underhill, Frank H. (1889–1971), 15, 21, 323

Union des écrivains québécois (UNÉQ), 94, 98, 107, 113, 129

Union des jeunes écrivains, 128

unions. *See* printers and printing

United Church of Canada, 95, 96, 285, 287, 288, 289–91, 319, 473

United Church Publishing House, 170, 284, 290. *See also* Pierce, Lorne; Ryerson Press

United States: agency system and branch-plant publishing, 42, 50, 163–8; book clubs, 408, 410; Canadian booksellers in, 397–8; copyright protection in, 111; literary agents in, 111, 149, 150; as market for Canadian authors, 104, 112, 131, 132, 135, 143, 157, 179, 224, 329; and mass-market distribution, 404–7; purchase of Canadian companies, 41, 167, 194, 223; textbooks, 229–30, 232

Universal Copyright Convention, 111

Université de Moncton, 211, 442

Université de Montréal, 46, 329, 333, 340, 355, 422, 436, 440, 450, 513

Université de Sherbrooke, 54, 333

Université du Québec, 333

Université du Québec à Montréal, 62

Université Laval, 18–19, 58, 62, 333, 335, 440, 442

universities: Canadian studies, 57, 60, 62–3; growth of, 21, 38, 110, 137, 383; libraries, 107, 114, 330–1, 439–45, 452; library education, 449–51; as market for Canadian books, 39, 46, 227, 229, 232–7, 239–41; as publishing centres, 179, 312, 315, 328, 331, 479, 482; student publications, 312, 323, 340, 371; writers-in-residence, 115–16. *See also* individual universities; post-secondary education; scholarly publishing; university presses

University College of Cape Breton (UCCB), 180

University of Alberta, 115, 439, 441, 443, 450; Rutherford Library, 439

University of British Columbia, 153, 331, 440, 450, 492, 508

University of Calgary Library, Rare Books and Special Collections, 113–14

University of Manitoba, 119, 345

University of New Brunswick, 115, 116, 127, 179, 312, 342, 440

University of Ottawa, 115, 116, 208–9, 287, 450

University of Prince Edward Island, 465

University of Saskatchewan, 441

University of Toronto, 87, 108, 109, 115, 287, 338, 439, 450, 451, 494

University of Toronto Library, 441, 442, 443, 444, 472; Thomas Fisher Rare Book Library, 443, 444

University of Toronto Quarterly, 482, 483

University of Waterloo, 447

University of Western Ontario, 440, 450, 451

university presses, 39, 195, 332–4, 341; Alberta, 61, 333, 335; British Columbia, 333; Calgary, 333; Carleton, 235–6, 333; Laval, 333, 335; McGill / McGill-Queen's, 297, 333; Montréal, 333, 335; New Brunswick, 179; Ottawa, 209, 329, 332; Sherbrooke, 333; Toronto, 173, 175, 194, 234, 329, 332–3, 335, 383; Wilfrid Laurier, 333

Urdu (language), 301

Vallières, Pierre (1938–98): *Nègres blancs d'Amérique / White Niggers of America*, 13, 22; *L'urgence de choisir / Choose!* 22

Valois, Charles (1924–), 477–8

Van Herk, Aritha (1954–), 110, 120

Vancouver, 489, 510; Aboriginal peoples, 294; allophones, 300, 305; authors in, 98, 102, 126, 127, 188; booksellers, 396, 398, 399, 400, 412, 468, 516, 517; libraries, 456, 496; magazines and newspapers, 326, 327, 469, 483; publishers in, 188–91, 213, 230, 313, 315, 321, 341, 342, 376–7, 517

Vancouver Public Library, 456

Vancouver Sun, 458, 481

Vaugeois, Denis (1935–), 51, 205, 438

Véhicule Gallery and Press, 177, 315, 374

Vézina, Medjé (b. 1896), 476

Vickery, Edgar J., 401–2; Vickery's Bookstore (Halifax), 401

Victoria, BC, 102, 312, 399, 430, 447, 495, 511, 516, 517

Vidéo Presse (Montreal), 218, 281

Vient de paraître (Montreal), 214, 414. *See also* book trade and review journals

Vietnam War, 8, 40, 313, 314, 327

Vining, Charles (1897–1974), 129–30

Wachtel, Eleanor (1948–), 320

Waldie, J. Kemp, 375

Wallace, Ann (1927–), 101

Wallace, W. Stewart (1884–1970), 139–40, 334

war. *See* First World War; Second World War; Vietnam War

War Measures Act, 24, 25, 188, 203, 299, 469, 471, 477

Wartime Information Board, 129–30

Waruszyński, Zbigniew, 101

Watters, R.E. (Reginald Eyre, 1912–79), 137, 188, 336–7; *A Check List of Canadian Literature and Background Materials, 1628–1950*, 331, 336–7

Wayzgoose, 376

Weaver, Robert (1921–), 155, 410, 483

Webb, Phyllis (1927–), 109, 137, 156

Weinrich, Peter: *Social Protest from the Left in Canada*, 323

Weiselberger, Carl (1900–70), 101–2; *Der Rabbi mit der Axt*, 102

West Coast. *See* British Columbia

Western Clarion (Vancouver), 469

Western Producer (Saskatoon), 182–3

Western Producer Prairie Books, 182, 184

Westmount (QC) Public Library, 431, 432, 436

W.H. Smith, 166, 397–9, 412; W.H. Smith / *Books in Canada* First Novel Award, 120

wheat pools, 433, 500–1, 561n27, 562n30

Whitehead, George, 188; Whitehead Library, 188, *189*

Whitehorse Star, 191

wholesalers, 166, 167, 173, 392, 402, 404–7; in Quebec, 199, 204–5, 392–3, 397, 413

Wiebe, Rudy (1934–), 97, 114

Wieland, Joyce (1931–88), 74, 79; *True Patriot Love / Véritable amour patriotique*, 79

Wilfrid Laurier University, 447

Wilson, Ethel (1888–1980), 127, 188; *Hetty Dorval*, 377

Winnipeg: associations in, 96, 127, 320, 344; newspapers and magazines, 243, 294, 298, 300, 303, 327, 483, 500; publishing, 101, 185–7, 224, 298, 299–300

Winnipeg Free Press, 139, 448

Winnipeg General Strike, 25, 469

Wiseman, Adele (1928–92), 97, 118, 307; *The Sacrifice*, 118

W.J. Gage (publishing house), 41, 167, 173, 194, 223, 227, 229, 230, 235

women: as authors, 96, 117, 147–8; bookstores for, 516, 517; and immigration literature, 274; and libraries, 433, 494, 498–500, 504; in the printing trades, 358–60, 362–8; and publishing, 68, 183, 189, 237, 244, 248–51, 288, 290, 318–22, 517, 545n51; and reading, 76–8, 474, 509–13; self-education, 513–14. *See also* feminism; gender

women's institutes, 433, 494, 498–500, 510

Woodcock, George (1912–95), 119, 331, 483

Writers' Union of Canada (WUC), 94, 97, 98, 100, 107, 113, 125, 126, 151–2, 398, 528n6

Writers' War Committee, 125, 129–30

writers-in-residence, 40, 107, 115–16, 125

Wrongfount (series), 375

Wyandot peoples, 30

Yearbook of the Arts in Canada, 72–3, 380
Yiddish (language), 299, 305–7
York University, 67, 443
Young, Scott (1918–2005), 105, 108, 132, 136, 143, 149; *Scrubs on Skates*, 144

Young-Ing, Greg (1961–), 295, 297. *See also* Theytus Books
Yukon, 189, 191–2, 435, 454, 494–5

Zeller, Ludwig (1927–), 101